AFRICANISM

First Published 2018

Published by Chukwueloka Obiamiwe
Printed in the United Kingdom

ISBN-13: 978-1-8381288-0-7

Cover design and layout by www.spiffingcovers.com

AFRICANISM

ACROSS AFRICA'S HIDDEN PSYCHOLOGICAL PARADIGM

DR CHUKWUELOKA
OBIAMIWE

DEDICATION:

This book is a dedication to all African people and their diaspora, who have lived in the chains of slavery, visible and invisible.

Bia Nnulu Onuanioh,
Come hear our voices,

Inna
Father.

Bia Nnulu Onuanioh,
Come hear our voices,

Onwere oge eke madu ga kali eke Chukwu.
There will never be a time when man's strength will ever surpass God's.

[Old Igbo spiritual song, from eastern Nigeria, West Africa.]

ACKNOWLEDGEMENTS

Africanism has taken almost twenty years to write and I have met so many people and debated the topics inside this book with over the years.

These people have helped influence my thinking along my book's journey and I do apologise, as they are too numerous to name. I remain extremely grateful to everyone for their deep insights.

However, I have to give an extra special thanks to a few people in particular, including Robin Walker, whose book 'When We Ruled' helped deepen my understanding of pre-colonial African history. I would also like to thank John Pilger, a world renowned investigative journalist, who I met at a book signing in London and who gave me encouragement both personally and vicariously through his many books and documentaries to inspire me to complete this work.

John Pilger put me through to Patrick Bond, a political economist and research professor at the University of KwaZulu-Natal School Development Studies in Durban, South Africa, who also deserves special thanks. He received me as if I was an old friend rather than a complete stranger.

Make no mistake, this book stands on the shoulders of giants; our African ancestors, African slaves, African freedom fighters, African icons past and present. It also draws from the fortitude and suffering of people globally — regardless of race, colour or creed. I salute the multitude of ordinary people, the unsung heroes, who have achieved so many extraordinary things.

Chukwueloka Obiamiwe

London

Contents

PREFACE

"My people are destroyed for lack of knowledge..."
Hosea 4:6

Africa is a continent of immeasurable beauty and immense biodiversity. The African people live on a continent endowed with an abundance of natural and human resources.

Unfortunately, Africa is also a continent scarred by a prolonged history of human suffering and strife. The endemic nature of poverty and deprivation begs the question: why so little in the face of so much?

There is no simple answer to this question. Like the metaphor about the elephant in the room, it cannot be addressed directly because the people who tell us about white elephants say so.

There was once a time when the white elephants openly rampaged and laid waste to the African continent. They proudly trumpeted their African spoils for all to hear.

Later, the white elephants decided they would rather lead their puppet African elephants on the rampage. Now, the white elephants sit quietly in the room, careful not to distract attention from their African puppets.

This book is a story about the living legacy of the white elephants' ravages across Africa. It is a story about the African people, so traumatized by their experiences that they have lost sight of who they are.

Generations of Africans, disconnected from their roots, physically and emotionally scarred by poverty and war, concentrate all their attention on surviving into the next day.

We all look at life through our 'personal constructs'. Personal constructs are perceptions drawn from our socialization: religious, intellectual and cultural beliefs. Owing to centuries of Western misinformation, it is safe to generalize that most people have negative personal constructs about Africa and its people. To deconstruct these entrenched negative perceptions, even among Africans, it is necessary to drill through their negative and hardened personal constructs on Africa, down to a spiritual level.

The true essence of human beings emanates from deep within the soul. Therefore, the veil of consciousness through which our personal constructs are manifest is merely a hologram and is consequently easy to manipulate. The ability of Europeans to manipulate our subconscious minds to determine our actions is a source of great wealth and power to the white supremacy power structure and a source of great suffering and deprivation to everyone else.

Following the transatlantic slave trade, Africa experienced a sharp reversal in its fortunes and a precipitous decline into a dependent and prostrate global position. Despite the complex and confusing modern African history bestowed upon them by their European colonial masters, a clear thread of exploitation is traceable from the tragedy of the transatlantic slavery up until present day.

Africa's problems do not require further elaboration — a cursory look across the continent from east to west and from north to south is sufficient.

In the west, people are literally bombarded with negative images and statistics emanating from the African continent. Every year, millions of Africans suffer and die needlessly from preventable causes like disease, famine and war.

However, behind all the doom and gloom is a vibrant, warm, resilient and creative people, still largely unknown to the rest of the world.

Pliny's comment, 'Ex Africa semper aliquid novi' [Out of Africa always something new] remains true, even today.

At first glance, it would appear that only chaos abounds across the African continent but a closer and more objective look into the struggles of the African people reveals a clear method to the madness. Africa's complex problems cannot be understood without reference to its global context. When Africa's problems are seen through the prism of Western geopolitics and strategic imperatives, it becomes clear that not only is the chaos 'organized' but it is also a necessary precondition for western domination in Africa. On further analysis, it is possible to conclude that Africans do not lack any intellectual or physical ability to improve their position nor is it due to Darwin's survival of the fittest theory as some Eurocentrics may argue. However, it is down to another vital but largely overlooked reason: western social engineering.

Since Africa was struck by the triple tsunamis of the transatlantic slave trade, colonization, and neo-colonization, its people have been blown wide off their natural course of development. It is important to note that Africans were not just physically enslaved and colonized; they were also mentally enslaved and colonized as an essential part of the subjugation process. African self-determination and actualization was not to be tolerated at any level.

Stripped of their identity, culture, and history, 'Africans' were redefined in Western culture and social hierarchy as its lowest common denominator.

Today, Africans urgently need to rebrand and reinvent themselves in order to re-establish themselves in the world.

Making this critical paradigm shift in the African psyche is not only the crucial first step but also the principal stepping stone for all other initiatives. All Africans individually and collectively must make a conscious choice to cross this paradigm. Once Africans become aware of the urgent need for psychological freedom they will, in time, become self-determining and actualizing. Africans who have made a conscious choice to become self-determining will naturally seek viable options for themselves and their people. Many Africans who have unwittingly acted in concert with the imperialistic designs of western powers to exploit their own people, may choose to reconsider their position.

In order to understand Africa's plight, it is necessary to stand back and form an objective unbiased opinion outside the paradigm created for Africans by the West. People of any race and colour who objectively challenge and reinterpret the long-held negative myths and misconceptions about Africa will soon realize the true state of affairs and the man-made nature of most of Africa's problems. This new understanding will help people reposition themselves to find constructive solutions.

Africanism explores the legacies of Africa's historical precedents and the impact on their psychology, science and religion. Africanism is about every African individual — how they perceive themselves, how much value they have for themselves and other Africans like them. It is about their desire to fulfil their dreams and ensure the future for themselves and their families — and to impact positively on the world in general.

For Africans living in the west, it is about how racial stereotyping and discrimination breeds low self-esteem, low confidence levels and underachievement in their children. It is also about childhood poverty, poor education, housing and health. Africans in the diaspora often experience no jobs, bad jobs, low income, unnecessary poverty, social injustice and even murder.

In Africa itself conditions are far worse — where life for many is no less than a struggle to secure and sustain the basics of life - food, clean water, health care and education. It is about unnecessary suffering and death from preventable diseases, conflict and many other causes. It is a story of extreme poverty and deprivation in the midst of plenty. It is also a story of inferiority complexes, lack of sovereignty, infrastructure and opportunities both locally and internationally. There is no African in Africa or in the Western diaspora or elsewhere who is not affected, in one way or another, by the white supremacy power structure.

I, like millions of others forming the African diaspora, grew up in the Western matrix. When my insatiable desire to acquire knowledge and the need to understand my personal and vicarious experiences of racism collided, this book was born. Unwittingly, my quest to get a better understanding of my personal experiences of racism uncorked a white supremacy system of global inequality.

This book does not claim to be a comprehensive study of African issues, neither could it be. Such is the length, breadth and depth of the subject matter that it would be an exercise in futility to try to cover it all in one volume. Many key points would easily be lost in the multitude of facts. However, it hopes to provide a basis for a better understanding of Africa's problems. It is written in a style aimed at reaching a wide readership while remaining well researched and relevant.

As human beings live not just as physical but also as intelligent, emotional and spiritual beings, it is necessary to address our problems on these different levels as well, hence the need for a unique approach.

The continuum of history is such that there is a significant overlap and interplay between the physical, intellectual, emotional and spiritual levels of all our lives. The west's heavily edited, revised and redacted version of African history needs to be vigorously challenged.

In order to develop a more accurate version of African history and the effects of slavery and racism, the first few chapters of the book deal with African prehistory. Then it follows the downturn of Africa and the evolution of racism through the transatlantic slave trade, colonization, segregation and apartheid. It goes on to explore the history of European Christianity and its effects on the African mind and journeys through the lives of Africans under colonization and in modern Africa and Europe. It dissects the psychology of racism and the psychology of freedom of the mind and touches on the socio-economic effects of globalization and neo-colonialism.

But Africa's problems are only microcosms of wider global issues such as the effects of globalization, world poverty, pandemics like AIDS and environmental problems like global warming. Therefore what transpires outside Africa and its diaspora has a great deal of relevance to the story and may help to balance the west's negative and distorted view of Africa.

A reversal in the fortunes of Africa could translate into a revival of the fortunes of the human race and the world as a whole. Every human being, regardless of race, colour or creed, thus has some moral obligation to make a positive contribution of sorts towards making the world a better place for all.

All that Africa and its people have achieved today has been through freedom alone - and this book is an attempt to expose and help break the chains of psychological slavery that has enslaved the minds of many Africans. It also hopes to release the awesome powers of self-determination that true freedom and equality can release, not just for Africans, but also for the hope of a freer and more equitable world.

PART ONE:
GLOBAL CONTEXT

CHAPTER ONE

THE CALM BEFORE THE STORM

'The world is made a dangerous place, not because of those who do evil, but because of those who look on and do nothing.' **Albert Einstein**[1]

The earth is steadily shrinking… metaphorically speaking. Advances in satellite and information technology allow us to be in touch with anyone, anywhere in the world, in real time. Air travel can transport you to any part of the globe in hours or days. The National Aeronautics and Space Agency [NASA] is currently searching for life on Mars. However, despite all our technological advances and burgeoning human population, we inhabit a world that is increasingly lonely and cruel.

Global poverty is on the rise, yet in the west, people spend millions of dollars yearly on acquiring luxury goods like chocolate, cars and jewellery — an expenditure that is well over ten times the amount required to provide food, clean water and medicines to billions of impoverished people around the world.

The world's population officially reached seven billion in September 2011, placing already constrained global natural resources in further jeopardy.

Unfortunately, Western capitalism penalises the 'perpetrators' and the 'victims' alike.

The word 'global', in modern times, has become an ominous prefix describing the complex challenges facing all men all over our planet. The greatest environmental challenge modern man has faced — global warming — is a direct result of the globalization of capitalism and conflict.

Therefore, the dark clouds that have gathered over what should be the shining example of human civilization on Earth should be the concern of every human being on Earth. Is it?

Even as these dark looming global forces conspire to unleash a 'perfect storm', in response to the unsustainable growth and expansion of human civilization, the vast majority of people still go about their business, content in their blissful state of ignorance and unawareness of their surroundings.

After all, for centuries doom-mongers have falsely predicted a dramatic, cataclysmic end to all life on Earth. When the predicted dates for Earth's demise come and go, we all breathe a sigh of relief — and life goes on as usual.

However, reality is more mundane because, in the last one hundred years alone, quietly unnoticed by modern man, thousands of animal and plant species have quietly slipped into extinction. Climate change has been gathering pace all around us and leading scientists to fear that we may have already passed the tipping point. The dinosaurs did not put up a gallant last stand before they became extinct.

Modern human beings have steadily alienated themselves from healthy interaction between themselves and their environment so that today many people find it extremely difficult to interpret the effects of these seemingly disparate events in their environment or their physical and psychological wellbeing. Out of sight is out of mind and in such a blasé state of mind many people are not even remotely concerned about the effects of global warming, nuclear weapon proliferation, increasing global conflicts and dwindling natural resources such as wildlife, land and water.

If there was any large group of human beings who are sailing uncomfortably closer to the seemingly unthinkable possibility of human extinction, it would have to be Africans and their diaspora. Many life-changing world events go unnoticed and unappreciated by many Africans, who have largely settled for a reactionary existence. They only respond, in knee-jerk fashion, to the most urgent and present contingencies they face.

This is largely due to Africa's near total dependence on the west and their general lack of preparedness to counter fabricated and natural events that threaten their survival. In order to understand why Africans have fallen from their former status as the origin of all men and progenitors of all human civilizations to their current prostrate condition, we must understand the links between our history, environment, modern-day civilization and the clear and present danger that all human beings face from global warming, war and poverty.

To do so, we must be as willing to accept the magnificent technological advances and conveniences that define modern human civilization, as we are prepared to accept the ugly underbelly of the methods by which they have been acquired and the effects of the globalization of capitalism and war on this global human village.

We must not glibly assign the global predicament human beings face today to mere happenstance or bad luck. We do not live in a vacuum and the world is closely interconnected. For every gallon of fuel we use, every piece of paper we write on, every item of clothing we wear, every time we fly to our ever-cheaper holiday destinations, a penalty is exacted somewhere else on the planet. The price of our consumer culture consists, not only of what we have paid for our material goods and services or the cost to the multinationals and airlines to acquire their products so cheaply. We must also consider the real price to another human being, far removed, and to the global ecosystem we call the environment. It is they who have paid for our conveniences and lifestyle.

No doubt Western capitalism has brought us many global technological advances. However, it has also facilitated the widespread habit of smoking which has brought us a variety of cancers, like lung cancer, bowel and bladder cancers and the proliferation of heart disease, diabetes and obesity. The reality is that the technological and other medical advances capitalism has delivered lags far behind the actual needs of over 90% of the world's population.

Western capitalism has always sought to procure goods and profits for the least possible investment leading to the creation of 'sweat shops'. These outsourced Western factories, mainly in Third world countries, are characterised by poor working conditions and safety regulations.

On December 3rd 1984, nearly 3,000 people died in Bhopal, India, after forty tons of lethal gas leaked from a chemical plant owned by a US company called Union Carbide. It was the worst industrial accident known at that time. Many more suffered permanent disability from blindness, kidney and liver damage. A further 15,000 deaths were directly related to the leak. [2]

Sadly, history often repeats itself. Death by 'capitalism' was again sharply brought into focus by the demise of nearly 1,200 Bangladeshi Primark sweatshop workers in a horrifying building collapse in Bangladesh in 2012.[3]

Today, capitalism driven industrial waste dump pollutants, including lead, mercury, chromium and pesticides, poison more than 125 million people in 49 different low and middle-income nations around the world.[4]

In addition, the countless wars waged by the west for acquisition of coveted resources have killed and impoverished billions of people.

The globalization of European capitalism is based around a hierarchical structure of western world hegemony. Every manufactured system, organization and hierarchy has a way of thinking that defines and propels it. The organized system of procurement of global capital is underpinned, defined and driven by the notion of white supremacy, superiority and racism.

As we shall see, western racism is, in real terms, a socially transmitted psychological disorder that underpins the only global and functionally active form of racism in the world today, the white supremacy global power structure. This complicated system of global apartheid is predicated primarily on race, colour and money.

Racism operates in all areas of human activity, including economics, politics, the military, social life, religion and sports. It manifests itself locally in the West mainly through the effects of institutionalized racism and globally via the capitalist system of imperialism or globalization. Virtually no human being or living thing is immune to its rapacity.

Even if you tried to seclude yourself on an uninhabited island, you would still be exposed to the sting in the tail of the white supremacy power structure — extensive environmental destruction and the effects of global warming.

Western imperialism does not seek or want your permission. As far as people of colour are concerned, what matters to the white supremacist power structure, are the human and mineral resources that they possess or represent.

Western imperialism does not care whether you submit to its rigid social hierarchy, voluntarily or involuntarily. It seeks to impose its will, either through mental slavery or by its most-favoured method - brute force.

Yet, despite the glaring inequalities and brutality of Western capitalism, many victims and perpetuators alike, accept its lexicon and logic. Human beings are inherently competitive and many will selfishly accept the suffering of other people as long as their own advantages and privileges are preserved.

However, Western capitalism goes much further. It encourages brutality and rewards the exploitation of the weaker and less privileged. It promotes and sustains every negative human trait known, as it relentlessly pursues the acquisition of material wealth to the exclusion of any other consideration.

Over time, Africans became assimilated and assigned the lowest rungs of the hierarchy of white supremacy. Critically, Africans are also in possession of virtually unlimited human and natural resources. For this reason, of all the non-white people in the world, this fact alone has singled Africans out for special treatment.

In general, Africans have reacted apathetically to the diverse and profound psychological and physical threats to their existence and wellbeing. This is a direct consequence of their marginal position at the base of the pyramidal hierarchy of the global system of white supremacy.

Why revisit slavery and racism now, some may ask? Apologists will argue that Africa is riddled with problems and that these problems are caused by Africans themselves. It is true that there is trouble everywhere - ethnic divisions, religious fanatics, tribalism, nepotism, corruption, war and poverty, to name but a few problems.

However, imagine for a moment, that Africa and her diaspora collectively was a severely injured trauma patient. On arrival in the emergency room the specialist doctors will rightly, not attempt to fix its broken bones or deal with its psychological stress first. Rather they will perform emergency cardiopulmonary resuscitation tending to the airways, breathing and circulation [ABC] first, knowing that failure to deal with either an airway, breathing or circulatory problem will lead to immediate death. Africa's problem is that Western imperialism and racism critically threatens all three.

A closer inspection will reveal the intimate relation the west has with Africa's most significant problems — war, poverty and corruption. Should Africa reverse these problems with bespoke democracy, development and the uplifting of its people from poverty, it would be remarkable how insignificant the differences between Africans will seem and how quickly many conflicts would be resolved.

Modern Western imperialism and racism have only changed suits and are very much alive today. The brutal, racially motivated, extrajudicial murder of African American men by white policemen in the US is being played out on social media for the whole world to see.

People who follow European football will be aware of several high profile cases involving racism - cases involving former top premiership footballers, John Terry and Luis Suarez, for example. In fact, racism in sports is quite common. Monkey chants dogged the black British players during the European Cup football finals in Poland and Croatia in 2012. The former FIFA president, Sepp Blatter's suggestion that the players should shake hands and forget the racial slights did no justice.[5]

In October 2019, during the Euro 2020 qualifiers in Bulgaria, racist Bulgarian fans greeted black players with monkey chants and Nazi salutes. Ostensibly, it is true that African people are no longer shackled and forced to work from dusk to dawn as chattel slaves. However, it is also true, that the expression of racism is now far more refined and less obvious than it used to be.

Racism used to be on the streets in the UK in the sixties and seventies. The words 'school run' had a very literal meaning when I was a child. While living in Liverpool, I remember being chased home through alleyways after school by gangs of white skinheads, offended by nothing more than the colour of my skin. It took the UK Race Relations Act of 1968 to gradually move racism off the streets into people's homes and institutions in the UK.[6] Signposts reading 'No blacks, dogs or Irish' have long come down but institutional racism is still very much alive.

Most Africans and their diaspora in the west can testify to the fact that modern-day institutional racism does not always involve the open use of racial slurs but rather centres around attitudes and behaviours that disadvantage and exclude them. Even the first black president of the United States, Barack Obama, was not exempt from racism. Given that modern America was built by immigrants, how bizarre that President Obama's Kenyan origins became a pivotal point in the run up to his re-election. Donald Trump's 'birther' campaign against Barack Obama whipped up so much negative emotion and doubt that Obama felt forced to publish his birth certificate online to quell doubters.[7] In September 2009, the shocking and disrespectful heckling of President Obama in the US Congress by a Republican representative, Joe Wilson, led former US President, Jimmy Carter, to state that Senator Wilson's actions were an act 'based on racism' and rooted in his fears of a black president.[8]

In February 2012, the killing of 17-year-old Trayvon Martin by George Zimmerman in Florida, USA, sent race-related shock waves throughout America. It was simply a case of being an African American male in the wrong place at the wrong time.[9]

Unfortunately, Trayvon's killing was only a prelude to what was to come. On August 9th 2014 another young African American was practically 'executed' by a white policeman for 'jay walking' on the street. Unarmed and with his hands up in the air, an 18 year old African American, Mike Brown, was shot several times and killed by Darren Wilson, a white police officer. Brown's last words were:

"I don't have a gun, stop shooting."[10]

The race riots that erupted in Ferguson, Missouri, and spread all over the USA, reflect the deep racial tension and distrust between the unrepresentative white police force and the largely African American population it polices.

On July 23rd 2014, in New York City, Eric Garner was killed after being put in a chokehold by white police officer for 'street selling'. He was heard calling out, "I can't breathe" several times before he became unconscious yet the white police officers surrounding him paid no attention and made no attempt to resuscitate him until it was too late.[11]

Sadly, the justified homicide of African American males has continued unabated despite all the negative images on popular social media.

On December 8th 2016, in the twilight of his Presidency, Obama in an interview with CNN's Fareed Zakaria openly admitted that he had faced racism while in office. President Obama asked Zakaria the rhetorical questions:

"Are there folks whose primary concern about me has been that I seem-foreign — the other? Are those who champion the birther movement feeding off this bias? Absolutely."

David Axelrod, a former senior advisor to President Obama, also appeared on the show and concurred that racial undercurrents had plagued Obama's presidency. He stated: *"It's indisputable that there was a ferocity to the opposition and lack of respect to him that was a function of race."*[12]

President Obama's presidency was marked by an unprecedented level of Republican party obstruction. A filibuster in the United States Senate is an obstructive tactic used to prevent a measure from being brought to a vote.

According to Senator Ben Cardin: *"We've seen more filibusters on judicial nominees by the Republicans under President Obama than we saw in the whole history of the United States Senate."*[13]

An author, Adam Albright-Hanna, stated:

"They did it 86 times to every other president combined. 82 times to Obama alone."

The Mother Jones Charts run by a non-profit organisation graphically illustrates the filibustering President Obama received at the hands of the Republicans compared to other presidents.[14]

Today, Africans and their diaspora suffer an all-pervasive white apartheid system of micro and macro inequities that blight their lives and the potential of their children from cradle to grave. For this reason, it is essential to explore the genesis and effects of institutionalized racism in order to deliver Africans from their eternal bondage.

CHAPTER TWO
DISSECTING EUROPEAN RACISM

'The black slave after receiving this indoctrination shall carry on and will become self-refuelling and self-generating for hundreds of years, maybe thousands.' **Willie Lynch**[1]

'If you do not understand white supremacy [Racism] - What it is, and how it works – everything else that you understand will only confuse you.' **Neely Fuller Jr.**[2]

Willie Lynch is thought to have been a white slave-owner based in the West Indies. To assist other white slave owners, he allegedly produced a handbook or guide on how to subjugate their African slaves. He graphically outlined the process of 'seasoning' slaves with the purpose of breaking them down physically, mentally, emotionally and spiritually.

The Willie Lynch story was widely circulated on the internet in the late 1990s. Excerpts of the Willie Lynch story were quoted by Louis Farrakhan during the one million-man march on October 16th 1995. Rapper Talib Kweli rapped about the Willie Lynch story in his song 'Know that'. However, the authenticity of the story has been questioned and it is now thought to have been a hoax. An African American Professor of Journalism at Colombia University, William Cobb, articulately outlined the inconsistencies in the so-called Willie Lynch account. [3]

However, while the Willie Lynch story does not stand up to close scrutiny, there is overwhelming anecdotal evidence to support widespread use of the tactics described in the discredited Willie Lynch story — hence its mention in this book.[4]

The French 'Code Noir' and the white apartheid system in South Africa, were based on a hierarchical system of racial discrimination, stratified on the basis of colour and minor physical differences, that characterises white supremacy all over the world today. Sadly, even the discredited Willie Lynch's guide does not scratch the surface when it comes to the actual physical, mental and emotional deprivation that African slaves endured.

The 'seasoning' method, as described in the Willie Lynch fable, were in fact, widely employed, in various guises, by white slave-holders and later by European colonizers. It was first applied to African slaves taken to the Caribbean and the Americas but it was also modified and used on African populations everywhere. The process of 'seasoning' slaves resulted in extremely harmful psychological effects on the physical and mental wellbeing and on inner psyche of Africans. Mental slavery remains the greatest obstacle in Africa's quest for the expression of true freedom and equality.

Within the Western paradigm, mental slavery is perhaps the most significant reason why African self-knowledge is of the utmost importance. Only Africans who have resigned themselves to a lifetime of unnecessary suffering — and by default, resigned the future generations of their children and grandchildren to the same — should ignore this. The only way Africa can begin to grow and regenerate is to break the perpetuating cycle of psychological inferiority and physical dependence.

Racism is essentially a socially transmitted psychological disease. Since the main repository of our social experiences and memories lies in the subconscious mind, it makes sense to have a basic understanding of how the subconscious mind works in order to understand how racism operates and how it is transmitted.

If the soul is the immortal everlasting essence of human beings, then our subconscious mind is the super biological computer that processes its wishes. The unfathomable essence we call life is translated into thoughts and physical actions by our subconscious mind.

Our subconscious and conscious minds are God's greatest gifts to man. The power of the human mind is what separates us from other mammals. The subconscious mind produces a subtle yet powerful drive that is required to sustain life and motivate one to seek a certain quality of life. Less than 10% of our subconscious motivations filter into our conscious minds yet we tend to think our conscious thoughts, plans and aspirations are the first time that we conceived of them.

Therefore, like a powerful genie, the subconscious mind can make our deepest wishes come true. However, we must be careful what we wish for because the genie leaves it up to the conscious mind to make the appropriate wishes.

Alas, despite being equipped with the most powerful supercomputer known to man, a creator and a transducer of life essence into physical form, thought and action, we know next to nothing about the subconscious mind and even less about how it works.

Unfortunately, we only use a limited portion of our subconscious ability. Just like many of the modern gadgets we buy, like our computers and mobile phones, the functionality of our brains is greatly underutilized. The human brain has evolved for over 500 million years and, even though it is an incredibly complex organ, it is still possible to break down its function into simple parts. When compared to other mammals, human beings have the biggest brain weight to body weight ratio — referred to sometimes as the encephalization quotient.

In the 1960s, a neuroscientist by the name of Paul D. MacLean introduced a Triune brain model to help simplify the understanding of brain structure and physiology.[5]

The oldest parts of the brain, the cerebellum and brain stem, are referred to as the reptilian brain and help to maintain basic body functions such as the heart rate, balance and body temperature.

The next part of the brain to develop is referred to as the limbic system and includes parts of the brain called the hippocampus, amygdala and hypothalamus. These parts of the brain regulate our emotions, motivations and short and long term memory. Finally, the most recent part of our brain to develop is called the neo-cortex and accounts for about 80% of our brain mass. The cortex is responsible for conscious thought, imagination, language and an almost infinite and flexible learning capacity.

The reptilian brain is shared with other mammals. The limbic system developed about 150 million years ago but remarkably the neo-cortex, which defines human beings, developed only two to three million years ago. A neurotransmitter called dopamine — of particular interest in the development of mental slavery — is largely located in the caudate nucleus in an area of the limbic system called the ventral tegmental area or VTA. Active in the dopamine reward system, dopamine plays a pivotal role in regulating our subconscious motivations around reward experiences like food and sex. Dopamine is a feel good hormone, like serotonin which is released during sex, compulsive activity and drug taking.

The dopamine system is extremely old and has been shown to have acted as a neurotransmitter as far back as five hundred million years ago in the Cambrian era. Dopamine is also referred to by neuroscientists as a 'teaching signal' as it modulates behaviour by subconscious learning. Human beings share this system with other mammals, fish and invertebrates.

Dopamine plays an important role in reward learning in all mammals, echinoderms, arthropods and even molluscs. Scientists have shown that it is possible to train nematodes, planarians, molluscs and vertebrates to repeat an action if it is consistently followed by an increase in their dopamine levels.

The dopamine reward system motivates us to seek things of biological value necessary for our survival, like food, water, sexual partners, and seek social relationships and social co-operation. Dopamine and serotonin binds to neuroreceptors in the brain that release opioid like endorphins that fill us with feelings of pleasure and mild euphoria. The fulfilment of these innate desires are 'rewarded' by the release of these hormones, which cause us to seek out the experience again and again. Food and drug addiction share a common pathway in the dopamine reward system.

However, the dopamine system does not only reward pleasure but also appears to motivate one negatively. The dopamine system therefore motivates us not only to seek what we need or like but avoid negative experiences as well. So powerful is the system that even recreating the imaginary conditions around the object of interest will release dopamine.

On balance, it is likely that over several centuries, in the face of the persistent hardships inflicted by the white supremacy system in the form of slavery and colonization and the neo-colonial system of global inequality, their natural dopamine reward system was distorted. This might have led to enslaved Africans sub-optimally accepting white domination and subjugation. Mentally enslaved Africans often seek temporary, meaningless consumerism and subservience to white dominion above the sacrifices and rewards of self-sufficiency and independence. The net result is an apathetic state of persistent poverty in which they can never free themselves from their suffering or the clutches of their white masters. Biological psychiatrists, Rachel Yehuda et al demonstrated an association of preconception parental trauma with epigenetic alterations that is evident in both exposed parent and offspring providing potential insight into how severe psychophysiological trauma can have intergenerational effects.[6]

It is only logical to expect that the longer Africans remain captive and downtrodden the more embedded these genetic and neurophysiological changes will be. These changes are most likely to be greater in the former African slaves and Africans in diaspora and be corresponding less in African's who only reside in the Western paradigm but were not former slaves. It stands to reason that African slaves who endured their capture, the middle passage and worked on plantations suffered more physical, mental and emotional torture than Africans who did not experience the full spectrum of European slavery.

However, the good news is that human behaviour can be modified quickly in the face of the right knowledge and environment.

Our ancestors from all races and colours around the world recognized the staggering potential of the subconscious mind and tried to access it using all forms of prayers, religious practices, transcendental meditation and self-hypnosis.

The subconscious mind also has the critical role of regulating our body functions and emotions and, what's more, it acts as the repository of our memories. When we recall an event, we are only tapping into the memory bank in our subconscious. Consciously learned skills are saved in the subconscious mind from where they can be accessed later, like walking, riding a bicycle or driving a car.

To a large extent, the filtering of external and internal stimuli by the subconscious mind is protective. Otherwise, the deluge of different types of stimuli would quickly overwhelm our conscious mind. The subconscious mind filters all our brain activity and presents our conscious mind only with sufficient information and, critically, only what it requests.

Over time human beings have developed an innate ability to instantaneously gather, process and utilize external information. This also means that we all instinctively try to reduce information down to a digestible size. Our subconscious mind tends to categorize data into powerful symbols and this can lead to stereotyping. The subconscious mind is also the seat of our imagination and intuition. When we intuitively deduce another person's thoughts or feelings, it is because we allowed our subconscious mind to interpret for us what we consciously do not know. The subconscious mind also provides us the 'symbol logic' of our dreams.

Occasionally people experience flashes of 'intuition' or 'genius' but by rights we should be experiencing a steady stream of inspiration. Unfortunately, modern man has learned to disable his subconscious mind and rely only on what he physically sees, feels or hears — in other words, rely exclusively on the conscious mind.

Unfortunately, the subconscious mind does not distinguish between reality and imagination and in co-operation with the conscious mind learns to classify information by deleting, distorting and generalizing from it.

As we have seen, because of the vast amount of information the subconscious mind processes, it provides information to the conscious mind on a 'need-to-know' basis, depending on our unique survival and socialization needs.

In so doing, the mind may distort information so that it conforms to its socialization or belief systems or delete information by concentrating on certain aspects of the information it receives in order to let it maintain the status quo and keep all rational thought processes pointing in the same direction. It may also generalize by drawing conclusions based on only two or three experiences, thereby readily stereotyping people it comes across socially.

Given these facts, we can safely conclude that racism is not the preserve of just Europeans. All human beings stereotype based on their cultural upbringing and have the potential to be racist to varying degrees depending on their social norms, religions and cultures.

We are primarily interested in white racism or supremacy because of the global impact of its racially motivated and determined social hierarchy and because white supremacy and the white-mediated capitalist system also affects Africans and their diasporas the most.

The Western capitalist system produces an intense, alienating and negative socializing stress that provides fertile grounds for the development and perpetuation of racism by placing modern man under the constant pressure of materialism. People are pressurized to conform to societal hierarchy and norms, as functional superiors or inferiors. They usually do not have time to explore healthy human interactions as they scurry around to meet the daily pressures of life. Under this intense social pressure, most people tend to be satisfied with superficial generalizations about one another. These generalizations, once inbred, are replicated from generation to generation.

Human beings, using only the minuscule powers of the subconscious mind they have been able to access, have been able to motivate themselves to extraordinary heights of achievement and endeavour. They have always tried to push their boundaries and accomplish the 'impossible'. Breakthroughs in science and technology, arts and literature have all come from a desire to push the boundaries of human existence ever further. Conversely, the misuses of power, the lack of motivation to survive, achieve, innovate and strive for more have mired others in unfathomable social depths.

Such is the power of our subconscious minds in determining our present and future that we are all exactly where we are, what we are and who we are today because of our motivation and drive — or, indeed, a lack of motivation. Nobody moves a single muscle in any direction without having the subconscious or conscious motivation to do so. As human beings are both the product of nature and nurture, we simultaneously bear the burden of our history and the promise of our futures as the prevailing environmental conditions mould our desires and ambitions accordingly, especially in the early stages of life. The most powerful product of the subconscious mind is the potential to be self-determining and actualizing. The subconscious mind provides the desire to compete as well as a clear picture as to what can be achieved. Our subconscious motivation provides the determination to stay on track.

This subconscious drive to achieve the near impossible not only separates human beings from other mammals, but has also given us the imagination and a clear vision of what we need to do to achieve it.

The Bible quotation: *'Where there is no vision, the people perish'* [Proverbs 29:18], remains as valid now as then. Eulogizing about the power of the subconscious mind, the famous scientist, Albert Einstein, was impelled to state: *"Imagination is more important than knowledge."*[7]

The saying that the eyes are the windows to the soul has more than a ring of truth to it because we see with our minds and not our eyes. Our eyes, which are sensory receptors, and the visual pathway collect visual stimuli and carry them to specific areas in the brain. In the brain, external stimuli are transduced and produced as images by our brains. This is no different to the way sensory receptors in our fingers transmit impulses to the brain where it is translated as touch.

What we call vision, is sensory stimuli and perceptions, translated in the brain. Many neurological experiments have shown that stimulation of the visual cortex can induce visions or hallucinations in the subjects. Seeing is not always believing. Therefore, of all the human senses, the sense of vision is perhaps the most powerful. Even so, the sense of smell, touch, hearing, and taste perform essentially the same function, namely, collecting external stimuli and transmitting them to the brain where they are processed into what we see, hear, touch, taste and smell. The reality is that human beings 'think' and not 'see'. After all, the eyes and the visual pathways are only a complex system of collecting visual stimuli for the brain to process.

A brain researcher, Dr. Win Wenger, suggested that over 90% of our processing of information is and less that than 10% verbal. It is often stated that we underuse our brain by over 90% of its capacity most of the time.[8]

However, there are exceptional cases were 'blind' people have been able to develop an acoustic vision or echolocation. They make clicking sounds and use acoustic vision, very much the same way a bat can fly in pitch-black nights using sonar. There was the incredible case of Benjamin Underwood, who lost his eyesight as a child due to a rare but dangerous tumour of the eyes, a retinoblastoma. However, he was able to compensate with using his hearing and echolocation to such an extent that he was able to ride a bicycle and roller skate on familiar streets.[9]

When our eyes are wide open, we call what we see vision. When we 'see' with our eyes shut, we call it imagination. There is no successful person in any field of life who has succeeded without having a 'vision' of success. Sport psychologists often advise top athletes to imagine winning at their chosen sports. The subconscious mind can shape our realities, like putty in the hands of a sculptor, and turn our vision from a dream into reality.

Human beings like to believe that they are all-knowing about their environment. In fact, we have enormous physical, psychological, emotional, intellectual and perceptual blind spots that prevent us from appreciating our surroundings for what they are. We do not see or smell the air we breathe. We cannot feel the earth's orbit, even though we can appreciate day and night. We all feel a false sense of stillness and stability as we stand on the surface of the earth yet it is wobbling and thundering along at sixty-seven thousand miles an hour as it orbits the sun. Human beings can only see light, hear sounds or perceive touch in specific bandwidths. It is common knowledge that the silent dog whistle is inaudible to humans because we cannot pick up low-frequency sounds like dogs do. Magicians and illusionists exploit the physical and perceptual blind spots of our visual pathway to create illusions. They use this knowledge to deceive their audiences. By using diversions and optical illusions, they can trick the brain into thinking what they are seeing is real. In Africa, 'native' doctors are also in this business to fool their unsuspecting audience into thinking these tricks are due to spiritual powers or witchcraft.

As we shall see, these physical and perceptual blind spots are also fertile hunting grounds for white capitalists.

Our perceptions are built around our socialization as personal constructs and more often blind us to reality rather than expose the underlying truth. There are distinct differences between the physiological process of seeing and the psychological process of perceiving. Human beings with sound eyesight simply have to open their eyes in order to see. However, our perception is coloured by a wide range of influences, such as the environment, culture and our socialization.

The illustrations that follow prove that when we 'see', our brains have to combine the existing physiological process of vision with the intellectual and psychological process of perception to interpret the visual stimuli:

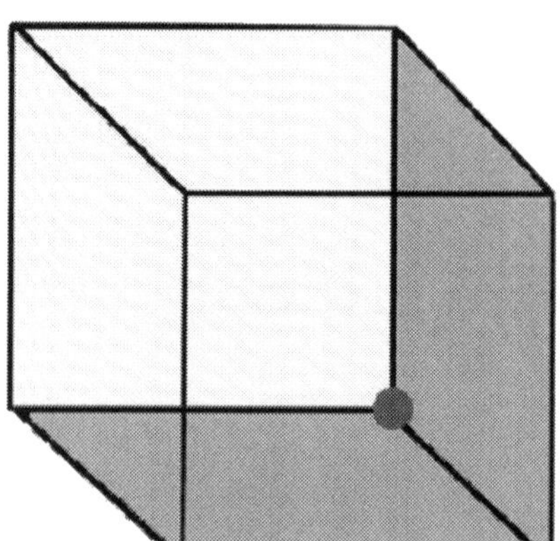

The Necker Cube: the cube appears to 'flip' so that the top appears to be in a different place after staring at it for about 30 seconds or more. The diagram does not give the brain enough perceptual information and it perceives a two-dimensional image as a three-dimensional object and flips it repeatedly to find the best interpretation.

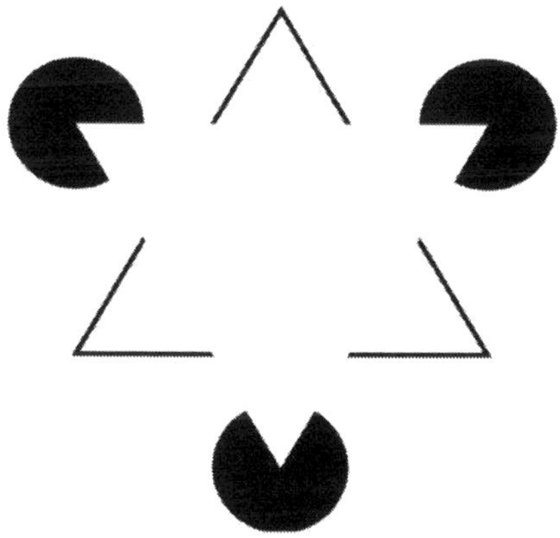

Kanza Triangle: based on the Gestalt laws of perceptual organisation an illusionary white triangle appears in the centre, as our brain tends to view objects that are linked together as a cohesive whole. Our brains close the gaps to create an image that is recognisable and understood.

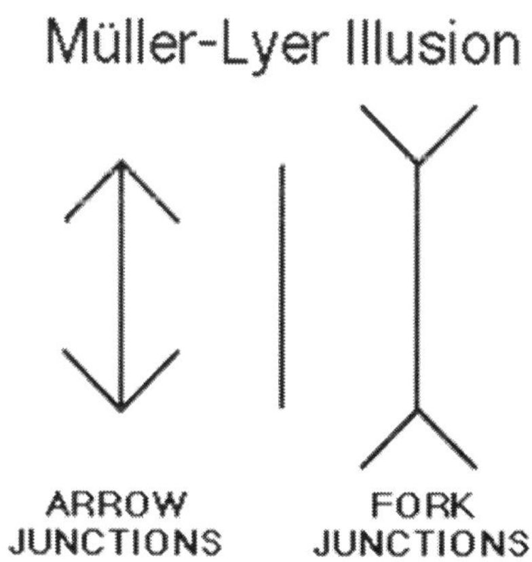

The Mulle –Lyer illusion: is one of these lines longer than the other? The lines with the arrow points inwards and arms out appear longer than the opposite even though they are exactly the same length.

These illusions confirm that our interpretation of external stimuli is subject to extensive modulation of our brains for it to conform to our definition of our surrounding and of whom we think we are.[10]

We are all familiar with the mirage of water as the hot sun reflects of off the hot sands of the desert or on hot asphalt. What about the beautiful vista of the sun dipping below the horizon during sunset? Many will be surprised to discover that it is actually an illusion. The sun's rays are bent by the curvature of the earth and, in addition, they only reach our eyes about eight minutes after they leave the sun. Therefore, in reality; the sun has already dipped well below the horizon while the mirage we perceive persists.

Psychologists Marshall H Segall et al concluded that the environment significantly affects the way we perceive our surroundings.[11]

The three main factors affecting our perception include:

Motivation: when we are hungry, pictures of food look better. Depressed people see more 'grey' than colour. Happier people seem to have a deeper and greater appreciation of colour.

Emotion: we are less tolerant of minor irritations when in an anxious and depressed mood than when feeling normal.

Beliefs: a religious person who believes in miracles is more likely to see one or assign a given outcome to a miracle than perhaps an atheist.

Thus, what racists 'see' when they look at the dark skin of a person is clouded by their perceptions and prejudices concerning those people.

The human brain is also functionally divided up into several parts or lobes. Each lobe has a number of functions. For example, the visual cortex in the occipital lobe converts visual stimuli into actual images. The frontal lobe located behind the forehead is the largest lobe of the brain and is the seat of human intellect, reasoning, and judgement. It presides over the moral and spiritual consciousness of humans. When the frontal lobe is damaged by trauma or disease, it produces remarkable changes in character, including disinhibition, aggressiveness, distractibility and amorality, lack of foresight and lack of abstract thinking among other symptoms.

Many psychiatric diseases like depression, mania, obsessive-compulsive disorder and attention deficit disorder have their origins in the frontal lobe.

It has been revealed by sophisticated brain scans [Positron Emission

Tomography or PET scans] that there is up to a 60% reduction to the frontal lobe blood flow in depression. When the activity in the frontal lobe increases, it enhances blood flow and the depression improves.

Conscious thought, or processing of information, produces beta waves, as measured with an electroencephalogram or EEG. In the quiescent state, like in non-REM sleep, we produce alpha brainwaves on the EEG.

During hypnosis, the frontal lobe and conscious thought are bypassed and a trance-like state ensues. The subject is open to manipulation as their capacity to logically reason or morally filter their actions is disabled.

Racism, is therefore, a socio-cultural filter that a racist uses to observe the world around them. Africans and other non-white people who get drawn into the Western paradigm get assigned roles and characteristics based on societal and cultural perceptions rather than the true character of the individual.

CHAPTER THREE
SUBLIMINAL PROGRAMMING

Television is the most common form of subliminal programming available, now followed closely by other means of mass communication, such as newspapers and increasingly, the internet. It has been shown that after two minutes of watching television, brainwaves were alpha in pattern, meaning that they were not 'reacting, not orienting, not focusing, just spaced out.[1]

In 1965, a brain wave researcher, Dr Herbert E Krugman, stated: *"Television is a communication medium that effortlessly transmits huge quantities of information not thought about at the time of exposure"*[2]

Another influential researcher and writer, Dr Erik Peper, wrote:

"The horror of television is that information goes in, but we do not react to it. It goes right into our memory pool, and perhaps we react to it later, but we do not know what we are reacting to. When you watch television, you are training yourself not to react and so later, you're doing things without knowing why you're doing them, or where they came from"[3]

This means that when children watch violence on television, they memorise acts of violence and even though they may never carry out violent acts, it does increase the possibility. A baby is a sensory sponge; even though babies are unable to communicate directly with adults, they possess a tremendous capacity to soak up visual and other perceptions that comprise that basis of their socialization. Babies stare intently at faces and memorize facial expressions and minor changes in tone, pitch, and intonations of voices.

It is well known that babies attempt to communicate with adults through crying, laughing and use of basic facial expressions through which parents can get some understanding of their baby's needs. The way babies communicate has been condensed into books like the *Baby Whisperer*, which helps new parents understand their babies more. In order to help children to bond quickly with their parents, nature has equipped them with billions of nerve pathways by which they get a grip on their surroundings.[4]

Equipped with an abundance of neural pathways, a six-month-old infant has the capacity to learn any human language and speak in any intonation, from English to Chinese. We all lose some of this incredible capacity to learn as large portions of unused nerve pathways in the brain disconnect as the baby develops socially.

Howard Bloom wrote: *"Social experience literally shapes critical details of brain physiology, sculpting an infant's brain to fit the culture in which the child is born."*[5]

It should not therefore be surprising to find out that scientists have proved that a person socialized in racist ideology has significant changes in their brain physiology which can cause permanent damage similar to the effects of depression on particular areas of the brain.[6]

Our memories are simply a collection of remembered perceptions. These memories, consciously and subconsciously, determine who we are today and what we are likely to do in the future. Thus, human mind can be programmed to think and act things out in different ways.

"Individual perception untainted by others' influence does not exist", says Howard Bloom.[7]

The manner and the extent to which subconscious influences affect our conscious motivations, has been further underlined by neurological studies. These studies have shown categorically that every conscious thought has its origin in the subconscious mind first.

According to an article based in a study led by Professor John-Dylan Haynes, brain researcher in the Max Planck Institute in Leipzig, Germany, and published in *Nature Neuroscience* magazine entitled 'Unconscious determinants of free decisions in the human brain':

'There has been a long controversy as to whether subjectively 'free' decisions are determined by brain activity ahead of time. We found that the outcome of

a decision can be encoded in the brain activity of the prefrontal and parietal cortex up to 10 seconds before it enters awareness. This delay presumably reflects the operation of a network of high level control areas that begin to prepare an upcoming decision long before it enters awareness.[8]

Professor John-Dylan Haynes added:

'The impression that we are able to freely choose between different possible courses of action is fundamental to our mental life. However, the findings suggest our subjective experience of freedom is no more than an illusion, and our actions are initiated by unconscious mental processes long before we become aware of our intention to act.'[9]

By exploiting how the human mind works, and knowing our natural blind spots, Western politicians and media have been extremely successful in influencing, manipulating and controlling people worldwide. Visual imagery has played a vital role in shaping the way we see others and ourselves. Every year, the advertising industry spends billions of dollars trying to influence our perceptions. Daily, advertisers try to persuade us to buy things we do not want or need. The advertising industry in the UK spent over £13.7 billion in 2009 and increased significantly in ten years to about £21.8 billion in 2019.[10]

Suggestive information about advertised products is fronted by symbolic societal embodiments of the rich, famous, wealthy, sexy and powerful. They present well-codified visual and auditory symbols seducing us to make the desired purchases. So powerful are these visual symbols in transmitting codified information that in many cases words becomes superfluous in achieving the set aim. Symbols usually represent the deepest cultural themes of people and reveal significant messages about a person and a culture's reason for being.

CHAPTER FOUR
STOLEN DREAMS

To achieve any ambition in life it is important to have a clear picture of the goal we want to attain and how to get there. All children are born with the innate potential to be whatever they choose to be in life, if the prevailing conditions are right. Ultimately, the degree of our success in our life ambitions is only limited by the size of our dreams. The conversion of our dreams to reality is directly proportional to their clarity and the determination to keep on course and succeed. Unfortunately, this is where, our environment or 'reality' steps in. Our dreams and ambitions are significantly affected by the prevailing conditions, in which we find ourselves as human beings.

As human beings are social creatures, we are naturally organized into families, communities and countries and through our socialization, we greatly influence each other. Babies and children carefully watch their parents and family's behaviour, verbal and non-verbal communication in order to seamlessly become assimilated into society. In so doing, they bear the unmistakable imprint of their surroundings, in their language, culture and customs. Every child's underlying motivations and aspirations are intrinsically intertwined with their wider social status and thus are indelibly marked by the nature of their upbringing and socialization.

Some psychologists assert that human beings have acquired the majority of their social skills by the age of ten.[1]

The early predetermination of whom we are by where we are is the reason why many people naturally want to be like their parents or are what their parents wanted them to be. For instance, many young people want to become professionals such as doctors and lawyers or go into the military as their parents did or wanted them to do. While it is also undoubtedly true that an individual can choose to differ and choose a different path, like the son or daughter of a priest becoming a rock musician, conforming to our parents' wishes tends to be the norm not the exception.

The 'child prodigy' is no 'accident of nature'. Usually, a child only attains a clear vision of their talents and what they want to succeed in by the combination of hard work, excellent nurturing by their parents and being in the right social environment, for their ambitions to be realized.

One example to illustrate the above was the case of child prodigies and chess sensations, the Polgar sisters.

Their father, Laszlo Polgar, an educational psychologist, claimed he could turn any child into a prodigy and wrote a manual called 'Raise a Genius!' The test cases for his theory, which was thought to be grandiose at the time, were his daughters. He raised his daughters in an environment of constant chess practice and the Polgar sisters stunned the male-dominated world of professional chess.

In January 1991, his eldest daughter Susan, at 15 years old, became the top ranked female player and the first woman to earn a grandmaster title calculated on the same basis as male players.

However, she was soon eclipsed by the youngest Polgar sister, Judith. In December 1991, Judith Polgar, at 15 years old, became the youngest player to earn the grandmaster title, breaking the record set by Bobby Fischer in 1958. In 2005, she became the first woman to be rated within the top ten grandmasters in the world when she reached eight in the rankings.

In 1987, Garry Kasparov, one of the most dominant world chess champions of all times, sparked outrage when he said that the idea of a female world chess champion "exists only in fiction" in his autobiography Child of Change. In 1989, in an interview with Playboy magazine, he went further and amongst many other derogatory comments described women as "weaker fighters".

However, retribution was not long in coming as in 2002, Judith Polgar, once dismissed by Garry Kasparov, as a "circus puppet" beat him in 42 moves at a show piece "Match of the New Century" event between Russia and the Rest of the World. Garry Kasparov has since admitted he was wrong about female chess players and has since become an ardent supporter of female chess.

Unfortunately, most of the productive years of Africans and their diaspora are spent living in, working for and trying to achieve social mobility in a white dominated supremacy system designed to keep them down. Africans and their diaspora who have not figured this out, have also condemned their children to a lifetime of toil for very little reward.

The prevailing physical and social environment can severely limit or enhance the innate ability of our subconscious and conscious mind to express itself. When faced with difficult prevailing circumstances we usually go into survival mode and deal with the most pressing problems to the exclusion of all others. Physiologically this is described as the fright, flight or fight response, when the body reacts by diverting blood away from non-essential organs given the circumstances — for example, from the digestive system to the muscles as we try to escape from a situation or fight. The surge of adrenaline intensifies in order to focus and concentrate on the object of fear or anger and the surroundings become blurry.

Physiologically and psychologically, there is a proven direct link between physical stress, suffering and depression in human beings. Under pressure, we produce other stress hormones to help our bodies deal with the situation. When we are put under pressure, the hypothalamic-pituitary-adrenal axis or HPA axis of the brain's hormonal regulatory system becomes activated. The hypothalamus produces corticotrophin releasing factor [CRF]. This stimulates the pituitary gland to secrete adrenocorticotrophic hormones and, in turn, the adrenal glands produce cortisol.

Cortisol is a known mood depressant and approximately 50% of people with severe depression have raised cortisol levels.[2]

Dopamine is also found to be depleted in people with depression.[3]

When people are under constant physical and psychological pressure, there is no time for lofty dreams and ambitions. Survival from one day to the next becomes paramount. People who are under stress, tend to prioritize their survival needs above their wellbeing and actualization needs.

We all need some external pressure to motivate us to do things. However, too much pressure demotivates and makes lack the energy to devote ourselves to anything but survival.

Our awareness of our surroundings fades into a blur. If the negative pressure persists, people can remain in this mode for their whole lives. The right psychosocial environment is essential to ensure self-actualization and self-determination. Rare though it may be, a some individuals are able to overcome seemingly insurmountable barriers and achieve success greater than their wildest dreams despite difficult prevailing circumstances. To these few, the word 'genius' can justifiably be applied. For the remaining more ordinary human beings, in the absence of the right psychosocial conditions, our dreams die first.

All African parents must attempt to provide their children with the necessary education and information needed to enable them reach their true potential and a grounding in true African history alone is an excellent start.

CHAPTER FIVE
PUPPET MASTERS

Through slavery, colonisation, negative policies and propaganda over the course of several centuries, the West has essentially destroyed hope in Africa. Western governments and politicians have long been extremely successful at influencing the thoughts and subsequent actions of their own people. The West has conducted social engineering on an unprecedented scale. Having cornered the lion's share of the world's resources and with ever advancing methods of mass communications, they can reach further still and penetrate deeper into societies all over the world.

No-one, black or white, living under the western paradigm, has been exempt from its social engineering. It is simply the case that Africa and its diaspora have the short end of the social engineering stick. In possession of a continent rich in human and natural resources, Africans are always in 'need' of Western capitalist intervention in one guise or another to control their resources through political, economic and psychological manipulation. It is no coincidence that wherever African communities reside in the western paradigm, they are uniformly downtrodden.

Racism, creates a self-regenerating and self-fuelling conundrum of psychological inferiority complexes and economic dependence. Thus, maintaining ideal conditions for exploitation for hundreds if not thousands of years to come. Once set on the wrong course, the mentally enslaved Africans will continue to propagate mentally enslaved children for generations to come. From a psychological standpoint, it is only through the prism of mental slavery that we can try to explain the somewhat puzzling actions of African subjected to the intense pressure brought to bear by the western powers.

For instance, why did many Africans sacrifice life and limb for their white masters in their wars of colonial conquest and global domination but not feel motivated enough to fight for their own freedom? Why do so many Africans and their diaspora continue to fight for recognition and acceptance into the wider white community rather than for true freedom and equality? The claims of the western superiority have immense psychological influence because they cut across all aspects of human endeavour and are buttressed by its prosperity and technological advances. No aspect of man's life is spared — neither science, technology nor religion. In Caucasians, it produces and supports superiority complexes, racism, xenophobia and paternalism while, conversely, in Africans it produces and supports inferiority complexes, hopelessness and self-hatred.

The gross distortion of Africans' dopamine reward systems and cultural values has led to former slaves seeking integration into the society of the white slave masters rather than their freedom. For the descendants of slaves to be proud of their white heritage and origins when these were forcibly raped into their great-grandparents when they were captured and enslaved were captured as slaves can only be the result of a severe distortion of self-value and self-worth. Many enslaved Africans were forcibly assimilated into Western culture through slavery and colonization. However, through western socialization or cultural imperialism coupled with ignorance of their own culture and history, many Africans have unsuspectingly plugged themselves into western culture. Their lack of true self-knowledge and understanding of pivotal historical precedents has allowed a disabling culture of psychological inferiority and physical dependence to develop. Assimilating western ideals and culture without filtering out the inbuilt ideas and notions of white supremacy and African inferiority has the same effect on Africans and their diaspora psychologically as being infected with a deadly virus or bacteria would have on the physical body.

Racism primarily operates at a subconscious level. It is not significantly altered by intelligence, societal status, wealth or poverty. This means an African and Caucasian child brought up within the same

Western environment will most likely develop and achieve differently due to the burden of societal expectation and pressures.

The process of assimilation of colonized people as a subculture in the colour-coded Western civilization, with all its attendant psychological complexes, accompanied the European colonization process all over the world. Africans, readily identifiable by their dark skin colour, were identified, classified and stereotyped on this basis.

However, there is a natural yin and yang of racism and inferiority complexes. For one person to assume superiority the other person has to openly or tacitly accept inferiority. Many social, religious, and economic factors based on a fallacious notion of European superiority help sustain this powerful psychological impact. Many Westernized African are, like their European counterparts, extremely sceptical and often quite disparaging about other Africans. On a conscious level, although they see through western hypocrisy, doublespeak and double standards, subconsciously, they accept racism as 'how it is' because their white peers and wider society accept it as 'how it is'. This is because inferiority complexes usually operate in the subconscious realm.

For example, many western socialized Africans often subconsciously express viewpoints and perceptions of African people that originate in and are disseminated by the western society. Consciously, they acknowledge that the West discriminates negatively against Africans but their subconscious actions remain influenced by the west. Many Westernized Africans clearly understand the importance of acting and organizing as groups. However, anecdotally, they subconsciously avoid being seen associating publicly with other African people because some white people frown upon it.

If you ask any African or descendant in the diaspora, the direct question: 'Do you feel inferior to the white man?' You are likely to get an angry and indignant denial. However, when these same Africans and their diaspora calmly sit back and objectively analyse their lives, the results may be much different from what they think. The language they want to speak, clothes they want to wear, food they choose to eat, what they want to look like, the African education curriculum, the value systems and culture they want to express are more western than African. Imitation is the sincerest form of flattery. As for African women and diaspora, many have taken to straightening their hair with toxic chemicals or using hair extensions or wigs in a bid to look as westernised as possible.

The human hair business is a multi-billion dollar business and most of the women involved in the use of human hair and fake wigs are African and African American women. In October 2014, an investigative BBC reporter found out that thirty-seven out of thirty-nine human hair traders in China were of African origin. In Guangzhou, most of the customers were from Africa and included Nigerians, Ghanaians, Congolese, South Africans, Angolans and Ugandans. They are able to sell their human hair extensions and wigs for triple the price they bought on return to Africa. However, the sting in the tail was that some unscrupulous Chinese traders have been supplementing their stocks of human hair with goats hair.[1]

Many African nations and thus millions of their people are dependent on the West for their basic needs, like food, medicine, and infrastructure. Across Africa, African education systems are Western and African languages and cultures take a back seat to Western languages and cultures. Not a single African nation speaks an African language as their only official language.

Generalization this may be but these psychological inferiority complexes are being expressed, not only on a personal level, but at all levels — individual, family, communal, national, continental and international. The problem Africa and its diaspora faces is not just finding themselves in a Western world and exposed to their racism and imperialism. It is now primarily a question of their tacit or even open internalization and acceptance of the psychological inferiority played out in their lives. Once Africans started to accept the Western hype and propaganda and started trying to be westernized, the die was cast.

Mentally enslaved Africans no longer require active cohesion to comply with the West's demands. Regular reminders by the Western media of their prostrate global position, buttressed by the reality of Africa's crushing poverty and dependence, is more than enough. This psychological inferiority complex, coupled with the loss of self-determination through slavery and colonization, has markedly diminished Africans' natural capacity for innovation and creativity, especially in the realm of technology and science.

All human beings are the product of nature and nurture. Like goldfish in a bowl, we can only see what is directly in front of us. What we see and experience is the greatest predetermining factor in what our motivations are, what we believe we can achieve, the situations we accept in life, the value we place on ourselves and on others like us. Simply put, our unconscious motivation is the greatest determinant of what we become or do in this life and the prevailing environment is the greatest determinant of our subconscious motivation.

If all that Africans see, hear, and believe about themselves is controlled by white supremacists, it stands to reason that their reason for being - the reason why human beings can stand apart from other mammals - their subconscious motivation is also controlled at source by white supremacists.

Anyone who controls what you see, what you think and your environment, controls what you can imagine - and holds the key to your soul.

Europeans did not stop at just defining 'black people' as inferior in Western society, they went much further. They maintained the pressure by 'setting the stage of life', by manipulating and controlling all aspects of human activity. In so doing, they have created the basis for a self-perpetuating pattern of African inferiority complexes, low self-esteem and low achievement. This creates the perfect environment for Western imperialists and capitalists to exploit. The wheels of this self-perpetuating cycle of psychological inferiority and oppression, are racism, globalization and imperialism. Today, Western racism manifests primarily as institutional racism and globalization, presented to Africa and its diaspora in the form of poisoned sugar-coated 'Aid' pills. Africans ingest these 'pills' unquestioningly as an integral part of their seemingly insatiable need to consume western products, culture and ideology.

The enormity of this travesty remains lost on millions of Africans, who spend an inordinately high percentage of their lives just trying to live into the next day. With their subconscious drive honed in on mere survival, most Africans have not been able to tap into their full potential. Severe limitation of their potential and vision results in widespread apathy, divisiveness and self-loathing at levels unparalleled in any other racial group of people.

Applying this basic logic, the seemingly inexplicable lack of African self-determination, cohesion and western dependence among African people and their diaspora becomes understandable even if it is still not acceptable. How else do you explain black African slaves fighting for their white masters against the abolition of slavery during the American Civil War? How else do you explain African people being mobilized by western nations to battle against each other during the western colonisation of Africa and in their global chess battles called the First and Second World Wars, when they could have used that opportunity to strike a blow for their own freedom?

During the First World War, thousands of African troops were mobilized to fight by the warring Western colonialists. The West African Frontier Force [WAFF] created by the British was used to invade and occupy the German colony Kamerun [now Cameroon].[2] The Germans mobilized their own African colonial army, the Schutztruppe, in Kamerun. The Schutztruppe even took part in the subjugation and genocide of the Herero people in Namibia and massacres in German East Africa.[3]

The WAFF, mobilised by the British, fought fierce battles in difficult terrain against their German-trained African counter-parts, the Schutztruppe, before the WAFF prevailed.

Sadly, even while Africans were fighting for their white masters and laying down their lives and their limbs for them, in a war they did not start or understand, many of them were still being exposed to the most heinous acts of racism and segregation.

There is only one reason that makes any logical sense of this illogical behaviour. These Africans were not just fighting for their Western masters' widely bandied tenets of freedom and democracy. They were also fighting consciously and subconsciously for acceptance into the European culture and society. The famous boxer, Muhammad Ali, appreciated this fact when he resisted being drafted into fighting the Vietnam war and stated:

> *"Why should they ask me to put on a uniform and go 10,000 miles from home and drop bombs and bullets on Brown people in Vietnam while so-called Negro people in Louisville are treated like dogs and denied simple human rights? No I'm not going 10,000 miles from home to help murder and burn another poor nation simply to continue the domination of white slave masters of the darker people the world over. This is the day when such evils must come to an end. I have been warned that to take such a stand would cost me millions of dollars. But I have said it once and I will say it again. The real enemy of my people is here. I will not disgrace my religion, my people or myself by becoming a tool to enslave those who are fighting for their own justice, freedom and equality... If I thought the war was going to bring freedom and equality to 22 million of my people they wouldn't have to draft me, I'd join tomorrow. I have nothing to lose by standing up for my beliefs. So I'll go to jail, so what? We've been in jail for 400 years*
>
> *I strongly object to the fact that so many newspapers have given the American public and the world the impression that I have only two alternatives in taking this stand: either I go to jail or go to the Army. There is another alternative and that alternative is justice. If justice prevails, if my Constitutional rights are upheld, I will be forced to go neither to the Army nor jail. In the end I am confident that justice will come my way for the truth must eventually prevail"*[4]

CHAPTER SIX

AFRICA'S CROSS: THE BURDEN OF WHITE SUPREMACY

The loss of vision, the inferiority complex and the struggle for acceptance into white culture, explain why the efforts of many knowledgeable but western-educated Africans get repeatedly frustrated. On the other hand, white imperialists or supremacists remain relentless, single-minded and driven to go to any lengths to keep African people down, wherever they are globally, namely, in their assigned positions on the lowest rungs of Western societies.

Africans, who have imbibed Western ideals and values to the extent that they create deep-seated psychological inferiority, are easily satisfied with platitudes and meaningless gestures of recognition or acceptance from their white masters. The result is that their true goals are never achieved. They lack the world vision, strategic thinking, motivation and commitment to keep on the course and win the biggest prize of all: true freedom and equality.

Two further cases in point highlight this dilemma, namely, the American civil rights movement and the dismantling of apartheid in South Africa. In the United States, institutional racism is still rife despite Martin Luther King's dream and in South Africa the power to vote was ceded to Nelson Mandela but black economic empowerment was not. Virtually all African nations have experienced the same steady roll back of their achievements since 'Independence' under the careful guidance of the leading Western imperialists of modern times — the United States, France and Britain. The implementation of the disastrous structural adjustment programmes of the International Monetary Fund [IMF], together with the deleterious effects of globalization, have resulted in the indices of health and wellbeing such as infant mortality, deaths from preventable causes and diseases and their gross domestic products [GDP], of many African nations failing to improve as expected. The political instability and economic weakness created by negative western policies means that African nations are unable to adequately care for or protect their citizens from pandemics like HIV/AIDS. In 2013, an estimated 1–1.3 million Africans died from HIV-related causes according to the Global Health Observatory [GHO].[1]

Of the estimated 3.1 million children worldwide who die daily from poor nutrition, one in four resides in Africa.[2]

Such are the depths of poverty and destitution in Africa that the life expectancy in some of the poorest African nations averages forty-seven years.[3]

In 2018, UNICEF reported that, approximately 84% of all the under-five deaths in the world occur in just two regions: sub-Saharan Africa (54%) and South Asia (28%).[4]

A psychological inferiority complex does not only result in lack of imagination or ambition. It is also intrinsically linked to how much value we place on our own life and wellbeing. By extension, it determines how much value African people put on the lives and wellbeing of other Africans. Self-hatred and the lack of African value for African lives is being manifested in ever-increasing levels. Black-on-black violence plagues the war-torn African continent and the black African communities in the African diaspora.

Africa and its diaspora need to ask themselves whose responsibility is it for the millions of starving Africans, HIV and AIDS sufferers, Africa's poverty and lack of development?

Despite all the western Aid, charities and NGOs, western leaders have almost all contributed in one way or another to Africa's poverty and suffering.

Despite Tony Blair, the former British Prime Minister, stating that 'the state of Africa is a scar on the conscience of the world', he duly added to Africa's scars by selling an unnecessary £28 million missile air defence system to Tanzania. By contrast, a civilian air traffic control system can cost as little as £3.5 million.[5]

While in office, the former American president George W. Bush, whose neoconservative credentials need no introduction, obstructed the fight against HIV/AIDS, global poverty and global warming, all of which would have had the most impact in Africa.[6]

It is safe to conclude that the wellbeing of Africa and Africans and their diaspora is primarily the responsibility of Africans and their diaspora.

The state of Africa and its diaspora today is a case study in what happens to people who have lost their vision and through that lost their self-determination because of social engineering, fabricated and driven by Western countries keen to facilitate the exploitation of Africa and its people. Africans and their diaspora are subjected to persistent and severe economic, political and social pressure from western countries and they endure constant denigration in the western media. As a result, the vast majority have not had the time to contemplate anything beyond survival — or so they think.

In trying to explain Africa's situation within the paradigm defined by the West, Africa's responses have in the main been unsurprisingly inappropriate and poor. Disunited and apathetic due to the alienating effect of the Western paradigm, many Africans who could otherwise make a difference, are happy to continue living in limbo in the west because of the individualism and dysfunction that western socialization tends to generate.

By definition, a paradigm is always less than a hair's breadth to a million light years away. A seemingly tiny paradigm shift, however, requiring only a little understanding and knowledge outside the western paradigm can result in a tremendous transformation from the present reality of African psychological inferiority, hopelessness and dependence to a state of self-determination, psychological, physical and financial freedom on a personal, communal and national level.

A revolution in thinking always precedes a revolution in action. However, to achieve revolution, Africans must be prepared to reassess the facts objectively rather than nostalgically or emotionally cling to unfounded but cherished and long-held falsehoods that lock their minds into the present paradigm.

Crucially, the white elephant of western superiority is largely a mirage in the desert sand. In an attempt to assign all human advances and progress unto itself, it has spread itself too thin and huge credibility gaps have become clearly discernible. The West's hubris does not stand up to any objective scrutiny nor is it compatible with real world history in general. It largely consists of a matrix of misinformation, omission, myths and lies creating a façade, which is hawkishly maintained by western media, politicians and academics for its much its treasured psychological impress.

As our unconscious motivation or rather lack of motivation ultimately determines whom and what we become in this life, it makes sense that the first step in Africa's long walk to freedom, self-determination, self-reliance and equality begins in the mind.

Africans must work together to deconstruct the effects of the western paradigm on their minds. They should revisit Africa's history from a non-Western perspective, and explore the links between their histories in the western matrix and their current predicament.

This tiny change in thought processing, which would however produce a massive paradigm shift in the African psyche, is not only the crucial first step but also the principal stepping-stone for all other initiatives. All Africans individually and collectively must at some point in their lives make a conscious choice, born of a dawning awareness of the need for psychological freedom, to strive to become self-determining and actualizing.

CHAPTER SEVEN

IN THE BEGINNING: THE EVOLUTION OF HUMANITY AND WESTERN CIVILIZATION

'There is very little that is important for people to know than their history and culture. Without this they stand naked and defenceless against the world.' **Cicero.**[1]

Survival has always been the sternest challenge that has faced all living things. All creatures have had to answer this most basic and fundamental question. While the choice and effectiveness of the response has differed, every mammal evolved complex ways of meeting nature's challenge.

Evolutionary adaptations to prevailing conditions ranged from the simple to the bizarre. While some species became specialized loners, others diversified and organized into families. For instance, some big cats, like the sabre-toothed tiger, became super specialized, while other big cats like lions formed groups or prides.

Surviving nature's fundamental question and thriving required the slow but steady distillation of successful adaptations and behaviours over millions of years. Without a shadow of doubt, the most successful adaptation for survival has been the collaborative approach to nature's problems. Organizing into groups or families and leveraging out the effort to survive, has been by far the most effective method of survival among all living things. The most successful groups of any species of living thing are usually gregarious and not solitary. Most of the evidence available has shown that species that grouped together coped better with the primary question of survival and continue to do so.

Human beings fall into this group, being organized into families and communities. However, the success of the human race cannot be explained by social structure alone. The power of the human mind has been God's greatest gift to humanity. The nearly effortless and unlimited ability the human brain endows us with differentiates man from all other mammals.

Given that the earth is estimated to be 4.5 billion years old and modern man around for only one hundred thousand years, the progress achieved by humans has been astonishing in what, by evolutionary standards, is a very short time. This has even led some to speculate as to whether humans have evolved by themselves or have had their evolution accelerated by outside influences.

The acquisition of knowledge and, more importantly, the application and dissemination of knowledge have been the key factors that underpin all human achievements. From natural disasters and the vagaries of weather, to wild beasts, disease and famine, the challenges facing humans have been sustained and varied over the centuries. In the face of these, human beings have correspondingly evolved linear coping strategies and technology to survive.

The ability to make and use fire revolutionized the human diet, making it possible to cook meat and vegetables, which helped shorten the digestive process. The faster acquisition of larger amounts of energy from cooked food in turn supported the development of bigger brains and allowed human beings the time to be creative and innovative. In comparison, some of our nearest animal relatives, primates like the mountain gorillas, still spend the best part of the day eating and digesting their food just to maintain the necessary energy levels. Given the above, it becomes clear that the simple innovation of cooking was a significant step forward on the human evolutionary ladder because it freed up time to contemplate other things.

Simple tools to facilitate the collection and storage of food were invented to support food production for families and communities.

Tools like knives, spears and the bow and arrow, all played pivotal roles in helping humans improve their ability to hunt and gather food. Another significant factor in human development was the domestication of animals and farming.

All these developments meant that families and social groups could settle and develop around reliable sources of food, leading to population explosions around these sites. Nature as well as necessity was truly the mother of invention because as human civilization developed exponentially under her often-harsh stimulus, further inventions like writing, the wheel and sophisticated communication through language, significantly enhanced and accelerated human development and brought humanity more time and comfort.

It is a common assumption that modern human beings far surpassed their ancestors in achievements and intelligence but this is not borne out by fact. The masses have only enjoyed the luxuries of modern living like electricity, mobile phones, cars and air travel for less than a hundred years. Deep within our brains the neuropsychological changes which evolution affected and which helped our ancestors survive, remain almost unaltered.

For example, our ancient neurophysiological responses explain why obesity is rife in the west. We still crave food like our caveman ancestors but we do not sustain caveman-like levels of activity with which to burn off the extra calories. No matter what nature's primary stimulus for development, the basic tenets for survival, and the acquisition and application of knowledge, remains true even today.

Human beings are deeply driven by an innate desire to survive but they also nurse the need to thrive and be free. It is certainly to our credit that we have not just survived nature's varied challenges and complexities of existence but have advanced rapidly to the point we are at today.

However, this stunning human survival success story has come at a potentially terrible price. In the relatively short duration that has defined human existence on earth, human beings have not only already forced the extinction of thousands of other species but currently threaten the existence of the entire planet as a whole.

Maintaining an identity in the group has played a highly pivotal role in our evolution by leveraging out the effort required for survival by the individual to the group. It is then no wonder that in ancient times maintaining an identity within a family, community, city or country was almost as essential to life as food and water. Banishment from a family group in ancient times was tantamount to a death sentence. This was because the chances of an individual surviving alone outside the group were exceedingly slim.

Human individualism has always been better expressed as part of a wider community. All individuals rely on their family and community to reach and express their full potential. This generalization still stands true today in spite of the incredibly complex world in which we live.

Our socialization and acceptance as part of a family, group or community has always been and remains an integral role in determining who we are and what we become later in life. The social pressure our children and teenagers deeply suffer from stems from their desire to be accepted among their peers, families, and other social groups. Failure to be accepted into one or all of these; family, community, nation or people, still represents a form of banishment and can have serious psychological, emotional, and even physical effects on an individual. While acceptance and integration into a different group or family is possible and has always happened, it not only requires patience and understanding but the support and willingness of the majority to allow integration of the minority to prevail. If acceptance is denied for whatever reason, it can lead to isolation of the individuals or minority groups.

The African diaspora and immigrants living in the west still suffer a form of banishment as they are denied full assimilation into western societies by the larger white collective.

Communal politics, hierarchy, diversity and leadership were always part of the human experience. This experience was not exclusive of the human weaknesses of greed, selfishness, and fear. As human groups multiplied and expanded their territories several times over, competition for available resources among groups of humans was almost inevitable. Competition between family groups would most probably already have raised the social consciousness of each group or community. This competition would have been more critical in areas where natural resources and living conditions were more difficult.

Competition for resources is natural and most mammals compete for available resources. However, furnished with an instinctive knowledge of the destructive outcome of uncontrolled violence, many mammals — with the noticeable exception of human beings — stop short of actual physical violence wherever possible. To achieve this restraint, many mammals have evolved a wide variety of warning signals, postures, sounds, smells and colours, which in most cases serve as sufficient deterrents to ward off most competitors and some potential predators. The lion's mane and roar, the dog's bark and growl, the cobra's hood and the rattling of the rattlesnake's tail of are some well-known examples in nature of warning behaviour designed primarily to ward off potential competitors or threats before actual physical violence is required. This allows animals to avoid unnecessary violence and possible injury, which could significantly reduce their chances of survival.

The vast majority of different human cultures all over the world developed symbiotically with their environment, i.e. the Khoisan bushmen of South Africa, Masai warriors of East Africa, Native Americans and Australian Aborigines. They understood our common humanity, and the need to respect the environment and each other. This in many ways meant that they did not develop in ways superfluous to the primary question of survival. It also meant that conflicts were relatively limited affairs, reducing the amount of damage to themselves and the environment due to a lack of sophisticated military technology and lack of motivation or reasons to develop it.

Unfortunately, in a significant aberration from nature's norm, some human groups developed differently. They demonstrated extreme cruelty towards each other and had a seemingly endless appetite for mindless, unwarranted violence towards other people and little or no regard for their environment.

While some aspects of this type of human development can be observed all over the world, it was in Europe that it became a highly refined art, sometimes euphemistically referred to as civilization. Perhaps, driven by the harsher climatic conditions, like the cold and the scarcity of natural resources compared to the comparative paradise of Africa and other parts of the world, Europeans needed to be resourceful and innovative to make the best of the harsher conditions in which they lived, in order to survive.

Possibly, over millions of years, the greater need to conquer nature and innovate technology to survive and the presence of albinism or pale skin, in contrast to generally darker-skinned people, may have sharply increased the levels of social awareness in Europe. Conversely, the African environment, where there was natural abundance, may have supported less aggressive, more static societies.

The severe environmental challenges Europeans faced may also have reduced their threshold to physical violence when compared to other races, leading to more conflict and wars.

For instance, when the Chinese accidentally discovered gunpowder its primary use for hundreds of years was to set off fireworks, especially after the Emperor of China, appalled by its destructive capacity, banned its use in China for hundreds of years. However, when Europeans belatedly came across gunpowder, through the Moors in Andalucía and their exploration in China, they quickly put its explosive properties to deadly use and accelerated the development of firearms and explosives. This development changed the course of world history.

It appears that nothing much has changed since then. In March 2003 the world watched in shock and horror as the American and British bombardment of Baghdad lit up the night sky and signalled the beginning of the invasion and occupation of Iraq. However, on August 8th 2008, a different type of firework display lit up the night sky. For the opening ceremony of the Beijing Olympics, China treated the world to one of the most spectacular and awe-inspiring fireworks displays the world had ever seen.

Therefore, in Europe, increased social consciousness forged through difficult environmental circumstances and competition against each other, bred not only a need to survive but also a need to achieve mastery over nature and exert their influence over all others.

Generally, human civilization is seen primarily, as the ability to cultivate the landscape and harness natural resources for use in accord with the environment. As the west developed, the word 'civilization' came to be synonymous with the degree of control over the environment and over other human beings. Western civilization is characterized by the use of technology to extract natural resources from the land and from people so as to accumulate wealth far in excess of what was required for survival or even comfort. Another important aspect of western civilization was the development of concentrated political and military power to dominate the people and to facilitate imperialism and the processes called capitalism today.

The desire for total domination of both the environment and other people can be considered an aberration in the human quest to survive in harmony with nature. Unfortunately, the west, in its desire for mastery over nature and other humans, simultaneously sowed the seeds for the destruction of the entire human race. This quest also drove the west to great lengths to innovate and develop military technology that would keep them one step or more ahead of their competitors. However, their desire for total domination directly threatens the potential for man or the environment to survive, even for a tenth of the time the dinosaurs survived, namely, over 100 million years compared to the 100,000 years of relatively modern man.

While the dinosaurs, renowned for their large size, large appetites and small brains, may not have been intellectually agile, they left behind a world that was still habitable. Despite their alleged minuscule brain size, it seems clear that the dinosaurs knew something that humans, for all our vaunted intelligence, do not.

Human societies or groups which did not seek to accumulate wealth and organize political power in this same manner were seen in the West as 'closer to nature' and therefore less civilized — in some cases even not quite human.

The west's quest for material wealth and political and military superiority led them to amass far in excess of that required for their survival and attempt to establish control over the world's resources and prevent their main competitors from doing the same. This drive established the seeds of imperialism and international conflict around the world.

It is important to remember that every group of human beings on the face of the earth, whatever their race, wherever they were in the world, had to develop different skills and basic technologies in order to survive the fundamental question of survival, which nature placed in front of every living species on earth. The main difference between different races was the degree to which and the purpose for which these innovations or technologies had been developed and utilized.

Therefore, the significant difference between the West and other people is that the technology of the West was used to fulfil its overarching aims of dominion rather than that the other races of people lacked technology.

The attempt to establish total mastery over nature and all other human beings is what defines Western civilization.

CHAPTER EIGHT
IMPERIALISM AND RACISM

The ideal precondition of Western capitalism is slavery or conditions as close to slavery as possible. This is why the globalisation of Western capitalism continues to create and foster the slavery or near slavery of its exploitable workforce in order to maximise its profits.

The West's technological advances, achieved primarily through war, have enabled it to establish a network of global inequality and privilege for the 'civilized' few in Europe and North America. In the minds of the Western elite this was justified by their erroneous belief in the superiority of the West and the inferiority of everywhere else. This forms one of the main underlying ideologies of Western civilization. This ideology encourages the domination of weaker so-called 'lesser civilized races' and their assimilation only up to the degree of permanent second-class citizens. In this state of perpetual servitude, 'second-class citizens' are only of value to the chosen ones – Westerners - by virtue of what resources they have or how they can benefit the 'master race'. Through institutionalised racism, attempts by 'lesser civilized people' to socially migrate in the west and achieve first-class citizen status are strongly discouraged.

What made Europe forge a different approach to many other people around the world? Were all these people all over the world, from Africa to Asia, Near East, Far East and Middle East, free of culture, religion and technology until their invasion by Europeans? It cannot just be better organization or military prowess alone. It is an established fact that virtually all mammals that are organized into groups, have some sort of hierarchy. An alpha female wolf often leads the wolf pack. Primates usually have dominant males and sometimes-dominant females. No human community could have survived for millennia without leadership and organization.

It is also important to state that while every social group requires some form of hierarchy to function, social hierarchy does not directly equate to racism or capitalism and neither is racism an inevitable consequence of different people encountering each other. It is on record that many of the societies the European explorers encountered as they sought out new land and resources were organized, peaceful and most importantly not racist. When the natural apprehension of meeting strangers of a different skin colour and custom was overcome, the European explorers were in general, treated with respect and kindness.

It is quite possible that European feudalism was the precursor of white racism, capitalism and imperialism. Feudalism promoted the idea of the innate superiority of the 'blue-blooded' aristocracy over the peasant masses.

In order to establish and maintain this artificial superiority, based only on birth and social status, material wealth and no intrinsic intellectual, moral, spiritual or physical superiority, feudalism the precursor to capitalism was born. Racism, became the illogical, but logical consequence of these developments.

In general, in the west, racism can be said to focus on the local society, while imperialism typically represents the export of racism and its tenets of exploitation to foreign people who are not directly a part of the white European culture but are, nevertheless, subjected to its rapacity.

Racism and imperialism thus became the central theme around which western societies were constructed and the way in which the oppression, exploitation and denigration of the vast majority the world's poorest was organized and justified. While tribalism can be considered a form of racism, there are clear differences. Tribalism seeks advantage over others, mainly through favouritism, but still recognizes the inherent humanity of others.

European nationalism largely grew out of the persistent conflict between European nations. In the middle Ages, witchcraft was widely practiced as a secret religion in Europe. It was also seen by some as a combination of nature worship and a nationalist revolt against the authority of the Church and the state. Famously, Joan of Arc was burnt at the stake for heresy and disobeying the Catholic Church. She allegedly was burnt alive for being a 'witch' and but in fact she was killed for leading a rebellion against the Church and the State. On her part, she had claimed to hear the voices of angels, which asked her to rise up against the establishment and install King Charles VI as king.[1]

Spain and Portugal may have been the first to recognize the power of nationalism following their long-running battles against the dark-skinned African Moors. Later, the French and the English also tapped into the power of nationalism to galvanize their people during their imperialistic Hundred Years War against each other. The English, much like the Germans and the French, had tried unsuccessfully to establish a European Empire on the back of this nationalistic fervour.

According to Lenin, imperialism was the *'highest stage of capitalism'*.[2]

Following the warped logic of imperialism, capitalism and the western superiority complex, the rulings classes in the so-called western democracies, applauded and supported fascism. When Mussolini invaded Ethiopia with much loss of innocent African lives, the US State Department praised Mussolini's bloody occupation for having *'brought order out of chaos, discipline out of license, and insolvency out of bankruptcy'*.[3]

Nazi Germany was considered by some to be the pinnacle of Western civilization in the 20th century. Through the eyes of Western imperialists, Germany was clearly 'superior' to their main rivals at that time, Britain and France, not only because Germany rapidly developed their country technologically but also by virtue of its military might and conquests.

The Western ruling classes, including Britain and the United States, initially, openly supported the Nazi regime, because fascist totalitarian regimes often facilitate the spread of capitalism. They viewed fascism favourably because it allowed extensive US and UK economic penetration into the German market and because it destroyed the much-feared labour movements [not to mention the Communist Party] and suppressed 'excessive' democracy, which impeded their freedom to function.[4]

Hitler's Germany, remained a model of strong leadership and the peak of Western civilization in sciences and art before the Second World War broke out. The US and UK governments, executives and their elites all supported the Nazi regime until it threatened their own interests.[5]

When Mussolini's fascist party came to power, it was described as a 'fine young revolution' in the US.[6]

The US even helped overthrow the fledgling Italian democracy in 1948 by withholding food from the starving Italians and helping to restore of the fascist police. They even threatened to do more if they faced opposition.[7]

UK and US investment boomed in Italy and Germany during the rise of fascism. When Hitler dismantled Czechoslovakia in 1938, it was with the approval of the American President Roosevelt. Big business also aligned itself with Nazi Germany and when Coca Cola could no longer operate freely in Germany due to the negative stigma of the Nazi regime, they began producing Fanta.[8]

These facts illustrate the ultimate greed of capitalism because it is amazing that even while Britain was facing its 'darkest hour' in the Battle of Britain against Germany, Germany continued to use the US, Britain's closest ally as an industrial base. It took the Japanese bombing of Pearl Harbour to induce America to enter the war and sever its links with Germany.

Following the Second World War, in a secret recruitment drive, code-named 'Project Paperclip', many German scientists were given immunity for war crimes and spirited off to the USA where they formed the backbone of American nuclear and space technology [NASA]. This was despite the fact that they had just worked for the most brutal regime in recent human memory [Project Paperclip].[9]

'Imperialism' only became politically incorrect, a name not to be associated with, after the defeat of the fascist Nazi regime and their 'axis of evil' as they had also declared themselves imperialists. Indeed, many former British Prime Ministers, Benjamin Disraeli and Winston Churchill, were proud imperialists and did everything within their power to maintain and expand the British Empire.

CHAPTER NINE

APPROPRIATING WORLD HISTORY

Nature has always operated in cyclical patterns, day and night, cold and wet seasons, being obvious examples. In the human body, at cellular level, simple cyclical activity drives individual cells, which together make up complete living creatures. These cellular cycles produce energy, excrete waste products, repair and protect against damage, and generate growth.

All these processes can be viewed in some way to be microcosms of nature. When an abnormal growth in a cell refuses to recognize normal cell-to-cell inhibition, develops its own growth factors and continues to divide and grow, the growth is called a cancer.

Imagine the whole body of humans across the globe as one living entity. Western imperialism can be considered a cancer that took hold in Europe as a primary site and grew until it breached the boundaries of the European continent, spreading to all parts of the world, just as a cancer spreads by metastasis in the human body.

As the effects of Western imperialism spreads rapidly in the global body of humans, feeding off a raft of negative human traits like greed, selfishness, corruption and murder, its rapid growth is to the detriment of the host, in this case the whole human race. The cancer of imperialism has also simultaneously signed its own death warrant, as the more successful the cancer, the more likely that it will kill the host and in so doing, be doomed to die along with the host which is essential for its survival.

The West is quick to point to the benefits 'Western civilization' has brought the rest of the world. While it is certainly true that Europeans have refined and redeveloped a great deal of the technology available today, the origins of civilization are not Western at all. Many presumed Western technologies came from alleged 'barbarians' and 'natives' like Africans and Asians at a time when the Europeans were living like barbarians.

Highly developed civilizations existed in Africa, the Middle East, India and the Far East that predate 'western civilization' by thousands of years. In 1620, Francis Bacon 1561–1626, one of the forerunners of modern science, remarked:

"[Three discoveries] w*hich have changed the whole face of things throughout the world... were printing, gunpowder, and the magnet — all of them invented by the Chinese at least a thousand years earlier and brought to Europe by the Arabs...*

Our letters had their origin in Western Asia and our numerals in India, and were, also brought to Europe by the Arabs".[1]

Imperialism is not just about resources and military technology. It is driven by a superego, a superiority complex that requires that it ascribe all human developments to itself.

In a remarkable process that has lasted over two thousand years, European countries would not only compete among each other for the world's resources but also make claim and counterclaim in intellectual circles, ascribing every human invention or development to one European country or the other. They have tried to achieve the impossible. They have tried to squeeze almost all the known human development and knowledge of 100,000 years from all over the world into the 2,000+ years of European development.

Today, the West has effectively rewritten the history of the world as their own, in their own image, placing themselves at its epicentre. No aspect of human endeavour or activity has been exempt from this process. Religion, social sciences, medicine, literature and the arts have all come under the influence of Western revisionists. Indeed, even current living history continues to be revised daily to suit the sensibilities of the Western audience, to reinforce their claim of innate superiority and therefore, by inference, the innate inferiority of all others.

The pervasiveness and extent to which this hoax has been propagated is astonishing. Millions, if not billions of people brought up in the west, or exposed to western ideology, religion and literature, wherever they are in the world have, to varying degrees, been influenced by it for over 2,000 years.

Our calendars are set by it, as Jesus Christ died on the cross 2,000+ years ago. However, Ptolemy named the days of the week after an incorrect interpretation of ancient astrology. Western science, technology and the European interpretation of Christianity have all evolved from this starting point onwards, effectively relegating over 80% of the total worldwide human experience and knowledge to antiquity.

Even though billions of people around the world have been born into, lived under, and died under the shadow of the two-thousand-year-old European broad claim to all the worlds civilization it does not make it correct and the human race as a whole will be greatly enriched by the truth.

The West not only needs to manipulate information, for example, history but it also needs to control the production and dissemination of information to its own people and the rest of the world. However, trying to squeeze over 100,000 years of global human experience into the two thousand year construct of Western civilization is not easy. Naturally, crucial omissions were made, and many other facts glossed over.

For instance, valiant attempts by Western academics to reconcile the biblical story of man's creation in the Garden of Eden remains at odds with the scientific interpretation of man's evolutionary development. How Egypt, the accepted progenitor of modern Western civilization, found its way into Africa, the 'dark continent', is still a mystery to many Western historians, archaeologists and scientists today. In many cases, it was necessary to plagiarize scientific ideas and religious ideology, music and art, from the original authors, change their identities to 'white' and even create fake inventors.

The West's redaction of world history does not stand up to close scrutiny, as it is incompatible with true world history and unsupported by objective archaeology, science and technology. The only way to maintain the illusion was to develop a pattern of 'layering' in which the original lie is coated several times over with pseudoscience and quasi-logical arguments, after which it is never revisited or challenged again. Once the spurious claim or deception has been repeated several times, it becomes the held truth in the minds of the unsuspecting recipient of this information and affects their whole perspective and even their lives.

Today, Western societies have had over a century's worth of practice at massaging history, omitting, inserting and fabricating factual events to create the right psychological impression. They have continued to evolve even more efficient ways of 'managing information' in order to shape the opinions of their own citizens and much of the world and to create the illusion of free speech and democracy, while in reality moulding public opinion such that it reinforces old and firmly held beliefs even when they are completely false. Some authors have described this phenomenon as the 'legendary lying lore'.

This complex matrix of misinformation, which includes lies, omissions and the truth only where it achieves the same end, is largely the preserve of the Western media and governments. As information flows through the matrix, it can change drastically in meaning and content, as it is doctored to influence the thinking of its target audience, the public or world opinion.

Another means by which the West has achieved this worldwide social engineering feat has been by the art of fragmenting world history into a kaleidoscope of well-packaged facts, presented piecemeal with the conscious and subconscious aim of gaining a psychological and material advantage. This practice helps cement certain perceptions and prejudices. It precludes other strains of thought and makes their historical narrative compatible with the sensibilities and ideologies of western societies.

Africans, who only identify themselves through the West's kaleidoscope, will only see the distorted and grotesque image of Africans that the West projects. Sadly, for Westernized Africans who only choose to identify themselves by Western ideals, it is as futile an act as trying to see yourself clearly through the smashed glass of a broken mirror.

The art of historical lying has been pleasantly called 'revision' by Western scholars and academics, which obscures the true meaning and intent from the minds of the people and provides the right hypocritical veil, not just to explain exploitation but explain it going forward.

The process can be exemplified by a euphemism in common use, namely, the term 'collateral damage'; a term which, when unpacked, in plain English, means killing innocent civilians but deflects the mind from the horror of brutal acts. In reality collateral damage brings about just the same terror, injury and death of ordinary and innocent people as the people they label 'terrorists' do.

Western hypocrisy, as breathtaking as it can be at times, is a necessary psychological by-product of racism and imperialism. To feed the superego of racism and imperialism, it was never enough to appropriate and claim to be the fount of all human knowledge, it must also simultaneously try to occupy the highest moral high ground around. In so doing, the mind conveniently fails to see or appreciate what the hands are doing.

For instance, transatlantic slavery was 'benevolently' employed to bring Christianity to the heathen and pagan people of Africa and the Americas. Colonization, realized by brute force, conquest and exploitative commerce, was a 'necessity' to spread Western culture. Today, Western globalization seeks to deliver freedom and democracy by massive bombing campaigns, military occupation, political manipulation and economic exploitation.

The Machiavellian means by which these lofty Western ideals are spread are of course insignificant for most westerners because, for the most part, they are the direct and indirect beneficiaries of the global power system of white supremacy and they are not exposed to the brutal truth of colonial and neo-colonial plunder. Genocide, plunder, subjugation, exploitation, lies and murder in support of their hypocritically stated aims of spreading Christianity, civilization and globalizing capitalism are all seen as legitimate and necessary means of spreading freedom and democracy. Otherwise the 'natives' in their ignorance, may actually resist change for the 'better'.

Adolf Hitler displayed deep perceptive insights into how the white imperialist system worked when he stated in his book 'Mein Kampf':

'The great masses of people in the very bottom of their hearts tend to be

corrupted rather than consciously and purposefully evil… therefore, in the primitive simplicity of their minds. They more easily fall victim to a big lie than to a little one, since they themselves lie in the little things but would be ashamed of lies that were too big.[2]

The result is that many Westerners are easily satisfied by the simple lies and obfuscation of their politicians as long as they fit in with their expected societal norms and their shallow, stereotypical understanding of the foreign people they exploit.

Thus, while Western governments scramble to appropriate the world's resources for themselves and make money hand over fist, there is a general lack of recognition amongst their people of the actual effects or 'collateral damage' caused by the pursuit of their 'noble' ambitions.

Fortunately, history leaves indelible footprints in the sands of time. True history is not only accurate but is consistent with the archaeological, geographical, genetic, linguistic and cultural finds of a place and people. A people's history, therefore, cannot be accurately told without a full understanding of all these parameters, how they interplay and crucially not without the input of the people themselves.

The West cannot change the laws of nature. Isaac Newton stated that energy is indestructible and can only be changed from one form to another. The laws of gravity still hold true for all on earth. Somewhere buried under the extensive Western rewriting of history and the false perceptions is a fundamental truth to all things.

Our daily existence is living history and is much like watching continuous live video footage. Without tampering with the tape, video evidence is therefore harder to manipulate. If one could borrow a time machine from Doctor Who and travel back in time, the observer from our time is likely to be completely confused. There may be little or no connection between true life history and what we believe as historical fact today.

CHAPTER TEN

CAPITALISM AND MILITARISM: THE RIGHT OF MIGHT

To reconstruct African history one must approach it in the same way detectives search for clues at a crime scene and weave them together to make a convincing case. The detectives work from the principle of an underlying truth.

Every race and colour of human beings on earth has at some point or another committed acts of cruelty and inhumanity. Unfortunately, history abounds with stories of human cruelty but the perpetuation of inhumanity and cruelty towards other human beings in concert and for so long has been the unique and exclusive preserve of the West.

No other race or people on earth could have imagined the intense and insatiate craving for a surplus of resources or for hegemony the European explorers embodied. The people the Europeans encountered were totally unprepared to deal with the well-armed, determined and ruthless men who confronted them, battle-hardened as they were from hundreds of years of incessant wars and wanton killing of each other, honed into a nationalistic need for hegemony over each other and anyone else they met. Nor could they have known that the Europeans fought 'total' war, using every means and every deception possible to further their aims.

Oliver Cromwell Cox, a Trinidadian-American sociologist, stated that European racism was uniquely associated with capitalist growth and expansion and in 1976 wrote:

'Racism, like race prejudice, is a relatively recent human development, it did not always exist... Racism as we know it in modern times, is not merely

verbal recognition of physical difference, ethnocentric comparisons among peoples in the design of creation, or invidious remarks by ancient conquerors about the physical and cultural traits of the conquered ...racism provides Europeans with a moral rational for their subjugation and exploitation of 'inferior peoples.'[1]

In 1913, the German socialist revolutionary and Marxist philosopher, Rosa Luxemburg, exposed the underlying brutality of Western capitalism, when she wrote:

'Force, fraud, oppression, looting are openly displayed without any attempt at concealment, and it requires an effort to discover within this tangle of political violence and contests of power the stern laws of the economic process. Bourgeois liberal theory takes into account only... the realm of peaceful competition, the marvels of technology and pure commodity exchange; it separates it strictly from the other aspect: the realm of capitals blustering violence, which is regarded as more or less incidental to foreign policy and quite independent of the economic sphere of capital.

In reality, political power is nothing but a vehicle for the economic process. The conditions for the reproduction of capital provide the organic link between these two aspects of the accumulation of capital. The historical career of capitalism can only be appreciated by taking them together. 'Sweating blood and filth with every pore from head to toe' characterizes not only the birth of capital but also its progress in the world at every step, and thus capitalism prepares its own downfall under ever more violent contortions and convulsions...

Militarism fulfils a quite definite function in the history of capital, accompanying as it does every historical phase of accumulation. It plays a decisive part in the first stages of European capitalism, in the period of the so-called 'primitive accumulation', as a means of conquering the New World and the spice-producing countries of India. Later, it is employed to subject the modern colonies, to destroy social organizations of primitive societies so that their means of production may be appropriated, forcibly to introduce commodity trade in countries where the social structure has been unfavorable to it, and to turn the natives into a proletariat by compelling them to work for wages in the colonies. It is responsible for the creation and expansion of spheres of interest for European capital in non-European regions, for extorting railway concessions in backward countries, and for enforcing the claims of European capital as international moneylender. Finally, militarism is a weapon in the competitive struggle between capitalist countries for areas of non-capitalist civilization.'[2]

Capitalism's modern expression, globalization, has brought about an even deeper integration of the western military, industrial and political complex, leading to the globalization of war and poverty.

For instance, Washington's 'fumigation programs' represented another phase of the historical process of driving the peasants off the land for the benefit of foreign investors and multinationals, practiced in Africa and South America in particular.[3]

Enforced through the privatization of the militia and paramilitary groups in the regions of interest, a great proportion of the atrocities they commit in the process are therefore 'privatized' according to Human Rights Watch.[4] Washington's neo-liberal policy of privatizing the fumigation process and conflicts means that fumigation is being taken over by 'private' companies consisting of US military officers under contract to the Pentagon.

The illegal act of 'rendition' or kidnapping people for torture and interrogation by the US government has been outsourced to private companies. Private civilian jets are used to fly kidnapped terror suspects to jails in foreign countries where they are subjected to 'enhanced interrogation techniques'. In some instances, these flights cost the US government over $30,000.[5]

The globalization of war was again in evidence in the American occupation of Iraq. During the Iraqi occupation, the second largest military force in operation, besides the American troops, was surprisingly not the British troops with 7,000 men, but private security contractors numbering over 16,000 men.[6]

This worldwide pattern has been useful in evading accountability for military atrocities committed and frees up the private contractors to use somewhat more coercive techniques than the US or UK military could get away with. Abdel Hakim Belhadj, one of the Libyan rebel leaders who helped the west topple Muammar Gaddafi, was earlier kidnapped under rendition sued Britain and demanded an official apology from the British government.[7]

The devastation and suffering caused by the globalization of capitalist war and poverty are enormous. As Noam Chomsky wrote:

'Peasant agriculture is based on a rich tradition of knowledge, and experience gained over many centuries, commonly passed from mother to daughter. Though a remarkable human achievement it is very fragile and can be destroyed forever in a single generation.'[8]

In places like the Niger Delta in Nigeria, Southern Sudan and Chad, this process has forced thousands of people from their homes into crowded city slums so that the multinationals can extract oil and other resources at will.

The west's imperialist drive continues to be the leading cause of environmental pollution, starvation, species extinction, war and genocide around the world.

CHAPTER ELEVEN

THE HIDDEN PSYCHOLOGICAL IMPERATIVE OF GLOBALISED RACISM

In his book, The Confessions of an Economic Hitman, John Perkins described America's global empire as:

'Self-centred, self-serving, greedy, materialistic system based on mercantilism, and it will use whatever means it deems necessary to help rulers gain more power and riches.'[1]

However, while capitalist expansion may be a plausible reason for the development of racism and imperialism, it is worth exploring a deeper layer of the white racist or supremacist psyche to have a better understanding of its motivations.

Dr Frances Cress Welsing, an eminent African American psychiatrist defined white racism as:

'...the local and global power system structured and maintained by persons that classify themselves as white, whether consciously or subconsciously determined; this system consists of patterns of perception, logic, symbol formation, thought, speech, action and emotional responses conducted simultaneously in all areas of people activity [economics, education, entertainment, labour, politics, religion, sex and war].'[2]

Welsing's 'Cress Colour Confrontation Theory' states that the primary subconscious drive emanates from a deep subconscious psychological sense of colour and numerical inadequacy as genetically recessive white Caucasians are a minority race in a world that is populated by an overwhelming majority of non-white, genetically dominant people [black, brown, red and yellow].[3]

Welsing postulates that the ultimate purpose of white racism and supremacy is the creation and maintenance of a global system of white domination to prevent white genetic annihilation. The resultant inherent hostility and aggression towards people of colour leads them to genocide or genocidal imperatives.

As Africans have the greatest colour potential of any people in the world, the black African race and the black African male in particular, have come under the most vicious and persistent attack of all. Psychologically, it is generally accepted that in most instances, the main cause of any neurotic drive for superiority is usually founded upon a deep and pervading sense of inadequacy and an inferiority complex. There is an abundance of evidence of white colour anxiety if one cares to look for it.

Without doubt, immigration, especially that of Africans, is a major concern for most right wing and far right groups in the West. On July 6th 2017, in his first speech in Europe, President Donald Trump played on white anxiety over the 'alleged clash of civilisations' in which the west is pitted against the rest. Addressing European leaders in Warsaw, Poland, Donald Trump asked the rhetorical question:

"The fundamental question of our time is whether the West has the will to survive. Do we have the confidence in our values to defend them at any cost?"[4]

Conflating the Nazi occupation of Poland during the Second World War with the 'state of the western world', Donald Trump answered his own question stating:

"Just as Poland could not be broken, I declare today for the world to hear, that the West will never, ever be broken, our values will persevere, our people will thrive, and our civilisation will triumph."[5]

During the 2017 Charlottesville riots in America, members of a violent neo-Nazi and openly racist white supremacy group, the Rise Above Movement [RAM] shared the meaning of their logo with journalists. Their motto, 'the 14' means 'fourteen words':

"We must secure the existence of our people and the future of white

children."[6]

Members of RAM came in 'uniform' — skull masks and grey clothes. They were extremely violent and when they were not chanting *"Kill. Kill. Kill"* while assaulting the anti-right demonstrators, they chanted: *"You will not replace us."*[7]

Dr Jonathan Metzl, a psychiatrist and sociologist at Vanderbilt University, postulates that white anxiety and white supremacy is at the key to understanding America's gun debate.

In his book, 'Dying of Whiteness, How the Politics of Racial Resentment is Killing America's Heartlands' Metzl postulates that the intensity and polarization of the US gun debate makes much more sense when understood in the context of whiteness and white privilege.

White Americans defend white privilege and the racial hierarchy by opposing issues like gun control, healthcare expansion or public school funding. One of the aims of the Ku Klux Klan was the disarming of African Americans. This is why there were widespread calls for more gun control when the Black Panthers tried to arm themselves but the National Rifle Association [NRA] refused to give up their own weapons.

Most southern states in America have permissive open carry laws. In states like Missouri and Michigan, open carry laws allow parades of heavily armed white Americans. They are allowed to walk into local shops like Walmart and Burrito restaurants and are generally viewed as patriots.

However, when African American gun owners open carried into Walmart, they were challenged, tackled and even shot.[8]

Many Africans and their diaspora, ignorant of the global white power structure, fail to make any connection between white supremacy and their current predicaments. Without appreciating the wider and deeper global imperatives of white supremacy, their actions will only confound and confuse the uninformed observer when trying to understand the multifaceted approach of the imperialists or supremacists.

Neely Fuller Jr. appreciated this when he wrote: "Racism is not merely a pattern of individual and/or institutional practice; it is a universally operating 'system' of white supremacy and domination in which the majority of the world's whites participate'.

He went further and stated:

"Most white people hate black people. The reason that most white people hate black people is because whites are not black people.

If you know this about white people, you need know little else. If you do not know this about white people, virtually everything else that you know about them will only confuse you."[9]

Imperialism thus represents the highest level of systematic social, economic and political, racial discrimination. It is organized and participated in by white nation states primarily against people of colour. One can generalize and state that Africans and their diaspora living in the west are exploited and dehumanized by white racism, while Africans in the African continent and other Third World countries, are exploited through its export product —imperialism and globalisation.

The global effects of racism and imperialism have caused death and suffering to billions of people worldwide. The wests desire to exploit people and the environment for power and profits has led to environment damage on an unprecedented scale globally. The endless western wars of material acquisition and environmental damage are on such an alarming local and global scale that it is putting the question of survival to life on earth, as we know it today.

There is no other functionally operative global system of oppression of anyone other than white racism or supremacy in the world today. There are certainly no examples in the world where there is an established pattern of direct or indirect oppression of whites by non-whites anywhere in the world in modern times. White racism is therefore, the most important phenomenon and existential threat facing the human race in general and African people, in particular, today.

Whether one accepts Dr Welsing's Cress Theory or not, the fact remains that generally Caucasians tend to express an unprecedented and almost uncontrollable sense of latent or overt hostility and aggression towards non-whites. The Caucasian drive towards superiority over all peoples of colour, its technological culture and dominant power structure are the cornerstones of the universal white supremacy culture, which according to the Colour Confrontation Theory is a response to their core sense of psychological inadequacy.

If the global human village is a jungle, then the West are the top human predators and Africans their most sought-after prey. Not even the Middle East comes close to experiencing the exploitation Africa has endured over the centuries. The hallmark of any top predator is its ability to study the physical and psychological characteristics of their prey, note their strengths and weaknesses and launch vicious attacks at an opportune moment.

This is the reason why European imperialists closely study foreign people, their geography, culture and customs, strengths and weaknesses and most importantly their natural and labour resources. Generalizing, it is often the case that Europeans and North Americans are aware of a country's natural resources but know precious little about the indigenous people.

Unlike jungle predators, human predators can easily manipulate the environment in order to flush out their prey or force them into compromising and vulnerable positions, especially when it is outside the conscious thought of their intended victims.

Imperialists always seek to divide people they oppress and use whatever means possible to set them against each other. Fear, desire, greed, ambition, pride and lack of confidence are all exploited in varying degrees to keep them weak and exploitable. Physical violence as coercion is the common denominator in the western imperial theme. Violence is invariably used, either directly or subcontracted indirectly, through proxies. Even while the imperialist tries to scatter non-white peoples like sand in the wind, they simultaneously try to rally their own people into supporting the exploitation process by taking an 'us versus them' stance and scaring them with a never-ending stream of 'imminent' threats to their people and nations.

It is for this reason that all Africans need to have a global outlook on their current predicaments and not just a local and personal one.

Once the impact and global context of white imperialism on Africa and its diaspora are clear it also becomes apparent that the African people and nations need to form a united front to stand any chance at confronting the exploitative aims of white supremacy as a whole.

CHAPTER TWELVE
GLOBALISING WHITE PRIVILEGE

White privilege is a modern day reality regardless of if you are white and have millions banked in your account or are a white person, broke and homeless on the street. Western governments plunder, cheat, lie and kill to provide and maintain white privilege, even if you might not be a direct beneficiary of their nefarious activities.

The concept of black privilege does not exist in the West. By Western design, non-white people must fight hard to survive and even harder to thrive. This is essentially the consequence of an inability to defend themselves or unawareness of the need to defend themselves...same difference.

Western civilization promotes a superficial, narcissistic approach to life. Selfishness, greed, callousness and exploitation are all handsomely rewarded — if carried out within the established societal norms. Crimes against humanity are not considered crimes if multinationals and governments can demonstrate clear profit margins. Even when Westernized people are not in a position to exploit others, they still show a high degree of alienation, apathy, callousness and a lack of consideration towards others, especially towards foreigners, just as their socialization demands.

It seems that the whole purpose of capitalist Western society is to get rich or die trying. As such, the most important ambition of the imperialist is to accumulate material wealth through the exploitation of others by whatever means possible. It is difficult to comprehend the level of destruction that Western capitalism is prepared to accept to achieve their aims. Ignoring the horrors of the transatlantic slave trade and genocide of the colonialism process for a moment, one is still staggered by the death and suffering that people endured during the two World Wars or European wars fought globally.

Official estimates of the First World War gives figures of over 50 million deaths made up of over 10 million civilians and 37 million men in arms in four years and three months. The Second World War was even more destructive and approximately 60–80 million deaths were recorded worldwide.[1]

The official estimated casualties may be much higher, as many people killed in Africa, Asia, and parts of Europe may not have been accounted for due to lack of records.

Western powers are now armed with nuclear missiles and bombs over ten times more powerful and destructive than ever before. When this terrifying fact is combined with a multitude of modern delivery systems ranging from killer robots, drones, supersonic aircraft, nuclear submarines and aircraft carriers and even satellites from outer space it means that a nuclear war would annihilate billions of people and end life on earth as we know it.

In order to facilitate exploitation, ruthlessness and a complete disregard for human suffering and life is an essential trait of an imperialist. You cannot prosecute wars of plunder at great cost to human life and the environment when you feel sorry for your victims. Most European pirates and colonizers were rewarded with high office and riches in recognition of their furthering of the imperial ethos. And this remains true even today. Former American president, George W. Bush, was named *Time Magazine's* man of the year in 2004, after the bloody occupation of Iraq in 2003.[2]

The United States of America has negatively affected virtually every economy in the world through its imperial neo-colonial foreign policies. Some form of negative American and British influence can be seen in most areas of conflict in the world. Andrew Simms, policy director of the New Economics Foundation [NEF] said:

"Over the last century, Britain and the US left a global trail of conflict, social upheaval and environmental damage as they sought to capture and

control a disproportionate share of the world's oil reserves."[3]

In 2012, a study by Stuart Laycock, revealed that Britain has at one stage or the other invaded nine out of every ten countries in the world. There were only twenty-two countries that had not been subjected to a British invasion [Copping]. The US has invaded 69 countries since the end of the Second World War in 1945.[4]

The Australian scientist, Dr Gideon Polya, stated that: "*American imperialism has made a significant contribution to the 1.3 billion global avoidable deaths between 1950–2005.*"[5]

Imperialism should also be seen as a war against the poor and defenceless. Even the poorer citizens of Western nations are not immune to manipulation and exploitation by their media and governments. Despite their own deprivations at the hands of capitalism, they are somewhat compensated by being constantly reminded of their innate superiority to all foreigners and Africans in particular. This is a form of cold comfort, to divert their attention from the actions of their governments and to unite them in xenophobia against everyone else.

The poorer the nation, the less likely they are to be able to defend themselves against the crippling effects of globalization and if need be Western invasion and occupation. Because of their defenceless nature, they are usually more likely to find themselves on the receiving end of racism and imperialism because of their vulnerability.

The imperialism that drives hegemony, sustains racism and xenophobia, creates divisions, sustains them, and starts wars, has impoverished over 70% of the population of the world. The inequality between the world's richest people and the poorest is so striking that the world's richest constitute less than 1% of the world's total population. Individual billionaires, like Warren Buffett and Bill Gates, are wealthier in monetary terms than several of the world's poorest countries combined.[6]

Racism and the imperialism it breeds have killed millions if not billions of people. Most of the world's population lives below the poverty line, suffers needlessly and dies often needlessly too, while the scourge of racism, imperialism and inequality continues, ensuring that the gap between rich and poor is ever widening.

CHAPTER THIRTEEN

DESTRUCTION OF THE ENVIRONMENT

Western civilization is unsustainable as it requires two main pillars to survive. The first, is widespread domination and exploitation of the vast majority of the world's poorest populations. The second is the indiscriminate destruction of the environment. Both these pillars are an anathema to the survival of the human race as a whole and to the planet, including that of the imperialists.

The need to maintain hegemony over the people of the world drives imperialists to destroy the environment as they continue to scramble for even more of the world's resources. The toxic emissions produced by developed nations is destroying the protective ozone layer and deforestation has damaged ecosystems and is leading to the extinction of many animals.

Major changes in the world's climatic conditions, heralded by the desiccation of the Sahara desert and the entry into the last the ice age, forced man to develop civilization accordingly. The drying of the Sahara desert stimulated human migration out of Africa to all parts of the world while the ice age, especially the formation of ice caps in the North and South pole, help maintain conditions favourable to the existence of man on earth.

Former US Vice-President and democratic representative for the Presidency against George W. Bush, Al Gore, won a Nobel Prize for his brilliant environmental film, 'An Inconvenient Truth'. His film was one of the first well-known environmental movies to articulate clearly the real and present danger that all human beings are facing from the dangers of global warming.[1]

In 2008 NASA geophysicist Scott B. Luthcke reported that more than half of the landlocked ice had melted within five years. Another NASA scientist, Zwally stated that the situation showed *'strong signs of warming and amplification'*.[2]

On September 16th 2009 medical chiefs in the UK, Ireland and around the world warned of a 'global climate catastrophe'. In an editorial in the British Medical Journal and the Lancet, they called on doctors to put pressure on politicians meeting in Copenhagen in a bid to secure a new global deal on cutting emissions. Heads of the Royal Colleges asked doctors to demand that world leaders listen to the scientific evidence and implement strategies to tackle emissions that will benefit the health of people around the globe. They stated: *'A failure to negotiate a strong deal could have catastrophic results with those in the poorest countries hardest hit by impacts on health, of drought and pressure on water resources, storms floods and conflicts.'*[3]

The Intergovernmental Panel on Climate Change Risks [IPCC] agreed with this assessment in principle and warned that 75–250 million people across Africa could face water shortages by 2020.[4]

In summary, the environmental damage caused by humanity over and beyond the effects of nature include the thickening of the ozone layer and the trapping of greenhouse gases, causing global warming at a rate that will soon make the earth unable to sustain human life as we know it. The natural absorption of carbon dioxide by trees has been severely impaired by wanton deforestation and industrialization is pouring out pollutants into the environment at a rate unparalleled in human history. Over 2,400 hectares of rainforest are being lost daily through deforestation.[5]

As a result of the increased global warming, the polar ice caps are melting rapidly and the albedo effect of the polar ice caps — their ability to reflect ultraviolet light or heat from the sun back out to space — is greatly diminished.

The immediate outcome of all of this has been dramatic changes in weather systems with a rise in sea levels and more frequent and severe flooding. Paradoxically, even though global warming has increased rainfall, it has also caused more droughts because the increased heat evaporates the water out of the soil rapidly, and moisture precipitates as a storm somewhere else causing flooding.

Clear signs of the effects of global warming in Africa due to climate change are the near-total evaporation of Lake Chad, the desertification of the Sahel and the ice caps on Mt. Kilimanjaro, which have been melting steadily.[6]

In Asia the drying up of the Aral Sea and effects of global warming on Lake Baikal are other depressing examples. Low-lying countries like Bangladesh have seen millions of people displaced by floodwaters due to rising sea levels. Severe flooding in Pakistan and China, heatwaves in Europe and droughts across Africa have destabilized the already fraught food and water supplies in some of these regions. The devastating tsunami's in Indonesia in 2004 and Japan in February 2011 caused enormous additional man-made disaster — in the case of the latter damaging nuclear reactors and releasing radiation into the air, soil and water.

The United States of America has been the largest producer of toxic emissions in the world for many decades yet when former US President, George W. Bush, was challenged about the United States pulling out of the Kyoto agreement in his second debate with presidential candidate John Kerry, he defended his position by stating that agreeing to the Kyoto agreement would lose America jobs.

During George Bush's presidency, in a move dubbed the 'no tree left behind policy', the Republican-controlled senate approved drilling for oil in Alaska's National Refuge. Bush also loosened pollution controls on coal-fired power plants and abandoned more than 50 investigations into possible breaches of the Clean Air Act.[7]

Long before Donald Trump became the 45th President of the United States he had made it clear that he did not belief in man-made climate change.

In November 2016 Reince Priebus, the incoming White House Chief of Staff, explained to the press that Donald Trump's default position is that climate change is a *'bunch of junk.'*[8]

The following year, as President of the United States, Donald Trump duly delivered. On June 1st 2017 he announced plans to withdraw the US from the Paris Climate Change Agreement, a pledge by almost 200 countries to reduce emissions linked with climate change. He also ordered the Pentagon to stop preparing for climate change.[9]

In stark contrast to this, the Kenyan Nobel prize-winning environmentalist, Professor Wangari Maathai, otherwise known as the 'Tree Woman', planted millions of trees in Africa to help combat deforestation and global warming.[10]

The effects of global warming in Africa will be more devastating when compared to other areas in the world as up to 70% of people depend on agriculture and are dependent on steady rainfall for good crops in the context of extremely fragile socio-economic systems.

CHAPTER FOURTEEN

GLOBALISING POVERTY AND WAR

Globalization is now a popular term, which in its technical interpretation is used to describe the integration of economic systems, capital movement and opportunities through improved information and communication technologies. However, the reality is that globalization has also come to mean the increased poverty, insecurity and powerlessness of the vast majority of the world's poor. In real terms, globalization is simply another euphemism to describe the process of accumulation or capitalism to sustain the west's military, political and economic domination of the world.

A classic illustration of this are the so-called structural adjustment programme foisted on many developing nations by the International Monetary Fund. These programmes were tied to funding for states who in most cases were already seriously in debt and the funding was only forthcoming if the SAP package was accepted. However, the real objective of the SAPS was to provide Western countries an economic platform through which poorer countries were economically plundered and controlled externally.

"Structural adjustment programs were organized globalization: Countries ensured capital mobility so that money of speculators; investors or creditors entered and exited a country with minimal risk. Capital mobility was facilitated through privatization of State assets [Utilities, health, investment, education facilities, and factories] and liberalization or deregulation of trade, investment and finance"[1]

Using this economic gunboat approach, the World Bank and the IMF used globalization to restructure the economies of Third World countries in the interests of global capital and maintain their dependence. Even though orthodox economists continue to claim that globalization through privatization stimulates economic growth and that the poorest countries have the most to gain from higher levels of trade and investment, this claim is theoretical at best, as evidence from independent academics, UN bodies, IMF and even the World Bank shows.[2]

The United Nations Development Program [UNDP] estimated the ratio of income of the richest 20% of the world's population to the poorest 20% has increased from 30:1 in 1960, to 78:1 in 1994. Other UN research showed that real GDP per capita in sub-Saharan Africa has halved in relative terms, and in Latin America it has fallen by 30% since 1979.[3]

The effects on poverty and health are tremendous, as the vast majority of Africa's poor remains impoverished due to poor economic growth. Incredibly, due to globalization, over half of the world's largest economies are now not countries but companies. The food giant Monsanto and oil companies like BP or Exxon are richer than many African nations.

The world's poor are being hit by globalization wherever they are and even though the US is the world's richest country, African-Americans, who constitute the bulk of its poor, are disproportionately affected due to racially motivated unequal distribution of opportunities and wealth in the US. While the US is still the 'richest country' in the world it is not the country that is rich but the 1% of the population who own 40% of the wealth: Unemployment runs at 12% and per capita income is falling for the majority.[4]

The late Fidel Castro, former President of Cuba, once said:

"Globalization is an objective reality, underlining the fact that we are all passengers on the same vessel, that is, this planet where we all live.

But the passengers are traveling in very different conditions. Trifling minorities are traveling in luxurious cabins furnished with the internet, cell phones and access to global communication networks. They enjoy a nutritional abundant and balanced diet as well as clean water supplies. They have access to sophisticated medical care and culture.

Overwhelming and hurting majorities are travelling in conditions that resemble the terrible slave trade from Africa to America in our colonial past. That is 85% of the passengers on this ship are crowded together in its dirty hold suffering hunger, disease, and helplessness.

Obviously, this vessel is carrying too much injustice to remain afloat, and it pursues such an irrational and senseless route that it cannot call on a safe port. This vessel seems destined to clash with an iceberg. If that happened, we would all sink with it."[5]

CHAPTER FIFTEEN

THE AFRICAN HOLOCAUST

Professor Sachs, an eminent economist, stated: *"Little surpasses the western world in the cruelty and depredations it has long imposed on Africa"*[1]

In whatever way or guise Europeans came to Africa with, it usually resulted in a net loss for Africa and their inhabitants. Be it as slave traders, explorers, missionaries, colonizers or, as now, neo-colonizers spreading globalization, the results have been uniformly disastrous for the vast majority of African people. Horror stories similar to the African holocaust — rape, murder and exploitation has followed Europeans wherever they set foot. Africa is unique in that no other continent or people have been raped, pillaged and plundered to the extent, and for as long, as Africa has been. The problem is compounded not just by the stripping of the people of their history, culture, land and people but also by the constant denigration of Africa and Africans in the Western media, the psychological basis of mental slavery.

Sadly, the story of European intervention in Africa is not just one of a holocaust in distant times. It is an unfolding series of holocausts, which continue to claim the lives and kill the aspirations of millions of Africans over the centuries until the present day.

Europeans, the very same people who maltreated and exploited the African continent have related much of what we know about Africa to us. Eurocentric Europeans have chosen to rewrite history in their own image and the true story of Africa and its people has not yet been told.

In order for Europeans to salve their consciences about the death, destruction, denigration and division they spread throughout Africa, African history must be rewritten. However, it was done not just to spare the conscience of the European perpetrators or justify the exploitation and enslavement of African people, it was done also to emphasize their alleged 'innate superiority' over them. This overwhelming hypocrisy in the west acts as a convenient shield to protect the mind from their actions and carry out their negative intentions on unsuspecting Africans.

Fortunately, through the efforts of many true scientists, archaeologists and historians, not all has been lost, and it is now possible to reconstruct a more accurate and less prejudiced history of Africa and its contributions to the whole world. The major impediments to renaissance in Africa and its diaspora are racism and its global version, imperialism. The roots of both are to be found deeply embedded in the fabric of Western and North American society.

Knowledge of true African history is a necessity for all Africans in their personal journey to rediscovering themselves and knowing how to defend themselves in this Eurocentric white man's world. A clear awareness of the deep, overarching motivation of white supremacy or imperialist, towards domination and exploitation in all areas of human activity is crucial for Africans and its diaspora in order for them to be able to re-establish themselves globally.

As a prominent historian Professor Clarke stated:

'History is the clock that people use to tell them their time of day. It is also a compass that people use to find themselves on the map of human geography. The role of history is to tell a people what they have been, where they have been, what they are and where they are. The most important role that history plays is that it has the function of telling people where they still must go and what they still must be'.[2]

The US, Britain and France remain the foremost proponents of imperialism and racism in the world today. France is also playing an important role in aggressively promoting western imperialism all over French-speaking Africa. These countries have erected huge empires and amassed great wealth based on the blood, sweat and suffering of vast swathes of the world's poorest people, especially in Africa.

The British, the past colonial masters, were the greatest slave traders of all times. When the British Empire was at its height, they colonized up to 70% of the known world. During its triangular slave trade, the US was the largest recipients of African slaves. It had the added advantage of not bearing the burden of direct colonialism. Today, it remotely controls the economies of practically all Third World nations. This large American neo-colonial empire is sustained through the destabilization of governments, subversion of economies and the instalment of puppet regimes. They achieve control of these economies via the globalization of capital and the use of military force whenever these controlling methods fail.

Utilizing the immense profits from the slave trade, the French, British and US Americans were able to develop their nations and their military to police their foreign policies and protect their economic interests.

A legacy of the British slave trade and the colonial era is that the vast majority of countries they colonized remain divided and continue to be exploited for their resources by their colonial masters until today. This is especially true in Africa, where flashpoints created by British colonialists left the colonized people deeply prone to conflict. Many have endured decades of great suffering through war, political instability and poverty as a result to this day. It is a pattern replicated all over the world — from Northern Ireland to the Middle East, across Africa into the Far East and Asia.

The underlying truth to Africa's prostrate position in the world today is the continuation of Africa's history of western exploitation from transatlantic slavery to the present day. The continuum of modern African history is also the continuum of the exploitation of Africa that all people all over the world must face up to. In order to penetrate back to the true African history and identity through the dense matrix of Western lies, Africa and its diaspora must deconstruct the effects of racism and mental slavery it has imposed on their minds. They must reconstruct their 'shaved' memories and cut through the matrix of the 'multiplicities of phenomenon' or the illusions, media lies and traps the white slave masters have placed in the path of Africans. The deception has predictably trapped many Africans and their diaspora in ineffective and circular patterns of behaviour which they have developed in order to cope with the brutality of the white supremacy system.

Understanding Western imperialism is by far the first and most important step in understanding and reacting appropriately to the situation that Africans find themselves in today. Africans must confront the myths, mysteries and lies in whatever shape they are, without prejudice or sentiment.

You do not have to be covered in burns to learn that fire is dangerous. The African people and their diaspora, wherever they are in the world, who choose to remain ignorant of or to ignore the white supremacist geo-political agenda around them, should prepare for a lifetime of unnecessary suffering, and in many cases prepare to die. Trying to fight the effects of racism and imperialism, using the construct and within the contexts given to us by European imperialists, is a strategy clearly doomed to fail. Until Africans and their diaspora are able to develop their own insight into the mind of the white supremacist culture of domination, they will remain exposed and vulnerable.

Westerners who genuinely want to help the starving and suffering people of Africa should start from the same stepping off point, albeit with a degree of difficulty because of their socialization in European ideology. They have to stand back and objectively reassess many notions in which they have been socialized, to appreciate what is really going on. Coming face-to-face with the true realities and brutalities of Western imperialism and capitalism is the first step for all people who really desire a better world.

They must be willing to place African history in its true context and honestly and accurately interpret the precedents to Africa's suffering today. They must also be prepared to take their lead from Africans, who are in the forefront of the fight, as only Africans can and should lead their people out of bondage.

There is much talk about 'giving back' in the West — and Africans are grateful for whatever aid and charitable initiatives that reach them from the west. However, Africa's problem is really about the disproportionate 'taking out' of essential African resources by western governments and multinationals. Westerners who want to make a difference should concentrate their efforts here.

Chinua Achebe wrote:

'If the hunter learns to shoot without missing, then the bird must learn to fly without perching.'[3]

True African self-knowledge is essential in understanding what is going on and true self-realization is the key to crossing into your own paradigm rather than the artificial and harmful one Africans currently inhabit, namely the western paradigm. The acquisition of knowledge is not enough and must be matched by an appropriate and reasoned response. The psychological paradigm may only be a hair's breadth apart but if not crossed the reality is all too harsh.

Noam Chomsky asked the rhetorical question on the cover of his book, Hegemony or Survival: America's Quest for Global Dominance. The question, 'hegemony or survival' can be extended to include most western nations, including post-empire Britain and France, who are the US's main allies in its quest for global dominance.

The evidence clearly shows that the west has chosen hegemony over survival. Africa and the rest of the poor and disenfranchised people of the world can only opt for survival.

Africa and its diaspora must wake up to understanding this and position itself to break the western hegemony. Rhetorically, do Africans continue to subsist to exist, or do they begin to strive to thrive? For millions of Africans and its diaspora the question posed by racism and imperialism is not just about quality of life, it is about life itself.

The stark reality is that Africans have no choice but to unite and bear the responsibility of their own survival — just as their ancestors did. To do otherwise would mean that Africans face the real risk of eventual extinction or worse still, perpetual mental, physical, economic, social and political slavery.

PART TWO:
DECOLONIZING AFRICAN HISTORY

CHAPTER SIXTEEN

AFRICA, THE BIBLICAL GARDEN OF EDEN

> *'Until the Lion tells its side of the story, the story of the hunt will always glorify the hunter.'* **African Proverb**[1]

> *'If I have seen further it is by standing on the shoulders of giants.'* **Sir Isaac Newton**[2]

Modern African history is the story of the 'hunter'. It is a story defined by asymmetric power structures that glorify the slave masters not the slaves, the colonizers not the colonized, and favour the rich and not the poor. Consequently, modern African history is more revealing of how westerners perceive Africans that about who Africans really are.

Africa was a rich, complex continent with highly developed people and sophisticated kingdoms and technology long before the Europeans arrived. Several great African civilizations and kingdoms had gone through their golden ages and were on the decline before the light of civilization illuminated Europe. Western propaganda and racist ideas have not only literally shaped the continent geographically but also created the present-day ideas and notions about the African continent and its people.

Europeans have identified Africans by several names over the millennia. The name 'Africa' originates from the Romans, who called it 'Aprica' meaning without cold, or sunny. The ancient Greeks called Africa 'Libya'. Africa was also known at some stage as 'Ethiopia' and at one time all Africans were called Ethiopians or Moors. The names used to describe

Africans are very important because it provides a name trail through which the true history of Africans and their contribution to European civilization is traceable through the matrix of white propaganda.

Geographically, Africa is the second largest continent in the world and covers about a fifth of the world's surface. It is only smaller than Asia. However, it is the richest continent in the world in natural and human resources, which include the world's largest store of fossil fuels, metal ores, gems and precious metals. Africa also has a great diversity of biological resources ranging from rich tropical rainforests to the famous wildlife of eastern and southern Africa.

Africans are blessed with an abundance of land. Africa only accounts for 10% of the world's population and is thus relatively under-populated when compared to other continents. With a population of an estimated 1.2 billion people, the African people and their cultures are about as diverse as their natural resources.[3] When you consider Africa's tremendous biological diversity, it is not hard to imagine that Africa could be the most likely geographical location of the biblical story of the Garden of Eden.

Africa has the highest birth and death rates in the world, with as much as 40% of the population less than fifteen years old.[4] Over 60% of the working population is engaged in subsystems of the culture and the production of food and cash crops.[5]

Africans come in every size and colour, from very dark skinned or 'black' to the very light skinned or 'white'.

During the European colonization of Africa, the continent was split, arbitrarily into smaller geographically-based units, reflecting the zone of influence of the colonizing country. The colonial divide did not consider the ethnic or other cultural distribution of people prior to their land-grab and this would leave a lasting legacy of mistrust, discord and disunity that still plagues many African countries today.

Scientifically, it is generally accepted that all human life originated in Africa. Over the millennia, Africans migrated to all other parts of the world. Fossil finds in southern and eastern Africa have shown human-type creatures spanning back over 6 million years. In 1959, Mary and Louis Leakey found an australopithecine skeleton [Australopithecus, which means southern ape] at the Olduvai Gorge in Kenya. The human-type fossil dates back 3 to 5 million years. In a more recent discovery a 7.5 million-year-old 'Toumai skull' was unearthed in Chad, which may just be the oldest human ancestor discovered yet.[6]

There has always only ever been one human race, even though racist Western propaganda has done everything within its powers to emphasize our minute differences rather than our overwhelming similarities.

Modern humans are thought to have appeared in sub-Saharan Africa about 200,000 to 100,000 years ago and migrated out of Africa. Remarkable advances in science have allowed us to use molecular biology to trace back human origins in Africa, utilising mitochondrial maternal DNA. Mitochondria are the engine rooms of cells and produce the energy required for cellular activity to take place. Maternal DNA, found in the mitochondria of cells is passed directly from mother to daughter in an unbroken chain and can be used to accurately trace our ancestral roots back for thousands of years.

In support for this 'Out of Africa theory' an article in the Washington Post stated:

'A small group of humans left Africa, the cradle of evolution, and went forth to populate Asia, Europe, and the Americas about 100,000 years ago, according to scientists who studied genetic patterns in worldwide groups… this pattern of variation suggests that all non-Africans derive from a single common ancestral population which has migrated out of Africa.'[7]

Thousands of years ago, land bridges joined some continental land masses and allowed human beings to migrate to all parts of the world. Over time, several major geographical events narrowed these land routes, preventing large land-based migrations. However, if one notes the proximity of Africa to Europe — Gibraltar and Spain — to Morocco or the United States of America to Russia across the Bering Strait, it is not hard to imagine that humans beings migrated across these routes throughout the millennia.

Against this backdrop we have the Eurocentric view, which concludes that the major migrations of black Africans have only been within Africa and not outwards. This view is entertained in order to bolster their claim that there was no civilization in Africa. Eurocentrics state categorically that the only major intercontinental migration was that of Europeans, who also migrated into Africa, but not Africans migrating outwards. In effect, Europeans isolated Africa away from the rest of the world and any civilizing influence. They maintain that the Europeans brought all the developments in science, arts and medicine to Africa. Fortunately, many eminent historians, archaeologists and geneticists have vigorously challenged the Eurocentric idea that Africa remained unchanged for thousands of years until the European explorers and traders came to civilize them.

It is now known that several legends on which Europeans based their historiographical ideology are false. One of these is the alleged 'discovery' of the Americas by Christopher Columbus. In his book, *They Came Before Columbus*, a prominent African historian, Professor Van Sertima, argues that Nile valley Africans, the ancient Egyptians and the Nubians all reached the Gulf of Mexico in the first millennium BC. He postulated that black African mariners from the Horn of Africa, Guinea, Mali and Senegal reached the Americas thousands of years before Christopher Columbus or any other Europeans did. They used natural drift routes in the ocean, based on the gravitational pull of the moon to create ocean currents, high tides and low tides, to find their way to the Americas.[8]

Anecdotally, in the coastal areas around the West African city of Lagos in Nigeria, it is local knowledge that the Atlantic drift routes from Lagos can take one to Brazil in South America. It may be more than coincidental that through early contact, in addition to the transatlantic slave trade, that many coastal Lagosian's bear Brazilian names.

Professor Sertima also showed that there was contact between the Mande-speaking West Africans of the Upper Niger Valley and native Americans, in areas now called the Caribbean, Mexico, Columbia, Panama, Ecuador, Peru and others, a whole millennium before the arrival of Columbus.

In his book, 'They Came Before Columbus', Van Sertima states that his claims are supported by the trail of African cultural and archaeological exports, like pyramid tombs and temples, scripts, alphabets, calendar systems and sculptures of all different shapes and sizes to South America.[9]

The Olmecs are the earliest recorded civilization in America and preceded the civilization of the Incas by thousands of years. They are thought to have migrated from Uganda, through northern Africa, and used the Atlantic drift routes to the Americas where they settled.[10]

The Olmecs built large pyramids and huge stone artefacts with the faces of black African men on them.

Incredibly, some Europeans have attributed the construction of large pyramids in Africa and the Americas to aliens from outer space. Erich von Daniken in his book, *'Chariots of the Gods?'* claimed the Egyptian pyramids could only have been built with the help of extra-terrestrials.[11]

In fact, it is not just Africans who are alleged to have reached the Americas before Christopher Columbus. The Phoenicians, who were in fact African Asians, are also known to have navigated to much of the known world before Columbus reached the Americas. It is now known, through authors like Professor Ivan van Sertima and David MacRitchie, in his book, *Ancient and Modern Britons*, that African mariners built seaworthy vessels and traded as far as China.

It is on record that there has been a presence of black African people in Britain dating back several hundred years, and it is also on record that Africans sailed to Scotland in search of metals like iron.[12]

Contrary to popular Western history, the Chinese and the Vikings also reached the Americas long before Christopher Columbus. The Chinese Admiral Zheng had sailed around the world, with hundreds of ships and thousands of men, and had already put down colonies in America by 1421.[13]

It is alleged that Christopher Columbus had a fairly accurate map of the world as produced by the Chinese and that he was also made aware of the drift routes from West Africa to the Americas, by Portuguese explorers who had come across the African mariners who had already made many voyages to the coast of Africa.[14]

In March 2013, scientists from Illinois found a rare 600-year-old Chinese coin in Kenya. The researchers state that this coin proves that trade existed between China and Eastern Africa decades before Europeans set sail for Africa.[15]

William Dwight McKissic Sr. wrote about the spread of Africans throughout the world:

'The darker races of India preceded the lighter Aryan races. The Etruscans who originated in Africa occupied Italy before the Romans. A short, swarthy [black] race initially populated France and Germany. The aborigine of Australia, the Maoris of new Zealand, the Ainus of Japan, the black Caribs of Saint Vincent, the Olmecs of Mexico, the Jamesis of Florida, and the Garifuna of South America[the list goes on] all represents dark or dusky complexion people who spanned the globe prior to recorded history.'[16]

Another respected African historian William Leo Hansberry wrote:

'Recent archaeological, anthropological, and historical inquiry has brought, and is bringing, to light evidence, which supports the conclusion that Palestine, Arabia, Persia, and India were once the seats of important groups of blacks or Africans, and the traces of this racial type, which are still to be detected in most of these areas at the present time, are but the surviving remnants members of the ones more firmly established ethnic group.'[17]

In 2010 a BBC documentary, 'Out of Africa' by Dr Alice Roberts showed how a relatively tiny group of migrant Africans could be the progenitor of all the races of the world.[18]

Anecdotally, the vast majority of the world population of the world today is non-white or dark skinned, in contrast to the relative minority of white people, who mainly live in Europe. Apart from European, North American and Mongolian people, every other human population on earth is either African or non-white.

Physiologically, the difference between white and non-white people is only skin-deep and rests primarily on the differing ability of the melanocytes in our skin to produce the pigment, melanin. Even so, histologically, the number of melanocytes in white and dark skin has been shown to be equal in number.

The African migrants to Europe, who became the progenitors of the people called Caucasians today, are known in literature as Grimaldi man or Cro-Magnon man. The Caucasian people are believed to have originated around 20,000 years ago, during the Ice Ages.

White skin evolved as a form of albinism which was a natural adaptation to prevailing climatic conditions. This is no different to other human adaptations such as the development of the sickle-cell gene in Africans and Mediterraneans in response to plasmodium falciparum that causes malaria, the deadliest and most widespread tropical disease in the world.

During the Ice Age, the land mass called Europe today was largely covered with a one-mile thick layer of ice that extended from Russia to and the British Isles. The Ice Age was characterized by reduced sunlight as well as cold. Light or 'white' skin became an evolutionary advantage, as it allowed better penetration of the ultraviolet light from the sun and facilitated the production of vitamin D in the skin to help proper bone formation. Deficiency in vitamin D leads to rickets in children and osteomalacia in adults, which makes affected bones become brittle and prone to fractures.

Dark or black skin, on the other hand, is more prone to frostbite and cold injury and even though melanin protects the skin from the damaging effects of ultraviolet light, it reduces the ability of the skin to produce vitamin D, especially in low sunlight conditions. This rendered dark-skinned people more prone to the effects of vitamin D deficiency and studies of the skeletons of prehistoric Europeans confirm the hypothesis.

Natural selection of 'albinos' or white people in Europe would have occurred, and with healthier and longer life expectancies the white population would have steadily increased in numbers as the darker skinned, environmentally disadvantaged people correspondingly receded in numbers. Other evolutionary adaptations developed to aid the survival of the original African migrants from the extremely harsh and cold weather conditions in Europe.

Dr Charles Finch, an author and specialist on human prehistory and origins wrote:

'Eighty-five percent of the heat loss from the human body comes from the head and the face. In equatorial Africa, kinky, and particularly the peppercorn, hair of the early human types would expose more of the scalp to the atmosphere and so promote heat loss. The typical Negro broad nose

and flaring nostrils would enhance the loss of moisture and, therefore, heat during respiration. The thick Negroid lips would increase the surface area of the face and further facilitate heat loss. Bodily leanness, so characteristic of East African Nilotic types, would also promote heat loss.

Among Caucasians of the frigid North, by contrast, body heat would have to be conserved. The characteristic Caucasian narrow nose and lips, by reducing surface area, would help conserve heat.

The narrowed nostrils would also help in warming inspired air. Caucasian straight hair falling down the back of the neck would help preserve heat in the head and neck region. The tendency in the Caucasian male to more profuse body hair may have also been an aid to heat preservation on the hunt away from his campfires. We have already noted that hominids, like other warm-blooded animals, are regulated by Gloger's Law, which states that the closer the animal is to the equator, the darker his coat; the closer to the Arctic Circle, the whiter his coat. The polar bear, the arctic fox, and snowshoe rabbit are all examples of winterized white-coated Arctic animals who illustrate Gloger's Law. The Caucasian phenotype among H. sapiens also follows it.'[19]

CHAPTER SEVENTEEN

THE SHAPE OF AFRICA

It is not just the name, Africa, which was bestowed upon Africans by Europeans but the shape of the continent as well. Europeans defined who Africans were and where they reside today, regardless of all the historical, cultural, geographical and archaeological evidence to the contrary. Therefore to appreciate ancient Africa and its people, it is important to conceptualize Africa outside its present parameters. We must begin to visualize Africa not in its present form but as a land mass that incorporates the area we know as the Middle East today. Prior to the building of the Suez Canal from 1859–1869, Africa extended up to the Tigris and Euphrates river.[1] On contemporary maps of Africa, the main body of the continent is shown with the artificially created Suez Canal as its north eastern border.

Cain Hope Felder of the Biblical Institute of Social Change [BISC] wrote:

'The ancient land mass of Canaan was but an extension of the African land mass and in biblical times African peoples frequently migrated from the continent proper through Canaan /Palestine to the east toward what was then included as Asia, namely the "fertile crescent" or the Tigris and Euphrates Rivers of ancient Mesopotamia.'[2]

Eurocentrics have tried to disconnect the main continent of Africa, not just from the biblical story of Christianity but also from ideas of Western civilization that have been appropriated from the Middle East or rather north-eastern Africa. The authors of the African Heritage Bible wrote of a map in the book:

'This map gives the ancient connection of continental Africa to the

neighbouring north-eastern land mass...Due to the manner in which western historians have taught about this geographical part of the world; students have been led to believe that Havilah [Arabia], Ethiopia, and Assyria [Mesopotamia], Persia and Syria were separate and disconnected in their historical and geographical context. However, during biblical times they were very much connected ...people migrated from lower Africa and journeyed to Northeast Africa [Canaan, Palestine] or Israel. There was no body of water to separate these two areas. The Suez Canal was not dug until the 19th century. And it was only during World War II that war correspondents began to refer to North Africa and North-eastern Africa as the "Middle East." The term "Middle East" required no mentioning of Africa.[3]

A respected scholar, Rudolph Windsor wrote:

'Ancient historians did not use names of continents such as Asia or Africa; they used national or tribal names, nevertheless, the African in the Middle East and the ones in Egypt, Ethiopia and Kenya were descended from the same family. In light of this old information, Palestine and much of the Middle East would seem to be an extension of the African continent just as Madagascar is part of Africa.[4]

The Arabian Peninsula is believed to have been originally inhabited by African people about 8,000 years ago. These African people were referred to as Sabaeans, who were the first known Arabs. Others occupied the south-western peninsula, a place known to the Romans as Arabia Felix and today as Yemen. The descendants of the Sabaeans are also called the Phoenicians of the southern seas.[5]

The Oxford English Dictionary defines an 'Arab' as *'A member of a Semitic people originally from the Arabian peninsula and neighbouring territories, inhabiting much of the Middle East and North Africa.'*

Thus the word 'Arabic' means mixed race and is an indication of the fusion of different races that has given us the racial composition of modern-day Arabs in the Middle East and Egypt. This point is elucidated by various sources. The late Professor Ali A. Mazrui, the renowned Kenya scholar wrote:

'Arabs as a "race" are impossible to classify by pigmentation. The range of colors of these people is from the white Arab of Lebanon and Syria, the

brown Arabs of the Hadramout, to the black Arabs of the Sudan and parts of Saudi Arabia. Large sections of the Arab populations of the Middle East are indistinguishable in physical features from Greeks, Spaniards, Italians and other Mediterranean people. On the other hand, many Arab Sudanese are as black as the non-Arab Sudanese and would certainly be indistinguishable from Hausa men and Jamaicans.[6]

The US historian and journalist, Drusilla Houston, stated:

'In the oldest recorded traditions, Arabia is the land of Cush, the celebrated Ethiopia of very remote times… traditions of the ancient world rightly interpreted that have no other meaning… we see how easy it is for superficial scholarship to have made the mistake of blending under the same name Arabian, two distinct races.'[7]

The African Heritage Bible states :

'The Cushites inhabited strategic parts of Arabia before the birth of the progenitors of the Arabs. Cush was the patriarch of all the Ethiopian tribes in Babylon, Arabia and India and along the Nile River. All of this area lies in northeast Africa in [the Middle East]. The Tigris-Euphrates region is located in northeast Africa. The southern section was known at different times by many names among which are Sumer, Akkad [or Accad], and Chaldea, but the name best known to us is Babylonia.[8]

This is significant because the European version of ancient history has attributed the origins of modern civilization to Phoenicians, who have then erroneously also been called Caucasians. Their land was known to have fertile soil, frankincense and myrrh, used by the three wise men as gifts at the birth of Jesus Christ, and was in close proximity to sea and trade routes. The fabled Queen of Sheba was a Sabaean. She is also known as Bilqis in the Koran and Makeda in the Kebra Negast.[9] The Assyrian King Sargon the second [721–705 BC] is another famous Sabaean.[10]

The Sabaeans built elaborate cities, urban centres, complex irrigation systems, domesticated cattle and they exploited the land, which was rich in natural resources, for frankincense and myrrh. They also built the Marib Dam, which was a formidable construction, requiring up to 20,000 workers. The mixing of African and Sabaean cultures led to the powerful African Kingdom of Aksum.[11]

The combinations of these cultures formed the foundations of the Ethiopian culture. The Ethiopian alphabet is derived from Sabaean. The name Abyssinia was taken from the Habashan, a powerful south-western Arabian family that settled in Africa. Ethiopia is also known as Habersha in Arabic scripts.

The Sabaean rulers adopted Christianity between AD 355–370 long before it was introduced into Western Europe and six Arabian bishops attended the first historic council of Nicaea in AD 325.[12]

The African Christians in Ethiopia used Ge'ez Coptic, an ancient Egyptian language, in which the original text of the Bible was written. According to the fable the Ark of Noah is thought to have been taken to Ethiopia.

It is significant that prominent classical European scholars place early Africans in the land mass we call the Middle East today.

Howard University language and literature and editor of the *Journal of Religious Thought*, Cain Felder wrote:

'According to Homer and Herodotus, the inhabitants of the following territories were Ethiopians: Sudan, Egypt, Arabia, Palestine, Western Asia and India.'[13]

'In the authorized version of the Old Testament, the term Cush, when referring to a land or country, has been translated, except in Genesis, as Ethiopia…Ethiopia, or Aethiopia, was for the early Greeks roughly equivalent to "the land of sun burned or black-faced.'[14]

Therefore Africa is not just the 'cradle of human evolution' but it is also the cradle of human civilization.

CHAPTER EIGHTEEN

THE AFRICAN ORIGINS OF HUMAN CIVILIZATION

The three most defining moments in the history of human civilization, the use of simple tools, the cultivation of crops and the domestication of animals, all began in Africa.

Archaeologists concede that the food-producing period, called the Neolithic Revolution, did not begin in the Middle East but in the highlands of East Africa and south-western Asia. The revolution in human evolution, which involved the invention of simple tools, the domestication of plants and animals, and development of further innovations, made it possible to substitute an existence of hunting and gathering for settled village life and occurred in Africa around 8,000–5,000 BC.

Improved nutrition and a more sedentary lifestyle led to population explosions in some areas. Food complexes that were transferred to the Tigris-Euphrates river valley, or modern-day Iraq, were initially situated in East Africa and South West Asia. The oldest known evidence of human culture is thought to have developed in Katanda, a region in north-eastern Congo. First described by Alison Brooks of George Washington University and John Yellen of the National Science Foundation in 1988, they discovered the existence of an old fishing-based culture. Initially, the artefacts were dated to 70,000 years old but, subsequently, revised dating of the Katanda culture revealed it to be 90,000 years old.[1]

The oldest known mathematical artefact in the world is the LeBombo bone and dates back to 35,000 BC.

The LeBombo bone, a bone tool fashioned out of a Baboon's fibula, was found near Border Cave in the LeBombo Mountains between South Africa and Swaziland during excavations in the 1970s.

It is marked with 29 well defined notches which may have been used as a lunar phase counter for African women to keep track of their menstrual cycles. Keeping track of menstrual cycles requires a lunar calendar. It resembles the calendar sticks still in use by Bushmen in Namibia today.[2]

Only four miles away from Katanda, in Ishango, another extremely important artefact was discovered. The Ishango bone, a tool handle, with notches carved into it, was excavated in Congo, near Lake Edward by a Belgian archaeologist, Jean de Heinzelin de Braucourt in the late 1950s. This tool was dated to approximately 25,000 years old, had three rows of notches that stimulated the greatest of interest amongst mathematicians, like Professor Claudia Zaslavsky.[3]

A black historian, Dr Charles Finch, also studied the Ishango bone. He believed that the notches represent an understanding of base 60, on which the mathematical concept of modern clocks and watches are based, i.e. 60 seconds = 1 minute and 60 minutes = 1 hour, and the basis of the decimal system of counting, i.e., 10 millimetres = 1 centimetre, and 10 centimetres = 1 metre.[4]

Evidence of the domestication of cattle in Kenya dates back 15,000 years and the oldest known evidence of the use of agriculture was discovered in the Nile valley region. In the floodplains of the Nile, now part of Egypt's Western Desert, the Wadi Kubbaniya people cultivated crops like wheat, barley, dates and peas among other things with ancient tools like grindstones, milling stones, cutting blades, hide scrapers, mortars and pestles. Their tools date to about 12,000 BC.[5]

The Egyptian or Ta-Seti civilization is probably the most well-known ancient civilization in the world. However, it is not Africa's oldest civilization, only its best-documented one. The Nubian Kingdoms of the Sudan region predate the Egyptian ones, which in turn are predated by Saharan cattle culture.

Egypt is widely known for its pyramids and mummies but it is not common knowledge that the ancient Egyptians who built them were black Africans. Africans were the first to keep records of their civilization through their writing, hieroglyphics. The Egyptians were well versed in astronomy, agriculture, and science. They even practiced advanced forms of medicine such as delicate surgery such as the removal of cataracts and brain surgery. It remains a mystery to modern science, how the Egyptians could build the pyramids with what they had over 10,000 years ago.

Egypt has always been a thorn in the flesh of Eurocentric Western historians. While the West has marvelled over the science and technology the ancient Egyptian possessed, many have been reluctant to give the great African civilization its true place in world history. Even in modern times, Western historians continue to oppose the black Egyptian theory without providing convincing evidence to the contrary. In 1997, a prominent British writer, Hugh Thomas, wrote in his book, 'The Slave Trade':

'Wild suggestions have been made that the ancient civilization in Greece had both an Egyptian and a black origin. That imaginative view, which, if true, might affect any history of the Atlantic slave trade, derives from a story reported by a Greek historian, Diodorus of Sicily, in the first-century BC. But there is no evidence of this claim, it is no more likely that the mythological first King of Athens, Cecrops, was black than that the lower part of his body was a fish.[6]

This view underlines the West's Eurocentric approach to African history and Africa's contribution to the world today. Initially, Europeans generally accepted that Egypt was the cradle of civilization upon which Europe drew heavily. After all, the great Greek philosophers Aristotle and Socrates pointed to Egypt as their source of knowledge and inspiration. However, things changed after the Greeks under Alexander the Great conquered and occupied Egypt and much of Egyptian science and technology was appropriated as their own.

Later European schools of thought decided to leave Egypt where it was but attribute their achievements to modern Egyptians, who had by now changed in complexion due to the Arab and Turkish invasions, western influx and inter-racial mixing, to the much lighter skinned Egyptians we have today.

Having accepted Egypt as the cradle of civilization, European scientists and historians not knowing how to explain its presence in Africa, have tried to 'move' Egypt away from Africa by distorting its history. They created the impression that western civilization developed independently of the science, technology and culture that were transmitted from ancient Egypt to Europe through ancient Greece.

In 1798, when Napoleon Bonaparte invaded Egypt, on finding that the sphinxes had a strong resemblance to black Nubians, he had his troops cut off the noses from the sphinxes, repainted the faces and defaced Egyptian artefacts bearing the faces and figures of black people.[7]

Earlier, Count Constantine de Volney visited Egypt between 1783 and 1785, and wrote unflatteringly of brown-skinned Christian Copts, who formed the great majority of the non-urban population:

'All have a bloated face, puffed up eyes, flat noses, thick lips; in a word the true face of the mulatto.'

When he saw the Sphinx, he noted:

'On seeing the head, typically Negro in all its features, I remembered the remarkable passage [of Herodotus]...The ancient Egyptians were true Negroes as the same type as all native Africans. That being so, we can see how their blood mixed for several centuries with that of the Romans and Greeks while retaining, nonetheless, the imprint of its original mould...what is a subject for meditation, to see the present ignorance and barbarism of the Copts, descendants of the alliance of the profound genius of the Egyptians and the brilliant mind of the Greeks!

Just think that it is this race of black men, today our slave and object of our scorn is the very race to which we owe our arts, sciences and even the use of speech!

Just imagine, finally that it is in the midst of peoples {whites] who call themselves the greatest friends of liberty and humanity that one has approved the most barbarous slavery and questioned whether black men have the same intelligence as whites.[8]

Another contemporary with Count Volney was Vivant Denon, an artist, who also accompanied Napoleon's army and made sketches. He wrote in his diary of his journey to Cairo:

'I had only time to view the Sphinx, which deserves to be drawn with

more a scrupulous attention than has yet been bestowed upon it.

Though its proportions are colossal, the outline is pure and graceful; the expression of the head is mild, gracious and tranquil; the character is African; but the mouth, the lips of which are thick, has a softness and a delicacy of execution truly admirable.[9]

Just as the redacted Western account of ancient Egypt, it is not common knowledge either that black pharaohs who held sway in Egypt also ruled the great Nubian Empires in Sudan. The black pharaohs of Sudan also built great pyramids that sadly have been left to decay by the Sudanese government and largely ignored by western historians. It is estimated that there are about 223 pyramids in the Sudan.

It was during the fourth dynasty, around 2750–2200 BC, that Nubian kings ruled as gods and the symbol of Osiris was adopted. It was during this period that the great pyramids were built, and when Egypt experienced a period of rapid intellectual growth and development.

The present ethnic composition of modern Egyptians is a result of cultural diversity and is not a true reflection of the demographics in ancient Egypt. Just as it would be inaccurate in the future to call South Africa a nation of white people, so it would for ancient Egypt, whose composition could be said to be up to 90% black African, with Arab, Asian and European influxes accounting for the present complexion of Egyptians today.

Oxford Professor of Anatomy, Arthur Thomson and an Egyptologist, David Randall-MacIver, carried out extensive surveys of Egyptian skeletal material. In 1905, they reported that up to 24% of the males and 19.5% of the females were pure Negro in the fifth dynasty. They also found steps between the sixth and eighteenth dynasty, 20% of males and 15% of females with pure Negro, and an even larger percentage were intermediates with Negroid physical characteristics.[10]

In general, Afro-Asian mulattoes made up northern Egypt while Negro-Africans made up southern Egypt. This sums up the racial picture of Egypt from about 3000 BC to just before the birth of Christ. The mulatto appearance of lower and north Egypt only took a few generations of interracial marriages to occur.

CHAPTER NINETEEN

THE CENTRAL SAHARAN CATTLE CULTURE

Perhaps the most compelling evidence of the African origins of ancient Egypt yet has been the discovery of the enigmatic central Saharan cattle culture. So widely spread was this Saharan cattle culture that it covered the entire North African region and part of western Africa, a land mass greater than Europe. This central Saharan culture existed long before ancient Egypt and the Mesopotamian civilization.[1]

These findings, well supported by archaeological studies, have clearly placed the origins of ancient Egypt in black Africa. Studies show that mummification was not just simply the embalming of the dead but a complex system of rituals and beliefs that existed in the region prior to the establishment of Egypt as the leading civilization in the ancient world.[2]

Archaeological studies in the Sahara and the Sudan have shown the majority of artworks and artefacts in the tombs of the pharaohs, like bird and animal deities, originate from among Negro-Africans south and West of the Nile. Saharan rock paintings showed chariots and wheeled vehicles of great antiquity.[3]

These Saharan people were mainly nomadic and formed the so-called 'cattle culture' as they revered cattle as a source of life in much the same way as the Masai and Hindus do today. The first clue to their existence was an abundance of rock art that was found throughout the central Saharan region, from Libya all the way to Mali.[4]

Archaeologists from different countries — Italy, England and Germany, working in different places at different times, have independently verified these findings. The rock art depicted funeral rites and mummification of their dead Puzzlingly, the rock art showed animals like lions, cattle, crocodiles and rhinoceros, not known to live in the desert.-

In 1958 a major breakthrough came with the discovery of a black mummy child in the Fezzan hills. He was named Uan Muhuggiag after the rock shelter he was discovered in by an Italian professor of archaeology, Fabrizio Mori.[5] Carbon-dated to 3500 BC, he wore an ostrich-shell necklace. This black African mummy is the only complete Saharan mummy that has ever been found.

From the rock art and the well-preserved mummy it became clear that the mummification process required significant technique and skill and had been practiced for over 1,000 years before it came to be used in ancient Egypt. The central Saharan cattle culture did not only leave rock art but also an abundance of pottery, which shed some more light on their culture, customs and practices.

The cattle culture people communicated with their gods in the heavens through various rituals and mummification. They clearly believed in life after death and elaborately prepared their dead for the afterlife, in the same way as the Egyptians.

Those who do not know the history of the Sahara may be wondering how all this happened when the Sahara desert is one of the most uninhabitable places in the world today? Fortunately, modern science and the technology of climatology have made it possible to reconstruct what the arid Saharan region would have been like over 6,000 years ago when these people lived and thrived. The science of paleo-hydrology, employing NASA radar technology, which is used to examine the surface of Mars for signs of life and water, was used to scan the surface of the Sahara desert.

It confirmed what archaeologists and historians had always suspected, that below the arid sand dunes lay an ancient system of river channels possibly over 10,000 years old. This meant that the Sahara region would have once been a lush savannah region similar to the Serengeti in Tanzania. It would have been like a Garden of Eden with an incredible amount of diverse wildlife. These facts explain the carved images and paintings of animals the central Saharan people produced — crocodiles, lions and elephants, into the rocks.

This staggering find is supported by scientific studies of desert flora, which are found to grow around oasis, also being depicted in rock art and on pottery. Perhaps more significantly they were carbon-dated back 10,000 years and proved conclusively the presence of a lush savannah in what is now a desert.[6]

The conversion of the Saharan region from a lush savannah into a desert it thought to have been caused by changes in the earth's axis that occurred about 6,000 years ago, resulting in the development of desert-like conditions and drought. Archaeologists have shown that when the Sahara started to dry, the central Saharan people offered elaborate ritual sacrifices of their most precious belongings, cattle, in an effort to bring about rain. The legs of live cattle were cut off and offered fresh, dripping with blood, to the dead in an attempt to transfer life essence.[7]

As the Sahara dried, the people followed the tributaries of the Nile into the Nile valley, evidenced by the presence of central Saharan pottery in the Nile region dated up to 6,000 years before the beginning of what is commonly called 'ancient Egypt'.[8]

The Nile valley with its source of water would have been a natural choice for people facing famine and drought, and they migrated there along with all their religious ideas, mummification and other rituals that are widely accepted as being Egyptian today.

British historian A. J. Arkell wrote:

'Black Africans moved north and east following the shrinking tributaries of the Nile until they reached the flood plains thereby colonizing Egypt.'[9]

The land they came to settle became the ancient Nubian Empire. African kings joined north and south or Upper and Lower Egypt.[10]

The Scorpion King, acted by Dwayne 'The Rock' Johnson in the movies was, in reality, a black African pharaoh called Khufu [2589–2566 BC]. He not only built the Great Pyramid of Giza but successfully united Upper and Lower Egypt.

Studies have found that ancient Egyptians were not just obsessed with the mysteries of life and death but the idea of divine kinship was not only African in origin but existed long before Egypt as a nation came into being. Pottery and ivory figurines dating back to 7000 BC found near Khartoum depict the rituals which were followed during the mummification process. These finds belong to the Badri, a Negroid race of ancient Egyptians.[11]

These African people were also able to depict the domestication of the cattle in art form from as early as 4500 BC. The land they came to settle became the ancient Nubian Empire. The world famous sphinx was alleged to be a portrait statue of the black pharaoh, Khafre or Chephren. The great pyramids were built during the reign of the African pharaoh Khufu, 2nd dynasty 2590–67 BC. The first recorded truly monotheistic religions of Ammon and Seth were African. The winged disc motif, now used on the American dollar, was developed as an Egyptian political symbol to signify the unification of the two lands, Upper and Lower Egypt.

African sciences of mathematics, mummification and agriculture and the concept of the divinity of kings laid the foundations for the first four Egyptian dynasties.

Another important fact to consider is that as the Sahara region was once green, it allowed easier migration of people across Africa. They are many African people scattered across north and western Africa who can trace their origins back to Egypt or the central Saharan culture. One such people are the Ashanti in Ghana. They claim to have migrated out of Egypt as black Jews during the biblical story of the Exodus.

Today, many Ghanaian people share many cultural practices and attributes with modern day Jews and are thought to belong to the so-called Ten Lost Tribes of Israel, who it seems were never lost at all but are alive and well in Africa. Many of these people, in Ghana and East Africa, still practice their customs in the traditional Jewish way today, like the practice of circumcision and the Passover feast.

Defined kinship and use of the Divine Stool in Ghana are identical with the practice in ancient Egypt. It is possible that as some African people left Egypt around the time of the biblical story of the Exodus and migrated to Europe but on balance it would appear much more likely that the vast majority of black Egyptian Jews would migrate into Africa and the Middle East. They took with them their science, technology, culture and religion.

CHAPTER TWENTY

AFRICAN SCIENCE AND TECHNOLOGY

Africans excelled at mathematics and science. How else could they build pyramids, ships, mine for iron ore and develop writing? Yet, according to Western academics and literature, Africa contributed little or nothing at all to world science and technology.

Euclid is regarded as the most prominent mathematician of Greek times. His treatise, 'Elements' is said in Western academic circles to be probably the most translated, published and studied book in the Western world, next to the Bible. The Encyclopaedia Britannica states:

'Almost from the time of its writing and lasting almost to the present, the Elements have exerted a continuous and major influence on human affairs. It was the primary source of geometric reasoning, theorems, and methods at least until the advent of non-Euclidean geometry in the 19th century.'[1]

There is a small problem though. Euclid lived around 300 BC in Africa and wrote 'Elements' for Ptolemy I, following the Greek invasion of Egypt. An eminent African mathematician Professor Emeagwali summed up the inconsistencies in the Western claim to Euclid's genius nicely when he wrote:

'In his one and only published book, called "Notes on Virginia", Jefferson explained why white men are intellectually superior to black men. Jefferson wrote that it would be impossible for a black person to understand the mathematical formula in Euclid's famous book called "The Elements".'[2]

Thomas Jefferson, a Virginian planter-scholar, hailed as one of the Founding Fathers of American democracy, helped draft the Declaration of Independence in 1792, the preamble of which declares:

'*We hold these truths to be self-evident, that all men are created equal.*'

Sadly, following this noble proclamation, for the rest of his life he was at pains to point out that this 'equality' did not extend to black Africans. A slave owner himself, he rationalized the enslavement of black people thus:

'*This unfortunate difference of colour, and perhaps of faculty, is a powerful obstacle to the emancipation of these people...I advance it; therefore, as a suspicion only, that blacks, whether originally a distinct race, or made distinct by time and circumstances, are inferior to whites in the endowments of both body and mind.*'[3]

Euclid authored his book 2,300 years ago and is considered to be the world's greatest mathematician of all time. To the ancients, Euclid's 'Elements' was a notoriously difficult textbook. The story is told about a discouraged student who asked Euclid: "What shall I profit by learning these difficult things?" Euclid, visibly angered, said to his assistant: "Give this boy a penny, since he must make a profit out of what he learns."

Because of its difficulty, Jefferson believed that 'Elements' would be too difficult for a black person to understand. He believed that only people of European ancestry could understand the subject of geometry.

Emeagwali stated:

'*As an African mathematician, I studied and understood geometry. There is nothing in my experience that could lead me to believe that whites have greater mathematical aptitude than people of other races. However, that stereotype persists among white mathematicians.*

While researching the origins of Euclid's work, I was surprised when I learned that Euclid never even travelled outside Africa.

"How could Euclid be Greek, if he was born, raised and educated in Africa?" I asked.

It occurred to me that Euclid, the greatest mathematician of all time, was neither Greek nor white. It occurred to me that he was probably black and a full-blooded Negro.

I found the best explanation in a book on the 'History of Mathematics'. The author explained that ancient Egypt was not in Africa. 'Egypt was part of Greece,' he added.

I was curious about how Euclid looked in person. As I probed further, I discovered a widely circulating photo of Euclid. It was the photo of a white male who seemed to be 90 years old.

I asked: "Is this a true portrait of Euclid?"

Upon reflection, I realized that it was a fictitious portrait. It was drawn 2,000 years after Euclid died.

Euclid died 2,300 years ago in Africa and we do not have any true portraits of any person that lived before Jesus Christ. We do not have any true portraits of any person that lived even 500 years ago.

I later learned that many Greek scientists of ancient times were born, raised and educated in Africa. And I still wonder if those Greek scientists were actually black Africans.[4]

This false portrait of Euclid as a white man reinforced Jefferson's view that only white people could comprehend Euclid's mathematics. Since there is no proof that Euclid ever travelled outside Africa it makes sense to assume that he is a full-blooded Negro.

Europe solved the issue of Euclid's race or colour by simply making the author 'white' and lavishing all the accolades for his achievements on the Greeks and Romans.

Several ancient documents exist which disprove the white supremacist view on African mathematics.

The Moscow Papyrus originates from the 13th dynasty in Kemet, Egypt. The papyrus was acquired by a Russian Egyptologist Vladimir Golenishchev in 1892 or 1893 in Thebes.

The Moscow papyrus is written in hieroglyphics and dates back to around 2000–1800 BC. The Egyptian mathematical papyrus contains 25 mathematical problems, some too damaged or unreadable. However, problem 14 shows an illustration with a formula of how to find the volume of a truncated pyramid. Finding the volume of a truncated pyramid is a very complicated mathematical process, even today, and cannot not be found by just trial and error.[5]

Similarly, the Rhind papyrus, is one of the most famous ancient Egyptian scrolls containing mathematical tables and problems. It was bought in 1858 in a Nile resort town by a Scottish explorer, Alexander Henry Rhind.

It dates from around 1650 BC and is also known as the Ahmes papyrus, named after the scribe Ahmes who copied it from an earlier document dated around 1800 BC.[6]

It contains 84 different mathematical problems including how to distribute 100 loaves of bread among workers in different ratios.

Timbuktu was once known as the city of books and the world's oldest universities, boasts the largest collection of manuscripts in the world. The Timbuktu Mathematical Manuscripts date back to 1200A.D. Held in libraries and private collections they are thought to number between 700,000 and 1 million. The manuscripts were mathematical and astronomical in nature.[7]

CHAPTER TWENTY ONE

THE FIRST SURGICAL TREATISE

When studying for my surgical fellowship, I noticed that a manoeuvre for reducing dislocated shoulders called the 'Kocher's manoeuvre' named after Professor Kocher, a German physician, was actually a method devised by ancient Egyptians and used for thousands of years before it was claimed as a European discovery.[1]

Today, there are almost over 7,990 eponyms in medical usage and over 99% are named after or associated with Europeans or North Americans.[2]

However, the world's oldest known surgical treatise is Egyptian and dates back to 1600 BC.

The ancient Egyptian surgical treatise is the most detailed and sophisticated of the extant medical papyri and the only surviving copy of part of an ancient Egyptian textbook on trauma surgery. Written in the hieratic script of the ancient Egyptian language, it is based on material from a thousand years earlier. It consists of a list of 48 traumatic injury cases, with a description of the physical examination, treatment and prognosis of each. When the papyrus was discovered it was about fifteen feet long in scroll form. In 1862 Edwin Smith, an American Egyptologist and collector and dealer in antiquities, purchased it in Luxor, Egypt.[3] Predictably, it is now known as the Edwin Smith Surgical Papyrus.

The Egyptian papyrus reveals that the ancient Egyptians are responsible for the oldest written record using a word for 'brain'. It is also the first written account of the anatomy of the brain, the meninges [coverings of the brain] and cerebrospinal fluid. This document was written around the year 1700 but is based on texts that date back to about 3000 BC. It is considered the first medical document in the history of mankind.

The 48 cases mentioned in the 'Edwin Smith Surgical Papyrus' concern:

27 head injuries [cases #1–27]
6 throat and neck injuries [cases #28–33]
2 injuries to the clavicle [collarbone] [cases #34–35]
3 injuries to the arm [cases #36–38]
8 injuries to the sternum [breastbone] and ribs [cases #39–46]
1 injury to the shoulder [case #47]
1 injury to the spine [case #48]

This papyrus contains the first known reference to wound closure by suturing, a statement translated as 'Thou shouldst draw together for him his gash with stitching'. Advice for infected wounds includes a recommendation to apply a decoction of willow [which contains salicin] and astringents of copper and sodium salts. There is also a mention of breast cancer in the surgical treatise.

Case #31 refers to the spinal cord injury as follows:

'If thou examinest a man having a dislocation in a vertebra of his neck, shouldst thou find him unconscious of his two arms [and] his two legs on account of it, while his phallus is erected on account of it, [and] urine drops from his member without his knowing it; his flesh has received wind; his two eyes are bloodshot; it is a dislocation of a vertebra of his neck extending to his backbone which causes him to be unconscious of his two arms [and] his two legs.'[4]

A mixture of grease and honey is recommended to prevent infection from occurring in an open wound.[5]

Most students and practitioners of modern medicine will instantly recognise that the Egyptians understood the basics of medicine and the presentation of complex spinal injuries even if their treatments were not as sophisticated as ours today.

The Egyptians were concerned about their dental hygiene too and frayed, fibrous chew sticks were being used by the Egyptians as a form of toothbrush. It is estimated that toothpaste was first used in Egypt around

2000 BC.[6]

In the Sibudu Cave in South Africa, evidence of the oldest known ancient mattresses and the use of medicinal plants has been found and dated to circa 75,000. Archaeologist Lyn Wadley of the University of the Witwatersrand, Johannesburg, South Africa, and team published an article entitled 'Middle Stone Age Bedding Construction and Settlement Patterns at Sibudu, South Africa,' in December 2011.[7]

How could it be that black African men, the Egyptians, who by Thomas Jefferson's declarations could not understand mathematics, could make such pivotal contributions to astronomy, medicine, science and technology? It is important to have a closer look at some of the Egyptians' other achievements in more detail to understand the depth of the Eurocentric fallacy.

Archaeologists discovered that the ancient Nubians built the world's first known archeoastronomy devices and megaliths at Nabta Playa that predate Stonehenge by over 2,000 years.

The authors stated:

'This complexity, as observed at Nabta Playa, and as expressed by different levels of authority within the society there, likely formed the basis for the structure of both the Neolithic Society at Nabta and the Old kingdom of Egypt.'[8]

Erected over 10,000 years ago, the great Egyptian pyramids have been listed as one of the Seven Wonders of the World but some facts are still necessary so as to comprehend the truly amazing scale of this achievement of the ancient Egyptians. The Great Pyramid of Giza is still the heaviest building in the world today. Weighing in at an estimated 6–7 million tons, it rests on an artificially raised platform, which is almost perfectly level.[9]

It consists of 2.5 million dressed stones, precision-cut, which range in weight from 2.0–2.5 tons for the limestone core blocks and 50–70 tons each for the huge granite monoliths. The polished limestone casing blocks were precision-carved, polished, and fit perfectly with one another.

The placement of the pyramids is no accident. The Great Pyramid is aligned to true north by one twelfth of a degree and almost exactly on the

30th parallel north. The sides of the Great Pyramid rise at a perfect angle of 52 degrees, the significance of which is that the pyramid embodies the mathematical constant pi. It is only at 52 degrees that the ratio of the height of the pyramid to its base is that of the radius of a circle to its circumference.

The Egyptians were gifted at astrology and aware of the planetary systems and of the presence of different planets in the solar system. Without astrology and mathematics how could the Egyptians have understood the earth's 25,920 processional cycles and the 'obliquity of the ecliptic' giving rise to the four seasons.

The earth does not only rotate around the sun; it spins like a top around its axis and wobbles, giving rise to an imaginary 360 degree circle when traced in the heavens over a very long period approximately 25,920 years. The wobble causes the start of the four seasons to arrive slightly earlier each year and this effect causes the seasons to arrive one month early every 2,160 years.

Conventionally measured from the point of the equinoxes, the 360 degree processional arc made in the heavens by the earth's wobble was divided into 12 sections of 2,160 years each, which were then associated with a house of the zodiac.[10]

The ancient Egyptians also noted that due to the Earth's processional cycle and observing the sun's rising and setting, there were four points of solar 'standstills'. The summer and winter solstices are marked when the sun appears to reach the outermost positions north and south and appears to stand still. The spring and summer equinoxes are the two occasions when the sun crosses over the earth's equator and day and night are equal.

In contrast, the way the Europeans named the days of the week is incorrect, due to the work of Ptolemy, a Greek philosopher, who thought that the sun, moon, and five planets revolved around the earth, hence the Latin names for the days of the week, Solis [the sun], Lunae [moon], Martis [Mars], Mercurii [Mercury], Jovis [Jove or Jupiter], Veneris [Venus] and Saturni [Saturn], which influenced the modern names in English and other European languages.[11]

African knowledge of astronomy and mathematics was transferred to other areas like ship building and, contrary to Eurocentric claims made it possible for Africans to reach many parts of the world, thousands of years before what is currently accepted by Western academics. Africans have been in Europe for millennia. Africans not only traded with Europeans but also occupied and settled in Andalusia, modern-day Spain and Portugal, living there for up to 700 years. The African presence in Spain is well documented by Ahmed al Makkari's 'History of the Mohammedan Dynasties in Spain'.[12]

The Africans came through western Spain and settled in Cadiz. They were expelled after the Spaniards defeated Batrikus in 1227.[13]

The first strong African presence in Europe was in AD 711 when the Moorish King Tariq ibn-Ziyad crossed the Straits of Gibraltar from North Africa into the Iberian peninsula, into Andalucia, Spain under the Visgoths. King Tariq ibn-Zayad is also known in Spanish chronicles as Tarraco.

Africans in Europe have been referred to by several names but the use of the term 'the Moors' was common. They were also called Aethiops, Nigritae, Moorens or Negroes. They brought with them advancements in all fields of science, medicine and social endeavour. At a time when the unenlightened masses of western Europe did not consider bathing and personal hygiene as important for good health and the prevention of disease, these Africans had built and used luxurious baths and saunas.

The libraries and centres of academic excellence the Moors built in Europe were not only the first; they were also the foundation of Western science and academia. Famous universities of Europe like Oxford and Cambridge began as translation centres for African or Moorish science.

'When one notes the period of Europe's oldest and finest universities established, note the proximity with Moorish Andalus [Spain] and the European centers for the translation of Moorish documents.'[14]

The first universities in Christian Spain had Muslim and Jewish teachers, who also helped them transcribe African and Arabic names into Latin. Constantinus Africanus, an African scientist, produced original works and texts that made the medical school at Salerno famous.[15]

Things changed dramatically in Europe when the Catholic Church adopted the official stance that the science and medicine brought by the Moors was witchcraft. When the Moors were driven out of Europe, the Catholic Church closed down Egyptian temples of mysteries and schools of philosophy, burnt books and executed scholars. The Catholic Church's rejection to African science and knowledge helped send Europe into the Dark Ages.

African science and technology has contributed so much to modern science that it is difficult to know where to begin. Unfortunately, many Africans and indeed Westerners are unaware of this, as both Africans and the Westerners rely solely on Western scholarship only from which Africa's contribution has been redacted.

Western scholars credit the Sumerians with having invented the wheel, which was one of the most important discoveries of modern man but fail to clarify their true origins of the Sumerians. As we have seen, Sumeria was a part of Africa and the Sumerians Africans. To date, no other historical and archaeological trail has been offered by western historians and archaeologists, to explain the mysterious 'disappearance' of the Sumerians, just like the mysterious disappearance of the Ten Tribes of Israel. Perhaps, the trail leads back directly to the black African people that lived and thrived there.

Apart from the pyramids, astronomy and medicine, Egyptians contributed to the development of science and technology in so many other ways. They developed complex irrigation systems by using floodgates, wheels and pumps. They had their own centres of academic excellence and there was a House of Wisdom in Cairo as early as AD 1005. Heron's steam engine, the first steam engine in the world, was built in Alexandra, Egypt around the 1st century AD.[16]

The US academic who specialised in African history and languages, Konrad Tuchscherer, wrote:

'Over 5000 years ago in Egypt Africans developed a system of hieroglyphic writing, the world's earliest known script. Scholars have traditionally access to it at the end is right and system's image at the end of the fourth millennium BC in Mesopotamia and that the idea of writing was borrowed into Egypt around 3100 BC at the onset of the first Egyptian Dynasty. The new evidence

uncovered by archaeologists in Egypt, however, revealed that Africans include a hieroglyphic system 150 years earlier than the Sumerians in Mesopotamia around 3250 BC.'[17]

According to Tuchscherer, this makes the Egyptian system the source for the development of Tifinagh and Ethiopic and it must have also inspired the Hebrew and Arabic scripts and indirectly the Greek, Roman and Cyrillic scripts.[18]

Many Africans are landlocked and like other landlocked people all over the world did not develop any significant seafaring capacity. However, African communities that lived close to water and in some delta regions built their houses over the water and fished for a living. They also built canoes and boats and learnt how to navigate the seas.

It is a historical fact that Portuguese seamen copied African Muslim navigators who had developed skills in shipbuilding and the use of the compass for navigation. The arts of cartography, astronomy and mathematics were also transcribed from African.[19]

When religious intolerance and xenophobia peaked in Europe in the 1500s, the Moors were expelled from Europe with much slaughter. An estimated 50,000 Moors were murdered on the Day of All Saints in 1570.[20]

Many Jews and Moors scattered into different parts of Africa to escape persecution and there transferred some of their science and technology in their new African settlements.

Under the rule of Queen Isabella and King Ferdinand and of Spain, over three million Moors were banished from Spain by the first decade of the 17th century.

Queen Elizabeth I of England is known to have had an African entertainer and a black page at her court. In 1596, there were so many Africans in England that she infamously demanded that all 'blackamoors' be expelled from England.[21]

CHAPTER TWENTY TWO

AFRICA: THE DARK CONTINENT

'I am apt to suspect the negroes, and in general all other species of men [for there are four or five different kinds] to be naturally inferior to whites. There never was a civilised nation of any other complexion than white, nor even any individual eminent either in action or speculation. No ingenious manufactures amongst them, no arts, no sciences. On the other hand, the most rude and barbarous of the whites, such as the ancient Germans, the present Tartars, have still something eminent about them, in their valour, form of government, or some other particular.' renowned English philosopher, **David Hume** [1]

'The darkest thing about Africa has always been our ignorance of it.' **George Kimble**[2]

What about the African interior? In those dark days Europeans referred to Africa as the 'Dark Continent' and imaginatively described Africa as a place of savage natives and acts of hideous barbarity. This is largely because of the romanticized misinformation peddled by European explorers and missionaries.

As Dr Vincent Robinson wryly noted:

'It is one of the paradoxes of history that Africa, the Mother of Civilization, remained for over two thousand years the Dark Continent. To the moderns, Africa was the region where ivory was sought for Europe and slaves for America. In the time of Jonathan Swift [1667–1745], as the satirist informs us, geographers in drawing maps fill in the gaps with savage pictures. Where towns should have been they placed elephant.[3]

However, the only darkness was the prejudice and the ignorance in the minds of Europeans about the lives and customs of the African people they barely knew. From the excellent work of many African historians, the evidence now available clearly shows that the great civilization of Egypt was only the tip of the 'pyramid'.

It is sad to note that there was a large amount of information available in Europe about Africa in the 15th and 16th centuries that could have mitigated this hugely erroneous impression of Africa. There are the classical observations of writers like Herodotus, Ptolemy and Pliny, the works of al-Idrisi, a Spanish Moor, from the 11th century, and Ibn Khaldun, a Berber from the 14th century.

In 1443 a Genoese merchant, Malfante, described his experiences in travelling to Tuat. His descriptions appear to have been used by the Florentines to establish trade routes with North Africa. In 1507 a Venetian, Cadomosto, sailed to Senegal twice and wrote an account of the country, the people and their customs, which he published. The famous Moor, Leo Africanus, visited Timbuktu and other states in Sudan in the early 16th century and gave eyewitness accounts of the splendour of Timbuktu, the Songhai Empire and 'his fifteen kingdoms of Negroes'. He became a protégé of the Medici Pope, Leo X, and wrote his accounts of African societies in Italian and taught Arabic in Bologna.[4]

In the 16th century Timbuktu was a city of exceptional learning. It was famous for its university and as a great store of knowledge in the Islamic world. Of the early 16th century Timbuktu, Leo Africanus wrote:

"Here are great store of doctors, judges, priests, and other learned men, that are bountifully maintained at the King's cost and charges, and hither are brought divers manuscripts or written books out of Barbary, which are sold for more money than any other merchandise."[5]

John Hatch quote on Africans in Europe prior to European renaissance stated:

'...Many well-educated, articulate Africans were sought after in Europe, not only to help them open up new trading opportunities in Africa, but also for their intellectual, artistic and military skills.

'From the 8th century through to the 15th, Arab–Berber slave trade

siphoned off blacks with military skills, political acumen and intellectual and artistic talent for the benefit of Muslim cultures stretching from Spain to Northern India.'

By the end of the 16th century, a Moroccan emperor employed English artisans and white Christian slaves were used in Africa. Some of them formed part of the Sultan of Morocco's army when he destroyed the Songhai Empire in 1590.[6]

In 1952, Thomas L. Hodgkin, a Fellow of Balliol College, Oxford wrote:

'It is no doubt flattering to our vanity to imagine that the peoples of Africa were "primitive"' and "barbarous" before the penetration of the Europeans and that it is we [i.e. Europeans] who civilized them. But it is a theory that lacks historical foundation. The Empire of Ghana flourished in what is now French West Africa during the dark ages of Western Europe. By the fifteenth century, there was a university at Timbuktu. The Ashantis of the Gold Coast [i.e. Ghana] and the Yorubas [of Nigeria] possessed highly organized and complex civilizations before their territories were brought under British political and military control. The thesis that Africa is what the Western European missionaries, traders, technicians and administrators have made it is comforting [to Western Europeans] but invalid.'[7]

Long before Europeans had penetrated Africa's interior, Europe could only trade with Africa through Arab intermediaries. These Arabs were African Moors, mainly of North African extraction, and formed the vital trade link as intermediaries between Europe and the rest of the known world.

Europe did not produce much that was of use to Africa in the 15th to 16th centuries. However, African gold, ivory, hides and other precious metals were in great demand all over the world, especially in Europe. This also coincided with a time when precious metals, like gold and silver, became established as the main currency for transaction and was in ever-increasing demand by most countries.

At this time, many African commercial cities conducted international trade with Arabs along the Trans-Saharan routes. East African port cities flourished with international trade from as far as Arabia, China and India.

Indeed, at this time international trade in Africa was far in advance of that in most parts of Europe.

In time, European reliance on the Arab and Moorish intermediaries and increasing religious fervour in the face of Islam, led to the Crusades. The Crusades greatly enhanced the Europeans' knowledge of geography and the sources of the Muslim merchants who controlled the Arab trade. They not only brought the Europeans new wealth from plunder and trade, but also gave them a new and wider geographical view of the then known world. This inspired kings and merchants all over Europe to employ traders, find maps and build ships in order to undermine the Arab intermediaries and access the sources of wealth directly.

The Venetians, Genoese and Pisans had not far to sail to reach Egypt and begin competing with the Arabs for the trade. From 1415 onwards Portuguese sailors, armed with knowledge from the Arabs and very often with the help of the Venetians and Genoese, explored the Atlantic coastline of Africa. By the end of the 15th century, Bartolomeu Dias had been blown around the Cape of Africa into the Indian Ocean, and Vasco da Gama had sailed around the African continent to India.

Much of the European exploration of Africa, to establish trade routes and secure monopolies, was carried out, or financed, by the English.-

When European explorers finally penetrated the interior of Africa, they did not find savage natives as they claimed but came across great civilizations and vibrant cultures all over Africa. Koumbi Saleh, the capital of ancient Ghana, flourished from AD 300 to AD 1240. Located in modern-day Mauritania, archaeological excavations revealed houses several storeys high. Some houses had up to nine rooms, underground staircases and connecting halls. One part of the city of was thought to have housed over 300,000 people, several times the size of medieval London.[8]

In the 15th century when the Portuguese first came across Benin City in southern Nigeria they found an established monarchy, good wide roads and fortifications that covered over 2,500 square miles, with more than five hundred interconnected enclosures.

In 1553 an English explorer, Thomas Wyndham, took an expedition guided by a Portuguese sailor to the Gold Coast and Benin in search of gold and pepper. They found that the Oba of Benin, could read, write and speak Portuguese.[9]

On arrival to the King's court the Benin King bartered with them for goods in Portuguese and even offered them credit against their return. Thomas Wyndham wrote:

'This gentleman beinge a blacke Moore [although not so blacke as the rest] sate in a great hall, long and wide, the wals made of earth without windows, the roofe of thin boords, opened in sundry places like unto louvers to let in aire.'[10]

In 1602, on reaching Benin City, a Dutch traveller recorded in his diary:

'The town seemeth to be very great when you enter into it, you go on to a great broad street, not paved, which seems to be seven or eight times broader than the Warmoes street in Amsterdam; which goeth right out and never crooks...; it is thought that the street is a mile-long [roughly equivalent to 4 English miles] besides the suburbs... When you are in the great street aforesaid, you see many great streets on the sides thereof, which also go right forth... The houses in this town stand in good order, one close and even with the other, as the houses in Holland stand... Their rooms within are four-square, over them having a roof that is not closed in the middle, at which place the rain, wind and light come in, and therein they lie and eat their meat; but they have other places besides, as kitchens and other rooms.'[11]

The surrounding wall of the medieval city of Benin City in Nigeria was built on a scale only comparable to the Great Wall of China. The vast system of defensive walling totalled 10,000 miles in all. In 1974, the Guinness Book of Records described the Benin walls as 'the largest earthworks in the world carried out before the mechanical era.[12]

Further evidence of Africans engineering skills can also be found in northeast Nigeria where Europeans found skilfully built stonewall terraces. Also in northern Nigeria, the royal palace of Daura dates back to medieval times. In fact, metallurgy, the use of iron in tool making, was first developed in Western Africa thousands of years ago.

In 1928 the Nok culture was accidentally discovered around the confluence of the rivers Niger and Benue in what is modern Nigeria today. The pottery that was found consisted mainly of sculptured human heads and figurines. The heads had triangular shapes with typical African features, wearing elaborate African hairstyles still used by the people in the region today. These figurines dated back to 500 BC proving that complex aesthetic African design dates back over 2,500 years.[13]

Other objects made of wrought iron and iron slag from smelting furnaces were also dated back to the 5th century BC making West Africans the first people on earth to how to extract and use iron ore and other metals.

The Igbo-Ukwu culture, discovered in 1938, has been dated back to 700–1000AD. Archaeological finds of hundreds of items of metalwork, weaving and pottery artefacts of very high quality and distinctive design signified the presence of a very highly developed civilization in the area.[14]

African works, in stone, ivory, wood and metal demonstrated the advanced technique and high artistic quality Africans possessed for thousands of years prior to the advent of western European culture.

When a German ethnographer, Leo Frobenius, acquired metal figures in the Yoruba settlement of Ile-Ife in southern Nigeria, such was their beauty that he could not believe that they were the works of black Africans and instead postulated that Greeks, from the legendary lost city of Atlantis, had made them.[15]

The Benin Empire is also famous for its bronze artwork. In 1898 the British attacked the Benin and looted the Oba's palace. They stole many of its great works of art, which can be found to this say still in the British Museum.

The Sungbo Eredo is a rampart or moat, located in the Yoruba town of Ijebu-Ode in Ogun state, South-western Nigeria and is thought to be the largest pre-colonial monument in Africa. This system of walls and ditches required more earth to be displaced than the Great Pyramid of Giza. Obscured by vegetation, most Nigerians are unaware of its presence. Estimated to be over 1,000 years old, it encircles the ancient territory that was once the powerful kingdom of Ijebu-Ode. It measures 160 kilometres long [100 miles] and in places 20 metres [70 feet] deep, as it snakes through swamps and forests. It has been carbon dated to the

10th century and suggests that a highly organized kingdom existed nearly three centuries earlier than previously believed.

According to Yoruba legend, the Sungbo Eredo was built in honour of the Ijebu noble woman, Oloye Bikilisu Sungbo. She was a wealthy and childless widow who hope that by constructing the great monument she would be well remembered after she had gone. She has also been connected with the legend of the Queen of Sheba, recounted in the bible and the Koran.

In the Koran she is referred to as an Ethiopian sun worshipper and incense trader named Bilqis, who converted to Islam. According to the Yoruba legend, she pilgrimages with a caravan of gold, ivory and other goods from her Kingdom to see King Solomon, fabled for his knowledge, to ask some questions. [1 Kings 10:2, 10:10] and [2 Chronicles 9:1–9]. While the link to the Queen of Sheba is tenuous as historians place the Sheba or Sabea in the middle East and the Queen thereof as living 2,000 years earlier, the Sungbo Eredo remains a melting point for the locals — Muslims as well as Christians, and animist believers, who all revere her grave and pilgrimage there to pay her homage.[16]

Even though the great archaeological structures like the Egyptian and Nubian pyramids in Sudan, the Lalibela churches of Ethiopia, Axum obelisks are much better known, they represent only a few of the many architectural and engineering feats that are scattered all across Africa.

In Southern Africa, there are at least 600 medieval stone built courts in the region of Zimbabwe, Mozambique and South Africa. They have been dated back to about 1335 AD. These ruins are called Shona in Bantu, the language of the builders, meaning 'great courts' and 'revered houses'.[17]

Just as in Europe and the Far East, many great African Empires or states rose and fell. The ancient empires of Egypt and Kush contributed immensely to human civilization. Later empires like the Mali, Songhai and Ashanti empires in Ghana also created international trading points with a fusion of cultures and religion.

The Malian king Mansa Musa might have been the richest man the world has ever known. His wealth in today's money could be estimated in trillions of dollars. So rich was Mansa Musa that when he travelled to Egypt on pilgrimage, he gave away so much gold that the price of gold in Egypt dropped significantly for over a decade.[18]

CHAPTER TWENTY THREE

THE AFRICAN COMMUNAL

A commonly held negative perception of Africans in the West is their inability to govern themselves. Nothing could be further from the truth. Africans have organized and governed themselves in political groups for millennia and long before Europeans ever set foot in Africa and for much longer than Europeans have. What is true is that African leaders have found it difficult to use western forms of government, imposed by their colonial masters, with anything approaching the degree of proficiency in which they used their bespoke African ones.

As with people all around the world, the need and type of political organization that they developed was itself largely based on the challenges that their geographical location and availability of resources created. For instance, African people who lived in savannah regions in Africa developed political organizations in ways similar to those in Europe, with recognizable large kingdoms or empires in which a King occupied the pinnacle of political power.

A council of chiefs who acted in similar ways to senators or members of parliament generally limited the king's powers. A striking similarity was that ascension to political power was largely through descent. In other words, ruling families produced the future king and chiefs. These chiefs had the job of supervising the collection of tax and annual tributes. The chiefs also organized religious and state events and processed disputes that could eventually reach the king. In some cases, the chiefs were kingmakers and held sway, some were even powerful enough to depose weak kings.

In the rainforest belts, large centralized governments were relatively uncommon. The communities were usually self-governing villages, run by a council of elders. There were kings but these kings were not as powerful as those found in the northern or savannah regions. Igbo societies in eastern Nigeria utilized this style of government and generally lacked a highly centralized concentration of political power.

The African social order was maintained largely through seniority and descent. The community was organized into different age groups, male and female members of the community all had well-defined and distinct roles to play in society. In non-nomadic societies, land rights were particularly important and land was typically inherited and passed on to the first son of the family.

If African communities were relatively stagnant scientifically, it was simply because the people where content with their lives. There was no pressing stimulus to seek scientific discovery to mitigate nature or to prosecute large-scale destructive wars with each other. Africans, in contrast to Europe, coexisted more or less peacefully with each other and with nature, in lands blessed with abundant food and wildlife. However, this does not describe the whole continent of Africa, and as pointed out earlier, science was applied where needed as in Egypt.

The prison institution was a rarity in ancient Africa because crime was not a predominant feature of society. Although Africans practised slavery, it was not chattel slavery but household slavery. In African slavery, the slaves had rights and were treated like human beings. They also formed part of the small labour force that was required by the kings' courts. Many slaves eventually did become part of the families or bought their freedom. The Malian emperor, Mansa Musa, is the most famous freed African slave of ancient times.

The African community was therefore, essentially a family, in which everyone had a role to play and had a responsibility for the welfare of others. African families produced food for themselves and a little extra for paying taxes and to exchange for simple implements. Skilled artisans, like blacksmiths, produced weapons and tools to exchange for food and a small surplus to contribute to their rulers.

The African people's religious, psychological and physical needs were met, even if this was in a rudimentary or basic form, and was always in harmony with the environment.

In the pre-western colonization period, African society did not seek to concentrate the wealth of the society in the hands of a few, while impoverishing the vast majority of its people. Nor did Africans generally seek to accumulate wealth beyond what was required for decent living, at the expense of other human beings or the environment. It was perhaps for this reason that ancient African societies did not generate high crime levels as seen in the west or in post-colonial Africa today.

The model of African socialism — its charity, freedom, democracy and social security with integration for all, even its slaves, is unsurpassed anywhere in the world. The communal approach to living in Africa created stability and continuity unknown in the west. It also created a robust system of social security, which comprised of the extended family and community that remains alive in Africa today. The stability of the community allowed free trade to flourish with very little crime. It is on record that many early European observers generally reported a peaceful and honest atmosphere virtually everywhere they went around Africa.

CHAPTER TWENTY FOUR
AFRICA'S DECLINE

The fall of Africa began with the Roman, Vandal [East German] and Arabian invasions of North Africa. The savagery and cruelty of these invaders set the tone for things to come. North Africa was the first African region to experience the detrimental effects of Western invasion, colonization and slavery. In fact, so severe was the destruction visited upon North Africa by Europeans, that the demographic appearance of North Africa was dramatically altered forever. Black African people, once the indigenous people of North Africa, were forced to migrate southwards, to avoid being killed or enslaved.

The tragedy of forced mass migrations meant that many African communities took to the hills, caves and swamps, some of the most inhospitable places they could find. Under intense pressure, communities disintegrated and splintered into smaller groups, and cut off from others, developed different dialects and culture with time. All African civilizations and culture degenerated, and in some cases, to the level of savagery. The deep mentality of distrust and tribalism that envelopes much of Africa today owes its origins to the forced migrations and slave raiding that pushed many organized African people into smaller splinter groups that precipitated and promoted cultural decline, technological stasis, new dialects and exclusivity.

Apart from the loss of human capital from the Trans-Saharan and transatlantic slave trade, the internal disruption from wars, killing, forced migrations, and natural disasters, there was a significant loss of technological skills and scientific knowledge.

Professor Ivan van Sertima eloquently explained the rise and fall of

African civilizations and how even highly advanced societies can decline rapidly. Van Sertima wrote:

'Thus a skilled African surgeon could be performing delicate eye-cataract surgery in the city of Jenne'[sic] in medieval Mali while a villager would be going blind with cataracts a few hundred miles away on the edges of the same empire, for lack of his fine medical instrumentation and expertise.'

Professor van Sertima continued:

'If we are to understand how a science or technology may rise and fall within a civilization, why the destruction of the center could lead to almost instant evaporation or disappearance of centuries of knowledge and technical skills.

'Thus, a nuclear war could shatter the primary centers of twentieth century technology in matter of days. The survivors on the periphery, although they would remember the airplanes and television sets, the robots and the computers, the space machine now circling our solar system, would not be able for centuries to reproduce that technology. Apart from the almost wholesale slaughter of the technocratic class, the interconnection between those shattered centers and the equal critical interdependency between the centre's and their peripheries, would be gone forever…A dark age would certainly follow. Centuries afterwards, the technological brilliance of the twentieth century would seem dream like and unreal. Until archaeology began to pick up the pieces, those of us who follow in the centuries to come will obviously doubt what had been achieved in the centuries preceding the disaster. This has happened before in the world. Not in the same way, of course, but with the same catastrophic effect. It happened in Africa… We are all familiar with the slave trade and the traumatic effect of this on the transplanted [B]lacks but few of us realize what horrors were wrought upon Africa itself.

'Vast populations were uprooted and displaced, whole generations disappeared. European's diseases descended like the plague, decimating both cattle and people; cities and towns were abandoned; family networks disintegrated; kingdoms crumbled; the threads of cultural and historical continuity were so savagely torn asunder that henceforth one would have to think of two Africa's: the one before and the one after the holocaust. Anthropologists have said that eighty percent of traditional African culture

survived. What they mean as traditional is the only kind of culture we have come to accept as African — that of the primitive on the periphery, the stunned survivor.'[1]

This was the internal milieu of Africa during the European invasion as defined as the transatlantic slave trade. It would create the ideal environment for modern white imperialists and white supremacists to exploit. The transatlantic slave trade and colonization would appear to put the final nail in the coffin of the fall of African civilizations from the heady heights of science, trade, and commerce to its prostrate position today.

Since the transatlantic slave trade Africa has been locked into a long-term and abusive relationship with the Europe and North America. From the slave trade to colonization and then on to neo colonization, the West has systematically plundered and exploited Africa for all its human and natural resources for over 600 years.

Today, Africa no longer produces any significant technology of note and has been forced into a position of dependence and perpetual consumerism. Much of Africa's skilled labour and expertise has moved to Europe and North America in the brain drain phenomenon. Poverty, crime and corruption have all grown in direct proportion to each other.

During the slave trade, Africans were kidnapped by western nations, to work as slaves for the rest of their natural lives. Their children were born into slavery and several generations later, form the bulk of black African people in diaspora who live in the west and north America.

When the colonial era arrived, Africans were forced to work their own land for their colonial masters in colonies and were stripped, not only of their land, but also their basic human rights.

Neo-colonialism, through dubious western economic initiatives like the structural adjustment programs, allows the remote control of the economies of poor African nations by Western governments, ensuring that they can continue to exert immense economic and political pressure, creating the conditions favourable for the continued exploitation and plunder of Africa's rich natural and human resources.

Political instability, wars and extreme poverty, all predictable end products of the Western capitalist process of globalization and exploitation, has created the massive brain drain phenomenon of Africa's intellectual elite, for various economic, political, health and psychological reasons, to the West.

Today, Africa's vital intellectual capital streams to the West. They largely become trapped on the lower rungs of the rigid western societal hierarchy and therefore, were they still continue to fulfil the Eurocentric capitalist ideals of cheap expendable labour. They also provide a negative psychological reference base on which the ideas of Western superiority are built.

For instance, every African doctor who migrates to the West is a source of massive savings to their health care systems because they have received the bulk of their training in their own countries. It is estimated that foreign doctors save Britain's NHS about £250,000 of training costs per doctor, because they are trained on arrival. Unfortunately, the vast majority of African and other foreign doctors who are able to break into the system are used to provide a cheap service for the NHS.[2]

In addition to providing a cheap service African and foreign doctors also suffer shocking levels of racism in the NHS. In 2015 one of the key findings of a study carried out by the Kings fund, was that black NHS employees reported the highest levels of discrimination. All other non-white groups were also far more likely to report experiencing discrimination than white employees.[3]

In another study by the King's Fund they found that on average, black doctors in the NHS earn £10,000 less and black nurses earn £2,700 less annually than white colleagues.[4]

Such have been the ravages of colonization and neo-colonization on Africa that millions of Africans are unable to access the basics of life: food, medicines, light and water, daily. The majority of the African people, who are surplus to the requirements of capitalist institutions and the puppet regimes, have to fend for themselves or die.

Deadly diseases, like HIV/AIDS and the Ebola virus, coupled with the effects of globalization and odious debts, have locked Africa into a deadly poverty and disease cycle.

One method of achieving this chaos was the subversion of Africa's food base by the west. One of the first targets of the Western colonial governments was the conversion of the traditional African subsistence farming to the provision of cash crops for the west.

Western farmers receive massive subsidies and when combined with the high tariffs imposed by the West on imports from Third World countries, keep a vice-like grip on the global world food markets. When you consider that 70% of the working population in Africa is engaged in subsistence farming, the switch to the production of cash crops strikes at the very heart of the economic wellbeing of Africa and other Third World countries.

In simple terms, western farmers are paid to overproduce. They are still paid if they have any downturn in fortune. High tariffs also mean that it is not cost-effective for Third World farmers to sell their produce abroad. These tariffs, sometimes over 100% higher, put a stranglehold on the economies of poorer countries. Through this means, richer countries can continue to dominate the world markets.[5]

Due to Western farming subsidies, European cattle receive more sustenance than the millions of poor sub-Saharan Africa people.

The unwanted surpluses produced in the West are, literally, forced down the throats of poor Third World countries. This practice creates a disincentive for these countries to produce enough food to feed themselves. It also creates an unnecessary dependence on Western food, aggravating the situation when natural disasters, like famines and floods strike.

Given that subsistence farming is the main means by which the vast majority of the African populace survives, it is not surprising then that unemployment in the agricultural sector is widespread, and famines are ravaging people across the continent. In addition, when natural, economic, and political disasters strike as they often do, by placing reliance on a market externally controlled by Western governments and conglomerates rather on feeding themselves, millions of Africans have starved to death, and many more suffer the effects of malnutrition and disease, a direct cause of their dependence.

Another alarming development on the African continent has been the grabbing of vast tracts of land by foreign countries, multi-nationals and rich individuals, further destabilising the continent and severely undermining Africa's food security.

Some African governments and individuals have been selling the land from under their people depriving them of a place to live and a means of livelihood in one fell swoop.

It is truly shocking that a famine ravaged country like Ethiopia continues to receive foreign aid for its starving people while its land under foreign irrigation produces enough food to export.

Many foreign nations are acquiring and leasing huge tracts of land to be used as an agricultural base to feed their own people and produce biofuels

Since the issue first came to prominence in 2008, 50.7% of the 79.9 million hectares of all the land grabbing deals across the world are in Africa as far back as 2011.[6]

In May 2004, another article in the Economist, noted the irony of Saudi Arabia spending as much money on Agricultural investments in Ethiopia as the UN World Food Program was spending on food aid there.

In 2009, the United Nations Food and Agriculture Organization [FAO] released a report called 'Land Grab or Developmental Opportunity' that was suspicious of the intents of these foreign interests in Africa and doubtful about the alleged gains to the indigenous African people.

In May 2011, the Economist appears to have justified their concerns. In Sierra Leone, farmers in Makeni signed a contract to grant a Swiss company 40,000 hectares of land to grow biofuels in Europe. The Swiss company promised 2,000 jobs and reassured the farmers that their swamps for growing rice would not be drained. Three years later, the exchange only produced 50 jobs and their irrigation had damaged the rice swamps.[7]

Given Africa's lowly status as a source of human and raw materials to the West, it is perhaps not surprising that the West has also used Africa as a dumping ground for toxic waste and expired medicines.

In 1988 thousands of barrels of hazardous waste disguised as building material was dumped in the village of Koko, in south western Nigeria.

This rendered the dumpsite and surrounding area uninhabitable and over 500 residents were evacuated.

This led a treaty of African nations setting up the Bamako Convention in 1998 prohibiting the import into Africa of any hazardous [including radioactive] waste.[8]

In August 2006, undeterred by the Bamako Convention, a cargo ship, Probo Koala, working for the European multinational, Trifigura, discharged 500 tons of toxic waste across 14 sites in Abidjan, Ivory Coast, killing 17 people and poisoning thousands more.[9]

Today, electronic waste or e-waste is the fastest growing type of waste from developed countries, especially North America and Europe. Researchers have found that alarming amounts of e-waste, from western countries, in the form discarded televisions, electronic devices and phones are being dumped in African countries.

In 2009, the Independent in the UK reported that toxic waste from Britain was being illegally sent to Africa.

The article stated:

'Tonnes of toxic waste collected from British Municipal dumps is being sent illegally to Africa in flagrant breech of this country's obligation to ensure its rapidly growing mountain of defunct televisions, computers and gadgets are disposed of safely.'[10]

Also in 2009, a joint investigation by the Independent, Sky News and Greenpeace used a tracking device to follow an abandoned, broken beyond repair television on a 4,500 mile round trip from a civic centre in Basingstoke, via Tilbury docks in Essex, UK to the Alaba electronics market in Lagos and back.[11]

The Global Partnership on Waste management outlined some of the health risks this practice poses to the locals at these e-waste dump sites.

'Harmful emissions come from lead circuits and cathode ray tubes glass, mercury in the liquid crystal display [LCD] backlights, cadmium, chromium, brominated flame retardants or polychlorinated biphenyls [PCB'S], and the accumulation of chemicals in soil, water and food. Inhalation of toxic fumes from reagents such as cyanide or other strong leaching acids to extract rare earth metals, copper and gold also cause health issues.'[12]

Another significant factor in the western suppression of democracy and development in African countries is the unrelenting pressure from odious debts, some accumulated as far back as colonial times brings to bear on the fragile African economies.

About odious debt that the West saddled Third World countries with, John Pilger stated:

'Their power derives largely from an unrepayable debt that forces the poorest countries to continue to pay $100 million to western creditors every day. The result is a world where an elite fewer than a billion people control 80% of humanity's wealth'.[13]

The World Bank projected that most African countries would remain shackled by these huge debts in comparison to their GDP, effectively killing of any glimmer of economic growth, by the year 2012. Unfortunately, several years on, the World Bank's projection came to pass and the gap between the rich and the poor continues to expand.

The Western media has exposed Africa's poverty and prostration time and time again, and many Westerners, based on their media spin, feel they have already given Africa too much through charities and aid. However, it is a known fact that for every one dollar given to Africa in aid, or through Western charities, at least ten dollars are recycled back to the West through debt repayments, capital flight and unfair trade rules.

It is worth remembering that these same Africans constitute the bulk of the poorest people on the face of the earth, people who in general live on less than a dollar a day. Ethiopians describe these poverty stricken people as 'people who cook water'.[14]

While Western backed African dictatorships, puppet regimes and governments donate their countries resources to the Western governments, every year, millions of Africans pay the ultimate sacrifice and perish because of preventable causes like hunger, diseases, accidents, or conflict.

The travesty of this inequality and injustice is that much of Africa's capital flight to the West only goes largely to finance the luxuries and excesses of the rich western elites. In the west, while the wealth of Western nations eventually trickles down to the poor, disabled and disadvantaged Europeans. However, in Africa, the bulk of Africa's looted wealth, is banked by corrupt African leaders and not put towards providing good schools, adequate health care or environmentally based projects to help reverse the effects of global warming.

Unfortunately many Africans are, directly or indirectly, complicit in their own abject poverty, through ignorance, apathy and greed, or all three. Many more are indirectly complicit in the Western exploitation of Africa through their apathy and disengagement from the real causes of Africa's poverty. The onus falls squarely on all Africans to initiate changes that will save their own lives, and the lives of their loved ones. Africans must strive to give themselves some quality of life, by galvanizing themselves cohesively, uniting, and utilizing the vast human and natural resource they have been blessed with.

As the famous reggae star Bob Marley said,

"Only a fool is thirsty in the midst of water."

By breaking the yoke of mental slavery and repositioning themselves locally and globally as a world force, Africa will, no doubt, return to its past glory.

PART THREE: THE EUROPEAN INTRUSION

CHAPTER TWENTY FIVE
THE SLAVE TRADE

'They are very simple and honest and exceedingly liberal with all they have, none of them refusing to anything he may possess when he's asked for it. They exhibit great love towards others in preference to themselves.' **Christopher Columbus** in letter to a Spanish patron about the Native Americans.

'They would make fine servants. With 50 men we could subjugate them all and make them do whatever we want.' **Christopher Columbus.**[1]

In 1492 Christopher Columbus and his expedition accidently landed on the coasts of Central and South America in their search for India. The Spanish exploration had grave short-term consequences for the Native Americans and for Africans in the long run. The exploitative mindset of the European explorers is exposed in Christopher Columbus's notes and contrasts starkly against the generosity and humanity of the unsuspecting Native Americans. In time European exploration changed the course of world history.

Slavery is almost as old as humanity and all races of people around the world participated in slavery and have been enslaved. Slavery is therefore a universal human phenomenon, not just an African one. Slavery or human trafficking is still practised in some form or another all over the world and the International Labour Organisation estimates that there are more than 40 million people in slavery in the second decade of the 21st century.[2]

An exposé on CNN of the slave auctions in Libya focussed the spotlight on modern day slave trading to the horror of the world. It attracted widespread condemnation.[3] However, the reality is that human trafficking and slavery have never stopped.

Slavery was a way of life in the ancient world and slaves were usually acquired as by-products of war and formed part of the warrior's booty. Slaves also consisted of members of a community or society who had fallen foul of the accepted societal norms and were enslaved as a result.

Serfdom, once common all over Europe, was a form of slavery. The land and the peasants who lived and worked on the land to all intents and purposes belonged to their masters. It is believed that at one point over 70% of Russians were either serfs or slaves. The word slave originates from Slav, from eastern Europeans enslaved, long before Africans were. The Latin word 'servus' meaning 'slave' or 'servant' also gave rise to the word 'serf'.[4]

Before the transatlantic slave trade, the trans-saharan slave trade run by Arabs had decimated Northern Africa for over eight centuries. The catastrophic Vandal [East German] invasions of North Africa in AD 435–534 were the first taste in Africa of the detrimental effects of western invasion, colonization and slavery. The savagery and cruelty of these invaders set the tone for things to come. In fact, so severe was the destruction visited upon North Africa by these Europeans that they dramatically altered the demographics of North Africa. The black African people, once the indigenous people of North Africa, were forced to migrate southwards to avoid being killed or enslaved.

After the Arab conquest of North Africa beginning in AD 647 the trans-saharan slave trade was established and had a distinct racial element. However, despite the gross brutality and depravities inflicted on African slaves by the Arab slave traders, it would pale into insignificance in the face of the dehumanization and human suffering that was endured by Africans during the transatlantic slave trade.

Domestic or rather indigenous slavery had already existed in Africa for centuries. Slaves in Africa were largely acquired through slave raiding, tribal wars and social outcasts. Some African slaves could eventually buy their freedom or earn freedom through manumission and become *bona fide* members of society, depending on the laws of the land. Slaves were sometimes assimilated into families via marriage and could rise to prominence. Mansa Musa, the great Emperor of Mali was born a slave.[5]

Other slaves were not so lucky and were offered as human sacrifices to appease various gods or in different ceremonies for their kings like in the Benin Kingdom in Southern Nigeria.

Despite the trials and tribulations of being a slave in Africa in ancient times, slaves were still recognized as human beings who had been unfortunate enough to be captured in battle or banished for crimes. Even though being a slave carried a great stigma in African society, there was no doubt about their humanity. Their captors may have considered them inferior but they were still human beings.

The transatlantic slave trade on the other hand was characterized by the global dehumanization of Africans. In order to salve their consciences, Europeans attempted to prove that African slaves were not human and therefore fit to be slaves. Mental slavery is a legacy of the transatlantic slave trade and is still very much alive among the African descendants of enslaved ancestors.

The transatlantic slave trade was one of the main pillars around which ideas of western superiority were built. In modern times, owing to transatlantic slavery, the word 'slave' is almost automatically associated with Africans and their diaspora. European feudalism was characterised by the cruel and indifferent exploitation of the poor by the landed gentry and royalty.

An English author, John Hatch, gives some insight into the origins of the callousness and brutality with which the African slaves were treated by their white masters when he wrote:

'In view of the ways in which English traders and plantation owners were to treat Africans in later years; it is instructive to observe how the poorer people of England fared at this time.

During the reign of Henry VIII, as unemployment grew from the effects of the enclosure movement, laws were passed for dealing with the unemployed. In 1536 those categorized as 'Sturdy Vagabonds' were ordered to have their ears cut off and, if arrested for a third time, to be executed.

The parallel between the English treatment of Africans was drawn even more closely by an Act of 1547, which decreed that those refusing to work should become the slaves of people who denounced them. They were to be whipped to work, if necessary in chains, and, if they escaped, they were to be brought back to their masters and branded.

By Elizabeth's reign, any beggar over thirteen without a license was to be flogged and branded unless an employer could be found for him, executed for a second offense, again unless someone would employ him, and for a third offense executed without an option.'[6]

Africa was certainly no Eden of peace and prosperity before the blight of the transatlantic slave trade. People differed in colour, languages, customs and traditions from one end of Africa to the other. Many African kingdoms, tribes and people naturally competed for territory and dominance in different areas. As in Europe, large African empires like those of Ashanti in Ghana and Oyo and Benin in Nigeria, conquered and assimilated surrounding people. It was no different to the way European empires, like the Greek and Roman Empires, conquered and ruled over surrounding European peoples for many centuries.

The coming of the Europeans to sub-saharan Africa derived from blocking the land routes to trade with India by the Muslims after the First Crusades. Europeans, initially the Portuguese, began to look in earnest for a sea route to India. They were the first to explore the possibilities. In 1418 Prince Henry sent an expedition to try to reach Cape Bojador on the Moroccan coast. The expedition was blown off course and ended up in the Madeira Islands. In 1433, several expeditions later, they finally reached their goal. They then concentrated on sending ships further and further along the coastline of Africa and in 1445 they reached the Senegal river. This was hailed as an important discovery at the time because it was thought that the river Senegal flowed out of the Nile, which in turn flowed out of the Garden of Eden.[7]

In 1492 the Portuguese, motivated by stories of magnificent African civilizations and a strong lust for gold, made landfall on the coastline of modern Ghana, a place which as a result they called the Gold Coast. On arrival they were excited to discover a gold-rich society. They called

Ghana 'Elmina' or 'The Mine'. Here they encountered the Fante people who lived in the area now known as Ghana and Côte d'Ivoire today. They observed that the African people wore flamboyant gold ornaments and routinely used gold for their religious festivals. The Portuguese forced the Africans to reveal to them under threat of death or torture where the source of the gold was. The Portuguese later opened a gold mine in the coastal town of Abrodi in Ghana.[8]

The story of Elmina is particularly poignant to Africans. It became a symbol of the genocide and inhumanity of the slave trade, the worst and longest running example of man's inhumanity to man. After the abolition of the slave trade, it also became a symbol and a bastion of white supremacy and the expansion of European colonialism in Africa.

The Elmina Castle, initially christened St. George's Castle, was situated on the rocky fringes of Elmina town. A Portuguese explorer, Don Diego D'Azambuja, built the Elmina Castle as a trading post which accommodated more than 200 soldiers and masons. The castle provided the Portuguese explorers with a safe haven from external and local aggression. The Dutch, who were also looking for gold and ivory, were only about 20km away in Moree or Mori, where they had built Fort Nassau.

The rear of Elmina Castle faced the sea and allowed the Portuguese to use the tides to cart off millions of Africans into slavery, while their cannons faced inland to deter other European slave traders and local African tribes attempting an assault from the mainland. In time, other Europeans converged on the Gold Coast and then spread their influence along the coast as the slave trade expanded.

In 1492 some Portuguese sailors captured four Fante men who were fishing near the Portuguese gold mine in Abrodi and took them back to Portugal and given as presents to their merchants and financiers. They were put on display and then forced into servitude in Portugal. Captured Africans slaves were soon to become a prized possession and a symbol of affluence in Portugal, so the sailors who went to the Gold Coast began kidnapping more Africans to meet this particular demand.

Back in Portugal, the Portuguese sailors portrayed the African people as subhuman and uncivilized and it was this that helped start the spread the myth of European superiority over Africans. The sailors and merchants argued that Africans were pagans and therefore enemies of Christianity and did not merit any Christian sympathy as such. This became one of the main platforms on which the notion of European superiority was built and would soon come to justify the further exploitation of Africans.

The Africans living around the gold mine, alarmed by the activities of the Portuguese and believing that the Europeans were cannibals, complained to the Portuguese governor. This prompted a change in tactics by the Portuguese, who then took to luring African people to the coastline with the promise of giving European goods to the African people who worked in their gold mines. However, when many villages sent able-bodied men, women and children to the mines most never returned. The Portuguese sheltered these people in dungeons that opened out to sea, and at night they were gagged and then taken by boats to ships waiting offshore, on which they were shipped as slaves to Europe.

As the demand for slaves increased, the Portuguese resorted to sending raiding parties inland. They attacked and destroyed many villages, kidnapping Africans as slaves and killing those they could not take. However, this move increased the tension between the Europeans and the local rulers who stopped sending people to work in the mines, as they never came back. In response, the Portuguese sold arms and supported rival tribes and villages to wage war against one another.

This vicious cycle of war, displacement and kidnapping of Africans set up by the Portuguese had the effect of generating and creating lasting strife amongst African tribes. This allowed the Portuguese to take advantage of the chaos and strife in order to capture more slaves. Thus the transatlantic slavery led directly to the creation of many militarized states within Africa, whose economies relied solely on the slave trade. The Ashanti and Abomey Empires of West Africa are prime examples of this.

In 1596 and 1626 the Dutch, who had begun to realize there were huge profits to be made from the slave trade, attacked Elmina Castle, making two unsuccessful attempts to dislodge the Portuguese. Eventually, on August 26th 1637, with the help of the local African people who were fed up with Portuguese exploitation and slavery, the Dutch managed to captured the castle — thus ending 155 years of Portuguese occupation. Tragically, the local Africans who had assisted the Dutch take the castle, turned out to be very short-sighted as the Dutch simply carried on the slave trade from where the Portuguese had left off.

The loss to the Portuguese of the Ghana slave trade by no means put them out of business. They continued to execute their heartless trade from their occupied land on the coast of West Africa, namely what came to be called Guinea-Bissau and the Cape Verde and San Tome islands. The Portuguese also went on to ship out Africans to Brazil in large numbers from their enormous possessions south of the Congo River in the region which came to be called Angola, baptising their captives on the shore before loading them into the slave ships and shipping them off to a lifetime of slavery.

Inside the Elmina castle, African slaves were packed into small cells and the slave dungeons could be crammed full with up to a thousand slaves at a time. Male and female slaves were kept separately in different dungeons. The female slave courtyards could hold up to four hundred slaves at a time. A trapdoor linked the female dungeon to the Dutch governor's bedroom on the top of the fort, allowing him to rape women of his choice at will. If a female slave was selected to satisfy the governor's sexual urges, she was scrubbed clean and led through a trapdoor into the governor's bedroom. If she resisted, she was dragged into the middle of the courtyard and chained in the sun until she relented.[9]

Occasionally, in some cases, if the forced encounter resulted in pregnancy, female slaves were freed and re-housed in the town of Elmina. The other female slaves crammed into their tight dungeon were expected to eat, sleep and answer the call of nature in the same dungeon. The floors of the dungeon were caked with human excrement and blood from their menstrual flow.

The situation of the male captives was even worse. Unlike the female slaves, the male slaves remained in chains, even within the dungeons. In addition to the stench of human excrement and sweat, the already fetid air was filled with the smell of putrefying flesh resulting from branding with hot irons. Many slaves who were branded died from shock and wound sepsis. Their bodies were simply thrown into the sea. The Portuguese built a special cell for disobedient slaves who refused to be subdued or tried to mutiny. These slaves were tortured, some slowly starved to death and their bodies also tossed out to sea.

Notwithstanding all the depravities the Portuguese and the Dutch visited on their captive slaves, the European slave traders were very religious people and in the middle of the courtyard stood the Portuguese church. It must have created one of the most unholy and eerie symphonies ever heard, when on Sundays the Portuguese slave traders raised their voices above the screams, groans and weeping of their captive slaves, to sing hymns in praise of their Lord. When the Dutch took over, the Dutch church, which was on the same floor as the governor's residence, bore an inscription in Old Dutch from Psalm 132:4 which read: 'Zion is the temple of the Lord and here is His eternal habitation.'[10]

Perhaps the saddest place in the Elmina Castle must have been the room of no return. This was the last point of the slaves' assembly before the smaller cargo boats came to carry their human cargo to the larger ocean-going ships, berthed in deeper waters some way out in the Atlantic Ocean. Realizing that this may be their last time to set their eyes on the land of their birth, many slaves wept bitterly. Led through separate tunnels for male and female slaves and squeezed, like cattle at the dip, through a narrow gate that could only admit one at a time, they would begin the long journey into a slavery which would not end even with their own death.

The Portuguese took most of their slaves to Brazil, while the Dutch took most of their slaves to the Caribbean, the West Indies, Haiti, Java, Guyana, and Suriname.[11]

When slavery was eventually abolished, the Dutch found it unprofitable to keep the Elmina Castle and in 1872 they sold it to the British. Of the 235 years of Dutch occupation, the Elmina Castle was used for slavery for 205 years.[12]

It is ironic that the Elmina Castle never stopped being the bastion of European imperialism in Africa after the abolition of slavery. The British used the Elmina Castle for their administration and as a training ground for African World War II recruits from all over Africa. It was here that the black face of the British imperial military forces, the West African Frontier Force, was trained.

In time, other Europeans converged on the Gold Coast and then spread their influence along the coast, as the slave trade expanded. In particular, the British extended their operations as far as the Cameroons, taking Lagos in Nigeria, Dahomey and coastal towns along the way. The British would later use these ports as the springboard from which the British colonization of West Africa was facilitated.

In light of the Portuguese success in acquiring foreign wealth, the Spanish also became involved in the search for gold in foreign lands and began sending explorers out to find the sea route to India and the Far East. This was the driving force behind the exploration led by Christopher Columbus and other Spanish navigators of the times.

It was inevitable that these two Catholic nations, Spain and Portugal would eventually come into conflict on foreign soil. Finally, they clashed in the Spice Islands in the East and the Catholic Church, which benefited from the foreign plunder and exploitation, decided to make sure they did not squabble over these lands. In 1494 the leaders of Spain and Portugal signed a non-aggression and non-interference agreement that protected their territories from each other, called the Treaty of Tordesillas. The treaty, arbitrated by the Catholic Church, divided the non-Christian world in two, with an imaginary line that ran through the Atlantic Ocean about 1,300 miles west of the Cape Verde islands. All lands to the west would be Spanish and all lands to the east Portuguese.[13]

The wealth Portugal and Spain were acquiring had made other European nations restive and the Dutch and the British soon joined them in their foreign quest for gold in Africa and the Americas. The British would go on to become the greatest slave traders of all time. A British slave trader, Sir John Hawkins, is credited with starting the 'triangular slave trade' after he acquired three hundred African slaves, in his own words, 'partly by sword and other means…' and sold them in the Caribbean. In the 1600s, the potential financial gains of the African slave trade had attracted the British, who had initially unsuccessfully tried to reach and form colonies in North America. In time, owing to their maritime dominance, the British would soon eclipse the combined efforts of all other European nations put together. They fought for, bought and took over European fortresses and trading posts all along the African coast, including Elmina Castle which changed hands from the Portuguese to the Dutch and finally to the British. These trading posts were to come in handy when the British colonized vast areas of Africa.

It is estimated that over 11 million slaves were shipped out of West Africa during the slave trade. The British alone are responsible for shipping at least three and a half million of them. Western history books do not do justice to the carnage, mass migrations, suffering and displacement, which were left behind on African soil. Millions of Africans died resisting capture into slavery. It is calculated that for every African slave that was captured and brought to the slave ships alive, an estimated ten others would die in the process. This means that over 100 million black Africans were killed or transported out of West Africa, as slaves during the four hundred years of the trade. Indeed, these figures may be underestimated.

The famous African historian and author, Basil Davidson, wrote:

'For the grand total of slaves landed alive in the lands across the Atlantic an eminent student of population statistics, Kuczynski, came to the conclusion that 15 million might be "rather a conservative figure". Other writers have accepted this figure, thought as a minimum; some others thought that the probable total was about 50 million, and others believed it was higher than this...But the sum of all the slaves landed alive was not, of course, the total of those embarked. Many died on the dreaded middle passage.'[14]

The transatlantic slave trade greatly increased slavery within Africa. Millions of displaced people were forced into mass migrations to avoid the slave raiders, from both the coastal and trans-saharan slave trade. Militarized African states came to power as African tribes sought to simultaneously defend themselves against slavery and profit from the slave trade in order to survive. This left behind deep tribal divisions and a legacy of mistrust between African people.

African civilization, economies, culture and communities ceased to develop under the siege of the slave traders. A large percentage of African history and culture that was verbally passed down through stories and songs became extinct. Today, many Africans cannot trace their ancestry beyond a few generations back owing to the mass migrations, kidnapping and incessant wars waged to acquire slaves. In return for African slaves and the widespread destruction of African societies, culture, economies and polities, Europeans brought outdated, faulty and obsolete firearms, gunpowder, mirrors, alcoholic spirits and shiny beads. While it is true that a handful of African monarchs and chiefs became very wealthy by the standards at that time, they constituted an insignificant minority, especially against the background of the widespread suffering that the trans-Atlantic slave trade created.

In contrast to the carnage in Africa, Western Europe, North America and Britain in particular were beginning to enjoy a period of great wealth. The transatlantic slave trade would rapidly accelerate the development of industry, science and literature in the West. The Industrial Revolution was capitalised and nurtured by the transatlantic slave trade and the exploitation of foreign lands by the West. Western science and literature, financed by proceeds of slave trade, would flourish and imperialistic ideas of superiority became firmly cemented in the minds of Europeans.

The slave trade also had a tremendous effect on British military might. The Royal Navy was the backbone on which the British Empire was built. Prior to the British involvement in the slave trade, the British navy and army were inferior to that of the Portuguese, Spanish and the French. However, during the Napoleonic wars, as the French fought against the combined forces of Prussia [kingdom of Germany] and Russia, Britain enjoyed a lull in its enduring hostility with France. The lull, coupled with the unlimited resources pouring in from the booming slave trade left Britain with the time and money to build a powerful naval fleet. The British navy not only protected the British Isles from attack but was also eventually able to crush the combined Spanish and French fleets. It was largely through her naval superiority that Britain was able to control and eventually dominate the slave trade and ultimately the known world. The position of the British navy in Europe came to occupy a dominant position that can be compared to the unparalleled might of the American Air Force today. Many British cities profited immensely from the slave trade. Liverpool and Bristol in particular are estimated to have made more than £13.6 billion each from the immoral trade.[15]

British slave traders, plantation owners and many others who were profiting directly from the slave trade used their wealth to buy political influence and social standing.

Without a shadow of doubt, the transatlantic slave trade laid the foundations of the British Industrial Revolution and the formation of the British Empire. Today, most tourists in central London do not appreciate that it was the sweat, blood and bones of African slaves that financed the stately buildings and structures they fly from all over the world to see.

CHAPTER TWENTY SIX

THE SLAVE EXPERIENCE

The brutality of the slave merchants to their slaves is well documented.

David Livingstone, a famous British explorer in Africa around this time, frequently came across slave traders and even travelled with slave raiders. He was appalled by the brutality of the captors and could not believe the amazing spirit of some of the slaves who, despite their suffering, showed him great kindness.[1]

Once on the coast, the slaves would be inspected and classified as goods. They spent varying lengths of time in the slave castles and those not considered good enough would be either killed or resold. Many slaves died from the very poor conditions in which they endured, while waiting for the slave ships to arrive. They saw little daylight when shackled in the slave castles or pens.

When the slave ships arrived, their prospective buyers would parade them on the beach naked for full inspection. After the transactions were complete, the slaves were then branded with hot irons. The Royal African Company used a brand that marked their company initials, RAC, out on their slaves. Many slaves developed severe infections and died from these burns inflicted by branding before they could reach the plantations. The high death rates following branding led to calls for modifications in branding techniques — to save 'human stock'.

Today, most of the information available about the slave trade comes from the European slave traders and sailors who ran the slave ships. However, there is a first-hand account of the dreaded middle passage by an African slave named Olaudah Equiano who was born around 1745 and lived in an Igbo-speaking area of South Eastern modern Nigeria.

When aged about 11 years old, Olaudah and his sister were kidnapped from their village and sold into slavery. Following his forced labour in Barbados and Virginia, Olaudah was bought by a British Royal Naval Officer, Captain Michael Henry Pascal, who renamed him Gustava Vassa. He worked as a slave for this Naval Officer for eight years in the British navy and served under Horatio Nelson. He may have been the first African in modern times to reach the North Pole, under the command of John Pipps, searching for an Arctic passage to India.[2]

Olaudah taught himself to read and write and embraced Christianity, he later became a prominent abolitionist and was employed by the British government in their failed attempt to repatriate the 'Black Poor' from London to Sierra Leone.[3] He also campaigned tirelessly as an abolitionist until he died in England in 1797.

He wrote a book about his experiences, including details of his capture, the middle passage and his life in England. His book, *The Interesting Narrative of the Life of Olaudah Equiano* became a UK bestseller. It was extremely popular and went through eight editions in his lifetime. He captured the message of the abolitionists and fired the imagination of the British people, which greatly helped the abolitionist cause. He also played an important role in helping to secure the freedom of African slaves not just in Britain but later all around the world.

About his capture and enslavement, Olaudah Equiano recounts:

'*While the adults were out of the village two men and women, climbed over the village wall and grabbed us...without giving us time to cry out, or make resistance they stopped our mouths, tied the hands and ran off with us into the nearest wood.*'[4]

They travelled for months until they got to the coast and came across many different people. He writes:

'*Thus I continued to travel, sometimes by land, sometimes by water, through different countries, and various nations, till at the end of 6 or 7 months after I had been kidnapped, I arrived at the coast.*'[5]

Equiano considered escaping during his trek to the coast but was faced by the natural dangers of the bush and uncertainty of being able to track back over such a long distance to his village. He decided to remain with his captors, not knowing what lay ahead. His first encounter with the Europeans, whom he had never seen or heard of before in his life, was terrifying:

"Their complexions too differing so much from ours, their long hair and language they spoke was very different from any I have ever heard."[6]

Once on the slave ships they would begin the terrible 'middle passage', crammed together into holds in chains with barely enough space to move. This is where the slaves were fed, where they defecated and urinated upon themselves and the stench was unbearable. Disease was rife and sometimes over 50% of the human cargo did not survive. Sharks and other predators followed these slave ships knowing they were guaranteed a good meal.

Of the conditions in the slave ship Olaudah wrote:

'The air soon became unfit for respiration, from a variety of loathsome smells and brought on a sickness among slaves, of which many died, thus falling victim to the improvident avarice... of their purchase. The screams of the women and groans of the dying rendered the whole scene [on the slave ship] of horror almost inconceivable.[7]

Death was a welcome reprieve for the poor slaves and suicide was very common as they threw themselves into the ocean at any opportunity they could get. Olaudah wrote:

'I wished for the last friend death, to relieve me.'[8]

This is as tragic as it is remarkable because it is important to note that he was only aged between 11 and 12 years old at the time.

Some slave captains resorted to beheading the drowned slaves, as some of the African slaves believed decapitation would hamper their progress to the afterlife. Wide nets were put around the ships to prevent the slaves from successfully reaching the water to drown. Slaves who failed to drown were hauled back on board the ship and severely flogged for their efforts. Those that refused to eat had their incisors knocked out and were whipped until they accepted to be force-fed. Many slaves went into catatonic depression and others descended into shrieking madness.[9]

Amidst the squalor and stench of the slaves' holds, the slaves fed themselves by hand and unsurprisingly diarrhoea from the unhygienic conditions was rife.

A prominent British slave trader, John Newton, recorded in his diary:

'Last 10 slaves died of dysentery a day before they caught sight of land in the Caribbean.'[10]

Through his writing Olaudah Equiano also gave Europeans an important glimpse into the lives and culture of Africans who lived around the time of slavery. Far from the alleged chaos and barbarity Europeans believed to be the case, the picture he painted was of a happy, stable, communal African life. He described a people who believed in one God, a creator of all things. They relied on priests and medicine men, similar in role to the Catholic priests and doctors in the west, as intermediaries between the people and their God and their 'medicine men' or 'doctors' dealt with both physical and spiritual matters. They had ceremonies and rituals covering all the important stages of life, birth, elevation into manhood or womanhood, marriage and death. They practised circumcision and were clean people who had firm cultural practices around cleaning and washing. Many habits of the Igbos were similar to those practiced by the Jews.

He also gave a first-hand description of slavery in an African community. African slaves were treated as human beings. Many lived in their own houses close to the family houses of their masters. Most African people were enslaved due to crime or as prisoners of war. They were allowed to dress decently and many freed slaves eventually became part of their master's family. Slaves had their rights, their duties and various methods of gaining freedom.

Equiano had led a happy life and his grief was total when he was wrenched away from his family and he also worried about the fate of his sister who was kidnapped along with him:

'I was left in a state of distraction not to be described. I cried and grieved continually; and for several days, I did not eat anything but what they forced into my mouth.'[11]

However, despite the terrible suffering and pain Equiano and other African slaves like him experienced, from the time of their capture and all they endured through the living hell of the middle passage, their trials had only just begun.

When the ships arrived at their destinations, usually in the Caribbean and North America, auctions would be held and the slaves sold to different plantation owners. It was said that on arrival in port the stench of the slave ships could be smelt from almost a mile away. On landfall, the slave traders tried to make the slaves appear presentable for the rounds of inspections by prospective buyers that were to follow. They were cleaned and rubbed with oil to give the skin a healthier gloss. The slaves were then split into separate groups for inspection. Many of them cried inconsolably, as they did not know if they were to be eaten or killed as human sacrifices by their captors.

'There was much dread and trembling among us and nothing but the bitter cries to be heard all night from these apprehensions.'[12]

Experienced slaves from inland were often sent amongst the new arrivals to ease their worries and pacify them. They had to learn the local patois quickly — to aid communication — or face spontaneous violence, the main language of slavery, as used by white slave owners. Families and friends were wrenched apart and the rape of slave women and children that began with their capture continued all the way to the plantations. Slaves that could not be sold for good prices were killed.

Sadly, this was only the beginning of a lifetime of torture and degradation. More than 70% of all African slaves shipped to the Caribbean and the Americas were destined to work on sugar plantations. African slaves took over tobacco farming from the Native Americans and Irish and Scottish indentured labour. African slaves perished in horrifying numbers; one in four of the newly arrived African slaves died within the first year in Chesapeake, Virginia. Of the 180,000 slaves imported into Barbados between 1700 and 1760, 50,000 died within the first three years.[13]

Many slaves were sold and then resold repeatedly, and Equiano was no different. He wrote:

'At a moment's notice, slaves were bought, and exchanged and transported to remote places, cast abroad, they knew not where, for reasons, they could not grasp, by people they did not know.'[14]

The 'lucky' slaves, who had survived the middle passage and made it to the plantations were worked from dawn to dusk. They were branded, kept in chains and fed on scraps. The slaves were organized into groups headed by other slave supervisors. They lived in wretched, inadequate accommodation and did not have enough or adequate clothing to protect themselves against the elements.

African slaves were treated worse than the pets of their white captors as they were considered to be 'humanoid savages' and well below their white captors on the scale of humanity. However, this characterization did not prevent white slave owners from repeatedly raping the female slaves. Male slaves had to endure watching their wives, mothers, sisters and children being raped, while they stood back helpless. The diary of a prominent British slave owner in Jamaica,Thomas Thistlewood, in the mid 1770's gives some insight to the sexual predation and brutality of white slave owners.

Thistlewood recorded 3852 acts of sexual intercourse with 137 enslaved women in his 37 years in Jamaica.

In his July 23rd 1756 entry, he described punishing a slave: *"Gave him a moderate whipping, pickled him well, made Hector shit in his mouth, immediately put a gag in it whilst his mouth was full and made him wear it 4 or 5 hours."*[15]

This sexual exploitation was not just done for its sake, it was also done in part to break the spirit and unity of the African family unit and to maintain psychological dominance in exerting power and control. Genetic studies today confirm the rampant sexual exploitation of slaves as up to 25% of Afro-Caribbean people have European genes.[16]

Paradoxically, the white slave masters lived in the perpetual fear of the male black African slaves sleeping with or raping white women. Several laws were passed all over Europe and North America preventing miscegenation. Miscegenation laws were firmly supported by the church, government and political institutions. Severe punishment was meted out to any black slave who was thought to have had any relationships with a white woman, whether the allegations were true or imaginary.

While working on slave ships Equiano observed:

'While I was thus employed by the master, I was often witness to cruelties of every kind, which were exercised on my unhappy fellow slaves. I used frequently to have different cargoes of new Negroes in my care for sale; and it was almost a constant practice with our clerks and other whites to commit violent depredations on the chastity of the female slaves; and these I was, though with reluctance, obliged to submit at all times being unable to help them.

When we had some of the slaves on board my masters vessels, to carry them to other islands, or to America I have known our mates to commit these acts most shamefully, to the disgrace not of Christians, but of men.

I have even known them to gratify their brutal passions with females not ten years old; and these abominations some of them practiced to such scandalous excess, that one of our captains discharged the mate and others on that account.

And yet in Montserrat I have seen a Negro man staked to the ground, cut most shockingly, and then his ears cut off bit by bit, because he had been connected with a white woman who was a common prostitute.

As if it were no crime in the whites to rob an innocent African girl of her virtue but most heinous in a black man only to gratify the passion of nature, where the temptation was offered by one of a different color, though the most abandoned woman of her species.'[17]

Another intriguing account from an African captive of the European slave trade was that of Omar ibn Said. Omar ibn Said's autobiography is the only known text written by an enslaved Muslim and is uninfluenced by abolitionists and slave owners.

Omar ibn Said was born to aristocratic Muslim parents in Futa Toro in 1770 in modern day Senegal. He received tutoring in maths, Arabic and translating the Koran until he was aged about 25 years old. He became a well known Muslin scholar in his town.

Omar was 37 years old when he was kidnapped into slavery from his village in Senegal and transported to Charlston, USA in the 1800s.

Describing his capture into slavery Omar ibn Said wrote:

"Then there came to our place a large army, who killed many men, and took me, and brought me to the great sea, and sold me into the hands of

Christians, who bound me and sent on board a great ship and we sailed upon the great sea a month and a half until it came to place called Charlston."

He was sold to a white slave owner who he described as a 'wicked man and complete infidel'.

After a brief failed escape bid from his slave owner, Omar ibn Said was jailed in Fayeltesville in North Carolina.

During his incarceration Omar wrote Arabic verses all over the walls of his prison cell. This caused great fascination and drew the attention of General John Owen who would later become governor of North Carolina. General Owen recognised that Omar Ibn Said was a highly educated man and purchased him and gave him to his brother James Owen.

A devout Muslim, Omar wrote his own biography, hidden in plain sight, as his European captors could not understand Arabic. He also wrote the Surah Al Mulk recital from the Koran completely from memory.

While Omar ibn Said outwardly accepted Christianity and the kindness hospitality of James Owen and his family, he remained a devout Muslim until his death in captivity, aged 94 years old, in 1864.

It is estimated that 20% of African slaves captured during the transatlantic slavery were Muslims.

Omar ibn Said resisted the institution of slavery and his choice of the Surah Al Mulk recital was no accident. The Surah Al Mulk is a recital in the Koran thought to save the disciple from the trials of this earth and the next.

About slavery, Omar Ibn Said quoted the Surah Al Mulk stating:

"Only God has ownership and possession of human beings or things".[18]

The greedy African chiefs who sold off other African men and women into slavery may have suspected that the lives of slaves were hard but it is doubtful that they knew quite how as bad they were. One must remember that communication was poor at those times — no mobile phones, text messages, television or internet facilities. There was poor and slow communication between the African interior and the coasts, and the sale of slaves was carried out by intermediaries, limiting the amount of contact between white traders and the people from whom the slaves had originally come. Most importantly, the slaves never returned to tell their story. In addition, most African nations at that time did not keep prisons and disposed of criminals and prisoners of war as slaves.

At this point in world history, the black African was adjudged by Europeans to be racially, spiritually, morally, and intellectually inferior to the white man. The only positive thing, if it could be deemed as positive, was that black Africans were thought to have great physical strength. Indeed, it was based on their physical strength that black African slaves were sought after on the plantations in preference to the weaker Native American slaves who could not keep up the rigours of physical work, reducing the amount of profit plantation owners could make.

This perception remains today, as you commonly hear Western media and sports pundits praise or recognize black African athletes and sportsmen and women in the West in reference to their physical strength only — without any mention being made of their intellectual ability to read a game, strategize and play the sport at a very high level.

From an African perspective, the legacy of slavery would leave deep psychological scars, which still breed inferiority complexes and divisiveness, right up to present day. The transatlantic slavery left the infrastructure in place for the West to start a new holocaust in Africa — colonization — but first the myth that slaves in the Western Hemisphere accepted their lot with docility.

CHAPTER TWENTY SEVEN
SLAVE RESISTANCE

The apparent docility of African slaves in the West is a myth peddled by Europeans to reinforce their negative depictions of African people. However, the truth was that the irrepressible and burning human desire to be free meant that slave revolts and rebellions started almost as soon as transatlantic slavery began, even in the face of almost insurmountable odds.

There are over 250 recorded slave revolts in America alone. Dr W.E.B. Du Bois, the prominent African American activist, compiled a list of over thirty-seven important slave rebellions from the onset of Spanish slavery in the Americas, i.e. from the revolt in Santo Domingo in December 1522 not long after their arrival — to the war in Cuba in 1895.[1]

Running away was the most common form of resistance to slavery, as was colourfully captured by the character Kunta Kinte in Alex Haley's epic film, *Roots*. In another Hollywood movie based on a true story, *Amistad*, African slaves took over the slave ship *La Amistad* and tried to make the ship's captain sail back to Africa.[2]

In response to slave resistance, the Spanish slave traders instituted fearful penalties and ferocious repression to deter the slaves from running away but it was all in vain. In 1535, the Spanish authorities in Lima decreed that:

'Runaways absent for up to six days were liable to be castrated, while those absent for longer were liable to be executed. Slaves who hid or otherwise aided runaways were subject to 100 lashes for a first offense, castration for a second, and death for a third.[3]

All over the Americas slave revolts broke out and one revolt led by

Andresote in the Yaracuy Valley in the 1730s annihilated a force of about 300 Spanish troops, before succumbing to another Spanish force of some 1500.[4]

In many parts of South America and North America runaway slaves were able to form large communities or 'mini Africas' that revived African traditions, languages, and religions. A Brazilian historian, Professor Abdias do Nascimento, wrote about one of the most impressive mini Africas in Palmares, Brazil:

'In early 1595, some of the enslaved Africans in Brazil broke the shackles of slavery and fled to the jungle between the states of Pernambuco and Alagoras. Initially it was a small band of escapees but this group grew little by little until it became a population of nearly 30,000 "rebel" Africans. They established the first government of free Africans in the New World, indisputably a true African state, known as the Republic of Palmares.[5]

He continued:

'The Republic of Palmares, with its immense population by the standards of the epoch, dominated a territorial area more or less one-third the size of Portugal. The land was the property of all. The fruits of collective labor were the property all. The free Africans planted and harvested a wide variety of products and bartered with their white and indigenous Brazilian neighbors.

They were effectively organized, both socially and politically, in their African manner and tradition, and were highly skilled in the art of war.

Palmares put the question to the entire colonial structure: the army, the land tenure system of the Portuguese patriarchs — the latifundo — and the Catholic Church.

It withstood some 27 wars of destruction, waged by both the Portuguese and Dutch colonial military structures established in Pernambuco. Palmares resisted for more than half a century: from 1634 to 1694.[6]

In Cuba professional slave catchers, or *ranchadores*, with specially trained dogs hunted down runaway slaves like animals. The *ranchadores* with their dogs, known all over the Caribbean for their ferocity, were paid handsomely to bring back slaves dead or alive. It was reasoned that the loss of property a dead slave represented was a much lesser evil than a free runaway one. In the US bounty hunters carried out a similar task. They hunted down and returned runaway slaves for their masters…dead or alive.[7]

Wherever slavery was practiced in the Americas, human cruelty was also carried out on alarming scales. In Dutch Guiana and Surinam, slave revolts broke out and spread rapidly across the region in response to the cruelty of the white slave owners. The Dutch responded by burning slaves over slow fires, breaking them on wheels and hanging them by hooks driven through the ribs. A narrator of the events in the Dutch colonies at the time, a captain in the Scots Brigade wrote about the sustained African resistance movement in vivid and gory detail:

'By such inhuman usage, this unhappy race of men are driven to such a height of desperation, that to finish their days, and be relieved from worse than Egyptian bondage, some have leaped into cauldrons of boiling sugar, thus at once depriving the tyrant of his crop and of his servant.

From these sketches can it be a matter of surprise, that armies of rebels are assembled in the forest, and at every opportunity thirsting for revenge?'[8]

The treatment of slaves in Haiti or France's Saint Domingue was probably the most murderous in the Americas. In just under 10 years from 1779–1788 about 317,000 slaves, or two thirds of the total in the colony, were landed to replace ones who had died.[9]

In 1791, a massive slave revolt swept through the island and an estimated 2,000 whites and 10,000 Africans were killed. Over 220 sugar plantations, 600 coffee plantations and 200 cotton and indigo ones were destroyed.[10]

The largest and most significant slave revolt during the transatlantic slave trade occurred in Haiti. François-Dominique Toussaint L'Ouverture, an exceptional African general, was born to African slave parents in 1744. He led a force of 5,000 former African slaves to a remarkable victory over the combined military might of the colonial slave masters, France, Britain and Holland. He established the first, totally free, African republic in the Americas.

By January 26th 1801 Toussaint L'Ouverture had captured the whole colony from the French and the British, abolished slavery in the colony and forced the slave ships in the harbour to surrender their slaves. The freed African slaves rebuilt the colony after waging a 10–year war of emancipation. They established towns, schools, bridges, repaired and built roads.

Despite the widespread destruction of the land and infrastructures, the freed Africans were able to bring about a sustained increase in agricultural production, prompting the English writer James Stephen to remark:

'So rapid was the progress of agriculture that it was a fact, though not believed at the time in England, that the Island already produced, or promised to yield in the next crop, one third part at least of as large return of sugar and coffee as it had ever given in its most prosperous years.

This, considering all the ravages of a 10 years' war and the scarcity of all necessary supplies from abroad is very surprising, yet has since clearly appeared to be true.'[11]

The British General Maitland, forced off the island by Toussaint L'Ouverture, had to compromise with trade treaties with the victorious Haitians in order to keep their ties with the island. However the French, under the leadership of Napoleon, had other ideas. Napoleon Bonaparte was determined to retake Haiti and restore slavery in the colony. Napoleon banned people of colour from entering France in 1802, and in addition, plotted to use Haiti as a military, economic and strategic base for expanding France's colony from Louisiana to cover all of what became the modern US. Napoleons plan to re-conquer Haiti was as devious as it was despicable. His four-stage plan of deceit would start with assurances that African slavery would not be restored, with further reassurance to Toussaint L'Ouverture and his generals that their posts were secure. When his troops had landed, he would then strip them of their authorities and disband the army, following which the African leaders would be deported and the population disarmed. In the final phase, they planned to reintroduce slavery.

In September 1801 Napoleon assembled an invasion force including a fleet of 86 warships and two successive armies of 20,000 men with monthly reinforcements to follow.[12]

It is of note that even warring European countries set aside their differences and agreed to support the war effort against the African slave uprising. The overarching aims of white supremacy simply could not tolerate a thriving independent African country in the western hemisphere. Britain, the arch-enemies of France at that time, promised supplies from Jamaica, despite a standing treaty with Haiti. Spain and Holland agreed to help with transport. The US also promised to take part in the 're-enslaving' of Haiti and revealed her willingness in a memo to Napoleon:

'Jefferson has promised that the moment the French army sets foot in the colony all necessary measures will be taken to starve out Toussaint and to aid the army.'[13]

The French invasion of Haiti ended in a terrible defeat for Napoleon and the French army. Over 50,000 French troops died in the battle, ultimately forcing Napoleon to give up any ideas of colonizing North America and led to Napoleon selling Louisiana to the US in order to recoup some of the losses France had incurred in the failed invasion of Haiti.

Unfortunately, General Toussaint L'Ouverture would not live to see the triumph of Haiti over the combined forces of industrialized colonialist Europe. On June 7th 1802 Toussaint L'Ouverture fell into a trap set by the French General Brunet. After receiving a letter laden with assurances of good faith and respect, he attended a meeting with the French general and was promptly arrested and shipped to France where he was jailed at Fort-de-Joux in August 1802. He died about seven months later from torture and maltreatment.[14]

His successor, General Jean-Jacques Dessalines, would prevail over the French and become the leader of an independent Haiti in 1804.

All over the Caribbean, white plantation owners took whatever steps they felt were necessary to reduce the chances and effects of slave rebellions. In Barbados the plantation owners took to deliberately buying their slaves from different parts of the West African coast in order to prevent a collective slave revolt because of the tribal and language difficulties the slaves would have.[15]

Many of the original black slaves in the Caribbean were deported to Belize in Central America where their descendants today constitute about 8% of the population.[16]

In Antigua, when a slave of the Governor was found guilty of inciting slave revolt, his tongue was cut out and his legs chopped off to provide, *'a living example to the rest'*.[17]

Yet, despite the vicious repression and cruelty which the white slave traders used to repress their African slaves, another major slave revolt was brewing. The story of the Jamaican Maroons began after the defeat of Spain by the British in 1655. The Spanish left their slaves for the British but the slaves had other ideas and fled to freedom in the hills. This started a gruelling guerrilla fight to the death for the runaway slaves. Other slaves called the Koromantyn slaves subsequently joined them. The insurgent spirit of the 'Koromantyn' slaves became well known. The Koromantyn slaves were shipped from dungeons located in modern-day Ghana, and consisted originally of mainly captured prisoners of war. The Koromantyn were highly skilled in the art of guerrilla warfare and made life difficult for the British plantation owners. A plantation historian, Edward Long stated:

'With the importation of slaves by the English, almost from the start the irrepressible spirits among the Koromantyn fled to the mountains and found refuge with the maroons in such numbers that they soon gained control of the entire body.'[18]

After 8 years of unsuccessful attempts to pacify the Maroons, incessant raids and the loss of slaves to the mountains, the British tried to lure their first leader, Juan de Bolas, to lead his people into a trap. They appointed him a 'colonel' in the British army and sent him back to his followers to sue for peace. The Maroons saw through the trap to re-enslave them and according to one writer, they ambushed Juan de Bolas and cut him to pieces. The Maroons of Jamaica were never defeated.[19]

In the Dutch colony of Surinam a similar Maroon community was established and it likewise was never defeated.

In many ways, similar resistance as the opposition to slavery carries on today as disenfranchised and oppressed people all over the world continue their enduring struggle for freedom.

CHAPTER TWENTY EIGHT

ABOLITION

'I have no purpose to introduce political and social equality between the white and black races. There is a physical difference between the two, which, in my judgment, will probably forever forbid their living together upon the footing of perfect equality; and inasmuch as it becomes a necessity that there must be a difference, I... am in favor of the race to which I belong having the superior position.

My paramount object in this struggle is to save the Union, and is not either to save or to destroy slavery. If I could save the Union without freeing any slave, I would do it; and if I could save it by freeing all the slaves, I would do it; and if I could do it by freeing some and leaving others alone, I would also do that.' Abraham Lincoln[1]

Abraham Lincoln is widely regarded as the great President who freed the black slaves in the United States of America. However, his statements above reveal his inner thoughts. In reality, Abraham Lincoln kept his promise and never freed any slaves at all. His declaration only freed slaves outside his jurisdiction, within southern controlled territory, with the aim of weakening the slave-based economy of the South. African slaves living in the North and in Southern states that agreed to the demands of the Union, namely Delaware, Kentucky, Maryland, Missouri and West Virginia were not freed. Lincoln did not live to see the abolition of slavery, as he was shot by John Wilkes Booth on 14th April 1865 and died the next day, and the Thirteenth Amendment, which abolished slavery, was not instituted until eight months later, nearly three years after his 'slave freeing' Emancipation Proclamation.[2]

While debating with Senator Stephen Douglas, Abraham Lincoln stated:

'I am not, nor ever have been, in favor of ... making voters or jurors of Negroes nor of qualifying them to hold office nor to intermarry with white people; and I will say in addition to this that there is a physical difference between the white and black races, which I believe will forever forbid the two races living together on terms of social and political equality.'[3]

What Abraham Lincoln was really worried about was not so much the immorality and inhumanity of slavery or the maltreatment of the slaves, as many abolitionists claim. What he was really concerned about was 'Slave power' or slavocracy; a term used by Northern states in 1840–1865 to describe the political power of the white slave-holding plantation owners in the South.

In June 1858, Abraham Lincoln in his famous 'House Divided' speech accused several leading Republicans at that time like Franklin Pierce, James Buchanan, Chief Justice Roger Taney and Senator Stephen Douglas of being part of a plot to nationalize slavery as proven by the Dred Scott decision.[4]

Thus, the American Civil War was fought over the right to maintain the economics of slavery and the political control and clout it gave the South over the North. The institution of African slavery was a necessity for the survival and continued prosperity of the Confederate Southern states in the US, an institution they were prepared to die for.

On March 21st 1861, after the secession and the establishment by the Southern States of the Confederacy, Alexander Stephens, the Confederate-Vice-President expressed the Southern States determination to maintain slavery:

'Our new government was founded upon exactly the opposite ideas; its foundations are laid, its cornerstone rests upon the great truth that the negro is not equal to the white man; that slavery, subordination to the superior race, is his natural and normal condition[5]

The American Civil War ranks as one of the bloodiest wars in recent human history and cost an estimated 1.5 million lives, including 620,000 fighting men or 2% of the US population at that time.[6]

Returning to Europe — up until the present day, Britain has never put moral and religious values ahead of its commercial interests and it was much the same with the slave trade. As in the United States, Britain's decision to abolish slavery was anything but altruistic as there were several important reasons why it was in her interest at this point in her industrial development to abolish the slave trade. Sugar and slaves were in those days as precious as gold and as significant a commodity as the crude oil that is coveted by the superpowers in our modern world.

The abolition of the slave trade was a pragmatic economic decision based on the needs of an industrializing Britain. Britain was already losing control of the slave trade, and the immorality and inhumanity of slavery was much less of a consideration to abolishing slavery than the commercial benefits to be gained by hamstringing their peer competitors and the eliminating the costs of remaining in the increasingly fraught transatlantic slave trade.

The British proponents of 'free trade' knew very well that 'free trade' would ultimately be controlled by Britain because of her naval dominance. Therefore, a rapidly industrializing Britain had everything to gain financially and morally by promoting the end of the slave trade and the institution of slavery, and spreading the 'free trading' system, based on low and wage-free labour.

As far back as circa 1610, Sir Walter Raleigh stated:

'Whosoever commands the sea commands trade; whosoever commands the trade of the world commands the riches of the world, and consequently the world itself.'[7]

Dissenting voices against the slave trade had been raised for many years, even while Britain was amassing great wealth from the triangular slave trade and the production of sugar in the Americas and West Indies. A pivotal case for abolitionists was the cold-blooded murder of one hundred and thirty-two slaves, thrown overboard by the captain of the *Zong*, a Liverpool slave ship. However, it is remarkable to note that the case surfaced in an English court not as a mass murder case, but as a disputed insurance claim for the loss of the murdered slaves.[8]

Along with the *Zong* incident, Olaudah Equiano's exposé on slavery helped the abolitionist cause at a time that coincided with increasing doubts about the viability and morality of slavery. However, the slave trade was still too profitable for the abolitionist moral and religious arguments to sway parliament. African slave labour made the establishment of large profitable plantations in the Caribbean and North America and the British market for sugar, rum and cotton increase dramatically. Between 1663 and 1775, English sugar consumption rose twenty-fold.[9]

Profits from the slave trade were reinvested in the emerging industries, as Britain prospered from the slave trade.

The slave ports of Liverpool and Bristol flourished and the city of Liverpool at one time was one of the most influential in Europe. The gun industry of Birmingham and copper industry of Swansea expanded on the back of the slave trade. Other industries grew, like coal and iron in South Yorkshire, and textiles in Lancashire, and the great rail networks were built — all on the back of profits from slavery.

The financial investment of the Royal family and aristocracy was central to the growth of Britain's slave trade. In 1660, the early days of the slave trade, the Company of Royal Adventurers Trading to Africa was formed. It relied on seven knights of the realm, four barons, five earls, a marquis, King Charles II and his Queen amongst its backers. The Company of Royal Adventurers Company later became the Royal African Company in 1672 and ensured that London was the only city to benefit from the trans-atlantic slave trade until 1698.

The city of London had already grown rich from the proceeds of slavery before it was overtaken by Liverpool and Bristol as the leading slave-trading ports. By 1698 London had already profited from the sale of over 100,000 African slaves and the importation of over 30,000 tons of sugar from the Caribbean plantations. The Barclay brothers, David and John, co-founders of Barclays Bank, provided credit for slave traders for periods ranging between 18 months and 3 years. All the big five British banks were established with the proceeds of the slave trade. Sir Francis Baring, owner of Barings Bank, claimed to have made his fortune as a slave dealer aged only 16 years old.

The Bank of England was also deeply involved in the slave trade. Sir Richard Neave, who was director of the Bank of England for forty-eight years, was also the chairman of the Society of West India Merchants. Thomas Leyland, founder of Leyland Bank, launched his banking house in 1807. He was one of the three richest men in Liverpool. Between 1872 and 1807, he trafficked almost 3,500 African slaves to Jamaica alone.

In Liverpool, the Heywood brothers, Arthur and Benjamin, made their initial fortunes from the transatlantic slave trade. In 1901, the Leyland and Bullins Bank became part of North and South Wales Bank, which was absorbed into Midland Bank in 1908, and later became taken over by HSBC.

The proceeds of African slavery produced the first British millionaire, William Beckford, who owned more than 22,000 acres of sugar plantations in Jamaica.

Many British slave traders 'legitimized' their status by becoming pillars of societal respectability and sought public office. They were often staunch supporters of the Church of England. For example, slave trader Thomas Johnson was knighted in 1708 and Ellis Cunliffe was made a Baronet in 1767. From 1700–1820 Liverpool had Lord Mayors in office all of whom were either slave traders or related to one.[10]

William Beckford, a wealthy plantation owner in Jamaica and who also had merchant interests in London, was an alderman of the City of London, sheriff [1755–1756] and Lord Mayor [1762–1763] and [1769–1770] apart from being the MP for Shaftesbury and London.[11]

Much of London's tourist attractions today, including Trafalgar Square and its famous underground train system, were built from the proceeds of slavery.

As the significance of Africa as a source of raw material for Britain's industrial revolution became apparent the pendulum slowly began to swing in favour of the abolitionists. The economic reasons for abandoning the trade took on a new importance. For instance, there was an ever-increasing challenge to British colonial sugar from different countries like France or Spain that were producing cheaper supplies of sugar, utilizing slaves acquired by British slave traders. Cotton manufacturers in

Manchester and ironmasters in Birmingham argued against the sustaining of the slave trade that produced commercial rivals in a system of closed colonial markets.[12]

In addition, many plantations were experiencing decreased productivity due to exhaustion of the land; requiring more slaves and more fertile land to produce the same amounts of sugar. In reality, widespread slave revolts and slave resistance, in particular the successful Haitian African slaves revolt in 1804, not to mention the Maroons in Jamaica, showed that significant material and human sacrifice would be required without any guarantee of success, to maintain the slave plantations based on the slave trade.

The British decision to abolish of the slave trade was also heavily influenced by the loss of the American colonies in 1783. This was a massive loss of territory and finance for the British. American independence was also a major disincentive for Britain to continue to support the American economic base with the slave trade.

Nearer home, the French revolution, fought over the basic ideology of the Rights of Man, had sent nervous shivers down the spine of British aristocracy and politicians for fear of how their own people, never mind their African slaves, might respond to this 'dangerous' ideology about freedom and equality.

Thus, the stage was finally set for the success of the British abolition movement led by the Quakers. Within twenty years of its foundation in 1787, they had 'won' the British parliamentary vote to abolish the slave trade. The powerful abolitionists' propaganda machine portrayed the abolitionists as good, versus the evil of slave traders. This is a perception that Western historians and commentators from successive generations have been keen to perpetuate despite their key role in the trans-atlantic slave trade and the globalisation of conflict and poverty.

Despite being the greatest slave traders of all time, Britain was able to claim the moral high ground when she embarked on a crusade to end the slave trade. Britain was able, through the dominance of the British navy, to prevent its commercial rivals from disrupting its trading interests and markets and from profiting from the vacuum created by Britain's withdrawal from the slave trade.

The simple fact was that the abolition of slave trading secured Britain's wider economic wellbeing and yielded obvious material benefits. The irony of Britain's abolition of the slave trade was not lost on her rivals, especially France and the United States, who clearly understood that Britain was simply protecting her economic interests.

Despite the hypocrisy of laying claim to abolishing slavery, Britain remains the greatest slave trader in human history.

However, for whatever reason the slave trade was ultimately abolished, it is impossible to ignore the moral courage and persistence of abolitionists like Elizabeth Heyrick, Granville Sharp and Thomas Clarkson, who despite much bitter vilification and every setback would never say die and continued the struggle. William Wilberforce, their voice in Parliament, also never wavered in his efforts to win the vote in the House of Commons. However, his limitations were laid bare not only in his opposition to Elizabeth Heyrick's participation in the struggle on the basis that women should not get involved in such things but also in his opposition to the immediate emancipation of the slaves. In a pamphlet written in 1807, he wrote:

"It would be wrong to emancipate [the slaves]. To grant freedom to them immediately would be to insure not only their masters' ruin, but their own. They must [first] be trained and educated for freedom."

The slave trade was officially abolished by the Abolition of the Slave Trade Act passed on March 25th 1807. However, the slavery itself was only really abolished with the emancipation of all slaves throughout the British colonies about 27 years later, on August 1st 1833.[13]

The transatlantic slave trade actually increased in volume following the abolition by Britain in 1807. In reaction to the Abolition Act, many slave traders placed emphasis on building faster ships to avoid capture by the British navy. They also resorted to carrying even more slaves per trip to maximise the financial rewards. This significantly increased the hardships of an already abominable middle passage of slaves from Africa to the Americas. Over 1.8 million African slaves are estimated to have been kidnapped and forced into slavery after the British abolition of slavery.

Remarkably, Portugal, the first European country to start the trade of African slaves, remained the longest European slave trader, partly because of the fact that British slave traders continued the trade indirectly in collusion with Portuguese slave traders. This was also facilitated, no doubt, by Portugal's dominance as a colonial master in Angola and their direct control of their own colony, namely Brazil.

In other words, the Portuguese controlled both the ports where they acquired slaves and where they were disembarked. They did this with the indirect, and sometimes direct, assistance from British slave traders.

Slavery was openly practiced in Africa up to 1930. Even today, forms of slavery persist in Africa as in the war-affected regions of Southern Sudan. Human trafficking continues unabated in many parts of the world. The International Labour Organization [ILO] defines modern-day slavery as debt bond, serfdom, forced labour, trafficking in people and the unconditional worst forms of child labour.[14]

Today, modern-day slaves are far more numerous than all the African slaves during the transatlantic slave trade.[15]

In 2005, the ILO estimated that there were at least 12.3 million people subjected to forced labour around the world.[16] They identified the root causes of modern-day slavery as poverty and discrimination. Other sources estimate the number of modern day slaves as being from around 21 to 29 million.[17]

Modern day slavery is a multi-billion dollar business that generates up to $35 billion annually. The numbers include economic slaves exploited by the neo-colonial activities of western capitalism. They consist of the bulk of the world's poorest and reside at the bottom of the human food chain, disenfranchised, exploited and controlled indirectly by western governments via puppet regimes and huge western multinationals. Whole countries like Haiti are used today as sweatshops to produce the luxuries and excesses of western capitalism and the African continent functions like a veritable farm and depot of cheap human and natural resources for the West.

Modern-day economic slaves do not have to be clapped in chains.

They instinctively follow the flight path of the human and intellectual capital from their communities to urban centres where many seek their 'survival' or 'fortunes' in the west. The hallmarks of modern-day slavery are poverty, deprivation, lack of representative African leadership, lack of infrastructure, wars, political and economic instability and, of course, western socialization. Western capitalism works hard to create and maintain the conditions of poverty and economic slavery all over the world, especially in Africa.

Modern-day economic slavers do not require the total physical captivity of the slaves as that which pertained in the days of transatlantic slavery because it can leverage its demands to millions of Africans using globalization, neo-colonization and information technology. Rich western nations can artificially create the noxious socio-economic and political conditions it needs to encourage the disenfranchised people naturally to seek and congregate around the only 'opportunities for social improvement' that reside under their control in the western paradigm. It took European slave traders over three hundred years of the transatlantic slave trade to capture 11 million African slaves and keep generations of their children, who they bred as slaves and servants.

In contrast, today, due to the unprecedented penetrative power of modern Information technology, control of African governments and puppet regimes and Africa's prostration through their odious debts and dependence on the west, the slavers have succeeded in making economic slaves out of virtually the entire African continent in less than 100 years.

The European imperialist agenda does not require every single African on the African continent or in the diaspora to be poor and disenfranchised. On the contrary, it actually requires a handful of Africans to do comparatively well and provide 'cover' for their exploitation of millions of other Africans. The European imperialist agenda plays a smart percentage game and makes far more from Africans now than it ever did during the transatlantic slave trade. With modern information technology, the white imperialists have been able to tap into a much wider global population. One should therefore not be surprised to see or hear of a handful of Africans who have become millionaires or even billionaires under western capitalism. As long as rich Africans remain a handful and disunited they will be unable to mount any effective challenge to the white supremacy power structure.

A key requirement of the transformation into modern-day economic slaves is mental slavery based on their Western dependence, socialization, miseducation and misinformation. Africans and their diaspora make up a disproportionately large percentage of the world's poorest and most deprived people today. All over the world they labour under the pressure of abject poverty and the dependence imposed on them by the west.

It appears that many Africans may have missed the latest sleight of hand in the continuing saga of their exploitation and slavery by the west — namely, the mass transformation from chattel slaves into the modern-day economic slaves of western neo-colonialism and globalization.

PART FOUR:
COLONIALISM

CHAPTER TWENTY NINE

COLONIZATION: CRIMES AGAINST HUMANITY

"The chronic bloodshed, which taints the West African season, is odious and disquieting; moreover the whole enterprise is liable to be misrepresented by persons unacquainted with imperial terminology as the murdering of natives and the stealing of their lands." **Winston Churchill,** as Undersecretary for the Colonies, 1906.[1]

'The white man is very clever. He came quietly and peaceably with his religion. We were amused at his foolishness and allowed him to stay. Now he has won our brothers, and our clan can no longer act like one...He has put a knife on the things that held us together and we have fallen apart.' Okonkwo in Things Fall Apart by **Chinua Achebe.**[2]

The Encyclopaedia Britannica defines colonization as a political-economic phenomenon beginning about the year 1500 whereby various European nations discovered, conquered, settled and exploited large areas of the world.[3]

More specifically 'colonization' refers to the process of colonizing, i.e. invading, conquering and settling. 'Colonialism' refers to the concept and phenomenon i.e. invading, conquering, settling, administering as well as the exploitation and the policies, economies, political systems and ideologies involved.

Though the British prided themselves in having abolished the slave trade and emancipated African slaves, they nevertheless then moved seamlessly from one form of slavery to another, namely colonization. With regard to colonialism, Gloria Emeagwali, Professor of History and African Studies, stated:

The process may be covert or overt, psychological, legal and military mechanisms. Colonialism inhibited the development of indigenous technology in Africa to a large extent; colonial domination brought with it a shift from subsistence farming to cash crop economy and destabilized some of the existing processes of technical growth."[4]

Historically, we are perhaps too close in time to appreciate the enormous psychological trauma European colonialism wreaked all over the African continent. The black Power activist Stokely Carmichael stated:

"Colonization deals with destroying the person's culture, his language, his history, his identification, his total humanity. When one is colonized, one is totally dehumanized. So that when the victims of colonization fight they are fighting for a process of humanization."[5]

The colonization and partition of Africa marked another important milestone in the orchestrated European downturn of African fortunes. The US author and academic, Daniel Headrick wrote:

'Among the important events of the nineteenth century, two were of momentous consequence for the entire world. One was the progress and power of industrial technology; the other was the domination and exploitation of Africa and much of Asia by Europeans.... In the year 1800, Europeans occupied or controlled thirty-five percent of the land surface of the world; by 1878 this figure had risen to sixty-seven percent, and by 1914 over eighty-four percent of the world's land was European-dominated.'[6]

The colonization of Africa would signal the beginning of another series of holocausts in Africa, the likes of which there are no historical precedents. Through colonization, the exploitative potential of white supremacy and imperialism was leveraged out to millions more Africans than those who were physically enslaved in the transatlantic slave trade. It is mainly during the European colonization of Africa that the terrible effects of mental slavery began to manifest themselves across Africa.

While many Western historians do not emphasize this, it is clear that when the Europeans colonized Africa, they did so with only one thing in mind: to exploit the African people and their land for whatever they could get out of it.

Unfortunately, many European and even African apologists fall in line with the Eurocentric view that somehow European colonialism was operated for Africa's benefit and cite, in ignorance, that it brought to Africa civilization and Christianity.

When Theodor Leutwein, Governor of the German Colony in south-western Africa, responded to allegations of the abuse of natives by German settlers, he told Berlin that German settlers were not risking their health in Africa to help the natives. They had come, like all colonizers, to help themselves to African land and labour.[7]

The Germans succeeded in annihilating over three quarters of the Herero people and at least half of the Nama between 1904 and 1908. Africans were herded into concentration camps, enslaved, beaten, raped and murdered at will.[8]

When the Herero revolted against German brutality, the German general issued a 'Vernichtungsbefehl' or an extermination order against them. Thousands of Africans were massacred and over 20,000 men, women and children were driven into the desert to die slowly.[9]

Clear precedents to the later Nazi holocaust of the Jews in the Second World War were set in German controlled African colonies. Many Africans were imprisoned in concentration camps and many more systematically slaughtered. The bones of thousands of men, women, and children still lie bleached by the sun today in open mass graves in the Shark Island concentration camp, one of five extermination camps set up by the Germans in Namibia as no attempt was ever made to cover up the genocide. Carefully documented German diaries remain that testify to the cold and cynical bureaucratic process of the industrialized murder of Africans. Over 3,500 Africans were killed on Shark Island alone and mass graves are still being discovered.[10]

The South African Khoi people, the Khoikhoi and San [formerly referred to as Hottentots and Bushmen] were the autochthonous inhabitants of the western and northern Cape in South Africa. In a series of encroachments onto their land, commando raids and broken treaties, they were annihilated by the Boers, farmers descended from the original Dutch settlers unhindered by the British colonial administration.

Unfortunately, the African killing spree was only a piece of the entire global jigsaw of genocide and oppression of non-white people in the face of white settlers and capitalist expansionism. The annihilation of aborigines on Tasmania in the so-called 'Black War' by the British was one such crime against humanity.[11] Deliberate attempts were made to exterminate the Aborigines on the Australian mainland too.[12] Whole populations of native peoples were annihilated in Central and South America by the Spanish and in North America by the British and later the US Native Americans, endured unbelievable suffering following wave after wave of European capitalist expansion and settlement. In addition to the wanton killings, the invading Europeans also brought new diseases such as smallpox and social problems like alcoholism which decimated whole people.[13]

In the mid 1870s, while India endured one of the worst famines to hit the country under British colonial rule, the British Viceroy of India threw a lavish party for 60,000 guests. While famine was killing off the Indians like flies, the British were stockpiling food at the docks awaiting shipment to the UK and the US. Thirty million Indians are thought to have starved to death in colonial British India.[14]

In later years, in Africa, the British employed the same tactics they had developed in India. Just as in India, the British dismantled the ancient systems of subsistence agriculture that had been the Africans' mainstay for millennia and supplanted them with cash crop farming for export to Britain and other Western countries.

Virtually all the main European powers took part in colonizing Africa. Powerful and ruthless individuals also competed to get a slice of the colonial African cake. At the Berlin Conference where Africa was partitioned among the European powers, King Leopold II of Belgium, schemed not just for his country but for himself as an individual, to lay his hands of a piece of African real estate. With some clever manoeuvring he managed to get the great powers, Britain, France and Germany, who were engaged in the frenzied scramble for African territory, to agree to him annexing the Congo for himself, a territory the size of half of Europe and the second largest country in Africa, rich in natural resources, including rubber and a wide range of minerals. He employed Henry Morton Stanley, a well-known British/American explorer, to help him secure the Congo region. Stanley became famous in Europe and North America for his expeditions and exploits in Africa. However, he was infamous amongst the Africans who suffered from his brutality. Stanley used bribery and trickery to get the Congolese chiefs to sign illegal treaties 'legitimising' King Leopold's claim to the Congo. The 'friendship treaties' that Stanley got them to sign were in actual fact the title deeds for their land. It is reported that in order to convince the Africans of the white man's superiority and persuade them to sign the illegal treaties, Stanley went so far as to tell them that the white man could control the sun.[15]

King Leopold turned the Congo with an estimated population of 20 million Africans, into a huge labour camp overnight. On July 1st 1885, King Leopold II declared the Congo to be *terra nullius* or vacant and stripped the native Africans of everything they owned. The African natives, who had inhabited the land for millennia, suddenly had no property, no rights, no justice nor freedoms under King Leopold's illegal act.[16]

The partitioning of Africa coincided with a worldwide boom for rubber which began after a Scotsman named Dunlop invented the pneumatic tyre for his bicycle. Thus, Leopold's capitalist project for the Congo could not have been better timed. Rubber trees grew freely and in great abundance in the Congo forest. The inhumanity, slavery, torture and exploitation that followed in the 'Congo Free State' as Leopold had euphemistically called it, inspired Joseph Conrad, to write his famous book, *Heart of Darkness*. In his book, Joseph Conrad described the 'Congo Free State' as,

'the vilest scramble for loot that ever disfigured the history of human conscience'[17]

Every Congolese community was forced to provide 10% of their population as full-time forced labourers and another 25% as part-time labourers. Henry Morton Stanley was known as Bula Matari or 'the breaker of rocks' by the natives, helped supervise the slave labour to collect the rubber.[18]

By 1902, the price of rubber had increased by 15 times and now constituted 80% of the export of Belgian imperial Congo. In order to ensure that enough rubber was collected to meet the rising international demand, the Belgian colonialists resorted to whipping, torture, and severing the hands of the native people that had not brought enough rubber. Belgian officers were so worried that their men might waste their ammunition hunting animals for sport; they required their soldiers to submit one hand for every bullet spent.[19]

A Baptist missionary, horrified by the savagery of the exploitation, wrote to *The Times* to say:

'The hands — the hands of men, women and children were placed in rows before the commissary who counted them to see that the soldiers had not wasted cartridges.'[20]

The soldiers collected severed hands by the basket load, both from the living and the dead.

The Belgian officers also ordered their men to:

'Cut off the heads of men and hang them on the village palisades, also their sexual members, and to hang the women and children on the palisade in the form of a cross'[21]

When the Congolese complained about the brutality they were experiencing, their complaints elicited only insults: said:

"Wild beasts — leopards — killed some of us while we were working away in the forest, and others got lost or died from exposure or starvation and we begged the white men to leave us alone, saying we could get no more rubber, but the white men and soldiers said; "Go — you are only beasts yourselves. You are only inyama [meat]."[22]

King Leopold II created a 16,000 strong force of gendarmes and armed them with the latest military equipment the Belgian army could provide. One of King Leopold's legacies was the recruitment of children as militants in the Congo region. Many of King Leopold's Congolese gendarmes were children who were abducted or forced to bear arms against their wishes.

The Congo was partitioned into districts which were administered by recruits from the Belgian Army. In order to increase rubber collection, King Leopold II personally supervised a system of bonuses paid to his Belgian agents. The inhuman tactics employed by these Belgian agents to force the Congolese people to increase rubber production would be too graphic to make a horror movie.

Apart from cutting off hands from the living and dead, Leopold's gendarmes resorted to cutting off and collecting the male genitals of their victims to prove that men, not just women and children, were being killed. European concession companies were awarded official hostage licences to incarcerate the wives and children of African male rubber collectors. The African rubber collectors faced losing their families, savage whippings, torture and even death if they did not hand in enough rubber after the fifteen day collection period.

Leon Fievez, the Belgian District Commissioner in the Equator region, boasted how he had killed 1,300 Congolese natives, burned one hundred and sixty-eight villages and cut down vegetable patches and gardens to drive up the rubber collection. He added: 'I only used 3000 cartridges or so'. The local Africans called him the 'Devil of the Equator.[23]

King Leopold II amassed a huge personal fortune as he enjoyed a monopoly on the world's rubber supply for about ten years. Edmund Dene Morel, a British writer and editor, had investigated the tales of horror from the Congo for some years and began to campaign for the dismantling of Leopold's Congo Free State. He started off as an anonymous writer in a paper called *The Speaker* and later wrote a moving book on the Congo called *Red Rubber,* which became a bestseller.[24]

Despite the genocide and killing of upwards of ten million Africans in the Congo, it took the hanging of a single British trader in the area, called Charlie Stokes, by a Belgian officer for the tide to turn decisively against King Leopold. Following the Casement Report into the genocide in the Congo, the Belgian parliament decided to annex the Congo Free State from Leopold and took over its administration.[25] In 1908, the Congo became a Belgian colony and the Belgian government awarded King Leopold II fifty million francs to compensate him for his 'sacrifices'.[26]

The legacies of the European colonization of Africa are all too evident and widespread to innumerate. African language, culture and customs were all irreversibly changed or altered to varying degrees. The present-day boundaries and borders, the names of African countries and people, hence who they say they are, the language they speak and what they refer to themselves as, all were all changed… and remains Africa's poisoned gift from the European colonial powers, who shared and partitioned the African continent like a piece of cake without regard for pre-existing historical, ethnic or language differences, creating chaos and bringing untold misery and suffering to millions of Africans, all over the continent.

CHAPTER THIRTY

AFRICA SCRAMBLED

'The conference, begun in November 1884, has come to be seen as the key moment in history of the colonization of Africa. Soon thereafter began the Scramble for Africa, and the Partition of the continent was completed.'[1]

'Every European country — with the exception of Switzerland — was there. Both the United States of America and the Ottoman Empire were also represented. Hung on the wall was a large map of Africa.'[2]

The pivotal moment in Africa's colonial history was the Berlin Conference, which began in November 1884. Just as the British had done in America and in Australia, Africa was regarded as 'terra nullius', in other words, vacant. Africa was therefore considered available to the colonial powers, underscoring the complete lack of consideration of the lives, culture and customs of millions of Africans who had lived there for millennia. Needless to say, there was no African representation or participation during the meeting.

At that point in time, the Europeans knew very little about the continent of Africa. To them it was little more than a coastline. Their maps of the continent were incomplete and wildly inaccurate. When they carved up the continent, which they considered as terra nullius or vacant, they took no account of the existing African societies on the ground. Colonial borders and frontiers were drawn as straight lines or arcs. Many borders followed the geographical lines of longitude and latitude, tearing living societies apart. For example, the Bakongo in Central Africa were partitioned between the French Congo, Belgian Congo, and Portuguese Angola. Somaliland was divided between Britain, Italy and France.

During the Berlin Conference the British Prime Minister at the time, Lord Salisbury, while addressing a London audience, told them:

'We have been giving away mountains, rivers and lakes to each other, only hindered by the small impediment that we never knew exactly where they are.'[3]

"Let them each have [that] big mountain," proclaimed Queen Victoria when dividing the land that is now Kenya and Uganda.[4]

African resistance to western colonization, like that of the African slaves, is something that tends to get written out of European history books. Regardless of religious or political inclinations, or whether they were initially hostile or friendly to Europeans, when and wherever Africans came to the understanding of the overarching strategic aims of Western imperialism, they uniformly fought back.

Unfortunately, ill equipped often with primitive muskets and outdated guns, spears and arrows, they soon found that leather shields and African 'juju' were no match or protection from European artillery, Maxim or Gatling guns or the Martini-Henry repeating rifles. Only Emperor Menelik of Ethiopia was successful in repelling a European invader, defeating the Italian invaders. Even so, the only two 'free' African nations, Ethiopia and Sierra Leone, the former American slave colony, could not lay claim to real sovereignty.

It took the Europeans over 30 years [from 1885–1914] of brutal, bloody, slow and grinding wars to subjugate the African nations. Notable African leaders that fought back against the western colonization process were Cetshwayo, King of the Zulus, Prempeh of the Asante in Ghana, Samori Touré of the Mandinka, Mwanga of Buganda, Béhanzin of Dahomey, Kabarlega of Bunyaro and countless others across the length and breadth of Africa.

It is no coincidence that Britain, the greatest slave traders of all time, eventually became the most powerful colonial power in Africa. The British simply converted their infrastructure and local knowledge from the transatlantic slave trade into the foundation of their African colonization.

This included the slave trading posts, slave castles and information about the people, their culture and their resources.

The process of colonization overlapped the abolition of slave trade, which, as we have seen, carried on well into the 1940s in some parts of Africa and still exists today. The British had barely freed their slaves from their shackles when began to exploit the Africans as free and cheap labour, as colonial subjects in their own lands. The British need to acquire and exploit vast expanses of foreign land and territory, was summed up by the arch Imperialist, Cecil John Rhodes:

"In order to save the 40 million inhabitants of the United Kingdom from a bloody civil war, we colonial statesmen must acquire new lands to settle the surplus population, to provide new markets for the goods produced by them in the factories and mines. The empire, as I have always said, is a bread and butter question. If you want to avoid civil war, you must become imperialists."[5]

The bulk of the missionary and exploratory expeditions to open up Africa were undertaken or sponsored by Britain. British missionaries like David Livingstone and explorers like Mungo Park had made great expeditions into Africa's interior, paving the way for European colonizers. The missionaries followed and helped provide the colonizers with detailed information about African people, the geography and natural resources.

David Livingstone talked about the three C's in opening up Africa, 'Christianity, civilization, and commerce', but he failed to mention the fourth C without which the other three Cs would not have got off the ground — conquest. Ultimately, it was military conquest that was the most significant factor in the colonizing of less technically advanced peoples all over the world. The Maxim gun [an early machine gun] was the favourite weapon of the British colonizers. It and the more readily available magazine rifles like the Martini-Henry along with artillery constituted their superior firepower which over and over again got the better of the fierce resistance and larger numbers insurgents they encountered and ensured the colonizers prevailed against the indigenous African people.

The flag followed the cross and the European colonizers rode into

Africa in the slipstream of their missionaries and explorers. To establish a foothold the colonizers employed a wide variety of tactics to dismantle African culture and belief systems. Even well-intentioned but paternalistic European explorers and missionaries felt that they had a moral duty to spread the European version of Christianity in Africa. These missionaries deliberately strove to destroy the African culture and belief systems in order to make Africans more readily accepting of Christianity and European values. Once they had infiltrated the African community, they would then seek to make the Africans subjects of the European monarchies and thus subject to European law.

It is on record that the European missionaries did very poorly at converting the pagan Africans to Christianity. David Livingstone documented his frustration at the low pace of African conversion to Christianity. Most of his converts were outcasts or slaves as was the case with many others missionaries. The missionaries also came across evidence of African Christianity and Judaism, as they sought to open up the continent to European commerce and eventual conquest.

'If the American white man fancies that he was the first to teach the bible to his black slave, he is quite mistaken… Mungo Park, as affirmed by Marion L Starkey, found that Fantooma, the Kaffir schoolmaster, had Arabic versions of the Pentateuch, the Psalms of David, and the Book of Isaiah. The unlettered Mandingoes entertained him with stories of Joseph and his brethren, Moses, David and Solomon. They gave out the stories as part of their own folklore and were very much surprised to learn that white men had heard them. If many slaves already knew a great deal of the Bible, the whole pattern of the origin and development of the backgrounds of the spiritual in America will have to be reconsidered.[6]

The prime aim of the European colonial countries was not to evangelise or even 'civilise'. The primary aim was to take over the land and use Africans as slaves, servants and free labour to extract its resources. This was in keeping with the main motive for the European expansion into all parts of the world — to obtain forced and cheap labour, raw materials and new markets for their goods.

Sadly, the real motives and process of European colonization went over the heads of unsuspecting African communities, who had no knowledge of what was to come, or any idea of the wider and overarching global European quest for territory and power. In many instances, fake treaties were signed in order to deceive African chiefs and convince the monarchy and financiers at home to continue to lend their support. Once the 'treaties' were signed, the African community was at grave risk of military intervention, as the Europeans would deliberately widen or change the remit of the agreement in order to create discord and then launch a punitive military operation against the Africans if they put up any resistance.

These so-called 'wars' were almost always one-sided and were only fought when the Europeans were confident that they had an overwhelming military advantage. In this way, the colonialists systematically destroyed African communities, killed or expelled their leaders, and installed puppet leadership.

When military force was not immediately available, then conversion to Christianity was employed, and if Christianity did not work, they would use trade as the form of entry into the community. For instance, when the Portuguese encountered the powerful Benin Empire in Nigeria, they failed convert them to Christianity or induce them sign treaties to make them subjects of the Portuguese monarchy because the Bini people were too strong and too far inland to bring their military superiority to bear. The Portuguese resolved to trade with them instead. The Benin Kingdom would later fall to a British 'punitive expedition'.[7]

Once the colonialists had established full control of the land and reduced the original African landowners to landless dependents, they imposed hut taxes payable only in British pounds, which the African natives could only get by working for the colonial administration, or white farmers or in the mines.[8]

These taxes raised additional revenue for the British government on top of the cheap labour, natural resources and land that they had already forcibly acquired.

It is common for modern western historians to try to compare the British Empire to empires like that of the Romans or Greeks but nothing could be further from the truth.

The British Empire is unique in that it started as an invisible empire of trade and was not in the first instance a product of direct military conquest. In Africa, it was based on the infrastructure it inherited from the slave trade. The British typically employed the 'smoke and mirrors' of stealth and deception first to reel in the African communities and then used its military superiority to kill off any resistance that it encountered.

It is surprising that the British, despite their success as colonizers, were late comers to empire-building, lagging many years behind the Spanish, who long since established their blood-drenched American empire and the Portuguese who had already laid claim to parts of Africa. The French and the Dutch had foreign colonies in Asia and the Far East, long before the British came to the game. Very much like the transatlantic slave trade, the British would be the last in and the last out. Britain created the largest colonial empire of all, which at it is height, covered three quarters of the world's surface.

Over time, Britain would annex and acquire colonies and territory from other European countries, including the Americas from Spain and France, much of Africa and Indonesia and Asia from the Portuguese, French and Dutch.

In the course of time, some colonies were forcibly taken and others ceded or exchanged, as part of the great global game being played out by the European powers who were all competing for the world's resources.

It is important to understand that it was not only African, American and Asian people were subjected to European colonialism. British colony occupation of Ireland was — and still is in the case of Ulster — probably the longest ever.

The first people to be colonized by the English were, as they saw them at the time, the 'barbarous people' of Ireland. The Tudor Queens, Mary and Elizabeth I, authorized this colonization, starting with Munster in the south and then Ulster in the north of Ireland. The systematic colonization of Ireland that began in the early 1600s was intended as a cure for the country's chronic instability and to expand English settlements, which had been limited to small areas around Dublin and Carrickfergus.

The early euphemism for 'colony' of Tudor and Jacobean England was 'plantation'. In the words of Sir John Davies, the settlers where called 'good corn' and the natives 'weeds'. The best land was to be taken for the colonies of the civil people of England and Scotland. King James of England argued: "Plant enough good English and Scottish corn, and the country will ever be happy settled."[9]

In real terms, the euphemism of planting good 'English and Scottish corn', and removing the 'native weeds' translated into a system of ethnic cleansing.

Even though religious and political reasons were provided as an excuse, i.e. to prevent the Roman Catholic Church of Spain using the Irish Catholics as a means of infiltrating Protestant England, the real reasons for colonization, as ever, were almost invariably economic and colonization, in most cases, led to conflict. The 'Printed Book' published in April 1610, detailed how this systematic colonization took place. The land was reallocated in parcels ranging from 1,000 to 3,000 acres with the biggest plots going to 'undertakers', who were charged with the job of building Protestant churches and fortifications. The walls of Derry, renamed Londonderry in 1610, were supposed to protect the colonizing Protestant English community, 'the good corn', while the original inhabitants or 'native weeds' and the Catholics had to live outside the walls, down in the Bogside.[10]

This graphically illustrates the religious intolerance and ethnic segregation in the policy of British 'plantation' colonialism.

CHAPTER THIRTY ONE

THE SHADOW BRITISH EMPIRE

Today, patriotic British historians describe Britain's colonization in heroic and noble terms but in reality it was a truly bloody and exploitative affair. It was driven by the insatiable capitalist greed for consumerism and trade. Pirates or buccaneers, missionaries and explorers cleared the colonizers path and had the full support of the monarchies, church and political establishments at the time. The full might of the military of the colonizing European nation was always on tap to meet their commercial requirements and strategic interests of the nation, be they pirates or priests. In England, their colonialist efforts were blessed and recognized by the monarchy and political leaders back in London.

In what could be compared to a modern-day Mafia organization, profits acquired from bloodshed, and all forms of coercion and deception, were laundered to acquire the veneer of respectability after they became recognized back in London, and would buy the pirates a promotion to the ranks of the nobility.

Buccaneering or piracy, developed as a way of waging a low-budget war against old enemies, like the Spanish and the French, and the English monarchy and government actively encouraged the English pirates to do so. The government recognized their activities and licensed them as 'Privateers' in return for some of the spoils of the robbery. Between the years 1585–1604, the English pirates were returning an annual income of about £200,000 a year to the crown.[1]

The huge profits made by the pirates also meant that the British began to increase not only the number of ships but also the quality of ships and navigation tools needed to maintain an edge over the competition.

A buccaneer, like Henry Morgan, made his fortune attacking Spanish ships and settlements. After making his fortune, he invested in Jamaican real estate and entered into the lucrative market of the cultivation of sugar using African slaves. He later became, Sir Henry Morgan, after being knighted by the Queen, and went on to hold the posts of Vice-Admiral, judge and Acting Governor of Jamaica.[2]

Another famous pirate was Sir Francis Drake, who started his career and made his fortune as 'privateer' or pirate, and would be later be knighted and elevated to high office for his efforts.

Regardless of how the fortune was acquired, if it yielded profit to the monarchy and the English government, it was recognized and rewarded. Perhaps, our modern-day Somali pirates may be following in the distinguished footsteps of British buccaneers before them in search of knighthoods.

For many years, the English had tried, unsuccessfully, to oust the Dutch from India and take control of the lucrative business of spices and textiles for many years. It resulted in several Anglo-Dutch wars but no decisive victory was achieved. In 1688, a compromise was reached and after the merging of the Dutch and English companies, the East India Company was formed.

As Indian states jockeyed and fought each other for power, British settlements responded by forming private standing armies and garrisons to protect themselves against hostile elements within India. They also had the French to worry about, as they were in direct competition with the French not only for commercial interests but also for overall strategic control of India.

As the British and the French vied for power and the Indian emperors fought against each other, Europeans started to intervene directly in Indian politics and affairs and played them off against one another. The Indian emperors also tried to use the Europeans to fight some of their battles but lost out in the end.

The Mughal Emperor granted the East India Company, civil administration or 'diwani' of Bengal, Bihar and Orissa and signed the treaty of Allahabad. This allowed the East India Company to raise extra money from taxing over 20 million people.[3]

This development ushered in the period of British company rule over India. It was a significant step in the development of the British Empire as the British would no longer satisfy themselves with the simple extraction of natural resources, harnessing cheap and free labour. The British were now into the business of government. By the time the British and other Western colonial empires became entrenched in Africa, their skills at running colonies as a business were already finely honed.

Newer and even more subtle approaches were fashioned and the English now proceeded to study the Indian culture and religion carefully, so as to gain a deeper and greater understanding of the people. The first Governor-General of British India, Warren Hastings, studied Persian and commissioned the translation of the Hindu religious book, the *Bhagavad Gita* into English.[4]

English scholars also translated Indian law and literature into English.

Many laws were established restricting Indian textiles to those that stimulated British manufacturing and soon Englishmen in good government positions in India were making huge profits. These Englishmen, rich from their Indian spoils, sent home vast amounts of money at those times and built large, imposing houses in England. They became known as 'nabobs', a corruption of the Indian title, 'nawab', meaning prince. Amongst the nabobs were Warren Hastings and Thomas Pitt, who bought the parliamentary seat of Old Sarum and whose grandson William Pitt would become Prime Minister of England.[5]

The British installed themselves as a superior race of colonial overlords in India and actively supported the Indian caste system as it helped keep the Indian people divided amongst themselves and therefore exploitable. However, the First and Second World Wars changed all that as the British had promised India its independence if they helped them fight in the World Wars. Of course, the British had no intention of relinquishing their grip on their Indian colony but Indian nationalism was growing, leading to increased social unrest and rising anti-British sentiments.

As in most of their colonies, the British had very little regard for the

Indian natives they lorded over. The low British opinion of Indian natives was articulated by a local British Commander, Colonel Dyer, in response an incident involving irate Indians attacking a British woman. On April 11th 1919, Miss Marcela Sherwood, an English missionary, was attacked by an angry Indian mob as she cycled home. She was stripped naked, beaten and left for dead but was later saved by some local Indians who knew her. Colonel Dyer issued an order requiring every Indian man using the street in which Miss Sherwood was assaulted, to crawl the length of it on their hands and knees. As Dyer explained:

"Some Indians crawl face downwards in front of their gods. I wanted them to know that a British woman is as sacred as a Hindu god and therefore they had to crawl in front of her too. [6]

Colonel Dyer, was also responsible for the Amistar or Jallianwala Bagh massacre. On April 13th 1919, he ordered his troops to corral over 20,000 unarmed Indians on a religious march into a blockaded street and shoot them. The British reports claimed that 379–1,000 Indians were killed but Indian officials claim the casualties were much higher, more likely in the region of 1,500 dead and over 1,200 wounded.[7]

Michael O'Dwyer, the Lieutenant Governor of the Province of Punjab at the time, endorsed the actions of Colonel Dyer which he described as a "correct action".

On his return to the UK, Colonel Dyer was absolved of wrong doing by the British Government and promoted for his efforts. This blatant disregard of Indian lives would have a significant knock-on effect.

In 1940, Michael O' Dwyer was assassinated in Caxton Hall, London, shortly after delivering a speech, by Udham Singh, who had been caught up in the Amritsar massacre and blamed Michael O'Dwyer for his role in the massacre.[8]

The revenge killing of Michael O'Dwyer was decried as a 'senseless murder' by the British Press and Udham Singh was later sentenced to death and hanged.

The acquisition of the Indian colony and its vast human and natural resources was the turning point in the development of the British Empire. It turbo-charged the creation of the British Empire and provided the model of indirect rule and taxation, which would be imposed on all other colonies. It is not surprising then that Queen Victoria referred to the Indian colony as the 'jewel of her crown'.

Many western revisionists claim that colonisation was beneficial to the natives they robbed. However, not only are these claims unsupported by facts, the native people always came off a lot worse.

Before the British colonised India, Indians enjoyed 27% global GDP in 1700 and about 23% in 1800. The growth rate of British India has been estimated as 0.001% between 1900–1947. In 1947, following 200 years of British exploitation, India was reduced to 3% of global GDP. Under British colonial rule, Indians had a life expectancy of 27 years and 90% of Indians lived below the poverty line.[9]

Even worse, was the chaos and upheaval the British caused in India as they hastily pulled out in the face of an incipient bloody colonial battle if they tried to forcefully hold onto India as the French did in Indochina and Algeria.

The British government gave a British lawyer, Cyril Radcliffe, thirty-six days to draw up a plan to divide India along ethnic and religious lines. He finished three days ahead of schedule. On the basis of this 'plan', drawn up by Radcliffe with no consultation with the Indians themselves, the British implemented a system which pitted Muslims against Hindus, Sikhs and Christians and vice versa. East Benghal, which had been a part of India for millennia, was cut out of India and renamed East Pakistan, resulting in the forced repatriation of over 7 million people. Over 1 million Indians were killed in the fighting that broke out between rival groups. Since then three wars and multiple skirmishes have been fought between India and Pakistan over Kashmir, a legacy of British colonial rule. Today, Pakistan and India, both nuclear armed countries maintain a tense standoff over Kashmir.[10]

One of the basic principles of the British Empire was, 'divide and rule', which was borrowed from the Romans, who had themselves colonized Britain. More accurately, the British employed a tactic of divide, fractionalize and rule, creating long lasting conflict and mistrust between different colonized peoples.

Christianity and trade were used interchangeably and together to unlock the colonized people and undermine their culture and economics. For all the religious fervour of Christian missionaries, they always deliberately set out to undermine the culture and unity of the people they converted to Christianity. European missionaries never treated Africans as their equals and always maintained a healthy 'superiority gap'.

CHAPTER THIRTY TWO

PALMGERIA: THE NIGERIAN EXAMPLE

Nigeria is a classic African example of how the British capitalist imperative became transformed from pure commerce into a country. The creation of Nigeria, the 'Giant of Africa', had more to do with vegetable oil than high-powered global politics, many Nigerians would be disappointed to know. As the industrial revolution took hold in Europe, the demand for vegetable oil, used to make lubricants for factories and soap, rose dramatically. Britain's interest in the oil-rich coastal strip of West Africa, running 300 miles eastwards from Lagos to the Niger Delta and Calabar, all the way to the Cameroon, grew exponentially, just as their interest in South Africa had increased after the discovery of diamonds.

Nigeria occupies a land area originally referred to as 'Negro land' in Joseph Conrad's map of Africa, giving credence to the claim that West Africa was colloquially called, 'Nigger Area' in Britain. Flora Shaw, who later married Lord Frederick Lugard, coined the name 'Nigeria'. Given the actual historical events, the country could easily, have been named 'Palmgeria' for Palm oil or 'Oilgeria' for crude oil, in line with the true intentions of the British colonialists.

In 1882, Edward Hewett, the British Consul to the West Africa area, sent a dispatch urging Britain to impose a formal protectorate over the whole region known as the Oil Rivers, in response to the territorial activities of their main colonial rival, France. To this end, the directors of the National African Company, led by Lord Aberdare, set about trying to achieve this ambitious plan, which would give Britain political control over a large proportion of the Niger and central Sudan region, whose population comprised about a sixth of the whole continent.

The man chosen for their job was an aggressive and eccentric, managing director, called George Taubman Goldie. He came from a rich family of landed gentry on the Isle of Man, whose family had made their fortune in the smuggling trade and had settled down as conventional squires and landed gentry.[1]

African vegetable producers and intermediaries had developed a sophisticated trade network. They controlled contract rates across the African coast, moving their palm oil in their canoes through the creeks, down to the British merchants who were trading with them close to the open sea. In a bid to lower prices and obtain a monopoly in the region, Goldie was eventually able to convince his rivals in the UK to merge their companies with his. After the merger, there remained only the competition posed by the African traders themselves.

For many years, the British had tirelessly looked for ways to forge inland in Africa, to control the oil trade from the source. Many European nations had set out to claim control of the West African coast, signing treaties with local African tribes. Some African leaders were plied with rum and others given cheap and flashy items like mirrors and costume jewellery as compensation for broad sweeping treaties, that in the eyes of the Europeans, especially the British and the French, gave them dominion over the land and its people. In many instances, the devil was not even in the details, many paper treaties were blank.

However meaningless these bits of paper would have been to the majority of African leaders, they would soon come to understand what the blank treaties meant to the Europeans when they unleashed their favourite coercion, brute force, to claim the conditions stated in their illegal treaties. Rejection of the blank treaties and European trade conditions almost invariably meant war against Africans.

Initially, thwarted by disease, especially malaria, and the difficulty of navigating forest creeks, British company steamboats were eventually able to push 300 miles inland to Bussa, exploiting the swollen rivers during the rainy season, to get their heavy steamboats afloat and cut out the African middlemen. When the African chiefs and intermediaries retaliated by sinking one of their steamboats, the British responded by burning villages, sinking their canoes and killing the natives.

Alarmed by the threat of competition from French trading companies, the British moved quickly to consolidate their monopoly of the region and to maintain control over the trade and exert political influence.

King Jaja of Opobo, who was brought to Bonny as a slave, had created the biggest African trading empire on the West African coast and was selling 8,000 tons of palm oil a year to white traders at Opobo.[2]

King Jaja had repeatedly outmanoeuvred the British Consul, Hewett. Even when Hewett tried to discredit him with lurid stories of atrocities he had allegedly committed, the Liverpool palm oil traders were reluctant to stop the lucrative business with him.

In a fine example of the 'free trade' that Britain used to acquire more wealth after the slave trade, the National African Company commissioned British gunboats to make punitive expeditions up the River Niger and anyone or anything that stood in their way was destroyed. The British methodically destroyed any town or village that had given any indication of trouble to British trade. They shelled Asaba, Onitsha and destroyed Abari with Gatling guns and artillery. They sacked the town of Torofani, killing many inhabitants, forcing the rest to flee the town. [3]

After Goldie had seized control of the palm oil trade in the Niger Delta thousands of African intermediaries were left to starve and their revolts bloodily put down. The African intermediaries were reduced to 'smuggling' their own palm oil produce — in their own country.

Taubman Goldie recruited Frederick Lugard, an English officer and gentleman who had lost faith in God after finding his fiancée in bed with another man, on return from active duty, and needed something to take his mind off it. Earlier, Lugard had been given the assignment to open up Uganda. In 1891, his employer, Mackinnon, sent him to make the teenage Ugandan king or Kabaka sign a treaty, granting Britain formal protectorate over Uganda. In his usual uncompromising style, Lord Frederick Lugard, got the treaty signed after he had threatened to use his Maxim machine gun. Lugard kept command with a heavy hand and flogging parades were a regular occurrence.

Military force was the main coercion used to establish the British will on the African leadership. African leaders were deposed or exterminated wherever necessary, and a British appointed African leader was imposed on the people. Through these African figureheads, the British were able to exploit vast areas of land and extract taxes from the indigenous people. Thus, the almost invisible British trade empire largely exercised its will remotely and only directly employed force when necessary.

These were some of the methods the British employed to successfully to colonize large proportions of the world. The vast majority of native Africans and Indians were blissfully unaware of the existence of the British Empire in those days even though many were indirectly taxed by it.

Eventually, the British colonial office fell out with Taubman Goldie, over his tactics of punitive expeditions against the African natives and his increasing militancy. To avoid Taubman Goldie steering England into open conflict with the French, the National African Company was taken over by the British government and Goldie was compensated. However, Taubman Goldie remained instrumental to the success of the British government and Frederick Lugard remained in charge on the ground.

Understanding how fragile the grip of the National African Company was on Britain's informal trade empire, Lugard set about attacking the caliphates of northern Nigeria and installing puppet emirs to form the basis of indirect rule that was used to run the protectorates which eventually became Nigeria.

From about 1914 onwards the British set out to amalgamate this trading area into a single protectorate, despite the fact that this immense tract of land mass was inhabited by people, who had been historically distinct and even traditional enemies for hundreds of years.

This led the first federal Prime Minister of Nigeria, Abubakar Tafawa Balewa, to state in 1948:

"Since 1914 the British government has been trying to make Nigeria into one country, but the Nigerian people themselves are historically different in their backgrounds, in their religious beliefs and customs and do not show any willingness to unite... Nigerian unity is only a British invention."[4]

Another prominent Nigerian of the independence era and Yoruba leader, Obafemi Awolowo, wrote in 1947:

"Nigeria is not a nation. It is a mere geographical expression. There are no "Nigerians" in the same sense that there are "English", "Welsh", or "French". The word "Nigerian" is merely a distinctive appellation to distinguish those who live within the boundaries of Nigeria and those who do not."[5]

The British process of divide and rule was especially facilitated where they found well-organized polities like monarchies or Islamic states. They only had to concentrate on changing the emirs or kings. However indirect rule was more difficult to achieve where less centralized forms of African governments prevailed such as in the South West of Nigeria.

The position of the European colonizers was vastly enhanced wherever they could undermine the culture of the indigenous people. This was largely achieved through introducing Western Christianity and Western re-education via missionary schools. African culture and practices were severely frowned upon and even ridiculed by British missionaries and colonizers, while British history and culture was promoted instead. This deliberate miseducation aided the European colonization process to the detriment of the African people. Western education made the African people less likely to reject their colonial masters, made them easier to exploit and made them more useful as servants.

Thus, the misguided notion of a British colony being part of the mother nation was created and many African people, unwittingly felt proud to be associated with what was the world's only superpower at the time.

Once the colonial masters had established themselves in Africa through slavery, trade and the efforts of missionaries and explorers to open up the continent, they needed some infrastructure in place to facilitate the extraction of resources and the harnessing of the labour that was available.

The British Empire, as most other European colonial empires, was run on the cheap. However, the indigenous people of the colonies paid a very high price in the loss of lives, liberty, land, workforce and culture. It is a commonly held but mistaken view in the West that the African colonies were better run by the British than they are today as independent countries. If this is actually true, perhaps it was because the colonial administrations basically functioned as parasitic skeletal governments that ran exclusively for the benefit of the British government and not the vast majority of African people who found themselves under the control of the United Kingdom.

To appreciate the immense wealth these parasitic skeletal western colonial governments were extracting from Africa, all one needs to do is to imagine how much the British or American governments would make if they did not use taxpayer's money to improve the health, economy or infrastructure of the country. This is exactly what the colonial governments did. Profits were invested only where it paid direct dividends into British companies or it was spent on infrastructure which was needed to facilitate the production of commodities which it would send to the Mother Country. The bulk of the Africa's wealth and raw materials was transferred out of the country.

To illustrate this point, in his book, *The State of Africa,* Martin Meredith wrote:

'Having expended so much effort on acquiring African Empires, Europe's colonial powers then lost much of their earlier interest in them. Few parts of Africa offered the prospects of immediate wealth. Colonial governments were concerned above all to make their territories financially self-supporting. Administration was kept to a minimum; education was placed in the hands of the Christian missionaries; economic activity was left to the commercial companies. The main functions of government were limited to maintaining law and order, raising taxation and providing an infrastructure of roads and railways. There seemed to be no need for more rapid development. Colonial rule was expected to last for hundreds of years.'[6]

The colonial principle of 'all for one and none for all' was put to use in the formation of Nigeria, as John Hatch wrote:

'Northern and southern Nigeria thus formed two separate administrative units of British Africa. But they shared common custom duties, the railway and river communications serve them both, the same detachment of troop's maintained security in both areas. Even the methods of governments were not

entirely dissimilar. Although direct rule was applied to the east and centre of the Southern Protectorate, in Yorubaland much the same methods were used as in the north. Here also, the chiefs were used as agents of colonial administration, their positions strengthened by its support of colonial authority, their functions blended into the colonial pattern.

It therefore seemed to the British government that amalgamation of the two units would be more efficient and less expensive. The people of the two areas had no common history, little common culture and some tradition of conflict, but this, if it was ever considered at all, appeared irrelevant to Whitehall.[7]

After Lugard had amalgamated northern and southern Nigeria in 1914, he retained separate administrations for the two sectors of the new country.

'Henceforth it was hoped that the British taxpayer would be relieved of the burden of supporting the north by making it reliant on the richer south. Services and communications were linked together with Southern ports now inviting produce from the north.[8]

It only took a few years for deep cracks to appear in the British construct of 'Nigeria'. The unequal yoking together of the disparate Nigerian people in order to facilitate British interests was a recipe for disaster. The Biafrian war broke out on July 6th 1967 and by the time the Biafrians surrendered on January 15th 1970 an estimated 2–3 million Nigerians had died.

CHAPTER THIRTY THREE

THE COLONIAL IMPERATIVE

The French African colonialists had the same aims as other Western colonizers but did it, as always with the French, in their own special way. The French presented the colonialism of their French African Empire primarily as a 'civilizing mission'. This was to be achieved by means of black Africans becoming fully assimilated into French society. To achieve this 'special privilege of Frenchness' native Africans would first have to reject their African heritage, family laws and customs in their entirety and cleave unto their superior mother nation, France.

Many of the black elite of L'Francafrique Noire obediently accepted the tradition of loyalty to France along with its language, culture, traditions, and most importantly, its government. The reward for this assimilation was allegedly not only the opportunity to enjoy the same rights and privileges as white Frenchmen but these small black elites would provide France with the necessary buffer of black middle-class puppet leaders through which they could continue to rule their African colonies. As a foot-note, by accepting France as their colonisers, French-speaking African nations also unwittingly ceded control of their natural and human resources to the 'Mother Nation' France in perpetuity.

However, in neither the British Empire nor the French African Empire, nothing was done altruistically or for the benefit of their African colonial population. Colonial governments only saw things in terms of how valuable or not the colony was to the process of mass exploitation. Infrastructure, like buildings, roads, and rail, were created with the sole the aim of facilitating trade, communication and movement of people and goods out of the colonies. Maps of India's railways link the subcontinent, whereas maps of Africa's railways only link areas of extraction of resources to the ports.[1]

The British colonial system was self-funding, meaning that entrepreneurs-turned-governors had to convince the English government of the profitable nature of their ventures in order to get government funding, just like the buccaneers and privateers before them had. In South Africa, it was the discovery of diamonds and the pressure placed by investors that stimulated the British government into action and led them to declare sovereignty over the Boers and black South Africans.

With the British at the helm of affairs, they needed to create a suitable subordinate workforce to ensure the smooth running of the whole operation and therefore were impelled to train Africans to fulfil several roles in the chain of command. This would also have another important advantage because in time it would put a black African face on British and other European activities in Africa, just as Britain had succeeded in masking their operations in India earlier.

The fact that no attempt was made to cater for the wider population significantly reduced the running costs for the colonial government.

The colonialists viewed Africans, their land and culture only in terms of how valuable they were or were not to the whole process of exploitation. When African nations began to demand and gain their independence, Europeans would have salvaged and removed the entire infrastructure they had laid down to facilitate the colonial process, if they had been able. And indeed this is exactly what they tried to do in Guinea. When Guinea refused to join the French Union, the equivalent of the British Commonwealth, the French stripped out as much infrastructure as they could, with the vindictive objective of crippling the country.[2]

In terms of education, most colonial schools equipped Africans with rudimentary skills that fitted them to perform a subordinate role in the colonial administration. Even in the churches, African converts served as subordinates who could never aspire to enjoy the same status their white brothers in Christ had, despite Christian teachings of equality in the eyes of God.

The combination of force and subtlety used by the British to achieve their colonial interests was greatly admired by Adolf Hitler, who wrote in his book Mein Kampf:

'The British were an admirably trained people, who had worked for 300 years to assure themselves that domination of the world for two centuries. They had learned the art of being masters and of holding the reins so lightly withal that the natives do not notice the curb.[3]

Hitler repeatedly expressed his admiration for British imperialism and their effective oppression of 'inferior races'.

"What Germany has do is to learn from Britain's example. The wealth of Great Britain, is the result of the capitalist exploitation of the 350 million Indian slaves."[4]

"What India was for England," he explained, *"the territories of Russia will be for us"*[5]

His main criticism of the English was that they were too self-critical and lenient towards their subject peoples.

In 1937 Adolf Hitler offered Lord Halifax, the British Foreign Secretary, a solution to deal with Indian nationalism that was simple and brutal. Shoot Mahatma Gandhi, he suggested, and if that did not suffice to reduce them to submission, shoot a dozen of the leading members of Congress and, if that did not suffice, shoot 200 more and so on until order is established.[6]

Despite Hitler's belief that the British were too lenient, they were not above the use of brutal methods of repression whenever they thought it necessary. In crushing the Mau Mau uprisings in Kenya, for instance, the British employed a 'shoot to kill' policy and murdering an African 'insurgent' earned a £5 reward. The fact is that the 'insurgency' in Kenya was blown out of all proportion by the British media and not a reflection of the reality on the ground. Thirty-two Europeans were killed compared to over 10,000 Africans who lost their lives in the immediate British repression of the revolution.

In 1948, the British governor of Kenya pronounced:

"As of right, the products of historical events which reflect the greatest glory of our fathers and grandfathers — the greater part of the wealth of the country is at present in our hands; that is because this land we have made

our land by right — the right of achievement, and Africans will simply have to learn to live in a world which we have made, under the humanitarian impulses of the late nineteenth and twentieth century."[7]

In 1955, in the British colonisers' usual high-minded but heavy-handed approach to Africans, the British governor in Kenya said:

"The task we have set our minds is to civilize a great mass of human beings who are in a very primitive moral and social state."[8]

Even after their experiences with concentration camps in South Africa during the Boer War and in Malaya, the British ran Kenyan concentration camps in very harsh conditions with up to four hundred inmates dying every month. During the 1950s, about an estimated 150,000 Africans died because of the British repression of colonial revolt.

In the end, the British Empire could not survive two World Wars and the agitation for independence that was on the rise in most of its colonies. It was terminally weakened by the First and Second World Wars and heavily indebted to the United States. The British had no choice but formally to dismantle the Empire.

However, in November 1956, the British Empire in its dying throes invaded Eygpt together with France over President Abdel Nasser's nationalisation of the Suez Canal. Unfortunately for Britain, the United States, fearing that an imperial military occupation in Egypt would drive Arab states into the Soviet camp, had warned against unilateral action in Egypt, so incensed by British and French deception, they withdrew their funds and vital support for the military operation.

Without the support of the US the French and British invaders were unable to prevent the Egyptians from blocking the Suez Canal and stopping all oil shipments going through it. As the pound fell in value, Harold Macmillan, then the Chancellor of the Exchequer, had to choose between devaluing the pound and asking for American aid; in the end, he chose American aid and lots of it. Prime Minister Anthony Eden was forced to eat humble pie and agreed to withdrawal from Egypt unconditionally. Only then did President Eisenhower arrange a billion dollar rescue package from the IMF and the export-import bank to bail Britain out.

The failed British and French invasion of the Suez Canal in Egypt substantially signalled the end of the British Empire. As nationalistic fever spread through the colonies, the British and other European countries scrambled out of Africa with almost as great haste as they went in. As the sun went down on the British Empire, its place would be taken by another western superpower, a superpower with the greatest economic and military might ever known to humankind...the United States of America.

PART FIVE:
SEGREGATION

"There is a natural disgust in the minds of white people about the indiscriminate amalgamation of black and white people."
Abraham Lincoln[1]

CHAPTER THIRTY FOUR
THE LEGISLATIVE AND IDEOLOGICAL ORIGINS OF SEGREGATION

The origins of segregation probably extend as far back as slavery itself, as the slave owners made clear-cut distinctions between themselves and their slaves. Slave owners enacted stringent laws in order to maintain the social gap and prevent their slaves crossing over into the mainstream of society.

Many old texts contain detailed instructions about slavery and the laws around it, for example:

Exodus 21:2 and Deuteronomy 15:12 in the Old Testament of the Bible both recommend that slaves were to be manumitted after six years, a law that was also followed in the Islamic faith.[2]

The ancient Mesopotamian Laws of Eshnunna [1900] and the Code of Hammurabi devote several articles to slavery.[3] In India, the Laws of Manu of the 1st century BC contain numerous articles on slaves.[4] Roman slave laws were very elaborate and were summed up in the great Pandects of Justinian of AD 533.[5] In the Koran, the starting point of Islamic law, and Sharia law also contained many laws on slavery from the acquisition of slaves from jihads to the treatment of slaves and their freedom.

The laws of the ancients legislated on the basis of the slaves' social and economic status, not on the basis of race or colour. The laws that have the most relevance to modern-day slavery and mental slavery are the laws that came into existence after the European powers set out on the road to Imperialism and accelerated greatly with the Transatlantic Slave Trade.

The earliest laws of this kind were the *Siete Partidas* of 1263–65 of Alfonso X of Castile and Leon and *Le Code Noir* of Louis XIV of 1685. Of special note were the slave laws of the Spanish-speaking colonies and countries based on the *Siete Partidas*, the Spanish slave code of 1789 and the Louisiana Slave Code of 1824, which too was based on the Siete Partidas.[6]

The *Code Napoleon* was based on *Le Code Noir* and defined the conditions of slavery in the French colonial empire. It ordered all Jews out of France's colonies and forbade all religions in the colonies except Roman Catholicism. However, it was primarily directed at black African slaves. It was the most detailed set of laws on how to manage African slaves in Europe.[7]

Under *Le Code Noir*, French priests focused the minds of the African slaves on particular Christian principles to help foster obedience and the notion of obedience to God was twisted to mean obedience to the white slave master and his rules. Slaves were made to believe they were pagans and their masters were holy. In general, black was bad and white was good.

Just how stringent the French book of codes was is highlighted by this piece — Article 38 of the *Code Noir* states:

'A fugitive slave who shall have escaped a month;...shall have his ears cut off and be branded with a fleur-de-lis on one shoulder; and if he repeats the offence for another month...; he shall be hamstrung, and branded with a fleurs-de-lis on the other shoulder, and for the third time, shall be punished by death.' [8]

Obviously the teaching of divine grace was rather limited as far as slaves were concerned. The priests deliberately promoted the New Testament teachings of salvation and freedom after death rather than the Old Testament account of the history of the people of Israel, who as slaves in Egypt gained their freedom from bondage.[9]

The South Carolina Slave Code of 1740 and the Tenth Amendment of 1791 were created for the basic protection of the institution of slavery in the United States of America and imitated the slave codes of Barbados.[10]

Prior to the American Civil War, the first American state to legalize slavery was Virginia. It was commonly accepted that Christians should not be enslaved. At this time, a lot of the free labour was indentured, mainly Irish and Scottish labourers, who had agreed to indentured labour in order to pay for their passage to America. A few free black slaves in Virginia actually prospered enough to own their own land and houses. However, as slavery became more entrenched, it was no longer enough for black African slaves to accept Christianity. Slavery in America became clearly defined by race and colour and was perpetuated by heredity.

As more slaves were brought to America, yet more stringent rules where devised to maintain control of the slaves. In June 1680, the Virginia General Assembly passed a law making it legal to kill any slave that was disobedient, ran away or resisted capture. In 1775, it passed another law that relegated all slaves to the state of property. Laws were passed to allow runaway slaves be captured and returned to their owners; an act that increased bounty hunting and kidnapping of free slaves in the North.[11]

Since county courts were paid more for the conviction and return of runaway slaves than for their freedom, it was exceedingly rare for slaves to be judged fairly or given their freedom.

In 1857, a few years before the outbreak of the Civil War, a case was tried in the Supreme Court [Scott vs. Sanford] to determine the answer to this question:

"Can a negro whose ancestors were imported in this country as slaves become entitled to the rights of the community?"[12]

The Chief Justice ruled that negroes were not intended to be included into the word 'citizen' under the Bill of Rights in the constitution and in the Declaration of Independence. It ruled that black people had no rights which a white man should respect and they should be reduced to slavery for their benefit.

Comparing of the slave laws promulgated in ancient times to those during the years of European colonialism and the Atlantic slavery era, a number of differences can be observed. Perhaps the most fundamental was the question of manumission. The earlier laws generally made provision for manumission. The African slaves who were taken to the West and to the Caribbean following their abduction from Africa were never given a chance to obtain their freedom. They and their offspring for generations to come would be born into perpetual slavery.

Once black African slaves were acquired there was a strong imperative to segregate them from the main body of the white population; not just physically but mentally, emotionally and socially. Apart from the sheer brutality of the punitive methods white slave owners used to keep the slaves obedient to their masters, very selective verses from the Bible were used to reduce the probability of slave revolts. Western Christianity promoted the idea of the innate inferiority of African slaves to their white slave masters and selective biblical verses were manipulated in order to quell any thoughts of equality in the minds of society and the African slaves themselves.

As the slave system became more entrenched, Western thinking moved even further away from the notion that black Africans were of the same human race as whites and several attempts were made to make a clear distinction between the races not only to prove how different they were but to maintain their innate superiority.

In an attempt to avoid any sense of shared humanity, certain thinkers hit on the idea of the 'pre-Adamites', which postulated that Africans and other races existed before the creation of the white man in the Garden of Eden. These ideas stemmed from obvious discrepancies in accounts of Creation in the biblical book of Genesis itself. There are two distinct creation stories in the Bible. In Genesis 1.1 to 1.31, God creates the world in six days and rests on the seventh. In Genesis 1.26 God creates man after the creation of the grass, herbs and trees had already been created on the third day. However, in Geneis 2.7, God creates Adam, then Eve from Adam's rib in Genesis 2.22. However, unlike the first narration, man is created before vegetation and not the other way around.

In the first creation story, time is defined and divided, i.e. the days of the week, in the second space is defined and divided i.e. the Garden of Eden, and the trees of life separated out from the rest of creation.

In Genesis 4.16, a further confusion also becomes apparent, as it appears as if there are people already inhabiting earth at the time of Adam's creation. After God banishes Adam's son Cain, for killing Abel, to the land of Nod, where he meets a woman and has a son named, Enoch.[13]

The obvious contradictions in the biblical creation stories led early Christian scholars to argue the case for two different creation theories. In the 17th century, a French Protestant scholar, Isaac La Peyrère [1594–1676], exploited this discrepancy and argued that the first creation story was of non-Jewish peoples, and the second was of Adam's particular race, the Jews.[14] This pre-Adamite theory apparently explained the obvious discrepancy between Bible chronology and the much older and longer chronology of world history and events.

This theory became widespread in Europe as it helped explain the presence of much older civilizations and people without detracting from the accepted Biblical creation story. The pre-Adamite theory helped liberate Western historians from their responsibilities of recounting world history as a whole but also created a natural schism that became the crucial 'biblical' support for the ideas of Western superiority and justified slavery of 'pre-Adamite' people.

One Matthew Hale, in his book, *Prae-Adamitae*, published in 1655, explained that there were only white people in the Garden of Eden.[15]

In 1847, a professor of biololgy Louis Agassiz lectured in New York on 'The Plan of Creation', with special reference to the animal kingdom, and maintained that Negroes had a different origin from whites.[16]

Nott and Gliddon, anthropologist and Egyptologist respectively, also proposed innate black inferiority in their work *Types of Mankind*.[17]

These ideas were floated with the sole purpose of creating a sense of superiority in the minds of the white slave traders and owners which helped to assuage the feelings of guilt that must have troubled the minds of anyone who had even the tiniest speck of a conscience in the face of the crime against humanity that was the transatlantic alave trade.

This legal and ideological framework defined the status of the African slave as not human, a chattel and the property of the slave-owner. The legal segregation of African slaves also underpinned western societies in which white priveledge was securely protected from any social incursion by African slaves. Thus, when the status of the slave changed with the emancipation, the segregationist parameters for maintaining white privilege were already in place.

CHAPTER THIRTY FIVE

THE EVOLUTION OF SEGREGATION IN THE UNITED STATES OF AMERICA

After the Civil War, black slaves in the United States faced a dangerous and uncertain future. Though technically free, they were not recognized as citizens of the United States by the Constitution or protected by laws of the land. This exposed them to the wrath of their previous white slave owners in the South and the apprehension and colour prejudice of white people in the North.

The American Civil War ended in 1865, leaving the defeated and discontented South with thousands of freed slaves who, at least on paper, had suddenly acquired the same liberties as their former owners. Some slaves had even fought against these former masters but even the slaves who did not fight must have quickly realised that the conquering North shared by and large the same feelings about the innate inferiority of the Africans as their former masters. The freeing of African slaves after the Civil War left the newly freed black slaves with no real social, economic or political base, completely destitute and at the mercy of white Northern and Southern Americans.

However, even in the chaos that followed the defeat of the Confederate South, the former white slave owners were not done with their freed African slaves. It is fair to state that the entire American criminal justice system colluded with white plantation owners, business men and even government holdings to entrap, convict and then lease out black people as prision labourers.

The Virginia General Assembly passed the Vagrancy Act on January 15th 1866. This law was specifically aimed at freed black men and defined a vagrant as anyone without a job or who appeared homeless. Freed African men were picked and criminalised on any pretext. In addition to the 'crime' of vagrancy, a black person could be assaulted for walking along the same pavement, towards a white person, instead of moving aside into the gutter. Looking at a white person the wrong way, was an offence. Seeking alternate employment or an increase in wages was an offence. A black owned convienience store, outperforming a competing white store was also an offence. A black man accused of looking at a white woman, talking to white woman or having a sexual relationship with a white woman, consensual or not, risked being brutally lynched. Freed male African slaves found guilty of vagrancy were forced into employment for up to 3 months. If a so-called vagrant ran away and was recaptured they could spend the rest of their lives in the prison system.

The Vagrancy law was enacted at a time when hundreds of thousands of newly freed African slaves were searching for missing loved ones, relatives, jobs and a place to live. In effect, the Vagrancy Act of 1866 functioned liked a dragnet to impose sanctions, incarcerate and criminalise the newly-freed African slaves who were trying to rebuild their lives.[1]

The Commanding General in Virginia at the time, Alfred H. Terry issued a proclamation declaring that the law would *"re-institute slavery in all but its name."*[2]

He forbade military and civil officials from enforcing it but there is no evidence to suggest that his order was adhered to. In fact, convict leasing became widespread in the Southern states and provided cheap and forced labour to farms, rail road and logging operations throughout the south.

Black American prison populations increased significantly with the combination of the Vagrancy laws and convict leasing.

In Georgia, the African American prison population increased tenfold between 1868–1908 due to convict leasing.[3]

Convict leasing was an extremely lucrative business for plantation owners, businesses and corporations. Large companies like US Steel and the Tennesse Coal and Iron Company exploited African labour through convict leasing. In 1898 about 73% of Alabama's annual state revenue came from convict leasing alone.

However, between 1866 and 1876, during the period of Congressional Reconstruction, the Federal government declared all such discrimination against blacks illegal. The passage of the Fourteenth and the Fifteenth Amendments, Civil Rights Acts of 1866 and 1875 and various Enforcement Acts limited the ability of Southern whites to formally deprive blacks of their civil rights.[4]

Several groups of former slaves were able to establish separate churches and schools from whites. They were able to make great strides towards building their own institutions, passing Civil Rights laws and electing African officials into public office. This period is often described as the first phase of Reconstruction.

In direct response to the progress made by freed slaves, the Southern whites began a vicious war of terror on African Americans and many right wing organisations including the Ku Klux Klan were formed. They terrorized freed African slaves via mob lynching, burning them alive on crosses and destroying their property. Thousands of African Americans were killed, maimed and terrorized in the late 1860s and early 1870s.

In 1872, President Ulysses S. Grant stated the true aims of the Ku Klux Klan:

"By force and terror, to prevent all political action not in accord with the views of the members, to deprive colored citizens of the right to bear arms and of the right of a free ballot, and to suppress the schools in which colored children were taught, and to reduce colored people to a condition closely allied to that of slavery."[5]

While lynching has been anecdotally associated with William Lynch who gave the alleged Willie Lynch speech on the Hudson River in 1712 and Charles Lynch, an officer in the Confederate army and Virginian magistrate or Justice of the Peace, this is thought to be inaccurate. It is believed that the word 'lynching' was in fact named after Captain William Lynch [1742–1820] of Pittsylvania County, Virginia. He was the author of an article, Lynch's Law, sent to the Virginia Legislature on September 22nd 1872.[6]

Brown [1975] described in macabre detail a 'typical lynching' ritual:

"Once a person was condemned, public notices were circulated a day or two in advance to whites in the locality and neighbouring areas. Some notices were sent to distant white communities. Trains made special trips, adding extra cars to meet the demands of crowds wishing to watch the gruesome spectacle of a man being lynched.

The number of spectators sometimes reached 15,000. The lynching was preceded by torture and mutilation, climaxed by what was euphemistically called "surgery below the belt".

Parts of the victim's body were dismembered and photographed for picture postcards, which were sold as souvenirs. The remains were then burned."[7]

White lynching of black African people was the most blatant example of structural, institutional and personal violence perpetuated by white supremacists on African people. The lynchings were carried out in the presence and in the full knowledge of white police officers and law enforcement officers but when the coroner's verdict on the cause of death was given it was declared to be lynching…by unknown persons.

The 'Mary Turner lynching' of 1918 was undoubtedly one of the most barbaric acts ever committed in a 'civilised' country. Though pregnant, the Negro woman was lynched in Valdosta, Georgia. She was hung from a tree, doused with gasoline and motor oil and burned. As she dangled from the rope, a man stepped forward with a pocketknife and ripped open her abdomen in a crude caesarean section.

"Out tumbled the prematurely born baby child," wrote Walter white. "Two feeble cries it gave — and received for answer the heel of stalwart man, as life was grounded out of the tiny form.'[8]

In another horrific example:

"George was burnt alive within one mile of the court-house at Greenville, in the presence of an immense assemblage of slaves, which had gathered to witness the horrid spectacle from a district of twenty miles in extent.

It was typical for "decent and respectable white folks" to pack basket lunches and spend their weekend afternoons participating and enjoying in these heinous acts.

"Lynching extra" editions of local newspapers spared no gory detail, and even carried society columns to report on who was there."[9]

The following graph gives the number of lynchings and racially motivated murders in each decade from 1865 to 1965. Data for 1865–1869 and 1960–1965 are partial decades.[10]

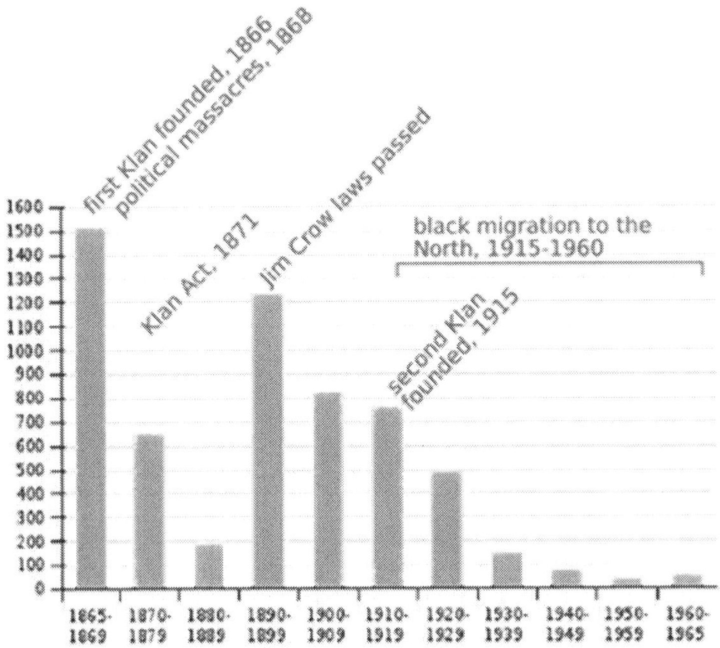

There are 2,805 documented victims of lynch mobs killed between 1882 and 1930 in ten southern states. Although mobs murdered almost 300 white men and women, the vast majority of the 2,500 lynch victims were African American. Of these black victims, 94% died in the hands of white lynch mobs. The scale of this carnage means that, on the average, a black man, woman, or child was murdered nearly once a week, every week, between 1882 and 1930 by a hate-driven white mob.

It is impossible to know how many African Americans were killed after the Civil War but nearly four thousand recorded lynchings [mutilations and burnings] took place between 1882 and 1968.

The same source gives the following statistics for the period from

1882 to 1951: 88% of victims were black, and 10% were white. 59% of the lynchings occurred in the Southern states of Kentucky, North Carolina, South Carolina, Tennessee, Arkansas, Louisiana, Mississippi, Alabama, Georgia, and Florida. Lynching was not uncommon in the West and Midwest but was virtually non-existent in the Northeast.[11]

The most common reasons given for the black lynchings were murder and rape but, as documented by Ida B. Wells, such charges were often pretexts for lynching blacks who violated Jim Crow[1] etiquette, or engaged in economic competition with whites. Other common reasons given included: arson, theft, assault and robbery; sexual transgressions [miscegenation, adultery, cohabitation]; 'race prejudice', 'race hatred', 'racial disturbance'; 'informing on others; 'threats against whites'; and violations of the colour line ['proposals to white woman'].

In truth, most black victims were the random objects of white rage, as in the bloody urban riots in which white mobs swooped down on black neighbourhoods, burning and killing any Africans they could get their hands on. This is buttressed by studies of Ida B. Wells-Barnett, a great anti-lynching crusader of the early 20th century. While many black individuals lynched were randomly picked, some of the targets of white rage were not quite as random:

All the mobs, by which people of colour have been hunted and persecuted, have been directed against their efforts and means of improvement. The negro brothel, or a dance house, might have stood... without being mobbed by the populace, or torn down as a nuisance,... but a negro church or school house, or a temperance hall, is not to be tolerated at all.[12]

---

1 'Jim Crow' as an expression originated in a song performed by Daddy Rice, a white minstrel show entertainer, in the 1830s. The entertainer blackened his face with charcoal, sang and danced in a routine to caricature a foolish black person. By the 1850s, the Jim Crow character, one of several stereotypical images of black inferiority in America's popular culture, was a typical act in the minstrel shows of the day. Jim Crow later became a name synonymous with the brutal disenfranchisement of the African Americans and by 1900 the term was usually identified with racist laws and actions that deprived the African Americans of their civil rights by defining blacks as inferior to whites and as members of a caste of subordinate people. A parallel show, the black and white Minstrel Show, which ran from 1958 to 1978 in the UK, was hugely popular. In the show white performers with blacked out faces performed songs and sletches based on racial caricatures and scenes of stereotypical behaviour.

The authors of 'A Portrait of the Lynching Era', 1880–1930 stated:

'The lynching era encompasses roughly the five decades between the end of Reconstruction and the beginning of the Great Depression. During these years, we may estimate that there were 2,018 separate incidents of lynching in which at least 2,462 African-American men, women and children met their deaths in the grasp of southern mobs, comprised mostly of whites. Although lynching and mob killings occurred before 1880, notably during early Reconstruction when blacks were enfranchised, radical racism and mob violence peaked during the 1890s in a surge of terrorism that did not dissipate until well into the twentieth century.

In addition to the punishment of specific criminal offenders, lynching in the American South had three entwined functions:

first, to maintain social order over the black population through terrorism;

second, to suppress or eliminate black competitors for economic, political, or social rewards

third, to stabilize the white class structure and preserve the privileged status of the white aristocracy.'

Lethal mob violence for seemingly minor infractions of the caste codes of behaviour was more fundamental for maintaining terroristic social control than punishment for what would seem to be more serious violations of the criminal code.'[13]

However, what determined a 'criminal offence'? What constituted proof? How many men were lynched based on false allegations? What about due process?

Between 1882 and the late 1980s, the annual number of black victims grew alarmingly: exceeding ninety in 1892 and 1893. From the zenith reached during the "bloody '90s," the number of blacks killed by lynch mobs began a protracted decline over the next three decades, reaching a nadir of fewer than ten victims annually in 1928 and 1929.

Lynchings were concentrated in a swathe running through Georgia, Alabama, Mississippi, and Louisiana: the region often referred to as the 'black Belt'.

Mob violence against African-Americans served four functions within southern society during the lynching era:

1. to eradicate specific persons accused of crimes against the white community;

2. as a mechanism of state-sanctioned terrorism designed to maintain a degree of leverage over the African-American population;

3. to eliminate or neutralize competitors for social, economic, or political rewards; and

4. as a symbolic manifestation of the unity of white supremacy.[14]

The Northern Federal government efforts to stop this murderous bloodshed were very feeble and the vast majority of investigations came to naught. The basis for institutional racism in America was firmly laid during these years.

Jim Crow laws legalized segregations and, in effect, achieved in law the type of white discrimination and segregation that the Klan's members and other white supremacy organizations' murderous campaigns were trying to establish.

The Plessy vs. Ferguson ruling of the US Supreme Court gave the go-ahead for full-scale legalized segregation.

America's legal systems, law enforcement, monetary institutions, housing and job opportunities remain clearly slanted in favour of white Americans over African Americans today. Today, African Americans are still more likely to be convicted of crimes without proper investigations and receive harsher sentencing, like the death penalty, more often.

Republican President Rutherford B. Hayes won the election based on his pre-election promise to end the Reconstruction that provided more favourable conditions to freed African slaves; but this brought even worse conditions for the newly freed slaves, as the Federal Government abandoned all efforts to protect their civil rights and liberties. This led to a marked increase in the white reign of terror in the Southern states and in the 1880s the vicious mob lynching increased, convict prison farms were created and chain gangs formed. The debt peonage of sharecropping evolved and the imposition of a legal colour line in race relationships and a vast variety of other laws blatantly discriminated against blacks.[11]

Legal segregation on public transport was imposed in several Southern states and blacks were made to sit in a special car on trains reserved for Africans that became known as the 'Jim Crow car', even if they had bought first-class tickets. In some states so-called 'miscegenation' laws banned interracial marriages. Their reasoning was simple. Africans were considered to be so inferior that any mixing of the two races would threaten the very survival of the superior white race.

Virtually all Southern states passed statutes restricting suffrage in the years 1871 to 1889 and introduced poll taxes in some cases. The devastating effect of these laws was that over half the blacks voting in Georgia and South Carolina in 1880 had vanished from the polls in 1888. Of those African Americans who did vote, many of their ballots were stolen, misdirected to the opposing candidates, or simply not counted.

In the 1890s, most Southern states started systematically to deny blacks their voting rights by imposing voter registration restrictions, such as literacy tests, poll taxes and the white Primaries, where only whites could vote. white registrars denied voting privileges to blacks at the registration place by using these new rules, rather than at the ballot box, which had previously been done by fraud or by force. By 1910 every state of the former Confederacy had adopted laws that segregated all aspects of life — especially schools and public places — where blacks and whites might socially mingle or come into contact.[15]

Fear of what Southerners referred to as 'uppity blacks' was rife. These were a new generation of blacks who were born after slavery who wanted their full complement of human rights as American citizens. This fear coupled with and reinforced by other fears, such as the risks of black people wanting revenge for the hardships they endured during slavery, was one of the driving forces behind the present gun culture in America today. It also explains the exodus of white Americans away from highly African American populated urban city centres to the suburbs.

With little or no police or judicial protection and under legalized segregation, it was very difficult for the former black slaves to resist the many injustices that they had to endure. The system of land tenancy, known as sharecropping at the time, left most freed African slaves dependent economically on the white planter-landlords and merchant suppliers, really a move from pure slavery closer to serfdom.

The white lynch mobs threatened all members of the black family — adults and children alike. This reality meant that any attempt to stand up to the prevalent injustice might bring down the wrath of the white mob on one's parents, brothers, spouse and children. Some blacks felt that appeasement of the whites would eventually stop with the disfranchisement of the southern blacks but as in all cases when one gives in to bullying, their situation deteriorated even further with more ritualized lynching and brutal acts of terror carried out by the Ku Klux Klan.

Unfortunately, the 1890s brought in even more stringent laws and clearer separation of the races. The white supremacists used legal racism and mob terror to deprive blacks of the vote and define them in life and popular culture as an inferior people.

The United States government continued to dither and remained weak and ineffectual regarding the white mob-terror that was being inflicted on the freed blacks. They refused to enact anti-lynching laws and when the Supreme Court sanctioned segregation in the Plessy vs. Ferguson case in 1896, this meant that blacks needed to devise many psychological ploys to survive.

CHAPTER THIRTY SIX
THE END OF LEGAL SEGREGATION

When dealing with white people, freed African slaves had to appear accommodating and they had to develop complicated psychological ruses to appear non-threatening and happy with the prevailing situation.

Many used 'dissembling', a ploy in which blacks assumed positions and appearances of non-confrontation. Sometimes this meant shuffling and feigning irresponsibility and sometimes it meant turning the other cheek and walking away. Another ply was playing the clown, always wearing a wide grin, to show your pleasure within dangerous and difficult situations, however hard. Unfortunately, some of these coping strategies became inculcated into mainstream popular culture and came back to haunt modern-day African Americans, who have for years now been locked into negative stereotypes which have done great damage to their current situation.

This 'putting on the man' or playing 'Sambo' was used in order to manipulate white masters and better control their otherwise helpless position in society. The Sambo character was supposed to be innately naïve, passive, cheerful, childish, lazy and submissive. This was interpreted as the true character of black Africans and became the commonly expected behaviour from freed African slaves in both northern and southern white Americans.

African customers were the last to be served in stores when white customers were present and had to patiently wait their turn and not speak unless spoken to rather than dare to address them directly. Adult African

Americans were disrespected by white people, who referred to them as 'boy', 'girl', 'auntie' and 'nigger'.

Over time this 'Sambo' character was immortalized in literature and film of the period, usually in the character of Uncle Tom, Uncle Remus, Jim Crow and 'Old black Joe'. D.W. Griffith's classic silent movie, *The Birth of a Nation*, released in 1915, depicts elected black Congressmen during Reconstruction as ape-like characters, eating bananas on the floor of Congress.[1]

Later, white-produced movies cast black actors as lazy, submissive, and innately docile characters who spoke in the same manner as black slaves did in front of their masters; that is, taking a posture of docility, holding their heads down, and smiling all the time with their hats in their hands when talking to whites. In short, freed Africans were forced to assume a multitude of personalities in order to cope with the prejudice and dangers of the Jim Crow laws.

The Thirteenth Amendment had officially ended legal slavery, in the United States.[2] The Civil Rights Act of 1866 acknowledged African Americans to be citizens of the US. Following this statute riots erupted in many southern states:

"In every southern state there was an assault on any activity that contested the privileges of whites or threatened to hinder white domination of the black population, including wresting the reins of political power from blacks, northern carpetbaggers, and sympathetic white southerners, know' as 'scalawags."

Booker T. Washington grew up in this environment. Washington was born into slavery and the author of the famous book, *Up From Slavery*, believed that accepting segregation for the time being and working hard in farming and community-based support groups would best enable southern blacks to avoid the violence and terror all around them. He helped found schools and colleges including the Tuskegee Institute, funded by white philanthropists. Washington argued that such tactics would bring them a measure of economic security and would in time enable them to challenge disfranchisement and the terror of Jim Crow.

His scheme of 'technical only education' for blacks to become economically viable was non-threatening to the whites and found support in both the southern and northern white Americans. His book was circulated widely and Queen Mary of England, wife of George V, was alleged to have read it as well.[3]

On the other hand, William Edward Burkhart Du Bois, a Harvard-educated New England-born intellectual, found Washington's appeasement strategy unacceptable and even though he understood that blacks could not end segregation immediately, he felt that they should insist upon all their constitutional rights as American citizens. He advocated among other things to educate a talented elite of African Americans to lead the masses in political and economic resistance to Jim Crow.[4]

Along with William Monroe Trotter, another critic of Booker T. Washington, Edward Du Bois founded the Niagara Movement which advocated vigilant protest and activism in place of Washington's gradualism and appeasement. Although this movement floundered, it helped set the stage for the National Association for the Advancement of Coloured People [NAACP], which emerged in 1909–1910. The organisation became the main voice of advocating legal resistance to segregation, disfranchisement and lynching in the nation.

During the 1920s, it conducted scores of lawsuits in the defence of black civil liberties and civil rights and lobbied the Federal Congress to pass an anti-lynching bill. Although it never achieved a Federal anti-lynching bill, it helped greatly reduce the number of incidents by 1940.

Perhaps, the most famous lynching in the US was that of a 14-year-old boy called Emmett Till.

Images of Emmett Till's mutilated body, broadcasted nationwide and worldwide, became the first mass-media images of the long-standing violence of Jim Crow in America.[4]

Emmett Till, [July 25th 1941–August 28th 1955], a boisterous 14 year old boy, was on his summer holiday in Mississippi from his mother's place in Chicago.

As he was born and raised in Chicago, he was unfamiliar with the strict codes of conduct for an African American male interacting with a white woman under Jim Crow in the South.

Trying to impress a group of African American boys outside a candy store, he boasted that he had a white girlfriend in Chicago. On a dare, he playfully flirted and allegedly wolf-whistled at the 21-year-old store proprietor, Carolyn Bryant, as she left the store and said "Bye baby."

However, Carolyn Bryant claimed in court that Emmett Till had grabbed her waist and muttered obscenities to her. None of this was witnessed.

In the early hours of August 28th 1855, Carol Bryant's husband, Roy Bryant and his brother-in-law J.W. Milam, armed with a gun, broke into Emmett Till's home in the evening and demanded that Emmett Till be given to them. They then abducted him despite the pleas of his great uncle, Mose Wright.

They drove around Memphis and probably tortured Emmett in a toolhouse behind Milam's house. They beat him and gouged out his eye, but according to Milam, Emmett remained defiant. They shot him in the head, attached a 75 pound cotton-gin fan to his neck with barbed wire to weigh the body down, and threw his corpse into the Tallahatchie river.

Three days later, Emmett Till's mutilated and decomposing body was discovered and retrieved from the river. When his body was repatriated to Chicago, Emmett Till's mother, Mamie Till Bradley, insisted on a public funeral service with an open casket.

In her words, she wanted the world to see the brutality and violence of Jim Crow in America, first-hand.

Jet magazine, marketed to black readers, carried an in-depth story and published the gruesome images of Emmett Till's corpse alongside pictures of him prior to his murder. Soon, mainstream papers including Time Magazine published the story and pictures too.

The images of Emmett Till's mutilated body shocked the world and became a powerful symbol and catalyst for the black civil rights movement.

Three months later when Rosa Parks refused to give up her seat on the bus, she stated that she had Emmett Till on her mind. Rosa Parks act of resistance became a one of the main rallying points of the civil rights movement, which in turn produced present-day America.

Unfortunately, on September 23rd 1955, Roy Bryant and J.W Milam were acquitted by an all white jury in Mississippi. The jury delivered their verdict of "not guilty" for abduction or murder in 67 minutes, despite the killer being positively identified by Mose Wright and other witnesses.

One white juror stated:

"If we hadn't stopped to drink pop, it wouldn't have taken that long."[5]

In 2017, Carolyn Bryant, in an interview with Tim Tyson, the author of the book 'The Blood of Emmett Till' changed her testimony, admitting that Emmett Till had never touched, threatened or harassed her.

She stated :

"Nothing that that boy did could ever justify what happened to him."[6]

In the aftermath of the black civil rights movement, other national organisations sprang up like the National Urban League, and the National Negro Congress and more radical ones like the Communist Party. The NAACP, through its constant agitation, won a landmark case of Brown vs. Topeka Board of Education. This decision not only reversed the 'separate but equal' doctrine but also opened the floodgates through which a sea of civil rights litigation and legislation flowed all over America in the 1950s and 1960s.[7]

During the slave trade many southern blacks had fled to the north, using the 'underground railroad' made famous by Harriet Tubman. During the Jim Crow years, thousands of blacks fled the south to Kansas and Oklahoma in the 1880s and 1890s — and even today there exist nearly all-black towns in these states.

In the 1940s, black Americans refused to accept a segregated military or lack of access to government jobs in the war industries. A. Philip Randolph, an African American leader, threatened a 50,000 strong black non-violent march in 1941 on Washington D.C. to secure fair employment in the war industries. President Franklin D. Roosevelt responded by opening the defence industries to equal employment, monitored by the Fair Employment Practices Agency. This and the Roosevelts support of labour, the various welfare benefit programs that aided impoverished blacks — and his wife, Eleanor Roosevelt's advocacy of civil rights attracted northern blacks to the Democratic Party in the

1930s–1940s. This switch in political parties represented a monumental shift from the party of Lincoln to the party of Roosevelt and laid the political ground for challenging Jim Crow in the 1950s.

In 1944, the Supreme Court struck down the white Primary, a measure used by white Americans to exclude blacks from the democratic parties in the South. The number of southern African Americans registered to vote rose from 150,000 to more than a million by 1952. The transition was complete when the NAACP lawyers convinced the Supreme Court to reverse the 'separate but equal' in the sphere of education.

This era of change heralded the activism that came to be known as the Civil Rights Movement. This era is frequently called the 'Second Reconstruction' because it effectively completed the civil rights revolution begun by Congress and embodied in the Fourteenth and Fifteenth Amendments passed in the decade of the Civil War.

The United States' Civil Rights movement also coincided with the decolonization of non-white nations all over the world, following the activism of Mahatma Gandhi and the black civil rights leader Martin Luther King.

With the passing of the Civil Rights Act of 1964 and the Voting Rights of 1965, legalized segregation and the disfranchisement of African Americans finally ended. It had taken over one hundred years of terror and discrimination to achieve this. Very few people today know or wish to remember what Jim Crow was. In a survey of students in American history classes at a major university, less than 20% recognized the word at all, and most of them had only a vague idea that the word once had something to do with segregation.[8]

While legal discrimination in America may have been reversed through the courts, the fact remains that white supremacy and the legacy of segregation and discrimination is still very much alive.

Freed African Americans are still haunted by institutional racism and the lack of equal opportunities to justice, jobs, quality education, and affordable housing which in itself remains a huge challenge today.

The bravery of Mamie Till Bradley in using her son's brutal murder to focus the attention of the world on the racism and the barbarism of black lynching by white people in the US with 'The blood of Emmett Till' literally improved the fortunes of all African Americans today.

It is important to remember that Emmett Till's mother Mamie Till Bradley noted that her fight for justice for her son's murder was beyond her as an individual and in fact was a fight for the African community as a whole.

PART SIX:
APARTHEID

CHAPTER THIRTY SEVEN

SOUTH AFRICAN APARTHEID

In 1488 Bartolomeu Dias, a Portuguese explorer, reached the southern tip of Africa, which he named the Cape of Storms, and was later renamed, owing to it being navigated by bolder sailors, the Cape of Good Hope. Vasco da Gama followed up, rounded the Cape and then sailed into the Indian Ocean. This opened up the sea route to India and the East Indies. The Dutch East India Company was formed to organise and of course profit from this trade. The ships of the company needed somewhere to take on water, fresh meat and vegetables. It was decided to establish a station at the Cape.

In 1652, a contingent of about a hundred Dutchmen under Jan van Riebeeck landed at Table Bay and founded what later came to be known as Cape Town, the first European settlement in southern Africa. Their arrival would change the course of the lives of indigenous South Africans forever.

By 1800, slavery in the Cape Colony had become so widespread that at least two thirds of the white farmers owned at least one slave. Here slavery was particularly brutal even when compared to other slave colonies and it was defined on very strict racial lines.[1]

In 1948, when the white South African National Party came into power it coined the word 'apartheid'. Apartheid means 'apartness' in Afrikaans, the language of the descendants of the Dutch settlers. This policy governed the relations between the white minority and the predominantly black majority of people living in South Africa.

The apartheid system legalised and sanctioned racial segregation: political and economic discrimination against non-whites. Race laws regulated every aspect of life for both blacks and whites. They prohibited the interracial sexual relations and marriage. Under what was called Job Reservation, certain jobs were reserved for whites, with blacks were only permitted to do relatively menial jobs.

In 1950, they passed the Group Areas Act, which established residential and business areas in urban towns for white people. Other races, especially Africans, were barred from living, working or owning land in these areas. The Population Registration Act required that all South Africans be classified into one of three categories, white, black [African] or coloured [of mixed descent].[2] The coloured category also included the major subgroups of Indians and Asians.

Two further acts were passed in 1954 and 1955 which collectively became known as the Land Acts. These laws completed a land grabbing process which had started with similar Land Acts in 1913 and 1936 of which the result was to set aside more than 93% of South Africa's land for the white minority.[3]

To enforce segregation the white apartheid government adopted the 'Pass' system, which required all black South Africans aged 16 years and above to carry a 'pass'. The pass or Reference Book, included a Polaroid picture and ethnic identity, work records, tax receipts, the employer's current address and the employer's signature. Passes governed the movements of black people in white areas and regulated the supply of labour in white areas. The pass restricted access to white areas without a permit or a job. The inability for a black South African to produce a valid pass was a criminal offence, punishable by a fine or imprisonment — and thousands of black South Africans disappeared into apartheid prisons after being arrested for pass offences; families had to search prison after prison to find where they had been incarcerated.

Many other laws were passed which forbade social contact between the races, authorized segregated public facilities, established separate academic standards, and curtailed non-white participation in the national government.

The white South African police, or any government official, could stop a black South African and demand that they produce their pass at any time or any place. So widespread was the white oppression due to the pass system, that at any given time African pass offenders constituted about 40% of the daily prison population. The police and government officials conducted frequent and impromptu raids to catch pass 'offenders', relying on the element of surprise. At a moment's notice, they carried out raids on the streets, at places of work and even in homes, late at night, while people were sleeping.

To further divide the communities, the Bantu Authorities Act of 1951 was passed. The apartheid government forcibly established tribal organizations for the black South Africans and the passing of the Bantu Self-Government Act of 1959 created ten new 'African homelands'.

The Bantu Homelands Citizenship Act of 1970 made every black South African a citizen of the Bantu homelands, regardless of their actual place of origin. The Bantu Citizenship Act also excluded black South Africans from the mainstream of South African economics and politics. Despite the fact that the apartheid white South African government claimed that the African states were 'independent', they were entirely politically and economically dependent on the white government. However, the reliance of the white South African government on black labour complicated the process and made it difficult for the white apartheid regime to carry out a clear policy of separate development.[4]

Concerning the Bantu[2], the Minister of Bantu Administration and Education, M.C. Botha stated in no uncertain terms:

Bantu individuals can be present in white areas solely for labour… There is a wall, a roof, and one cannot get past that… The Bantu cannot strive towards the top on equal footing with whites in our policies, social matters, labour, economy and education in South Africa.[5]

Dr Henrik Verwoerd, the theoretical and ideological architect of the formal apartheid, stated when he was Minister of Bantu Education:

"My department's policy is that education should stand with both feet in the Reserves and have its roots in the spirit and being of Bantu society… there is no place for him [the Bantu] in the European community above the level of

2 Previously, earlier white governments had referred to black Africans as 'kaffirs' and Natives. The apartheid government referred to them as 'Bantu', which is a short form of the Nguni word for 'people'.

certain forms of labour."

The African National Congress [ANC], first founded in 1912 as the South African Native National Congress, was the major organisation of the African people that fought against white discrimination and segregation. The founding fathers of the ANC included John Langalibalele Dube, its first President, and Sol Plaatje.[3] Others who over the years played key roles in the ANC's long history of struggle include Chief Albert Luthuli, Oliver Tambo, Thabo Mbeki, Walter Sisulu and Nelson Mandela, who was to become the first President of democratic South Africa.

Thousands of black South Africans lost their lives in the struggle for freedom against the white apartheid regime. Through the sustained struggle, brave actions and sacrifices of thousands of black South African men and women — many less prominent but no less influential black activists, including Robert Sobukwe, Steve Biko and Chris Hani, black South Africans were able to secure the right to vote in their own country and, in April 1994, after the first democratic election in the nation's history, legal and formal apartheid came to an end and South Africa attained majority rule.

---

3 Dube founded the first newspaper in Zulu, iLanga laseNatali, still going today, founded the Ohlange Institute and wrote the first novel in Zulu, Insila ka Shaka. Sol Plaaitje founded a number of newspapers in seTswana and wrote a number of articles and books including *Mhudi, An Epic of South African Native Life a Hundred Years Ago* [1930]

CHAPTER THIRTY EIGHT

THE BRITISH EXPROPRIATION

The British influence on the formation and the institution of white apartheid in South African cannot be overstated. The British Empire's interest in southern Africa had increased dramatically after the discovery of diamonds and gold in the Northern Cape colony, Bechuanaland, and Matabeleland in the 1860s and 1880s. British Imperialists rationalized their greed for resources and the genocide of innocent Africans with their 'strategic imperative theory'.

Christopher M. Paulin stated:

'The "strategic imperative" theory argues that British expansion in southern Africa aimed at protecting one of two primary routes to India. To keep this route around the Cape of Good Hope open, Southern Africa had to be kept free from foreign influence. Not only must the Germans and the French be prevented from obtaining ports in southern Africa, but the Boers must also be kept from gaining an outlet to the sea. If the Boers obtained a harbour, they might invite a hostile foreign power to protect that harbour.

Economic theories of imperial expansion generally focused on the desire of British capitalists to find new areas to sell their products. Once Africans were conquered and ruled by British civil servants, they would see the benefits of civilisation. British goods would be demanded since these Africans would come to recognise the cultural superiority of their conquerors. If Africa was lost to the Germans, French, Belgians, and Portuguese, British goods could be restricted from trade on the continent. British markets needed to be protected. Once southern Africa was found to be rich in diamonds and gold this economic imperative became an even greater driving force. Diamonds and gold must be secured for British capitalists to exploit.'[1]

Clearly, no thought was spared for the inhumanity meted out to the indigenous Africans who it would seem were just fodder in the acquisition of the material wealth.

'While the combination of these factors may have played a role in British expansion in southern Africa, scholars have largely neglected one aspect of the economic forces at work. This was the role played in late nineteenth-century southern Africa by the constant need for a cheap, stable, supply of labour to work the mines, farms, and public works projects of this emerging area. The building of industry in southern Africa required a huge work force. This work force was to be found amongst the African population. However, when these potential wage labourers proved reluctant to abandon their traditional means of subsistence, coercive measures was employed.

One by one, independent African polities were conquered, disposed, restricted to 'native reserves' and taxed into becoming a cheap and readily available supply of labour for European enterprises.'[2]

To achieve their strategic aims the British instigated and conducted a series of 'wars' against every independent African society in southern Africa. The sole aim was the break up the African social structures, such as communal farming, cattle rearing, and military structures. The natural structure of the African society was seen by the British as an inhibiting factor in freeing up able-bodied men to work as wage earners in the employment of Europeans in the mines and on their farms.

Lord Carnarvon also authorised the annexation of the independent Boer Transvaal state in an attempt to increase the labour force in the diamond mines. The British wars against South African natives like the Xhosa, Zulus and the Pedi were all conducted with this goal in mind.

According to Paulin again:

'The conquered African state was then forced to accept treaties that required land possession and cattle confiscation in order to make these people dependent on European paid wages for their survival. The treaties also contained clauses which forced the Africans to become apprentice miners or farmers and forbade African military organisations and African chiefs or leaders to encourage able bodied men to seek labour with European employers.'[3]

Another ploy used by the British to raise revenue from the Africans they had subjugated was the imposition of 'hut' and 'poll' taxes, which were only payable in British coin. The hut tax meant that every homestead was liable to pay a tax. Poll tax was levied on every individual. British coin could only be obtained by working on European farms or mines. This left the subjugated African chiefs and their people with no choice but to seek employment in the mines and on the farms in order to be able to pay the illegal taxation in British currency. By so doing, they were able to pressurize the Africans out of their communal and rural lifestyle, into becoming migrant workers.

Insight into the projected revenue the colonial masters expected from the hut tax is revealed in the comments of Hicks Beach, then Secretary of State for the Colonies to the British Treasury:

"It is to be remembered that the natives at present contribute nothing to the revenue.... But the taxes are now beginning to be paid regularly; and the successful termination of the Zulu war and of the contest with Sikikuni [sic] will enable the government to impose taxation on the natives which is estimated to produce from 50,000 to 65,000 pounds a year."[4]

Britain's illegal hut and poll taxation in South Africa netted the British government nearly £2 million per year in today's money.

In general, the exploitation of black South Africans was justified by a plethora of racist arguments.

In 1899 British control of the natural resources and the wealth of southern Africa was frustrated by the discovery of gold on the Reef in the Boer South African Republic. When the British had found a *casus belli,* they moved in to try and annex the republic and gain control of the gold fields. This precipitated the Anglo-Boer War.[4]

The Boers inflicted a number of embarrassing military reverses on the British initially but in the end the Boers could not match the full might of the British army in open combat and resorted to extremely effective guerrilla tactics. Irritated by the Boers' successes, Lord Roberts, the general commanding the British forces in South Africa, thundered:

"Why can't they [the Boers] stand and fight like men?"[5]

---

4 Or Boer War. The Boers themselves called it the Tweede Vryheids Oorlog [the Second Freedom War].

He ordered his men to burn down every house within a one to ten mile radius of any act of rail sabotage. He then took the wives and children of the Boer commandos, including any black servants that happened to be in the area into custody, creating the modern concept of the concentration camp, which the British and Hitler later employed with terrible effect. The wives of the Boers were sometimes sent as emissaries to the Boer fighters to ask them to stop fighting under the threat to burn down their farms and take their land.

When Lord Kitchener took over from Lord Roberts as commander of the British troops, this policy of total war was continued. Over 1,500 people were incarcerated in these concentration camps. Many were kept without food and water for many days and Boer wives whose husbands were known to be fighting got half the meagre rations or none at all.

The concentration camps were built with no regard for the weather and were situated on flat, open terrain. The prisoners were unable to protect themselves from the heat by day and the cold by night. They were also extremely unsanitary with one lavatory to about 300 people. It was not therefore surprising that they had an overall mortality rate of over 25%, the hardest hit being the women and children. For children aged between one year to five years old, the mortality rate was nearly 100%. It is estimated that 20,000–28,000 Boers and about 14,154 black South Africans died in the camps.[6]

By October 1901 the harsh winter, coupled with a major typhoid epidemic, wreaked havoc in the camps, some families losing up to twelve of their children to disease and the prevailing conditions.

While the fate of the of the white Boer families has been well documented and written in history, the fate of the black South Africans who were incarcerated in the camps is much less known. The Africans were separated from the whites and put into separate camps and at first were given no rations and did not have access to any medical treatment at all. They were forced to clean the white prison camps and dispose of the excrement from the lavatories in return for food. The elderly and the young, unable to work for their food, naturally starved to death. The life expectancy of black South Africans incarcerated in those harsh and dirty surroundings would have been brutally short.

Many able-bodied black African men were carted away to perform gruelling menial tasks like building railway lines for the British army in South Africa, which at its largest numbered in the region of 500,000.

When Emily Hobhouse, a humanitarian nurse, visited the South African concentration camps at Bloemfontein she was appalled and exposed the inhumane conditions to the British press. In June 1901 she wrote a report entitled 'Report of a Visit to the Camps of the Cape and Orange River Colonies' detailing her findings to the British Prime Minister and calling for an immediate improvement in the standards of the prison camps.[7]

Emily Hobhouse's findings were later investigated and verified by a formal commission and official investigators headed by suffragist Millicent Fawcett. The British government reacted by labelling her a liar. On her return to South Africa, Lord Kitchener placed her under arrest and sent her back to England without allowing her to set foot on South African soil.

It is interesting to note the parallels between the response of the British media at that time and the way the British media react to events today. Some British newspapers wrote articles in support of the concentration camps, suggesting that that was how Boers lived anyway. An English doctor, Dr Kendal Franks, sent to South Africa to study why the death rates in the camps were so high, wrote in his recommendations that 'Boer women needed sharp discipline and soap!'[8]

The British press set about demonizing the Boers. They carried stories and made movies in England that depicted the Boers treacherously killing British prisoners and nurses. A fake movie called *The Dispatch Rider* was circulated showing Boer prisoners begging for water, only to shoot the bearer or stab him or her in the back.

Essentially, the British public was not told the true story of what was going on in South Africa and was largely uninformed about the harshness and cruelty of the camps. The British government exercised tight control of any reports coming out of South Africa and it was able to deceive the British public. Even when Emily Hobhouse blew the whistle on them, they simply denied it.

When other European countries like Russia, France and especially Germany began to receive reports about the British concentration camps, it started a propaganda war in Europe. German newspapers carried grim news about the British 'Hellkampke' in South Africa. The European news stories collectively succeeded in putting the British government under enough pressure to shut the camps down. Sir Henry Campbell-Bannerman, Liberal leader and a Member of Parliament, openly condemned the camps and wrote an article about the British concentration camps called 'methods of barbarism' that was keenly debated in the House of Commons and helped convince the British government, in the light of the bad international press, into closing the concentration camps.

COLONIZING ZIMBABWE

The British colonization of the East African region called Zimbabwe today was Britain's attempt to form a white settler colony in Africa. Just like Southern Africa, East Africa was much desired by Europeans for its sub tropical climate and vast natural resources.

The British insinuation into Zimbabwe is also notable because it clearly demonstrates the how the British colonial imperative works and the fine interplay between all its protagonists.

The process that began with British missionaries and explorers and then moved through its entrepreneers, politicians, royalty and military.

The rich African territory that is Zimbabwe today belongs mainly to the Shona and Ndebele people. Early British reconnaissance through their explorers and missionaries had given Britain a good idea of its potential. The British were particulary interested in the area which lay between the Limpopo and Zambezi rivers. During the Berlin conference in November 1884, the principle of effective occupation was enacted meaing that a European country could acquire the rights to an area only if they already possessed them or had "effective occupation". This meant they needed to have treaties with the local leaders, flew their flag there or had treaties with the local leaders. The principle of effective occupation ignited the European scramble for Africa with representatives from various European nations desperately seeking to sign treaties with local African leaders by whatever means possible.

The British imperialist and financier, Cecil Rhodes, had the vision of building a railway between Cape Town to Cairo and saw the British as foremost imperialists in the world. Cecil Rhodes believed that the Anglo-Saxons were the most superior human race in the world and stated that they were *"the first race in the world"* and claimed that *"the more of the world we inhabit the better it is for the human race"*.[9]

Rhodes described the Africans in the Cape Colony as living largely "in a state of barbarism" and as a leading architect of the South African Apartheid system recommended that Africans should be politically and economically marginalised. He was also a leading advocate for British Settler colonialism and in order to grab the territory called Zimbabwe he had tried and failed several times to convince the influential King of Matebeland, King Lobengula, to sign various treaties.

In 1888 he dispatched John Moffat, son of a British missionary, Robert Moffat, who was trusted by Lobengula, to sign a friendship treaty with Britain and consider Rhodes proposals. Lobengula was assured by Cecil Rhodes that Britian only wanted mining rights and was not interested in acquiring land like the Boers or other European states.

He then sent a delegation consisting of his associate Charles Rudd, Francis Thompson and a lawyer Rochfort Maguire to Lobengula to draft the treaty for alleged mining operations.

Still suspicious about Cecil Rhodes intentions, Lobengula had brought a European missionary of his own to the meeting, Charles Helm, as an interpreter. Lobengula was reassured by Charles Rudd that no more than ten white men would mine in Matebeland.

However, this limitation known as the Rudd Concession was left out of the final treaty. Had Lobengula not brought Charles Helm as an independent interpreter, the truth about Cecil Rhodes' dubious treaty with Lobengula may never have been known.[10]

In addition, the treaty was one sided and only imposed restrictions on Lobengula and stated that the mining companies could do anything necessary to maintain their operations.

Not long after Lobengula signed the treaty he realised the full ramifications of the treaty and desperately tried to renounce it. He put out a public statement and even sent two of his chiefs to London as emissaries to meet Queen Victoria who Lobengula described as 'White Queen', but both the British government and the royalty ignored him.

In 1889, on the basis of Cecil Rhodes' flawed treaty, Queen Victoria signed a royal charter which empowered Cecil Rhodes, now backed by the British government and royalty to march on, police and rule Matabeland from the Limpopo River to the Lake Tanganyika in Central Africa.

THE WHITE ZIMBABWEAN LAND GRAB

In 1890, in order to seize Matebeland, Cecil Rhodes raised a company of troops that consisted of members of the British South African Police force and and volunteers called the Pioneer column.

The white colonisers and settlers were promised a minimum of 3000 acres of Matebeland each in addition to mining rights as the spoils of war. They hoped to exploit the Shona's ancient gold mines but later found that the gold deposits were not as much as they believed. However noting that the land was extremely fertile and they became farmers instead.

The original African owners were driven of the land and the white settlers carved out huge swathes of the most fertile and productive land of Zimbabwe for themselves.

Predictably, the Shona and Matabele people rose up against the white occupation and this led to the First and Second Matabele wars. The African landowners were defeated in the Matebele wars which further cemented the white settlers / British colonizers grip on the land.

In May 1895, the vast area of land, that was originally Matabeland and Mashonaland, approximately 1,143,000km squared, which was originally called "Zambesia" after the Zambezi River was renamed "Rhodesia" by the white settlers and colonisers in honour of Cecil Rhodes.

In 1923, Cecil Rhodes company's charter was revoked and company rule was replaced by self governance supervised by Britian.

Under white minority self rule, the largely British white settlers enjoyed significant political and economic advantages over the colonised

Africans. British settlers and Europeans from many different countries flooded Rhodesia to take advantage of the high standard of living conditions of white Rhodesians. The Rhodesian economy was based on farming, agriculture and mining.

The white population in Rhodesia grew to nearly from a population of approximately 1500 in 1891 to nearly 300,000 in 1975. Despite this population explotion the white settlers never constituted more than 7.3% of the population, even though they had appropriated over 90% of the land.

In 1930 the white colonial South Rhodesian government passed the Sothern Land Apportionment Act that was based on race and divided the land into 5 regions. The most fertile regions I, II and III were reserved for minority of white settlers only while the least fertile region — region V — was reserved solely for the majority black population.

Region V was further divided into the Tribal Trust Lands (TTL). This led to the enforced overuse of the TTLs due to overpopulation while large swathes of white only farmlands lay idle.[11]

Between 1945 and 1955, over 100,000 Africans were forcibly driven from farmland designated for white ownership only.[12]

Rhodesian society was racially segregated and the white settlers lived in separate areas of town. Schools, hospitals and recreational facilities were kept racially segregated to avoid the intermingling of the white settlers and the native Africans.

Because of the the inequal distribution of land, black labour costs were very cheap, and in 1975 the average income of a White Rhodesian was one of the highest in the world.[13]

THE RHODESIAN BUSH WAR

In addition to the total annexation of Zimbabwe's most fertile land, the white settlers enjoyed many other privileges.

The white settlers dominated all the political, military and socio-economic structures of the country. Senior positions in all public services were reserved for the white minority. White settlers working in manual occupations enjoyed legal protection against job competition from their

Black African colleagues.

As time went on, it became clear that the oppression of black Africans by the white minority and the living conditions of the black majority was untenable and drew criticism locally and internationally.

In addition, African was rapidly being decolonised and Britain was keen to keep its leverage over its former African colonies through the Commonwealth organisation.

However Ian Smith, a Zimbabwean born white settler and the Rhodesian Prime Minister at the time, was determined to maintain white minority rule at any price.

On November 11th 1965 Rhodesia made a Unilateral Declaration of Independence.

In so doing, Ian Smith stated:

"The mantle of the pioneers has fallen on our shoulders to sustain civilisation in a primitive country."[14]

This move not only put Rhodesia and Britain on a collision course but it incensed the African nationalists who had been applying political pressure for over 20 years prior to seek a military solution instead. The unequal distribution of Zimbabwe's land lay at the heart of the conflict.

In 1979 Ian Smith tried to defuse the tension by pushing for the 'internal settlement' changing the country's name to Zimbabwe-Rhodesia and appointing Bishop Abel Muzorewa as the first Black head of government. It was to no avail, as Zimbabwe-Rhodesia was not recognised internationally, by Britain, or accepted by the African nationalists.

The Rhodesian Bush war was fought between the Rhodesian government on one side and the Shona tribes represented by Robert Mugabe and ZANU movement and Ndebele people represented by Joshua Nkono and the ZAPU movement.

The Cold War deeply complicated the Rhodesian war and the African nationalists were supported by Russia, China and North Korea while South Africa clandestinely provided military and financial support to the Rhodesian government.

Many European volunteers came from Britain, Ireland, Poland, Australia, New Zealand, Canada and the US to help the South Rhodesians maintain white minority rule.

After Mozambique won its independence from the Portuguese, Ian Smith's Rhodesia found itself surrounded by hostile neighbours on three fronts. Even, its main supporter, Apartheid South Africa, advised a negotiated settlement.[15]

LAND REFORMS

On December 21st 1979 Britain brokered a ceasefire and a negotiated settlement of the Rhodesian Bush War at Lancaster House in England.

Rhodesia was briefly put under British rule while supervised multiracial elections took place. On 18th April 1980, Robert Mugabe and the ZANU party won by an overwhelming majority and Robert Mugabe became the first Prime Minister of the newly created and internationally recognised Republic of Zimbabwe.

One of the key demands of Robert Mugabe and his followers was immediate land reforms and an equitable redistribution of land ownership in Zimbabwe. However, Britain pressured Robert Mugabe and his ZANU party into waiting 10 years before instituting land reforms.

The British and the US government offered to compensate white Zimbabweans for any land they sold to aid the process of reconciliation. The "Willing buyer, Willing seller" principle was set up and refunded white Zimbabweans for any land sold between 1980–1998.

However, in the late 1990s the Prime Minister, Tony Blair, terminated the "Willing buyer, Willing seller" arrangement claiming that a predecessor's administration, Margaret Thatcher's Conservative government, had exhausted the funds to support the scheme. In addition, Tony Blair repudiated all the British government's commitments toward the land reforms scheme.

In response, Robert Mugabe's Zimbabwean government embarked on a "fast track" redistribution campaign, forcibly confiscating white farms without compensation.

Between 1980–1998, under the "Willing buyer, Willing seller" scheme white farmers had voluntarily given up about 3,498,44 acres of land. However, by 2013, 10,816,886 acres of white farmland had been expropriated by black Zimbabweans.[16]

In 2002 Tony Blair's Labour government imposed crippling sanctions on Zimbabwe. The US and the EU also applied targeted sanctions to Zimbabwe which are still extant.

The Zimbabwean economy was virtually destroyed by the crippling sanctions and the impact of reduced farming.[17]

CHAPTER THIRTY NINE

APARTHEID THROUGH BLACK AFRICAN EYES

It is important to see apartheid South Africa through the eyes of black South Africans in order to understand what it was like to be black and living in South Africa under the white apartheid system.

"All the wages and housing schemes will not change the native. He will remain dirty, lazy, and thoroughly dishonest... If we want the natives to be law-abiding, let us speak to them in the language they understand: the language of the sjambok, administered freely and with vigour".[1]

Thus lamented a white South African farmer in 1947. It is as good an index of the way in which South African whites regarded those they oppressed and exploited and what black people had to suffer.

Nelson Mandela, in his book *Long Walk to Freedom,* gave some insight into the difficulties black South Africans faced at that time and some still face today.[2]

Following his circumcision, which marked his transition to adulthood, the main speaker of the day, Chief Meligqili, a son of Dalindyebo, Paramount Chief or King of the abaThembu. He gave the young Rolihlahla his first real inkling of the struggles that lay ahead. He began conventionally, remarking how fine it was that they were continuing a tradition that had been going on for as long as anyone could remember. Then his tone suddenly changed:

"There sit our sons, young, healthy and handsome, the flower of the Xhosa tribe, the pride of our nation. We have just circumcised them in a ritual that promises them manhood, but I am here to tell you that this is an empty,

illusory promise, a promise that can never be fulfilled. For the Xhosa, and all black South Africans, are a conquered people. We are slaves in our own country. We are tenants on our own soil. We have no strength, no power, no control over our destiny in the land of our birth, they will go to the cities where they will live in shacks and drink cheap alcohol, all because we have no land to give them where they could prosper and multiply. They will cough their lungs out in the bowels of the white man's mines, destroying their health, never seeing the sun, so that the white man can live a life of unequalled prosperity.

Among these young men are chiefs who will never rule because we have no power to govern ourselves; soldiers who will never fight for we have no weapons to fight with; scholars who will never teach because we have no place for them to study.

The abilities, the intelligence, the promise of these young men will be squandered in their attempt to eke out a living doing the simplest, most mindless chores for the white man. These gifts today are naught, for we cannot give them the greatest gift of all, which is freedom and independence." [3]

The British laid down the framework for the white South African apartheid system. Systematic racial segregation led to the dispossession of Africans of land and material possessions. The white South African National Party fully exploited the system, codified and focussed it as 'apartheid' in order to further deprive Africans, the original owners of the lands, the power to vote and influence the politics and laws of the land. The white apartheid system also facilitated the British-instigated breakup of African societies so as to provide a cheap source of labour and illegal taxation to provide another source of revenue.

As Nelson Mandela grew up he came to the full realization of the scale of the problems that lay ahead and described the grim choices that faced black South African at the time:

"I cannot pinpoint a moment when I became politicized, when I knew that I would spend my life in the liberation struggle.

To be an African in South Africa means that one is politicized from one's birth, whether one acknowledges it or not. An African child is born in an Africans Only hospital, taken home in an Africans Only bus, lives in an Africans Only area and attends Africans Only schools, if he attends school at all.

When he grows up, he can hold Africans Only jobs, rent a house in Africans Only townships, ride Africans Only trains and be stopped at any time of the day or night and be ordered to produce a pass, without which he can be arrested and thrown into jail. His life is circumscribed by racist laws and regulations that cripple his growth, dim his potential and stunt his life. This was the reality, and one could deal with it in a myriad of ways."[4]

In 1980, under the white apartheid regime, a report from the Institute of Criminology at the University of Cape Town showed that South Africa had the highest prisoner to population ratio among Western countries. The comparative statistics were: South Africa 440/100,000, the US 189/100,000, UK 75/100,000 and France 52/100,000.[5]

Unsurprisingly, apartheid South Africa also had the highest rate of executions in the world. 'The rate of executions in South Africa has at times accounted for about 50% of all the legal executions in the world'.[6] A white political prisoner of the apartheid regime of South Africa, Harold Strachan, exposed to the public some of the horrors of the apartheid prison system. "The most terrible and prolonged screams you ever heard came from the African section of the prison." He reported that African prisoners were forced to stand naked in the cold winter: *"They had to stand with the frost thick on the ground, barefoot, clutching each other to keep warm, shivering."*[7]

The inequalities of the white apartheid system also extended deep into the South African mines. The ratio of white to black wages was around R20:1. In 1978, the average wage of the African miners was R119 compared to the white miners' R840.21. Mine work was difficult and dangerous as well. Accidents were frequent in the mines but the distribution of accidents also mirrored the inequalities of wider society:

In the three decades from 1936 to 1966, no less than nineteen thousand miners, more than nine-tenths of them black, were killed in the gold-mines, an average of 3 per shift.[8]

The legacy of the white apartheid regime still lives on, as even though black South Africans won the right to vote in 1993, economic power and, as such, much political power remains with the white minority population. The World Bank uses the Gini coefficient is an economic standard for measuring income inequality. A zero Gini coefficient means absolute equality and 100 absolute inequality. Post-apartheid South Africa has one of the highest levels of income inequality in the world. The World Bank calculated South Africa's Gini coefficient at 63.1 in 2009. In 2012, the US Census Bureau calculated the Gini coefficient in the US to be 47.[9]

According to journalist Nicholas Kristof, 20 years after the end of apartheid in South Africa the white minority population [9%] is richer than all black South Africans [80%] put together. A 2013 survey between white and black incomes revealed that income inequality in South Africa was greater in 2013 than it was at the advent of 'non-racial democracy' in 1994.[10]

Black South Africans remain very much under-represented at the higher levels of multinational organizations, the workforce and landownership. The ANC won them the right to vote but the fight for full socio-economic equality for all has yet to be won in South Africa.

While apartheid, in formal and legal terms, has been dismantled, in its other manifestations, it is remains as active as ever. Thus, there are many black South peoples whose plight has not changed and whose suffering is little known.

PART SEVEN:
THE FORGOTTEN PEOPLE

CHAPTER FORTY
AUSTRALIA'S FIRST INHABITANTS

On the evidence available, it is clear that there is a global oppression of people of colour all around the world. When looking at the global effects of racism and imperialism it is quite common to concentrate on the most well-known examples, while the experiences of many others are simply lost to posterity.

Australia is one such place where the suffering and exploitation of one of the oldest races of human beings in the world continues largely out of sight and out of the minds of most people around the world. Australia, the land of sunny beaches, rugby, cricket and the breezy television soap *Neighbours*, hides its dark secrets and racism behind its bright sunny and cheery exterior.

The Aborigines have been exploited and disenfranchised ever since Captain Cook planted the Union Jack in Australia in 1770 and declared the land *terra nullius*. About the time Captain Cook declared it *terra nullius* it is estimated that there were over four hundred different nations and 750,000 Aborigines in Australia where they had lived for millennia.[1]

The Aborigines lived a simple life in harmony with the environment and their natural habitat. They fished and hunted in the surrounding waters and the bush and harvested food from the abundance around them. They led a rich complex spiritual and ritualistic life. They handed down their history by word of mouth, through dances, myths and legends called the 'dreaming'.

The dreaming is the Aboriginal history of the creation of the world.

Aborigines believe that every meaningful activity or event in life leaves behind a vibrational residue in the earth and that everything, the shape of the mountains, rocks, riverbeds and waterholes in the natural world, is a symbolic footprint of the metaphysical beings whose actions created our world.

The Aborigines, isolated from the rest of the world and Europe in particular, had like the native Americans North and South never been exposed to European diseases like smallpox, syphilis and influenza, They too had no immunity to these foreign diseases and died like flies when they came in contact with the Europeans.

The arrival of the British upset the balance of nature, damaging the natural habitat by depleting fish sources, shooting the kangaroo population and clearing the land. The net result was to push the Aborigines to the brink of starvation.

The British regarded Aborigines as close to vermin and ruthlessly hunted them down to pave the way for the creation of their penal colony, Australia. In 1845 the Catholic Archbishop [1794–1877], John Bede Polding, stated:

"I have myself heard a man, educated, and a large proprietor of sheep and cattle, maintain that there was no more harm in shooting a native, than in shooting a wild dog. I have heard it maintained by others that it is the course of providence, that blacks should disappear before the white, and the sooner the process was carried out the better, for both parties.

I fear such opinions prevail to a great extent. Very recently in the presence of two clergymen, a man of education narrated, as a good thing, that he had been one of a party who had pursued the blacks, in consequence of cattle being rustled by them, and that he was sure that they shot upwards of a hundred. When expostulated with, he maintained that there was nothing wrong with it, that it was preposterous to suppose that they had souls. In this opinion he was joined by another educated man present."

The deeply racist British attitude — and the genocide that it supported — created a legacy of a racial system similar to that of the South African apartheid system, which still operates in Australia today.

"If you were a "full blooded Aborigine...[or] any person apparently

having an admixture of Aboriginal blood", a half-caste being the "offspring of an Aboriginal mother and other than an Aboriginal father" [but not an Aboriginal father and other than an Aboriginal mother], a "quadroon", or had a "strain" of Aboriginal blood you were forced to live on Reserves or Missions, work for rations, given minimal education and needed governmental approval to marry, visit relatives or use electrical appliances."

In 1993 the claim that Australia was *terra nullius* was 'reversed' by the Native Title Act passed by Australia's Federal Parliament, 233 years after it was first proclaimed. However, despite this, the Aborigines continue to suffer severe discrimination and racism based on the appropriation of their land rights. A successful land rights claim by Eddie Mabo, called the Mabo Decision, prompted the Australian High Court to take a compromise position in 1993. The judges decided that Aborigines may have a title to crown lands where they have lived continuously, but then added an escape clause. Aboriginal land rights could be extinguished by the existence of freehold and leasehold of huge pastoral estates many of which were acquired by the sons of nineteenth century English aristocrats simply by squatting on them.

In simple English, if your land had been stolen by the English, aristocrats or transported convicts, you have lost your rights to the land.

Even so, successive conservative Australian governments have also gone out of their way to attack the Native Title Acts and reverse any gains the Aborigines made. One of the most damning reports on Australia's hidden past was chronicled in the Human Rights and Equal Opportunities Commission report called 'Bringing Them Home'. The report concluded that up to a third of Aboriginal children had been forcibly removed from their families between 1910 and as late as 1970. As many as 100,000 children — 'the stolen generations' — were involved.[2]

This heartless, fascist policy stemmed from the eugenics movement that started in the early nineteen hundreds. The eugenics movement widely promoted 'swamping' fear as Australians were told that women from the superior white race were not reproducing at an adequate rate and this would allow the 'white race' to be swamped by the Native Autralians. The idea was widely inspired by a professor of anthropology at the Sydney University, A.P. Elkin, who speculated that the Aborigines were the 'lowest race' and 'parasites' that should not be allowed to be absorbed into the white race.

White Australian police officers snatched Aborigine children and placed them in white mission stations and foster homes. Most of the kidnapped girls were sent to the Cootamundra Domestic Training Home for Aboriginal Girls. Some of the stolen girls were given hysterectomies without their consent, even as early as the age of eighteen years old. At the Training Home they were used and trained as domestic servants and then indentured to 'white masters' in middle-class homes. It was phenomenon very similar to the use of black slave girls as domestics in white southern American homes before the emancipation.

A film documentary by Alec Morgan, *Lousy Little Sixpence,* was the first film to expose the story of the stolen children to the world as recently as the early 1980s.

Sir Ronald Wilson, President of the Australian Human Rights and Equality Commission, said:

"Genocide is the attempt to destroy a people and culture. The first act was the dispossession of Aboriginal people of their land.

The second act was the dispossession of Aboriginal people of their children. The land was stolen. The children were stolen.

What is the third act going to be?"

Aboriginal children were barred from attending public swimming pools for many years. Over 40% of Aborigines lack the most basic needs. Life expectancy of Aborigines was found to be lower than in most countries in the world, matched only by India and central Africa. Aboriginal infant mortality rates were three times higher than the white Australian children and higher in West Australia than in Bangladesh.[3] In 1997, the Federal Health Minister for Australia, Michael Wooldridge, stated that there had been no improvement in the health of Aborigines over the space of ten years. The President of the Australian Medical Association, Dr Keith Woollard, stated that 'much of the poverty and disease in aboriginal communities is a result of the dispossession of their lands.[4]

While the eyes of the world were on South Africa's apartheid system in 1986, an Australian newspaper, the *Sydney Morning Herald*, pointed out that the rate of black deaths in police custody in Australia was thirteen times higher than in South Africa at the same time.[5]

When the Royal Commission was asked to investigate Aboriginal deaths in custody in the late 1980s, some of their conclusions were that Aborigines were sixty times more likely to be arrested than whites in Western Australia and even though Aboriginal children made up only 2.7% of the state's youths, they constituted about 58% of juveniles in detention.[6] The Royal Commission took two years to complete its report at the cost of $30 million Australian dollars. It made 339 recommendations. Not one recommendation alleged any foul play and no criminal charges were brought against the police or prison officers or any other white Australian.[7]

White Australia's openly racist policies not only discriminated against Aboriginals; they also discriminated against Jews. In de-classified reports following the demise of Nazi Germany, Australian governments went to great lengths to prevent the immigration of Jews into Australia while they did everything possible to attract British nationals to emigrate to Australia.[8]

The Australian Aborigines have been a forgotten people. But their trials and tribulations must never be ignored or swept under the carpet until reparation for all these injustices are made and these injustices have been righted.

CHAPTER FORTY ONE
HAITI: THE FIRST BLACK REPUBLIC

Haiti survives today as a symbol of black slave resistance and the first enslaved people to govern itself.

The stirring story of Toussaint L'Ouverture, the brilliant African general who led a slave rebellion which defeated both the combined might of the British and the French armies, has already been told. An estimated 50,000 French soldiers died fighting in Haiti — more than those killed at the Battle of Waterloo.[1]

However, the significance of Haiti goes much further than being a symbol of slave resistance. Haiti was directly responsible for the dismantling of slavery in South America and indirectly responsible for the abolition of transatlantic slavery as a whole.

The renowned and revered Venezualan military and political leader Simon Bolivar could not have succeeded in liberating Venezuala, Ecuador, Bolivia, Peru and Colombia from Spanish colonial rule without the help of Haiti.

Alexander Sabès Pétion [April 2nd 1770–March 29th 1818] was one of the founding fathers of the Republic of Haiti and was the first President of Haiti from 1806 until his death in 1818.

Alexander Pétion gave sanctuary to Simon Bolivar in 1815 and provided him with financial and military support.[2]

Pétion shared his virtues and ideals of freedom and democracy for the whole world, especially for slaves, with Simon Bolivar and extended Haitian support to him in return for a promise to secure the freedom of all slaves. Simon Bolivar had set out to liberate South American countries or "Gran Colombia".[3]

Gran Colombia, or the Republic of Colombia, was a short-lived republic, [1819–1830] that included the modern nations of Colombia, Panama, Ecuador and Venezuela.

In 1816, with Haitian soldiers and vital financial and material support, Simon Bolivar liberated Venezuela. On June 2nd 1816 Simon Bolivar fulfilled his promise to Pétion and freed all Spanish American slaves within his jurisdiction.

In deference to Alexander Petion, Simon Bolivar stated:

"Should I not let it be known to later generations that Alexander Petion is the true liberator of my country?"

Since then Haiti has paid a high price for its presumption, a black nation that humbled the armies of the most powerful Eorupean armies and had the cheek to govern itself for generations thereafter, free from white suzerainty and interference.

The West never forgot or forgave Haiti for its temerity to free itself from white domination. The West never forgives those who refuse to do its bidding or bow to its power. At last, little Haiti could not withstand domination at the hands of the hemisphere's rising power — the United States of America in the hemisphere. In its more recent history, there has not been a time when Haiti has not been dominated by the USA. The result is that Haiti is the poorest country in the Western Hemisphere.

In 1825 France demanded that Haiti pay 150 million Francs because of the liberation of Haiti. Even though this was later reduced to 90 million Francs, it took Haiti 125 years to pay France for their freedom from French colonial slavery.

In 2010 Ammi Sarfo wrote:

"If you want to see what unconstrained US power looks like —look at Haiti."[4]

In 1862, the US accepted Haiti as an Independent state. The US's dominance has been characterised by exploitative neo-colonial relations. Haiti has become a sweatshop for American multinational businesses.

Between 1890 and 2009 the United States intervened in the

sovereign states of Central America, South America and the Caribbean around fifty-five times. Hardly a single country has been immune to its illegal violations in order to protect its economic and political interests. It has invaded Haiti three times, in one instance occupying the country for nineteen years.

In 1915 President Woodrow Wilson occupied Haiti with 2000 US troops. The US military occupation did not end until 1934. According to Haitian sources, over 3000 civilians were killed during the US military occupation.[5]

Under US President Woodrow Wilson, the Haitian Constitution was rewritten so as to permit US corporations to take over Haiti's land and resources following the dismantling of its parliament by marines.[6]

As a direct result of the so-called 'free market system' imposed by the US half of Haitian children die of poverty related causes before the age of five years. A child of two is called a 'youn to chape', which means in Creole, a 'little escapee' from death.[7]

In the intervening years, Haitian leaders were changed on the whim of the American presidents. Coup d'états were organized by Haitian military generals who trained in the USA and were paid by the CIA. Between 1957 and 1971 Francois Duvalier, known as Papa Doc, presided over a vicious and corrupt regime only to be succeeded by his son, Jean Claude Duvilier, known as Baby Doc. Much like Mobutu of Zaire, the United States and the West were embarrassed by his brutality but found his anti-communist and obliging pro-Western stance comforting.

Under the oppressive US-sanctioned regime of 'Papa Doc' Duvilier, it is estimated that over 50,000 Haitians were killed.[8]

'Baby Doc' Duvilier became president for life of Haiti aged only 19 years old. He ruled Haiti with fear, enforced by the infamous Tonton Macoute, his personal terror squad. Poverty and suffering as well as the indigence of the state increased in leaps and bounds until finally his regime became so scandalous that Pope John Paul II visited the island and called for a change. Eventually, Duvalier fled the country in an aeroplane full of riches. In general elections in 1996, a priest by the name of Father Jean Bertrand Aristide became the first democratically elected president in Haiti's history.

Aristide pursued popular policies aimed at reducing poverty and improving services for the poor. Under 'Baby Doc' it was estimated that there were well over a hundred security thugs for every teacher in the country. In short, Aristide's policies were not those which big business and corporations appreciated and he was told by Big Brother, namely, the US, to stop trying to redistribute the nation's wealth and embrace an IMF structural adjustment program instead. When he proved recalcitrant, he was simply bundled out of office and deported to Africa by the CIA.[9]

In more recent years, Haiti has also been subject to severe economic duress by the US and remains one of its main neo-colonial projects.

The UN military force [MINUSTAH] controlled by the US military maintains oversight in Haiti while an NGO created by Bill Clinton in 2010, the Interim Haiti Recovery Commission [IHRC], effectively administers Haiti's economy.[10]

Despite all this, Haiti remains one of the poorest and most undeveloped countries in the world.

PART EIGHT: RELIGION

CHAPTER FORTY TWO

RELIGION: THE OPIUM OF THE PEOPLE

'What profit has not the fable of Christ not brought us!' **Pope Leo X**[1]

'Negros of goodlie stature, shape and personage, and yonge of yeres beinge the choise and Principall of all the Negros gotten.'
Master John Hawkins, ESQ., Captain, Slave ship JESUS commenting on his cargo in 1564–1565[2]

In the Bible, Genesis 1:1, God created the heaven and the earth and in Genesis 1:26 and 27, God created man and gave him dominion over the all other creatures on earth.

However, in Europe, the beginnings of the Western Renaissance saw another creation story unfold. The Catholic Church reinvented Christianity in Europe but in this case, God and all the angels were cast in the image of the white man and, in addition, the white man's dominion was extended from over all creatures to include all other men as well. This subversion of Christianity from its primary purpose of glorifying God to one of widespread exploitation and political control laid the foundations of racism and imperialism and continues to fuel Bible and religious-generated racism and intolerance today.

Right at the very core of European racism lies one of its most powerful drivers, the white man-god principle. It acts as a powerhouse of the heart of white supremacy and imperialism. It produces superiority complexes in whites and inferiority complexes that paralyse the psyche of Africans and other non-whites that have internalised the white racist ideology. It is no coincidence at all that in the United States the calling card of the terrorist white supremacy organization, the Ku Klux Klan, is a burning cross.

The most significant lie told by the Catholic Church was the conversion of Christianity from its African origins to a Western European religion. The three main religions of the world today, Judaism, Christianity and Islam, all owe their historical origins, in that order, largely to ancient Egyptian religion.

All three religions believe in the Old Testament of the Bible. The Jewish Talmud, the Christian holy Bible and Islam's holy Koran all have Abraham as their founding father. Their main point of division is not they believe Jesus Christ existed but of his significance.

In Christianity, Jesus is the Son of God, sent to save the souls of mankind and in Christianity he is the only way, the truth and the light. However, in Judaism and Islam, while the story of Jesus Christ is not challenged, they believe he was simply another of a long line of prophets.

This difference in belief has resulted in centuries of war, suffering and bloodshed that has engulfed the whole world, as men try to use religion to justify their need to exploit and dominate others.

The most powerful claim of authenticity and power any author can lay claim to, is to assert that a book was written by God himself or through direct inspiration from God. This is why the holy books of the world are so revered by their followers and blindly adhered to by billions. This in no way undermines the significance of these religious books, as they are the theosophy of man condensed in book form and they have helped lay the foundations of many civilizations around the world.

As the ideas and theosophy of Christianity were transferred from Africa to the west it underwent significant changes in its eytomology and iconography.

The iconography of western Christianity chrystallized in the art form of Michelangelo's famous Renaissance frescoes on ceiling of the Sistine chapel in the Vatican in Rome. Michelangeloes frescoes depicts the essential story of Christianity from the creation story to the last judgement. God and the most important characters and events in the Christian story; Adam, Moses, Noah, Jesus, Mary, the disciples and the angels are all white.

The Sistine chapel is one of the most consecrated places in the Vatican palace. It was named after Pope Sixtus IV who oversaw its restoration in the late 15th century. It is used as a gathering place for cardinals and for great events in the Vatican like the electing or inaugurating new popes.

In 1508 Pope Julius II commissioned Michelangelo to draw the frescoes and he continued until 1512.

Between 1534-1541, about 25 years after painting the Sistine ceiling, Michelangelo was directed to draw the Last Judgement fresco on the altar wall in the Sistine chapel by Pope Clement VII.

Realizing the nascent power in the Bible, the Catholic Church not only committed name sacrilege, by changing the names of certain important biblical characters, they also went even further and committed identity sacrilege as well, by changing the identity of the original Christians. Once they had recreated Western Christianity, they placed their priests as a buffer zone between the true Bible story and the fervent but ignorant and unsuspecting masses. This created an artificial vacuum of religious information and an immense source of power by which they could control the masses and the monarchies at the time. Inadvertently, the Catholic Church not only set the ball rolling for the development of European racism but it also succeeded in facilitating the exploitative capitalist process that concentrated an enormous amount of the world's economic, political and military power in the West. In other words, the Catholic Church also succeeded in laying down the foundations of Western exploitation, genocide and environmental destruction, which have ravaged the world all over and continue to accumulate the wealth of the world in the West to the detriment of all others.

Today, the writing is on the wall for the Catholic Church. It is no longer the potent tool of mind control and white imperialist expansion that it once was. It is faced by ever-dwindling numbers of its congregations and has been forced to close down many churches. It is also constantly challenged by the rapid growth of Protestant evangelism and its old enemy: science. Furthermore, there is growing public knowledge of its dark past for it to contend with. Books and movies like *The Da Vinci Code*, which fictionally sensationalized aspects of the Catholic Church's murky past have done it no favours. In response, the Catholic Church has started to recant and put some of its records straight in an attempt to bring itself in line with the fast-changing modern world of information.

In what can only be described as a monumental admission, Roman Catholic bishops published a document confessing to their followers that some parts of the Bible are not true. In a book, *The Gift of Scripture*, they have stated that certain verses in the Bible, for example, Genesis 2:21–22, Genesis 3:16, Matthew 28:25 and Revelations 9:20 are untrue.[3]

The Catholic Churches admission would have come as a real shock to the system of ardent followers. It a survey in America revealed that 48% of US Americans considered the book of Genesis to be literally true.[4] In July 2011, a in a later Gallup poll survey by Jeffery M. Jones found that three in ten Americans view the Bible as the literal word of God. There has been a steady movement away from religion towards secularism in the West, perhaps brought on by disillusionment in the church. In the secular West, sports like football, in particular, have arisen as the new 'religion' because as the churches' pews empty, the football stadiums are packed to overflowing.

In his documentary, *Hallowed be Thy Game*, Mark Dowd, a former footballer now pundit, explored the increasing transfer of devotion and passion in ways not exhibited in other spheres of Western life, from the church to the football field.[5] Robbie Fowler, the former Liverpool striker, was sometimes called 'god' by some of his staunch Liverpool supporters. Some football fans in Argentina took the deification of footballers to its logical conclusion when they established the church of Diego Maradonna.[6]

Anglican Canon Edward Bailey, author of *The Secular Faith Controversy*, believes that in the modern Western society, people increasingly organize their lives around football the way they once did around religion.[7]

Former Manchester United Football Club manager, Alex Ferguson said:

"The great thing about football is that it can attract the sort of emotion and passion that becomes a sort of religion in people's minds."[8]

Africans and their diaspora are united in their profound spiritual connection to God, whether they are Christian, Muslim, animist, juju or voodoo worshippers. There is something about Africans' warmth of spirit and character, coupled with a deep spirituality, that drives them to ponder spirituality and the afterlife in ways that are perhaps not as widespread as amongst other people.

Like all strengths, African spirituality also comes with a corresponding weakness. The 'white man-god' psychological complex, and the symbolism it engenders appears to have affected Africans the most. African preoccupation with religion is the main reason why the pious fraud of the founding fathers of European Christianity strikes deep into the hearts and minds of gullible Africans who have not sought to know or understand the roots of Christianity and have blindly followed the white man religion wherever the white man leads. The psychological bondage it fosters resides several layers deep in the subconscious and unconscious psyche of the deeply religious and spiritual Africans.

The image of God as white man is pervasive and permeates all layers of western culture and all areas of the world that western culture has been projected. The negative effect of the 'white man god' complex on the fortunes of Africans and their diaspora is so great and widespread that it prompted the African American author Edward Blyden[5], to write:

'Wherever the Negro is found in Christian land, his leading trait is not docility but servility. He is slow and unprogressive. Individuals here and there may be found of extraordinary intelligence, enterprise and energy, but there is no Christian community of Negroes anywhere, which is self-reliant, and independent.'

On the other hand, there are numerous Mohammedan [sic] communities and states in Africa, which are self-reliant, productive, independent and dominant, supporting without the countenance or patronage of the parent

5 'The Father of Pan-Africanism' he is sometimes called, Blyden, a native of the US Virgin Islands, went in later life to live and teach in Liberia. He wrote prolifically of Pan-Africanism and the Bible. One of his publications was *Africa for the Africans,* echoing the slogan of Marcus Garvey's political movement.

country Arabia, whence they derived their political, literary and ecclesiastical institutions.[9]

Written nearly 150 years ago by a Christian theologian, it is sad to note that this view is still pertinent today.

In actual fact, it was Africans who created the basic concepts of 'the religions of the book' that hold sway today. This can be verified by tracing back the historical, cultural and archaeological evidence.

The continuum of history not only applies to inanimate things that can be traced through hard scientific facts, like carbon dating, archaeological digs and discoveries, but also linguistically and culturally through the tracing of language and cultural habits and norms. The power of religion to shape our destinies should not be underestimated as all the major religions and eventually man's corruption of these religions have played a central role in shaping the lives of billions of people who have been exposed to them over the years.

Unfortunately, nothing evokes a more emotional and irrational reaction than the discussions, debates and exploration of religious ideas and practices. From the completely illiterate to the eminent professors in the highest institutions of human education and endeavour, the reaction is in many cases identical — a complete shutdown of logical and rational thinking. This is because many have been taught that to try to intellectualize their faith is not to have faith at all.

Perhaps it is a subconscious bid to retain an area in our minds that can roam free of logic — a place where anything can happen. No matter how hopeless a situation may seem we try to retain this logic-free space at all costs. To do otherwise might means that we will have to face up to some really unpleasant and harsh facts about life. This belief system is aggravated by the human ego, which operates mainly in the subconscious mind and seeks to ascribe all knowledge to itself. Many people will quite happily compartmentalize religion into the realm of the unfathomable, therefore walling it off from conscious, logical and objective speculation. However, it remains obvious that despite all our advances in science and technology, we actually still know very little about the environment and ourselves.

Religion, in many ways, serves as a buffer zone from reality in our minds and keeps us feeling optimistic, hopeful and willing to go on — in the expectation of the great and miraculous things to come — despite the daily turbulence we call life.

When Karl Marx said religion was the opium of the people, he had a point. Anecdotally, it is worth noting that the wealthier the people of whatever race, colour, or creed, the less religious and the more pragmatic they are in their approach to life and its trials. It is almost as if they rely less on their religious faith than poorer people and are often more likely to seek a empirical solution to their problems rather than a spiritual one.

For poor people, the converse is true. As they often do not have the material means to resolve many of the problems they are faced with, they look to God for a solution. In the face of grinding poverty, poor health and no access to funds, they actively seek a miraculous solution that resolves all their problems; personal, financial and health, in one fell swoop. In biblical times, tithes of all sorts, mostly in the form of flocks and fruit were made and in modern times monetary tithes are made out of the same biblical principle.

The religious of a more fundamental type tend to approach life as an out-of-body experience. In their view, their physical presence here on earth is temporary and so they tend to their spiritual needs and callings. Then there are the others, perhaps in the majority, who tend to be more materialistic and rely more on 'Sunday – Sunday medicine', having their spiritual top-ups weekly.

However, for the vast majority of us, whatever our religious inclinations, atheist, agnostic or spiritual, we have to grind out a living, in the very same fashion for our families and ourselves to maintain our lifestyles. For the very poor, it is more than a struggle to maintain a lifestyle; it is a struggle to stay alive. No one has been exempt from this earthly struggle for survival or lifestyle based on his or her spirituality or religious inclinations. The harsh reality of life casts some doubt on the philosophy of religious fanatics who choose to live on this earth as if they are not really on it. I have not come across any firm scientific studies that show any major difference in the life expectancies or wellbeing of religious fanatics as compared to atheists but it would seem that people primarily focused on the afterlife tend to be the poorest in life.

When God created man, he created a whole human being — a complete being, who comprised of the mind, the body and the soul. To experience life fully as human beings, we therefore need to fulfil all aspects of our makeup. In other words, if we concentrate solely on the physical aspects of life, we will suffer in aspects of life related to the mind and the soul. If we concentrate just on our soul then we will find that living in this world as a poverty-stricken human being very difficult. If we neglect the physical or the mind, it usually translates to illiteracy, poor health and poverty. As our spiritual progress is believed to be assessed in the afterlife, we have no objective means of knowing how well we are progressing spiritually on earth. However, our physical and intellectual progress, or lack of it, on earth becomes apparent rather quickly. In other words, the secret to a wholesome life is balance in all aspects of living.

If we truly believe in God, it should be patently obvious that the absolute limits of human intelligence do not even approach the beginnings of the knowledge of God. When we expand our minds, it is sobering to appreciate how little we know or understand of ourselves or of our surroundings. It is a clear sign of personal development when we begin to expand our consciousness after breaking out of the natural human tendency to egotism, bigotry and narrow-mindedness.

About 2,000 years ago the Roman historian Polybius wrote:

'Since the masses of the people are inconstant, full of unruly desires, passionate, and reckless of consequences, they must be filled with fears to keep them in order. The ancients did well, therefore, to invent gods and the belief of punishment after death.'[10]

In order to facilitate mind control, the Catholic Church once persecuted scientists for saying that the world was round and not flat. Scientists and philosophers of the European Dark Ages lived in fear of persecution and execution owing to the vice-like grip the Catholic Church had over religion, science, the monarchies and the masses. Nicolaus Copernicus was a 16th century astronomer whose findings were condemned as heretical by the catholic church. Copernicus' major treatise- "On the Revolutions of the Heavenly Spheres" was published shortly before his death in 1543 but later came under attack by the Vatican.

The European Dark Ages are so-called because no scientific progress could be made, owing to the almost complete shutdown of thought or ideas beyond existing Christian dogma. Anything that did was considered heretical. The Catholic Church rightly feared that free thinking could break the powerful mental bind they had on the masses. If their minions were allowed to think, they might challenge the priests and that would not be easy to control. The uncritical acceptance of all the major religions around the world still hold sway and is the common practice today all over the world.

Many Christians today still practice their faith in the firm belief that to question their religion is an affront to God and an indication of no faith. However, if you love something and hold it dear, it is logical that you expend some effort in trying to get to know and understand more about it.

The human brain is a wonderfully complex and extremely important part of our make-up. Such is the complexity of the brain that modern medicine deems severely brain-damaged people to be brain-dead and therefore to be dead, even if they linger in a vegetative state. A vegetative state where only basic bodily functions like eating and excreting can be carried out, without any capacity to process information, move or communicate cannot be equated with normal human life.

Human thought is what separates us from other mammals and defines us as human beings. We do not voluntarily stop using our hands or refuse to walk with both legs, so why do we decide to stop thinking when it suits us?

The philosopher René Descartes summed up the central role human thought plays in our lives when he stated:

'I think, therefore I am.'[11]

Many people perhaps fear that they may lose their faith if they question their religion in any way but the best converts to any religion are those who soberly consider their chosen religion and do not simply rely on a rush of religious fervour or emotion to decide. Obviously, there is less than no danger of humans beings out-thinking God. If we did, then we would obviously become gods ourselves.

When it comes to religion, many of the faithful's ideas and actions, looked at through sober, cold and unemotional eyes, cannot be fathomed or explained. The inability to think about religion clearly and logically has been — and continues to be — a source of human conflict and war. Millions, if not billions, of people have died directly and indirectly from the religious intolerance and racism that have been spawned through willed ignorance.

The Bible is one of the most influential books in the world today. It continues to influence the hearts and minds of many across the world and has played a pivotal role in creating the bedrock of Western society. It has inspired man to great heights but has also been used to justify some of the greatest acts of genocide and man's inhumanity to man.

Some religious authors have tried to put into words what the Bible means to them and others explain perhaps why many hold it in such awe. The authors of the Gideon New Testament, Psalms, and Proverbs wrote:

'That religion is held as the most sacred and revered part of all human exigencies cannot be disputed in any way. Every race, colour or creed has sought to in different ways establish his area of human endeavour by embracing the spiritual side, a side of our nature that runs deeper than the deepest waters. The Bible as a religious book can be considered as one of the greatest efforts by man to compile the philosophies of life to form a repository of spiritual knowledge for all men.'[12]

And:

The Bible contains the mind of God, the state of man, the way of salvation, the doom of sinners, and the happiness of believers. Its doctrines are holy. Its precepts are binding. Its histories are true, and its decisions are immutable. Read to be wise, believe it to be safe, and practice it to be holy. It contains light to direct you, food to support you, and comfort to cheer you. It is the traveller's map, the pilgrim's staff. The pilot's compass, the soldier's sword, and the Christian's charter. Here paradise is restored. Heaven opened, and the gates of hell disclosed'.[13]

It is for reasons like these that an enormous blind spot is created in the minds of many, allowing them to be easily manipulated by a devious few.

Despite its influential position in world history, it is still not entirely clear who actually wrote the books of the Bible. However, it is not that the true origins of most of our religious texts are not known, rather that they have been hidden from the people, with the aim of using the knowledge concealed to influence, misrepresent, misinform and manipulate people's minds to achieve the goals of control that the Catholic Church used, similar to the Dark Ages.

Unbeknown to most Christians, there have been serious doubts in secular academic circles for hundreds of years about the facts some take for granted about the Bible. Under this cloud include the origin of the Bible, its authors, and characters — even the contents. There are many inconsistencies regarding the historical versus biblical timing of events and many more misrepresentations, and omissions. Many narratives were crafted in such a way so as to mislead the innocent believer and create the wrong impressions. Unfortunately, many of these ideas have crystallized, in the West, into their version of Christianity as we know it today — in that part of the world, at least.

When I was about seven years old, I developed a passionate love for reading and acquiring knowledge. At one point, I embarked on a mission to read all the books in our library at home. This was one of the most exciting things I had done I had ever done as a child. I read literature, science, history, fiction — just about any book I could lay my hands on.

About a year later, I decided to read the Bible from cover to cover just as I had read the other books. I would lock myself away in my father's room for hours and read my way through from Genesis to Revelation. One of the strongest impressions I had was a deep and worrying feeling of injustice in the Old Testament. It is a very difficult feeling to explain because we were practicing Catholics and I, like most children my age, had quickly and almost subconsciously learnt to adopt an unquestioning attitude towards the things of God. However, locked away in this room I had serious doubts about what I was reading.

It just did not seem fair to my childish mind that the Israelites would be told by God to take over lands already occupied by other people. Why didn't God just create more land for everyone? I also worried about the somewhat vengeful nature of 'God' as portrayed in the Old Testament — angry, jealous, and partial. These seemed closer to the emotions you would ascribe to a man, not the creator of the whole universe, who could in the blink of an eye wipe out and recreate it again.

My parents told me that God loved everyone; why then did he ask the Israelites to destroy several people they came across? It made me very worried not to transgress by processing these thoughts because I feared that it would mean eternal doom! However, these nagging doubts lingered. As I read through the Bible, it made me more discerning and less likely to embrace the Bible text and Christianity blindly. It made me seek out more truths and set me on the journey that culminated in my writing this book.

CHAPTER FORTY THREE

ANCIENT RELIGION

Religion represents man's attempt to answer the fundamental and primordial questions of life — who we are, where we are from and where we are going to in the afterlife.

In the beginning, the need for religion probably arose from the fear and the superstition that developed in human beings as they faced the multitudes of uncertainties and problems of survival nature posed. Religion became the medium through which humanity's inner spiritual void was filled.

In pondering nature's cycles of life and death and man's eventual mortality, the ancient people developed concepts about religion that followed remarkably similar pathways at different times and places, all over the world, even though they were quite ignorant of each other's development. In effect, the wise men and women who pondered these religious questions and principles became the first priests and priestesses of ancient religion. They became the intermediaries between their people and their gods. They closely studied and observed nature and human behaviour and noted certain constant cycles, principles and laws of nature and the universe. Through these studies, they began to understand the great significance these laws and principles of nature had on human lives. Thus, the philosophy of religion was created. Life and death, night and day, the seasons and the tides, were all believed to be governed by theology in ancient times.

The ancient Egyptians appear to be the first people to conceive of the in-depth sacramental practices of theology. Everything the Egyptians did was driven by their spirituality, religion and culture — from the building of the pyramids to the invention of writing, science and technology. Religion was the engine that drove the Egyptian civilization to the heights it attained.

For the ancients all over the world the worship of the sun, the most visible source of life for all living things on the face of the earth, was the natural focus in their religions. God, 'the Sun', was a universally common myth and the starting point of practically all ancient religions. The fact that Christians worship on Sunday is an ironic but simple fact that is largely unappreciated by millions of Christians around the world as their minds have been deflected away from the historical fact of ancient 'sun worship' by the story of Genesis, which designated 'Sunday', the Sabbath as a day of rest.

The Christmas season today is another throwback to ancient sun worship. The origins of Christmas or the Yuletide season are enshrined in the eternal cycle of the seasons or the 'Wheel of the Year'. We now know that ancient astronomers could work out the winter and summer solstices by the old science of astrology. Ancient Neolithic people, who were hunter-gatherers and farmers, formed out of pure necessity an intimate relationship with the natural cycles of the seasons. They followed the movements of the sun and the moon closely and plotted their movements in the heavens quite accurately. In so doing, they could work out the summer and winter solstices.[1]

Ancient people did not seek this knowledge for frivolous reasons. Their very lives depended on accurately understanding nature's rhythms and cycles. It is believed that the Polynesians could navigate at sea by using astrology and reading the wave patterns of the sea.

For millennia, people have celebrated the winter solstice or Christmas period and there are many customs associated with it. The winter solstice is unique because it is the shortest day of the year and for many customs worldwide it represents the birth of light from the womb of darkness. Native Americans called the winter solstice the 'Long Nights Time'. In many ancient traditions, a saviour, the Sun child, is born to a virgin mother during the winter solstice.

The modern commemoration of Christmas Day can be traced

directly back to ancient Egypt. The Egyptians observed a ceremony to worship the birth of a sun god, Horus, from his mother, Isis. In fact, the statues of Mary carrying the baby Jesus on her lap in the Catholic church derive their form from an ancient statue of Isis holding the baby sun god, Horus, on her lap and showing him to the world. So the Winter solstice was celebrated to mark the birth of a son of god, who brings light to the world.

In Europe, many customs celebrated the winter solstice from December 17th–25th. During the same period, the Romans celebrated Saturnalia. Named after Saturn, Saturnalia was the gloomy, moody god, who ate his own children rather than let them surpass him. For new life to flourish, dark gave way to light and feasting and merriment were religiously mandated, to combat the forces of gloom. The social order was reversed and masters waited on slaves. All work was put aside for feasting and gambling. The day following Saturnalia was Juvenilia, a holiday in honour of children who naturally, were feasted, entertained and given gifts.

December 25th was not always Christmas Day. The birth of Jesus was celebrated on January 6th for over four hundred years after the death of Christ. January 6th was the same day that the Holy Virgin goddess Kore, the Greek goddess of Spring and queen of the underworld, gave birth to the sun god. This was celebrated in Alexandria in a festival called the Koreion.[2]

"As far back as the second century the eastern Christians celebrated the Nativity on January 6th. In 354, some western churches, including those of Rome commemorated the birth of Christ on December 25; this was erroneously calculated as the winter solstice, on which the days begin to lengthen; it was already the central festival of Mithraism, natalis invincti Solis, or the birthday of the unconquered sun. The eastern churches for a time clung to January 6, and charged their western brethren with sun worship and idolatry, but by the end of the fourth-century December 25 had been adopted also in the East."[3]

Authors of the Christian Calendar stated:

"A second group of festivals developed around pagan celebrations of winter solstice. The earliest of this was the feast now known as Epiphany…

The birthday of the Invincible Sun, established by Aurelian on December 25 in the third century, was Christianised as the feast of Jesus's nativity ca. 336."[4]

As we see from the above, the modern concept of recognizing Christmas Day, December 25th, as the birth of Jesus was started in 274 based on the widespread cult of Mithra, the Persian/Indian god of light. December 25th was the well-known and widely celebrated. The Roman Emperor Valerian declared December 25th, the birthday of Sol Invictus, the 'Unconquerable Sun'.

According to the Persian myth, Mithra sprang up from a rock, fully grown, armed with a knife and carrying a torch. Shepherds who saw his miraculous appearance flocked to greet him with their first fruits and harvests, echoed in the story of Christ by the angels appearing to the shepherds as they watched their flocks by night.[5]

There are many historical and archaeological findings that prove that many Biblical myths are not Jewish in origin and predate the Bible by many thousands of years. The Assyrian story of the creation and fall of man is practically identical to the Biblical creation story in the book of Genesis. Archaeological evidence in the form of the Assyrian clay tablets found in Mesopotamia between 1873 and 1874 have been dated to 1500BC to 2000BC and predate the compilation of the Bible by at least 1,700 years[6] In the Enûma Eliš, a Babylonian ritual text, the Babylonian god Marduk creates heaven and earth. The myth of paradise, the flood, and the town of Babel are all to be found in ancient folklore in places as diverse as Egypt, India, Iraq, Iran, Greece, and Mexico.[7]

The story of a universal flood is known to almost all ancient civilizations and over five hundred versions exist. In the Bible, the flood hero is Noah; in the Babylonian text, the Epic of Gilgamesh, the flood hero is known as Utnapishtim or Ziusudra. The flood hero of the Aztecs is called Nene and in the Near East he is called Atra-Hasis.[8]

By the time Moses received the Ten Commandments directly from God on Mount Sinai, according to Genesis in the Bible, the ancient laws of Egypt had been given to the Egyptians by their gods. Thoth, and Zoroaster, the Persian patriarch, had already been given the 'Book of Law', by Ahura Mazda or God, who appeared to him amid thunder and lightning.[9]

Certain numbers have always played a significant role in all ancient sun myths. The numbers 3, 7, 12 and 40 all appear repeatedly in relation to several myths. The number 12 is a sacred number in many religions worldwide. For instance; the zodiac has 12 signs and the number 12 is used repeatedly in the Old Testament and New Testaments of the Bible, for example, the 12 gates of heaven, the 12 disciples, the 12 months of the year, Jacob's 12 sons and the 12 tribes of Israel.

The number 40 is another important number in ancient traditions. Moses was on the mountain with God for 40 days, the Jews were in the wilderness for 40 years, Jesus fasted for 40 days and nights and his ascension took place after 40 days.

There was no shortage of virgin mothers in ancient times. The stories of virgin births are found in nearly every culture and country around the world. The virgin birth of Jesus through Mary or the Madonna is a recent version of a very old and universal myth of a virgin birth. All over the world, from Egypt, Greece and Rome to India, Iraq, Iran, and China divine beings have always selected the purest and most beautiful daughters of men to serve as a means of entry into the world of mere mortals.

In China, a beautiful nymph, bathing in the river is selected to give birth to the divine being, Fohi.[10] In India, Buddha descended on his mother, entered her womb and came to save the world.[11] In Greece, Apollo visits the beautiful Athena and Plato is born.

European Christianity borrowed the symbolism of kneeling down and folding hands in prayer, ringing of the bells, burning incense and the use of vestments and vessels in the church. Holy water, candles and even the word 'mass' were all adopted and adapted to European Christianity from the religious practices of the ancients. The idea of the Trinity itself is as pagan as it is Christian and so too was the idea of a Son of God that came to save the world.[12]

The physical sun in some of the ancient religions became, in the course of time, represented as the Son of God and heaven is personified as his father on high. Even the halo depicted in traditional icons around the head of Jesus and the saints is not unique. Rays of light are seen radiating around the heads of Hindu and pagan gods, evidence that all these gods were at one time the physical sun in heaven.[13]

Legend has it that when the Roman emperor, Constantine, went into battle against German 'barbarians', he saw a vision of the sign of the cross. He asked his troops to put the sign of the cross on their shields and went on to be victorious in battle. Following this victory, Constantine adopted Christianity, which became the official religion of Rome and eventually Europe. In reality, Rome adopted Christianity for its unifying theme more as a political tool to quell unrest and the breakup of the Roman Empire than for purely religious reasons. Emperor Constantine continued to persecute Christians throughout his reign and only became a true convert on his deathbed.[14]

The sign of the cross has been of great significance since prehistoric times. It is possible that the significance of a cross from these times stems from the fact that primitive men used the friction between two sticks placed across each other to create fire. Signs of the cross in Stone Age monuments can be found all over Europe. The sign of the cross has been found on coins and in altars, dating back to prehistoric times, all over the world.[15] From ancient Egypt, China, India, Korea to Europe, the cross was considered a charm of great power. Specimens of the prehistoric, pre-Christian crosses can be found in museums in Paris. In the Louvre museum in Paris, a 'heathen god' carries a cross on its head.[16] In the Saint-Germain museum, an ancient divinity of pagan Gaul is seen wearing a garment on which the cross is woven and the sign of the cross is found carved into the altar.[17] On Captain Cook's second journey to New Zealand, they found that the natives marked the graves of their dead with a sign of the cross.[18]

Perhaps one of the most well-known and controversial crosses in our time is the swastika. The word swastika originates from the Sanskrit word, *sva'stika*, which means luck or wellbeing. The swastika is the sacred symbol of Hinduism, Buddhism and Jainism, religions with a worldwide following of over one billion followers.[19]

Evidence of the use of the swastika sign has been found dating back to the Neolithic period. People of Indo-Aryan origins used it extensively and it has been a Hindu symbol for luck for over 5,000 years.

However, luck ran out for the swastika in Europe when the Nazis adopted it as a symbol of Nazi Aryan ideology and its use is now banned in Europe.

CHAPTER FORTY FOUR

BLACK AFRICAN CHRISTIANITY

Africa and the African people were main players in biblical history, even though it requires some critical thinking in order to appreciate this.

If you add up the number of times that African people and places are mentioned in the Bible, you will find that references about African people exceed more than a thousand times.[1]

Black African people are referred to in biblical history on numerous occasions. Zipporah, Moses' Midianite wife, was black. This means that Zipporah's father, Jethro was black.

In his book, *The Early Church in Africa*, Dr John Mbiti asserts that the message of Jesus penetrated Africa long before it ever reached Europe — "Christianity in Africa is so old that it can be rightly described as an indigenous, traditional, and African religion".[2]

Historical documentation of the church in ancient Africa shows that Christianity was the dominant religion of North Africa and most notably in Egypt. By the year AD 300, Egypt had over one million Christians.[3] Egyptian and North African scholars like Origen, Clement, Tertullian, and Athanasius were all widely recognized as fathers of the church.[4] In the 6th century of the Christian era, Christianity spread to the Nubian kingdoms and soon became the dominant religion. The Christian Nubian kingdom survived for seven hundred years and resisted domination by Muslim conquerors for six hundred of those years.[5]

The Catholic Church originally accepted the African origins of Christianity. However, as racism and xenophobia grew in Europe, it was no longer deemed acceptable to concede the origins of the religion as great as Christianity to alleged 'barbarians'. In the recreation of Christianity in Western Europe, the Catholic Church resorted to all forms of pious fraud and deception.

It began with the conversion of the important Christian figures and people from black to white or from Africans to Europeans. The early white catholic priests combined dubious and doubtful evidence with the destruction of so-called 'pagan' works in order to obscure the truth from the followers of Christianity.

Early Christians were heavily persecuted in Europe, and this drove them into becoming an underground religious movement. Many Christians were slaughtered for entertainment in the Coliseum in Rome. As a result many early Christians sought refuge in the underground Catacombs where a glimpse of the true identity and origins of the religion can be discerned. Even today, depictions of a phenotypically African Jesus and Mary can be seen on the walls where the early Christians had worshipped in hiding.

There is strong evidence of the long-standing presence of Christianity in the Nile Valley and present-day Ethiopia. Egypt and then Ethiopia were the centres of Christianity in Africa before it spread to southern and western Africa.[6] The first two Catholic Popes were Africans and were based in North Africa and Ethiopia:

'Christianity reached Ethiopia in the first century. Moreover, the spiritual authorities of the Ethiopian Orthodox church are unequivocal in their teachings that Ethiopia had accepted the Old Testament and was living by the laws of Moses for several centuries before Christianity reached that land. The general contents of these teachings is, in fact, confirmed and supported by scholars and historians.'[7]

Ethiopia was known throughout in the Middle Ages as the country of Prester John and was supposed to be the habitat of the Ten Tribes. The ceremonial centre of Lalibela, with its Church of Golgotha, its Jordan River, and Mount of Olives [among other holy sites], was conceived as a model of the Holy Land.[8]

Back in Europe, even the Pope of the Catholic Church recognized the African origins of Christianity as this article from the Washington

Post reveals:

'The mysterious black Madonna of Czestochowa is the most sacred icon in Poland...Pope John Paul II, a strong advocate of devotion to the Virgin Mary, will travel to the hill top monastery in June to show his special devotion to the strange painting depicting Christ's mother as a black woman...Many of the Madonnas painted in the earliest centuries of Christendom were black, according to historians, and it wasn't until the renaissance that it became popular to give the mother of Christ the features of a Florentine maiden.'[9]

In Western Europe evidence of black Christianity was hidden away from the masses and virtually all images and text that proved the African origins of Christianity removed by the Catholic Church.

In February 2005, two sacred paintings were returned to Ethiopia 137 years after British soldiers had ripped them out of Holy Books, 'The Miracles of Jesus and Mary', venerated illuminated manuscripts in the Ethiopian Orthodox church. Hundreds of items were stolen from Ethiopia during a British military campaign in 1868.[10] Unfortunately, this information is still not mainstream knowledge and the vast majorities of African Christians are unaware of their great heritage and find themselves led by the theology of Western capitalism.

CHAPTER FORTY FIVE
PIOUS FRAUD

The early Christian missionaries carefully studied the indigenous people to understand their belief systems and to gain their trust. They perfected the practice of converting people by associating their local gods with the closest corresponding Christian saints or deities. For instance, the practice of drinking of animal blood by pagans was presented as a version of the Holy Communion.

The idea of the trinity for instance is, as we have seen, as pagan as it is Christian and so too was the idea of a Son of God that comes to save the world. The physical sun in the ancient religions became in the course of time, represented as the Son of God and heaven is personified as the father on high.[1]

The white Christian missionaries did not stop at this but, as we have seen, also borrowed heavily from other established religions: kneeling down and folding hands in prayer, ringing of bells, burning incense and the use of vestments and vessels in the church, holy water, candles, and even the word 'mass'.

It was a commonplace practice by early Christian missionaries to place their churches and cathedrals on local pagan 'power spots' and ley lines, not because the priests believed that these locations offered any magical leverage but because the people believed that they did.[2]

The priests disarmed the 'heathen people' by claiming that every word in their version of the reworked Bible was written or authenticated by God. They convinced the 'pagans' to attend the church because they built the new faith on the foundations of their own worship.

Ironically, this led to 'black masses' carried out by non-converts, not just in an attempt to defile the church but to carry out their own ceremonies in the place where they believed they would work. It is interesting to note that devotees of Wicca[6] [witchcraft] celebrate the feast of Yuletide around December 21st during the Christmas season.[3]

The celebration of Christmas with Christmas trees began as a German winter solstice ritual to light up the darkest night of the year.

The white Christian missionaries understood that the ritual was developed to address the superstitious fear of the darkness of winter and the fear of lack of rejuvenation coming in the following spring season. They redirected the pagan belief in their own rituals and the hope they fostered towards the birth of Christ and Christianity, and thus Christmas Day was born.

Overall, white catholic priests and missionaries reworked the early African Christian religions. They copied the early Christianity in ancient Egypt, and gradually absorbed many of the rituals and the beliefs of the people they converted.

The Yuletide or festival of Yule derives from the old tradition of burning Yule logs around the winter solstice and was usually selected earlier on in the year and set aside for Christmas. Many decorated their Yule logs with evergreens, ivy and holly. The earliest evidence of an evergreen being used comes from Latvia in 1519.[4] Large Christmas candles, usually red, were also decorated with evergreens. Animals such as wild boars were killed and eaten. Riddling tournaments were held and alcohol consumed in large quantities. Seasonal gifts were exchanged and songs were sung.

Many old European traditions were woven into the tapestry of European Christianity.

For instance, the tradition of kissing under the mistletoe is probably a surviving remnant of an early Celtic fertility ritual. The ancient Druids believed mistletoe to have magical powers and bore the soul of the tree from which it was harvested. It was believed to be an aphrodisiac and a charm to ward off natural disasters, dangers and evil spirits. Branches of mistletoe were distributed to villagers who hung it above their doorways as a charm against thunder, lightning and wind. A sprig of mistletoe was

6 Wicca is the modern sect of pagan witchcraft

placed in the cradles of infants to protect them from being stolen by fairies.[5]

The act of taking down the Christmas tree after the twelfth day began as a pagan ritual to prevent bad fortune.

The modern customs and Christmas traditions do not stand up to scrutiny either; according to the accepted Western legend, Santa Claus comes from the Dutch adoption of the patron Saint Nicholas of the Catholic Church or 'Sinter Klaas', a 4th century Catholic bishop. According to a St. Nicholas historian, Charles W Jones "the cult of St. Nicholas was the most intensive of any non-biblical Saint in Christendom". The Christian Almanack states:

"By the height of the Middle Ages, St Nicholas was probably invoked in prayer more than any other figure except the Virgin Mary and Christ himself".[6]

Surrounded by mystery and legend, Saint Nicholas not only allegedly saved three poverty-stricken girls from prostitution by providing gold for their marriage dowry, he was also alleged to have brought back to life three children who had been murdered and their bodies chopped to pieces. He gave gifts to children and became venerated as the patron saint of children in the Middle Ages.

Called 'Sint Nikolaas' in the Dutch language, this name was later anglicized into Santa Claus. The modern-day Santa Claus was born when Dutch children started placing their shoes by the fireplace on December 5th in expectation of the gifts they hoped to find in them the next morning. When Dutch settlers in America formed their colony New Amsterdam, later to be called New York, they brought this tradition along with them.

However, just like most of the preceding examples of pious fraud, there is very little evidence of the existence of Saint Nicholas and most reputable sources of information have distanced themselves from the claim that a Saint Nicholas actually ever existed:

Nicholas' existence is not attested to by any historical document, so nothing certain is known of his life except that he was probably a bishop of Myra in the fourth century.[7]

And another:

Unfortunately, very little is known about the real St. Nicholas. Countless legends have grown up around this very popular Saint, but very little historical evidence is available.[8]

In 1969, the Catholic Church finally decided to pull the rug on the Saint Nicholas legend and Pope Paul VI officially decreed that the feast of Saint Nicholas should be removed from the Roman Catholic Calendar along with forty other saints because of *'doubt that they ever existed'*.[9]

The reality is that the Sinter Klaas legend most likely derives from the old Scandinavian or Nordic cosmology. The god Thor, a jovial, elderly and heavily-built man with a long white beard that rode in a chariot, was known as a Yule-god or the Christmas god. His element was fire and his favourite colour was red. Two white goats drew his chariot, and he was fabled for coming down the chimney into his element, fire. The modern image of Santa Claus was in part the creation of Coca-Cola, who capitalized on the Christmas legend for commercial purposes.

Some Christians ponder the deeper spiritual significance of the pious fraud concerning white Christianity and Christmas Day. It worth considering, that every year, on December 25th, white Christianity and their huge corporations lead the world in a capitalist media and commercial binge based on pagan worship and the ancient sun ritual. Christmas is very much capitalism's big annual retail opportunity — and therefore possibly in homage to the devil himself. After all, Santa is simply an anagram of the word Satan.

It is common knowledge among Bible historians that none of the Gospels, Epistles or Acts of the Apostles existed within 120 years of the crucifixion of Christ.

In the Gospels, Matthew suggests that Jesus was born in King Herod's time, who, upon hearing that the King of the Jews was born, set out to destroy him. In order to escape the baby being killed by Herod, Joseph and Mary fled with the infant Jesus to Egypt. However, in the Gospel according to Luke, there is no mention of this escape to Egypt nor of King Herod planning to kill Jesus. Luke suggests that Jesus was born when Quirinius was King of Judea, historically approximately 14 years later than the date given by Matthew. If Joseph and Mary were trying to escape to save Jesus from being killed by King Herod, why was he publicly presented at the temple after forty days of purification where he could have easily been arrested and killed?

As Jesus had to manifest himself in a human form, there should have been some historical and archaeological evidence that placed him around where he lived and died. He would have had a family, and so would his parents Joseph and Mary. If one was unable to pinpoint Jesus himself, it is logical to think that he could possibly be traced through his family or his immediate community. Similarly, his disciples should be traceable historically and archeologically to where they lived and died. The fact that there is no such evidence suggests pious fraud and manipulation of the facts to deceive and enslave the minds of millions of followers of Christianity.

Historically, when an early Christian writer, Origen, was questioned by Celsus, as to the validity and reality of Jesus and he could give no historical evidence. Rather, Origen argued that the story of Jesus was no more incredible than the stories of the Greek and Roman gods. He stated:

"Before replying to Celsus, it is necessary to admit that in the matter of history, however true it might be it is often very difficult and sometimes quite impossible to establish its truth by evidence, which shall be considered sufficient.".

His main argument for the existence of Jesus, when deconstructed, was that stories similar to those told of Jesus are admitted to being true when told of pagan divinities, why then should they not be held true when they are told of the Christian Messiah? He also argued the theological viewpoint that they must be true because they are the fulfilment of Old Testament prophecies.

Josephus, another prominent historian in the time of Jesus, wrote extensively on the eminent men and events of his day but does not directly mention Jesus at all.. Bible historians exposed the only apparent mention of Jesus by Josephus as a forgery inserted into the Armenian version of the text of Josephus between the time of Origen and Eusebius.

Another great historian at the time of Jesus was Philo, an Alexandrian Jew. He visited Jerusalem around the time of Jesus but did not mention him at all. His only mention of the word Jesus was when he described the difference between the Jewish names Hossaih and Jesus in his works. The name Jesus, he explained, means 'saviour of the people'.

Perhaps the greatest and most important discrepancy in the New Testament about the life and works of Jesus Christ and the cover-up from its African origins, are the works of St Paul. St Paul has come to be accepted as the greatest apostle of Christianity and the author of its theology. The New Testament largely consists of the thirteen Epistles of St Paul.

St Paul never met Jesus. Unsurprisingly, in his teaching, Paul does not capitalize on the miracles of Jesus Christ, healing the sick, awakening the dead and giving sight to the blind, as he travelled around foreign lands to convert unbelievers and lay the foundations of Christianity. It would have significantly increased his worth and made his task much easier if he had emphasized that Jesus was the Son of God, and detailed his life and his miracles.

CHAPTER FORTY SIX

THE ICONOGRAPHY OF JESUS

Is the white, blue-eyed and long-haired hippy called Jesus Christ in Western iconography a racial, mythical creation? Are the white Jesus and his white followers simply a clever way not only to deflect the minds of the followers away from the real Jesus but also to claim the religion as 'ours'? And was Jesus Christ really the son of God or was he simply a sun god?

Despite extensive archaeological and historical research, neither the exact place nor time of Jesus' birth is known. The place of birth or death of his disciples remains unknown as well. However, it can be safely said that most of the disciples of Jesus were not Europeans.

The Orientals told the story of a god in the manager, surrounded by animals in the Far East several thousand years before the advent of Christianity.[1] Dating back over eight hundred years before Jesus Christ, a picture of the annunciation, conception and birth of king Amenhotep III was carved on the walls of one of the great temples of Luxor. The story carved into the walls, is practically identical to the birth, death, and resurrection of Jesus Christ.[2]

Remarkably, it was not until 800 years after the crucifixion of Jesus, that depictions of the crucifixion included a human. The disciples Matthew, Mark and Luke, say nothing about Jesus being nailed to a cross, and rather give the impression he was hanged. In the Gospel according to Luke, when writing about the two thieves, who were sentenced to receive the same punishment as Jesus, he mentioned '…one of them a malefactor that was hanged with him'.[3] This may be consistent with the historical fact that the early Christians were called 'the followers of the god who was hanged'.[4]

It is only after the first three Gospels that we see the beginnings of the legend of the cross in the Gospels. For a long time, a lamb with a cross, or a lamb on the cross, was the symbol of Christianity, as defined by John the Baptist at the start of Jesus' misistry and in the book of Isaiah. Even today, it is a lamb and not the human form of Jesus, which we see entombed in the Holy Sepulchre, the alleged burial site of Jesus Christ, and holiest Christian site in Jerusalem. Jesus is still described as the Lamb of God in Catholic literature and Catholic masses today.

If Jesus Christ was not the white, blue-eyed and long-haired character depicted to us by some religious art and icons, does this mean that Jesus Christ never existed?

Historical and archaeological evidence does point to the existence of a real 'Jesus', one that would be unrecognizable to millions of Christians today.

"His parents gave him the quite common name Yeshu'a [our Joshua], meaning "the help of Yahveh," the Greeks made this into Iesous, the Romans in Jesus."[5]

However, the problem is compounded by the fact that the Romans may have crucified several people by the name of Joshua or 'Jesus' in the time when Jesus was meant to have lived. Patricia Eddy explains:

"Before Christianity could grow into a major religion, it had to be shaped to appeal to the gentiles, and chief among these were the Romans… this was no small task for a single institution, and re crafting its centerpiece, Jesus, needed to be successfully accomplished to ensure survival in the hostile political environment of the Roman Empire…Not only the man must be reshaped, but the very ceremony and mystery of the religion required redrafting to move into the gentile mainstream…Adapting pagan imagery and phraseology went a long way toward ensuring the Christian triumph in the Roman Empire. Just as important were the adaptations of pagan ceremonies that became Christian sacraments."[6]

People generally accept that the Jews wrote the Bible but strangely, they have not wondered why recantations of the scriptures in the modern-day Catholic church are in Latin and not in Hebrew.

"During the first three centuries after Christ, though they retained the scriptures of Israel, Christians began to adopt Greek ways of thinking and speaking… they also adopted Roman ways of governing and acting."[7]

The following author gives a clue to the real identity of Christianity:

"In the early days — less than two decades after the Crucifixion of Jesus — Christianity was a sect of Judaism. Its members went to synagogue and lived by the Torah — the rigid law revealed by Moses and the prophets as the way to get right with God. Yet few gentiles were willing to have themselves circumcised and accept Judaism's many other onerous requirements to become Christians.

Paul's bold solution was to preach a new doctrine: Salvation can be gained without following the Mosiac Law—all it takes is faith in Jesus as the Son of God… When Paul was not raising the synagogue roof with his doctrine of salvation by faith alone, he was raising other tent poles of Christian theology—many, with, at best, only faint antecedents in the words of Jesus.

It was Paul, who proclaimed that all humans are born with the original sin deriving from Adam.

Paul preached that although Jesus was God, he allowed himself to be put to death to atone for mankind's wickedness. It was an idea to which the gentiles were receptive. Many pagan gods were said to have died to redeem man. Perhaps most important, Paul offered believers the promise of life after death…"[8]

It is believed, in some theological circles, that John the Baptist and possibly Jesus Christ belonged to a radical group of zealots called the Essenes. They believed in the imminent arrival of the Messiah, one who would lead them, as prophesied, to overthrow the Roman occupation of their land.

In Roman times, many different 'Messiahs' emerged from the oppressed masses and the Roman Empire looked upon them as troublemakers. The Romans set out to crush the religious zealots and hanging was as commonplace as crucifixion. Romans particularly favoured crucifixion, as their victims would endure slow painful deaths and while hanging on their makeshift crosses serve as a deterrent to all aspiring criminals. According to this theory, in today's modern American Empire, it most likely that Jesus and his disciples would have been described as 'insurgents'. [yet he showed no sign of anti-Roman sentiment or agitation]

In a documentary entitled, 'The Secret Family of Jesus' aired on Channel 4 and hosted by a black professor, Robert Beckford, this lead was pursued even further.[9] Historical and biblical evidence shows the fact that Jesus had brothers and sisters, cousins, aunts, uncles, nephews and nieces. Jesus had deep friendships with devoted disciples such as Mary Magdalene, Mary of Bethany and her sister Martha.

The documentary asserts that the sect that Jesus grew up in, which was said to be led by John the Baptist before Jesus was baptized, may have been a strict group of the Essenes who believed that the essence of the original Christian message was a renewed version of Judaism, and was committed, first and foremost, to persuading the Jews to join their movement.[10]

It is accepted by both the Catholic, Orthodox and Protestant churches, that the first leaders of the Early Church were Jesus' brother, James 'The Just', St Paul and the apostle John.

St Paul, although he never met Jesus, claimed to have met him in miraculous visions or dreams and placed more emphasis on Jesus' divinity than his humanity. St Paul's preaching of Christianity won out in the end, not only because of its universal appeal and mysticism, but mainly because the Roman Empire and the Catholic Church adopted it as the official version of Christianity.

Following the Council of Nicaea, the Catholic priests made several Gospels and books of the founding fathers of modern Christianity apocryphal. The book of James, by Jesus' own brother, who not only grew up with him but led the movement after his death, was removed to make sure that the human story of Jesus was written out of the Bible. Evidence of this redaction is supported by the fact that none of the present-day biblical Gospels, Acts or Epistles existed within 120 years after the crucifixion of Christ.[11]

Another unpleasant side effect of the nefarious activity of pious fraud was the generation of a seam of anti-Semitism, which would persist down the ages. The concept of monotheism was popularised by Akhenaten, an Egyptian Pharaoh. It is thought that his followers, led by Ahmoses, became the religious zealots called the Essenes.

The Nazarean Essenes reflect some of the earliest teachings of modern-day Christianity, before it was revised by the school of St. Paul. The word 'Essenes' is an Aramaic word meaning 'healers'. Around the time of Jesus, the Essenes were numerous and the sect had a followership that numbered in the thousands. Today, the relatively small Gnostic Mandaean sect of Iraq is what survives of the Essenes.

The Essenes believed in living simple communal living and shunned the acquisition of material goods. They gave away their worldly possessions and gave profits to their leaders. They considered themselves to be chosen from God and criticized some of the Jewish practices at the time as unholy. They were a radical group that was prepared to die for their cause. The Essenes were the only religious sect around that period to condemn the practice of slavery.

It is unclear from the available literature, whether the Essenes were Jews or not and it may be that St. Paul's school of Christianity tried to make the Essenes, Jesus and John the Baptist, fulfil the Jewish prophecy of the return of a Messiah, and made up the story of a virgin birth to Mary. According to Essene historians, Jesus was born in and lived in Yeshu and not Nazareth. The Essenes are accredited with writing the Dead Sea scrolls, found at Qumran but there are no references to the name 'Essenes' in the Dead Sea scrolls.

On balance, it is obvious that the historical Jesus was not blonde, blue-eyed with long hair. It is interesting to note that when a documentary in England was done into researching the real identity of Jesus Christ, the final image that was created to be Jesus appeared to be a dark-complexioned man, of Middle Eastern or African origins.[12] The shroud of Turin, another more modern myth designed to promote the idea that Jesus was a Caucasian, was alleged to have mysteriously retained the image of the face of Jesus after it was wrapped around the body of Jesus. It was kept as a sacred religious symbol and physical proof of Jesus Christ's existence on earth. Thousands of fervent Christians have flocked to see the garment over the centuries. The garment strongly divided opinion between believers and sceptics. The controversy was eventually put to bed by carbon dating and other tests which proved the shroud to be a fraud.[13]

Ben Ammi summed up the deliberate cover-up by white Christian founding fathers:

'Any literal search for Jesus will always lead to a Roman/Hellenistic mythical personage, rooted in European paganism. The correct name of the Historical Hebrew Messiah was Yeshua... rooted in the Hebrew land, language and culture. The Roman/Hellenistic name Jesus Christ [os]; is a deliberate mistranslation and deculturalization that disallows the researcher from finding the true origin of this person and this era and keeps you from connecting with a nationalistic whole in Africa.

The Euro-gentile Greek interpolators, while attempting to crush rebellion, always sought to prevent the rise of a Messiah in the midst of the Israelites. They inaugurated a process of 'name sacrilege'. They had been well taught by their spiritual mentors that men of high, spiritual sensitivity should always pronounce the name of the anointed with profound accuracy. Their first test of 'name sacrilege' was initiated with Yeshua the Messiah. They transformed his name, thus successfully transforming his character [in the minds of the people] and amputated his message from the prophetic body...By calling Yeshua Ben Yoseph 'Jesus Christ' the Euro-gentiles successfully transformed the spirit of the man and his message to conform to their scheme. How was this accomplished? They gave him a Greek name and created an image and personality that would be in agreement. Very few people are aware that in spelling and pronunciation, of the name 'Jesus Christ' is totally Greek. The English derivatives are in harmony with the Greek, not Hebrew, syntax.'[14]

CHAPTER FORTY SEVEN

ORIGINS OF MONOTHEISM AND THE TEN MISSING TRIBES OF ISRAEL

Ideas of monotheism, which is the hallmark of Christianity and subsequently of Islam, do not come, as is widely thought, from the wise old Jews who transcribed the modern Bible. They can be traced to back even further to ancient Egypt, long before monotheism was claimed to be the brainchild of the Jews, who transcribed biblical text from the Egyptians.

In 1853 the Epic of Gilgamesh, an ancient Sumerian, text was discovered by Hormuzd Rassam.[1]

The epic, written by ancient Sumerians clearly outlined a story of creation, which is similar to the biblical story of creation. These ancient stones on which the stories are inscribed have been displayed in the British Museum, and clearly show that the ideas of creation of the world and monotheism originated long before the Jews allegedly went to Egypt and eventually transcribed scrolls, which were put together to form the Bible as we presently know it. These ideas existed in and around the Middle East possibly for thousands of years before the advent of Christianity and Islam.[2]

Another interesting fact is that modern-day archaeologists, historians and people have not been able to clearly identify who many of the ancient people mentioned in the Old Testament of the Bible were. The Sumerians, like other people should have left a genetic, cultural, archaeological and linguistic trail behind. These clues can be traced, if objectively and carefully followed up. Historically, as things stand, the Sumerians and black Jews simply vanished off the face of the earth.

However, there is some anecdotal evidence to the contrary suggested by historian, Charles S. Finch, who wrote:

'In Sumer, so often touted as the world's "first" civilization, the African derivation of the original inhabitants is betrayed by their name for themselves, "the black heads",...Furthermore, Sumer's first capital was Kish, the same as the Egyptian KESH, a name for Cush or Ethiopia.'[3]

It is interesting that the Sumerians whose lineage cannot apparently be clearly traced are also credited with the origins of mathematics and the wheel. This sleight of hand was done with the sole intent of deflecting people's minds away from the fact that science and religion were created by Africans, who are not credited with contributing to the development of the world in the West.

Recent historical and archaeological finds suggest that the 'missing people', including the 'missing' ten tribes of Israel, were black African people who occupied this region for centuries. Due to famine, wars, and persecution, especially slavery, they migrated in vast numbers across Egypt through North Africa and down towards West Africa, all the way to Senegal. It is logical, therefore, to think that these people may have been the pyramid builders, who through the western tip of Africa, Gambia and Senegal, found their way through drift routes to the South Americas and began the South American civilization known as the Olmecs.

Roman exploitation, taxation and ruthlessness caused a lot of the original Africans in North Africa to move further into the body of Africa. The question is often asked; what happened to North Africa's black population? This is part of the answer.[4]

Around 1300 BC Akhenaten, an Egyptian pharaoh, suddenly changed from worshipping in the usual polytheistic manner of ancient Egypt, to the doctrine of one god. It is possible he was attracted to a monotheistic doctrine that was actually not novel in the region at the time. This pharaoh, whose name was originally Amenhotep IV, established a new monotheistic religion and worshipped just one god called Aten. He then changed his name to Akhenaten meaning 'one useful to Aten'.

Prior to Akhenaten, the Egyptians had worshipped a multitude of gods and goddesses. The Egyptians even some borrowed gods from the foreigners they met or had conquered in battle. They had already established the concept of heaven and hell and worshipped Osiris, the god above and Isis, the god below. They conducted elaborate rituals concerning the present and the afterlife, made famous by Egyptian Book of the Dead.

Central among the many gods that were worshipped was the sun god Amon-Re, the prefix meaning 'Amon is satisfied', which was added to the names of the pharaohs. This idea of an all-encompassing and unified nature of their gods must have been the precursor to monotheism.

Encyclopaedia Britannica states:

'Hymns before Akhenaten's reign show that the spread of the empire meant the spread of religion. Gods became universal. Egypt had already combined gods, with Amon and Re [the sun god] becoming Amon -Re or even Amon -Re Harakhte. This permitted the Egyptians to think of the gods as a unified force, which was the prelude to monotheism.[5]

The extent and detail to which this Egyptian pharaoh Akhenaten went to promote monotheism in ancient Egypt was amazing. Akhenaten was so inspired by this new religion that he moved the thriving capital of Egypt at that time to Thebes, 200 miles away. He built his new desert city from scratch, in a position to receive the sun's rays at sunrise, in honour of this new god, the sun disc Ra. This involved the relocation of over 10,000 people to help create his dream. This new city was called Amarna.

However, Akhenaten also angered many Egyptians when he ordered the wide-spread desecration of the shrines and artefacts of the multitude of gods that the Egyptians worshipped at the time.

Comparative studies by many writers have shown that the European idea of monotheism was also borrowed from ancient Egypt and formed the bedrock of both Christianity and Islam today. For a book as influential as the Bible, in the development of civilizations around the world, particularly Western, it is simply shocking that the millions of practicing Christians do not know who the real authors are. The concept of a hierarchy among the gods was known in ancient Egypt long before the creation of the main monotheistic religions today. In other words, the concept of God, heaven, hell and angels was not new.

Sir Wallis Budge, a renowned Egyptologist, wrote in his book, Egyptian religion:

'A study of ancient Egyptian's religious texts will convince the reader that the Egyptians believed in One God, who were self-existent, immortal, invisible, eternal, omniscient, almighty, and inscrutable, the maker of heavens, earth, and the underworld, the creator of the sky and the sea, men and women, animals, and birds, fish and creeping things, trees and plants, and the incorporeal beings who were the messengers that fulfilled his wish and his word.[6]

Akhenaten and his wife, Nefertiti a black woman whose beauty was fabled, promoted the worship of their only god, Aten. This was the first fully documented practice of monotheism known to man. The King Akhenaten wrote beautiful hymns to Aten, which were found inscribed in the walls of the temples of worship, Ai, during excavations in archaeological digs in Amarna.

The king addressed a beautiful hymn to his god, expressing gratitude for the benefits of life.

'The Aten, says the hymn, gave these blessings not only to the Egyptians but also to 'Syria and Nubia' and to 'all foreign countries to 'all men, cattle, and wild beasts, ' to the lion coming from his den, the fish from the water, and the chick within the egg.'[7]

Men live when the sun has risen, but at night the dark land is as if dead.'

It has often been pointed out that this hymn has a remarkable similarity to Psalm 104 in the Bible. Both the hymn and the psalm reflect a common family of ideas, according to which god is praised for his bounties.

The Jewish scholars of Alexandra took the Ancient Egyptian perception and epithets of God, his form, and power and included them in the biblical narrative, exactly as the ancient Egyptians conceived and verbalized them. Sir Wallis Budge also presented a summary of the ancient Egyptian epithets pertaining to the most ancient concept of God and the practice of religion, long before these epithets and concepts got into the Christian and Muslim religions. Sir Wallis Budge wrote:

When classified, these ancient Egyptian epithets read thus:

'God is One and alone, and none other existeth with him.

God is the One, the One who hath made all things.

God is a spirit, a hidden spirit, the spirit of spirits, the Great Spirit of the Egyptians, the divine spirit.

God is from the beginning, and he hath been from the beginning; he hath existed from of old and was when nothing else had being.

He existed when nothing else existed, and what existed he created after he had come into being.

He is the father of beginnings.

God is the eternal One, He is eternal and infinite; and endureth for ever and aye; He hath endured for countless ages, and He shall endure to all eternity.

God is the hidden being, and no man hath known his Form. No man hath been able to seek out his likeness, He is hidden from gods and men, and He is a mystery unto his creatures.

No man knoweth how to know Him. His name remaineth hidden; His name is a mystery unto his children. His names are innumerable; they are manifold and none knoweth their number.

God is truth, and He liveth truth, and He feedeth thereon. He is the King of truth, He resteth upon truth, He fashioned truth, and He executeth truth throughout all the world.

God is life, and through Him only man liveth. He giveth life to man, and He breatheth the breath of life into his nostrils.

God is father and mother, the father of fathers, and the mother of mothers. He begetteth, but was never begotten; He produceth, but was never produced, He begath himself and produced Himself. He createth, but was never created; he is the maker of His own form, and the fashioner of His own body.

God Himself is existence, He liveth in all things, and liveth upon all things. He endureth without increase or dimunition, He multiplieth Himself millions of times, and He possesseth multitudes of forms and multitudes of members.

God hath made the universe, and He created all that therein is: He is the Creator of what is in this world, of what was, of what is, and of what shall be. He is the creator of the world, and it was He Who fashioned it with his hands before there was any beginning; and He established it with that which went forth from him. He is the Creator of the heavens and earth; the Creator of the heavens, and the earth, and the deep; the Creator of the heavens, and the earth, and the deep, and the waters, and the mountains. God hath stretched out the heavens and founded the earth. What his heart conceived came to pass straight away, and when He had spoken His word came to pass, and it shall endure forever.

God is father of the gods, and the father of the father of all ideas. His made His voice to sound, and deities came into being, and the gods sprang into existence after He had spoken with His mouth. He formed mankind and fashioned the gods. He is the great Master, the primeval Potter Who turned men and gods out of His hands, and He formed men and gods upon a potters table.

The heavens rest upon His head and the earth supporteth His feet; heaven hideth His spirit, the earth hideth His form, and the underworld shutteth up the mystery of Him within it. His body is like air, heaven resteth upon His head, and the new inundation {of the Nile] containeth His form.

God is merciful unto those who reverence Him, and He heareth him that calleth upon Him. He protecteth the weak against the strong, and He heareth the cry of him that is bound in fetters; He judgeth between the mighty and the weak. God knoweth him that knoweth Him, He rewardeth him that serveth Him, and He protecteth him that followeth Him.[8]

There is historical evidence to show that Akhenaten was gradually increasingly intolerant of the old Egyptian gods and goddesses. After a plague in the east and a series of personal tragedies including the death of his beloved Queen Nefertiti, two of his six daughters and his influential mother-in-law, the queen mother Tiy, he ordered the name of the old god Amon to be hacked out of all the inscriptions in Egypt.

He even went as far as removing the name Amon from the tomb of his father, the late pharaoh Amenhotep III. The Amarna letters discovered in the ruins of Tell el-Amarna show that he ignored the affairs of the state leading to the disintegration of the Egyptian Empire in Asia, Syria and Palestine. When Akhenaten died, Egyptians did all they could to deface him and his religion, as he was considered to ultimately have been the cause of the decline of the golden age of ancient Egypt.[9]

Most people who have read the Bible will agree that apart from the theosophical messages, the Old Testament of the Bible also represents the history of the Jews as they journeyed out of Egypt. It is therefore, important to establish that the ideas of monotheism were already established in Egypt before the Jews ever arrived there, as slaves or migrants. The Jewish history in the Bible is closely intertwined with that of the ancient Egyptians.

If the Jews as we know them today were not ancient Egyptians, then why is the very basis of their religious ideas, practices and culture so similar to that of the ancient Egyptians?

It is also quite remarkable that every major Jewish figure in the Old Testament like Moses, Abraham and Joseph, invariably had something to do with Egypt.

However, Moses who supposedly wrote the first five books of the Bible was a Hebrew, brought up in an Egyptian household.

In the biblical narrative, Abraham went to Egypt with his wife Sarah during a famine and later Joseph was sold into slavery by his jealous brothers and ended up in Egypt. Later, Joseph was made a ruler by the Pharaoh.

The connection with Egypt does not end in the Old Testament; Jesus is linked to Egypt following his birth.

According to the Old Testament, the Jews were Egyptian slaves for up to 400 years, surely long enough to have imbibed the religious ideas, customs and practices of the Egyptians.

'Long before the destruction of Jerusalem by Titus, the Mediterranean shore of Africa had become lined with influential Jewish Colonies, which undoubtedly were in constant mercantile relations with the interior of the Dark Continent. But Egypt especially had been the haven of refugees from Jerusalem at the time of the Babylonian captivity, and for many subsequent centuries, the Jewish element in the land of the Pharaohs continued to increase and prosper.'

'Ethiopian Hebrews point out…that black Hebrew themselves included were in Africa 1500 and years before Islam and that wherever the Arabs travelled in Africa, they found Hebrews. According to their sources, the Kanuri Hebrews were located in central Sudan along trails hundreds of miles north south, east, and West of Senegal from where they had apparently migrated.

'Others came to the Sudan from the north and converged with those who were heading to four countries along the Niger River. They were settlements on the West Coast as well as in the interior of Africa in communities reaching from Morocco to Angola. They gave a number of tens of thousands of black Hebrews, who were also in Morocco and the Sahara desert area, including the group known as the Beni-Moussa ["Sons of Moses"].

'They also point out that in 1484, under the reign of King John II of Portugal; hundreds of black Hebrews were deported to the island of Sao Tome, off the West coast of Africa.'[10]

Doubts exist about the Jewish claim that Moses wrote the first five books of the Bible, known as the Pentateuch, have existed for centuries and has been the subject of much investigation by Bible scholars.

When an early Jewish scholar, Isaac ibn Yashush, declared that Moses did not write the first five books of the Bible, his colleagues branded him a heretic.

The early Catholic Church also played a strong part in the conspirational protection of the origins of the Bible and rejected the work of Bonifils of Damascus, deleting passages of his work that questioned if Moses had written the first five books of the Bible. The church relegated the work of Andreas van Maes on the same topic to the Index of Prohibited Books, the most powerful index of religious censorship ever known.

Isaac La Peyrère was arrested, jailed, and forced to recant after he published a book suggesting that Moses never wrote the Pentateuch.

Not only was there doubt that Moses wrote the first five books of the Bible, there are also a lot of doubts as to the claim by Jewish scholars, that he was a Jew.

In the Encyclopaedia Britannica, scholars of Jewish history expressed their own doubt and stated:

'The central figure of the exodus [13th century BC] and the wanderings in the desert is Moses, whose life story recorded in the Bible reads like an epic. In the consciousness of the Hebrews and the Jews at all times, Moses is the great liberator, leader, man of God, and father of the prophets. Although no external evidence proves such a man lived, the subsequent history of Israel cannot be conceived without Moses, and his existence must be taken as a fact.'[11]

These same scholars went on to write in the Britannica that:

'Stripped of legendary embellishments, such as the ten plagues, the miraculous crossing of the Red sea and the Revelation in Mount Sinai, the historicity of the exodus is vouched for by the psychological impress it left on the consciousness of the Hebrews and the Jews. The Exodus became the corner stone of Jewish history, religion, and nationhood.'[12]

In other words, they assert that because the Moses story left a strong psychological impression on the Jews, it had to be historically accurate.

Among Western scholars, it has long been established that Moses was not a Jew but an ancient Egyptian. In his book, The Ancient Lowly, C.O. Ward pointed out that the name Moses was ancient Egyptian, he hypothesized that the name might have been shortened from the Egyptian royal name Ahmoses.[13]

It was intriguing to find out how Moses, who is thought not to be a Jew, ended up being the cornerstone of the Jewish religion.

The famous psychoanalyst, Sigmund Freud, was of Jewish origins, and spent a lot of his time researching who Moses really was. Freud wrote a book, Moses and Monotheism, and postulated that Moses must have been an Egyptian noble and a follower of Akhenaten's.[14]

Gary Greenberg, a modern Jewish author, wrote the book, 'The Moses Mystery: The African Origins of the Jewish People'. Taking an ancient Egyptian perspective, he concluded that Moses served as a chief priest in Akhenaten's cult. After the death of Akhenaten, the new pharaoh, Horemheb, eradicated all the vestiges of Akhenaten's heresy, eliminating the evidence stone by stone and word by word. This resulted in Akhenaten's legacy being lost to history until the 19th century when Egyptologists discovered the ruins of his capital, Amarna. He postulates that Moses led the followers of this cult out of Egypt after a failed coup. He concluded that this mass movement of people was the real Exodus.

Greenberg also showed that the biblical chronology was based upon the exact ancient Egyptian chronology of the kings.

'Many of the descendants of Abraham followed Moses from Egypt, but some remained in Egypt, while others migrated south and westward… Those migrating Hebrews explain why traces of Hebrew culture can be found throughout West, central, and east Africa. Many scholars believe the ancestors of the Fulani, Ashanti, Ewe, Yoruba; Bantu and other peoples were, in fact, early Hebrew Israelites.'[15]

'Today there are still millions of African Jews… in many tribes in Kenya, Zaire, Zambia and the Congo, there are people who are circumcised, respect the Sabbath, and have a tradition of using succot for a week. My father taught me the Tora, and he was taught it by his father who was taught by his father, and on and on.'[16]

Yoruba folklore claims that the Yoruba people descended directly from Egypt and some scholars believe that Yoruba people in West Africa descended from the Middle East

'Another major African group whose origins have been traced to the other side of the Red Sea are the Yoruba are now mainly concentrated in Nigeria and Benin. One legend has it that Yoruba are the remnant of the children of Canaan, who were the "Tribe of Nimrod."'[17]

'Yoruba scholars have advanced diverse ideas as to the origin of the Yoruba, some even suggesting a relationship to Middle Eastern countries.

'The staff of Oranyan, said to be a thousand years old that is a symbol of the Yoruba, and has the Hebrew letter yod, carved near its pinnacle.'[18]

In Uganda, it is well known that African Judaism survived several centuries virtually unchanged. It is interesting that the leader of the Lord's Resistance Army, fighting a long running battle with the Ugandan government, claims that he wants to run the country by the Ten Commandments of Moses.

'Speaking of Uganda to the West of Lake Victoria and north-east of Belgian Congo, it has an organized native government with tradition of the 33 Kings and legendary line that traces back to King David.'[19]

Some of the most remarkable and most recently studied group of east African Jews must be the Lemba of Zimbabwe. Thousands of black Africans claim that according to their ancient tradition, they are the descendants of Abraham, Moses and Solomon.

CHAPTER FORTY EIGHT
WHO WROTE THE BIBLE?

Too few Christians have stopped to consider the critical question: who wrote the Bible? However, this knowledge is central to their understanding of their Christian faith.

Bible scholar Lawrence Livingston wrote:

'Immediately, some persons will suggest that the racial background of the biblical characters doesn't matter… Apparently, it has mattered enough, until now, to comprehensively exclude all people of color, particularly in the light of the last four hundred years of racialist history.'[1]

'Contrary to popular opinion the Bible is not a white man's book. The widely used authorized or King James Version is action in actuality 66 different books. They are not a complete representation of the inspired writings of the prophets and scribes of ancient Israel. European church leaders neither found, had access to, nor accepted every ancient manuscript as part of the church canon, hence the Apocrypha, the Dead Sea scrolls and other texts.

'While Europeans may have been involved intimately with the Bible— in its compilation [as with the Kings James scholars in 1661], publication [as did the German Johann Gutenberg in 1451], or interpretation [as do many religious denominations today] they were not its authors! As for the translation of the scriptures from the Hebrew and lands men of Europe, we're certainly unable to accurately convey, the true Hebrew thought and cultural context.[2]

"'I [King James] could never yet see a Bible well translated in English…" These few dissident words started the greatest writing project the world has ever known and the greatest achievements of the reign of James I — the making of the English Bible, which has ever since borne his name.

'The day was Monday January 16 1604. The scene was the palace at

Hampton's court… the air must have been heavy and stale for there is no record of baths in the palace, though the courts used perfumes and pomanders and the King kept his hands soft as sarcenet by never washing them, merely dipped the royal fingers into bowls of attar and other balm….. James at 37 an old young man who sputtered because his tongue was too large for his mouth… having spoken James went on about his royal business, which had nothing to do with translating scriptures.[3]

'What the King James men had and what we have today in greater variety, cysts of copies derived from former copies and so on backward. The text as it stands in any scholarly edition must by the very nature of the problem be in respects corrupt. We can only trust that what we have is a reasonably accurate text of the 66 books, which through the ages of the churches came to accept as Holy Scriptures. It should be obvious. Therefore, that no English rendition is, or can be from any literary standpoint the precise word of God.'[4]

King Henry VIII's desire to translate the Bible to English and make the known Bible available to the common man had more to do with his desire to marry more wives and have a son and male heir than his religious fervour to spread the word of God.

Ancient Egypt is known to have existed over 6,000 years ago and the Jews were known to be in Egypt around 1300 BC not long after Akhenaten. If the Bible was compiled then, it had to have been compiled in ancient Egypt. Historical records confirm that the books of the Bible were edited after the 7th century BC or even later, nearly 700 years after the Jews left Egypt and wandered around in the wilderness.

This genealogy is consistent with the fact that the modern-day Bible, which reads from Genesis to Revelation, only became a single book about 600 to 700 years ago. Prior to this, the Bible was an amorphous collection of scrolls whose origins are over two thousand years old.

Old Testament texts were made of papyrus, parchment and leather. In the time of Jesus, the Old Testament revelations were widely known, and though there was no collection of biblical texts called the Old Testament, the scrolls were known variously as the Law of Moses or the scriptures. Jesus therefore, grew up among people who had scrolls and texts but no Bible.

Texts of the Hebrew Old Testament were composed between the 8th century BC and the mid-2nd century.

According to Bible historian Robin Lane Fox, a further 200 years would elapse before the texts of the Christian New Testaments were composed around AD 60 and AD 100. [5]

From a historical standpoint, none of the books of the Bible existed in its present form before the 8th century.

Archaeology has helped clarify the situation further, after a landmark discovery of texts written on papyrus and animal skins, the Dead Sea scrolls were recovered from a cave near the ruins of Qumran, south of Jericho, near the western shore of the Dead Sea. When the texts were deciphered, they included bits of every biblical book except Esther.[6]

The Dead Sea texts, dated to between AD 73 and AD 132, reveal an ancient Masoretic Hebrew text which form both the Jewish and Christian Bibles.[7]

History also shows that the Greek king who ordered the compilation of the Bible as we have come to know it, did so in Egypt. This Greek compilation, tà bibla, was the beginning of many translations and editions to come.

One of the first translations was written in the language of the ancient Egyptians, Coptic, and found its way to Ethiopia. It is also interesting that the Ark of the Covenant also allegedly went to Ethiopia.

Other old texts form the basis of the Greek Orthodox Church and Russian Orthodox Church.

Throughout the Greek-speaking world, early Christians adopted the Septuagint or 'seventy', named after the 70 Alexandrian Jews who translated tà bibla, as the first Bible.

As time passed, the Septuagint and new documents [the New Testament] were combined and became the foundation of the modern Bible. The spread of Christianity across Europe necessitated the translation into different languages and this could have left the Bible open to translation errors and linguistic corruption; however, any study of hermeneutics will reveal the extraordinary accuracy of scribes and their competence in copying scripts. The Greek Bible was translated into Latin and Syrian in the 2nd century and later allegedly re-translated into Coptic in the 3rd century and Armenian in the 5th century.

In the 6th century, Saint Jerome translated the original Septuagint into the Latin Vulgate, and it was the Latin Bible that spread across Europe.

The English translation of the Bible is one of the most popular books in the world today. However, English was of one of the last European languages into which the Bible was translated.

The first copy of the English Bible is believed to have been translated by John Wycliffe, but it was the work of William Tyndale, who translated the New Testament part of the Old Testament that was compiled to form the King James Authorized Version or Authorized Version in 1611. [8]

In Europe, the Bible was first translated into Anglo-Saxon in the 8th century, German, Slav and Frankish in the 9th century and French in the 12th century.

The invention of printing in 1450 greatly facilitated the printing and distribution of the Bible in Europe. In addition to the translations of the Bible, there have been numerous revisions, including a revision of the King James Version in the 1960s. The new Revised Standard Version appeared in 1989 to satisfy the needs of American Protestants.[9]

Many of these translations and revisions were to suit the social-political sentiment of Europeans and obscure the true African origins of Christianity.

For instance, where King Solomon said, 'I am black but comely' in the Song of Solomon; the Revised Standard Version reads, 'I am very dark, but comely.' Song of Solomon 1:5[10]

In 325 AD, the First Council of Nicaea convened by the Roman Emperor Constantine I, apart from settling the dispute over Aryanism had to decide which biblical books were considered apocryphal.[11]

The First Council of Nicaea also attempted but failed to set a uniform date for Easter.

There are over 14 books of the Bible considered apocryphal by the Catholic Church, including the Gospel of St. Thomas, Gospel of Philip, and even the Gospel of Mary Magdalene.

CHAPTER FORTY NINE

CATHOLICISM AND CAPITALISM

Christianity and Islam have both played significant roles in African history but Christianity would be a major tool in the physical and mental subjugation of black Africans by Europeans.

It was a cruel twist of fate that Africans, who developed the ideas of monotheism and indeed, the first recorded practice of it in Egypt, would find themselves called pagans. Africans found themselves subjugated and exploited in the name of and by Western Christianity.

After the death of Jesus, Orthodox Christianity was practiced in Ethiopia for more than 2,000 years before it reached and was accepted in Europe. The spread of Western Christianity was used as justification to explain white superiority, slavery, and the plunder and pillaging of the African continent, citing the subhumanity, inferiority, and paganism of Africans as their excuse.

When the Muslims took over Jerusalem, the perceived centre of Christendom or the 'Holy Land', it triggered the first Christian Crusade, to wrest control away from the 'infidels'. At the same time, Islamophobia provided a central rallying point for Christian Europe and the Catholic Church was able to intertwine itself very closely with politics and government. The Catholic Church called for the first Christian Crusade in 1096.

Pope Urban II called a meeting of Church leaders in Clermont, northern France in 1095. This followed a pilgrimage to the Muslim-controlled land two years earlier by Peter the Hermit, who alleged that he had seen Christians chained, beaten and killed. He would promote armed pilgrimage and led over 20,000 peasant men, women, and children, in what would become the first preliminary wave of the Crusades.

'Let hatred therefore, depart from among you, let your quarrels end, let wars cease, and let all dissensions and controversies slumber. Enter upon the road to the Holy sepulchre, wrest that land from the wicked race, and subject it to yourselves.'[1]

When the crusaders finally made it into Jerusalem, they shed the blood of the 'infidels' with all the religious fervour they could muster. It is estimated that up to 60,000 inhabitants of Jerusalem were slaughtered in this holy Christian onslaught. It is ironic that these 'infidels' did not just include Muslims but also Jews and Orthodox Christians as well.

The Christian historians wrote:

'Crusaders rushed through the streets and into houses and mosques, killing everyone they met—including women and children. All Friday afternoon and night, the killing and looting continued as the soldiers and pilgrims rushed through the city.'[2]

Through the exposure to foreign lands and people, Europeans were able to set up political and economic links with many nations and obtain gold, precious stones, silk, ivory, and spices that were much sought after in Europe. They were able to trade with the Far East through Asia and although the Mongol Empire created by Genghis Khan controlled large areas of this land, they did trade with Europe. Magellan explorer who stayed in the Far East for years and brought back stories of great wealth and civilizations.

The Crusades, which lasted around 200 years, though initially successful, eventually failed. Europe and Christians lost access to these lands because the Muslims under the Ottoman Empire attacked and defeated the overstretched Mongol army and eventually not only blocked the access of the Christians and Europeans to Jerusalem but also cut off the land route through which this lucrative trade was done to Asia and the Far East.

Despite the failure of the Crusades, they did succeed in firmly linking the Catholic Church with the monarchy in Europe, making sure they were part of every major political decision that was taken by the monarchy.

In a bid to discover a sea route to India and the Far East, to get round the land route blocked by the Muslims, European explorers struck out to sea hoping to find a route that skirted the coasts of Africa and led on to India and the Far East.

St. Augustine had written that humankind *'has sprung from one protoplasm'* but the discovery of people from other lands forced the Church to rethink the idea of 'one humanity' in order to accommodate its policy of capitalist expansionism and exploitation.[3]

Despite the atrocities meted out on the poor people of these lands who had the misfortune to come into contact with European explorers, especially in Africa and the Americas, the Catholic Church was convinced that the 'pagans' were more than adequately compensated by the introduction to Christianity and civilization in these foreign lands.

The Catholic Church even went as far as blaming the Dark Ages on the pagan barbarians but many of these so-called pagans were already Christians and were not illiterate. The open exploitation of 'pagans' in foreign lands by Christians from Spain and Portugal was fully endorsed by the Catholic Church.

Pope Nicholas V permitted slavery in a Papal Bull in 1454. As the Church began to get rich from the proceeds, it became increasingly difficult to oppose slavery.'[4]

The relationship of divine disfavour, sexual immorality, and black skin, themes from Greco-Roman times, were revived for the present.

Christian theology marshalled two main theological themes; prominent in England and America was the Curse of Ham theory.

According to the popular myth this was Noah's curse; in Genesis 9:20–26, Noah was found drunk and naked by Ham, who did not cover his nakedness, but Shem and Japheth, who are believed in white Christian circles to be the ancestors of Europeans, covered him up. This lead to the drunken Noah cursing, not Ham, but his grandson, Canaan, condemning his descendants to servitude and slavery. This fabrication was used by white churches all over the world to justify slavery and in spite of all the evidence to the contrary, some churches, and surprisingly, some Africans who interpret the Bible believe it literally too.

Many Church scholars argued that colonialism ought to go hand in hand with evangelism of the infidel.

This viewpoint was supported by Christopher Columbus and Giné de Sepulveda [c. 1490], who argued that war was necessary against 'native Americans' of Latin America as a prerequisite for later evangelization. As a result, European capitalist expansion instigated horrifying levels of violence towards foreign people by European explorers that was justified and sanctioned by the Church.

'There is no single philosophy, no single movement or author who can be considered as having paved the way for 19th century racial theory. Instead, it grew out of the combination of previously rather distinct traditions — a liberal, lay, anti-monarchical political outlook, phrenological and physiognomical fortune telling; a political interest in finding a scientific justification for slavery; the philological investigation of languages as a mirror of national character. Nineteenth century racial theory resulted in a unification of various approaches to the study of mankind, which has evolved in the preceding age.'[5]

As science marched forwards so did the European expression of racism but its roots were deeply entrenched in the Catholic Church.

The biological argument: Two broad schools of thought existed.

The monogenesis idea, which recognizes a single human species and the polygenesis viewpoint, albeit a minority view, which argued for the plurality of species, naturally with whites being superior to blacks.

Polygenesis gave intellectual support for the horrors of genocide in America and Australia.[6]

Physiological Arguments:

'*Pseudo sciences like Craniology and Phrenology in the nineteenth century supported the belief in the superiority of European character, culture, and morality due to their superior skulls and facial features.'*[7]

Phrenology, a pseudoscientific study of the shape and size of the skull as a supposed indication of a person's character and mental abilities, justified European expansion of empire because it supported the concept of British rule over 'lesser races'; the African was lazy and in need of brutal subjugation for the best civilizing results. Phrenology cheapened the value of African lives — expressed in the brutal repression of Paul Bogle and the Morant Bay rebellion in Jamaica in 1865.[8]

To salve the conscience of the Christians in Europe, they then needed to somehow explain away the plunder, rape, murder, enslavement and exploitation of these 'pagans' and began to search for reasons to justify their actions, while of course, continuing to enjoy the wealth, status and free labour these foreign lands provided them.[9]

For many European Christians, European inhumanity and racism to foreign races may have contradicted the core Christian and biblical principles of morality. However, they perceived the economic gains through plunder of African wealth, and the free labour of African slaves, were to be good for Europe's economic development and survival. As a result, Christians in Europe were forced to make a choice between their religious morality and economic greed, and they chose to reinterpret the Bible to justify their morality and greed at the same time. To do so, Christian Europe had to prove through the Bible that Africans were pagans and inferior sub-humans, therefore enslaving them did not violate Christian or human morality.

To prove the African was a pagan was easy. However, proving that he was inferior and subhuman was more difficult. In the Bible story of creation, Christianity preaches the equality of all humans through the Adamite theory of monogenesis. This theory suggests all human beings were equal because we all came from the same ancestors, Adam and Eve.

The author continued:

'To be able to prove that Africans were inferior and sub-human, Christian Europe had to first reject the biblical theory of human origins, and it did.'[10]

The theory of polygenesis was the first attempt of the Catholic Church to justify slavery and the inhumanity that was being perpetrated against Africans and others foreign people whose lands white 'explorers', who were often financially backed by the Church, were visiting upon them.

If the Bible asserts that all men were created equal, how could the Church justify the conduct of European explorers in foreign lands?

Europeans had to prove that Africans and Europeans were created at different times, with the African the inferior human being and therefore, at the mercy of their white counterparts. The Christian theory of polygenesis was seized upon by scientists and pursued with great vigour.

Bory de Saint -Vincent, an anthropologist and advocate of the theory wrote:

'Revelation...nowhere prescribes that we are to believe exclusively in Adam and Eve...'[11]

Another claim is the difference of our origins explained from the biblical flood; according to Europe, they accept the first humans originated from Adam and Eve but then claim they were wiped out in the flood. They then claim that a new group of humans emerged, from the sons of Noah; Shem, Japheth and Ham.

These false assertions by the European churches were the foundations on which racism took hold in Europe. It also provided the motive for the Catholic Church to expunge any trace of the black origins of Christianity out of the church and records. At a time when Christianity was not yet accepted in the West during Roman times many practiced their religion under the threat of death.

Once the ball was set in motion, it no longer mattered if the origins of racism began on baseless claims of European's superiority and black inferiority. It did not matter if Christian Europe's claims of polygenesis or Noah's curse were totally unfounded. Europeans now felt justified in their greed and exploitation, as their actions had the seal of approval from the Church and royalty.

Upon this foundation, European academics and scientists began to build their assertions. It is entirely likely that many of these pseudo scientists never considered the basis of their beliefs, as in their eyes, African inferiority was simply a fact, and they were just trying to put it in a scientific format. They always worked from the 'fact' of African inferiority backwards to their hypothesis.

Motivated by a subconscious drive to assert superiority, placed in their minds by the Catholic church, they went to great lengths to prove that Africans were not just inferior, from a religious standpoint but also from a physical, intellectual, moral and emotional one too.

The drive of anthropologists to prove European superiority was taken to extreme lengths by Hitler and the Nazis who believed Germans were descended from a superior race of Aryans from Atlantis. This fabled city of Atlantis was supposed to have been created by an advanced group of humans who were light years ahead of the rest of the world in terms of their technological and other achievements.

The Nazis conducted the largest ever search for the lost city of Atlantis which was supposed to have sunk under the sea. They also conducted grotesque experiments on captive people, especially the Jews, to support these claims. They pushed eugenics as far as they possibly could before their defeat in the Second World War. Many Western scientists and scholars still hold fast to flawed premise of eugenics even though the ideas and 'scientific and biblical proof' are flawed.

When the Spanish arrived in the Americas, they treated the American natives with such savagery that it prompted an outcry from a Catholic Dominican friar Bartolomé de Las Casas. He reported to the Church in Spain that it was wrong to enslave the pagans they were trying to convert to Christianity, and that they were human beings that must be converted to Christianity and treated as free men. Conversely, a Spanish slave merchant, Juan Sepulveda, quoting Aristotle, argued that the Native Americans were barbarians and could therefore be taken as slaves.

However, the Catholic Church agreed with Bartolomé de Las Casas, and in 1537 issued a papal bull, Sublimis Deus, proclaiming that Native Americans were human and could receive the Catholic faith and sacrament. Unfortunately, Bartolomé de Las Casas also argued the case for using Africans as free labour in the Americas as the Native Americans were now entitled to the Catholic faith, and sacrament could not be used as free labour in the plantations of the Americas. This move was to spawn the transatlantic slave trade that took over ten million Africans into slavery.

In AD 323 after Constantine defeated Emperor Licinius, he decided to unite the Roman Empire under the banner of Christianity. When the Arian Controversy threatened to divide the Catholic Church, he decided to settle the differences which were destabilizing the Roman Empire as a whole. Fighting had even broken out between the different factions and the stability of the empire could not be jeopardized by this.

In a letter to the warring bishops, Arius and Alexander, to persuade them to settle their differences, Constantine wrote:

'This contention has not arisen respecting any important command of the law, nor has any new opinion been introduced with regard to the worship of God; but you both entertain the same sentiments, so that you may join in one communion.

'It is thought not to be indecorous, but altogether unlawful, that so numerous a people of God should be governed and directed at your pleasure, while you thus emulously contending with each other, and quarreling about small and trifling matters.'[12]

The Aryanism movement essentially believed that even though Jesus was the Son of God, he was a living human being, while the Nicene Creed held that he was purely supernatural. This was, in fact, the same schism between the old or early Christians and those who followed the teaching of St. Paul.

In 325 AD, Emperor Constantine called the Council of Nicaea, attended by nearly 300 bishops from around the world. At the council, Aryanism was defeated and important dates in the Christian calendar, like the date to celebrate the Resurrection and Easter were debated. The Nicene Creed of Catholicism is still read in churches all over the world today.[13]

Christianity thus became the official religion of Europe and was spread as the Romans expanded their Empire. Constantine, who had earlier prosecuted Christians terribly before his conversion, only allegedly became baptized as a Christian on his deathbed.

The corruption in the Catholic Church was so staggering that it stimulated the backlash that eventually led to its break up. Yet, in the 7th century, during the most corrupt period of its existence, the Catholic Church supplied more than 800 saints to the Roman calendar.

Although the Catholic Church finally unified Europe, the Catholic Churh itself would later split into three main branches, Catholic, Anglican and Protestant.

In 1517, Martin Luther levelled his list of accusations of corruption and nepotism against the Church and would lead to the splintering of the Church and the origin of the Protestant Reformation. When King Henry VIII of England was refused permission by the Catholic Church to divorce his first wife, he broke away from the papacy in Rome and renounced the Pope's authority over the newly formed Church of England.

Despite the fact that their differences were now less fundamental they would still lead to several bitter European wars.

Modern African people have largely followed whichever way Western Christianity has turned.

Today, many black African Christians are completely ignorant of the history of Western Christianity and cannot appreciate the impact it has had on their lives and the lives of their forefathers.

The sword always followed the cross, as the European missionaries preached Christianity, European explorers swept through Africa behind them in search of minerals, like diamonds and gold, and land suitable for European settlement. Missionaries set up schools, built hospitals, and then employed the African locals, converted Christians as soldiers, office workers, clerks and servants. However, they never employed a single African person as an equal. white missionaries and explorers helped form the basis of European colonial rule in Africa. When Lord Lugard defeated the northern Caliphates in Kano, Nigeria, to establish the Northern Protectorate, he did so with 3,000 troops, and of these numbers, only 250 men where white.

Most Africans were not allowed into the churches, hospitals and schools just for Christianity or civilization's sake. It was a necessity of the colonization process to create enough semi skilled, 'educated' African workers who would form the basis of 'divide and rule', which was the only way the Europeans could rule over vast areas of Africa, holding political and religious sway while they extracted limitless resources.

These Christian missionaries would teach the African natives to have great pride in the British Empire, to which, by virtue of their civilization and conversion to Christianity, they now 'belonged'. The assimilation into the lower rungs of Western civilization would also signal the end of the development of their own African cultures.

Christians usually state that 'we had all sinned and were not worthy of the Kingdom of God,' and being black at that time was seen as a living embodiment of sin. This was a simple but very powerful psychological message. Black was bad and white was good. God is white, and the Devil is black. Everything Africans believed in was deemed bad or inferior, and conversely everything the white man believed in or did was better and superior. This method of brainwashing was far superior than just the terror instilled via a gun and torture. This simple but powerful message still continues to persuade people today through the mass media, education systems and in people's attitude.

To the African, already deeply religious by nature, these were serious indictments of their core self-identity, and many were convinced of their inherent inferiority. The white man and his wealth, guns and manner may have impressed them, but the white Christianity absolutely clinched it. If God, Jesus and all the angels in heaven are white people and the Devil, and his followers were black or non-white, then what did that make a black person?

African culture, history and moral values all became irrelevant to the African convert to white Christianity. Today, African evangelist, 'spirit–filled' believer churches are the fastest growing in the world, far outstripping the European orthodox churches, which are in decline. Unfortunately, many black African pastors and their followers totally ignore the history of the Western Christianity they follow so fervently. The core message of Christianity transcends race, colour or creed, but the problem has never been with his message, but with the interpretations formed by white missionaries. Today, being religious is quietly breathed upon in Europe and many are frankly irritated by people who identify themselves with religion, be it Christian or Muslim. Christianity established Europe as a dominant force in the world, but today, they simply have no more use for it.

Football now has more pulling power than the church in Britain today, and it is the most likely place to see the normally restrained English people show any sort of emotion.

The role of Christianity in the entrapment of the minds of black slaves cannot be overstated. Western orthodox churches supported the slave trade and the colonization of black Africans through Christianity. Many Catholic bishops owned plantations, which used slaves and were very profitable for the church. The money realized from the slave trade would build more churches, schools, hospitals and fund the expeditions of missionaries into Africa. African slaves were from different tribes, countries and beliefs — kidnapped, placed in chains and transported to foreign lands. Possibly their first contact with Christianity would have been from their white captors who told them about a white God in heaven and about Jesus Christ. They would have been told about the paradise called heaven, which they may or may not attain if they worked hard and remained obedient slaves to their white masters. Being in chains, the slaves genuinely felt their reward and freedom would be in heaven, and this calmed some of the desperation they felt about trying to escape or revolt against their captors. In other words, Christianity became and still is a legitimate way of coping with the physical and mental stress of being oppressed.

In time, the white kidnappers and colonizers combined the twin objectives — the use of the Christianity to calm and brainwash the minds of the African slaves into feeling inferior to whites and control of their land and resources. In so doing, the white slave traders, missionaries and colonizers exerted a vice- like psychological grip and control over their African captives.

On the other hand, the black African slaves and colonized people to struggling to cope with the desperate conditions they found themselves in, embraced white Christianity that on one hand, psychologically vilified them but on the other, offered some psychological comfort in the hope that they would be validated by a white Jesus, if not on earth, then in heaven — which has resulted into today's state of uneasy symbiosis.

During the years of legal segregation in America, the Southern white church was at best silent and at worst active in supporting and defending the conduct of the Klan's people who were marauding, intimidating and lynching black people.

Missionary efforts were allowed among slaves because it was believed that it would make them better workers, but the slaves saw through the contradiction and found a liberating dynamic instead.[13]

The Southern American churches began to limit and restrict missionary activities among slaves, forbidding reading instruction and limiting preaching by slave preachers.[14] Most of the white colonialists, explorers and missionaries to Africa were Christians. In the name of Christianity, they brought wave after wave of genocide and suffering to Africans. Such is the hypocrisy of Western Christianity that even as they were preventing freed black slaves from worshipping with them in churches in the West and moving away from the inner cities to the suburbs to get away from the poor black in the West, they were sending flocks of white Christian missionaries to Africa to go and save more African souls.

Segregation and apartheid were sanctioned by white churches and in 1909 Reverend William Montgomery Brown, a bishop of the Protestant Episcopal Church asked the question, *'How shall the colour line be drawn'?*[15]

The white author of the popular Deake's Bible wrote:

'Races must stay separate, especially black and white.' He went on to quote 30 reasons supporting the segregation of black and white people'.[16]

In churches around the Western world today, black churches remain predominantly black and white churches predominantly white. Sunday is still the most segregated day of the week in the West among Western Christians. When the Jamaicans, who settled in England after the Second World War, tried to attend churches to pray with their white Christian folk, they were turned away and asked not to come back by the white priests, who did not want to upset their congregations. These same white missionaries forayed into Africa and India to spread the Gospel.

The post-war African immigrants to Britain had to form their own churches and places of worship, and thus we have Western churches split along colour lines today.

Given the above situation, it is not surprising that when white evangelists visit Africa that they are treated with the utmost respect and command followership far greater than that any indigenous black preacher can command in the west. It is sad to note that many black preachers would fail dismally if they ventured into Europe to spread the Gospel to white folks exclusively, not due to a lack of understanding of the Bible, eloquence or difficulty expressing themselves in English but simply due to colour and race considering that it is the same message of Jesus that they are preaching The inferiority complex or self-hatred, sown by the first Christian missionaries to come to Africa, continues in the sub-conscious indebtedness which black Christians still feel towards white people today.

Since the ideology and practice of Christianity were African in origin, it explains some way why many Africans identified with the Western version of Christianity that had been reworked in the image of the white man, not of God, and brought back to Africa about 1,500 years later. Already familiar with the concepts of monotheism, heaven and hell, Africans took to it like ducks to water.

This new brand of Christianity did not suffer questioning lightly and took a dim view of anyone who questioned the way and manner it was practiced. Hypocrisy was allowed to flourish in the European version of Christianity as it justified slavery, serfdom, and the Spanish inquisition.

Unfortunately, many African evangelist churches continue to exploit the poor and defenceless people and turn a blind eye to societal injustice in general.

Many African pastors have refined the use of modern Christianity to exploit and impoverish their own people. The self-styled Bishop Deya was found guilty of allegedly human trafficking while claiming to miraculously make infertile couples have children. Wanted in Kenya for human trafficking, DNA tests run on the babies and children he was supposed to have brought to life miraculously were not found to match those of the parents in the UK and the real parents in Kenya are still waiting for answers about the whereabouts of their children.[17]

Unquestioning Africans, unaware of the true history of Christianity, allowed the Europeans to use it as a weapon to strip them of their culture and history. The net has been the creation of a permanent inferiority complex towards white people who had visibly cast themselves in the lead roles of the new religion the Africans worshipped.

Sadly, this process is ongoing, as both black and white Christians across the globe have continued to worship in much the same fashion and regard any discussion of the history of Christianity as heresy.

However, while Christianity in the West is clearly in decline, in Africa and amongst its diaspora abroad it increases steadily with time, in almost direct proportion with increasing poverty.

This is not surprising as Western Christianity covered its hands with the blood of innocent people all over the world and was used as a political tool of mass control rather than to create a worldwide family of love under the umbrella of Christianity.

Today, the West relies more on the geopolitical tools of the globalization of capital, puppet governments, of installing 'democracy' and 'humanitarian' interventions which are more relevant means of justifying exploitation.

Even though Western Christianity has fallen from its lead role in subjugation and exploitation of foreign people, it still plays a very powerful behind the scenes role. The Catholic Church is yet to fully publicly apologize for slavery and other atrocities and has continued to shape the ideology of imperialism and lend it their support, both financially and through their extensive political clout.

Unfortunately, many African churches have not been the rallying point that they could have been to stimulate black African growth. Content to remain caricatures of European Christianity, they have diluted their potentially powerful influence by squabbling endlessly over trivia and stimulated division and subdivisions in the African church. In Africa, churches spring up almost daily as many unscrupulous 'pastors' recognize they can personally escape from poverty by fleecing their hapless but hopeful congregations.

This is in sharp contrast to the way churches developed in Europe, where influence and power were concentrated in Rome, allowing the body of the Catholic Church to wield even more power than all the monarchies across Europe.

While black churches and their people are caught up in these endless diversions and subdivisions, they become easy prey for the white imperialists who control the agenda; after all, they have no agenda of their own.

Many African Christians' religious schools concentrate on producing more African people to work in the Western framework of religion, helping to maintain the vice-like grip Western Christianity has on the minds of many black African people. Very little effort has been made to set up African schools of Theology that reflect African culture or practices. Modern black Christians have advanced not a single thought as a working principle in theology to modern European Christianity.

Controlled remotely from Rome, the UK and the US, many Catholic Africans fall in line with the white supremacy agenda for African people without as much as a whimper and usually, unless directed to by their white masters, they do nothing or say nothing to alleviate the glaring suffering and injustice fellow Africans endure.

The Western form of Christianity justified slavery and allowed white Christians to keep black Christian converts as slaves. During slavery, 'good' white Christian folk wore fine clothes, lived in beautiful houses and drove cars while the black African Christian converts toiled as slaves in fields, their mouths padlocked to prevent them from eating any sugar cane.

While white Christian slave owners lived in on earth in relative luxury, and in the knowledge that they had access to opportunities to fulfil their potential if they tried, their black African slaves who became Christians lived in abject poverty, constant fear and waited only for the time when they would be released from the life of physical and mental torture into heaven that afforded them full equality and the pleasures the white Christians slave masters had denied them in life. In time, they would also know that their children and grandchildren would face a similar fate on earth.

Modern white imperialism is still driven by the fundamental tenets of white Christianity which are subjugation and exploitation — and not the real ideology of Christianity which preaches love and equality.

Today, many white Christians sleep comfortably, knowing that they can feel safe in the knowledge that their white privilege can provide in excess of what is required for their needs and those of their families. The fact that these needs are fulfilled through the bloodshed and suffering of innocent people of different countries around the world, appears irrelevant. Many Christians are well aware that what their countries call 'foreign policies' can be distilled down into two words: exploitation and murder and many western right winged Christian groups are actively involved in the process. Without the support of the right-wing fundamental Christian groups in America, George W. Bush nor Donald Trump would never have made it into the white House. George W. Bush claimed to have heard from God before he unleashed his war in Iraq.[18] Many fundamental Christian groups in America are consistently pushing a right-wing neo-conservative message, thinly veiled with biblical verses and end time apocalyptic proclamations and associations all supposed to come from Revelations in the Bible.

Many of the West's foreign policies kill and impoverish millions worldwide yearly, but Western nations have long since given themselves a license to kill.

Operation Iraqi Freedom, or more accurately 'Operation Iraqi Freedom by Death', has taken the lives of over 2 million Iraqi civilians and counting. Only the West has practiced this unsolicited right to enslave, civilise and now 'free' other people, by killing them for many centuries now.

It is important to remind our fundamentalist white Christian brothers and sisters that it was expressly written in the Ten Commandments given to Moses, 'Thou shalt not kill', and another central figure in the Bible, Jesus, never freed a single soul by killing them, rather he gave his own life so that others may be free.[19]

White Christians do not even have to look abroad to find inequality and exploitation; the Western societies in which they live are skewed most definitely in their favour across the board when compared to Africans and other ethnic minorities, from the legal systems, police and financial institutions.

Many of their so-called black Christian brothers and sisters live well below the poverty line, unable to compete fairly whether they are the

African diaspora in Western countries or in African nations impoverished by exploitation by Western countries.

Many African churches have got in on the exploitation act too as they try to emulate their white Christian brothers and strive after a life of luxuries obtained through the exploitation of others and in particular, their own congregations, with no regard to the suffering of Africans like them all over the world.

Crucially, the black converts and imitators of false white Christianity have subconsciously and sometimes consciously led the charge for acceptance into the white community, rather than the fight for true equality, thereby stringing out the suffering of Africans and their diaspora for hundreds of years. It is not surprising that, they too are largely silent about the suffering of millions of their own in Africa and their diaspora all over the worldat the hands of white imperialists.

Pentecostalism is the fastest growing branch of Christianity in any part of the world today and particularly in Africa. In southern Nigeria, churches are mushrooming up all over the place, in parlours, living rooms and even bedrooms. Some streets in Lagos have several churches less than a few doors apart, singing and playing their music louder and louder in an effort to drown out each other and the rival mosques that have begun springing up too.

Unfortunately, despite of Nigeria's obsession with religion, it is still known internationally as one of the most corrupt countries in the world.

In true capitalist style, many pastors and televangelists are exploiting the desperation these poor people feel about their constantly worsening socio-economic situation, in their 'one miracle cures all' approach to life.

Several self styled African pastors and bishops have gone as far as claiming to miraculously raising the dead in the face of widespread problems with disease and poverty of their flock.

It is ironic that the suffering masses have failed to understand that empty promises of material wealth like money, job success and good healh, the main staple of some modern-day pastors in Sunday worship, are all the same things a good government with a stable economy would provide them. Like desperate gamblers in a saloon, they continue to ask these self-serving pastors to roll the 'miracle dice' over and over again.

Miracles; raising the dead, demonic warfare, and exorcism of witchcraft come as intangible extras that can only be found in the churches.

The significance of these intangibles cannot not be underestimated because they give many poverty-stricken Africans an outlet or an excuse for their poverty. However, it wilfully deflects the mind from the culpability of poor government and rampant corruption as the main causes of their ill health and prostration.

So desperate have some Nigerian people become that even after a pastor was arrested for burning alive a member of his congregation as a witch, after she had allegedly 'confessed' to her iniquity, alarmingly, this murderous pastor's congregation was still growing.

The antiquated belief in witchcraft in children, believed to be widespread in southern Nigeria, combined with abject poverty, has led to the most frightening and appalling epidemic of child abuse. Many self-appointed pastors, male and female alike, have attacked the most vulnerable and defenceless members of society…the children.

These children who are alleged to be 'witches', are accused of everything from the poverty of their parents, illness and death in their immediate and extended families, to their own illness and failure to develop. The abused children are not in a position to defend themselves or argue their case. These children are then systematically physically and emotionally abused into 'confessing' being a witch following which they are further tortured, maimed and even killed.

A 'Dispatches' documentary by Channel 4 titled, 'Africa's Witch Children', painfully exposed this practice to the world.[20]

Many church members refuse to acknowledge that it is hardly miraculous that their prosperity-preaching pastor is getting richer on the tax-free proceeds of the church, while the congregation is correspondingly getting poorer. They hold on in vain for their own personal miracle buoyed on by the apparent 'success' of their prosperity pastor and continue to tithe and donate the little they do have, freely. The truth is that the prosperity pastors are being paid to give their congregations what they came there to get: hope.

In return for providing 'hope', these selfish pastors live lavishly and travel around the world in private jets.

Some Africans, miseducated in Western Christianity, can be some of the most obedient servants to the West and even the most dangerous members of the African people for their own people. They constitute some of the most dysfunctional and mentally inferior Africans on the African continent and in the diasporas. They often openly despise other Africans for their lack of Westernization and are prone to religious fundamentalism. They cherish and love the white supremacy system to the point of which they will, and have in the past, taken up arms against their own people in the defence of and support of Western culture and ideology.

All people were created equal in the eyes of God. Yet the reality is that inequality and intolerance spawned by the Catholic Church and practiced in virtually every Western country is truly alive and well. The seed of hypocrisy and greed that was grown in the Catholic Church blossomed into racism and imperialism, which is devastating the lives of billions of people all over the world.

Africans created the true concepts of modern Christianity, and it is perhaps time they took back ownership of this great religion of deep and great ideologies, that has been subverted by the West for other means. All true Christians of whatever race or colour, who believe in being their brother's keepers and in the true equality of all men, must wrest Christianity back from the hands of white imperialists or supremacists, by staying true to the real teaching and works of the real Jesus Christ. We need not mourn the demise of European Christianity, as many of the original founding principles of Christianity remain sound, and they give us the foundation we need to redevelop and build up this African theosophy anew.

We are all the children of God and therefore have God consciousness within us. It is futile to seek and identify or express our spirituality solely in the temporary materialism of the world today. The spiritual fulfilment we all cherish in our various religions and belief systems already resides within us and following the middle path of life will lead us inexorably to the God consciousness within.

We have glimpsed the past, now we must order our footsteps for the future and reconstruct Christianity into the great vessel of inner spiritual development and the great civilizing tool it once was.

PART NINE:
SLAVERY ENTRENCHED

CHAPTER FIFTY

EUROCENTRISM

"As historians, it is our responsibility to convey an accurate account of what has transpired in our past. We must at all costs refrain from the same tactics employed against us by the European historian for, as we have seen this approach leaves a void which is easily filled with the truth, making it easy to refute all lies and scholarship which is based on deception." **Wayne. B. Chandler.**[1]

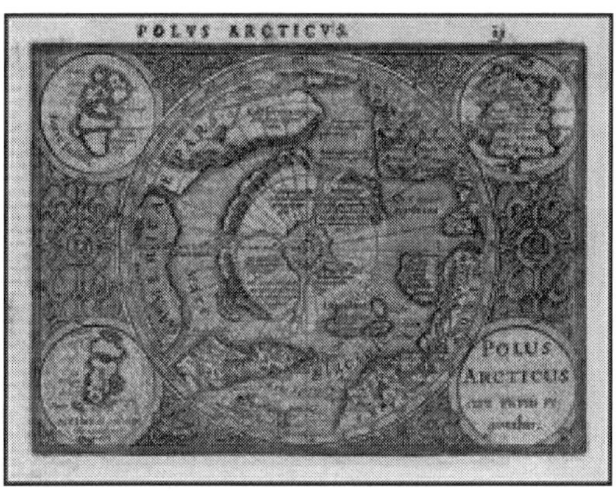

A picture is worth a thousand words and the European Mercator map of the world graphically illustrates how the European mind at a time visualized the world. Europe, a land mass less than half the size of the African continent, was seen as the 'world' not just graphically but also in the minds of the Europeans at that time. Other continents and geographical sites were barely represented so that the expansive map of Europe could take centre stage.

Ward L. Kaiser wrote:

'Maps send powerful messages. If a picture is worth a thousand words, a map of the world is worth a thousand pictures as we try to understand our place in the world. The Mercator map… enlarges those areas of the world historically inhabited by whites, shifts those same areas to the heart and centre of the world's stage, where they do not belong, and minimizes the importance of… what we designate the Third world.'[2]

Even when the geography of Africa became better known, Joseph Conrad's map of Africa depicted vast swathes of the African continent as occupied by either wild animals or the location of strategic resources.[3]

In the modern parlance of today, it is not uncommon for Western media to refer to the opinions of a few Western countries as 'world opinion'. It is usually sufficient to describe the US and UK position alone, as the 'West's or 'world opinion'.

As early as the 13th and 14th centuries, Africans were already regarded as repulsive and inferior in Europe, no doubt aided by false and negative impressions related to them by early sailors and explorers.

The Spanish referred to Africans as 'Moreno savages' with temples of gold and English sailors spoke of 'blacke Soules' with mounds of glistening ivory.

When some Britons finally initially encountered some Africans on their expedition, they wrote:

"And entering in [river] we see

A number of blacke Soules,

Whose likeliness seemed to be, their captaine comes to me as naked as my naile

Not having witte or honestie to cover once his tail."[4]

In the Middle Ages, negative views and impressions of black African people from the classical period became accumulated and expressed from the prevailing religious cultural viewpoint of the Catholic Church.

During the Middle Ages, a new phenomenon emerged, where deformed births and unfamiliar, strange people from foreign lands were referred to as 'acts of God' or 'monstra'.

Friedmann stated:

"In the early middle ages, monstra defined whole populations of people with physical appearances and phenotypes that differed from those found in Europe."[5]

It was highly significant for Africans, whose skin colour was considered by many in Europe, as a form of monstra.

"When filtered through Christian belief, with its light/dark, good /evil symbolism it was really easy to think of blacks as monstra."[6]

In addition, Malik buttressed this point and stated:

"…in the isolated, ignorant world of feudal Europe, Africans were often portrayed as devils, monsters or apes."[7]

Paul Freedman wrote:

"The medieval writers commonly describe the serfs as stupid, malformed, grotesque, dwelling in filth and excrement, and closer to beasts than humans."[8]

Thus, the word 'black' became a byword for negative attitudes and negative black imagery all over Europe.

The word 'black' is a highly symbolic code for negative or evil in the West, and Europeans have always sought to hold on to the term 'black' when describing Africans. The Oxford English dictionary describes at least ten negative adjectives connected to the word black [Black mood, black humour, black deeds, black lies, black look, black-amoor, black death, black- guard, black-leg, etc.]. It is important to note that whether they called Africans, Negro, nigger, Moreno, blackamoor, or even just black, as is commonly used today, they all mean the same thing and are highly concentrated and symbolic codes for everything that the European and North American feels is negative.

Modern Western societies today still universally hold the colour black as symbolic of undesirable objects, situations, and emotional and psychological states.

The devaluation of the colour black predisposes African people and other non-whites who live within Western societies to negative stereotypes and attitudes towards non-white people. The description of people as black or white in itself polarizes the Western society because the very words 'black or white' describe polar opposites.

In medieval Europe a commonly held belief was that all humans were originally white, and the black skin of Africans was seen as a form degeneration of humankind.

Some believed that Africans had a special skin layer that turned black after birth; others thought that African mothers painted themselves black, which had caused a prenatal influence on the colour the offspring. Europeans took white skin as the universal Caucasian standard of beauty and described Africans as ugly, disfigured and cursed.

Africans, on the other hand, possessed little bias towards Europeans and largely saw them as foreigners who had lost their way. The Yoruba name for Europeans translates into 'peeled man'.

West African poetry reveals evidence of African hospitality and generosity:

"The winds were roaring and a white man fled
The rains of the night descended on his head
The poor white man sat down beneath our tree
Weary and faint, and far from home was he
For him, no mother fills with milk the bowl,
No wife prepares the bread to cheer his soul,
Pity the poor white man who sought our tree;
No wife, no mother and no home has he."

Omosegbun 1995.[9]

In time, Africans would come to regret their open-door policy, hospitality and generosity.

The roots of white supremacy and Eurocentrism were firmly established by the deception of old Jewish scholars and the founding fathers of the Catholic Church, by giving Caucasians a false sense of moral and spiritual superiority over people from other lands.

Ideas of European superiority grew on the foundation of the Jewish legend of Noah and curse of Ham. This story began with Josephus, a Jewish scholar of the 1st century BC. This legend became firmly established in the Catholic Church of Christian Europe by the 5th century.

This legend describes Europeans to be the descendants of Japheth, who was promised dominion over the children of Shem and Ham, then considered Asians and Africans. Africans were defined as the Hamites and according to this legend were destined to serve both Europe and Asia.

However, during the Greek and then the Roman Empires, it was clear that black African people were seen as human beings, if not equals. Tales of great African empires, with limitless wealth were rife, and trade was taking place between Africans and Arabs through the trans-Saharan routes, and goods including slaves were on sale as far as India.

The Greeks and then the Romans were fascinated by the great empires of Egypt, the cradle of civilization, and for several centuries ruled by black Nubian pharaohs. Black Nubian women were fabled for their beauty, and Nubian warriors were feared, respected and sought after as mercenaries to help fight battles.

Septimus Severus, emperor of Rome, was an African man, originally descended from Libya. In AD 250, some black Roman soldiers were said to have been in Britain defending Hadrian's Wall.[10]

Many black African people had filtered into Britain as musicians, workers and slaves. When Queen Elizabeth I decreed that the blackamoors should be deported from England as they were becoming too many, there may have been up to twenty-five thousand black Africans in Britain.

The first Europeans to encounter African people and kingdoms did not find a rabble but large organized cities, not too dissimilar to those they had left behind. However, as the European countries developed, they became increasingly race conscious and nationalistic. In particular, England, Spain, Germany and France strove to establish dominance, expand their territories to different countries, by becoming nationalistic. This would result in increasingly bitter and bloody wars with each other as European countries ranged further afield in search of resources. Their quest for resources took them to the Americas and Africa with grave consequences for the original inhabitants of these lands. European wars stimulated an arms race leading to the production of more lethal weapons and battle-tested troops.

The European wars developed their self-image and a sense of nationalism. Europeans, therefore, drew not only the notion of being the 'chosen ones of God' but also on their claims to nationality, superior geography and biological superiority.

Europeans set about making distinctions between themselves and all others in all aspects of life, religion, culture and biology. Naturally, this tendency would translate into systems of legal discrimination and eventually led them to genocide. From as early as the 14th century European cities and towns would begin to be discriminate against their native populations, especially in Eastern Europe, Wales, and Ireland.

Laws were made to segregate people by race, language and cultural practices. The languages and cultural practices of these native populations were banned and marriages between the 'superior' European conquering races and the natives were prohibited.

The systematic denigration of Africans, described as the descendants of Ham and an inferior and savage race began in earnest after the mid-15th century. Dark or black skin would become the main symbol of all negative racial characteristics in European eyes. When Spain introduced the ban on enslavement of Indians in 1542, it was not extended to Africans.[11]

The systematic denigration of Africans has not stopped until present day; the West has accumulated an enormous number of derogatory references to black Africans in all spheres of their lives.

As European ideas of superiority developed, it was only logical that Europeans would decide to find a way to attribute to all human development to themselves.

In the old conventional view of the origins of ancient Greek culture, much credit was given to the Egyptians and Phoenicians.

However, from the 18th and 19th centuries, for European racists and anti-Semitics, this was simply intolerable, and many scholars worked to destroy the ancient model of Greek civilization.

Karl Orfried Müller, a German scholar, discredited the clear links between the language and culture of the ancient Egyptians and early Greeks.[12]

"If it had been scientifically proven that blacks were biologically incapable of civilization. How could they explain ancient Egypt, which was inconveniently placed in Africa."[13]

The first impulse was to deny that Egypt created a true civilization, and later that Egyptians were black. By the 19th and 20th centuries, most European historians denied both.

European scholars began to systematically move the origins of civilization away from Africa and the Middle East. In so doing, they had extended European history backwards over 5,000 years and had managed to appropriate technology and innovations from all over the world. In fact, the European history of development following the Renaissance only lasted about two thousand years.

The appropriation of knowledge would, in European minds, reinforce the idea that Europe had been the only centre of development and technology in the world. This view supported the European notion that the majority of the people around the world were passive recipients of Western technology. The European version of world history in our literature and culture has been used to create and to sustain this myth. This process undermined an equal and fair assessment of the global multiregional origins and history of science and technology.

The transfer of technology from the Africans in Egypt to ancient Greeks has been omitted from Western history. Euclid was described as a Greek instead of an African. Thales, the declared father of science, and Pythagoras, who both have partial Asian parentage became honorary Europeans.

Today, there are over 8,000 medical eponyms in use since modern medicine developed, and 99% are named after Europeans.[14]

In many cases, the names of outstanding scientists were westernized, in order to hide their non-Western origins.

The ancient Egyptian arithmetical and medicinal documents became known as the Rhind, Ebers and Edwin Smith papyri.

A procedure to relocate dislocated shoulders, described by Egyptians over 2,000 years ago, was named the Kocher's manoeuvre, after a German professor.

Halley's Comet is named after a European, even though the Chinese identified the comet over 2,500 years ago

In some cases, fictitious European inventors were created to accommodate the rewriting and reworking of history. Important historical dates were manipulated to fit all this within the time of the European Renaissance.

Dr Emeagwali wrote:

"The stirrup, the stern post rudder, the lateen sail, the abacus, the pendulum, the game of chess, the axle, the bow drill, the chisel and the wedge are all of non-European origin. The latter did for building technology what the Mesopotamian and the African sail boats, barge, freight and wheeled vehicles date for navigation and communication. Add to this the Persian [Iranian] Windmill, the predecessors of the modern water turbine, and we have an array of devices, which constitute important landmarks in the history of power generation. Glass, cement, enamel and porcelain; the nail and saw, the printed book and the compass, all join this list. The check [cheque] is not of European origin. Arab traders pioneered this important commercial device."[15]

Of no less importance was the development of military technology. The gunpowder acquired from China, navigation skills and shipbuilding from North Africans and armour from Mesopotamia, built up the military capability of Europeans.

The West has always defined itself as civilized because of their technological mastery over nature and this in itself was simply borne out of a necessity to survive the harsh conditions that they lived in.

However, the drive for technological mastery over nature was accelerated by the incessant European wars fought to establish dominance over land and resources. For several centuries, Europe had not seen up to five consecutive years of peace, and engaged in all forms of warfare.

Some European wars were more famous than others were, like the Napoleonic Wars and the First and Second World Wars.

The so-called 'World Wars' were basically European wars, fought on a global scale, using foreign people, their land and their resources. These wars resulted in a tremendous loss of human life and human suffering, but they also resulted in much Western military and civilian technological advancement. Technological advancements, primarily for military use, have been adapted for civilian use in the last century, through the drive to modernize warfare and produce newer and more lethal weapons of mass destruction.

European wars also forged the use of closer union of organized political and economic power into the industrialized production of military equipment, into the industrial-military complex that prevails today. This development also facilitated Western capitalism, economic theories and banking.

Older civilizations around the world, like Africans and the Native Americans, dovetailed their development with nature. They respected the environments and included worship in some of the wildlife and fauna around them. The Native Americans, for instance, had a great deal of respect for the wild buffalo on which they depended.

When they killed the buffalo for meat, they utilized virtually every bit of the carcass. They used the meat for food; the bones were shaped into hunting implements and hides for clothes. In contrast, when the American cowboys came along they drove the buffalo nearly into extinction by wanton mass slaughter.

Western societies defined civilizations that did not seek technological mastery over nature as inferior. The alleged inferiority of non-whites has been touted as justification of the global system of inequality and privilege for Europeans and North Americans.

Westerners remain convinced that the ability to cultivate or improve the landscape, process the natural resources and use the technology to accumulate wealth and build their military, constitutes superiority. They were also able to develop concentrated political power which they used to dominate the social environment. Other societies, which were not based on the drive to accumulate wealth and power and develop technologies for that purpose, were then classified as being closer to nature, less civilized and less fully human than those which were. This ideology of imperialism and euro centrism has dominated the minds of Western civilization for over 500 years and justified in their minds their imperial ideology over non-Western civilizations of whom they believe they have the God-given right to dominate and exploit at will.

What the West has conveniently overlooked is that many of the civilizations, where necessary, have developed according to the challenges they faced. For example, Egypt centred its civilization around the river

Nile and developed complex irrigation systems in order to harness the rich soil and water the river provided. They also went on to develop complex astrological geometry in an attempt to understand flooding some of the Nile to prepare for times of possible famine.

Non-Western people who lived by the sea became seafaring and built ships with which they traded as far as China and India. The Moorish sailors who occupied Spain would leave behind the blueprints of shipbuilding and navigation on which Europe would develop their own.

It appears that the ancient Greeks were the first to acquire consciousness of their distinctness from so-called barbarians. A sense of superiority would begin to develop in later years during their battles with the Persians.

The famous philosopher Aristotle argued in his book Politics:

'That Barbarians are deficient in reasoning and lacks the ability to govern, and hence they are by nature fit to be slaves. The Greeks were born to be free and govern others.

He continued:

'the Greeks combined the virtues of Asians and Europeans, while avoiding their defects. If only they were united they would rule over everyone.'[16]

In the modern interpretation of Western superiority, the control of the production and dissemination of knowledge are key mechanisms through which it works. This facilitates the globalization of Western capitalism and the control of the media, through which they can manipulate the minds of billions of people around the world.

In defining their self-image, the West not only drew on differences in religion, culture and geography. Early in the development of racism, the claims of superiority have been framed in biological metaphors, which gained greater salience over time.

Natural differences in ideology would in time translate into systems of illegal discrimination and genocide. Christianity, initially an African religion, would acquire European identity, starting around the 7th century.

This was largely the result of two parallel processes. Firstly, even though the German invaders destroyed the Roman Empire, they embraced

Latin Christianity and carried it to the northern regions of Europe. As a result, the political unity of the defunct Roman Empire was replaced by a deeper cultural unity based on Christianity, a common language [Latin], and a hierarchy of priests centred in Rome. At the same time, the Islamic empire conquered Christian domains outside Europe. A politically segmented Europe increasingly emphasized its Christian identity as a means of unifying against a common enemy. This new Christian identity found expression in the wars against heretics, persecution of Jews, and the *'demonization of Islam.'*[17]

As ideas of Western biological and spiritual superiority flourished in Europe, they crystallized into movements that expressed themselves through religion, science, literature and arts.

One such movement was that of the 'Aryans' made infamous by Nazi Germany. They were supposed to be a white, blue-eyed and blonde race of people descended from the mythical land of Atlantis.

The supremacy of the Nordic Aryan was first proclaimed in a book [Inequality of Human Races, 1854] 35 years before Hitler was born, by a French author and diplomat Count Joseph Arthur de Gobineau. Gobineau picked up the ideas set out 60 years earlier by the English philologist, Sir William Jones, who stated that in antiquity there had been a great and pure Aryan race.

Gobineau postulated that Aryans were superior in the past and therefore they were still so in the present. He propounded the doctrine that different races are innately unequal in talent, worth and ability. Gobineau argued that only the *'white Aryan races'* were capable of creating culture and that the *'darker races'* only borrowed. He proclaimed that races change their innate character only by crossbreeding and that the white race was *'exhausted'* because their racial composition was no longer pure.

The prevalence of right wing nationalism at the time led most white intellectuals to accept Gobineau's view. Each attempted to prove that their own national group had preserved its pristine racial purity and virtue the most. In France, racialist interpreters [Pictet in 1859 and Lapouge in 1899] *'proved' the innate superiority of the 'French race'*. In Great Britain and the United States, there were, 'numerous supporters of the view that the *'Anglo-Saxons'* were the human cream of the *'racial'* crop; among these were the British historians, J. A. Froude [1818–1894] and J. R. Green [1837–1883], and the later American writers, Madison Grant, Homer Lea, and Lothrop Stoddard.'[18] In Russia, racialist publications like Nicolay Danilevsky's pan-Slavism 'Russia and Europe' [1869], coupled with a nationalistic populist movement, proclaimed the *'Slavs as one of the finest products of civilization'*.[19] In Germany and Austria, pride in their alleged Aryan origins also found its proponents in men like Wagner, who declared the superiority of the German race.

During Hitler's period in Vienna, race theories numbered in the hundreds. However it was the Aryan ancestry theory which would attract a wide and popular following. It was held that prehistoric, *'Nordic Aryans... were the chief ancestors of most Europeans and most white Americans'*.[20] These ancient people spoke a primary language called Aryan [now called Indo-European] from which all dominant European languages originated. Since it was acceptable to experts at the time to deduce that people who had once spoken the same language were of the same race, it was concluded that these, *'taller and fairer Aryan-speaking people'* originated in the northern part of today's black Sea area around 9000 BC. Around 5000 BC these Aryan tribes had moved into North Russia and Central Europe. By 2500 BC, they had spread throughout all parts of Europe, breeding with the thinly spread tribes of shorter *'dark white'* races and in time developing their own customs, religion, appearances and different versions of the Aryan language.

It was estimated that only 7% of Europe was populated by non-Aryan language, race groups, such as Ural-Altaic [Hungarians, Turks, etc.], Semitic [Jews, Arabs, etc.], and other *'darker-skinned'* types who, for the most part, had followed the Aryans into Europe. However, it was propounded that *'three great racial groups'* accounted for 93% of the total population of Europe. First were the Nordic or Germanic races, which, for the most part, consisted of the Germans, English, Dutch, Swedes, Norwegians, Danes, some Swiss and *'probably'* the Albanians and the *'hopelessly mixed'* Greeks. Second was the *'Latin race'*, which included the French, Italian, Spanish, Portuguese, and Romanian. And finally, the *'Slavic races'* consisting mainly of the Russians, Czechs, Yugoslavs, Bulgarians, and Poles.[21]

Joseph Arthur de Gobineau wrote:

"Indeed, the human species seems to have a very great difficulty in raising itself above a rudimentary type of organization; the transition to a more complex state is made only by those groups of tribes that are eminently gifted. I may cite, in support of this, the actual condition of a large number of communities spread throughout the world. These backward tribes, especially the Polynesian Negroes, the Samoyedes and others in the far north, and the majority of the African races, have never been able to shake themselves free from their impotence; they live side by side in complete independence of each other. The stronger massacre the weaker, the weaker try to move as far away as possible from the stronger. This sums up the political ideas of these embryo societies, which have lived on in their imperfect state, without possibility of improvement, as long as the human race itself. It may be said that these miserable savages are a very small part of the earth's population. Granted; but we must take account of all the similar peoples who have lived and disappeared. Their number is incalculable, and certainly includes the vast majority of the pure-blooded yellow and black races.

'If then we are driven to admit that for a very large number of human beings it has been, and always will be, impossible to take even the first step towards civilization; if, again, we consider that these peoples are scattered over the whole face of the earth under the most varying conditions of climate and environment, that they live indifferently in the tropics, in the temperate zones, and in the Arctic circle, by sea, lake, and river, in the depths of the forest, in the grassy plains, in the arid deserts, we must conclude that a part of mankind, is in its own nature stricken with a paralysis, which makes it forever unable to take even the first step towards civilization, since it cannot overcome the natural repugnance, felt by men and animals alike, to a crossing of blood.

'Leaving these tribes, that are incapable of civilization, on one side, we come, in our journey upwards, to those, which understand that if they wish to increase their power and prosperity, they are absolutely compelled, either by war or peaceful measures, to draw their neighbours within their sphere of

influence. War is undoubtedly the simpler way of doing this. Accordingly, they go to war. But, when the campaign is finished, and the craving for destruction is satisfied, some prisoners are left over; these prisoners become slaves, and as slaves, work for their masters. We have class distinctions at once, and an industrial system: the tribe has become a little people. This is a higher rung on the ladder of civilization, and is not necessarily passed by all the tribes, which have been able to reach it; many remain at this stage in cheerful stagnation.

'But, there are others, more imaginative and energetic, whose ideas soar beyond mere brigandage. They manage to conquer a great territory, and assume rights of ownership not only over the inhabitants, but also over their land. From this moment, a real nation has been formed. The two races often continue for a time to live side by side without mingling; and yet, as they become indispensable to each other, as a community of work and interest is gradually built up, as the pride and rancour of conquest begin to ebb away, as those below naturally tend to rise to the level of their masters, while the masters have a thousand reasons for allowing, or even for promoting, such a tendency, the mixture of blood finally takes place, the two races cease to be associated with distinct tribes, and become more and more fused into a single whole.'"[22]

Even though Christianity became the established European religion, many European battles would be waged around issues of religion; for example, the English Civil War, or the Wars of the Roses. Science was steadily making a comeback in Europe after the Dark Ages and its progress would be greatly accelerated by the incessant wars.

Science became closely linked to religion and European scientists categorised people by race, placing the white man at the top of the ladder. Motivated by religious imagery, biblical texts and anecdotal stories of brutal, barbaric, cannibalistic races, they placed the black man at the bottom of their list. Jews, gypsies and the Irish also shared the lower rungs of this scientific ladder.

Taking all this into account, the unsuspecting Africans were thus met by a racist European explorer, filled with national pride and confident of his racial superiority. The European explorers were keen on establishing a name for themselves, greedy for the untold treasures yet to be tapped by them. They were well armed and battle-hardened in ways the unsuspecting Africans could never have imagined.

To clear their conscience for the plundering, pillaging and raping that was to follow, they claimed they were civilizing *'barbaric African rabble'* and introducing them to Christianity, which meant saving their souls. In the religious-based societies that existed in Europe at that time these were truly noble ideals. Despite the savagery that they wrought upon foreign people those who executed the exploitation occupy prominent places in European history today.

There was no way these Africans could have had any idea about the global European wars for world domination and the scramble for foreign territory that was going on in Europe. It is most likely that the Africans would have assumed that these European expeditions were just for trading purposes only, just like they had done for hundreds of years before.

They would have had no knowledge of the demise of the Native Americans, first to the Spanish and later to other Europeans, to the extent that some of the civilizations like the Maya would become extinct.

As warm and friendly people, most Africans welcomed these early European explorers. They were also in awe of their white skin, which many tribes felt had spiritual connotations. European weaponry would also have been impressive in helping reinforcing these ideas of Western superiority. In tow were the white missionaries who spread Christianity with the *'white'* Jesus Christ; white imagery; in essence, the message was: become Christians, obey these white men and go to heaven. WhereverAfrican natives did not accept the European overtures, they were killed and those remaining made an offer they could not refuse. Many African people unwillingly took up Christianity but their descendants would later become staunch Christians. It is not surprising that many of these African natives, though Christian, continued to practice their own forms of religion largely out of sight of their colonial masters. European explorers presented a difficult problem for the African indigenes, powerful *'white man'* with a strong God, with strange but lethal firearms and resources to back them up. It is no wonder an African inferiority complex soon developed.

The Islamic states, having their own unifying religion, would be 'divided and ruled' by European-imposed puppet leaders.

CHAPTER FIFTY ONE

THE PSYCHOLOGY OF SLAVERY

"When you control a man's thinking, you do not have to worry about his actions. You do not have to tell him to stand here or go yonder. He will find his "proper place" and will stay in it. You do not need to send him through the back door. He will go without being told. In fact, if there is no back door, he will cut one for his special benefit. His education makes this necessary." **Carter G. Woodson**[1]

"Fear, awe, and obedience became interwoven into the very nature of the slave." **Frederick Douglass,** My Bondage and My Freedom[2]

Simply put, a slave is a human being who lives under the complete control of another human being. This definition of slavery has remained constant in both the ancient and modern practice of slavery because all the characteristics of a slave, including the loss of personal identity, liberty, lack of social freedom or political expression and total dependence on the slave masters for sustenance have remained the same. In chattel slavery; the slaves, their children and all that they produce belong to the slave masters, to be used and abused, as they choose.

However, in reality, living in another person's paradigm, with limited opportunities for freedom of expression, self-determination and self-actualisation represents actual or relative slavery. It is no wonder that the International Labour Organization [ILO] has described the socio-economic conditions of the world's poorest people living in underdeveloped countries as a form of modern-day economic slavery.

It is important to appreciate that the process of slavery only begins with the loss of physical freedom and is characterized from start to finish by the psychological process of bringing the mind of the slaves under the control of their slave masters. white slave owners called the process of facilitating physical and psychological control, 'seasoning'. Without the proper 'seasoning process' the slave is no longer a material asset but could even be a dangerous liability.

Today, white imperialism is the only global, effective and functioning form of racism in the world today. white racism forms the basis of the white supremacy power structure and modern-day economic slavery. It operates in all areas of human endeavour — social, political, economic, religious, sexual and military.

During the transatlantic slave trade and the colonial era, white imperialism and racism was a badge worn with pride. Europeans openly viewed imperialism as proof of their innate superiority over non-white people and the outward symbolic expression of an advanced civilization.

The 'political correctness' of today's world requires the white global system of racism and imperialism hypocritically to masquerade behind revolving euphemisms. It constantly shapes itself and shifts to suit the prevailing conditions and sentiments. In so doing, it avoids provoking an intense reaction to the harsh reality of their exploitation and denigration from the exploited masses. white imperialism has always remained single-minded about fulfilling its desired objective — the creation and maintenance of a global system of white domination and exploitation.

The system adapts cleverly, not just to avoid producing an intense adverse reaction on the part of the people it is exploiting but also to create a hypocritical veil for the perpetrators to wear — so that 'the mind does not appreciate what the hands are doing'. Without appreciating the overarching objectives of white supremacy or imperialism, many non-white and white people alike, fail to see the real picture of the jigsaw of white supremacy. They have difficulty seeing its complex mosaic as one cohesive whole.

Racism or prejudice can be defined as a rigid attitude, which is usually negative, towards a particular group of people, based on characteristics which are assumed to be common to all members of the group. However, not all prejudice is negative, and anecdotally it is possible to generalise that many Africans have a positive prejudice towards white people. Many Africans automatically attribute a host of positive attributes to the possession of white skin. They make an automatic assumption of Caucasian honesty, integrity, morality and technical ability however unrealistic and unfounded in the face of facts. Correspondingly, many Europeans harbour negative prejudice towards Africans and judge the ability of all Africans based on their skin colour alone. They often generally assume Africans to be lazy, loud and late, without knowing anything about them.

A stereotype is only a mental image of a person. It may not relate to the individual's character but rather to what we infer about that person. All human beings are prone to stereotyping because our brains need to structure and compartmentalise a wide range of information in order to allow effective and prompt decision-making.

As social creatures, human beings are quick to categorize other people into 'us' and 'them'. The phrase 'first impressions count' originates from this old human tendency spontaneously to jump to conclusions about another person's character and ability. Even though it is possible rapidly and roughly to assess people and situations, the caveat is that instant assessments and 'stereotypes' only provide a 'guesstimate' rather than an accurate assessment of another person's ability and character. The mental image of the person or people we are trying to assess is more about what we infer about them than who they really are. For instance, when Europeans generalise that blonde-haired women are dumb and redheads are hot-tempered, they are expressing a flawed but commonly held stereotype.

Given this human predilection, we all develop our own highly personalised way of looking at the world, something which is called 'personal constructs'. People often interpret other people's behaviour and draw conclusions about them based on their own personal construct. Our personal constructs are a distillation of our own socialization within our families and the wider society and can be as rigid or as flexible as we choose them to be. In general, a narrow-minded or bigoted view of the world suggests a narrow personal construct and a broad-minded view of life and the world around would suggest a broader personal construct.

People also tend to develop 'event scripts' or schema. These are knowledge structures based on previous experiences or events. Personal experience can often be generalized to assume the behaviour of a whole group. For instance, a Caucasian mugged by a black youth begins to extrapolate that all black youths are muggers or robbers.

Psychologically, racism tends to express itself in three main ways: affective, behavioural, and cognitive. An example of affective expression would be the negative emotions we feel. How we treat others or discriminate against them is a behavioural expression. What we think about others or how we stereotype them is a cognitive expression. Stereotyping overrides the affective and behavioural expressions of racism because it pre-sets or primes the subconscious and conscious mind and dictates how these inner feelings are expressed.

Many psychological studies have been carried out with a view to unmasking the latent prejudice or racism in Western societies. In one study, psychologists asked the participants to watch a video of two people having a conversation in which one pushed the other. The psychologists manipulated the race of the actors — two whites, two blacks, or a white and a black. Participants who saw the black actor doing the shoving rated his behaviour as more violent, compared with those who saw the white actor doing the shoving.[3]

These results provide evidence of prejudice because they show that participants interpreted the behaviour they saw based on the actor's colour or race. This single feature was enough to affect their judgement or perception.

Outwardly, it would seem that the economic imperatives of financial gain and material wealth sufficiently explain why Europeans industrialized the process of slavery. However, on closer analysis, there are psychological drivers for this imperative that run much deeper. The neurotic drive of white imperialism to achieve superiority and dominance at all costs masks a deep, inner sense of psychological inadequacy. This psychological inadequacy is often expressed as an almost uncontrollable aggression towards and an irrational hatred of all non-white people in general, black

Africans in particular.

Dr Frances Cress Welsing, a prominent African American psychiatrist, argued in her book, Cress Theory of Color and Confrontation, that even though the outward stated and apparently obvious economic and political motivators for Western capitalism appear to drive their quest for technological, military and political hegemony, this is not so. Instead it resides much deeper. Dr Welsing postulated that it stems from a deep sense of psychological inadequacy related to an anxiety over colour and numerical inadequacy. This has repeatedly driven white imperialists and supremacists to genocide and genocidal imperatives against non-whites in the relatively short period of truly global human interactions.[4]

White anxiety about being 'over-run or swamped' by non-white races has been repeatedly articulated as a major concern by most white conservative and right-wing political groups and parties for over two hundred years. Paradoxically, it is quite clear that having dark skin colour is very important to the conscious and subconscious psychological wellbeing of many Caucasian people. A survey in Britain claimed that up to 50% of the British population felt that having a tan made them look healthier. Every year, billions of dollars are spent by white people on make-up, creams and lotions, all with the aim of acquiring some colour. [6]

In support of her 'Cress' theory Dr Frances Cress Welsing cited the 'Freudian slips' made by two well-known American authors, Mark Twain and the Edgar Rice Burroughs, in relation to skin colour. Mark Twain, the iconic American author, who wrote the popular classic, The Adventures of Tom Sawyer, gave some insight into the workings of white minds and the power of our external appearance to shape their minds. In a collection of articles called 'Mark Twain on the Damned Human Race', he cited:

"Nearly all black and brown skins are beautiful, but beautiful white skin is rare. How rare, one may learn by walking down a street in Paris, New York or London on a weekday – particularly an unfashionable street – and keeping count of the satisfactory complexions encountered in the course of a mile. Where dark complexions are massed, they make whites look bleached out, unwholesome, and sometimes, frankly, ghastly. I could notice this as a boy, down South in the slavery days before the war. The splendid black

satin skin of the South African Zulus of Durban seemed to me to come very close to perfection. I can see those Zulus yet… handsome and intensely black creatures, moderately clothed in loose summer stuffs whose snowy whiteness made the black all the blacker by contrast. Keeping that group in mind, I can compare those complexions with the white ones streaming past this London window now… the advantage is with the Zulu I think. He starts off with a beautiful complexion, and it will last him through. And as for the Indian, brown – firm, smooth, blemish less, pleasant and restful to the eye, afraid of no colour, harmonizing with all colours, and adding grace to them all – I think there is no sort of chance for the average white complexion against that rich and perfect tint."[7]

This deep sense of colour comparison was also inadvertently articulated by Edgar Rice Burroughs, author of the bestselling Tarzan of the Apes series in 1929. As the story goes, 'Tarzan', which he explained meant 'white skin' in the language of the apes, was a British baby, Lord Greystoke, who was abandoned in the African jungle aged just nine months when his parents died. He was adopted and taken care of by the great 'apes' in Africa. He wrote:

"The sun beating upon his naked body had no such effect upon his skin as would the sun of the outer world under like conditions. But it did impart to him a new confidence similar to that which he would have felt if he found his lost apparel. And in this fact he saw what he believed to be the real cause of his first embarrassment at his nakedness — it had been the whiteness of his skin that had made him seem so naked by contrast with other creatures, for this whiteness had suggested softness and weakness, arousing within him a disturbing sense of inferiority; but now as he took on his heavy coat of tan and his feet became hardened and accustomed to the new conditions, he walked no longer in constant realization of his nakedness."[8]

While a deep-seated sense of numerical and colour inadequacy may drive the white quest for supremacy, many other psychological interactions exist around the phenomenon of human slavery. In 1807, the famous philosopher, Hegel, outlined the main psychological master-slave paradigm that governs the interactions of slaves and their masters everywhere. His thesis, 'Phenomenology of Mind', has influenced the thinking of many philosophers, including Karl Marx, Sigmund Freud, Jean-Paul Sartre and Frantz Fanon. Hegel argued that man only becomes conscious of himself through the recognition of another person. The one who is recognized but does not recognize becomes the master; and the one who is not recognized but recognizes, becomes the slave.

He also argued that the master in gaining the recognition of his slave but not recognizing him or her, reduces the slave to a mere instrument of his will. Thus, the slave, lives only as an extension of his master and is a convenience to help fulfil his material and psychological needs. However, in so doing, the master becomes alienated from human labour and loses the critical means of transforming himself and the environment. The slave is forced to work on objects and transform them with his labour, which in turn crystallise and reflect his humanity. Hegel argues that ultimately, it is the slave not the master, who is the real victor, and is self-actualised.

This is arguable, as the slave masters may also feel self-actualised by the labour of the slaves. The slave master not only owns the slave but all the output of his or her labour. The clear outline of Hegel's slave master and slave paradigm can be seen in the relationship between the West and the rest of the world, especially in Africa. The struggle of the white slave masters and their African slaves, white colonial masters and their colonised people and our present paradigm of neo-colonialism, is encapsulated in the master-slave dialectic.

From the outset, the process of European slavery, colonialism, and capitalism was a struggle of adversaries unequal in military strength, ideological motivation and intent. The white imperialist adopted the first principle — conquer or die — while their victims, the African slaves, were forced to adopt the second principle — become a slave and live.

While the white imperialists took great risks in circumnavigating strange lands and coming into contact with foreign people, they always had the advantage of surprise. This was because they primarily presented themselves as missionaries, explorers and traders, and not as invaders or conquerors. Employing subterfuge, when establishing first contact with foreign people, was an essential part of the creeping imperial process. The European explorers bided their time as they knew all along that they needed this front in order to win the Africans' trust. It was essential to understand what and where the African's natural and human resources were and assess the strengths and weaknesses of the cultures and religions of foreign peoples before showing their hand. In time, they would deploy their second and deadliest advantage of all, overwhelming military superiority. Even so, they would only apply the use of force after their intended victims and their society had been sufficiently undermined through commercialization and the culturally imperialist activities of their missionaries and explorers.

This smoke and mirrors approach meant that in most cases, when the European colonisers eventually applied military force, it was usually the case that the colonised people had only two stark options: become subjugated as slaves or die.

Frantz Fanon believed that the oppressors and the oppressed, colonisers and the colonised, lived in a Manichaean world and described it as:

"Two camps inhabited by two different 'species', in perpetual conflict."[9]

This underlying Manichaeanism still holds true all over the world today. Even in our technological modern age of neo-colonialism, the dark underbelly of capitalism maintains its grip on the world's resources using the same methods. Power is maintained by the threat and use of military, economic and political force. Acts of violence on a structural, institutionalised and individual level are carried out daily by white imperialists, against the poor, exploited and denigrated people of the world, especially in Africa.

In 1982, Orlando Patterson further described this Manichaean world when he outlined three distinctive conditions that govern the slave–master relationship. Firstly, there is the establishment of the slave–master relationship, based on the use of interpersonal and institutional violence. The second is the master's absolute power and the slave's powerlessness, resting mainly upon the use and the threat of violence. The third feature of the slave-master relationship is the slave's generalized state of dishonour. In the eyes of the master, the slaves have no redeeming features, no integrity, no worth, and no autonomy.[10] This was emotional and psychological violence in itself because the devaluation of the slave from a human being to a mere object helped reinforce the conditions of slavery and helped the slave masters gain total control of the slave's psyche.

Throughout human evolution, the mind has developed extremely complex subconscious coping mechanisms, called 'ego defence systems'. Ego defence systems protect our conscious minds from the consequences of our actions and recognition of the true state of affairs. Over several centuries, Caucasians have evolved a complex social, political and economic structure of domination and exploitation of non-white people.

Psychologically, in addition to its myth of innate white genetic superiority, white supremacists also claim to be the apex of human morality and integrity. This is psychologically necessary in order hypocritically to block out the reality of their actions. Ego defence mechanisms in part help us to understand how people are able to adapt and live under very difficult conditions like war zones. These ego defence systems not only act to shield the oppressors from the barbarity of their actions, but also to help the oppressed to block out the true extent of their exploitation and denigration. In the master-slave paradigm, the slave masters' ego defence mechanisms are clustered around justifying their claims of superiority and rationalising their inner fears of inadequacy and immorality, while the ego defence mechanism of their slaves centres on coping strategies to stay alive and rationalise their slavery or even simply to formulate strategies to block it out altogether.

Many ego defence mechanisms exist, but some of the most important regarding the master and slave dialectic include the following: reaction formation; projection of their inner feeling of hostility and aggression towards non-white people; and 'displacement' or hostility towards people who are perceived to be weaker.

Reaction formation is one of the main psychological responses to the deep-rooted sense of colour and numerical inadequacy in Caucasians. In this response, the mind converts something desired and envied but unattainable into something to be hated and discredited. Thus instead of acknowledging a desire for darker skin colour, they associate the possession of dark skin colour with an inferiority status and the lack of skin colour or white skin a superiority status.

Anecdotally, in most Western societies it generally holds that the darker the skin the more 'inferior' the person, and a myriad of negative human traits are ascribed to dark skin. Conversely, a host of positive human qualities are ascribed to white colour or skin. In every Western country and all aspects of human activity affected by the white supremacist system, the deeper the melanin pigmentation the more pressure the racist system applies.

The second psychological defensive response by Caucasian people is a projection of their inner feeling of hostility and aggression towards non-white people. Instead of acknowledging their inner hatred of non-white people, they state that non-white people hate them. This allows them to mitigate their guilt feelings, when trying to rationalise their hostility and hatred of non-whites.

The third psychological defence mechanism in the behaviour of white supremacy is 'displacement,' or hostility towards people who are perceived to be weaker. Freud identified 'displacement' as an ego defence mechanism employed by people when they have consciously unacceptable feelings towards others.

The frustration and aggression that build up towards Africans and other non-whites is 'displaced' when, for example, Western politicians blame ethnic minorities for rising crime levels or other aspects of social decay, predisposing them to an almost predictable rise in race-related attacks. This displacement of frustration and aggression on to the more vulnerable in the society is also called 'scapegoating'.

A classic example of 'scapegoating' was Hitler's displacement of German frustration and anger following the loss of the First World War and the spiralling economic crisis on the Jews, which lead directly to their genocide.

While ego defence mechanisms play an important role in determining the life experience of non-white people living under the global reach of white supremacy, there are many other significant psychological factors in play.

Three important side effects of Western capitalism are the psychosocial states of alienation, materialism and narcissism.

Alienation is a powerful, centrifugal, psychological and societal dynamic pressure that capitalist Western societies produce, that drives human beings further and further apart and away from all meaningful, emotionally supportive and truthful communications among one another. It also pushes human beings away from respectful and harmonious relationships with the physical environment, leading to the pollution and destruction of the planet.

Materialism is an essential part of the human existence, necessary to fulfil bodily and mental requirements of food, shelter, relaxation and recreation. This is fine, as long as the society is driven forward by a higher purpose or ideal. However, when materialism itself becomes the primary goal of the society, to the exclusion of all else, the society becomes a living death.

Very early in the development of the white capitalist system, many prominent sociologists, in the late 19th and early 20th centuries, expressed concern at the alienating effects of the process on society. Sigmund Freud postulated that alienation involved a separation or schism in the different parts of the human psyche. Hegel defined alienation as the 'externalisation' or 'objectification' of a society. Georg Simmel and Ferdinand Tonnies wrote critical articles on 'individualisation and urbanisation'. Karl Marx analysed the alienation theories of his time and produced theories of his own in his, 'Economic and Philosophic Manuscripts of 1844'. He defined four principal aspects of the alienation process of Western capitalism: alienation of human beings from nature, alienated from their own productive activity, alienation of their characteristics as members of the human species, and finally, the alienation of human beings from each other.[11]

Even though social alienation is 'self-imposed', the pressure society places on people to conform and to avoid being ostracized, is immense. The mainstream media, promoted by the government, financial institutions and huge corporations, constantly reinforce societal norms. These views become the accepted norms, even though they may be based on mere fiction, inaccurate or incomplete information. People who challenge these views, risk being stigmatized and ostracized by the wider society, who in real terms are now prone to fundamentalism. The fear of social alienation encourages self-imposed ignorance and dependence on external authority.

Materialism has become the goal of the Western capitalist system and money is the key to all materialistic ambitions. Money has become the symbol of the capitalist system of domination. Displaying incredible foresight our Christian forefathers described the love of money as, 'the root of all kinds of evil'. Globally, on a daily basis, people lie, cheat and kill for money. Most Western movies or dramas involve, to varying degrees, plots that revolve around killing and/or cheating for money. They extol the pleasures money can buy and expose the deprivation of poverty. They celebrate desperate people stealing and killing for money and the power it can give them. In real life, virtually every local or global Western war of domination, including the two World Wars, has been primarily fought for the acquisition of material wealth. Prostitutes sleep with strange men for money, wives divorce their husbands for money and millions of the children of the world's poorest languish in abject poverty for the lack of money.

In a social system designed to achieve and maintain white domination and exploitation, the key factors in determining the potential of success in the racist system are colour, identity and money. For instance, in the colour-coded, institutionally and racially segregated American society, it can safely be said that the only colour white Americans love more than white, is the green of the American dollar.

Racial prejudice creates unique views in a society. It is a known fact that Caucasians tend to exaggerate the differences between the races because of race prejudice. To many Caucasians, all black people tend to look the same, regardless of shape, size or place of origin. Because of racism, Caucasians also have a tendency to want to make the white race appear more homogenous than it actually is in order to support their narrow personal constructs. This results in a tendency to increase or favour the status of their own group, while simultaneously denigrating and belittling races or ethnic minority groups.

In white societies, through institutionalized racism, the ethnic penalty of 'black skin' carried by the bulk of the African diaspora significantly reduces their access to money, and/or opportunities to make money. The same applies to Africans on the African continent, who pay a severe price for blindly inhabiting the lowest rungs of the white global power structure and thus have the least chances of anyone in the imperial global hierarchy of having access to the common denominator of the capitalist system — money.

In the highly materialist and pressured Western societies, depression due to social pressure is threatening to overtake physical ailments like heart disease and cancer as the most common illness in the West. The National Institute of Mental Health in the US estimated the prevalence of depression as about 1 in 18 people or about 14.4 million US Americans.[12] In the UK, it is estimated that about 5–10% of the UK population suffers from clinical depression but up to 30% of the population — one in three people — have symptoms of depression that do not meet the criteria for major depression.[13]

Unfortunately, many mental health professionals in the West concern themselves primarily with the individual or sick patient's mental health while ignoring the systemic effects of societal alienation or the 'sick society', as the root cause of the problem. It is very much like treating a caged animal with tranquillizers for stress, rather than simply setting it free. Undoubtedly, releasing the animals from bondage would immediately reduce their anxiety. It is for this same reason that many treatments and therapies for mental health problems will have limited success in reducing mental health problems like anxiety and depression when the primary causes of the illness — the 'sick society' — remain unaddressed.

In a Western society, defined more or less by the acquisition or possession of money, it becomes apparent that the alienating effects of such a society will hit the poorest the hardest. It is for this reason that Africans in urbanized African cities, on the African continent and the African diaspora living in the West, who occupy the lowest socio-economic rungs of the white social engineering project, display many of the negative characteristics of alienation — be it black-on-black violence, single parent units, a lack of positive male role models or high poverty rates.

Another significant cause of psychological slavery is the effects of narcissistic white religious and other iconic imagery on the subconscious minds of the non-white people, who live under the umbrella of global white domination.

Imagery plays a very important role in determining how people turn out and whom they define themselves as. It is very important for all Africans to understand the immensely powerful and negative effects white religious and other iconic imagery have on their psyche so that they process this information at a conscious, rather than a subconscious, level.

The most important iconography is the white man-god complex that derives from all the false images of European Christianity and its powerful impact on the psyche of Africans, who have consciously and subconsciously accepted it. The subconscious, the driving force of the white supremacy system, is the white man-god complex, which breeds the loss of humility and humanity necessary to maintain healthy and productive relationships with each other and with the environment. The Caucasian, seeing in himself the same physical attributes as his 'gods', makes the natural leap to assuming a superiority status over other non-white human beings and also a disregard of the environment.[14]

Africans who accept and internalize the idea of a Caucasian man/ woman or white deity, as nearer to the 'God' they worship, have automatically made the natural leap to an assumed inferiority status. They will begin to see themselves as somewhat deficient and inferior to the Caucasians, who are in their eyes 'closer to God'. This inferiority complex permeates all aspects of their lives, and is socially transmitted through their children in a self-perpetuating cycle. Therefore Africans who have imbibed this miseducation see nothing wrong in being dependent on Caucasians and seek to caricature them in all aspects of their lives. They try to look, talk, act, eat, live and behave like Caucasians.

Many years ago Edward Blyden lamented this fact and stated:

"Wherever the Negro is found in Christian land, his leading trait is not

docility, instead it is servility. He is slow and unprogressive. Individuals here and there may be found of extraordinary intelligence, enterprise and energy, but there is no Christian community of Negroes anywhere which is self-reliant and independent. On the other hand, there are numerous Mohammedan communities and states in Africa, which are self-reliant, productive, independent and dominant, supporting without the countenance or patronage of the parent country, Arabia, whence they derived their political, literary and ecclesiastical institutions."[15]

The Caucasians, on the other hand, develop a narcissistic and paranoid sense of entitlement and divinity. It is no accident of nature that several 'paranoid' rulers emerged in Europe over the centuries, obsessed with their own divinity and hell-bent on the domination and exploitation of others by their divine rights of conquest. Alexander the Great from Macedonia, Julius Caesar of Italy, Napoleon Bonapart from France, Richard the Lionheart from England and Adolf Hitler from Germany all fall into this group of Western leaders. White nations such as Britain, France, Germany, and the United States are totally obsessed with their divine right to rule because they are God's people and 'innately superior' to the people they sought to dominate.

While love of self is natural and necessary to maintain self-esteem, when it overflows, it manifests as a variant of the Narcissistic Personality Disorder and creates a personality primarily concerned about 'me, myself and I'. Thus the motto of the narcissistic white imperialist is: "What's mine is mine and what's yours is mine too."

It is not surprising that many of the core character traits of the Narcissistic Personality Disorder — lack of empathy, arrogance, a strong sense of entitlement, a grandiose sense of importance and taking advantage of others to achieve their own ends - accurately describes white supremacists and imperialists.

According to Christopher Lasch, social critic, historian, and author of the book, The Culture of Narcissism:

"The hedonistic need to acquire symbols of spiritual wealth is the only overt expression of a rigid, yet covert social hierarchy."[16]

One of the aims of imperialism is to create a superior race of white rulers, superimposed on the large base of non-white 'inferior' and even 'subhuman beings', who they can then exploit. A clear hierarchy in society developed in the West through the subdivision of human beings by their ethnicity, colour and race.

Exposure to this implied superiority is almost as damaging psychologically as growing up in Western society itself, where people become stereotyped and defined by their colour and race in society. This holds true in all former European colonial countries. This global hierarchy is exported by Western capitalism under the smokescreen of freedom, democracy and globalization.

The institutionalized racial hierarchy places an almost impenetrable social mobility barrier in the paths of their ethnic minority communities, especially Africans, because of their added colour-related ethnic penalty.

It is for this reason too, that white racist or imperialist systems cannot be expected to provide equal opportunities for non-whites, especially Africans. The white supremacy system, by definition, must produce different levels of social functioning for whites and blacks. Western society must thus always extract an ethnic penalty, based strictly on ethnicity and colour. Where apparent equality is granted in one area, it is taken away in another:

If apparent equality is granted in the area of education, it is denied in the family background. If it is given in income, it is denied in housing opportunity. If it is granted in health services, it is denied in terms of father's income levels. If it is granted by law, it is denied through social practice. In most cases most Africans are uniformly denied most privileges.[17]

Since a child's social status has already been predetermined by that of their parents, everyone, including children, has an assigned status in society. While it is evidently true that every child has the inherent potential to be whatever they want in society, the true power to be self-determining lies with the oppressors or 'functional superiors'. In the white supremacist society, there are only two real functional roles, the oppressors and the oppressed. white children, with the 'true power' of self-determination and social mobility, will therefore be socialized in the role of functional superiors, while children from oppressed families will be forced to play the role of 'functional inferiors' by the alienating pressures of Western societies. It is critical to appreciate that the mere acquisition of material wealth is insufficient to grant black Africans equality in Western societies, because it does not address the institutionalized nature of the Western society. Rather, it grants the wealthier Africans, the 'privilege' of operating as higher level servants, of the white supremacy system.

Socialization into functional inferiority is achieved by the imposition of a stressful, negative, non-supportive social/ environmental experience on the non-white people, who are to be dominated from birth to death.[18] Erik H. Erikson, author of Childhood and Society postulated that the psycho-social development of a child could follow two main pathways, functional and dysfunctional. When the social environment adequately supports the development of the child, its psycho-social development advances functionally through eight stages: basic trust, autonomy, initiative, industry, identity, intimacy, generativity, and finally, integrity.[19]

When society exerts excessive negative pressure on the developing child, its psycho-social development becomes dysfunctional. It develops dysfunctionally, through a mirror image of its functional peers: mistrust instead of trust, shame and doubt instead of autonomy, guilt ['I cannot'] instead of initiative ['I can'], inferiority [or lethargy] instead of industry, role confusion in place of identity, isolation instead of intimacy, stagnation in place of generativity, despair in place of integrity.[20]

Racism is a socially transmitted disease and social manipulation is the key means by which the racist attitudes of the oppressors and the oppressed are passed from generation to generation. Human beings are not born racist. they become racist by exposure to racist behaviour and ideology. Racism helps perpetuate the social transmission of corresponding superiority and inferiority complexes, which are simply different ends of the same spectrum. It also means that the vast majority of Caucasian people will, in certain circumstances, display or harbour racist or paternalistic tendencies unless they and their parents have been raised outside the all-pervasive blanket of white societal superiority complexes.

Johnny Lee Perry, later to become the leader of the Ku Klux Klan, shed some light on the social transmission of racist ideology within families as he recalled:

"One day, when I was 5 years old, sitting in the car with my father in 1964, first time I saw a black person, I exclaimed, look daddy a chocolate-colored man.

Say Nigger, son, say Nigger my dad said. I leaned out of the car and called, nigger, nigger, nigger."

Observed learning is the main way of transmitting human behaviour and sociologists estimate that we absorb most of our cultural etiquette, culture and moral values before the age of ten.[21] Many people erroneously believe that what they say to their children is all they know. They cannot be further from the truth as non-verbal communication accounts for more than 90% of human communication. The process of inferiorisation is therefore, inadvertently also taught in part by the oppressed parents, as well as the wider racist society — even if they do not verbalise it.

The greatest determinant of who we are and what we become later in life is our socialisation and our main psychological drivers of fear, love, greed and security, are manipulated by the prevailing society and culture. If this hierarchy remains unchallenged, it will predictably produce differing levels of social functioning, depending on ethnic origins, sex, and background. Dr. Welsing describes the social process through which the genetic potential of the black child is destroyed as 'inferiorization'. This social process profoundly influences their total life experience.

Inferiorization is the conscious, deliberate and systematic process utilized by a fascist [white supremacy] social system, as conducted through all its major and minor institutions [including the institution of the family], to mould specific peoples within that system [namely, all people classified as non-white] into "functional inferiors" in spite of their true genetic potential for functioning.

Under the white supremacy system, the more melanin present in the skin, and thus the darker the individual, the greater the "inferiorization" pressure imposed by the racist system. Consequently, among all non-white peoples, blacks are most victimized by this process. Particularly, darker black people receive extreme victimization — even amongst black people themselves. The skin colour code established by the global white collective, like other methods of black subjugation, is essential to white genetic survival.[22]

The sceptical may wish to turn their noses up at this theory but there are several examples in history that firmly support this. The French Code Noir was primarily designed to segregate black slaves. The caste system in India, promoted in British colonial India, clusters their dark-skinned 'untouchables' at the very bottom of their social hierarchy. During the slave trade in South America, it was declared that a single drop of African blood made one an African. During the white South African apartheid system in South Africa, the presence of any African ancestry put a Caucasian under suspicion. It could result in severe economic penalties, including being socially excluded and stripped of all their rights of being white.

It is nothing short of amazing to note the tender age at which the inferiorisation process begins to take effect. In 1939, a study carried out by Dr and Mrs Clark was published in the Journal of Social Psychology, which showed that pre-school African American children as young as three years old had major psychological problems with their African identity. The Clarks gave three-year-old African children black dolls and white dolls and asked them: "Which of these dolls is pretty?" The children chose the blonde-haired, blue-eyed Caucasian doll. When asked: "Which doll is smart?" they picked the Caucasian doll. Asked; "Which doll would you like to look like?", again they picked the Caucasian doll. When asked: "Which doll is ugly?" they picked the black dolls.[23]

For people exposed to Western ideology from the colonial period onwards or even just constantly exposed to its media and literature without any other balancing views, all the key human psychological markers are occupied by the 'snowy peaks' of symbols and figures of white people. The asymmetric domination of all indices of human success by white people, as depicted by the global system of white supremacy, is no accident. It is deliberately constructed for its powerful psychological impression, especially on the children of non-whites, exposed to white socialization.

It sets non-white children the alluring but unattainable psychological task of becoming 'white'. It then sets them up to fail by placing before them the relatively impenetrable barrier of institutional racism.

From religious figures like Jesus and Moses, to classic literature, music, political leaders, experts in science and technology, all are white-dominated. This deprives African children, whose true history is untold or unknown, of essential positive role models at the most crucial stage of their psychosocial development. Even today, despite a smattering of blacks and ethnic people in politics and science, there is still dramatically unequal representation of ethnic minorities in Western societies.

World history, as recorded by the West, is dominated by white people who occupy virtually all of the highest peaks of human achievement. There is, therefore, no need for the press and politicians to remind people daily of where they belong in society. They simply gravitate towards their assigned positions.

Thus, when exposed to this great psychological impress, Carter Woodson wrote in his book, The Miseducation of the Negro:

"No systematic effort towards change has been possible, for, taught the same economics, history, philosophy, literature and religion, which have established the present code of morals; the negro's mind has been brought under the control of his oppressor. The problem of holding the Negro down, therefore is easily solved."[24]

Many psychological tests have shown quite clearly the effects of negative stereotyping upon black African people. Yet, many people underestimate the power of their psychological state of mind. Even more are completely unaware of the impact that negative stereotyping has on their ability to perform. Claude Steele and Joshua Aronson, both psychologists, carried out a famous study, using African American college students, and asked twenty questions taken from the graduate record examination, the standardised tests used for entry into graduate school.

When the students were first asked to identify their race on the pre-test questionnaire, that single question was enough to prime them with all the negative stereotypes associated with African Americans and their academic achievement. It was surprising to observe that the simple pre-test question about race was sufficient to reduce the number of correct questions they got by up to 50%.

Remarkably, when the students were asked if they felt anything had reduced their performance, they could not identify any reason. When asked if the question about their race affected them directly, they all said it did not. Some even went on to say they did not think they were smart enough to get a qualification.[25] What they did not reckon with was the immense power negative stereotyping had on their lives, as it operates mainly in the subconscious.

Western miseducation and a negative social life experience restructures the thought patterns of African people. Virtually every aspect of human activity is affected. The profoundly negative experiences of poor education, health care, housing, schools, broken homes and low incomes lead predictably to their development as functional inferiors — and a myriad of dysfunctional ways of expressing this frustration.

Once the slaves have lost their consciousness of self and their self-determination, they have also lost sight of their own goals and ambitions, as individuals and as a collective, and begin to internalise the values, norms and prohibitions of their masters.

In order to fractionalize and divide the oppressed people among themselves, a system of rewards and punishment based on loyalty to the oppressor is instituted. The result is a conflicted and divided people, who compete among themselves for the affections and rewards of their slave masters, rather than engage in a cohesive fight for their own freedom. Many are willing to fight to the death for their masters but will not lift a finger to assist or support any plan for the emancipation of their people or struggle against any injustice meted out by their slave masters.

In his review of Frantz Fanon's work, in understanding the psychology of the oppressed, Hussein Abdilahi Bulhan wrote about the paradigm the oppressed people find themselves in:

'*Prolonged oppression reduces the oppressed into mere individuals without a community or a history, fostering a tendency to privatize a shared victimization. Thus one observes contrasting attitudes and behaviours between the two protagonists in situations of oppression.*

When a member of the oppressing group meets a member of the oppressed, the first always acts as a majority; while the latter behaves simply as a minority of one. The former demands more space and privilege; the latter tends to settle for less.

The former exudes confidence and a sense of entitlement; the latter betrays self-doubt and a readiness to compromise. Consciously, and subconsciously, each knows that their personal encounter is also an encounter of two collectives with unequal power. The prevailing ideas, values, and rules of conduct serve the former; they entrap and frustrate the latter.

The one who is a member of the oppressing group exploits all this; the other compensates with his personality and individual resources[26]

The slaves must learn to hide their true feelings from their masters to avoid eliciting punishment and must wear different 'masks' for different situations. They must learn to detect the moods and wishes of their masters and develop contingencies for all these occasions in order to survive.

Mental slavery was the main weapon of the slave master and was the worst form of slavery black African slaves had to deal with as they arrived as captives from Africa as it destroyed the very essence of their humanity. With the rising population of black African slaves in proportion to the white slavers, white slave owners did everything within their power to crush the free spirit and will of the African and the black slaves in order to render them completely malleable for their use.

Even though physical violence was the main tool used to subjugate black slaves, many other more insidious methods were used in order to gain full control of not just the bodies but also the minds of their slaves in order to facilitate their manipulation.

The African diaspora and Africans on the continent suffer, not because of any inferiority in intelligence, spirit or physique. They suffer, primarily, because of the legacy of the psychological inferiority towards their colonial masters, coupled with their physical dependence on them. The inferiority complex means they do not have the courage and confidence to challenge the white man and their dependence ensures that they lack the means to stand up for themselves. Inferiority complexes sap the motivation and confidence of many African people, preventing them from aspiring to great heights in many fields.[27]

To understand how the self-replicating viruses of inferiority complexes, psychological and physical dependence on their white slave masters became implanted into the subconscious minds of many Africans, we must explore the 'seasoning process' employed by white slave masters and colonialists in more detail.

CHAPTER FIFTY TWO

THE SEASONING PROCESS

Thomas Jefferson, famous for his role as a founding father of American independence wrote:

"The alleged inferiority of the black slaves means that slavery was for their benefit."[1]

Instilling in blacks a fear of freedom is essentially what the 'seasoning process' was all about. The seasoning process was the breaking down the physical and psychological resistance of African slaves through unmitigated, gratuitous, physical and emotional violence. Most white slave owners did not need much encouragement and took Thomas Jefferson's advice with relish. To really understand the seasoning process, we cannot simply regurgitate the historical facts. It is important to transport yourself mentally and emotionally into the mind's eye of a black male or female slave to fully appreciate the terror and mental anguish they would have experienced before we can make any judgements about their fortitude and later actions.

The 'seasoning process' of slaves, whether kidnapped and exported to the Americas in the transatlantic slave trade or exploited in their own land during the colonisation of Africa, was practically identical.

The process of establishing mental slavery can be broken down into phases. The first phase consists of intense physical and mental torture and abuse. This induces fear and hopelessness. The predominate emotions inculcated are anxiety, depression, worthlessness, despair and suicidal tendencies. Phase two is the stripping of identity and culture, inducing a lack of direction, re-enforcing hopelessness and a sense of powerlessness stemming from loss of self-determination and actualization. African slaves were deliberately miseducated in Western history, culture and ideology. The vacuum created by the destruction of the family unit and the loss of identity and culture was filled by a denigrated identity of inferiority in Western culture. Predominant emotions in this phase were fear, awe and obedience.

Phase three involved the psychological acceptance of denigrated identity. The slaves no longer seek to be free but now identify with their oppressors and want to integrate with them. They identify and define themselves by 'buying' through oppressive system of white supremacy. They deal with the oppressive system with a range of circular, often self-destructive and self-denigrating behaviour. Even though the system imposes negative stereotypes on them and oppresses them, they still seek its acceptance and want to integrate into it. Fear, awe, obedience and dependence now predominate.

Phase four is the social transmission of the inferiorizing process. Cut off from their history and culture by their oppressors, they see nothing better than to remain dependent on them. Fragmented individualism predominates. They now see themselves as individuals in the larger white collective, rather than part of the African collective. They secretly or openly hate their African identity, which inhibits their assimilation into the white society. Fear, awe, obedience and dependence on the white society remain and become embedded.

As the repeated attempts of the psychologically fragmented Africans to successfully integrate into white society are blocked and frustrated by the rigid white supremacy power structure, numerous self-destructive or negative circular behaviours develop. Physical and emotional black-on-black, violence, promoted by the self-hatred and poverty created by the system develops. However, this violence is directed at themselves or other Africans like them not at their oppressors because of their inbred fear of white people and internalised hatred of black people. Children born to miseducated and psychologically broken Africans grow up socialised as functional inferiors by their oppressed parents and the wider oppressive white society and are doomed to repeat the cycle with their own offspring if not re-educated.

Today, many miseducated Africans, especially in the older African diaspora, have an intangible but real fear of white people. It paralyses their thoughts and actions to such a degree that they cannot fathom any alternative view, thought or action not sanctioned by or generated by Caucasians.

Unfortunately, many modern-day Africans and their diaspora have regressed through the psychological phases of mental slavery and reside in the latter phase of mental slavery. They do not have a full conscious awareness of self because they do not know their history and do not appreciate their own cultures. They no longer strive to be free of slavery like the initial captive African slaves, and live to caricature their white masters.

In this almost childlike state, dependence comes naturally in much the same way that prisoners become institutionalized and accept the rigours of their imprisonment as a means of getting through the sentence. Many ex-inmates confess to finding the consistency of prison life much easier than the uncertainty of life in the wider society.

It is hard to imagine or describe, the terror, the intense, soul-destroying degradation and suffering the Africans slaves endured from the moment of capture. Even after they had survived the horrors of the middle passage, they ended up in a life worse than death on the plantations or in the slave masters' homes. The psychological and emotional trauma of the slave trade is hardly mentioned in Western history books, even though a former slave, Olaudah Equiano's account sheds some light on it. The omission of the suffering of African slaves is deliberate because it shields both the perpetrators and the victims alike from the enormity of the genocide and man's inhumanity to man being perpetrated.

In addition to the individual suffering of the African slaves, many African societies were thrown into a state of almost perpetual terror and chaos and their populations were forced to migrate en masse in order to escape Arab slave traders, the Trans-Saharan slave trade across North Africa and the European transatlantic slave trade. It is important to revisit the trials and tribulations of the slaves whose only release from bondage was death. To understand how the deep psychological scars were created and are still carried in the psyche of Africans and their diaspora, we must revisit the slave trade.

Many African societies have been shown, through the passing down of information, historical documents and artefacts, to have been in a continuous state of flux during the slave trade. Africans fleeing slavery had to migrate deeper and deeper into the interior of Africa to escape these slave raiders. It would not be conjecture to imagine that the people lived in constant fear of the slave raids and had to evolve elaborate means to keep their family units together to avoid falling prey to these inhuman predators. Facial scarification marks were just one way the tribal people tried to identify each other, and avoid being infiltrated by slave raiders from other villages or lands.[2]

Once the unfortunate slaves were captured, it marked the beginning of a slow descent into a living hell, previously unimagined by the captured slaves. The slaves were chained together like a string of cattle and marched for hundreds of miles, depending on the area of capture, to the sea. They were beaten, starved, branded, raped, tortured and some killed at the whim of their captors. They were often sold and resold along the way. These trips to the coastline or across the desert could take up to three months and many slaves died during this phase of their transport to the slave ships that waited for them off the coasts, like the castle Elmina in Ghana or the Gold Coast, as it was known then.

On arrival at the coast, their potential white purchasers then subjected them to the most degrading forms of inspection. This included stripping them naked and examining their bodies, including their genitals, breasts and orifices, to determine their state of health. The white slave owners with a hot iron branded them like cattle for identification purposes, such as the emblems of the Royal African Company. Then they were herded into the holds of the slave ships.

The closest thing to being branded in a domestic setting is being burnt with a hot iron. In my practice as a doctor, I have seen first-hand the pain, infection and the subsequent scarring these burns cause. It does not bear thinking what the African slaves went through without any analgesia or antibiotics. It is clearly documented that many slaves died from the infections caused by the branding, leading to a change in the practice in order to save more of their human 'cargo'. As Horace Campbell writes:

'The capture and middle passage crossing, where at least 30% of the cargo was fed to sharks, was reinforced by the seasoning process, or the struggle to break the spirit of resistance among Africans. But it took three years of seasoning with the whip to fully break the will of stronger Africans. During this period of 'adjustment', which lasted between one and three years, between one-quarter and one-third of Africans died.'[3]

Having inflicted the harshest and cruellest induction to the Western world possible, the white slave owners did not stop there. Into the vacuum in the slaves' minds, created by their wrenching out of their own society, history and way of life, the slave owners then proceeded to denigrate everything African — from their physique, hair, colour, lips and nose, to their names, languages, culture and history. Without the reference points of religion and culture, it was obvious the slaves had to adapt to their new surroundings quickly or die. They were then re-educated in the ways and history of their white slave masters in such a way that their continued subjugation and alleged inferiority was carved out in stone.

The very limit of the Africans' ambition in this new and hostile Western society, was a place of servility and docility. The slaves were doomed to remain in a state of perpetual childlike dependence on the goodwill of their white captors for acts of benevolence and kindness, as seen fit by their captors. African slaves were subjected to intense physical, verbal and sexual abuse from the moment they were captured in Africa. The abuse continued during the middle passage and long after being sold on to different plantations. Many African slaves were worked to death and those who survived, and their descendants, remained in perpetual slavery.

The process of destroying the African culture, identity, language, and self-esteem continued on the plantations. This deliberate process was aimed at bringing about the total loss of self-identity and the creation of captive people, whose physical and emotional needs could only be met by their captors.

To create obedience to the slave masters, the male and female roles were reversed. Docility, obedience and dependence were beaten into the slaves and then subsequently inbred so that the offspring of slaves would be easier to manage and more of an economic asset than the original slave. Faced with death, many slaves had no option but to accept the slave masters' value system, which then totally devalued their own. Once kidnapped into slavery, one of the first things to go would be their names.

The African male was especially singled out for extremely harsh treatment by the white captors, who knew that by symbolically and systematically denigrating the head of the African family and social system, they fostered the growth of self-hatred and frustration.

The slaves were kept dirty and poor and humiliated by public beatings. They were branded like cattle and paraded naked in the streets. They had their private parts publicly examined, and wives and children were raped and abused in front of the partners/husbands to emphasize the impotence of the male slaves to protect their own. Slaves who resisted were drawn and quartered publicly to warn other slaves of pursuing a similar path. Some slaves were slowly roasted to death over fires to prolong the agony before death.

Newborn infants were taken from their mothers and prolonged breast feeding was discouraged to minimise bonding. Slave families were constantly split up and sold separately. All in all, these heinous acts were generally aimed at preventing the natural love and bonding between the slaves, which could in the future foster the kind of self-respect and unity which could bring about resistance.

Open communication and the practice of any African religion or Islam was forbidden so as to prevent slaves from unifying around a belief or having a common cause. This ensured the total loss of traditional values, names and customs.

Natural African leaders were targeted for special treatment and punishment. Many were tortured and killed for trying to instigate any unity of cause among their fellow slaves. They were then replaced by African stooges, who did exactly as they were told by the slave masters, in return for favours and a sense of power over their fellow slaves. These African taskmasters were obliged to be just as brutal as the while slave owners or they were subjected to the same punishments. Others vented all their pent-up self-loathing on their hapless fellow slaves.

The white-appointed black foremen also acted as a ready source of information about what was going on among the African slaves and helped put a black face on the death wishes of white people towards black people. Unsurprisingly, white-appointed black leaders are still treated with a high level of mistrust, among black people today.

Slaves were made to work from dawn until dusk and the work did not end until they were disabled, old or dead. This meant that the white slavers had to replenish their slave stock regularly.

"Nearly two-thirds of the African slaves ended up cutting cane on sugar plantations [in the West Indies]. During harvest, it typically meant 14 hours of back breaking labour six days a week in extreme heat for men, women and children...The combination of hard labour, exposure to new diseases and inadequate food meant that approximately one in three Africans died within three years of arriving in the Caribbean."[4]

Slaves learnt how to work slowly so that they could conserve their energy and preserve their health, and it was also a way of working to rule, preventing the slave masters from getting all that they could out of them.

Many white slave owners actively practised slave breeding. Child-bearing age for females began around the age of thirteen years and by the age of twenty a good childbearing slave was expected to have delivered around four to five children. Some plantation owners promised their female slaves freedom after producing fifteen children. It was a common practice in those days to see young African slaves advertised in the local papers as *'good breeding stock'*.[5]

In order to endure living and working work under the threat of constant mental and physical abuse, beatings, torture, humiliation and death, the slave reacted in a variety of ways. One of the main psychological reactions was identification with the slave master. Denied access to their true identities, lithe slaves lived vicariously through the slave master and modified their responses in the form of passive self-defence. This behaviour developed primarily to avoid the violent repression that was the lexicon of white slave masters.

The slaves had to accept the complete authority of the slave master and they maintained attitudes and responses that reflected this. When the master was happy, they too were happy and when the master was sad, they also felt sad.

Playing the clown was one way of presenting a non-threatening front to the slave master. In so doing, they could to some degree control and manipulate the slave masters in order to avoid punishment or get favours or leniency. Even though it became a successful survival mechanism, it would later give rise to the black stereotypes, 'Sambo' and 'Uncle Tom'.

Many slaves reacted to their living hell by choosing to run away from the slave master, in spite of the almost negligible chances of success and the severe punishment that was meted out to them if recaptured. Incredibly, some white slave owners struggled to understand why the slaves ran away, in spite of the obvious suffering the slaves had to endure. Some white Christian slave owners believed that servitude was God's chosen position for the African and the American South provided the 'right atmosphere' for black slaves. The basis of this lay in the quasi-medical portrayal of black slaves as not having an aptitude to organize themselves beyond the ability of a child and the so-called curse of Ham, which, in their eyes, had condemned all Africans, the alleged descendants of Ham, to serve as slaves to all the other races.

In trying to explain the African slaves' behaviour, some pseudoscience theories emerged; Dr Benjamin Rush, one of the co-signers of the American Declaration of Independence, also referred to as the father of American psychiatry, declared that Africans suffered from a peculiar illness called Negritude Another white physician, Dr Samuel Cartwright, went on to claim that runaway black slaves had a mental disorder called 'drapetomania', which he said was common to black Africans and cats. His suggested cure was a thorough whipping. He also labelled black slaves with another disease, which he called Dysaesthesia Aethiopis, or 'Herbitude' of the mind or obtuse sensibility of the body — what slave overseers termed 'rascality', which he said affected 'free Negroes' more than slaves.[6]

Even in the face of certain torture and death many African slaves also revolted — a revolt led by a literate slave, Denmark Vesey, in South Carolina in 1822 and Nat Turner's revolt in Virginia in 1831 being the most prominent. Ultimately unsuccessful, these revolts led to the promulgation of harsher laws, forbidding reading, writing and arithmetic among black slaves.

The net result of the suffering of the African slaves was the development of a sense of inferiority, a lack of knowledge of their distinguished past, achievements and contributions. They were also deprived of opportunities to develop in the future as equal and worthy partners.

To cope with the 'total captivity' of slavery, African slaves developed many other mechanisms. The slaves did not own anything, even the clothes on their backs. In sharp contrast, the slave masters lived in opulence and owned everything, including the slaves. This created a dual approach to materialism on the part of the slaves, who yearned to have the wealth and riches of the white slave owners and the urge to destroy these symbols of slavery. They knew that the fruit of their daily toil went into the pockets of the slave owners. Work, therefore, was looked upon as slavery and freedom was associated with the avoidance of work and became hated among African American slaves.[7] This may explain to some degree the reason why many African American or West Indians seek out and respect material possessions. African American rap stars have popularised the glorifying of money and other material possessions as a means of showing that they have escaped from the 'hood'. Some like to be showy and expensive to the extreme and do not take a long-term view to acquiring material wealth. They do not have an authentic identity in society and reject the tag of inferiority the white man has placed upon them. They seek, if only for a short while, to experience the material pleasures they saw across the fence like clothes, jewellery, cars and houses. Unfortunately, living for the moment in an unforgiving Western society ultimately takes its toll.

Today, we see many African slave descendants still have a sense of deep rooted fear and mistrust of white people and are spending much of their efforts acquiring material wealth, rather than seeking real social and political power — the only way to real equality.

CHAPTER FIFTY THREE
COLONIZING AFRICAN MINDS

Transatlantic slavery remains the greatest act of man's inhumanity to man. Mental slavery has, on top of physical slavery, served to perpetuate and prolong the suffering of the African people.

In Africa, instead of individuals, whole nations are exhibiting traits of white psychological manipulation and following a path of self-destruction they were set on by their white colonial masters. The aim of Western colonialism was the extraction of forced, cheap labour and raw materials from Africa. In order to achieve their objectives, European colonisers had to understand African geography, pinpoint the resources and undermine African culture.

One of the most far-reaching psychological effects of colonialism on the African psyche was the disruption of the continuity and synchrony of social identity, cohesion and culture. Fanon noted that in the stable societies of Europe there was synchrony between the three main domains of their society — the nation, the family, and the individuals. The same principles, laws and values governed all three areas.

In Africa, due to the socio-economic, cultural and psychological effects of colonial deracination, there was significant disruption in social continuity. Africans under colonial rule and even in neo-colonial rule, display a significant disruption in all three, promoting individualization above social cohesion, as people competed for the recognition and rewards from their colonial masters.

Once again, the key instrument used in achieving African social disruption and compliance with the demands of the colonial and neo-colonial masters was violence.

In his preface to Frantz Fanon's book, The Wretched of the Earth, Jean-Paul Sartre wrote:

"Violence in the colonies does not only have for its aim the keeping of these enslaved men at arm's length; it seeks to dehumanize them. Everything will be done, to wipe out their traditions, to substitute our language for theirs and to destroy their culture without giving them ours.

"Sheer physical fatigue will stupefy them. Starved and ill, if they have any spirit left, fear will finish the job; guns are levelled at the peasant; civilians come to take over his land and force him by dint of flogging to till the land for them.

"If he shows a fight, the soldiers fire, and he's a dead man; if he gives in, he degrades himself, and he is no longer a man at all; shame and fear will split up his character and make his inmost self-fall to pieces."[1]

The idea to open up Africa to Christianity and commerce was not just David Livingstone's. Leading British missionaries, in particular Thomas Fowell Buxton and Henry Venn, had already described the strategy:

"The only way to destroy the slave trade was to introduce simultaneously Christian values and legitimate commerce. To achieve this in West Africa required communications with the interior so as to provide the means for tribal societies there to produce and sell goods, which the European needed, and, which would produce higher profits than the sale of slaves.

For this purpose an African middle class must be created, instilled with Christian moral and ethical values, convinced of the virtue of labor, imbued with all the certainties of Victorian Britain.

Then West Africa could follow Britain's lead, producing industrialists, merchants and modern farmers, though perhaps concentrating on the production of those committees needed by British industry — like cotton."[2]

Overall, white Christian missionaries in Africa were largely unsuccessful in their attempts to convert native Africans to Christianity. True African conversions to Christianity were very few and often superficial. The bulk of those converted were usually the weakest and most insecure individuals in the African community. Many were people excommunicated from their tribes or communities for different reasons and a large number were slaves who had been released or had escaped.

They were more than grateful to express their newfound freedom, and embrace Christianity. Other converts continued to practice pagan rituals or modified European Christianity to suit their own culture and communities.

David Livingstone wrote about his great disappointment in not being able to make African converts at the desired rate.[3]

In actual fact, many white missionaries did not have much time for saving African souls — their immediate and most pressing task being self-preservation. The next was the maintenance of racial and cultural superiority. The missionaries often had to rely on land and gifts of food from the local chiefs. They also needed African labour to help them erect houses and plant food where possible. In some cases missionaries even had to resort to violence to extract compliance from their African converts, following Lugard's recipe of *'thrash them first, conciliate afterwards'*.[4] Flogging was the accepted method of keeping porters obedient. Without using violence, even the white missionaries would not have been able to extract the labour required for building mission stations, as in many instances the African helpers and converts showed little loyalty to the Christian church or its missionaries.[5]

Because the missionaries needed to communicate clearly with their intended converts, they learnt their languages.

Overall, the European Christian missionaries helped open up the African communities to trade, materialism and consumerism, and worked hand in hand with the European military to physically and psychologically undermine the minds and culture of many Africans. It was only under these conditions that European Christianity eventually flourished in certain parts of Africa.

The missionaries created an African quasi-middle class, which was and still is the vein through which African resource are drained by the West. Many Africans were completely blindsided by European Christianity and Western materialism. They did not understand the far-reaching implications of Western imperialism and were willing agents for the colonialists as they stripped Africa of its workforce, culture and resources.

Bishop Ajayi Crowther was a well-known example of an African who assisted the insinuation of British colonialism into West African societies. He was taken into slavery as a child but was lucky to be freed by a British patrol in Freetown. He was educated at the Church Missionary Society from where he went to study in England and at Fourah Bay. He became a teacher and later a missionary. When the Church of England decided to create a new diocese in West Africa, Bishop Ajayi Crowther was the obvious choice as its first African Bishop.[6]

It is significant that he was a disciple and a close friend of Henry Venn, a British missionary and one of the main proponents of undermining African culture with European Christianity and commerce. Bishop Ajayi Crowther had so deeply imbibed British attitudes that his remedy for African 'backwardness' was the introduction of more British habits into Africa and to allow Britain to have a greater and deeper participation in African affairs.

In 1868, Ajayi Crowther played a leading role in persuading the Yoruba king to give over Lagos to the British government, even though British troops had shelled Lagos with much loss of African life. Despite the British invading, occupying his own country and killing his people, Bishop Ajayi Crowther's journals and his general attitude towards the future of Africa mirrored that of his English mentor. In one of his entries, he wrote:

"The country abounds with produce; labor is cheap: if the youths are only taught to prepare them for European markets, our work is done… when trade and agriculture engage the attention of the people and with the gentle and peaceful teachings of Christianity, the minds of the people will actually be won from war and marauding expeditions to peaceful trade and commerce."[7]

In French-controlled African colonies the process of creating an inferiority complex was even more profound. The lure of 'Frenchification' and the hope that they could become worthy of assimilation into the French society was a tempting incentive. A small black elite helped administer French African colonies as proxies for the French. They were given, at least on paper, full French citizenship, which allegedly afforded them equal rights to white Frenchmen. It was from this elite of black 'Frenchmen', that the first black leaders of French-controlled African territory arose — for example, Leopold Senghor of Senegal and Houphouet-Boigny of Côte d'Ivoire or Ivory Coast.

Leopold Senghor was born in 1906 into a prosperous Serer trading family. A gifted poet and intellectual, he was well socialized in the French culture and familiar with a vast range of Western literature and philosophy. He recounted that his Catholic missionaries in Senegal taught him that his African ancestry was worthless. He left Senegal for France on a government scholarship at the age of 21 to pursue his literary studies. It took about seven years of study in Paris for him to become the epitome of an alienated but 'civilized' black Frenchman. In 1961, he recalled:

"With docility we accepted the values of the West; its discursive reason and its techniques. Our ambition was to become photographic negatives of the colonizers: "Black skinned Frenchmen". It went even further, for we would have blushed, if we could have blushed, about our Black skin, our frizzled hair, our flat noses, above, all for all, the values of our traditional civilization... Our people...,secretly, secretly, caused us shame."[8]

Ultimately, 'Frenchification' was not enough because black Frenchmen and women continued to experience widespread racism, and many, like Senghor, began to search for their true identity. Senghor remembered:

"Paradoxically it was the French, who forced us to seek and then to reveal ourselves. We had been able to assimilate the French language and mathematics but we weren't able to slough off either our Black skin or our Black soul."[9]

Even though Senghor and his companions in Paris promulgated the philosophy of Negritude, a black consciousness movement that asserted the unique contributions, values and characteristics of black people and civilization, he nevertheless remained committed to the French empire.[10]

Houphouet-Boigny, another black 'Frenchman' who rose through the elite in the French colonies, even resisted calls for African colonial independence from France at a time when the independence fervour had gripped the whole of West Africa.

In his book, Decolonizing the African Mind, Chinweizu wrote:

"The Europeanized African, for his part, is overwhelmed by the fantastic achievements of industrial civilization. But having accepted the European propaganda that industrial civilization is the genetic property of its European pioneers, he fails to distinguish industrial civilization as a type from European civilization as an instance of a type. His desire for the former is therefore perverted into a wish to assimilate himself into the latter. He overlooks the fact, which the Japanese and Chinese have demonstrated, that industrial civilization can be replicated by non-Europeans, and so cannot be somehow intrinsically European. And he is usually ignorant of the fact that Europeans were latecomers to scientific culture, and that their pioneering of the industrial revolution was based on scientific heritage borrowed from others — including ancient Egyptian and Mesopotamian civilizations.

Obviously, he can't resist European imperialism if he believes that Europeans are the sole owners of the paradise of industrial civilization; or that European languages, which are colonial languages in Africa, are indispensable for participation in industrial civilization. Any invitation to de-Europeanize his culture would be viewed as an invitation away from the industrial paradise and back to some pre-industrial hell."[11]

The late one-time Prime Minister of Ghana, Kofi Busia, declared himself a European by virtue of his European education and culture.[12]

Without understanding the great psychological impress that Western culture, Christianity and materialism had on Africans or indeed other colonial subjects as in India, it seems inexplicable that hundreds of thousands of Africans fought and died in the First and Second World Wars, even against each other, for their colonial masters.

Thousands of Africans fought and died for the British, against thousands of Africans fighting and dying on the German side during the First and Second World Wars. This is remarkable because by 1914 the colonial masters had not fully yet imposed their authority on Africans. The mental colonization of Africa only truly began in real terms when sufficient numbers of Western-educated and socialised middle class Africans had been firmly indoctrinated in the virtues of their white colonial masters and had tacitly or openly accepted the roles as psychological inferiors to their white masters.

The psychological imperative for millions of Africans to sacrifice their lives and limbs in European wars of dominion over them was well articulated by Chinweizu:

"The reason is simple. The colonized mind, like a well- conditioned slave, is incapable of initiative independent of its master. Initiative in pursuit of the slave's own interests would be tantamount to a revolt."[13]

The white supremacy system conditions many Europeans to aspire to positions of power and correspondingly it conditions miseducated Africans to aspire to positions of servility in the white society. The miseducated African revels in the external attributes of Westernization, which they value very highly indeed — speaking in an English accent, displaying English or Western customs and attitudes. These are valued far more than their African identity, language, customs and culture.

The impact of Western cultural imperialism on the minds of Africans is profound. Once Africans are 'plugged' into the Western paradigm from their formative childhood years, the die is cast. The Western miseducation they receive orders their footsteps, from childhood and onwards, for the rest of their lives. It determines their cultural values, their religious beliefs and even their eating habits and preferences. It makes miseducated Africans insatiable consumers of Western goods.

The Western paradigm defines Africans as a dysfunctional inferior in the hierarchy of the capitalist process, pegging them down to the lowest rungs of its socio-economic ladder. It encourages psychological and physical dependence of African people, allowing their white masters to exploit them for all their human and natural resources without giving them commensurate reward or access to achieving their monetary ambitions. Psychologically, it may be that the prevailing African culture of accepting something for nothing made it easy for Africans to fall into the European trap. This attitude is in sharp contrast to the European attitude of not giving anything unless for something.

In many African communities there is the culture of the 'big man', or 'Oga', as he is called in Nigerian culture. These big men or women are rich, influential and successful people in the community. Many African people who are less financially well off in the community see nothing wrong in taking money or gifts from these big men. Indeed, they will continue to take as long as the big man continues to give.

These 'big men' reinforce their position by how much wealth they can show or give. The less financially well off people, usually somewhat envious of these big men or women, are prepared to eat humble pie as long as its results in them getting what they want. In so doing, it is not customary to question how these big men or women acquired their fortune or the real motives behind their apparent generosity.

Into this environment came the Europeans in whose culture there is nothing like a free lunch. The Europeans did not invest the time or money in Africa without expecting to reap back the rewards at least tenfold. The attitude of some Africans to take money or position without questioning the underlying motives or reasons and long-term effects was then quickly exploited to the Europeans' benefit. To boot, the humility and servitude of Africans towards Europeans, to whom they were effectively selling, or handing over, their birthrights, was interpreted as inferiority and weakness.

The colonialists also deliberately set about dividing the people against themselves, very much like the slave owners did. They exploited every major and minor difference amongst African people to help maintain the country in a state of perpetual conflict. Puppet African leaders had to be installed, whose sole aim was grabbing as much material wealth for themselves as they could. In return for Western military and financial support, they provided the colonialists with the right conditions to fleece the country. The West acted as the 'Mafia' protection wing that could apply external pressure ranging from sanctions, financing rebels to destabilizing regions and, if that failed, covert and then overt military assistance.

The vacuum created by denuding the colonized African people of their identity, culture, religion, government and economy was filled with ideas of Western culture, history and identity. The economic benefits of colonialism went straight to Europe, leaving the African people militarily defenceless and economically dependent on their colonial masters for any development. Thus, a young child growing up in Nigeria will learn a great deal about British history, culture, science and technology to the detriment of their own history and culture. Nobody cared to mention the contributions Africans had made and were still making to all spheres of life, not just in sports and music. Nobody cared to mention that the so-called classical civilizations of the Greeks and Romans borrowed heavily from the Egyptians and the Africans that had once colonized the land mass known as Greece, Italy and Spain. African youth are not taught that the origins of science and religion are African.

The lack of knowledge of their own cultures in the face of that provided by our colonial masters naturally created a bias in the minds of the African recipients. This Western education led quite logically to the perception that their culture, history and peoples were inferior. Without background knowledge, they accepted as fact the propaganda of the white man and just as the captive slaves of North America and the West Indies they were then left without culture, history and identity. They lost belief in the value of their own culture and were denigrated by the Western culture they craved.

Today, the net effect is that the average African citizen does not have much faith in his or her government. Africans saw quite clearly that many African politicians had no interest in their betterment but simply went into government to enrich themselves. They did not have the power to challenge them because of the 'Western Mafia' who ensured that corrupt African politicians could fleece their countries almost at will. Today, the more despotic and brutal an African regime, the more desirable to the West.

Therefore, it should not come as a surprise that the majority, if not all, despotic African leaders were at some time or are still in close collusion with the West. Idi Amin of Uganda was installed and protected by the United Kingdom while Mobutu Sese Seko of Zaire was anointed by the United States. Despite the fact that these despotic leaders butchered thousands of their own people, they still found much favour with the West and had the red carpets rolled out for them on many occasions. In many cases, corrupt African leaders colluded with the West to accept morally bankrupt contracts, which ran their governments into massive debts which are still crippling their countries today. This practice led directly to the death of millions of Africans through the lack of adequate health care, drugs, roads and infrastructure.

Unfortunately, today many Africans still see their governments as a means of enriching themselves and their families, rather than an opportunity to serve their people and bring about change for the good. Corrupt politicians are the scourge of the African continent because they still facilitate the Western plunder of African countries, which fall further and further behind in all areas of development in spite of their abundance of raw material and manpower.

In summary, the alleged superiority of the white slave masters was not one of higher intellect, moral codes or physical characteristic of any kind. It was based primarily on psychological manipulation wrought by physical and emotional violence. It required the total dehumanization and exploitation of African slaves and people in every way they could imagine possible.

CHAPTER FIFTY FOUR

SOME LEGACIES OF MENTAL SLAVERY

The first legacy of mental slavery is poverty.

Poverty can be seen as a disease of the mind as well as a physical lack of money and material goods. While poverty exists in every human society on earth, the state of poverty is also relative to one's perceptions and accepted social norms of what is of value or not. The paucity of money and material assets in a Western society that is defined by materialism is clearly poverty but it cannot be extrapolated so easily to a society that does not value materialism in the same manner.

When African and other foreign societies are assimilated into the Western global power structure but denied access to its money and material wealth, poverty is the only outcome. The white supremacist global power structure socially engineered mental slavery as a means of assuring itself access to the natural and human resources of African people and their diaspora wherever they are. They created and maintained material wealth for themselves while simultaneously restricting the access of non-whites to do the same. Even blindfolded, if you spin a globe of the world and stab your finger at almost any Western society, you will win no prizes for guessing that the African segment of the ethnic minority population occupies the lowest rungs of their society. The smattering of prominent or rich Africans who make the headlines is statistically insignificant.

Typically, in the West, African diasporans usually end up in positions of servitude, low and poorly paid unskilled work. They will also, by virtue of their lowly economic positions, be more exposed to the alienating effects of capitalist societies in addition to their poverty. In comparison with the local white population, they suffer disproportionate rates of crime, poor health, poor housing, reduced education and job prospects,

Africans became a huge resource to the West during the transatlantic slave trade and have remained so until today. Only a clear understanding of the imperatives and aims of the white supremacy power structure — essential knowledge for every African — will help them come out of poverty. Many Africans fail to understand or appreciate that they work for a system, designed from its inception, to use and impoverish Africa. True knowledge will make Africans rethink and begin to reorder their footsteps in the direction of self-actualisation and knowledge.

Africans, however rich or poor, if dependent on the white capitalist system for their livelihood and existence, have a degree of exposure and vulnerability. Africans armed with the right knowledge must remember that social alienation is self-imposed. Therefore a knowledgeable African can mitigate the effects of the Western capitalist system on their mental and physical wellbeing.

Africans who start cultivating and nurturing their inner selves through true knowledge and association with like-minded Africans, will find that they begin to experience a definite increase in self-worth that is not associated with the possession of material wealth. The reorientation and centring of self will develop and foster both psychological and material wellbeing. These Africans will find that they neither need — nor indeed want — the acceptance of white supremacists, an unnecessary burden that skews the thought process of many in the African diaspora. They will be able to develop normal and healthy relationships with themselves and other people.

The second legacy of mental slavery is Fragmented Individualism. Many miseducated Africans concentrate all their attention, efforts and emotions on negative African traits and behaviour, just as their miseducation in Western ideology leads them to do. They rationalize that the African condition and position in the capitalist system is justified — without considering the effects of white social engineering.

The unsuspecting miseducated African then finds himself in a dilemma. After internalizing the hatred, bias and low self-esteem projected to him from the white community or his colonial masters, he expresses his hatred and self-loathing towards himself and any other African or descendant he comes across. Walled off from his history, past and future, he lives only in the distorted present.

Fragmented individualism is a psychological response found mainly in non-whites who at all costs seek acceptance and validation in the white supremacy culture. In what is almost a mirror image reaction to colour anxiety and numerical inadequacy in whites, most fragmented individuals are black Africans or non-white people, who form ethnic minority groups within a majority of white people. These people want to integrate by losing their own identities and reinventing themselves in the white community.

Subconsciously and, in some cases, consciously, miseducated Africans know they can never attain the status of a first-class citizen in Western society. They are aware that they will never receive the full recognition and remuneration of their white peers. However, this does not deter them in their quest to whiten themselves as much as they can. They make a great effort to speak with the 'correct accent', adopt the correct 'etiquette' and usually try to distance themselves from all things African or black, especially in the presence of the white folks they need to impress.

Unfortunately, many Africans and their diaspora fall into this trap. They have struggled against terrible odds in the white society, and feel justifiably proud of their achievements. Even so, they realize they have paid an extremely high price for the 'success' of serving their white masters.

Many of these black people, especially the more successful ones, can be savagely critical of other black people. While writing this book, the author had informal discussions with many successful African men and women and found that almost uniformly many expressed extremely negative views of Africa and Africans. Paradoxically, many felt they were alone in their achievements and did not see themselves as part of the overall black problem, even though they had very positive comments to make about their own sacrifices and achievements. When asked pointedly if they felt that they themselves embodied some of the negative traits of black people, they again almost all denied having any. In other words, they could not see many positives about Africans in general, despite their own achievements, and the fact that they were Africans themselves.

This exposes one of the main ways human beings express subconscious and conscious negative thoughts about themselves and others. Criticism is one of the ways the human mind deals with its own psychological stress by comparing and criticising others. The criticism produced is projected on to others rather than self and is usually unfair and unbalanced.

A healthy critique, on the other hand, emphasises the two sides of the story and is aimed at building people up rather than simply tearing them down. Criticism is usually accompanied by constructive advice on how to improve things and is always better received.

Fragmented individuals invariably find themselves in a no-man's land, rejected by the white community they seek to integrate into and self-isolated from the black community and people who remind them of their inner self-loathing or hatred of blackness.

The third legacy of mental slavery is black-on-black violence, one of the worst legacies of the slave trade and colonization. Young Africans fight each other to the death for a myriad of petty reasons that primarily stem from their poor socio-economic position in the global Western hierarchy.

Many of the problems facing black African individuals, communities and countries can be explained by poverty. The high levels of self-hatred are fostered by their social deprivations and lack of avenues of self-development and expression. Under Western domination, African self-hatred separates Africans and their diaspora from other impoverished people.

In his book, Black-On-Black Violence, a prominent author on black American issues, Amos N. Wilson, tried to explain the high degree of self-hatred and violence in the African American situation. He wrote:

"The bane of the African-American community is the exploitative White American community which projects a so-called civilised, fraternal, egalitarian, liberal face while concurrently seeking to maintain while supremacy.

This means that the White American community must maintain African subordination while appearing not to do so. It must cannibalistically sacrifice the vitality, autonomy, and if need to be, the life of the African-American community while posing as its benefactor and saviour.

It pleads innocence while washing its hands of the blood of African people.

This duplicitous task can only be accomplished by making it appear that the African community is dying of natural causes, not of an ingenious attempt on the part of the White American community to strangle it to death.

This means that African American hands must be used to plunge White American manufactured dagger into the hearts of African American citizens.

This is the assigned role of the Black on Black violent criminal."[1]

This analogy is quite apt in Africa too, where the equivalents of the 'black-on-black' criminals are the defunct puppet governments. They only act in self-preservation and in protecting the interests of their European financiers. Corrupt African politicians act as the European channel into the affairs and economies of African countries. This is very much the same way a parasite may require a carrier to infect the host.

By necessity, Western nations have to disseminate negative information about Africa, Africans, and their descendants. The negative stereotyping creates a negative reference point for members of the white communities. It provides the West with a heightened sense of moral superiority, better living conditions, achievements, ideals and goals. This negative portrayal also provides the West with the basis for taking punitive action against African countries. Under the guise of perceived threats to their security and the installation of false democracy in Africa, the West can exploit the African people and their economies, time and time again while pretending to help them.

The negative stereotypical image of a black African in the West is so powerful that it can dramatically alter an African child's capabilities and potential.

Crime is a social phenomenon and not simply the preserve of the black community but the black American male has been so heavily targeted and stereotyped that they are treated as living symbols of crime in America today. The black male is guilty of being a criminal just by the mere fact of his very existence. Wilson wrote:

"In the context of White American domination there are no innocent

Black males, just criminals who have not yet been detected, apprehended or convicted."[2]

To 'help' the white communities reach these conclusions, the media continuously beams made-up, alleged and actual infringements committed by any black person to cement the idea of the black community's inherent criminality in the minds of all white and black people. If there are no juicy crime stories or notorious black celebrity stories then the focus is usually on the deprivation that is ravishing the African communities and countries. Few of these stories are balanced as they never point out what has caused the deprivation. In so doing, they fulfil their real objective, which is to reinforce their superiority and better economic status. The deprived African community then provides negative reference points and the smokescreen duplicitous Western governments need in order to carry out more depraved acts to maintain status quo.

White-on-white and white on any other race of people crime constitute the main forms of crime in the United States, Europe or, in fact, any part of the world today. However, due to the effectiveness of the stereotyping the Western media has managed to convince not only their own citizens but paradoxically even the victims of these crimes that the opposite is the case. This is no small achievement. This is like an apprehended burglar convincing his victims that their belongings have not been stolen but misplaced by themselves.

Corporate crime in America robs Americans of billions of dollars, endangers the health and destroys the lives of millions of Americans and non-Americans, yet these activities are not even perceived as crime. Rather 'street crime', the preserve of African-Americans is perceived as crime. As reprehensible as some of the street crimes that are beamed on the TV are, they are not even as much as 1/100th as damaging to the nation as corporate crime.[3]

The judicial, police and prison systems are also geared along these lines. Administration of justice is grossly biased against the Negro and the poor.

Arrest and imprisonment are a process reserved almost exclusively for the black and the poor; the major function of the police is the preservation, not of public order, but of social order — that is the inequality between man and man.[4]

White policemen, empowered by the knowledge of the racist wishes of the wider society, also want to preserve — not only protect — white privilege and tend to resort to brutality and other draconian methods in the process.

Many European and North American courts violate and suspend the due process of the law and show clear double standards when dealing with Africans. In general, the law comes down much harder on Africans, who generally receive longer and harsher sentences. The white American community is prepared to pay more taxes, build bigger prisons, and incarcerate prisoners at a cost of over $30,000–40000 per head per year.[5]

The money would be better spent bringing schools and infrastructure up to scratch in deprived areas. This would give black African youths a constructive outlet and help them become meaningful members of society later in life. It is well known that many prisons are merely training grounds for criminals and many former inmates come out and repeatedly re-offend in one way or another.

Western communities have not been set up so that Africans or their descendants can ever achieve full integration or first-class citizenship, psychologically or economically.

It is crucial that Africans and their diaspora, before anything else, re-establish their lost identity, true sense of history and achievements and adopt an Afrocentric based plan of economic and psychological parity. Every single African and the descendants of the diaspora must take this step as individual, communities and countries. Today, the main function of the black man in the Western world is to be a source of free or cheap labour and their countries to be exploited for their natural resources and manpower. In this dependent position, they remain trapped in negative social, economic and political positions in relation to Caucasians, who fulfil their twin goals, namely the subjugation and domination of all other races, especially Africans.

The lack of appreciation of this fundamental fact has left Africans and their diaspora struggling to achieve any real development. In the case of the African Americans and the West Indians in the UK, they are dependent on the same Europeans who kidnapped their descendants from Africa as slaves for all their psychological, social and economic needs.

Today racism is now largely institutionalized. The glass ceiling which aspiring black people come up against determines the limits of their aspirations and achievements. It significantly diminishes the capacity for black people, aspiring to excel in the Eurocentric model they find themselves in, to effectively contribute to their own communities, as they only become well trained in the fulfilment of the white man's agenda, dreams and plans.

Africans have drawn the short end of the stick, be it on an individual basis, as communities, or as the former colonies, in all their dealings with Europeans. From an African perspective, Africans have lost an enormous amount of resource and manpower to the West. The transatlantic slave trade and colonization left Africans the poorest people in the world. In addition, Africans have suffered immensely from the loss of culture, history of their own achievements, control of their own polities and destinies.

History dictates that Africans and their diaspora should not trust their futures, economies and polities to influences that do not have their best interests at heart. This is not advocating total disengagement with the West or Western societies, in which many now reside, but it calls into question the gullible way in which Africans have lived, expecting the white communities to 'do the right thing' and give them back their identity, redress the economic and political imbalance and establish a free and fair society for all.

Unfortunately, the utopia of a Western-instigated redress and equality will never happen and Africans need to take control of their own destiny, economies and politics. Africans and their diaspora must rediscover the great achievements of their forefathers, who set the stage for human civilization, and plot their own path to the future. A resurgent Africa will lay the framework for a better world in general.

"No African living in the 20th century has escaped the taint of the colonial experience. None has freed himself from the colonial mentality in

every department, or from the structures, which maintain and reproduce that mentality. The decolonization of the African mind must therefore be seen as a collective enterprise, as a communal exorcism through an intellectual bath in which we need one another's help to scrub those nooks of our minds which we cannot scour by ourselves."[6]

CHAPTER FIFTY FIVE

YOUR COUNTRY NEEDS YOU BUT DOES NOT WANT YOU

'This is our basic conclusion: Our nation is moving towards two societies, one Black, one White, separate and unequal.' — Summary, Report of the National Advisory Commission on Civil Disorders[1]

'These two nations, these separate societies, have existed from the start.' **Andrew Hacker**[2]

'There ain't no Black in the Union Jack.' **Paul Gilroy**[3]

'Representatives and direct taxes shall be apportioned... according to their respective numbers, which shall be determined by adding to the whole numbers of free persons,... three-fifths of all other persons.' — Article I, Section 2 [3], the Constitution of the United States of America, 1787[4]

During the First World War the British army recruitment ran adverts to rally the British public into enlisting for the war. Lord Kitchener's advert, a British war veteran and hero himself, was one of the most imposing. His dramatic poster read: *"Your Country Needs You"*.[5] This must have been very compelling to impressionable British youths at the time, who wanted to defend their country against the threat of the Germans. Unfortunately, today, like then, the current state of affairs is that while most countries need their people, eventually, they do not want them.

It is an absolute necessity for the Western capitalist process of exploitation to create and maintain a social hierarchy on which it thrives — the rich and poor, lords and peasants, haves and have-nots. Therefore, most of the people Western capitalism oppresses fall into a peculiar state of being needed by their countries and foreign taskmasters for the cheap labour they provide but not wanted or appreciated for who they are as people or individuals.

John Pilger aptly described them as 'unpeople' in his book Hidden Agendas. Most 'unpeople' live in the Third World but they also occupy the lowest rungs of the social hierarchy in the developed world.[6]

Unpeople are simultaneously essential and incidental to the capitalist process of accumulation. Even though their collective efforts are of great value to the system, individually they have no intrinsic value in the eyes of the capitalist system and in essence are readily dispensable commodities.

It is a sad fact that most ethnic minority groups living as immigrants in the West and North America can be described as unpeople. Despite being much needed for their contributions and taxes, they often find themselves excluded from mainstream opportunities. In the UK, they are still made to feel like an uninvited intruder who has gate-crashed a tea party at Buckingham Palace.

In 2016 former British Prime Minister David Cameron referred to immigrants as 'swarms' threatening to overrun Europe.[7]

Later, in October 2016, Freuke Petry, leader of the German far right party ADP described immigrants as 'compost'.[8]

Ironically, many 'unpeople' and immigrants are forced into seeking refuge from war, human rights abuse and the crushing policies brought about by the foreign policies of the very same Western nations, like the US, UK and France, who despise them so much. Iraq, Afghanistan, Libya and Syria are examples of recent Western military interventions in foreign countries that have directly led to wave after wave of immigration towards Europe and North America.

It is true that the life and fortunes of African and other immigrants to the West can be dramatically changed by their access to Western societies and the possession of proper immigration status like citizenship, passports and other relevant papers. However, the single most determining factor in deciding the outcome of the life of an immigrant in the West is institutional racism.

Institutional racism is the invisible force that maintains social hierarchy in Western societies and severely limits the access of ethnic minorities to equal opportunities in all areas of social activity. Institutional racism utilises a wide ranging system of micro and macro inequities to blight the life experience of ethnic minorities.

Racism has undergone a significant metamorphosis since the transatlantic slave trade, as it keeps abreast with the times. Thus, institutional racism is the proverbial glass ceiling aspiring immigrants come up against in the West. At best, institutional racism can severely limit the capacity for black African people aspiring to excel in the Eurocentric model. At worst, it can exploit the biased judicial systems and is responsible for the extrajudicial murder of the immigrants and ethnic minorities. In addition, immigrants are unable to contribute to their countries of origin or communities as their efforts become channelled either into survival or the fulfilment of the goals of Western capitalism.

Scholars have described racism as old and new. Old racism is dominative and is based on two main theories. The first of these is ideological. This identifies individuals as superior, based on some real or imagined biological or inherent characteristic. The second is common sense racism, namely life experiences which guide us as to how the world works. When we build a picture of how things should be, it constitutes an ideology. An ideology, when taken for granted, becomes 'common sense'. However, common sense reasoning is neither consistent nor systematic; neither is it stable as it may change when tested.

In its modern expression, institutional racism suppresses the debate about race-based inequality, making it is easier for racist practices to be denied and persist in Western societies. *"Once race as a factor is silenced, it is possible to continue practices that exclude people."*[9]

In modern day Britain, racism has become so elusive and subtle that it is almost a diagnosis of exclusion. Crude racist behaviour, like open name-calling, is frowned upon while more measured racial abuse, behaviour and racially motivated exclusion is generally interpreted as non-racist. This presents ethnic minorities in the UK with the burden of proof when claiming they are treated in a racist manner and allows the behaviour to persist.

After the racially motivated murder of Steven Lawrence in 1993, the Macpherson Report into the murder of black teenager Stephen Lawrence set out to provide grounds to help clarify the amorphous nature of racism in the UK and surmised that:

"The link between institutional racism...is clearest when the link between race and practice is determined when there is a collective failure of an organization to provide an appropriate and professional service to people because of their skin colour, culture, or ethnic origin. It can be seen or detected, in processes, attitudes and behaviour which amounts to discrimination through unwitting prejudice, ignorance, thoughtlessness and racist stereotyping which disadvantage ethnic minority people."[10]

New racism marks a shift from old, dominative racism to new aversive racism. The social and political context of post-war, post-industrial Britain has led to a re-articulation and reconfiguration of British racism. Enoch Powell was the key spokesperson for re-articulating racism in Britain by reconfiguring the myth of the British nation as homogeneous and fixed:

Aversive racists can appear liberal, tolerant and even supportive of black liberation, but this expression is just a veneer — beneath this outer appearance the aversive racist is keen to maintain their dominant position.[11]

In Britain, institutional racism is focused mainly on the entry of ethnic minorities, especially black Africans, into a mythically homogenous British nation. Margaret Thatcher and her new right Conservative Party helped to develop strategies for articulating racism without the mention of race.

The immigration card is one of the favourite ploys used by the British press to whip up feeling of xenophobia among decent white people, who are constantly scared of being swamped by immigrants. The strange thing is that the alleged homogeneity of the British people is itself a myth. Many Britons have Gaelic, British, German and Scandinavian roots. With the transatlantic slave trade, many Europeans acquired African genes as well because sexual exploitation was widely practiced.

In 1917, in response to growing anti-German sentiment, King George V changed the name of the British Royal family, descendants of the German House of Saxe-Coburg and Gotha, from Saxe-Coburg and Gotha to Windsor. Admiral von Louis Alexander of Battenberg also changed his name, at the behest of King George V, to Admiral Louis Mountbatten to disguise his German origins.[12]

During the First World War anti-German sentiment peaked in March 1917 when an ironically-named heavy German aircraft called the Gotha G.IV became a household name after it crossed the English Channel and began bombing London directly.

Sadly, the diverse origins of the British people do not stop politicians from capitalizing on the frequently employed 'race card'. Edgar Griffin, a long-standing Conservative councillor and father of the one-time leader of the British National Party, Nick Griffin, claimed that immigration, especially black, was turning the UK into a 'mongrel nation'.[13]

The myth of white homogeneity and quintessentially English culture therefore is exactly that — a myth. The iconic St George, fondly remembered by the white flag with the red cross, adopted by King Richard, the 'Lionheart' in the 14th century and much loved by xenophobic, right wing, anti-immigration groups in the UK, is purely fictional and is thought to have originated from Turkey. It is highly unlikely that the real St George, a Roman soldier of Turkish and Syrian descent, ever slayed a dragon. If St George were to set foot in modern Britain today he would probably be languishing in a detention camp for illegal immigrants while awaiting imminent deportation. British Prime Minister, Boris Johnson, the quintessentially English and maverick Conservative MP's paternal grandfather, Ali Kemal, is Turkish.

Other quintessentially English cultures have their origins in other countries too. Tea was adopted by the British from China and taken to India, the game of polo from the Assam state in India and the signature fish and chips dish from Jewish refugees from Portugal and Spain, who introduced fried fish to the UK.

Nevertheless, immigration continues to be viewed by a minority as an attack on the natural and homogenous white British nation and a corruption of its 'purity'. The new British concern over her territory was expressed in immigration controls and attacking anti-racism as reverse racism. There was no need to express racism in the crude socio-biological terms of the past. Rather simplistic assumptions about human nature were made instead:

"Contemporary British racism deals in cultural differences rather than crude biological hierarchy. It asserts not that blacks are inferior but that we are different, so different that our distinctive mode of being is at odds with residence in this country".[14]

Cultural racists recast the language of cultural diversity, in order to promote exclusion and hegemony; culture is something you are born into, not something you acquire, the conservatives argue. Viewed in this fashion culture inherits the role of race in the nineteenth century, and the history of biology.

Culture becomes particularistic and exclusive, delineating a common past to which some can belong, and some cannot. And the past becomes determinist and teleogical, holding power over the present through tradition and rootedness.[15]

By living according to this xenophobic theory the problem for blacks and other foreign immigrants is that true integration becomes unattainable:

"They are forever locked in a bastard culture of their enslaved ancestors, unable to break into the mainstream alternative."[16]

Thus, institutionalised racism became a way of life for both the immigrants and the local British indigenes and this was reflected in the difficulties the first African arrivals experienced after the Second World War. As Britain rebuilt itself after the Second World War, it desperately needed cheap labour from wherever it could get it. Naturally, it turned to its colonies and people from British colonies were allowed to come to England, not philanthropically in order to better themselves as the immigrants might have thought, but to help fill a vast labour shortage in British industries.

Enoch Powell achieved the pinnacle of infamy with his anti-immigration 'Rivers of Blood' speech.[17] However, even while decrying British immigration while Enoch Powell was Health Minister in charge of the newly formed National Health Service, he still saw the sense in attracting Indian and African medical personnel — doctors and nurses — from British colonies to the 'motherland'.

Between 1950 and 1960, the average rate of unemployment in the UK was below 1.7%. This meant that British industry had to look abroad for extra workers, because most people were already gainfully employed. Citizens of British colonies were granted UK citizenship under the British Nationality Act of 1948, allowing migrant workers to come to Britain and stay as long as they liked.

Conversely, unemployment was high in the African, Indian, Pakistani and West Indian British colonies, especially after the McCarran-Walter Act of 1952 had blocked the traditional outlet for West Indians to the US.[18]

The trickle of foreign immigration to the UK soon became a flood and the pressure on local resources like housing, schools, medical care and social services rose as did the resentment and prejudice among British locals.[19] The net result was a reluctant British government allowing 'British citizens' to immigrate into the UK while a resentful British public had to put up with the steady influx of foreign people, who were, in their eyes, racially inferior and in competition with them for available jobs and housing.

In 1948, reacting to the anxiety being caused by the reality of foreign immigration into Britain, Clement Attlee, British Prime Minister when ithe Empire Windrush arrived in the United Kingdom with a contingent of West Indians looking for work and to resettle in the UK, wrote in response to a letter from some backbenchers:

"I am replying to the letter signed by yourself and ten other members of Parliament on 22 June about the West Indians, who arrived in this country on that day, on board the Empire Windrush.

I note what you say, but I think it would be a great mistake to take the emigration of this Jamaican party to the United Kingdom too seriously.

It is traditional that British subjects, whether of Dominion or colonial origin [and whatever race or colour], should be freely admissible to the United Kingdom, that tradition is not, in my view, to be lightly discarded, particularly at a time when we are importing foreign labour in large numbers. It would be fiercely resented in the colonies themselves, and it would be a great mistake to take any measure, which would tend to reduce the goodwill and loyalty of the colonies towards Great Britain.

If our policy were to result in the influx of undesirables, we might, however, unwillingly, have to consider modifying it. But I would not be willing to consider that except on really compelling evidence, which I do not think exists at the present time."[20]

In actual fact, British anxiety about the presence of foreigners in their midst goes back many centuries. Given the manpower needs of the expanding British navy and merchant fleets at sea in the 18th century it was inevitable that African enslaved labour would be drawn upon. In 1786, Governor Parry of Barbados wrote to the Colonial Office:

"The numbers of negro slaves employed in navigating the trading vessels in the seas seems to me to increase so much as to require the attention of the British legislator, as it throws so many English seamen out of employment."[21]

As the influx of foreign migrant workers into Britain increased, it did not take long for the latent British racism and xenophobia to express itself. Even as the West Indians disembarked from the ships, signs like 'No blacks, No dogs, No Irish' awaited them.

However, taking an immigrant's perspective, there seemed nothing more logical than returning to the 'mother nation', as described by their British colonial masters. Most British immigrants were taught English language and culture, as most of the British colonies modelled their educational curriculum on that of England. Apart from their foreign location, the facilities and people, it was essentially the same education, transposed to different parts of the former British colonial empire.

Human beings have always migrated in search of better living conditions since Neolithic times. Therefore, the desire to follow the flight path of the resources of former British colonies back to England was a logical and natural response by people denuded of their own culture, natural resources and opportunities.

Caught between the crossfire of their puppet neo-colonial governments and their Western puppet masters, many immigrants left their countries, ravaged by the effects of globalisation, corrupt and brutal puppet regimes, hardship and poverty, in search of greener pastures. During the British colonial era, many people in the vast outreaches of the British Empire believed that the streets of London were literally paved with gold.

Unfortunately on arrival in the West most of the immigrants ended up as cheap, expendable labour, employed in menial tasks, often far beneath their qualifications and ability. Disillusioned, they became firmly stuck for generations on the lowest rungs of the Western socio-economic ladder.

Thus, like an act of bad karma, the British people have been unable to shake off their colonial past. Despite all the xenophobia, racial prejudice and discrimination shown to foreigners, the influx has continued. As the saying goes:

"The foreigners are here because you were there."

Having imbibed English education, culture and ideologies in their colonized countries, the immigrants had been suitably trained to serve Her Majesty and country — and where better to do so than in England. In fact, many Africans who had internalized most of the English ideals, instinctively felt out of place in their countries of origin as their English socialisation clashed with the culture and ways of the African 'natives'.

For many ethnic minorities, following this 'natural urge' has led to a lifetime of suffering. The English and other 'parental colonial nations' in the West wasted no time at all in making the immigrants feel as unwelcome as possible. The proverbial glass ceiling was quickly erected to prevent any real upward mobility of ethnic minorities. The notion that ethnic minorities have to work ten times as hard for ten times less was no myth at all. It fitted in perfectly with the overall strategic objective of imperialism that assimilates 'foreigners' up to second or third class citizenry at best. It maintains a significant labour force of cheap but highly skilled foreigners. It also fosters a superiority complex in the privileged whites, uniting them in xenophobia against the 'constant threat' of being overrun by immigrants.

In the United States, the 'problem' of black slaves becoming free people triggered off widespread radical extremism, mainly in the slave-owning South. However in the UK the response was far more subtle. Whether it was open or covert racism, institutionalised racism or other forms of racism, it was clear right from the start that an ethnic minority in England's status in society had largely already been predetermined, namely, as a lower-class citizen. There was less than no chance of ever being fully accepted in society, no matter what you achieved.

To the English public it became accepted that every conceivable obstacle would be thrown in the path of ethnic minorities to ensure they remained ethnic minorities. British society is very hierarchical in its structure. Even among white Britons, it is obvious that many socio-economic barriers prevent its own citizens from being the best they can. One of the first obstacles placed in the way of Jamaican immigrants was the lack of accommodation, not due to a lack of housing, but an unwillingness of white landlords to rent to black tenants.

Fast forward to 2013 when, undeterred by historical precedents, the ex-British Prime Minister David Cameron authorised the Home Office to start a highly controversial 'Go home' campaign, which involved a program of arresting and repatriating illegal immigrants.

In July 2013, the Home Office wheeled out its program titled 'Go home or face arrest'.[22]

'Racist government vans' warned illegal immigrants to 'go home or face arrest' and offered a phone number which users could call or text for assistance on returning to where they had come from.

Unsurprisingly, it is widely reported that the British police and immigration officers were racial profiling and were stopping and searching people based on their skin colour and place of origin.

In a separate move the Home Office plan to force visitors from Asian and African countries to pay a £3,000 bond before being allowed to visit the UK was not agreed by the coalition government.

Knowing Britain's xenophobic nature, it was surprising that David Cameron decided to gamble his political future and the future of the country as a whole, on a referendum about staying in, or leaving the European Union. The Remain campaigners appealed to the intellectuals while the Leave campaigners, spearheaded by Nigel Farage, the leader of UKIP, a far Right party, Boris Johnson and Michael Gove, whipped up people's deep rooted fears and sentiments on the thorny issue of foreign immigration.

On June 23th 2016 Britain's decision to leave the European Union sent shockwaves throughout the world. The British people were split between 'Leave' and 'Remain' supporters,, old and young. Scotland and Northern Ireland, that had overwhelmingly voted to stay in the EU, found themselves seriously compromised by the results. It soon became clear that neither the Remain nor the Leave Campaigns had made any adequate contingency plans. David Cameron's Remain camp had assumed it would win with the full backing of the establishment and big business and the Leave campaigners who had expected to lose were suddenly thrust into the limelight. Britain had decided to check out of the European Union without a passport or a destination.

In the eyes of the British people on the street, the EU referendum results were a decisive victory over the 'foreign invader', who was 'taking' their benefits, jobs and housing. The white racists and xenophobes felt vindicated by the popular vote and the incidence of racial abuse and attacks soared following the referendum vote. However, David Cameron's debacle was nothing compared to the political earthquake across the pond.

In the 2016 presidential election in the United States, the Republican candidate, Donald Trump, defied the pollsters to achieve an unprecedented victory against Hilary Clinton's well-oiled and established political machine. Political pundits argued that the American electorate were disillusioned with the political establishment that Hilary Clinton embodied. Some argued that people just wanted change but, very much like the British vote, the American election was marked by strong racial undertones.

It did not seem to matter to Donald Trump's Republican

supporters that he had evaded tax for many years, been found to be a xenophobic, misogynist, racist Islamophobe and that he had lied about almost everything. His support grew stronger and stronger amongst the conservatives and right-wing groups.

Few political pundits concentrated on how Donald Trump divided the American people along racial lines and exploited the deep-rooted and widespread racial anxieties that plague the whites most Western countries. What most pundits failed to dwell on was just how strong Donald Trump's credentials were as a white supremacist. His campaign message to 'Make America Great Again' was a thinly veiled call for white privilege to supersede all. The Ku Klux Klan openly applauded the fact that Donal Trump shared similar views with them. In a radio message to his audience, the former Imperial Grand Wizard of the Ku Klux Klan, David Duke, warned his followers that voting for any candidate other than Donald Trump would be *'treason to your heritage'*.[23]

Following Trump's election victory the former Wizard tweeted: *"This is one of the most exciting nights of my life, make no mistake about it, our people have played a huge role in electing Trump."*[24]

It is true that Donald Trump's election machine was far more social media savvy than Hilary Clinton's. It is also true that Hilary Clinton was struggling to energise and motivate her Democratic followers and the undecided. However, it is also true that Donald Trump's racial escapades were not limited to his election campaign. He has a proven track record of racism and misogyny that goes back many decades. In 1983 and 1986, the Justice Department sued Donald Trump's company, Trump Management Cooperation, for not renting apartments to black people in the Brooklyn, Queens and Staten Island boroughs of New York City. In 1989, Donald Trump helped fuel the public outrage and politicizing of the judicial process that sent five innocent black men to jail following their alleged assault and rape of a female jogger in Manhattan's Central Park. Donald Trump took out full-page adverts in four New York City area newspapers calling for the return of the death penalty and an expansion of police authority. Later known as the Central Park Five, the black men's convictions were overturned in 2002 after DNA evidence proved that they were innocent. Donald Trump remained unapologetic that he had called for their execution and that the five black men had been wrongly sent to jail. He maintained that the men were guilty even after they were released.

As if to confirm his credentials as a white supremacist and racist, Donald Trump's appointments to office as President Elect were revealing: Steve Bannon, his Chief Strategist and Senior Counsellor was the former executive chairman of a white Supremacy group, Brietbart; his choice for Attorney General of the United States, Senator Jeff Sessions was refused confirmation as a Federal Judge in 1986 following allegations of racially insensitive remarks he had made; including that he had stated: *"The only reason he had not joined the Ku Klux Klan was because their members smoked marijuana"*; Steve Munchin, Donald's Trump's choice for Treasury Secretary had been previously found guilty of profiteering from black and ethnic minority communities and refusing to rent apartments or lend money to them via his bank; and Donald Trump appointed Retired General Mike Flyn as National Security Advisor, who had been criticized for his anti-Islamic stance and comments for many years.[25]

Very few Caucasian people really appreciate what it is like to be black or a foreigner in the West. It is not surprising as in their own lives they do not, or rarely do, suffer racial discrimination at work, in shops, hotels or by the police and justice system. For black African people living in the West, it is the opposite. They are exposed to a constant barrage of conscious or subconscious prejudice in the very same institutions that act so courteously to their white colleagues, workers or citizens.

In the late 1950s, racism and segregation was legal in the States. Black people were still being lynched and segregated on buses, in restaurants and schools. There were 'whites-only' restrooms, hotels and residential areas. The colour line was effectively drawn in blood in the southern states of Alabama, Louisiana, Georgia and Mississippi.

A white American journalist, John Howard Griffin, decided to take the considerable risk of finding out what it was like to be black in the US at that time, by changing the colour of his skin. With the help of a dermatologist, he darkened his skin colour using medication and ultraviolet light. To complete the look, he also used some black paint. His racial change was only superficial, because he kept his name and spoke with his normal accent. To his horror, he immediately began to experience an almost intolerable level of racial hatred and discrimination everywhere he went.

When Griffin retraced his steps and visited places he normally frequented as a white man, he was shocked to find people he knew in the shops and restaurants discriminated against him — the same people who had been very pleasant and courteous to him as a white man. He found that he was discriminated against everywhere — in the shops, in the restaurants, on buses, etc. He could not use the toilets in white owned shops and restaurants and had to look for the odd and awkwardly situated black only restrooms where he could find them.

He met and befriended several African American people and was amazed at their fortitude and generosity despite their suffering. He also glimpsed the other side of the psychological inferiority complex. He was astonished when seemingly intelligent black people, or Negroes as they were called then, intimated to him that the lighter the skin of a Negro the more trustworthy he was. He witnessed first-hand the destructive tendencies of this internalized self-hate and black-on-black violence.

As he toured the southern states, he kept a diary that was as chilling as it was gripping. His book, Black Like Me, was to become a bestseller as it exposed the predicament of African Americans in the Deep South. In one incident, he thumbed a ride from a white man, a married 53-year-old father of grown children and a grandfather of two. He was mortified to hear how his host talked casually of how he forced the 'coloured girls' he hired to have sex with him or lose their jobs and how troublesome blacks were shipped off to a different state or killed. After he thanked him for the ride and was about to leave the car, his white host said:

"'I'll tell you how it is here. We'll do business with you people [Black people]. We'll sure as hell screw your women. Other than that, you're completely off the record, as far as we're concerned. And the quicker you people get that through your heads, the better off you'll be."[26]

In the end, all it took was one more 'hate stare' from a white complete stranger and he decided he could carry on no longer. After three weeks as a 'black man', from November 7th to November 28th 1959, he became so despondent that he decided to change back to his real identity.

His book aroused great anger and hatred from the white community. As he spoke publicly about his experiences on television and wrote articles in the newspapers, he and his family began to receive death threats and his effigy was burnt in the streets. Eventually Mr Griffin and his family fled to Canada after they were inundated with threatening hate calls, hate mail, death threats and intimidation.[27]

Everything changes, but everything stays the same. In essence, while white racism has changed, much of the change has been superficial. white supremacy still conditions the lives of Africans all over the world today. It is ironic that John Griffin could only last three weeks as a 'black man' but black people have to suffer racism, personally and vicariously all their whole lives.

John Griffin's three-week experience of being an African American was, of course, only a microcosm of the life experience of African Americans, at that time. White racists do not need to know a black person's personality, abilities or aspirations or even names. All that concerns them about Africans is in the colour of their skin and the negative stereotypes which are attached to dark skin colour and have been socially transmitted in the West for centuries.

It is worth exploring some key social issues to get a clearer picture of the impact of institutionalised racism.

PART TEN:
SOCIAL EFFECTS

CHAPTER FIFTY SIX

SOCIAL MOBILITY

It is truly surprising that countries like the United States and Britain, which remonstrate about freedom and democracy, are also the two countries with the lowest social mobility in the West.

Social mobility is an economic index that shows how the prevailing socio-economic and political environments allow or prevent people from being upwardly socially mobile, thus improving their lot in society. Low social mobility is, therefore, also an indication of how oppressive and discriminatory a country is to its citizens. The black African communities in the States and Britain have the lowest social mobility of all the ethnic groups in the West.[1] An update of the same OECD report in August 2016 showed a slight improvement in the US's position to 31st, even when the criteria was altered favourably.[2]

In February 2014, Gregory Clark of Princeton University and author of The Son Also Rises reckoned that societal divisions in the US were far more entrenched than earlier suggested. He tracked the wealth of rich surnames and noted their over representation in elite positions. He wrote:

"Birth has predicated of the tracked ones income or educational status. Erasing the legacy of past prosperity takes 10–15 generations rather than 3–4 implied by sunnier estimates."[3]

In defence of this situation, Western apologists usually accuse the black African people of being lazy and unwilling to strive but they stubbornly refuse to look at the prevailing ingrained institutional racism and racial stereotyping that stifles their aspirations from birth to death.

In January 2018, during an immigration meeting with a bipartisan group of senators, Donald Trump described some countries populated by black and Latino people as 'shithole' countries.

According to the Washington Post, President Trump asked:

"Why are we having all these people from shithole countries come here?"

Prior to this comment, the New York Times reported that during a different White House meeting Trump had said that Haitians *"all have AIDS"* and that people from Nigeria would never *"go back to their huts"* if they came to the United States.[4]

Yet, several studies show that the Nigerian community in the US are the most progressive ethnic minority groups and contribute enormously to the America economy.

The impediments to upward social mobility in the West are numerous and in many cases almost insurmountable for many black and ethnic minority citizens. In addition, there is the ever present and less publicised threat of downward social mobility. As the African diaspora ages most will experience significant downward social mobility, far in excess of the ageism experienced by the elderly white population.

Western societies effectively have two main social mobility escalators: one, which appears to move young white people seamlessly upwards, and the other for blacks and other immigrants who are constantly rolling downwards. For white people, it seems that just making enough effort to get on the social mobility escalator is enough when compared to their black counterparts.

For Africans, again the opposite is true. The social mobility escalator they have to ascend is the one running downwards, not upwards. This means ethnic minorities, especially Africans, need ten times or more the required effort to run up their unique social mobility escalator. They also have to negotiate tricky bends and narrow bottlenecks. They must take care not to make a single mistake as the white system is ready at any time to haul them off the escalator and pin them down, most likely never to rise again.

The harsh reality for many blacks and immigrant people is the daily risk of unfair treatment at work and unfair dismissal. They often have to look on in frustration as they are repeatedly passed over for promotion. Conversely, their white colleagues rise, almost effortlessly, through the same system.

As an ethnic minority, they have usually taken much longer to achieve the same level of success as their white colleagues. The amount of time they have to earn and be productive is also significantly reduced. They are more vulnerable to becoming redundant if there is a dip in the fortunes of their company. This also means that they are always hit much harder, financially, than their white colleagues. The chances of finding another job becomes slim and they slide down the social ladder, with mounting debts and all the social and psychological problems, like the anxiety and depression that it brings with it.

While underachievement instantly dooms any progress, 'overachievement' has also been a problem for some immigrants and black African people. In Britain, where maintaining social hierarchy and skin colour appears to be infinitely more important than ability, being 'too good' usually brings out the resentment of white colleagues who, lacking any legitimate reason to stifle the progress of their black or foreign workers, resort to bullying tactics and intimidation to try and force the ethnic minority person out of their job. Sadly, these practices are very common in the public services like the NHS, where foreign doctors have to maintain a reasonably high standard just to get and keep their jobs. It is also quite common in other fields, like in the civil service, or in more competitive areas, like law. Most of the bullying and discrimination experienced by ethnic minorities goes unreported, as the recipients of this treatment are often too scared to lose their jobs and source of livelihood.

Many ethnic minority professionals suffer from lack of career progression despite turning in performances that are well beyond the call of duty. Most African and Asian doctors in the UK have at one time or another experienced discrimination, harassment, bullying and lack of progression at work. Many African people have become severely depressed, even suicidal, as a result of this, in addition to the social and financial burdens they have to carry through loss of earnings. For black people further down the social ladder the situation is predictably much worse.

Generations of black Britons have been exposed to discrimination from as early as their nurseries and are socially conditioned to have low expectations and consequently, achieve much less. Many ethnic minorities only have menial work to look forward too, which is very dependent on physical health and age. As they get older, it becomes harder and harder to acquire work or keep the work and they begin the steady decline down the social ladder into poverty and an increasing reliance on state benefits to survive.

It is for this reason that a disproportionately high number of black youths get mired in crime or socially unacceptable behaviour. They look to music and sports as a way out of their social trap. Alas, less than 0.1% of black youths will be lucky enough to break through despite their obvious talent because of limited opportunities. Many black youths decide not to even try, due to the seemingly inevitable prospect of failure.

In contrast, African children coming from families where they are taught to strive against great odds have high expectations and overall are more successful. Many have not been indoctrinated with a psychological inferiority complex in their formative years and are correspondingly less defeatist in their attitudes.

About the institutional racism in the United States, Michael Moore wrote in his book Stupid White Men:

"We've rigged the system from birth guaranteeing that black people will go to the worst public schools, thus preventing them from admission to the best colleges and paving their way to fulfil in life [please check] making our lattes and picking up our trash.

Oh, sure a few slip by — but they pay an extra tariff for the privilege — the black doctor driving his BMW gets pulled over continually by the cops; the black Broadway actress can't get a cab after the standing ovation, the black broker is the first to be laid off because of 'seniority'"[5]

In a 2008 report on intergenerational social mobility, the Brookings Institute and Pews Charitable Trusts teamed up and concluded:

"Cross-country comparisons of relative mobility aren't always based on perfect data. But the US is distinct from the other countries, research shows, in having 'less, not more intergenerational mobility than do Canada and several European countries."[6].

Upward mobility is particularly uncommon for children who are born into families at the lowest income bracket. In 2012, a UNICEF report on social mobility put paid to the myth of America being the land of opportunity. In a study of 35 developed countries, the United States ranked 34th in terms of its social mobility. It only ranked higher than Romania, a non OECD country.8

Never mind the American dream, the American reality is the nightmare that the United States was built on a slave economy that is maintained by their slave descendants, immigrants and the economic slaves of globalisation today.

CHAPTER FIFTY SEVEN
HEALTH, EDUCATION AND HOUSING

Prevalent psychosocial stressors and poverty predictably lead to more health problems in the African diaspora. This is compounded by late presentation, less access to treatment and therapy, poor health education and prevention of disease. Overall, the net result is a reduced life expectancy and poorer quality of life:

"The average life expectancy of African-Americans is 70.3 years, much less than the 76 years that white Americans can expect...the gap between white and black has remained stubbornly wide, and it increased sharply during the Reagan years."[1]

The extent to which blacks experience higher cancer mortality than whites is striking. Not only do blacks have higher mortality rates than whites, but the mortality rates are increasing faster.[2]

African American heart attack patients are far less likely than whites to undergo cardiac catheterization, a common and potentially life-saving procedure, regardless of the race of the doctors. Black and white doctors together referred white patients for catheterization about 40% more times than black patients.[3]

White Americans are five times more likely than African Americans to receive emergency clot-busting treatment for stroke.[4] African American women are four times more likely than white American women to die while giving birth.[5]

Commenting on the US health care system, Lori Smith who works with the Poor People's Economic Human Rights Campaign stated:

"My home state of Tennessee is the model for a national political campaign to dismantle vital social programmes for sick and poor people throughout the US, and whatever is the model for the US, unfortunately, becomes the model for the world.

There has been a tendency to believe that poverty, hunger, homelessness, and lack of health care are nearly non-existent in the US. After all, the US is the richest country in the world. However, human rights violations and suffering are prevalent and growing rapidly. For example, in Tennessee 42.1% of children under the age of 19 live in poverty.

Memphis, Tennessee, has a higher infant mortality rate than Vietnam, El Salvador, or Iran."[6]

Remarkably, a doctor led some of the largest health cuts of US national health programs in US history — Dr Bill Frist, former US senate majority leader at the time under the Republican-controlled senate of George W. Bush. *"Senator Frist, a doctor, is from Tennessee and supports TennCare cuts"*, wrote Lori Smith.[7] Senator Frist and his family own the largest hospital chain in the US, which generated revenue of $21.8 billion in 2003.

Mental health problems and incarceration in mental health institutions are significantly higher among the African diaspora and immigrant populations than their white counterparts.[8]

The schooling system is one of the most obvious illustrations of the social divide in the West. It is common knowledge that black African people disproportionately occupy the poorest and most deprived areas of the US and the UK. The 'social apartheid' becomes immediately obvious once one understands how schooling or education systems work in the West.

It is common knowledge in the UK and US that if you attend 'public' or Ivy League schools then your child is likely to access prominent positions and affluence in society later. Privileged children go to the best schools and get into the best universities. This, in turn, means they get the best jobs, access to high political office and earn huge salaries reserved for the select 1% of the society. In America, Ivy League schools are over-represented by the children of rich, famous, and politically connected people.

A US economist, John Roemer, estimated that to compensate black children for all the other disadvantages associated with growing up in the US, it would be necessary to spend at least ten times as much per capita on the education of black children as white children to equalize future earnings.[9] Early Childhood Longitudinal Study data researchers in the US have shown that most African American children underperformed in school when compared to their white counterparts. However, when just a few variables were controlled; the parents' education and income bracket and the age at which the mothers had their first child, this gap was virtually eliminated. When data from African American children and their white peers from the same socio-economic background were analysed it was found that there was no difference in the maths and reading abilities upon entering kindergarten.

This proves conclusively that African American children perform poorly at school because they come from low educational and low-income households, not because they were black. However, due to the effects of institutionalized racism, the gap between the black and white pupils from the same or even more affluent backgrounds, becomes evident again by the end of the first grade and widens steadily by the second and third grades.[10]

As 95% of white American children go to largely white schools and 95% of African American children attend schools with over a 95% black child predominance, it is clear that schooling in the US is still very much segregated. This means that the civil rights movement only managed to desegregate schools in the US by about 5%.

CHAPTER FIFTY EIGHT
CHILDHOOD POVERTY

Social capital consists of the values and networks of contacts which parents pass on to their children. This invaluable resource means that the young not only have the motivation to succeed but also access to an extensive and diverse social network of people who can offer information, jobs and support.[1] Without this socio-economic support, it has been proven repeatedly that children from poor backgrounds fare considerably worse in all areas of human activity, compared to their more privileged peers.

Nothing captures the true level inequality in the UK more than the statistics on landownership despite the UK's façade of equality.

In a shocking revelation in his book 'Who owns England' the author, Guy Shrubsole, wrote:

"A few thousand dukes, baronets and county squires own far more land than all of middle England put together. Land ownership in England is astonishingly unequal, heavily concentrated in the hands of a tiny elite."[2]

At least 30% of the land is owned by aristocracy and gentry while the crown and royal family own about 1.4% of the land.

A Shadow Minister for the Cabinet Office and Labour MP called for a full debate on the issue stating:

"The dramatic concentration of land ownership is an inescapable reminder that ours is a country for the few and not the many. It's simply not right that aristocrats, whose families have owned the same areas of land for centuries, and large cooporations exercise more influence over local neighbourhoods — in both urban and rural areas — than the people that live there.

Land is a source of wealth, it impacts on house prices, it is a source of food and it can provide enjoyment for millions of people."

In 2003, UNICEF [the United Nations Children's Fund] produced the first study of childhood poverty across the world's industrialized nations called 'Child Poverty in Perspective'.[3] This was an overview of child wellbeing and a league table of rich countries consisting of 21 of the world's leading industrialized nations. UNICEF looked at 40 indicators between the years 2002–2003, including poverty, family relationships and health. In this league table, the Netherlands came top, followed by Sweden, Denmark and Finland. The United Kingdom was rock bottom in 21st position, followed by the US in 20th position.

Other UK report findings show that UK child poverty has doubled since 1979 and children living in homes earning less than half the national average ranged at about 16%.[4] Several economic studies in the UK and US have shown repeatedly that institutional racism has severely limited the potential of generations of black African children, crucially preventing them from actualizing themselves in society.

In the US African Americans fare even worse as African Americans have been on the lowest rungs of the economic ladder since slavery and they have not made it off that rung for even a single day. A study conducted by economists, Richard Vedder, Lowell Gallaway and David C. Clingaman showed that the average income for a black American is 61% fewer pay years than the average white income, that is the same percentage that it was in 1880![5] The average income for a black American family has been shown to be 61% less than the average white income.[6] This is the same approximate difference in earnings between white South Africans and black South Africans. Other studies have shown that the average black family in the US holds only a tenth of the assets of the average white family.[7]

These shocking statistics are a testament to the brutal efficiency of institutional racism, an all-pervasive system that automatically inhibits and freezes out black African people from the system.

In order to boost World War II efforts by enlisting young black men and encouraging them to lay their lives on the line during the war, Franklin D. Roosevelt's New Deal attempted to create more opportunities for black people, but it had little impact. Under immense pressure by the black Civil Rights Movement, President Lyndon B. Johnson introduced civil rights measures that proved no match to the institutional racism and iron will of self-serving whites, to keep the descendants of slaves down and out.[8] Worse still, the gap has been slowly and steadily widening after taking a sharp turn for the worse under the Republican President Ronald Reagan.

A similar pattern of discrimination and exclusion has also emerged from the UK. Even though there are few studies on the social mobility patterns in ethnic minority groups it has been shown that the first generation of black migrants to Britain generally experienced downward social mobility. Many white collar position holders were forced to take manual jobs. Studies by Cheung and Heath concluded that Indians, Pakistanis and West Indians suffered a significant 'ethnic penalty'.[9]

Apart from the physical effects of childhood poverty, like diet on brain development, childhood poverty also has several psychological and behavioural effects. Behavioural qualities like anti-social behaviour, peer relations and attentiveness and extraversion at the age of ten are all strongly associated with social class and background. Childhood poverty is associated with low self-esteem and behavioural problems as early as age ten and affect labour market outcomes in later life. Candidates with more self-esteem are likely to be more confident and do better at job interviews. They also get on better with their colleagues at work, are better team players and so on. These young adults had more self-esteem and a greater sense of control over their destinies.[10] People from middle-class families also have the added advantage of financial capital, which significantly enhances their job opportunities and prevents downward social mobility.

Gavin Kelly and Rachel Lissauer, quoting a study from the National Child Development Study, found that someone aged three in 1981, who had received a £5,000 inheritance [at 1981 prices] was approximately twice as likely to be self-employed as someone who received no inheritance.[11]

Childhood poverty also carries a severe and increasing labour market penalty and young adults from low-income households faced greater disadvantages in terms of the probability of finding work and the size of earnings than the young adults in the 1958 cohort.[12]

A study by Bernard Coard, an Inner London Education researcher, put forward three reasons why black children in the UK, particularly boys, underachieved. The first two were low expectations and aspirations by the black students and the third, low expectations by their schools.[13] Another study by the SWANN Committee 20 years later reached the same conclusions.[14]

UK government figures show that black students start primary school with some of the highest scores in baseline assessments of initial ability. After two years, they begin to slip behind the other pupils. By GCSE just 37.5% of black Caribbean children and 43.5% of black African pupils scored at least 5 C grades, compared with a national average of 52.3%. This discrepancy is reflected later in life when even though ethnic minorities in the UK make up 8% of the population, they only occupy 3% of senior positions. 7.2% of university students in the UK come from ethnic minorities but are three times less likely to be offered top jobs in top companies.[15]

In 2016 several reports noted that childhood poverty in the UK had trended upwards sharply, up 200,000 from 2015 alone. Current estimates suggest that 29% of children in the UK live in poverty. The Institute for Fiscal Studies and the Resolution Foundation projected that childhood poverty is set to rise to 30% or more by 2020.[16]

CHAPTER FIFTY NINE

JUDICIAL SYSTEMS AND EMPLOYMENT

Many Western police and judicial systems appear to assume black people are guilty regardless of the available evidence. In the eyes of Western law enforcement organisations, African people are guilty persons only waiting to be caught, rather than innocent until proven guilty as stipulated by the law.

Nearly one million Afro American males have been jailed in the US, a startling statistic considering African Americans make up only about 8% of the total population.[1]

Once they have been incarcerated they are denied voting rights and have great difficulty reintegrating into the larger society, forcing them either to re-offend or experience a sharp decline in social mobility into near absolute poverty.

In the UK, a criminologist at King's College London, Professor Ben Bowling, revealed that Africans are 27.5 times likely to be stopped and searched than their white counterparts, especially under Section 60 of the Criminal Justice and Public Order Act. In the UK, black African and Caribbean people, especially males, are seven times more likely to be stopped and searched by the police than their white counterparts.[2]

It has even been suggested that the white supremacy system is trying to prove the presence of a 'criminality gene' in Africans and when the British Metropolitan Police revealed that they hold the DNA records for about 37% of African men on the national database compared to 13% for Asians and 9% for whites, it only added fuel to the fire.[3]

The 'ethnic appearance' of the crime suspect is also recorded. A Home Office spokesperson accepted that black men were disproportionately represented and explained that the DNA figures were 'based on the operational judgement of the arresting officer'.

Dominic Bascombe, of the Voice, a black newspaper said: *"The revelation exposed biases in the criminal justice system that begins with ethnic minorities being more likely to be arrested. It is simply presuming if you are black you are going to be guilty – if not now but in the future."*[4]

In the United States inequality in justice and law enforcement has been enshrined in the legal and police systems. Rosa Parks, Marcus Garvey, Malcolm X, Martin Luther King and thousands of other African Americans have been unlawfully and unjustly arrested and/or killed in open miscarriages of justice in a consistent pattern of unequal arrest and biases judicial proceedings. Since 1930, 455 men have been executed for rape and 89.1% of them [405] were black men.[5] In Dallas, Texas, an African American man was sentenced to one thousand years in prison for stealing $73.10 whereas white executives convicted of a price conspiracy involving over $1 billion were sentenced to 30 days in prison. Countless black people have been arrested and sentenced to death for crimes against whites, 'in the history of the US In Florida, for over 170 years no white person has ever been executed for murder, rape, or other capital crimes against a black person'[6] —an incredible fact when considered only in the light of the officially accepted figure of over 3,500 lynchings of African Americans.

There have been numerous studies into the effects of racial profiling in America. In one such study published in the Journal of Personality and Social Pyschology, the researchers used a video game to test the effect race has on a split decision to shoot or not shoot where there are African American and white American targets holding guns or non-threatening objects. The participants where told to shoot armed targets and not to shoot unarmed targets. In terms of response time the participants were quicker to shoot the armed Afroican Americans than the white Americans. Conversely, the participants were quicker not to shoot the unarmed whites.

The most common errors were shooting the unarmed African Americans and 'not shooting' the armed white Americans. All the results were consistent with a Black-Crime bias and this bias was found in both African Americans and white Americans.[7]

In 2015, US policemen killed twice as many black unarmed people as white.

A group called 'The Counted' monitoring US police killings produced the following statistics showed that the risk of the different ethnic groups in the US being killed while unarmed broke down as follows; White 15%, Hispanic/Latino 25.4% and Black 31.9%.

Steven Hawkins, Executive Director of Amnesty International, USA described the racial imbalance as 'startling'.

Hawkins stated:

"*The disparity speaks to something that needs to be examined, to get to the bottom of why you're twice as likely to be shot if you are an unarmed black male in 2015*".

Unfortunately Hawkins' rhetorical question is easily answered. Racial profiling has dogged African Americans since they arrived as slaves.[8]

On November 23rd 2012, Jordan Davis was murdered at a Gate Petroleum gas station in Jacksonville Florida in the United States following an argument over loud rap music being played in car in which Jordan and his three teenage friends were travelling.

Michael Dunn, a white American, took out a handgun from his glove compartment and fired 10 shots into the teens SUV and only stopped firing when the car was out of range. He and his fiancée, Rhonda Rouer then went back to their hotel and ordered pizza.

Jordan Davis was killed in the shooting but the three other black teenagers were unhurt.

After his arrest, Michael Dunn and his defence team argued that he repeatedly fired at the teenager's SUV because felt in imminent danger; however the four teenagers were unarmed and no weapons were found inside their car.

The precise numbers of African American men that have suffered a blatant miscarriage of justice and have been wrongfully jailed are too numerous to mention.

Three black men — Alfred Chesnut, Andrew Stewart and Ranson Watkins, dubbed the 'Maryland Trio' were wrongfully sentenced and jailed for life in 1984 for alledgely killing a 14 year old boy in 1983.

Freed after 36 years when further evidence came to light, the Baltimore State Attorney stated:

"These three men were convicted, as children, because of police and prosecutional misconduct."

It transpired that the police had ignored and withheld reports from mutilpe witnesses identifying another person as the killer and that trial witnesses failed to identify the three teenagers in photo line-ups.

Many other Afro-American men have suffered similar and even worse cases of wrongful incarceration.

Richard Philips was freed in Detroit in 2008 after spending 45 years in jail for a murder he did not commit.

Ricky Jackson was put on death row and served 39 years in various prisons in Ohio before a witness recanted claiming that the police had pressured him.

Walter Lomax served 38 years for murder and received $3, the largest payout ever made by a state for wrongful jailing.

Robert James was released in 2015 after serving 23 years in New Orleans for crimes including the murder of a British tourist, when another man was proven to have committed the crime.

The 'Central Park Five' served 6–13 years in wrongful imprisonment before they were released.[9]

The Marshall Project, a study into the killing of black Americans by whites, confirmed what most people suspected anecdotally. Most of the killing of black men and women by white people in America are most likely to be ruled as 'justifiable'. The Marshall Project examined 400,000 homicides committed by civilians between 1980–2014.

In almost 17% of the cases when a black man is killed by a white or non-hispanic over the last three decades, the killing was categorized as 'justifiable'. This is a term used when a police officer or civilian kills someone committing a crime or in self defence.

The use of deadly force by white policemen and civilians in most cases has been been based on the belief of imminent danger whether it was real or imagined.

This the most commonly used excuse to justify not only the blatant murder of African Americans but to help secure their release or reduced sentencing by a corrupt and racially biased judicial system in the US.[10]

This inequality is just as evident in the employment sector. In the UK, the Trades Union Congress [TUC] produced a paper which used official data to analyse the link between the poverty of people from black and ethnic minority groups and the labour market discrimination that they faced. It revealed that black workers were more likely to be poor and unemployed than most white people and that unemployment stood at 11% among black workers, compared to 5% among whites. It also revealed that even though the gap in employment between black and white workers had improved slightly since 1997, the improvement remained very slow and, unless this changed, black children would be the hardest hit.

The ethnic penalty for being black was clearly demonstrated as it was shown that skills or qualifications were not respected. The Ethnic Minority Employment Task Force showed:

For any given level of qualifications, a black minority person will be less likely to be employed than a white person with the same qualifications. For instance, 81.4 % of BAMEs with degrees are employed compared with 87.4 % of white people.

In fact, a white person whose highest qualification is GCSEs at grade A–C is substantially more likely to have a job than a black or minority ethnic person with A levels. [The gap in employment rates is more than 10 %.]

While the employment rate between ethnic minority people of working age and white people of working age has fallen by 2.3% since 1997, a modest improvement but nowhere near enough to plug the current 15.4% gap. If black and Asian workers continued to find work at the rate as in the previous seven years, the TUC calculated that it would take 46 years before the employment rates were the same.[11]

Professor Anthony Heath and Dr Sin Yi Cheung, sociologists at Oxford University and Oxford Brookes University respectively, wrote about ethnic penalties:

"Overall a number of ethnic minority groups, notably Pakistani, Bangladeshi, black Caribbean and black African men continue to experience higher unemployment rates, greater concentrations in routine and semi-routine work and lower hourly earnings than do members of the comparison group of British and other whites."

They went on to add:

"These differences cannot be explained by the age, education or foreign birth of ethnic minority groups. Even for the second generation, born and educated in Britain, we find significant net disadvantages [after statistical controls] for black African, black Caribbean, Pakistani and Bangladeshi men in the labour market with respect to unemployment, earnings and occupational attainment.

We term these ethnic disadvantages, 'ethnic penalties'. The ethnic penalties experienced by black Africans, both men and women, are especially high.

Within the private sector, there was a clear pattern for ethnic minorities to be under-represented in professional and managerial occupations and over-represented in semi-routine and routine occupations. Ethnic minority men also tend to have lower earnings than whites in the private sector."[12]

It was also noted that UK towns and cities with the highest unemployment rates tended to be home to large ethnic minority communities.

In the US, many African Americans have gravitated towards service in the military as a way of escaping the unemployment and lack of social standing that dogs the African American community. Unfortunately, the US military is only a microcosm of the wider society and has always mirrored the practices and attitudes of the times. African Americans who served in the US military during the Second World War were all officially segregated and the US Army was only legally desegregated in 1948. African Americans were over-represented in high-risk combat units, non-technical and unrewarding jobs. Many had great difficulty reintegrating into civilian society after the war because they lacked skills and re-enlisted because army life was all they knew.

In 1966 African American combat deaths peaked at over 20% of all combat deaths in Vietnam. The public outcry that followed forced the US Defence Department to issue an order to reduce the number of black deaths in combat. Today, the military still recruits African Americans disproportionally from poor deprived areas to fight its wars.[13]

The stark reality is that Africans and African Americans in the West have not come close to attaining equality in the white judicial system. Alienation of the black African community, rather than any gain in security or safety is the result.

Poverty, violence and premature death has remained a constant companion of the African slaves acquired during the slave trade and their descendants, the African Americans today. They suffer more fatalities, disabilities, unemployment, incarcerations and indignities than white Americans. Studies have shown that cases of 'justifiable homicide', whereby a police officer on duty kills a civilian, reveal that African Americans were killed at a rate of 6–20 times higher than whites.[14]

CHAPTER SIXTY

BROKEN FAMILY UNITS

The effects of institutionalised racism on the African family unit in the diaspora have been nothing short of catastrophic. The single or lone parent family unit has been inadequate in meeting the needs of the children of the African diaspora and several studies on the socio-economic effects of this have been made. In 2007 the UK Education Secretary, Alan Johnson, made this point in a speech: *"Children of lone parents are 70% more prone to psychological illnesses later in life"*.[1]

The African male child is particularly vulnerable and the lack of adequate adult male models at home leads them predictably to seek role models from their peer groups and possibly from street gangs. Unfortunately, some African men view their positions in the family as an optional extra but the presence of an adequate adult role model plays a vital role in their children's emotional wellbeing.

In 1944 Nobel Prize-winning economist, Gunnar Myrdal, wrote a book called, An American Dilemma: The Negro Problem and Modern Democracy, and proved that the founding principles of the States were meaningless and a mockery for blacks systematically locked out of equal participation.

The southern States were the worst, and he wrote:

"The observer is frequently told by white southerners that whatever blacks get is a charitable gift for which they should be grateful. There is no sense in talking about discrimination, it is held as Negroes have no right to anything but to get something out of the white's benevolence."[2]

The vast majority of people of all extractions in Western societies have been socialized as functional racists especially in the UK and US.

Both these Western countries have relatively large African populations compared to other European countries. Perhaps it is only natural that their endemic milieu of institutionalized racism throws up obstacles and problems on a daily basis for Africans and other ethnic minorities in the form of covert and overt discrimination and sometimes startling and 'unprovoked' attacks, which have claimed the lives of many innocent victims. One does not have to search hard to find the endemic racism that is expressed in practically in all areas of social contact between Europeans and Africans.

Casual racism, in whatever area of social contact between the wider white population socialized in racialism; work, school, play in social or formal setting, whether recognized or not by the victims, unsuspecting Africans or unwitting casual racism by the wider white population, racial prejudice and its many manifestations and effects are part of the daily experience of the African diaspora.

In its extreme expression, many African people have lost life and limb to these unprovoked racist attacks. The Metropolitan Police continue to search for the killers of Stephen Lawrence in South East London, while Anthony Walker, a model African student was killed with an ice pick driven about 6cm into his skull by racist thugs in Liverpool. A website set up in memory of his life was desecrated by a white Liverpudlian, Neil Martin, who posted comments under the pseudonym Genuine Scouser, urging white people to celebrate the murder and suggested that Anthony's family should be burned. He also made frequent references to slavery and 'banana ships' less than a week after his murder.[3]

Sentenced on the February 23rd 2007, John Laidlaw, a former amateur boxer from Holloway in London, while on probation for an earlier racist attack, vowed to 'kill all black people' and went on a random shooting spree in Islington and Finsbury Park in May 2006. He shot Abu Kamara, an African social worker, in the neck and an African woman, Emma Sheridan, in the back after firing more than two shots at another African man, Evans Baptiste.

In October 2004, he had racially abused and assaulted a motorist, Ayandele Pascall, because he beeped his horn at him. While in police custody according to a police document, he had 'foamed at the mouth' and stated he was a member of the BNP. He had also stated he was going to 'kill all black people' and referred to them as 'niggers'.[4]

Sometimes it takes manmade errors and at other times natural disasters to uncover the true state of affairs of a nation. When Hurricane Katrina ripped through New Orleans, it also ripped open America's hypocritical façade of freedom and equality and exposed the true depths of America's urban inequality to the whole world, there was a combination and synergy of both the natural disaster and the manmade disaster factor in action.

It was not just that most of New Orleans lay about ten feet below sea level and as much as 20 feet below the surface of Lake Pontchartrain or that in spite of repeated warnings, there was no adequate contingency plan in place.

It was the live pictures of human suffering, and needless death played out on television screens all over the world that exposed levels of destitution and a bankruptcy of empathy not seen even in the poorest Third World countries.

The poor black African people disproportionately represented in the disaster, unable or unwilling to escape to safety, mainly for simple reasons like a lack of transport or the means to pay for transport and therefore constituted the bulk of poor people, were condemned to a watery death in the fetid, polluted waters of submerged New Orleans.

When help arrived, it was in the shape of guns and security forces, not the food and water that most of the hurricane victims were crying out and dying for. It was more important to stop black people 'looting' supermarkets for much-needed supplies than it was to deliver life-saving food, water and medicines.

Perhaps it is an American approach to a crisis, as they do have a tendency to export military hardware to Third World countries with the poorest and neediest people in the world.

Perhaps and most importantly, it showed that a downtrodden person, who still looked to the state for their survival, even when they had been let down repeatedly, was a state that really could not be bothered if they lived or died.

It is completely erroneous based on the simple historical and socio-economic facts elucidated for black Africans in the West to refer to themselves as black Britons or African Americans, until the barriers of institutional racism and societal colour prejudice are eliminated, not just on an individual basis but most crucially on a general one too. However long, or however many generations of the African diaspora are born into the racist society — until all the racist structures and institutions that prevent real assimilation and integration of the vast majority of black African people are dismantled, and true freedom and equality prevail — they remain black Africans, whose primary role in the West as defined by white supremacists through transatlantic slavery, is a generational lifetime of servitude and denigration.

Unfortunately, many Africans and their diaspora do not see through the hypocritical veil of white supremacy and define themselves through the white supremacy power structure. They are proud to be described as 'the first black man/woman' to be appointed to, or hold positions in, the white imperial system rather than to be known as courageous African men and woman who dedicated their lives to the fight for freedom and equality of the African people. It is not uncommon to hear our African brothers and sisters boast about being the only 'black man/woman' in the establishment, or how their children, isolated and discriminated against, are the only 'black children' in a school.

This behaviour is no doubt stimulated by the Western media who are quick to point out the 'achievement' of finally reaching a degree of acceptance into the Western mainstream by elevating their status of being the only 'black' or 'first black' person to hold office among their white peers. These appointments are usually long overdue, are scarcely representative of the number of African people who are able to perform at that level, and who are usually overqualified for a similar appointment. When the Western press refers to their 'first or only black status' it does appear as a somewhat backhanded compliment or to be reaffirming just how hard it is for Africans to hold a position in the white supremacy power structure.

This is not to take away the achievement and success of prominent Africans in the Western hemisphere, but we all must judge their achievements by how much they contribute to the regeneration of our own communities and continent in contrast to the effort expended in making sure the power structure that exploits and denigrates African people runs smoothly. When Africans and their diaspora are 'born again' into true African history and knowledge by stepping across the Western paradigm into their natural African one, they bring much-needed expertise and experience to the regeneration of the African continent.

As the main white institutions of power in the Western society are run by the white people in power, the politicians, financial institutions, police, judiciary, academics, etc., it stands to reason that it is really they who stand watch over the possibility of a truly integrated culturally diverse Western society or the ones which prevail currently, are those with reflections of the hierarchy of white supremacy and imperialism. It is important to note that laws, which can be promulgated to affect change, and more importantly, these laws can be upheld and enforced immediately, radically changing the landscape and eradicating institutional racism from the society within a few years.

Many Africans in the diaspora do not understand just how fragile their positions are as they are protected by laws which are subject to the whims of imperialists who can change them at will with a significant downturn in their financial and psychological wellbeing. For instance, without much warning the former British Prime Minister, Tony Blair, produced a white paper on the NHS that literally forced thousands of foreign doctors out of work and made it almost impossible for them to get jobs.

African people often miss the point regarding racism, money and actual power. The power to effect change comes from conscious African people organizing themselves in such a manner that they can counter white imperialism and supremacy. The mere individual accumulation of material wealth is insufficient in itself to re-establish them as a force in society.

It does not come as a surprise therefore, that many rich and successful black people, even though somewhat insulated from racism, still find themselves on the receiving end of it.

When Luis Aragonés, the Spanish national coach, called former French international and Arsenal star, Thierry Henry, a highly talented footballer and multimillionaire, a 'black shit' he was fined a paltry £2,060 by FIFA, prompting Henry to comment:

'It is laughable. They fined him for the sake of it, not because they felt he had done something wrong.[5]

Man has often used sports as an expression of human ability and achievements. In ancient Greece, athletes were venerated and celebrated, in sculpture and in literature. Before the West came to appreciate the natural ability of Africans to excel at all kinds of sports, sportsmen and women were highly regarded. For many in the African diaspora, a sport represents one of the key routes for individuals to escape from racial discrimination and deprivation to fame and fortune in the institutionalized racism of the white global power structure.

At the 1936 Olympic games in Berlin, Hitler who was keen on displaying the racial superiority of the 'Aryans' over lesser human beings was bitterly disappointed by the string of victories by African American runner Jesse Owens. Jesse Owens was the highlight of the Berlin Olympic games, and he won four gold medals, including the long jump with a new world record. Three other black athletes won gold medals as well, prompted Hitler to say; *'People whose antecedents come from the jungle were primitive, their physiques were stronger than those of civilized whites. They represented unfair competition and hence must be excluded from future games'.*

Throughout the West, the African diaspora experienced significant racism when it came to sports and only broke through very recently. Sports in the West represent one of the areas where the African diaspora can express themselves more fully. In the US, black tennis players were excluded from the US Open championships by the requirements of competitors having to win the qualifying tournaments of the country clubs, and there were no black players invited to take part in the qualifying tournaments. African Americans responded by forming their own tennis association from which Althea Gibson emerged. In 1950, Althea Gibson became the first black player allowed to compete at Forest Hills and in 1957 and 1958, she won both the US open and Wimbledon singles titles.[6]

In Britain, Larry Gains, a black Canadian boxer who held the heavyweight British Empire title from 1931 to 1934, was repeatedly refused the right to fight for the World Championship.[7]

As the Thierry Henry case and other innumerable examples of racism in sports have shown, individual success does not necessarily protect one from institutionalized racism of Western society and does not in itself solve the problems that the majority of Africans face individually or collectively if no active steps are taken to help their people develop.

It is also very important to note that no matter how successful an African or their diaspora is in the white dominated supremacy system, they have and are contributing immensely to the upkeep and maintenance of a global system of oppression that primarily oppresses their own people. Many have worked ten times as hard and ten times as long as their white peers in order to achieve a comparable level of success. For a foreign doctor who takes over ten years to attain a consultant post or become a GP this could amount to over £1 million in lost earnings, which have been donated to the white supremacy power system.

Many Africans and West Indians wear their badge of achievement in the West with immense pride, and even though any personal achievement is to be celebrated, one cannot help but note that when viewed from a more detached and objective position, it does in some ways amount to an own goal.

The alienating effects of Western socialization make many Africans and their diaspora fail to appreciate the widespread nature of white supremacy and racism. They fail to see themselves as part of a larger African collective and are blind to the big picture. Each African is like a piece of a large jigsaw puzzle, and you cannot claim to see the whole picture until nearly every piece of the puzzle is slotted together. The fragmented individuals and Westernized Africans tend to judge the situation, mainly from a personal perspective, which is wholly inadequate considering white supremacy operates globally and in all areas of human activity.

While Western society, to some degree, also alienates Caucasians from each other as well, there is no real love lost between the English, French or Germans; they, unlike Africans, have their governments, media, military, and multinationals working tirelessly for their benefit ensuring that the society remains socio-economically slanted in their favour.

Fragmented African individualism has also meant that most of the socio-economic gains made by Africans in the West is temporary. In most cases is eroded before it has time to be passed on from a single generation to another, like from father to son, because institutional racism is constantly working to disenfranchise Africans, who do not pay any attention to it.

Even though Africans must strive to be financially able to meet the demands of the modern world, we must all have a way of translating it into a direct practical benefit, to the African community and diaspora without which we are only strengthening the hand of our oppressors.

Viewed collectively, based on the socio-economics of Western societies, there are no African Americans, black British or other black Europeans to mention. None of the socio-economic or political statistics supports this fanciful notion. The reality has been that descendants of the African slaves have on the whole failed to integrate into the white community over a hundred years on from slavery and not for want of trying. Kidnapped, and brought in chains as a cheap and expendable labour resource, the bulk of the African diaspora has remained in the lowest echelons of Western society, pegged down by institutional racism.

No matter how painful the exploitative natures of these societies are to accept or confront, there can be no turning a blind eye to the fact that while this goes on and some people can benefit and get away with it, it will continue. The onus is on each, both black and white, to seek to correct this injustice in order to build a better, safer and fairer world for the generations to come.

The poverty gap between Africans and their fellow European 'countrymen' is widening daily. Africans are being discriminated against, exploited and disenfranchised, in all areas of human activity. All African indices of socio-economic wellbeing, like life expectancy, infant and maternal mortality, poverty, housing, education, jobs, etc., are drifting back to a position of relative slavery, slowly but steadily, and the silence of these damning statistics is deafening.

PART ELEVEN: GEOPOLITICS

CHAPTER SIXTY ONE

FAILURE TO THRIVE

"American imperialism is all the more dangerous because it comes to Africa elaborately disguised...It masquerades as the leader of the so-called free world." Nelson Mandela[1]

In medical terminology, 'failure to thrive' is taken to describe neonates and infants that have not reached their appropriate developmental milestones due to disease and malnutrition. Individuals who have reached adulthood but remain dependent on their parents and families and have not embraced the responsibilities of adulthood can also be described as failing to thrive in a social sense.

Like people, so nations. All countries evolve slowly through their own developmental milestones until they become a single cohesive functional unit. However, unlike individuals, self-sufficiency is a core-defining feature of a nation state at whatever state of development it might be — be it at a low level where the people are only able to meet their basic needs or a higher level where they are able to do so and even produce a surplus. Perpetual dependence is not a feature of a sovereign nation.

Historically, the idea of African sovereignty has been meaningless to the West. The US has deployed drones, aircraft and helicopter gunships to kill hundreds of people and displace many more in African nations that are not even at war with them. Since January 2007 the US has arbitrarily fired cruise missiles into Somalia and Sudan and conducted military raids within African countries against suspected Islamic terrorists without any legal mandate.

In April 2011 the French government sent troops into Côte d'Ivoire, and forcefully deposed the Ivorian leader, Lawrence Gbagbo, closed the country's airports and shot Ivorian protestors dead in the streets.

In 2011, following NATO's illegal onslaught on Libya and forceable regime change, spearheaded by the US, UK and France, its Head of State, Muammar Gaddafi was brutally murdered and Libya destroyed as a nation state. When asked about Gaddafi's murder, the US Secretary of State at the time, Hillary Clinton, laughed and notoriously gloated:

"We came, we saw, he died..."[2]

With the primary objective — unrestricted access to Libya's oil wealth — secured by the Western invaders, Libyan society has since spiralled into chaos. The world market signalled a job well done for the West as Libyan oil was back under Western control. However, Libyans — the 'unpeople' — suffer and die as their country is torn apart by the various warring factions.

Apart from Ethiopia, modern African nations were born as the illegitimate children of Western colonialism. The African people who found themselves contained in these artificial constructs were arbitrarily assigned countries based on their geographical location and which colonial master claimed ownership of that area. Even though many of these African people had coexisted in those areas and had traded with one another for centuries, they had not coalesced into nation states. Many of these African people, unequally yoked with one another, were even traditional enemies. Virtually all African nations have failed to thrive, or make any significant economic, political or infrastructural developments since their illegitimate births to their colonial masters.

As a consequence of the slave trade and colonialism most African nations have experienced severe cultural and technological reversals owing to the trauma and the effects of slavery and colonialism. Some African nations took a few hopeful but somewhat unsteady steps after their creation, but many soon descended into conflict and chaos. Most African nations have returned to the false comfort of economic and political dependence on their Western masters.

For a brief period following the Second World War Africans tried to engage in global politics as the 'independence fever' started in India by

Mahatma Gandhi swept throughout the world. The result of this brief global engagement was almost 90% of the infrastructure, development and intellectual capital that Africa has today. The rate of progress and development that African countries enjoyed under 'independence fever' has not been maintained. The drive for African independence also stimulated and motivated the American Civil Rights Movement in their quest for freedom.

Unfortunately, over the last 40 years, there has been a steady erosion of those gains by the white capitalist process, and the resulting poverty and unrest, the main underlying reason for the brain drain phenomenon of Africa to the West.

Given the many years of Western misinformation and suppression of Africa's real history, it is not surprising that modern-day impressions and expectations of Africa stem almost entirely from its colonial history. This biased and incomplete account of Africa permeates all Western history books, education curricula and media outlets. To understand Africa, we must clearly disentangle the low expectations and the poor conceptions of modern Africa from its glorious past. African history dates back to the origins of modern man over 200,000 years ago while Africa's colonial history is barely 100 years old.

Africa's failure to thrive following nominal independence can be summed up in a few words: lack of knowledge, poor geopolitical awareness, inferiority complexes and colonial dependence.

It is a poor analogy to try to compare the leadership of Africa's politicized tribalism and Western puppeteers to actual leadership in a truly sovereign nation. The political direction of many of Africa's leaders cannot be really described as 'leadership' but rather Western followership. The key to successful colonialism and 'divide and rule' has always been to control the head. After all, if you control the head, the body will follow. Historically, groomed, weak African leadership has always been largely harvested from the miseducated Europeanised African elite and middle class.

Following colonial independence, the white colonial masters expanded the puppet role of many illiterate, unelected African military dictators and politicians whose only mandate often came from their colonial masters and not from their own people. Many African leaders, through ignorance or apathy to global politics and a clear inferiority complex, let their white colonial masters set the fledgling African nations on a slippery slope to nowhere. Colonial policies were based on economic principles and strategies that did not balance the books. This allowed their colonial masters the luxury of bleeding their colonial countries of their resources from a distance while the long-term economic prospects and the sovereignty of the new nations were fraught.

Undoubtedly, white colonial masters placed their puppet African leaders under immense pressure. However, the bottom line remains that African leaders should have placed the wellbeing of the people they claim to serve first before the money and the white masters they sought to follow.

In 2008 while on a visit to Algeria the French President Nicolas Sarkozy admitted:

"The colonial system was profoundly unjust, contrary to the three founding words of our Republic: freedom, equality and brotherhood."[3]

Unfortunately, Sarkozy's specious words flew in the face of the West's geopolitical strategy in Africa. The real importance of Africa to Western policy is summed up by these comments:

'Control of the African continent, in other words, unrestricted access to its vast mineral wealth, remains a cornerstone of Western policy — to do otherwise would be to commit geo-political suicide'.[4]

It is abundantly clear that the way Africa's human and natural resources were reorganized was in such a manner as to meet the needs of the Western nations' industries and multinationals and could only be practically achieved by colonial occupation and domination.

A light on the economic cost of Western dependence to Africa was shed by a Christian Aid report of March 8th 2005 which estimated that the African continent had lost $1,440 billion to the rich world in the previous three decades.[5]

The white colonialists have always used the carrot and the stick in their relations with Africa, the carrot being the mirage of an equal participation in the Western global economic and political structure. The stick being open or covert military, political and economic destabilisation.

All African nations have uniformly been let down by their previous European colonizers. According Ngugi wa Thiong'o:

"To participate in the global economy and access the "free" market, African nations have to pay exorbitant fees in the form of cheap labour, raw materials and high consumption. But the competition promised by global capitalism only applies to the rich and powerful countries. African leaders also have to make commitments to pro-Western standards of democracy measured by good governance, accountability and transparency — standards that Western nations themselves do not meet."[6]

To have a deeper appreciation of the failure of African nations to meet the expectations of their own people and their dependents, we must look again at the effects of the triumvirate of Western colonialism — the miseducators [Western teachers and missionaries], the Western military, and the multinational companies — have had on the African continent.

Unlike the parents of newly born children, the Western colonialists were filled with great expectations of what their newly acquired illegitimate African nations could do for them and not what they would do for their newly acquired African colonies. To achieve their aims, they had to create the necessary environment, and groom them so they would follow their expected paths of development and deliver unto them the limitless human and natural resources they craved.

The first role fell to the white miseducators, the missionaries and teachers, whose aim was to 'civilise' their African subjects and in so doing deeply undermine African culture and cohesion. Western missionaries and explorers were largely responsible for the almost complete erasure of pre-slave trade African history and achievements, and the reprogramming ofAfrican minds in Western ideology and history.

They had the task of grooming enough Africans for positions of servitude, converting them to Western Christianity and the creation of inferiority complexes in them. The vast majority of these Western educated Africans were used to run the colonial system, allowing their colonial masters the luxury of a cheap and simple chain of command, overseen by a skeletal staff of white colonialists.

The military and political wing of the triumvirate of Western imperialism was the strong-arm of the process. They instigated wars against independent African nations and used African proxies to create perpetual conflict and social unrest. These wars were always unequal, due to the clear military superiority of the colonialists. Punitive wars were fought to exterminate and persecute natural African leaders, dominate the land and the resources and ensure that weak unstable African leaders, with little or no popular mandate, eventually prevailed over the conquered African people.

Western colonialists promoted and rewarded conflict, tribalism and puppetry. Conversely, they punished African nationalism, leadership, cohesion and progress among Africans. Keeping the African people down, divided and conflicted, helped facilitate the colonial process.

The commercial arm of the Western colonial process undermined the economic and food base of the African people.

They switched African economies from subsistence farming to cash cropping for Western nations. Just like in India, Western multinationals ran both as companies and as governments, and were extremely powerful. Many African nations initially had company rule, which was overseen by politicians back in Europe.

These Western companies-cum-governments stifled any local African competition, industry, and technology, creating dependence on the West all across Africa.

Therefore, weak, ineffectual, and undemocratic African leadership was inherited from the colonial master following 'independence', because it was a prerequisite to secure effective control of the native population. Unfortunately, the framework of this type of leadership has remained, providing the nexus for overwhelming corruption, at all levels of these unrepresentative African governments.

The role of African agents remains crucial to the whole process of Western plunder in Africa. Walter Rodney scathingly wrote about them:

'The minority in Africa which serves as the transmission line between the metropolitan capitalists and the dependencies in Africa. The importance

of this group cannot be underestimated. The presence of a group of African sell-outs is part of the definition of underdevelopment. Any diagnosis of underdevelopment in Africa will reveal not just low capita income and protein deficiencies, but also the gentlemen who dance in Abidjan, Accra, and Kinshasa when the music is played in Paris, London and New York.[7]

Western colonial masters groomed African agents to facilitate the process of extraction or primitive accumulation, of human and natural resources.

Alternatively called slave agents, African middle class, or comprador allies, put an African mask on the white face of Western capitalist accumulation, in order to avoid widespread resistance from the African people.

By African nations remaining compliant with the wishes of their colonial masters and dependent on them for their development, it was only natural that a crop of African leaders who were amenable to the wishes of their previous masters eventually emerged post-independence.

Given the legacy of colonialism — superimposed on a background of the conflict, mistrust, and suspicion created by the slave trade between Africans — it is hardly surprising that African societies, at the first sign of unrest, fracture along tribal lines due to deeply imbedded colonial divisions. In most African nations, political position and national resources are fought over and the nation splinters along tribal and religious lines.

African tribalists have no allegiance to any nation state, and their tribal and religious affiliations always come before national interests. This is why most disputes over stolen elections, allocation of resources and positions of political power, almost invariably end in tribal or religious warfare in Africa.

The legacy of colonial divisions led directly to the terrible genocide in Rwanda in 1993 and the ethnic cleansing in Kenya in 2008. Ethnic divisions, nurtured by the Belgians in Rwanda and the British in Kenya during their respective colonial rules, resulted in the respective post-colonial African societies disintegrating along tribal lines.

While African tribalists and religious fanatics usually deeply distrust each other they are often, naively, completely open to manipulation by their European and 'foreign allies', who in most cases, are the source of their conflict.

Given this mindset, African tribalists do not see anything wrong with being European puppets as long as it secures their immediate interests and aids their power struggles against other enemy tribes in the short-term, even if the whole nation, including their own tribe loses heavily in the long run.

Despite of all the fervour, good intent and feelings that the securing of nominal colonial independence created, the leading political African elite did not substantially challenge the ingrained inequalities of the colonial era. In addition, African leaders were generally unsuccessful in bringing their people along with them in order to create the right atmosphere for the fledgling countries to implement exciting new nationalistic ideas of development. In many instances, they not only depended on the previous colonial masters, but also even looked imploringly to help them to develop their countries. As a result, many detrimental and unequal political, economic and social structures, which characterized the colonial period, were left in situ and some even strengthened in the post-independence period.

In the 1980s, the concentrated economic power of Western agencies led by the World Bank and IMF was brought to bear on African nations, and the recruitment of African agents, witting or not, gathered pace across Africa. According to Patrick Bond:

"Home grown' neo liberal technocrats began to flourish especially in the finance ministries and central banks in Africa.

'Ministries of Finance, central banks, bureau with oversight mandate for privatization and commercialization often became the first-line soldiers for the emergent neo liberal orthodoxy. "Capacity building" projects by the Bretton Woods institutions and similarly orientated Western agents focused on reinforcing this ideological commitment."[8]

Thus, in the post-colonial era, the role of corrupt African politicians and dictators with the West became clearly defined. They existed as conduits for the extraction of African natural and human resources to the West. These African agents were handsomely rewarded, in cash and in kind, for assisting the West in its exploitation of Africa. Just like colonial rule, wealth and power was unevenly distributed around the country to a relative minority of people, whose task was simple: to enrich themselves and their Western allies at the expense of the nation, while simultaneously providing cover for Western activity. African puppet leaders are often reviled in the Western media as incompetent, brutal and corrupt; however, this is only a small price to pay, considering the kind of wealth they can accumulate.

Fanon noted the neo-colonial process of divide and rule, in his book, The Wretched of the Earth:

"We know the colonial administration has marked certain regions out for privilege. The colony's economy is not integrated into that of the nation as a whole. It is still organized in order to complete the economy of the different mother countries. Colonialism hardly ever exploits the whole of a country. It contents itself with bringing to light the natural resources, which it extracts, and exports to meet the needs of the mother country's industries, thereby allowing certain sectors of the colony to become relatively rich. But the rest of the colony follows its path of underdevelopment and poverty, or at all events sinks into it more deeply."[9]

Dependent on their Western allies as their source of power, wealth and personal protection, these African compradors have always operated from a relative position of weakness. Their natural tendency has always been to place personal gain above national interests. In so doing, they became deeply committed to maintaining the corrupt infrastructures and practices that have ravaged the African continent and consequently become even more dependent and pliable to their Western collaborators.

Many of these African agents also embody the crippling psychological inferiority and physical dependence syndromes that have swept through Africa, and who have, through Western manipulation, undeservedly found themselves in positions of power.

Fanon elaborately captured the psychological insecurity of these African neo-colonial agents:

"The national middle class which takes over at the end of the colonial regime is an underdeveloped middle class. It has practically no economic

power, and in any case, it is in no way commensurate with bourgeoisie of the mother nation, which it hopes to replace. In its willful narcissism, the national middle class is easily convinced it can replace the middle class of the mother country. But the independence which literally drives it into a corner will give rise within its ranks to catastrophic reactions, and will oblige it to send out frenzied appeals for help to the former mother country."[10]

The politicized tribalism of the African nations' post-colonial independence has been so pervasive that some Western academics have even begun to peddle the theory of African patrimonialism, or rule through personal patronage, rather than through ideology or law, based upon relationships of loyalty and dependence with a blurred distinction between private and public interests.[11]

Apart from the psychological trauma of slavery and colonization, fledgling African nations inherited an economy which was wholly dependent on the colonial masters. Western colonial economies were conditioned to spectacularly fail the African people but be immensely profitable for their previous colonial masters.

Long before Europeans had set foot in Africa, Africans were trading virtually throughout the world, and had established international trade centres as far as India and China.

Much of Africa's population at that time was dependent on subsistence farming and many African nations were organized into stable self-sufficient societies.

Overall, Africa was not organized into nation states like in Europe. Africa's modern borders were arbitrarily created by Europeans during the scramble for Africa.

This is a very significant point as millions of Africans, especially in West and Central Africa, did not live in large nation states and therefore, did not have a 'national identity' to reach back for, after colonial independence. This fact made it easier for Western colonialism to take hold, as the colonialists did not have to face a large group of African people organized along national lines, and found it easy to play traditional enemies and tribal rivals against one another. These shallow divisions, amplified by colonialism, have lingered on and have made it difficult for the relatively young African nations to cohesively face the challenges before them.

The slave trade was not just significant because it kidnapped African children and young adults, the future of any growing society, depleting an essential workforce. It also stimulated wars, created division, forced mass migration of people and left a legacy of lasting suspicion between people all over Africa.

Europeans created the colonial economies of African nations against this backdrop. It was an unequal relationship from the very start as the main aim of Britain and other European countries, in Africa was not to further the interests of Africans, but their own.

European companies whose political power resided in Europe, directly controlled the extraction and sale of African natural and human resources.

As was the case in India and in China, indigenous manufacture was firmly discouraged, Africans were moved from subsistence farming for themselves, to producing cash crops for Europe.

The undermining of African subsistence farming and switch to the production of cash crops, goods and textiles for Western consumption rather than trade and barter with other African people and nations had already begun to take place because of the slave trade. Just like in British colonial India, millions of Africans died from famines and starvation when they moved away from their traditional subsistence farming to cash cropping.

Driven by the 'gun slave cycle' and the terrifying reality of the slavery, many African societies that had participated in the slave trade found it much easier to depend on foreign goods and guns in exchange for slaves, rather than rely on any production of their own goods. The primary aim of Europeans was the extraction of natural resources using the African natives as slaves or cheap labour. To achieve this they deliberately subverted Africa's agricultural base, subsistence farming, which was the mainstay of living for over 90% of the people, towards the introduction and production of primary crops for export. Thus, African food insecurity which had begun during the transatlantic slave trade was accelerated under Western colonial rule.

This development severely undermined the food security of African societies and created the conditions for conflict, famine and starvation, which would inevitably follow.

On the other hand, Western colonialists profited immensely from their colonial conquest. The First World War left Britain weakened by several factors; it had to divert a large part of its industrial efforts towards the war. This also included its international trade in machinery. Britain had lost a large number of young men during the First World War, further aggravating its economic problems. Due to the high costs of waging the world wars, Britain was forced to sell the important sections of its overseas investments in order to pay for the war efforts.

As Europeans scrambled for control over Africa's land, people and natural resources, the role of Africans as primary producers became firmly entrenched. Apart from the economic cost of colonialism, thousands of Africans were recruited as 'cannon fodder', to aid the colonial master's World War Two efforts.

During the Second World War, the demand for primary products had risen exponentially. However, after the war the commodity prices fell just as rapidly. This exposed the fragile and unreliable economic base of the newly formed African nations that relied on a few primary exports as the main means of growing a viable economy.

In the developed countries, the manufacturers and industrialists could maintain price levels by organizing cartels and reaching price-fixing and agreements.

In contrast, the African colonies had to accept the wild price fluctuations that they were powerless to resist. Only European firms operating in the colonies had the economic leverage necessary to resist the instability and stockpile goods when prices were low.

British and European companies like Imperial Tobacco and Unilever created almost total monopolies, using low prices of raw materials to secure high profits by selling price agreements.[12]

The possession of the colonial empire was an indispensable asset that provided a cheap supply of human resources and raw materials that helped Britain to rebuild after the ravages of the two World Wars. It provided British industry with an outlet, by giving them special preference for empire goods and preferential agreements of import tariffs between Britain and the colonies. When British exports were rejected in the world markets, they were sent to the colonies instead. In so doing, Britain was thus able to continue exporting textiles, iron and steel to markets in its colonial empire.

Britain's colonial empire came to the rescue of Britain again after the world economic collapse of 1937. This was also a period of mass unemployment around the world. The British colonial empire provided jobs for over 20,000 administrators and members of the armed forces.[13]

To further compound African economic woes, large companies created subsidiaries, for example; Unilever developing the United Africa Company, which entered the retail trade, thereby handicapping the development of a West African entrepreneurial class.

In South Africa, the white colonial government did succeed in creating an economy that could take off on its own, but this was run by white South Africans for white South Africans, who widely practiced apartheid. This also meant that the British government had to pay some dividends and royalties back to its workers.

In 1937 North Rhodesia was paid £5.5 million in dividends and royalties from mines and the British government collected only £700,000.[14]

In contrast, in Nigeria, where British companies had a monopoly, dividends and royalties of £1.3 million were paid, while in the Niger mineral outputs were £2.5 million.[15]

It was bad enough that Africans were forced into a cash economy and their means of self-sustenance, subsistence farming, destroyed; much of the African labour was cheap or forced. In many instances, slave labour was utilized to meet the required tasks, and some of the African labour was used as a tax liability to the colonial government.

South African mineworkers carried out their jobs in atrocious conditions and contracted debilitating diseases, like tuberculosis and pneumoconiosis. Up to half of the African mineworkers were infected, and were allowed to transmit the disease back to their families, as they were deprived of adequate medicine, health care or education.

Their colonial employers would not provide any social security for their workers, and African workers were expected to retain their roots in their villages or tribal societies with their families and homes.

The average wage of African miners remained unchanged for 50 years, from 1890 to 1940, at two shillings per day and subsistence.[16]

The main European objective of building infrastructure in Africa was to assist the process of exporting crops and raw materials out of Africa. To buttress this point, when comparing maps of India's rail links with Africa's, it becomes apparent that the Indian railways link the subcontinents, whereas African rail lines link areas of extraction to the ports.[17]

Under the colonial masters, very little if anything was done to tackle endemic tropical diseases like malaria and bilharzia, or malnutrition in the population. The vast majority of colonial children remained illiterate. Proportionately, only a handful of Africans were groomed to take up some subordinate positions, to facilitate the running of the colonial empire. It is also from these insignificant numbers that the ruling class was selected.

When African countries gained nominal independence, their economic power remained with the colonial masters. African economies never diversified and relied on a few primary commodities for the bulk of their foreign export. Africa suffered, not just because of the change to cash crops, but also because they had no control over the crop prices. African countries remain producers of primary commodities for industrialized Western markets and continue to remain dependent on Western imports to sustain their economies today.

The World Trade Organization has been manipulated by the West to aid the neo colonization of Third World countries. Even though the World Trade Organization was created to abolish trade barriers, the only trade barriers that it demolishes are those in poor countries. The US, EU, and Japan continue to subsidize their farmers with millions of dollars every year, and while placing very high tariffs on African goods.[18]

In 2002 developed nations spent more subsidizing the agribusiness than the equivalent income of all the people in sub-Saharan Africa combined.[19]

Having forced Africa into cash crop farming during colonial times, these heavy and unfair subsidies almost guarantee that African farmers cannot compete for world trade in the agricultural business.

For example, the US customs agricultural subsidy was $3.9 billion in 2002, driving down world prices by 10–20%. This caused an estimated $250 million annual loss in West African cotton producing countries.[20]

The European Union continues to subsidize European cotton production, destroying the incomes of ten million West African people who rely on cotton production in Africa.[21]

Another façade in the saga of the Western underdevelopment of Africa was a project called the New Partnership for Africa's Development [NEPAD]. It is abundantly clear that the uneven relationship between Africa and the West was enshrined into the organization, but it poses as an equal partner of its Western allies while, in reality, is simply another vehicle for Western power to control and maintain their agenda across the continent.

In his book, Looting Africa, Patrick Bond wrote:

"In attempting to disguise their role in amplifying uneven development within Africa, projects such as the New Partnership for African Development [NEPAD] pose a unified African Partnership with the North. In the process, their proponents suffer from a psychological sense of grandeur and collaboration, rather than displaying the tougher mentality of struggle and material analysis which, according to Fanon, won liberation in the first place."[22]

The result is that the African farmers cannot compete with their Western counterparts while African countries are flooded with cheap Western produce further stifling growth and development.

The 2001 trade round in Doha was torpedoed by the rich countries that even went as far as bypassing African leaders and bribing their ministers. The IMF and World Bank forced negative conditions on poor countries in order to get much-needed funds.

In 2004, Kenya lost $60.2 million in aid from the US because it championed the WTO cause.[23]

The fragility of African dependence on cash crops and primary commodities to grow and support their economies can clearly be outlined by the steep changes in prices since their independence.

From 1982–2000 the price of primary commodities dropped dramatically across the board: sugar by 77%, cocoa by 71%, coffee by 64%, and cotton by 47%.[24]

Most puppet African governments, rather than seek to have developed the agricultural business in order to feed their own people, no doubt pressurized by their colonial masters, decided to follow the path of reliance on exported food.

In the space of twenty years, Southeast Asia increased its land under irrigation by up to 40% within that same period while African land under irrigation remained static.[25]

Southeast Asia was also able to increase its production of manufactured goods from 22% to a staggering 80%. Today, African manufacture is relatively negligible.

Even though Africa does not produce much by way of manufacture, the West has placed impossibly steep import tariffs as a barrier that not only prevent African goods from reaching the Western markets at reasonable prices but also indirectly suppresses the African manufacturing industry itself.

For instance, export tax of African goods into Europe is about 23% and into the United States, a staggering 132% tariff on peanuts exists. In addition, as trade barriers are removed, others are erected in its place. Africa's share of world trade fell steadily from 6% in 1980 to just around 2% in the year 2002.[26]

A Christian Aid report showed that unfair trade laws allowed rich nations to plunder almost £150 billion from Africa's poorest in June 2005 alone.

"Struggling countries in Sub-Saharan Africa have been the victims not the beneficiaries of "Free Trade"'.

'The 150 billion pounds lost would be enough to wipe out the continent's debt and would have still been enough to vaccinate every child and send them to school."[27]

Ghana has been importing rice from the mid–1980s despite rice being a major crop produced by its own farmers. Christian Aid calculates that without 'free trade' Ghana's national wealth in 2000 would have been £466 million more than the £2.7 billion it actually produced.

Ghana lost the equivalent of £24 per person in potential income but only received £17 per person in aid.[28]

The story of Africa is not just about exploitation — it is also about the wanton waste of natural resources.

Shell has become embroiled in a lawsuit from Niger Delta communities in Nigeria and Western environmentalists over allegations of causing pollution and global warming by flaring gas in Nigeria.

Up to 2.5 billion cubic feet of gas a day is flared instead of harnessed for its energy, losing Nigeria about $2.5 billion or £1.5 billion in potential revenues and producing 70 metric tons of CO_2 a year.

These deadly toxic gases have been flared for more than 40 years. The Nigerian government had promised to stop it by 2008 but Shell stated that it would not meet that target.[29]

Nigeria is the most populous black African nation on earth, and the tenth most populous country in the world. Sadly, Nigeria ranks as the 19th poorest country in the world, despite its vast wealth of natural and human resources.[30]

With a population estimated at 170 million people, it is also unfortunately the largest failed state in the Third World, and the best African example of failure to thrive.

With a life expectancy of 52 years of age, only one in five children live above the age of five years.[31]

Its infant mortality rate as at the year 2000 was 77/1000 births. Over 40% of Nigerian children, or about 32.5 million, are chronically malnourished, and only 56% of mothers received antenatal care according to UNICEF.[32]

3.5% or 5.95 million Nigerians were living with HIV/AIDS in 2013 according to UNIAD.[33]

Home to over 300 ethnic groups with different cultures and languages after the British amalgamated them into a single nation, this bewilderingly rich and diverse nation is also bewilderingly dysfunctional.

Even Nigeria's famous national football team, the Green Eagles, sometimes mirrors the nation in the way they play their football. Eleven immensely talented footballers, laden with national expectation, who are often largely dysfunctional as a team.

Since winning its neo-colonial dependence from Britain in 1960, Nigerians have endured over 30 hard years of military rule.

Nigeria may be the largest 'failed state' in the world, but if you understand the workings of the white imperialist's minds, then you must conclude that 'Nigeria' was set up to fail its own people, just like all the other postcolonial African states. However, in its role as a portal for extraction of vast human and natural resources by the Western capitalist process, it has been a tremendous success.

Nigeria was born of the desire of its illegitimate colonial parent, Britain, to serve the British Empire, and not the Nigerian people. Ever since colonial Nigeria came into being in 1914, it has been plundered directly by Britain during the colonial era and indirectly by Britain and other Western nations via corrupt African leaders, since it acquired it neo-colonial dependence. To get a better understanding, try and imagine that after Nigeria's creation or 'birth' the umbilical cord made up of the strong vines of political, economic and military control were never cut. The new country named 'Nigeria' was effectively created as a bus, painted in the colours of the Union Jack and driven by British colonial governors under the guidance of the British colonial empire. Its sole aim was to collect its own natural and human resources and deliver them to via the unsevered umbilical cord to Britain, in particular, and the West in general. Come 'independence' in 1960, the colour of the bus, the British Union Jack, was repainted in the colours of the Nigerian flag, and British approved Nigerian drivers also called military and political leaders, given the wheel of the bus.

Today, the bus called 'Nigeria' still delivers a disproportionally large proportion of its natural and human resources to Britain in particular and the the West in general. Even though the drivers may have changed, its set aim and direction has remained the same.

The proof of this is remarkably simple; it is enough to track the direction of Nigeria's capital flight, whether it is from failed Western instigated economic policies like SAP [the Structural Adjustment Programme], Nigeria's odious debt, or money stolen by corrupt Nigerian politicians or military leaders, stashed away in Western bank vaults.

Since oil was discovered in the 1950s, Nigeria has made over $600 billion from oil revenue alone. It is estimated that Nigeria has lost over $200 billion worth of oil revenues to Western governments and large oil companies like Shell and Chevron alone. During British Colonial rule, Nigeria retained only 50% of the profits from oil derived within its own territory; over 40 years on Nigeria retains an underwhelming 60% of its oil revenue.

In December 2002, the New York Times wrote:

"40% of Nigeria's oil revenue goes to Chevron alone and 60% to the Nigerian government."

In 2005 Britain made over £5 billion in profit from the sub-Saharan region of West Africa and most of that profit came from Nigeria.[34]

It is clear then, that even in postcolonial independence or rather in its neo-colonial dependency, Nigeria is still performing the function it was set up to do; serve the West and not its own people, whether it is described as a failed state or not.

Nigeria, like many other colonial countries, started as a corporatocracy rather than a true nation. Just like colonial India, Nigeria began its existence under company rule, that later transposed into the British colonial rule. George Taubman Goldie was the true founder of 'Nigeria' and first conceived of the idea to form a British controlled commercial empire extending from the Niger Delta river to the river Nile. What and how Taubman Goldie did was largely up to his own ingenuity, as long as he made a profit for the British government. The British claims to the Niger River basin were enhanced after the Berlin conference in 1884–1885.

At its very inception, many prominent Nigerian leaders voiced their concerns about the way the country was stapled together by the British, to facilitate cheap colonial government and 'divide and rule'.

When Lord Lugard amalgamated the Northern and Southern

territories in the name of the British Crown, it was not because of the interests of the Nigerian people, or for nation building. Rather, it was for the simple reason that the North's colonial budget was running at a deficit, and the losses could be rectified by incorporating the more profitable Southern territories, thereby eliminating the need for subsidies from the British government.

Nigeria has a rich mosaic of people, languages and cultures and has an estimated 300 ethnic groups. Even though many had co-existed for over 1,000 years, there was very little cohesive interaction and in fact, some were traditional enemies.

In order to administer such a vast land mass as Nigeria, the British favoured indirect rule through a northern elite, consisting mainly of a Fulani aristocracy which ruled over the Hausa populations. Indirect rule allowed the emirs to continue running their affairs more or less as they chose, but they had to defer to and pay taxes to the British colonial administrators.

When indirect British rule was extended, largely through Muslim emirs, over the Christian southerners all living together in a country abundantly blessed with natural resources, modern Nigeria today was born.

It was clear that the federal structure inherited by Nigeria post-independence was problematic and trouble flared almost immediately between the three largest ethnic groups in the country: the Hausas, Igbos and the Yorubas.

Just over six years after independence, a bitter civil war engulfed the country. On May 30th 1967, late Biafran leader Chukwuemeka Odumegwu Ojukwu declared the secession of the state of Biafra. Over two million Nigerians died in the Civil War, and mostly Igbos.

Since the British colonial times, a deep aversion for the 'government' became embedded in Nigerians who were used to being preyed upon and let down by their so-called 'governments', be they colonial or postcolonial. A system of politicized tribalism developed alongside normal government. It is within the murky backdrop of Nigeria's politicized tribalism that most of the corruption in government is hatched. Unfortunately, even today, many Nigerians still go into government to 'chop' their share of the national cake and not to serve the people of Nigeria.

The combination of bad leadership and politicized tribalism ensured the blatant corruption of successive governments, mostly military regimes, filtered all the way down to the grass roots.

Nigerians fight and kill each other to get into government, to pawn off the country's great wealth, for a relative pittance, to the West.

This could not have worked out any better for Britain and other Western countries, who no longer needed to subsidize colonial administrators and infrastructure, to reap the rewards, they set the country up to extract in first place.

In 1993, Nigerians had barely begun to contemplate a fresh change in direction after Chief Moshood Abiola won the elections. Nigerian and Western external observers considered the elections as the freest and fairest in the nation's history. Sadly, to general dismay, the military President Babangida arbitrarily annulled the elections and threw Abiola into detention.

Abiola was jailed for four years, but he never relinquished the mandate he had received from millions of Nigerians all over the country. Despite his victory at the polls, even after Babangida left office, Abiola remained behind bars. The then Chief of Army Staff, Abdulsalami Abubakar, who had assumed office after the demise of Sani Abacha, allegedly in the arms of a pair of Indian prostitutes on June 8th 1998, tried in vain to make Abiola relinquish his claims. He called on the then UN Secretary General Kofi Annan, and the Commonwealth Secretary-General Emeka Anyaoku to convince him to drop his claim, on the absurd basis of potentially destabilizing the country. Rather, it would have been logical for them to be lobbying the Nigerian government to fulfil its promise of returning to civilian rule, by reinstating the election results and giving Abiola, who had won the popular vote, a chance to lead the country.

With Abiola set to be released from detention, almost a month to the day that Sani Abacha died, on July 7th 1998 the US Under Secretary of State Thomas Pickering and a delegation of US officials, paid him a visit at a guest house in the capital, Abuja.

Within minutes of meeting with them, Abiola fell ill and was dead ninety minutes later of an alleged heart attack.[35]

The highly tribalized politics of Nigeria creates a government whose only aim is to plunder the country and not serve the people. It is not surprising that when the potential benefits of corruption are enormous compared to the abject poverty that well over half of its population has to endure, corruption is hard to eradicate.

It is sad that many Nigerians see the giving, demanding and taking of bribes as part of everyday life. People go into government to embezzle government funds, egged on by their families and even their villages, which have been starved of government funding.

Bilikisu Yusuf, an internationally acclaimed leader of the anti-corruption organization Transparency International of Nigeria, urged Nigerians to take some personal responsibility for the mess they are in and stated:

"The whole thing starts with the people themselves and their expectations. A minister's family will expect him to do things that are impossible on a minister's salary; they make spurious demands such a expecting them to buy a new car or take them on trips. Where does the money come from? When an honest aspirant for public office comes along, his village and family will say, 'No, not that one because he will not eat, and he won't let us eat'."[36]

Many Nigerians educated to university level are able to discuss British and American politics intelligently. However, due to their colonial miseducation, many Nigerians know very little about each other, bar a few negative stereotypes about other tribes.

Despite Nigeria's vast cultural heritage, when Nigerians travel on holiday it is typically overseas, either to the UK or the US.

As a child, on my return to Nigeria from the UK, I had to do the latter half of my primary school education in Nigeria. It was commonplace for Nigerians to laugh at each other's broken English and strained attempts to speak Queen's English. Many teachers threatened their students with punishment if they spoke vernacular or their own native languages in school.

Having an American or British accent and etiquette is highly valued, and is thought to improve the social standing of many Westernized African people. So valued is this Western miseducation, that the wife of a friend vowed only to speak English in her house, and not teach her toddlers their native language, in order to improve their English. During my practice in medicine in the UK, I once had a Yoruba woman attend with a middle-aged Nigerian woman as an interpreter. To my utter amazement, perhaps to impress me with her spoken English, when I spoke to the interpreter, she would turn to her Nigerian client and speak English instead of Yoruba, to try to force some broken English out of her. I had to remind the interpreter several times that I needed her to speak Yoruba, not English, so that the consultation could be facilitated.

A Nigerian, Elechi Amadi wrote:

"The Nigerian intellectual is an expert in foreign ideologies. Take the Marxist, for instance. Although he defends Marxism with fanatical zeal and is sure it can be transplanted over here, he is quite ignorant of the indigenous political system that has kept his people going for millennia. What is more, he does not want to know.... Socialism was here long before Marx wrote the Capital.

'But the Nigerian Marxist lacks the initiative to research into how our socialism and extended family system operated."[37]

Nigerians are also fond of criticizing otherNigerians, especially the government, even when they play an active role in it. So much so, that Nigerians tend to harbour very low expectations of each other and always seem to expect the worst from one another. In some ways, it becomes a self-fulfilling prophecy, because most Nigerian politicians and military dictators do not carry even the most modest burden of expectation, which any discerning electorate, could place on their governments. In fact, in can be argued that they carry almost no expectation to deliver any aspect of leadership; economic or political, and they are almost invariably expected to help themselves to the national coffers...which they duly do.

Bilikisu Yusuf tried to explain the corruption and stated:

"We are the majority, and the elite who manipulate all these things are a tiny minority, powerful, yes, but they cannot compete with us. Civil society must hold them to account and refuse to let them get away with it.

'Corruption – "the degree of insanity," she called it – had reached down to the lowest levels, to the local government and even the village."

She continued:

"It is very un-African in the sense of traditional society. There is supposed to be this moral suasion, which stops you misbehaving in your locality. But now Nigerians are looting money from their own people. It is not enough for us to say, ah; the leadership is corrupt, government is corrupt'. We have not internalized the message of probity, accountability, and transparency. If we are going to hold people to account and really make meaningful change in Nigeria, we must first start with ourselves."[38]

Despite Nigeria's infamy for corruption, thousands of professional Nigerians work for Western institutions, multinationals, banks and conglomerates at home in Nigeria and overseas, without practicing bribery and corruption. Thousands of Nigerian professionals in the West hold down responsible positions as doctors, lawyers, accountants and engineers without having to rely on bribery and corruption. When in the West, Nigerians do not jump queues or run red traffic lights because the Western countries they live in do not tolerate that type of behaviour. Unfortunately, as soon as some Nigerians reach home, they are happy to ditch the discipline they displayed in the West and can be as corrupt and law breaking as the next Nigerian. What this exposes is that people conform to the prevailing culture, whether they live in Nigeria or abroad.

Nigeria is corrupt because the Nigerian people collectively have let the country become so.

Chinua Achebe pointed this fact out in the late 1990s:

"It is totally false to suggest, as we are apt to do, that Nigerians are fundamentally different from any other people in the world.

'Nigerians are corrupt because the system under which they live today makes corruption easy and profitable; they will cease to be corrupt when the corruption is made difficult and inconvenient… the trouble with Nigeria is simply a failure of leadership. There is nothing wrong with the Nigerian character. There is nothing wrong with the Nigerian land, climate, water, air, or anything else. The Nigerian problem is an unwillingness or inability of its leaders to rise to the responsibility, to the challenge of personal examples,

which are the hallmarks of true leadership… I am saying that Nigeria can change today if she discovers leaders who have the will, the ability and the vision."[39]

There was a glimmer of positive change on the horizon in 2016. In a landmark stance against corruption, Nigerians voted in President Mohammadu Buhari, whose victory against the incumbent President Goodluck Jonathan was on an anti-corruption and reforms platform. This signalled a sea-change in the psyche of Nigerians who are fed up with the blatant corruption and mismanagement of their politicians. Sadly, corruption is fighting back. Despite Buhari's claim to be fighting corruption many Nigerian's perceive his government to be ineffective and determined to re-establish the Fulani ruling classes' authority over southern Nigeria.

If Africa's failure to thrive could be distilled into a bottle of wine it would be called L' Francafrique. France's grip on its neo-colonial African Empire of French speaking African countries is so strong that surpasses all old colonial arrangements.

Unlike the British, the French pushed for the amalgamation of French-speaking African countries as part of the French Republic. This meant that French-speaking Africans could look forward to 'exceeding' their African culture and language and become French citizens instead.

However, what French-speaking Africans failed to recognise is the fact that African human and natural resources were explicitly exploited to keep the French imperial dreams alive. Several former French Presidents underlined Africa's importance to France's survival and fortunes ;

In 1957, former French President Mitterrand stated:

"Without Africa, France will have no history in the 21st century."[40]

And in March 2008 former French President, Jacques Chirac reiterated this view and stated:

"Without Africa, France will slide down into the rank of a third[world] power."[41]

Even in modern times, these comments seem to have more than a ring of truth to them. In 1998, France won the football World Cup with the help of a large contingent of French/African football stars, including

Zinedine Zidane and Thierry Henry and France repeated in 2018 with stars like Kylian Mbappe and Paul Pogba which appears to buttress Jacques Chirac's point.

During the Second World War, the German Blitzkrieg had outflanked the French Maginot line via the Ardennes forest and the combined elite French and British forces were routed with weeks. It was only Hitler's indecisiveness at Dunkirk that allowed the crop of British and French troops that had not already surrendered to escape back to the England. During the Second World War, the exiled French leader, Charles De Gaulle, relied heavily on their African colonies to support the French resistance in German occupied France between 1940–1944.

As 'Independence fever' swept across the Africa after the Second World War. France, like Britain, was severely weakened by the war and could not hold to its African colonies like it used to. France needed to find a new colonial arrangement.

In 1945, in order to arrest France's waning international influence and access critically needed resources, France created the CFA franc with the aim of formalising its ties and maintaining its colonial assets in Africa.

President Charles De Gaulle proposed that French-speaking African colonies enter a 'colonisation pact' with France to repay France for the benefits of being colonized by them.

However, given the brutality and greed of European colonizers, it was arguable that the African colonies deserved to be compensated by France for their suffering and exploitation under colonial rule rather than colonial France being compensated. As such, many leaders of newly independent African countries were wary of Charles De Gaulle's intentions and rightly felt that it was a trap.

In 1958, Sekou Toure of the newly independent Guinea decided to lead Guinea out from French colonial rule.

Sekou Toure's slogan was :

"We prefer freedom in poverty to opulence in slavery."[42]

Sekou Toure's rejection of French colonial rule enraged the French colonial elite and before the 8,000 or so French people left Guinea, and in a hissy fit of French imperial indignation, they set about taking all their property and destroying anything that could not be moved.

Schools, museums, public administration buildings were torn down. Cars, books, medicines, research instruments, tractors were crushed and sabotaged. Horses and cows on the farms were killed and food in the warehouses were burned or poisoned.

No doubt, the purpose of their outrageous behaviour was to send out a clear message to their other French African colonies that the consequences for rejecting French colonial rule would be severe.

Sylvanus Olympio, the first elected President of newly independent Togo also refused to sign Charles De Gaulle's colonisation pact. However, fearing French reprisals, he agreed to pay an annual debt to France for the alleged benefits Togo derived from French colonization, to deter them from destroying the infrastructure before leaving.

President Sylvanus Olympio planned to build a fully independent and self-reliant country but soon found that Togo's 'annual debt' to France accounted for up to 40% of Togo's small budget.

To facilitate his plan he decided to take Togo out of the Franc for French African Colonies [CFA] and issue Togo's own currency.

On January 13th 1963, only three days after Togo had started printing its own currency, a squad of illiterate soldiers led by an ex-French Foreign Legionnaire army sergeant called Etienne Gnassingbe assassinated Olympio. Sergeant Gnassingbe was allegedly paid $612 by the local French embassy to carry out the assassination.

On June 30th 1962 Modiba Keita became the first President of Mali, another former French African colony. Like Sylvanus Olympio, he saw the French colonization pact as a hindrance to his countries development and decided to withdraw from the French colonial pact too.

On November 19th 1968 Keita was assassinated by another ex-French Legionnaire, Lieutenant Moussa Traore.

During Africa's struggle for independence from European colonization, France repeatedly used ex-French Legionnaires to carry out coups against elected Presidents in French speaking African countries.

Over a period of 50 years, a total of 67 coups occurred in 26 African countries with 16 or 61% in Francophone Africa.[43]

On January 1st 1966, ex-French Legionairre Jean–Bidel Bokassa carried out a coup against David Dacko, the first President of the central African Republic and on January 3rd 1966, ex French Legionnaire Aboubacar Sanguale Lamizana carried out a coup against Maurice Yamego, the first President of the Upper Volta, now Burkina Faso.

On October 26th 1972 the first President of the Republic of Benin, Hubert Maga, was ousted by a former security guard, Mathieu Kerekou, who had attended French military schools from 1968–1970.[44]

Some years later, French troops intervened directly in the overthrow of the former Ivorian President, Laurence Gbagbo from office and collaborated with the US and UK in the murder of Colonel Ghaddafi in Libya.

The French currency, the CFA, was created as a necessity on December 26th 1945 due to the weakness of the French franc following the Second World War. 'CFA' originally stood for Colonies Francaises d'Afrique ["French Colonies of Africa"]. The CFA franc is composed of two currencies, the West African franc and the Central African franc, which are guaranteed by the French Treasury and are effectively interchangeable.[45]

Following the Bretton Woods Agreement in December 1945, the French franc was set to a fixed rate with the US dollar. However, the French ratification of the weak franc was sold to Africans as an act of generosity rather than a means to fight French insolvency.

The French Minister of Finance at the time, Rene Pleven stated:

"In a show of generosity and selflessness, metropolitan France, wishing not to impose on her far-away daughters the consequences of her own franc poverty, is setting different exchange rates for their currency".[46]

The CFA franc is currently used in 14 Francophone African countries, including twelve former French colonies, Guinea Bissau [a former Portuguese colony] and Equatorial Guinea [a former Spanish colony].

The 14 CFA African countries pay in 85% of their foreign reserve into the French Central Bank and under the direct control of the French Finance Minister.

Through the CFA arrangement, France collects $500 billion per year from Francophone African countries. This puts France in control of the economies of over 154 million Africans living in Francophone Africa.

Even though the CFA franc was disguised as a noble gesture to protect French African colonies, the converse was true.

In 1994 when France suddenly devalued the CFA by 50% it led to a sharp rise in the cost of living in Francophone countries and widespread civil unrest, including riots in Dakar, Senegal's capital, in which six policemen were lynched.[47] During the world financial crisis of 2008–2009, Francophone CFA funds were exploited for France's benefit.

Gary Busch, a political analyst who has extensively written on the subject, alleged that the CFA funds in the operations account were pledged against huge loans made for failing Eurozone countries, such as Greece and Italy.

In other words, the foreign reserves of some of the world's poorest people in Africa were risked to protect European states from bankruptcy.[48]

For over 70 years the CFA arrangements have remained unchanged. The Central African CFA banks have no monetary policies of their own.

Quite apart from collecting 85% of the foreign reserves of CFA countries, the French Treasury stipulates many other conditions that stifle any growth and development in Francophone countries.

The 14 CFA countries collectively pool together a minimum of 65% of their international reserves and a further 20% is set aside in an 'operations account' held by the French Treasury. CFA members do not know and are not told, how much of the pool of foreign reserves held by the French Treasury belongs to them individually or as a group. CFA members cannot use their deposits as collateral to obtain credit because the money is held in the name of France.

The French treasury limits CFA countries' access of only 15% of their deposit each year. If CFA countries need to 'borrow' than 15% of their deposits it has to be at commercial rates from the French Treasury.

In addition, France imposes a cap on the amount of money the CFA countries can borrow. The cap is set at 20% of their public revenue from the preceding year. France can veto any CFA country from borrowing more than 20% of their own funds.

As part of the strict conditions of the French colonial arrangement, France has the first right to natural resources found in CFA countries. CFA countries can only seek other international partners after France declares that they are "not interested."

When awarding government contracts, CFA countries must consider French speaking countries first even if they can get better value for money elsewhere. As a consequence, all the major assets of CFA countries are in the hands of French expatriates.

Under the "Defence Agreements" of the French colonial pact, France has the legal right to intervene militarily in CFA countries, and station their troops permanently in bases and military facilities, run solely by the French.

France forbids CFA countries to have any regional or international military alliances other than the ones France has sanctioned.[49]

In 2008, Mamadou Koulibaly, an economics professor at Aix-Marseille University and a former speaker at the Ivorian National Assembly stated:

"The CFA franc is financially repressive, unfair and morally indefensible."[50]

The French grander scheme of La Francafrique between France and its former African colonies is one of the most corrupt in the world. The puppet African political elite in Francophone countries rely on France's support to stay in power while the natural and human resources of their respective countries are drained at source by France.

In return, French leaders stretching back to the Second World War including: De Gaulle, Mitterrand, Chirac and Sarkozy solicited campaign contributions from their African leaders or 'senators' as they are referred to in France.

In an interview with Africa in Fact, Simon Mbaye, a Senegalese Development consultant and a former senior official at the African Development Bank stated:

"The CFA franc arrangements keep West African countries involved in the same economic shape as in colonial times. They provide raw materials

to France and import all their manufactured goods. The convertibility of the CFA franc and its free transferability, combined with high interest and exchange rates, keep the franc zone countries in a state of structural deficits that render any development policies irrelevant."[51]

Crushing poverty in Africa is the outcome of failed African leadership combined with the sapping effects of neo-colonialism.

Poverty is the world's greatest killer, and it exacerbates all other health and environmental problems. About 161 in 1,000 African children will die before their fifth birthday.[52]

Over 50% of the sub-Saharan population lives on less than one dollar a day, and poverty-related diseases, such as malaria, tuberculosis and diarrhoea claim about 5 million lives a year.[53]

Seren Boyd, in the BMA News, grimly summarized the enormity of the tragedy unfolding in West Africa in an article: Money, Medicine and Mortality:

"The biggest obstacle to development is HIV/AIDS. Some 70% of people living with the disease around the world live in sub-Saharan Africa…28.5 million people, according to UNAIDS. It kills two million Africans every year and is indirectly responsible for spiralling death tolls from related illness, such as TB.

'Poverty makes people more vulnerable to disease too. In the case of HIV/AIDS, the United Nations Development Programme [UNDP] notes that poor people's low health status means they are more likely to have undiagnosed or untreated sexually transmitted infections, 'a very significant co-factor in the transmission of HIV'.

'Poverty brings with it social exclusion and lack of involvement in safe sex education programmes. The need to move in search of work makes poor people join mobile populations, where more risky sexual behaviour is common.

'Worse still, disease drives people further into poverty. Medicines sap scarce financial resources and being incapacitated with a life-threatening disease means loss of income. In Zimbabwe, the UNDP estimates that communal agricultural output has fallen by 50% over a five-year period, due largely to HIV/AIDS.

'And at a national level, money spent on health means cash diverted from areas such as education — a key factor in lifting people out of poverty.'"[54]

The effects of global warming are worse in Africa because of the fragile socio-political ecosystem that can barely sustain the lives of its people without the added complications of natural disasters, precipitated by man-made global warming.

When poverty co-exists with corrupt, ineffectual government and HIV/AIDS, any slight precipitating factor, like drought or famine, can lead to a vicious downward spiral in the health and socio-economic wellbeing of the nation.

"Famine exacerbates disease, which deepens poverty, which makes countries even more vulnerable when the rains fail the next season."[55]

In 2002,when famine hit southern Africa, the trigger was a seemingly insignificant 'erratic rainfall and a relatively modest fall in food production' according to the Commons International Development Select Committee.[56]

In spite of all the obstacles placed in their path by the ex-colonial masters, many African people have valiantly tried to make the best of what they have. This has not been easy because undemocratic puppet African governments have provided the West with their main entry points to which they can control the resources and lives of Africans. These brutal, undemocratic and repressive regimes have been crucial in extending and maintaining Western hegemony over Africans.

These oppressive and corrupt regimes perceive African intellect as a threat and stimulate the brain drain to the West due to instability and repression. It is estimated that about 70% of Ghanaian medical officers trained in the 1990s have left the shores of Ghana for greener pastures.[57]

Studies have shown that more African scientists and engineers are working in the United States of America alone, than on the African continent.[58]

This leaves African nations without a vital section of its workforce which it needs to stimulate the growth of an economy and direct the country towards true democracy, without which Africa cannot develop.

Many African communities and leaders have not questioned why they are divided. They have not questioned inequalities created by the divide and rule system employed by the colonial masters. Colonialists magnified artificial differences and encouraged corrupt tribalist African governments to sell off their national assets to Western nations and multinationals, without batting an eyelid.

In so doing, many African governments today perform the tasks that African intermediaries played during the slave trade, by selling off the continent's human and natural resources to the highest bidder.

These unscrupulous African puppets do not represent Africa's suffering multitudes. It is imperative that all Africans and African diaspora must unite in weeding out these elements, as corrupt African governments will continue to provide the instruments through which the West reaps its deadly harvest of the lives and aspirations of the African people.

For millennia, African people had been able to feed themselves, manage their socio-political affairs and develop civilization at pace with their own particular needs. In less than 30 years of postcolonial dependence, most African nations are now almost completely dependent on the West.

Today, African nations rely on Western food aid to help feed their people, and Western loans and charity to run and maintain the little infrastructure that there is. They are impelled to take political and economic direction from the West, be they their former colonial masters or their new neo-colonial master, America.

Even when one accounts for the disruptive effects of natural disasters like flooding, droughts, famines, desertification, population explosion and wars, the main cause for Africa's shift from self-sufficiency to dependence has been the undermining effects of the imperial grand strategy of colonialism and white supremacy.

Instead of feeding its starving and poor people, Africa produces and exports cash crops at a pittance. To further compound the problems many African nations import food from the West at an exorbitant price.

Africa is awash with the natural and human resources it needs to develop and grow, but it also exports it vital natural, human and intellectual capital to the West in return for virtually nothing.

To cap it all Africa and its diaspora are one of the greatest consumers of Western products and goods in the world.

This is a predictable pattern of behaviour and consumption predicated on the miseducation and Westernization of African's and their diaspora into dysfunctional inferiors, whether at an individual, family, community, country, continental or global level.

It is naive to view Western aid as a form of altruism. Western aid to Africa has always been a means of promoting and maintaining the Western interests in Africa, instead of focusing on the plight of the poor and deprived people it was supposedly aimed at.

During the Cold War, Africa became a Cold War battleground by proxy for the West. Western aid was given with the primary aim of creating and maintaining allies and protecting self-interests.

Aid was an essential weapon in America's strategic arsenal, and military aid and neo-colonial dependence was a necessary precondition for any reconstruction or aid packages. As the Cold War ended, so did the imperative to shore up African nations as allies, and aid to Africa in general fell dramatically.

All Africans have played a part in Africa's failure to thrive, whether by intent or omission. Many have contributed nothing or not enough to the African cause through either ignorance or apathy. A plea of ignorance or apathy is unacceptable in court. This is because it provides a loophole for people to abdicate their social responsibilities towards each other, their communities and the wider collective. Apathy and ignorance, therefore, is not justification for African people and their diaspora's lack of engagement to sort out its own plight.

Africans must develop inter-African and Caribbean trade deals to facilitate their own economic growth. By demolishing intercontinental tariffs, the increase in intercontinental trade could trigger a bespoke industrial process that is as effective in stimulating economic growth, as it is ecologically friendly and humane.

All Africans on the continent and in the diaspora must realize that they have a crucial role to play in the regeneration of Africa, individually and collectively. The onus is on all Africans and people with a conscience to contribute whatever they can, however big or small, to the uplift and regeneration of that once glorious African continent.

CHAPTER SIXTY TWO

NEO-COLONIALISM

"The souls of nations do not change; they merely
Stretch their hidden range
Just as rivers do not sleep the spirit of empire still runs deep.
Into a river, many waters flow the merging and conquest that is history's glow.
A gathering of homely and alien streams
A tumble of turbulent and tranquil dreams
Classes overflow their rigid boundaries slowly stirring mighty quandaries;
Accents diverse ring from the land's soul
A richer music revealing what is whole;
New pulses from abroad shake the shores.
Troubling the sleep of the lands resonant bores.
But the gods of the nation do not change; their ways are deep and often strange.
History moves, and the surface quivers, but the gods are steadfast in the depth of the rivers." **Ben Okri**[1]

"We have fifty percent of the world's wealth but only 6.3% of its population. In this situation, our real job in the coming period ... is to maintain this position of disparity. To do so, we have to dispense with all sentimentality.... We should cease thinking about human rights, the raising of living standards and democratization." **George F. Kennan,** US strategic planner 1948.[2]

"Control oil and you control nations. Control food and you control people." **Henry Kissinger,** 1974.[3]

The name neo-colonialism was coined by the late Kwame Nkrumah, Ghana's first Prime Minister and President. He was also the first African leader to achieve independence from Western colonial rule. The myth created by the Europeans is that Western colonisers relinquished all control of their colonies, and left it all to the African leaders to pick up the pieces as they scrambled out of Africa. This commonly peddled Western idea has no basis in fact, and shifts the responsibility of Africa's post-colonial development solely onto the shoulders of Africans. It deflects one's mind away from the European involvement in controlling Africa's economies and political affairs, down to even minute details.

Many people in the Third World labour under the illusion of being self-determining and free, simply because they have little or no contact with their white puppet masters.

However, the fact that Western neo-colonialists methods and means are subtle and well masked does not diminish to any degree the severe effects Western influence has on the African population of people under their remote control.

In 1965, Kwame Nkrumah, quick to recognise the shift from colonialism to neo-colonialism wrote:

" In the place of colonialism we have today neo-colonialism.

The essence of neo-colonialism is that the state subject to it is, in theory, independent and has the outward trappings of internal sovereignty.

In reality, its economic system and thus its political policy is directed from outside.

The result of neo-colonialism is that foreign capital is used for the exploitation rather than the development of less developed parts of the world.

Investment under neo-colonialism increase rather than decrease the gap between the rich and poor countries of the world. Neo-colonialism is the worst form of imperialism. For those who practise it, it means power without responsibility and for those who suffer from it, it means exploitation without redress.

In the days of old-fashioned colonialism, the imperial power had at least explain and justify at home the actions it was taking abroad.

In the colonies of those who served the ruling imperial power they could at least look to its protection against any violent move by the opponents.

With neo-colonialism neither is the case."[4]

In truth, Western colonial powers cultivated poor African leadership and African economic dependence from the start of colonial rule. Most African leaders, with the exception of a few, did as they were told by their Western masters, whether they were corrupt and despotic or not.

Another reason why the West loves to support brutal dictatorships is their ability to create a cheap labour force for Western multinational organizations and to this end, no level of repression has been deemed too excessive to employ in order to achieve the desired aim.

In so doing, corrupt unrepresentative African leaders handed over the reins of their country's vital socio-economic, political, and natural resources to the external control of their former Western colonial and neo-colonial masters.

Today, no matter how unrepresentative and corrupt African elections are, they are closely monitored by 'Western observers' and the 'selection' process rather than election, still has to receive a seal of Western approval. Western support is guaranteed, once the 'right' person is selected, even if they do not have popular mandate.

The result is that most Africans are merely passengers in the back of the 'bus' called their 'countries', driven along a pre-determined route by their Western controlled African leaders.

The most important change the Western colonialists made was the shift from direct colonial government to indirect neo-colonial governance through puppet leaders. Thus the triumvirate of Western politics, big business/banks and the military was only slightly altered. Western political and military control has not changed much, and they still depend on African proxies. Today, large Western companies and multinationals now share some of their territory with Western charity organisations. All in all, due to the power of the Western media and education, the West has penetrated much deeper into African societies and culture than their missionaries and explorers ever could achieve.

In reality, the white colonial masters have always been around the corner, just out of plain sight of the African governments and their people. Direct colonial rule of the colonial era was exchanged for the indirect economic rule of the present-day era of neo-colonialism, which meant that the colonial masters never really left Africa in the real sense of the word. They maintained extremely close ties with the fledgling African governments that inappropriately adopted, almost in entirety, the failed systems placed by their white colonial masters. This allowed the former colonial masters to maintain a significant amount of control over the economic and political development of the newly 'independent' African nations.

In so doing, Western colonial masters remained very influential on the type of government that was formed and the system that was chosen to govern, whether capitalist or communist. They controlled the wealth of African nations through their economic policies, extracted raw materials through their massive multinationals and stifled technological growth through the promotion of dependence on Western products and aid.

Starting from an invisible trade empire to formal colonial rule, former Western colonial masters have continued to refine running their African empires by remote neo-colonial control. Just like changing television channels, they had gone from direct pressing of buttons or turning of dials on the TV, to channel surfing from across the room, in the comfort of their sofa, with the remote control in their hands.

African economies, politics, military, food, water, medicines, import and exports, and are all subject to remote Western control. Indeed, practically every aspect of African lives has remained within the sphere of control of white imperialists, who still wield enormous power and continue to make life or death decisions on their behalf.

New African nations had to grapple with the problems of governing diverse people; whose only common history was, primarily, having the same colonial masters. They had to smooth over the deep divisions that

the colonialists had created and maintained to keep the African people scattered and ineffective as a group.

Most former colonial masters, including Britain, pressurised the newly independent African governments to adopt economic policies, which continued to provide them with the same resources and access to resources that they had before they granted 'independence'. Indeed, in many of Britain's former colonies, the economic base of their colonial system was virtually untouched by the conferring of 'independence' to their colonial subjects. In some cases like in the Far East, Malaysia, the economic base was even strengthened because the outward symbol of British colonial occupation had been visibly retracted, taking the wind out of the sails of nationalist and anti-imperialist groups fighting for independence. Most former colonial Western nations would adopt similar strategies as they moved from direct control to remote control or neo-colonialism.

In addition, they encouraged these fledgling African governments to buy many unnecessary Western goods which did not meet the needs of the African people but provided outlets for Western businesses to sell their goods. This legacy of pointless Western consumerism is still very much alive in Africa, a practice continued by most corrupt Africa leaders. They enrich themselves by accepting to buy millions of pounds and dollars' worth of unnecessary Western goods and military hardware. They also take unnecessary Western loans, while the national debt increases exponentially.

It would be erroneous to believe that the West employed only remote means. Most previous colonial masters have also played a direct role wherever and whenever force was deemed necessary to steer the course of the African nations in their preferred direction.

Since African nations acquired 'flag independence', from South Africa to Senegal, there has been countless Western, covert and open, military interventions all over Africa.

In the late 1960s, during the Biafran War in Nigeria, Harold Wilson, the British Prime Pinister intervened and supported the federal government with munitions to ensure that Britain kept close control over the destination of Nigeria's oil and natural resources.

In Uganda, Britain helped Idi Amin crush the fledgling Ugandan democracy in a military coup. After Idi Amin's use by date expired, Britain alleged that Idi Amin killed thousands, if not millions, of his own people, and enriched himself at the expense of the country. It was even claimed that he ate the body parts of his rivals raw, which he stored in his fridge after having them killed. These issues had not previously caused any concern for British politicians while Idi Amin toed their line.

When the inspirational Congolese leader Patrice Lumumba tried to break ties with his former colonial master, Belgium, and put his country on the road to recovery, another Western-backed African dictator Mobutu Sese Seko, sponsored by the West, was unleashed on his people. After Patrice Lumumba was killed, Mobutu Sese Seko, much loved by the West and the darling of America, built massive houses in Paris and Belgium and had the red carpet rolled out for him in the United States several times. Mobutu Sese Seko,with the support of the West, crippled the Congolese economy and impoverished his people for decades.

Kwame Nkrumah, who led Ghana to become the first independent post-colonial African nation, was thrown out of power by a CIA backed coup and exiled until his death. Nelson Mandela was declared a wanted terrorist by the US and UK because of his struggle against the white apartheid regime of South Africa. Nelson Mandela was only caught after a CIA tip-off and was jailed for 27 years.

Traditionally, the West has long supported puppet and cruel African military regimes, which only become vilified in the West after they begin to toe their own line or are no longer fit for purpose. Due to close Western support, the impoverished African people are almost powerless to remove the African puppet dictators, because they have the full military backing of Western forces, and have not hesitated to brutally and bloodily repress their own people.

Where more legitimate African governments exist, they are often undermined by Western backed 'rebels'. They usually succeed in widening the artificial gaps between the African people created by the Western colonialists. These 'rebels' whose cause usually solely begins and ends with their acquisition of power, are armed and funded by Western countries and serve the function of undermining legitimate African governments, and creating a constant flux of instability across the region.

However, neo-colonialism is not just about Africa's natural and human resources; it is a global phenomenon, which projects itself in all areas of human activity.

To have a meaningful understanding of this phenomenon, we must seek to understand neo-colonialism in its full manifestation and global projection. As the sun set on the British Empire following the Second World War, another empire would rise in its place...the American empire.

It is possible that a huge part of America's success as the leading neo-colonialist of our time is its lack of a colonial history. America became an economic giant from the proceeds of the transatlantic slave trade, and the vast territory it had forcefully acquired from Native Americans. Even while America rode to Britain's rescue in the Second World War, it already had expansionist ambitions of its own. Realistically, it was never going to hand back power to a severely weakened Britain, as a new era in human history beckoned.

As the saying goes, you start as you mean to go on. Contrary to the popular myth, the American neo-colonial empire was built not on the lofty ideals of high morality, freedom, and liberty. The reality was far more brutal; in fact, it started out as an orgy of bloodshed. The arrival of Europeans to the Americas spelt doom for the native Americans. The native Americans were literally wiped out by the early European settlers by a combination of genocide and Western diseases, to which they had no immunity. Millions of Native Americans lost their lives and land. Those who survived were later herded into settlements, which many survivors still inhabit today.

Far removed from the redacted fairy tale stories of the European conquest of the Americas, like the tale of Pocahontas, research from the Smithsonian Institution National Museum of Natural History revealed that the first British settlers at Jamestown even resorted to cannibalism, in the face of starvation during the severe winter of 1609–1610.

Forensic studies of the bones of a 14-year-old girl corroborated written accounts of cannibalism that have been previously found.

Douglas Owsley, a Smithsonian forensic anthropologist stated:

"The desperate and overwhelming circumstances that faced the James Fort Colonists during the winter of 1609–1610 are reflected in the post-mortem treatment of this girl's body.

The recorded bone fragments have incisionally patterned cuts and chops that reflect tentativeness, trial and error and complete lack of experience in butchering animal remains."[5]

He added:

"Nevertheless, the clear intent was to dismember the body, removing the brain and flesh from the face for consumption."[6]

Written accounts of cannibalism in an old letter from the President of Jamestown, George Percy, were reprinted in a Smithsonian magazine.

George Percy wrote:

"And now famin beginneinge to Looke gastly and pale in every face, that nothienge was spared to maiteyne Lyfe, to doe those things which seame incredible, as to digge upp deade corpes out of graves and eate them. And some have Licked upp the Bloode which hathe fallen from their weake fellowes."[7]

During the triangular trade with Britain, America made immense profits from the slave trade and in the process, acquired a large population of black African slaves, who were the forefathers of most African Americans today. Like Britain, America profited from the wholesale and widespread human suffering and exploitation of the transatlantic slavery.

Despite its dark beginnings, America has long viewed itself as possessing the moral values commonly regarded as the core Western principles. Paradoxically, Britain and America have also always claimed the highest moral high grounds of liberty, equality and freedom of any nations in the world.

In 1630 John Winthrop, the first governor of Massachusetts, articulated this puritanical view. He warned his fellow Americans that should America fail to make their 'city on the hill' a model of hope and virtue and should they 'deal falsely with our God', then they would be cursed.[8]

The idea of America being the model of society in the known world was bolstered the convictions of American supremacists. They placed

America first and regarded American culture and ideals to be the model that the rest of the world mustaspire to. For several centuries, America's vision of being the moral beacon of the world explained, to some degree, American's isolationist tendencies when dealing the rest of the world.

This core American ideology holds true today, as America still seeks to force its democracy and ideals upon diverse people of the world, regardless of their own beliefs or culture. In the face of the Second World War and urged on by Britain, America's isolationist stance did not last long. As the dust of the Second World War settled, America emerged as the dominant political force of the day. Today, white, right wing, American neoconservatives continue to play on the so-called 'clash of civilizations' interpretation of history, based on the conviction that the Judaeo-Christian transatlantic culture, constitutes the epitome of human civilization.

By the 19th century, America felt threatened by the great European powers of the time, France, Spain, and Russia, who had wanted to recolonize the South American countries of Venezuela, Bolivia and Colombia. America was supported by Britain, who wanted to protect their trade monopolies in these countries but needed the help of America to do so.[9]

On December 2nd 1823, President James Monroe addressed Congress and outlined American foreign policy, which stated that America would not intervene in European politics and hemisphere and similarly prevented European countries from intervening in the Americas. This became known as America's Monroe Doctrine. Manifest destiny, was a phrase first used by Jackson Democrats in 1840, to promote the annexation of the present-day Western USA [Oregon territory, Texas annexation and Mexican regions].[10]

It was popularized by a journalist called John L. O'Sullivan. He articulated the feelings of American exceptionalism and romantic nationalism based on a belief of the natural superiority of the 'Anglo-Saxon race'.[11]

The Anglo-Saxons, descended from the Germanic Angles and Saxon tribes that had dominated England before 1066.[12]

The ideology of manifest destiny believed that 'Providence' or God had given the United States a mission to spread Republican democracy in the 'great experiment of liberty', and that manifest destiny was a moral ideal or higher law that superseded all other considerations.

The Republicans revised the term in the 1890s to justify US expansion outside North America.

The strong racial undertone of the manifest destiny and Monroe doctrine was clearly articulated by Senator John C. Calhoun of South Carolina as he spoke out against the planned annexation of all of Mexico:

"[W]e have never dreamt of incorporating into our Union any but the Caucasian race — the free white race. To incorporate Mexico, would be the very first instance of the kind, of incorporating an Indian race; for more than half of the Mexicans are Indians, and the other is composed chiefly of mixed tribes.

'I protest against such a union as that! Ours sir, is a government of a white race... We are anxious to force government on all; and I see that it has been urged...that it is the mission of this country to spread civil and religious liberty over all the world, and especially over this continent. It is a great mistake."[13]

Unfortunately, this strong racial undertone was also clearly articulated by successive American presidents. In 1779, the first American President, George Washington, and the 'father of the American nation' instructed Major General John Sullivan to attack the native American Iroquois people.

He stated: *"lay waste to all the settlements around... that the country may not merely be overrun, but destroyed".*[14]

In 1783 George Washington stated:

"The 'Indian' he said, have nothing human except the shape... the gradual extension of our settlements will as certainly cause the savage, as the wolf, to retire; both being beasts of prey, though they differ in shape."[15]

In justifying his decision to annex the Philippines, another American President, McKinley stated:

"There was nothing left for us to do but take them all, and to educate the Filipinos, and uplift and civilize and Christianize them..."[16]

This statement by the American president gave birth to the poem by Rudyard Kipling, 'The white Man's Burden', subtitled, 'The United States and Philippine Islands'.[17]

However, the Filipinos fiercely resisted their 'civilization' and the Philippine/American war broke out in 1899. This prompted an opponent of overseas expansion, William Jennings Bryan to write:

'Destiny is not as manifest as it was a few weeks ago.'[18]

In time, the Monroe doctrine would be extended to justify American aggression and imperialism globally. The Monroe doctrine is not recognized in international law but has guided American foreign policy and successive American presidents to date.

Its definition, expanded from the prevention of European intervention in the Americas, was extended to mean any non-American power. It was first interpreted to allow America to intervene in Latin American countries and then later rearticulated to mean all over the world.

American supremacists have always viewed the world as the West against the rest, and American foreign policy has always reflected this thinking.

President Woodrow Wilson expanded America's policy of interventionism and redefined both manifest destiny and America's 'mission' on a broader, wider, worldwide scale.

In 1904, President Theodore Roosevelt redefined it yet again. Roosevelt's corollary to the Monroe doctrine rejected territorial expansion, but declared America's new role as an 'International Police Power'. Territorial expansionism was replaced by interventionism, in an attempt to uphold the new definition of the Monroe doctrine.

America had emerged as the world's most powerful nation after the Second World War, and was only counterbalanced by the Soviet Union. The United States wielded great military and economic power and had amassed an enormous surplus after the war. The United States had used its industry to provide machinery for both warring sides, Germany and Britain, before it was drawn into the war by Japan. By the end of the Second World War, Britain had exhausted its gold reserves and was effectively broke. Following the Second World War, Winston Churchill, keen on preserving the British Empire, formed the Atlantic Charter with President Franklin D. Roosevelt. However, America had no intention of staying out of world politicsin its primacy and forced the UK to open up the British Empire to US trade, as a precondition for receiving much-needed US loans.

The colonial and commercial British Empire was effectively taken over by the 'American Empire', which we have today. Stringent conditions attached to the loan made sure that the UK would never regained its place as the pre-eminent colonial empire in the world.

Following the Second World War, it was clear that Europe was in great need of reconstruction. After all, it was the neglect of Germany after the First World War which allowed the Nazis, led by Hitler, to come to power, by taking advantage of the difficult socio-economic situation at the time.

America used 'the Marshall Plan', to reconstruct post-war Europe, by giving conditional loans to European countries, with a view to opening up Europe to American business. This also allowed America to maintain close to control over the affairs of Europe.

Britain's 'special relationship' with America came into being after the Second World War, when British leaders realized they had to give up the baton of empire to the United States. Britain, effectively became America's '51st state', crucially situated in Europe. In 1948, Israel was created and became the '52nd state', also strategically well placed, in the Middle East.[19]

Following the Second World War the United States and UK oversaw and encouraged 'mass ethnic relocation' in Europe, which in today's terms can also be described as ethnic cleansing.

This forced relocation saw the borders of many European countries change with the forced repatriation of millions of people.

About 12 million people of German origins were forcibly repatriated back to Germany, regardless of the length of time they had spent in neighbouring European countries. Some of these families had resided in these countries for several centuries.[20]

Parts of Poland and the Ukraine became incorporated into Russia, and parts of Germany became Poland.

Following the Second World War, America also created several international institutions as a political means of controlling the nations of the world.

The United Nations was created and only five countries were given permanent seats and veto power. These countries included the United States, the UK, France, China and Russia.

In 1992 Francis Fukuyama of the US State Department articulated the true function of the United Nations when he stated:

'The UN is perfectly serviceable as an instrument of American unilateralism and indeed may be the primary mechanism through which unilateralism will be exercised in the future.'[21]

When the UN fails to toe the American line, it becomes irrelevant and useless and in other instances, America goes to war in 'defence' of UN resolutions. Paradoxically, prior to the Iraq war in 2003, America and Britain saw the UN as both as irrelevant and relevant. Saddam Hussein's failure to comply with UN Security Council Resolution 1441 was cited as one of the US and UK's main justifications for invading Iraq. However, the UN almost unanimously rejected this and the bogus claim of weapons of mass destruction, as a premise for war.

In blatant disregard of the UN, President Bush, British PM Tony Blair and the Spanish PM José Mara Aznar had a meeting in the Azores and issued an ultimatum to the UN, asking them to capitulate in 24 hours, or they would invade Iraq whether Saddam Hussein and his family left Iraq or not.[22]

The world's financial institutions were created at Bretton Woods. They include the World Bank, and the International Monetary Fund, IMF. These are the institutions through which the United States controls the world's economy today.

The International Criminal Court was also created, in order to try the Nazis for war crimes. The Nuremberg Trial was widely publicized in order to deter other world leaders, from following the Nazi example.

Laws prohibiting the invasion and occupation of countries by others were written, to prevent and reduce the incidence of war in the world; unfortunately, only to deter non-Western nations from going to war. Western nations have simply re-interpreted the laws, employing doublespeak and legalese to get around invading and occupying a sovereign nation, to appear to remain within the international laws against aggression and wars. It is ironic to note that the US military is exempt from trial at the International Court of Justice.

The Cold War actually started long before World War Two. In effect, the 'Cold War' was 'put on ice', until the Second World War ended. The Cold War, in effect, began after the Western invasion of Russia in August 1918 by the Western allies, including America, Britain, Canada and France.

At this time Russia, and much of Eastern Europe, was regarded by the major European powers, Germany, France and Britain, as Europe's Third World.

Coupled with this was the fact that Russia possessed vast oil and labour resources, surpassing that of the Middle East. Over the centuries, European superpowers made many attempts to seize the 'Russian prize'. Famously,attempts by Napoleon Bonaparte of France and Hitler's Nazi Germany both failed.

When the Russian Revolution swept away the Western-backed tsarist monarchy, the US and UK felt obliged to invade Russia. The reason for the West invading Russia, as Churchill put it, was 'to strangle the revolution at its birth.'[23] Millions of Russians died in the failed Western invasion to restore the Western allied Russian monarchy.

The Allied invasion set the stage for the Cold War. Russia and the Western countries, suspicious of each other's intentions, then embarked upon an arms race, which was to threaten the safety of the whole world. The threat of nuclear war has increased exponentially over the years and still remains a possibility, even after the break-up of the Soviet Union following perestroika, in 1992.

For over 60 years, until the break-up of Russia, Westerners lived in fear of the hyped up 'Red Threat' of the communists and NATO, was created to 'protect' Western nations from a Russian invasion. With hindsight, it appears that the Russians have been at far greater risk of invasion or attack from the West, as America aggressively militarily and economically isolated Russia from the Western world.

When John F.Kennedy provoked the Cuban missile crisis by invading Cuba, Russia was blamed in the Western media, and Kennedy went on to achieve a hero's status in the 1960s.[24]

In time, America's unilateral and isolationist posture, and its international establishment of global hegemony, transformed into its foreign policy. America also emerged from the Cold War as the only neo-colonial power in Africa that did not carry the 'white man's burden' of Europe's colonial past, yet it exerted the most influence over the politics and finances of Africa.It fought the communists on the battlefield and in the marketplace. However, it was in the marketplace, through their global economic might, that America forced the break-up of Russia. The Russian 'Vietnam' or the Soviet occupation of Afghanistan, coupled with its arms race with America, proved too much for the Russian economy.

During the Cold War, many Third World countries were used as pawns in the manoeuvring of these two superpowers and Africa was a pivotal battleground, between the communists and the capitalists. Just as the Axis forces, the Germans and Italians, had battled over territory in Africa with the Allies, Britain and America, the communists and capitalists battled over and split up African territory for their own interests. For example, the West [America, Belgium and Britain] orchestrated the murder of Patrice Lumumba, allegedly due to his affiliations to Russia, and the Congo was then ruled for over a decade by a military dictator, Mobutu Sese Seko, who was backed by the West. The foreign interests of Britain and America were preserved, but the Congolese people suffered immensely and continue to do so.

Throughout Western history, their interests in Third World countries stem directly from economic and political motivations, designed to control resources and exert policies, which usually do not have any benefit for the indigenes, and in most cases leads to widespread loss of lives, enduring poverty and disease in these countries.

George F. Kennan of the US State Department, when briefing US ambassadors in Latin America on the need to be guided by pragmatic concern, stated:

"For the protection of our raw materials, ours, wherever they happen to be located to which we must preserve our inherent "right of access", by conquest if necessary, in accord with the ancient laws of nations."[25]

When Iran sought to gain control of its own resources, the US and Britain instigated a military coup to install an 'obedient regime' that ruled with terror in Iran for about 25 years.

The New York Times wrote:

"Underdeveloped countries with rich resources now have an object lesson in the heavy cost that must be paid by one of their numbers, which goes berserk with fanatical nationalism."[26]

In a further article, they wrote:

"Iran's experience may strengthen the hands of more reasonable and more far-seeing leaders elsewhere who will have a clear-eyed understanding of the principles of decent behaviour."[27]

On September 11th 1990 President George H. W. Bush gave a speech titled a 'New World Order' which outlined America's position in the world. Even though President Woodrow Wilson had first explicitly employed the phrase, 'New World Order' after World War I, the deeper subtext of the speech was the outlining of America as the sole superpower in the world.

The LA Times reported that the speech had far greater significance than rhetoric about superpower cooperation and described America as 'the single greatest power in a multi-polar world.'[28]

The US was unconstrained militarily for the first time since World War Two and was determined to cement their place as the world's leading superpower.

Even while American politicians publicly stressed a US–Soviet partnership, the US precipitated an economic disaster in the Soviet Union, fostered Russian dependence on Western aid, deployed troops to Saudi Arabia only 700 miles from the Soviet border, forced the unification of Germany and the withdrawal of Soviet support for former Third World clients and prepared for war against Soviet client states.[29]

President Woodrow Wilson used the phrase 'New World Order'

not only to justify US national interest, but also in moral terms 'to make the world safe for democracy'. In reality, this meant opening up opportunities for the US to extend its military and economic hegemony over the world. One of the first things the US senate did at that time was to reject membership into the League of Nations. In its place the UN, World Bank, International Court of Justice and NATO were created.

The New World Order is really the triumvirate of Western supremacy that includes Western governments, huge multinationals and financial institutions, and their military. These sectors have become so closely interwoven that John Perkins in his book 'Confessions of an Economic Hit Man' defined it as 'corporatocracy'.

Many Western economists and academics either refuse to acknowledge, or do not understand the macroeconomics of globalisation. Capitalism promotes a system that resembles medieval feudal societies, as they create rigid hierarchies with top-down control over the masses of poor deprived people, who are relatively, in economic terms, slaves.

Robert McNamara, former Secretary of Defence under President Kennedy and Johnson, was one of the founding fathers of modern 'corporatocracy' as his own career testifies. He was instrumental in forging strong links between politicians, military and industry, and grooming successors to maintain continuity.[30]

Robert McNamara's first major appointment was as President of the Ford Motor Company, at the time, one of the biggest car companies in the world. He moved on to become the Secretary of Defence under Presidents Kennedy and Johnson following which he was appointed head of the World Bank.

The former American vice President in the Bush administration, Richard Cheney, was also former president of Halliburton, one of the largest oil companies in the world. He became Secretary of Defence under George Herbert W. Bush and then American vice President under George W. Bush. George W. Bush's father, George Herbert W. Bush, began his career, as a founder of the Zapata Petroleum Corporation, became the US ambassador to the United Nations under President Nixon, the CIA director under President Ford and finally US president.[31]

Paul Wolfowitz, an arch neoconservative and one of the main architects of the 2003 Iraq war, was nominated to be the head of the World Bank by George W. Bush.[32]

Tony Blair, former British Prime Minister and other main architect of the Iraq war, following his exit from office became the lead Western envoy to the Middle East, illustrating the close links between Western politicians, industry and their military.

America and Britain's interest in the Middle East and the war on Iraq demonstrates the modern idea and implementation of neo-colonialism.

This blatant annexation of Iraqi's resources mirrors the West's 'nation building' that is also taking place in Afghanistan. Afghanistan's resources are under America's control and where, apart from Kabul, the country is in chaos. Afghan warlords remain in control of literally the rest of the country. Following the September 11th 2001 attacks that killed about 3,000 people in the Twin Towers George Bush declared war on 'terrorism'. Between Ariel Sharon, Tony Blair and George Bush, over three million innocent civilians, men, women and children have been killed since September 11th 2001, including the occupation of Iraq and Afghanistan and the nearly daily killing of unarmed Palestinians in Israel.

The death toll will only continue to rise, as not even one of these areas of conflict have even come close to any form of lasting resolution. The bitter truth is that the civilian death toll exacted by the West far exceeds that exacted by terrorist groups such as al-Qaeda, Isis or others, all put together.

Unfortunately, the only way Western foreign policy can be maintained in the Middle East and the rest of the world is by creating and supporting puppet governments and destabilizing legitimate and well-meaning governments. Any non-Western foreign government that acts by their people, for their own people and with their own resources is an existential threat to Western capitalism. The West then conspires to promote state-sponsored terrorism and rebel groups, which not only destabilize the regions but also provide a source of Western arms sales to both sides.

The peculiar method to the madness of imperialism requires it to develop a split personality and mask the untoward effects of their actions, not only from their own people, but from the world at large. The victors of wars have usually taken liberties with history and revised it to suit the sensibilities of their captive audiences, both at home and abroad. The British, in particular, have developed this into a fine art. With complex combinations of doublespeak, lies and omissions, and euphemisms to mask their real intentions, they have plundered almost at will and yet claimed the highest moral ground that any living or dead people ever could.

During the Second World War the Western Allies deliberately firebombed civilian homes in Dredsen, Germany, to try to crush the spirit of German resistance. Thousands of civilians were killed in the firestorm that resulted.

This tactic was repeated again by the American Air Force in Tokyo, which was bombed with incendiaries in order to set the civilian areas alight, as it was known to be made of combustible materials. Over 100,000 civilians died in one night of bombing, prompting the American general who ordered the bombing to remark that if he had been on the other side, he would have been tried for war crimes.

It is not commonly known that the first atomic bomb was dropped on Hiroshima five weeks after Japan had sued for peace.

The Nagasaki bomb killed about 70,000 people in the initial blast. Thousands more died from the effects of exposure to radiation. US General MacArthur banned the Western media from covering the aftermath of the atomic bombs, and was infuriated when an American journalist and reporter George Weller smuggled himself into the city and took dozens of photographs.

When the story broke, Weller was ordered to give his photographs to censors who have never released the originals. George Weller's son finally released his papers in 2005, after his death in 2002.[33]

In Okinawa, after the fierce battle to take the island from the Japanese, the US Marines mutilated the bodies of dead Japanese soldiers, and took their body parts home as souvenirs. In Vietnam, the American 1st Infantry Division rounded up 500 Vietnamese civilians in My Lai and gunned them down in cold blood; they only stopped to have lunch.[34]

The US has, since the break-up of Russia in the late 1980s and 1990s, persistently blocked attempts at reducing the proliferation of nuclear arms contrary to its public stance of reducing nuclear arms proliferation. This stance sharply increases the chances of a nuclear attack from terrorists and 'rogue nations' that get their hands on nuclear weapons. Unfortunately, the sad fact is that 'rogue nations' already have their hands on nuclear weapons.

Western nations, in particular the United States, have continued to develop their nuclear armament programs while preventing Third World countries from acquiring any. Since the US and Britain have repeatedly flaunted international law and attacked, intervened and occupied nations at will, it would seem logical that they fit their own description of rogue nations who are threatening the wellbeing of all living things, bringing the reality of a nuclear holocaust ever closer.

The most well-known nuclear disaster is the Chernobyl disaster in Ukraine, but the West has had many close shaves with nuclear holocausts without the majority of their own citizens being aware. Called 'broken arrows', nuclear weapons have gone missing, been accidentally dropped from aircraft, and caused explosions, fires and exposure to radiation has claimed the lives of many of their own citizens.[35]

On October 10th 2006 it was widely reported that North Korea had successfully tested a nuclear bomb at a secret underground location. This was in the face of US threats and sanctions which convinced North Korea to seek possession of a nuclear weapon in order to protect itself from Western aggression.[36] North Korea has remained in a tense stand-off with the US ever since.

In 2002 George W. Bush unilaterally tore up the 1972 anti-ballistic missile treaty between Moscow and the US to allow America to start the 'son of Star Wars' missile program. This pre-9/11 national missile 'defence' program meant that the US could no longer honour NATO's post-Cold War pledge not to build bases on former Warsaw Pact territory.[37]

With the US trying to ringfence Russia and install military installations in Poland and the Czech Republic, Russia responded by building 120 silo-based and mobile Topol-M SS-27 intercontinental ballistic missiles specifically designed to penetrate any defensive missile shield.[38]

The Bush administration justified its actions in terms of the global war on terror.

Other evidence of America's aggressive expansion of the empire under President Bush's administration has been the indiscriminate abduction, incarceration and torture of 'terror' suspects from all over the world, called 'extraordinary rendition' by the CIA.

In February 2007 a report from the Members of the European Parliament reported that the US operated 1,245 covert rendition flights in Europe, some of which took suspects to states where they could be tortured.

The collusion of EU countries was required to carry out rendition at this scale, and the report stated:

'Britain, Germany and Italy were among 13 EU countries that turned a blind eye to the CIA's secret movement of terror suspects.'[39]

As José Padilla found out, the CIA does not always need to delegate torture to other states because they are very well versed in it themselves. Padilla, an alleged Brooklyn born former gang member was arrested at Chicago's O'Hare airport in May 2002 and classified as an 'enemy combatant'. He was locked in a navy prison in Charleston, South Carolina, measuring 9 feet by 7 feet, with no natural light, no clock or calendar. He only left the cell shackled and suited in heavy goggles and headphones. He was injected with 'truth serum', most likely LSD or PSP, his lawyers believe. Padilla was imprisoned without charge in this state for 1,307 days.

In truth, the CIA has perfected the art of psychological torture for several decades. It is known that sensory deprivation causes personality disintegration, the whole point of the torture. By depriving their captives of sensory stimuli with the outside world, they induce regression, forcing the mind in on itself and at the same time the calculated provision of stimuli during interrogation makes the person view the interrogator as a father figure.[40]

Extracts from a declassified 1963 CIA manual for interrogating 'resistant sources' outlined the methods used to break down the prisoners.

In the 1950s the CIA funnelled about $25 million through its MK-ULTRA program to scientists to carry out research into, 'Unusual techniques of interrogation'.[41] Under this program infamous psychiatrist Dr Ewen D. Cameron subjected hundreds of psychiatric patients to large doses of electroshock and total sensory deprivation treatments and drugged them with LSD and PSP.

In 1960 Dr. Cameron gave a lecture at the Brooks Air Force Base in Texas, in which he stated that sensory deprivation *"Produces the primary symptoms of schizophrenia."*[42]

Figures obtained by an organization called Human Rights First from the US Pentagon revealed that nearly 98 prisoners have died in US custody since August 2002, as the 'war on terror' that is being waged in Iraq and Afghanistan rages on according to the BBC Newsnight program.[43]

William Blum wrote: *"If love is blind, patriotism has lost all five senses."*[44]

Paralyzed by misguided patriotism and miseducated by their media, some Americans have not been impressed by the millions of people that have been killed by America's frequent bloody interventions worldwide. However many American neoconservatives would like America to deploy even more destructive weapons of mass destruction in the pursuance of their strategic goals regardless of the disastrous consequences.

During the Iraq War, an extremely popular US radio commentator, Paul Harvey, appealed to President Bush to deploy weapons of mass destruction aggressively:

"We sent men with rifles into Afghanistan and Iraq, and we kept our best weapons in our silos. Even now we're standing there dying, daring to do nothing decisive, because we've declared ourselves to be better than our terrorist enemies — more moral, more civilized. Our image is at stake we insist.

'But we didn't come this far because we are made of sugar candy. Once upon a time, we elbowed our way onto and into this continent by giving small pox infected blankets to Native Americans. Yes, that was biological warfare! And we used every other weapon we could get our hands on to grab this land

from whomever. And we grew prosperous. And, yes, we greased the skids with the sweat of slaves.

'And so it goes with most nation states, which, feeling guilty about their savage pasts, eventually civilize themselves out of business and wind up invaded, and ultimately dominated by the lean, hungry and up and coming who are not made of sugar candy.'"[45]

CHAPTER SIXTY THREE

AN ANATOMY OF MODERN WESTERN COLONIZATION: COLONIZING IRAQ

Many Africans and inhabitants of previous western colonies tend to view western colonisation globally as a historical event that has no bearing on their present situation. The West's subversion, invasion and occupation of Iraq stands as a living example of the West's use of military force to exploit a nation of its resources. All non-western nations that are richly endowed with natural and human resources, and most African nation fall squarely into this category. The Iraqi people have suffered and endured a great deal at the hands of the West for over a century now. Iraq's greatest 'crime' was committed a long time ago, not by Saddam Hussein and his mystery collection of weapons of mass destruction, but by Iraq being 'caught in possession' of the second largest and 'highest quality' oil reserves in the world.[1]

Judging by the endemic levels of suffering and poverty in oil rich, developing countries also 'caught in possession' of oil by the West, like Nigeria, Sudan, Libya and Venezuela, we can see why the Iraqi people cannot be let off lightly. Over a period of several centuries, Russia was repeatedly invaded by European imperial powers, not just for their abundance of land and manpower but also for their vast oil reserves. Today, the Russian 'crime' of being in possession of large oil reserves has been mitigated somewhat by their possession of the world's largest arsenal of nuclear weapons.

Like a golden goose, Iraq sits upon the second-largest oil reserve in the world, an impressive projected 112 billion barrels of crude oil. Iraq's light, low-sulphur oil is considered to be of very high quality, and often lies just beneath the surface. This facilitates production costs as low as $2.00 a barrel. With a $20 billion investment, Iraq's oil output could, theoretically, within a few years increase up to 7 million barrels per day. This would constitute one tenth of global oil consumption.[1] The abundant supply of cheap oil under Western control would not only reduce the price of oil globally but also critically uplift the ailing economies of Western nations.

The ex-economic adviser to President Bush, Larry Lindsey explained in 2002:

'When there is regime change in Iraq you can add 3–5 million barrels to the world supply [per day].'[2]

Lord John Browne, the CEO of British Petroleum, publicly warned the British government that British oil companies would lose out against their American competitors if London did not participate in a war on Iraq.[3]

Digressing slightly, access to crude oil decided the outcome of not just the First World War but also the Second World War. Germany lost the First World War, mainly because it ran out of petrol. Starved of fuel, Germany eventually surrendered on November 11th 1918. Lord Curzon, a member of the British war cabinet and future foreign minister, stated quite explicitly:

'The Allied cause had floated to victory upon a wave of oil.'[4]

It was a case of déjà vu for Nazi Germany when, yet again, the lack of access to oil forced the German war machine to grind to a halt. Some Western historians would have us believe that Hitler attacked Russia in error instead of Britain, but Hitler was desperate to get his hands on the Caspian oilfields as part of 'Operation Blue'.[5]

Even when his prized German 6th Army was encircled by Soviet troops, and faced total annihilation in winter of 1942/3, a desperate Hitler refused to withdraw them from the Caucasus. He reportedly told Field Marshal Erich von Manstein:

'It is a question of the possession of Baku, unless we get the Baku oil, the war was lost.'[6]

The German offensive ran out of oil in the Caucasus Mountains and by January 1943, Hitler belatedly gave them the order to retreat. Within two years, Soviet tanks entered Berlin and the dream of the 1,000 years Reich had died.

Iraq's strategic importance, however, far exceeds just its vast oil reserves. The battle for Western dominance in Iraq is also about water and geopolitics. The two main rivers of the Middle East, the Tigris and Euphrates, flow through Iraq to supply all the Middle Eastern countries.

Geopolitically, Iraq is very strategically located in the Middle East as it borders Iran, Kuwait, Saudi Arabia, Jordan, Syria and Turkey. It also has a coastline — the Persian Gulf. It is within easy missile striking distance of both Israel and Russia.[7]

Military strategists compare the strategic importance of modern Iraq to the significance of the Hudson River during the French-Indian wars and the American Revolution.[8]

Like in Africa, Western companies since the 1980s have been fighting to privatize water resources in the Middle East and Latin America.

Thus, whoever controls Iraq controls the increasingly critical water resources of the Middle East. Iraq is, therefore, the geopolitical key for controlling the Middle East.

The same way gold, slaves, and silver had stimulated the appetites of European countries to exploit and plunder, the discovery of oil in the Middle East in the late 19th century initiated the frenetic drive by the major European powers to gain access and control of the Middle East.

Iraq came into being in the early 1900s when Britain carved it out as a country and at the time took care to remove the oil-rich Kuwait as a separate country, which remained under Western control until 1961.

T. E. Lawrence, a flamboyant orientalist, was a British Oxford graduate turned undercover agent. Fluent in Arabic, an archaeologist and a guerrilla fighter, his aim was to break up the Turkish Ottoman Empire by stirring up Arab nationalism among nomadic tribes that resented centuries of Turkish rule.

Capitalizing on the Arab discontent and dislike for the Turks, he energizing them with empty promises of securing Arab freedom and independence and succeeded in mobilizing the Arabs and waged highly effective guerrilla warfare against Turkish installations laying the groundwork for the occupation of Jerusalem and the break-up and colonization of Mesopotamia, now Iraq, by the British.

Lawrence of Arabia calculated:

"The Arabs should be our first brown dominion, and not our last brown colony. Arabs react against you if you try to drive them, and they are as tenacious as Jews; but you can lead them without force anywhere, if nominally arm-in-arm. The future of Mesopotamia is so immense that if it is cordially ours we can swing the whole Middle East with it."[9]

In 1945 the US state department described the oilfields in the Middle East as;

"a stupendous source of strategic power, and one of the greatest material prizes in world history."[10]

However, it was not only the British that sought after this stupendous source of strategic power; the French and the Germans had aspirations for Middle Eastern oil too. Hitler had planned to take the great prize of the Caspian oilfields in Russia and then swing south for the even greater prize of Persia [Iran] and Iraq.[11]

By 1918, European imperial powers had colonized all Arab countries including Iraq, despite their empty promises of independence. Kuwait, Baghdad and Basra were placed under British control. France controlled Northern Iraq, Lebanon and Syria. As soon as Iraq was colonized, the 'Iraqification' of the colonial process was initiated, with the puppet King Faisal installed to cover the tracks of the imperialists in their time-honoured fashion.

In the 1920s, Britain tried to occupy the entire country of Persia [Iraq] but was forced to leave because of the widespread Iraqi resistance, which accounted for more than 2,000 British lives. The British were brutal in their attempts to crush the Iraqi insurgency. Iraqi nationalist movements to achieve independence were bloodily smashed and villages bombed with artillery and phosphorus bombs.[12]

When the Kurds tried to rise up against the British, Churchill mused, *'I do not understand this squeamishness about the use of gas. I am strongly in favour of using poisoned gas against uncivilized tribes'.*[13]

Robert Fisk stated:

'Britain set up a colonial regime in Iraq after a long military campaign during World War I. In response to Iraqi resistance, including a country-wide uprising in 1920, British forces battled for over a decade to pacify the country, using airplanes, armored cars, firebombs and mustard gas. The French and British reached this secret Sykes-Picot Agreement in 1916 dividing Mesopotamia into zones of British and French influence in the event of the collapse of the Ottoman Empire. This division of spoils —which also included a share for Russia — demonstrates the Allies' attitude towards the people of the Middle East and reflects their lack of sincerity when they promised self-rule. The British later ignored the agreement when they seized the oil-rich province in 1918.'[14]

The 2003 US and UK Iraq invasion 'shock and awe' tactics were nothing new. In 1916, air attacks were used to shock and awe, to teach obedience and to force the collection of taxes. Winston Churchill, as responsible cabinet minister in the early years, saw Iraq as an experiment in high-technology colonial control. Though officials in London sometimes had qualms about the violence, colonial administrators on the ground like Gertrude Bell expressed enthusiasm for the power of the imperial military enterprise.

Iraq remained a British colony in all but name until the Suez invasion in 1956, and their oil resources remained under the control of Western powers ever since.

In 1958, the puppet Iraqi monarchy was overthrown by a nationalist called Abd al-Karim Qasim. His new organization called itself the Arab Socialist Union and threatened to nationalize the foreign consortium that exploited Iraqi's oil in 1963. At this time, the United States, not Britain, was the new imperial power, and the CIA promptly organized a coup which allowed Saddam Hussein's Ba'ath Party to come into power.

Saddam Hussein became the leader of the Ba'ath Party in 1979 and through financial aid from the United States and intelligence support from the CIA, they protected him from an internal coup d'état and he attained a vice-like grip on power.

Saddam Hussein became America's man in the Middle East from 1979 to 1990, as his secular Iraqi state was vital to securing America's Middle Eastern interests, especially against the virulently anti-American Iran.

John Kelly, the US assistant Secretary of State, on his visit to Baghdad in 1989 told Saddam Hussein, *'You are a force for moderation in the region, and the United States wants to broaden her relationship with Iraq'.*[15]

The Anglo-Persian Oil Company, later to become British Petroleum [BP], controlled the output of oil in Iraq. Such was the exploitation of Iraq's oil resources that even as late as 1973 British Petroleum took over 40% of Iraq's oil, while the rest was split between European powers. Iraqis only got 5% of their own oil resources.[16]

It is also interesting that as late as 1970 the Iraqi oil company revenue was distributed as follows: 47% British, 24% USA, 5% Iraq and the rest amongst other European countries.[17]

The fact that so little of Iraq's oil revenues went to the Iraqi people caused so much unrest in Iraq.

In 1972 Saddam Hussein nationalized the Iraqi oil company by collaborating with Russia, and then later France, instead of the UK and US, and this led to a period of immense prosperity for the Iraqi people, similar to what happened in Egypt, with rapid development in all areas of life; social, economic and military.

Following the revolution in Iran, which threw out American-backed leaders and saw the rise to power of Islamic fundamentalists, a nervous USA and Britain, keen on stopping Iran's 'Islamic backslide', supported Saddam Hussein to fight — but crucially not to win— the eight year war with Iran. The idea was to maintain the balance of power in the Middle East. This meant the West supported both sides with arms that killed and maimed millions of people on both sides. *'Too bad they both can't lose.'* Henry Kissinger stated.[18]

During the eight-year war with Iran that resulted in over a million casualties on both sides, the United States and Britain supplied Saddam

Hussein with everything he needed. Ironically, the West supported Iran too, because the Western powers did not want an outright winner but wanted to attenuate the power of both nations by keeping them supplied with enough arms to continue fighting but not enough to win the war.

When human rights groups presented evidence that Saddam Hussein had used mustard gas and nerve gas against Iranian soldiers and Kurdish civilians, the US and the UK turned a blind eye.

In fact, British and American based companies supplied Iraq with the ingredients of biological weapons, including botulism developed at a company in Maryland USA, which was licensed by the commerce department and approved by the state department.[19] Anthrax was supplied by a British government establishment in the full knowledge of Saddam Hussein's use of nerve gas against the Kurds.[20]

Even after the news of Saddam Hussein's human rights abuse and use of mustard and nerve gas was made public, Britain and America continued to supply him via illegal arms shipments through different countries. In 1992, a congressional inquiry found that George Bush Senior and his top advisers had ordered a cover-up to conceal their secret support for Saddam Hussein and the illegal arms shipments that were sent to him indirectly thought other countries.[21] The arms were being shipped to South Africa and Chile, and then 'sold on' to Iraq.

In Britain, the Thatcher government covertly and illegally channelled arms to Iraq using a British arms company called Astra.[22]

To give the tyrant his due, after Saddam Hussein had succeeded in securing a higher percentage of the Iraqi oil proceeds, he did redirect some of the oil profits into internal development, and within ten years pulled half of the country's population into the middle class. Under Saddam Hussein, Iraq became the most highly developed and secular country in the Middle East, with one of the highest levels of literacy in the world.

Following Iraq's costly war with Iran, the Iraqi economy took a further battering by the oil-rich Western run Kuwait draining Iraqi gas and oil offshore.

Donald Rumsfeld, Defence Secretary to President Bush, and another main architect of America's 2003 invasion and occupation of Iraq, was a key arms dealer on behalf of the USA. The bloody Iran-Iraq conflict, which lasted about eight years, finally ended in 1988 with a peace treaty. Iraqi Kurds supported by Iran tried to break this treaty but were put down with chemical weapons by Saddam Hussein, resulting in the deaths of up to 5,000 civilians. These chemical weapons were directly supplied by Britain. In fact, the USA and UK provided Iraq with the chemical weapons it used during the Iran-Iraq war.

The West, by manipulating the oil prices in Kuwait, damaged the Iraqi economy even more and provoked Saddam Hussein into a pre-emptive strike against Kuwait. This was their chance, not only to crush Saddam Hussein's military apparatus but also formed the premise for the invasion and occupation for Iraq. Saddam Hussein seriously miscalculated his popularity in the West as he insisted that the Americans knew about his invasion plans and had allowed him amass troops on the Iraqi-Kuwaiti border under direct US vision via satellite. He fell straight into this trap set for him by the United States and Britain.

In 1990, Saddam Hussein decided to attack and occupy Kuwait in an attempt to recoup some financial losses following the eight-year Iran-Iraq War as Kuwait was a puppet oil state that regularly increased its oil production to keep the price of oil low and cheap for the West.

Saddam Hussein's invasion of Kuwait led to the first Gulf War. In the build up to the second Gulf War, the sanctions imposed by the United States and Britain resulted in the deaths of over 500,000 Iraqi children and caused untold suffering to many more.

Iraq has been the only country in the world to date to have been defeated at war and disarmed. Partitioned by a no-fly zone, over which Britain and America flew bombing raids for over ten years, and then occupied under the guise of liberation and the possession of weapons of mass destruction, which has been proven to have been completely false.

The current situation in Iraq remains one of complete anarchy and unrest and so far the only consistent event is that America and Britain have secured the Iraqi oil wells and have been annexing of Iraq's resources. This annexation of a nation's resources mirrors the West's 'nation building' that is taking place in Afghanistan, where once again their resources are under America's control and apart from Kabul, the country is in chaos and Afghan warlords remain in control.

The cost to Iraqis has been immense; over 250,000 Iraqi civilians and military died in the first Gulf War, including the soldiers who were buried alive by American troops with bulldozers.

In an orgy of killing, American pilots indiscriminately slaughtered Iraqi men, women and children after refugees became gridlocked on the road from Baghdad to Jordan. Saddam's troops, who had clearly given up the fight, were mown down with machine gun fire and missiles from planes, firing depleted uranium into tanks, trucks and civilian vehicles.

Much of the slaughter was not aired, as the little that was shown was 'too stomach-churning' for Western viewing. The killing was so one-sided that virtually all the of American and British troops that died in the first Gulf War were killed by 'friendly fire' from their own troops.

This was a concerted attempt by the West not just to defeat Saddam Hussein but also to destroy the infrastructure of the country.

Depleted uranium is 'a weapon of mass destruction' that is internationally prohibited but was used liberally by American and British troops.

The effects of depleted uranium have yet to be fully assessed but there has been a marked increase in the occurrence of cancerous growths among children and adults.[23]

The Shiites in southern Iraq, long oppressed by Saddam Hussein's ruling party, tried to take advantage of the first Gulf War to start an uprising. Unfortunately for them, the Americans stood by and allowed Saddam to crush the uprising with tanks and helicopter gunships. The reason: they had not come there to liberate the Shiites and establish an Islamic state partial to Iran, but to establish control over Iraq's oil resources.

After the first Gulf War the United States and Britain imposed sweeping sanctions on Iraq, which resulted in an even greater loss of life. According to human rights bodies, the sanctions placed on Iraq from 1991–2003 cost over one million lives and by 1996, the lives of over 500,000 children.[24]

By any description available, these actions can only be described as genocide.

Several members of the UN resigned their appointments in protest of the inhumane sanctions as the UN was created, at least theoretically, to prevent conflict and save lives, rather than administer the genocidal wishes of their creator.

Even after Iraq had submitted to a humiliating weapons disarmament program and allowed the weapons inspectors led by Hans Blix to conduct ever more intrusive and aggressive searches, the UK and US refused to lift the sanctions.

The weapons inspectors were also allegedly used as spies, to gather information about Iraqi installations and this culminated in Saddam Hussein expelling them in 1998.

President Clinton and Prime Minister Tony Blair responded to the expulsion of weapons inspectors by bombing Iraq in 1998, claiming to be destroying weapon facilities. As usual, the truth was scarce, and the bombing claimed the lives of innocent civilians and did nothing to deplete military capacity of Saddam Hussein.

What the consenting Western public did not realize was that the plan to attack and occupy Iraq had existed since 1991, after the first Gulf War.

Neoconservative Republicans held the view that Iraq should have been occupied following the first Gulf War in 1991, despite negative public opinion. It was widely felt that George Bush Senior did not complete the job at the time.

Several right-wing neoconservative groups have existed in America, but one that became pivotal to the neoconservative agenda was called the 'Project for the New American Century [PNAC]'.[25] PNAC declared that while America was at the pinnacle of its military and economic might, it should take advantage of the absence of a peer competitor, i.e. a superpower like Russia, and aggressively expand its hegemony in a manner unseen since Roman times.

It called for the aggressive military destruction and economic crippling of competitors, and the occupation of countries like Iraq and Iran which had large reserves of natural resources like oil. American military bases, deployed around the world, were to be increased to allow tighter control of Third World and special interest economies. It proposed several swift and decisive military responses in order to maintain hegemony.

Iraq and other countries in George Bush's 'axis of evil' were all high on the hit list. Oil-rich countries would be closely policed and run remotely from Washington, much like in the British colonial empire.

This aggressive military stance, coupled with with globalization of capitalism, would keep the dependent countries so economically weak that they would not be in a position to resist, even if they wanted to.

Popular signatories to the Project for the New American Century include Donald Rumsfeld, Jeb Bush, Colin Powell, Paul Wolfowitz, Condoleezza Rice, and many other members of the former Bush Republican administration.[26]

The American plan of attack had strong similarities to the German Blitzkrieg in World War Two, and involved using a relatively small force, backed by the best and latest technology available. With total aerial superiority, rapid mobile mechanized units and artillery, the idea was to decisively defeat opponents before they could mobilize.

Therefore the plan to attack Iraq had been on the shelf since 1991, just waiting for the best opportunity, and a willing American President to implement it.

By 2000, Iraq had been severely weakened by its eight-year war with Iran, the first Gulf War and nine years of Western sanctions. The UK and US had used the weapon inspectors to further reduce Iraq's military capability. Iraq was monitored by satellites via space, and their planes grounded by the illegal UK and US no-fly zones. The entire country had been mapped from within and from without.

To put it simply, Iraq was a sitting duck, only this 'duck' was not sitting on water but on the world's second largest reservoir of oil.

When George W. Bush came to power it was only a matter of finding or creating an excuse for war. The excuse was dramatically provided by the September 11th 2001 attacks on the Twin Towers in New York.

In 2000 the United States organized the largest and most expensive war games in history. By 2001 it was clear that President George W. Bush was publicly preparing for war against Iraq, long before Saddam Hussein was alleged to have weapons of mass destruction.

Called the Millennium Project 2002, and at a cost of $250 billion, the United States prepared for the eventuality of a virulently anti-American rogue military commander in the Persian Gulf, allegedly harbouring and sponsoring four different terrorist organizations, who would challenge American strategic resources in the Middle East.

The US was preparing to fight an unconventional war in the Middle East, as the lessons of the first Gulf War showed it was clear that no nation had the military might to face the United States head-on in conventional warfare.

In the words of the US Joint Forces Command, [JFCOM] Commander General William F. Kerman at a Pentagon press briefing:

"We looked at the full array of what we can do to affect our adversaries' environment. Political, military societal cultural, institutions...all the things looked at very comprehensively.

They are things that the agencies have right now that can interrupt people capabilities. There are things you can do to disrupt the ability to communicate, to provide power to the people, to influence their national will... to take out the power grids."[27]

"Instead of going after war fighting capability, we have to go after war making capability. The military is connected to the economic system, to their cultural system, to their personal relationships. We have to understand the links between all those systems."

Another JFCOM analyst put it like this:

"The next war is not just going to be military on military. How many tanks you kill, how many ships to sink and how many planes you shoot down, the decisive factor is how you take apart your adversary's system."[25]

This account clearly defines what 'collateral damage' really is. It fairly obvious from the above description that Saddam Hussein was the rogue leader the US had been preparing to use as an excuse for war since 1991, after the first Gulf War, but Saddam Hussein and his ruling party were not the 'collateral damage'.

The real aim was to achieve complete control of Iraq's vast oil reserves and resources, and the real targets were the Iraqi people, their systems, their culture, their way of life and ultimately, their lives.

When you take a closer look at the type of weaponry in use, it is hard not to draw the same inference.

Cluster bombs are effectively landmines dropped from the air and essentially target the civilian population.

During the US/UK led occupation of Iraq in March 2003, thousands of cluster bomblets were dropped. The British forces used the RBL-755 air delivered cluster bomb; each bomblet contains 100 grams of explosive. As the weapons fall through the air, the tail fin causes it to spin and the canister opens at pre-set altitudes from 300–3,000 feet. Each RBL-755 contains 147 sub munitions and depending on the rate of tailspin can cover an area the size of four football pitches. The bomblets contain a copper cone for piercing armour and a ring of incendiary zirconium for starting fires.

Two thousand bomblet shells were fired by British artillery and 68 cluster bombs dropped from the air in March 2003 alone, according to the Ministry of Defence.[28]

A landmine clearance expert and acting director of Landmine Action said:

"The BL-755 sub-munitions bomblet is one of the nastiest munitions I have ever cleared. The effects are blast, shrapnel, molten metal and fire. It would fit in your hand."[29]

No doubt the thousands of unexploded bomblets dropped will leave a terrible legacy in Iraq and the small size of bomblets makes them particularly attractive and deadly to unsuspecting children.

When the atomic bombs were dropped on Hiroshima and Nagasaki, the civilian population bore the brunt of the attack and has suffered the radioactive fallout for over 70 years now.

Napalm and Agent Orange were used to deadly effect in the Vietnam War, denuding the forest and polluting the land for years.

In the First Gulf War, and in the Iraq War, depleted uranium was used causing widespread death and ongoing genetic malformations.

Even while Saddam Hussein was on trial for the use of chemical weapons against his own people, the United States and Britain used chemical weapons, in particular, white phosphorus, in the pacification of Fallujah, in 2003.[30]

There were more human rights abuses and murders in Iraq during the US and British occupation than during Saddam Hussein's reign, according to Ayad Allawi, the first interim president of the occupied Iraq.[31]

It is striking that, despite all these atrocities, American troops have been exempt from being tried for war crimes in the International Court of Justice in The Hague. It was only after the cruel treatment of Iraqi prisoners in the Abu Ghraib prison scandal that the United States offered to relax their position of being exempt from war crimes.

Today, Iraq faces the dire prospect of losing over $200 billion of its oil wealth since an American installed Iraqi government handed over of the development of its oil reserves to American and British multinationals.

Long before the US invasion of Iraq and the September 11th 2001 attacks, production sharing assessments [PSA] by multinationals sought rates of returns on their investments of 42–162% far in excess of the typical 12% rates a report by Crude Designs stated.[32]

Ever since large Western oil companies were being ejected from Iraq in 1972 following Saddam Hussein's nationalization of the oil industry, the world's four oil giants, BP, Exxon, Chevron and Shell, had been desperate to get back into Iraq.

The new Iraq constitution was practically written by the US and British Foreign Office advisers, and they guaranteed themselves a major role for their oil companies.[33]

Saddam Hussein must have made a decision to remain in Iraq long before the American and British invasion began, after all, where could he have gone? Surrounded by enemies on all sides, Iran was out of the question after his 10-year war. Kuwait, he had invaded in 1991. Saudi Arabia, Turkey and Jordan were all close allies of the West. The usual safe havens for ousted tyrannical dictators in the West were out of the question.

Eventually, flushed out of his bunker by a cash reward of American dollars, he played out his last scenes in the farcical trial that was supposed to demonstrate to the world, the 'true process' of Western democracy, which it duly achieved.

Despite his request not to be hung 'like a common thief', he was sentenced to death by hanging. Saddam Hussein's trial was a macabre exhibition of reality television, in which his fate had been decided long before. Saddam Hussein was sentenced to die in the run-up to the US mid-term elections, an obvious move by George W. Bush to win more votes at home.

Iran's Resalat newspaper wrote:

"Saddam is playing out the last scene of the White House scenario after 40 years of being at their service. Now he is the Republicans trump card … in the run-up to the US midterm elections."[34]

CHAPTER SIXTY FOUR

PLUNDERING THE CONGO

The Congo is facing one of the greatest humanitarian crises in the world today. Over 6 million people have died since 1996, an estimated 45,000 people each month. Hundreds of thousands of women and children have been raped as both victims and a strategy of war. However as tragic as these terrible figures are, they are merely a distraction to the American-led Western scramble for the Congo's huge mineral and agricultural riches and resources.[1]

The Congolese holocaust started by King Leopold's annexation of the Congo has progressed seamlessly through Belgian Colonial rule to American neo-colonial control of the their governments and resources today.

The Congo is perhaps the most mineral and agriculturally rich country in the world. It has vast reserves of diamonds, gold, copper, tin, cobalt, manganese and even oil. It has about 64% of the world's reserves of coltan, a mineral used in cell phones, computers and other electronic devices. The US military relied heavily on Congolese minerals to develop its nuclear and space technology during and after the Second World War.[2]

The Congo has the agricultural capacity to feed the entire world up to 2050 and the hyrdrocapacity to supply the entire African continent, Southern Europe and parts of the Middle East with electricity.[3]

Even though the US did not directly receive African territory during the partitioning of the African continent during the Berlin's conferences of 1888, they did support King Leopold II and made it possible for him to carve out the Congo for himself. In return, King Leopold II granted America concessions and access to the agricultural and mineral wealth of the Congo. After the Belgian government took over from King Leopold II, American interests and companies in the Congo continued to have access to the resources they needed.

However, following Congo's independence, Patrice Lumumba came to power as the first democratically elected leader of the Democratic Republic of Congo and made it clear that he would further the interests of the Congolese people above that of the previous colonial masters, Belgium and other Western countries, including America.

In June 1960, during the colonial handover speech, the Belgian King, Boudin, extolled King Leopold II's achievements and his 'civilising of the Congo'. Patrice Lumumba then made an unscheduled speech in which he outlined the suffering of the Congolese people and systematically criticized Belgian colonial rule. He described Congolese independence as the crowning success of the nationalist movement.[4]

His speech angered the Belgians and Western powers and immediate steps were taken to undermine his leadership.

Merely 5 days after Congo's independence, a revolt broke out after a white Belgian officer, Lieutenant-General Emile Janssons, the Belgian Commander for the Force Publique refused to recognise Congolese independence and hand over command to African officers.

The day after the independence ceremonies he had assembled the African non-commissioned officers and told them that things would stay the same under his command. He emphasized his point by writing on a blackboard "Before independence = After independence".

By July 1960, several units mutinied against their white officers and the unrest spread across the country.

On July 11th 1960, Moise Tshombe, leader of CONAKAT declared the mineral rich Congo's southern province of Katanga an independent state. He was backed by the Belgian government, rich Belgian and South African mining companies and America, who feared that Patrice Lumumba's MNC would nationalise the company's assets.[5]

Moise Tshombe was supported with money and arms from the US, the Belgian army and white mercenaries from South Africa and Rhodesia to supplement his Katangese soldiers.[6]

Patrice Lumumba appealed to the UN and US for help to no avail. He even made an unscheduled trip to America but was not received by the US government. The 'UN troops' who first arrived in the Congo were in fact largely US troops, barely disguised as UN troops, with a much smaller contingent of UN troops from other countries, like Ghana. The real UN troops had specific orders not to intervene in the unfolding crisis in the Congo. In desperation, Patrice Lumumba turned to the Soviet Union for help but this was to be the excuse America needed to label him as a communist and eliminate him. Code named 'Project Wizard', it is alleged that the order for Patrice Lumumba's assassination came directly from President Eisenhower in memo to the CIA.

A CIA operative called Larry Devlin was allegedly paid $100,000 to liquidate Patrice Lumumba. However, the killing was orchestrated to appear as if he was killed by his African opponent, Moise Tshombe, to deflect blame from the West.

In the end, Patrice Lumumba and two other close associates were arrested, taken to Katanga and handed over to his African opponents. Supervised by Belgian officers, they were shot, their bodies hacked to pieces and then dissolved in sulphuric acid.[7]

With Patrice Lumumba out of the way the US installed the unelected Joseph Mobutu Sese-Seko as a military dictator. Mobutu was in power for 30 years and looted over $7 billion out of the Congolese economy. Mobutu renamed the country Zaire and became a multibillionaire while his people lived in abject poverty. Human rights abuses were rife in the Congo and whenever Mobutu's dictatorship was threatened by an uprising, the US reacted strongly to ensure that his dictatorship continued.[8]

In 1977 and 1978, President Jimmy Carter sent US troops to the Congo to assist Mobutu quash attempts of the Congolese people to remove him from office.

On a visit to the US, President George H. W. Bush described Mobutu as the US's 'Best friend in Africa'.

All attempts for the Democratic Republic of Congo to find its feet following Mobutu's reign of terror have been systematically undermined by the US.

The US also played regional forces against the DRC to ensure it remained chaotic and exploitable. The Rwandan leader, Gen. Paul Kagame was trained in the US like Uganda's Museveni and invaded Rwanda through the north of Rwanda. It is alleged that Paul Kagame's rebel forces, in collusion with foreign Western forces, shot down the plane that killed the Hutu president of Rwanda, Burundi's president and the Rwandan Army chief of staff on April 6th 1994.[9]

This single act was the final spark in the unrest and turmoil of Kagame's and Musoveni's invasion of Rwanda that triggered of the Rwandan genocide that killed about 800,000 people.

Following the genocide in Rwanda in 1994, the US simply looked the other way when the US backed leaders of Rwanda, Paul Kagame and Museveni of Uganda, invaded the DRC in 1996. Over 200,000 men, women and children were killed and the UN described invasion and rape of the Congo resources as a war crime.

On July 16th 1997, the US Committee on International Relations about the Democratic Republic of Congo revealed evidence to the House of Representatives that showed that Rwandan forces led by Gen. Paul Kagame's Rwandan Patriotic Front [RPF] were massacring Hutu refugees who fled to Eastern Congo-Zaire after the Rwandan genocide in 1994.

In 2006, as a senator, Barack Obama was credited with the passage into law of Public Law 109–456. Some even refer to PL 106–456 it as the Obama Law. Obama and Hillary Clinton forced the Republican government of George W. Bush to pass a comprehensive law that promised to support the Democratic Republic of Congo and prevent any destabilizing interventions from neighbours, especially Rwanda [10]

In 2008, the Spanish National Court indicted 40 Rwandan military officers with crimes humanity and genocide against Congolese Rwandan and Spanish citizens. The presiding judge, Fernando Andreu, stated that he had enough evidence to implicate Gen. Paul Kagame but could not indict him because of his presidential immunity.[11]

However, despite a thorough and detailed Mapping UN report in 2010 that heavily implicated Rwanda and described in detail mass murder, ethnic cleansing, mass rape, recruitment of children into militant groups, abduction and torture, President Obama turned a blind eye like his predecessors did earlier and refused to bring an alleged war criminal, but important US ally, Paul Kagame to book. The US continues to provide Rwanda with $ 1billion worth of aid and military support yearly.

So wanton is the US supported Rwandan pillaging and plunder of the Democratic Republic of Congo mineral resources that Rwanda is now a major exporter of Coltan despite the fact that Rwanda has no Coltan reserves of its own.

In 2012, a Rwandan militia force called the M23 invaded the Democratic Republic of Congo. This may have been linked with the DRC's president Paul Kabila's decision to lean towards China and sign a $9 billion mining and infrastructure package in 2013.

Despite the fact that there are 17,500 UN peacekeepers and US special forces permanently stationed in the DRC, no action was taken to protect the people and stop the M23 militias who number around 3000, from mass murder, rape and torture.

The UN stated official reason for not beating back the M23 rebels is that they do not have sufficient forces and are worried about collateral damage. This echoes the inaction of the UN forces when Patrice Lumumba's newly independent DRC was being torn apart by US and other Western backed forces right under their nose.

CHAPTER SIXTY FIVE
A WAR WITHOUT END

Under the rubric of a war against terror, the Bush Republican administration aggressively and militarily expanded the American empire all over the world and not just in Iraq. It is important to note that George Bush's Republican administration expanded into the space that President Clinton's Democratic administration created for them, while President Obama only refined Bush's foreign policy to make it more palatable and presentable to people.

In hindsight, the September 11th 2001 attacks on the Twin Towers was the new 'Pearl Harbour' for the Bush administration. It provided them with an excuse to take the American public along with the expansion of its imperial empire, while fighting the so-called war on terror. It may not be a coincidence that the Twin Towers attack in New York occurred ten years to the date after Bush Senior, President George H. W. Bush, outlined the New World Order, on September 11th 1991.

We now know there were no weapons of mass destruction in Iraq and there was no link between Saddam Hussein and the terrorist who carried out the September 11th 2001 attacks. There was no 45-minute capability, of Saddam Hussein firing weapons of mass destruction into Europe as claimed by Tony Blair, the former British Prime Minister. There were no nuclear weapons in Niger, and no chemical or nuclear weapons depot in Iraq, as claimed by Colin Powell in his now, infamous, United Nations presentation.

What we are left with is the reality of an American and British led occupation, of both Afghanistan and Iraq, their acquisition of material and strategic resources and millions of civilian deaths. In Afghanistan, some years after the Taliban regime was toppled from power, the country remains desperately undeveloped and significant numbers of Western troops remain even though they 'officially pulled out', perhaps to protect their multinationals while they secure the oil pipelines that Western multinationals have been laid across the country.

In Iraq, Western occupying troops led by America and Britain, have secured Iraq's oil wealth and maintain a military base in probably the most strategic country in the Middle East.

The estimated one million Iraqi casualties of the bloody occupation are only collateral damage of the imperial grand strategy. The vacuum in the Iraqi leadership that followed the US invasion and occupation of Iraq has now been filled by the mediaeval Islamic Caliphate called Isis. Just like Al-Qaieda, Isis are in fact a another creation of the US foreign policies, as they started off as American backed rebels who were armed and trained by the US, to topple Bashar Assad of Syria, but had plans of their own.

Thus, successive US administrations have systematically attacked any remaining shackles, to the expansion of its hegemony and empire.

America tore up the antiballistic missile proliferation treaty, the nuclear non-proliferation treaty and anti-chemical and biological warfare treaties. In 1972, the US withdrew from the biological and toxics weapons convention and exempted itself from the chemical weapons convention in 1997.

It is common knowledge that the US opposed the Kyoto agreements to reduce carbon emissions. Less well known is American opposition to the outer space treaty of 1967, to reserve space for peaceful purposes.[1]

In his book, 'Rogue State', William Blum pointed out the imperial grand strategy of the American empire. American foreign policy is not driven by any form of morality, or even simple decency, but rather by the necessity to serve other masters. American officials have no problem walking the moral high ground, if they have to.

He broke this down into four imperatives:

1. Making the world open and hospitable for — in current terminology — globalization, particularly American base transnational

corporations.

2. Enhancing the financial statements of defence contractors at home who have contributed generously to members of Congress and members of the White House.

3. Preventing the rise of any society, that might serve as a successful example of an alternative to the capitalist model.

4. Extending political economic and military hegemony, over as much as the globe as possible to prevent the rise of any regional power that may challenge America's supremacy and create the world order in America's image as befits the world's only superpower.[2]

It can easily be argued that racism and imperialism are forms of mental illness, and this impression was reinforced by a study produced by the US Strategic Command responsible for the US Strategic Nuclear Arsenal in 1995 in an essay titled 'Essentials of Post-Cold War Deterrence'.

The 'Madman philosophy' as proposed in the study stated:

'Because of the value that comes from the ambiguity of what the US may do to an adversary if the acts we seek to deter or carried out, it hurts to portray ourselves as too fully rational and cool headed. The fact that some elements may appear to be potentially out of control can be beneficial to creating and reinforcing fears and doubts within the minds of an adversary's decision makers. This essential sense of fear is the working force of deterrence. That the US may become irrational and vindictive if its vital interests are attacked should be a part of the national persona, we project to all adversaries.'[3]

No matter how powerful the drive for wealth, expansion, power or glory, none of the previous empires; the Roman Empire, Ottoman Empire or even the British Empire, could even conceptualize it, let alone make plans for it.

In what can only be described, as a terrifying development, the American empire is not only seeking to control earth-bound mortals: it wants to fight wars from space too.

The US Space Command and the Pentagon stated:

'US space command-dominating the space dimension of military operations to protect US interests and investments. Integrating space forces into war fighting capabilities across the full spectrum of conflict.... Any

portion of the 21st century space power will also involve into a separate and equal medium of warfare... the emerging synergy of space superiority with land, sea and air superiority will lead to full-spectrum dominance... development of ballistic missile defence is using space systems and planning for precision strikes from space offers a counter to the worldwide proliferation of weapons of mass destruction... space is a region with increasing commercial, civil, international and military interests and investments. The tractor these vital systems is also increasing... control of space is the ability to assure access to space freedom of operations within the space medium and PDC to deny others, the use of space, if required... control of space is a complex mission that casts USCINCSPACE [US commander in chief of space] in a classic war factor role and mandate and established AOR [area of responsibility].... With regard to space dominance, we have it; we like it, and we are going to keep it.... We will engage terrestrial targets someday — ships, airplanes, land targets —from space... we're going to fight in space. We're going to fight from space, and we're going to fight into space.[4]

As the US is the only country militarizing space, they seek to have total military hegemony. US space forces will be like no force ever seen before. Using space-based strike weapons with conventional and nuclear capabilities, they could strike and kill individuals, communities and even wipe out whole countries at will.

A military analyst, William Arkin stated:

'No target on the planet or in space would be immune... the US can attack at will, without warning or credible pretext.'[5]

With this in mind, the US refused to join the rest of the world in reaffirming and strengthening the Outer Space Treaty of 1967, to reserve space for peaceful purposes. In recent times, they have continued to reject calls for the non-militarization of space. In January 2001, the US rejected the call of the UN Secretary-General Kofi Annan to overcome their lack of 'political will' and work towards a comprehensive accord to bar the militarization of space.[6]

The United States remains the only one of the 66 member states to oppose the launching of informal negotiations on outer space.[7]

As globalization, the economic arm of the imperial grand strategy, continues to widen the gap between rich and poor countries, the need for full-spectrum dominance increases, not only, to maintain capital flight from Third World countries but also to actually increase it. The income ratio of one fifth of the world's population in the wealthiest countries to the fifth of the world's population in the poorest went from 30 to one in 1960 to 74 to one by 1997.

The increased need for full-spectrum dominance, as explained by the US Space Command, is that the globalization of the world economy is expected to widen the economic gap between the poor and the rich countries. The deepening economic stagnation, political instability and cultural alienation will lead to unrest and violence among the 'have-nots' much of its directed against the US.

By monopolizing this domain of warfare, the US will be ready to control the anticipated social disorder in reaction to their policies, by using space systems and planning for precision strikes from space, as a counter to the worldwide unrest anticipated through the capitalist process of globalization.

There is nothing futuristic about these plans, as American and British drones continue to kill thousands of 'suspects' in Pakistan, Afghanistan, Sudan, Somalia, Yemen and beyond, at the click of a computer mouse. Today, the UK and US are still eliminating individuals and groups of people, deemed to be a real threat or potential threat to their capitalist process, via drone attacks well outside the boundaries of international law.

Drone attacks have killed thousands of innocent civilians; men, women and children, all acceptable collateral damage of the capitalist agenda.

Wedding parties, schools, council meetings and hospitals have been struck by 'accidental' deadly drone attacks. At best, a generic apology is issued; otherwise they are labelled as 'insurgents' in the Western newspapers and life goes on.

The legality of the process of killing innocent civilians and suspected insurgents around the world without civil or military legal process is being challenged and is further radicalizing societies which America and Britain claim to be trying to reintegrate into the global community.

Bradley Manning, a former American intelligence analyst, found infamy for being responsible for leaking over 700,000 battlefield reports and diplomatic cables to the anti-secrecy site WikiLeaks. Villified as a traitor and a whistle-blower in America, it is interesting that Mr Manning stated that he leaked the material to expose the US military's 'bloodlust' and disregard for human life, and what he considered as American diplomatic deceit'.[7]

Mike Marqusee wrote in his article, 'A four-year nightmare' in the Guardian November 4th 2004, it is not anti-American to reject this imperial power.

"People rebel against US hegemony for the same reasons they rebelled against the dominance of earlier imperial powers, not out of a distaste for the culture of the rulers but out of an objection to undemocratic, unaccountable, self-serving rule by remote elites of whatever culture."[8]

CHAPTER SIXTY SIX

SMOKE WITHOUT FIRE

'All warfare is based on deception.' **General Sun Tzu** ca. 500BC.[1]

'Who controls the past controls the future. Who controls the present controls the past.' **George Orwell,** 1984.[2]

"It is possible to deceive all the people all the time when the government and press cooperate." **George Seldes,** 1938, in reaction to spreading fascism in Europe.[3]

When George Orwell wrote his best selling novel 'Nineteen Eighty-Four' in 1949, he problably did not realise he would prophetically capture the essence of modern western societies.

The main message of George Orwell's fictional futuristic dytopian society was centred on totalitarianism, mass surveillance and repression of independent thinking and individuality. In Orwell's fictional work, by the year 1984, the world is dominated by three perpetually warring super-states; Oceania, Eurasia and Eastasia. Great Britain is a province in Oceania called Airstrip One. Oceania is ruled by the Party, led by Big Brother, who may not really exist, and they use the Thought Police to persecute individuality and independent thinking. Oceania has four government ministries which use their stated names as facades or (doublethink) for their true intentions.

"The Ministry of Peace concerns itself with war, the Ministry of truth with lies, the Ministry of love with torture and the Ministry of Plenty with starvation."

Many words from George Orwell's novel are now common parlance like; "Big Brother", "doublethink" and "newspeak".

It is thought that Soviet leader Joseph Stalin and the totalitarian communist government in Russia preceeding and following the Second World War may have been George Orwell's inspiration to write his book.

Unfortunately, the three slogans that dominated the fictional dystopian Oceania society in his novel now also dominate the modern western society:

'War is peace, freedom is slavery and ignorance is strength'.

In dissembling this Orwellian fact, John Pilger stated:

"Today's slogan, 'war on terrorism', also reverses meaning.

The war is terrorism. The most potent weapon in this 'war' is pseudo-information, different only in the form that Orwell described, consigning to oblivion unacceptable truths and historical sense. Dissent is permissible within 'consensual' boundaries re-inforcing the illusion that information and speech are 'free'.[4]

How is it that human beings remain so psychologically vulnerable in this age of information? The internet, Facebook, Twitter, YouTube and a multitude new information platforms, in addition to the traditional ones, provide a wealth of information and has improved communication significantly.

However, the vastly enhanced communication and availability of information has left the majority of people even more apathetic and psychologically malleable than ever before.

For instance, people remain lonely and depressed even though they may have hundreds of Facebook friends. The secret lies in the subconscious manipulation of the mind by the implantation of agenda's, views and opinions couched as news and information, much like a bacterial or viral infection will infect and affect the physical body.

What we refer to as 'reality' is our conscious appreciation of the world around us. Our conscious minds filter the immense amount of external and internal information we receive through our brains and in essence creates a 'hologram' through which we make sense of the world around us. While our conscious mind helps us understand and process the huge amount of information we receive, our 'conscious reality' is heavily influenced by our socialization and cultural upbringing.

The cognitive dissonance people of all races suffer from daily is a direct result of our socialisation.

The process of creating and understanding our environment is largely a function of our memories. Once sensory stimuli are received, it is processed into memory in our brains. This is a highly complicated process involving different types of neurons and receptors in our brains. Memory is thought to be a brain wide process but the frontal cortex and the hippocampus are mainly involved.

Human conscious reality consists of the interplay of millions of memories and perceptions that weave together to help form the tapestry of 'reality'. These 'blocks' of memory are interspersed by important 'keystones' we call symbols. These symbols can contain simple or highly complex information that gives meaning to one or millions of memory blocks simultaneously.

The memory blocks and symbols are like condensed video and photographs clips of our lives and can generate any range of emotions or combinations of our senses, like pleasure, pain, happiness and sadness.

The perceptual gaps in between our memory blocks are 'doctored' by our brains to fit our concept of reality.

The concept of free will and uninfluenced human agency has been repeatedly been challenged by researchers and neuroscientists who discovered that the brain shows recordable Electro-Enchephalogram (EEG) activity before people become consciously aware of their thoughts or subsequent actions.

The EEG signals reflecting this build up is known as the Bereitschaftspotential or the readiness potential.

The readiness potential was first reported by two German researcher's Hans Helmut Kornhuber and Luder Decke from the University of Freiburg.

These findings were built upon by Benjamin Libet et al, a Virtual Nobel prize winner in Psychology from the University of Klagenfurt in Germany.[5]

Advances in modern medicine have facilitated research in this area and using functional magnetic resonance imaging (fMRI), neuroscientists were able to read brain activity to accurately predict their subjects decisions 11 seconds before they acted.[6]

The readiness potential suggests that subconscious processes in the brain are the true initiators of volitional acts of consciously assumed 'free will'.

Therefore the modern human world is extremely illusory but our perceptions make it appear real. As our brains attempt to process and codify information according to our socialization can often has to distort 'reality' to ensure it fits and remains comprehensible to our conscious minds.

Symbolism is the glue that holds the individual and collective psyche of people and their culture together. Therefore decoded symbolism is the key to understanding that system or culture.

From ancient times until the present day, the power of symbols on the human psyche has been immense. All over the world, from the great pyramids in Egypt, coliseum in Rome and the statue of Liberty in America, large structures were erected as symbols of worship and achievements.

Symbols create an instant messenger system for transmitting, highly codified information. At a subconscious or unconscious level, they aid the processing and evaluating information within that social setting or culture. Symbol stimulate or evokes thoughts, emotions, and subsequently actions and behaviour that define us in that society. Symbols provide the brain a short circuit in decoding the physiological and psychological perceptual process of understanding visual and other types of information based on an individual's socialization.

It is no wonder then that Western societies constantly seek 'heroes' and 'icons' as symbols of Western intellectual, technological and moral advancement to buttress its claim of innate superiority.

Thus, the modern human world is a house of cards built on shifting sand. The price of modern Western civilization is to inhabit a world that constantly bombards all of our senses with stimuli, conscious and subliminal, intended to sell us products, services, and political agendas.

In addition, Western society utilises a wide range of chemical agents and additives, pharmaceuticals, street drugs, and even sodas to chemically distort our thoughts and suppress our minds.

From baby food to cars, advertisers use every trick in the book to catch our attention and then suggest to us directly or subliminally to buy their goods. Exploiting the universal and powerful appeal sex has on all peoples, advertisers commonly use sexual themes and innuendo to attract our attention.

Politicians who employ the well-used psychological ploy of problem, reaction, solution, and deploy fear as their main tool of manipulation. Politicians and the media deliberately create fear amongst people, who react by running to the same authorities for the solution.

Several studies have shown that people drink and smoke more when anxious.

Exploiting this fact, huge cigarette multinationals play on the human mind's deep-rooted and subconscious awareness of sexual and fear themes. They insert subliminal messages of sex and scary images in their adverts, in the hope that it turns people to smoke and drink to relieve their anxiety and fears.

Advertisers do not stop at catching our attention once but keep repeating the adverts, like mantras, so the information slips deeper and deeper through our conscious minds and into our subconscious. Once this has been achieved, people find themselves going out to buy things they may consciously not feel any great desire for. How many times have you bought something from the shops just because you liked the advert, or have seen the advert so many times that you simply buy the good the next time you see it? You may have also caught yourself tapping your feet or humming to music you do not like, simply because you have heard it so many times that it has slipped into your subconscious mind.[7]

If it takes an advert less than ten repetitions to sink into the subconscious mind, then it is easy to understand why continuous negative imagery and portrayal of black people perpetuated over several centuries has developed into the socially transmitted racism and hatred that are woven into the fabric of Western societies.

Europeans have denigrated black African people in all aspects of their society, literature, science and politics for many years. It is clear that if one has been socialized in racist ideology from birth, it is more than likely that one would consciously or subconsciously act in ways and manners socially accepted by the wider community. For example, miseducated African people brought up in the same Western environment are internally no different from Caucasian. They consciously appreciate that they are the objects of racial discrimination as minorities in the white society, but they still harbour self-hate and a hatred of African people, almost as much and sometimes even more than white people do.

Children are naturally obsessed with belonging to groups and being accepted. This is an entirely normal part of growing up and socializing, but they react to the perception of difference with a brutal honesty that only adult socialization helps grown-ups to mask. When white children bully black African children and other racial minorities in school playgrounds, it is not just the fact that the children they bully are different or have dark or black skin that they do so, but it is because it is socially accepted in wider society.

The constant denigration of black people all over the world must be seen for what it really is: a weapon used to foster white hatred of black Africans and impose white supremacy. It simultaneously generates black hatred and contempt of each other between black Africans. Such is the hatred that white imperialism fosters that it does not matter that they do not even really know the African or non-white people they have elected to hate. After many years of being filled with negative stories and portrayals of the non-white people, many Caucasians do not go as far as open hatred but harbour an irrational and deep resentment of black people.

There are countless adverts in the Western media that promote and support the widely-held negative stereotypes of Africans — from seemingly innocuous adverts claiming to help starving children in Africa to other stereotypical adverts or clips on black people designed to reinforce their lowly status in Western societies.

Before his second term, the incumbent American President, George W. Bush ran an extremely negative campaign against the Democratic presidential challenger John Kerry. While John Kerry focused on policies and issues, Bush concentrated his efforts on damaging John Kerry's character and ran millions of dollars' worth of negative adverts aimed solely on crippling his opponent and keeping the American people scared of a terrorist attack. It worked like a dream, as Americans forgot the issues; bad management of the economy with record deficits, the fact that millions of Americans had slipped below the poverty line and could not afford health care, and the lies about weapons of mass destruction leading up to an immoral and pre-emptive war against Iraq, which contravened international law, cost over $200 billion and had claimed the lives of over 100,000 Iraqis and over 1,200 coalition troops at the time.

It only took George W. Bush one election year to savage John Kerry's character. Consider the fact that Europeans have portrayed Africans negatively for over 1,000 years. The West's negative portrayal of black Africans has affected the Europeans, and the rest of the Western socialized world sees black Africans and the way Africans see themselves.

If there was any defining moment in the establishment of white supremacist symbolic ideology in the social fabric of Western countries, it was the conversion of Christianity into a white Caucasian religion.

One of the biggest psychological ploys used by the Catholic Church was the use of false religious iconography to reinforce the notion that the Christian God is white. When you see all the Western art dating from the Renaissance, one striking fact is that none of the drawings showing God, the angels or Jesus and his disciples represents anyone other than Caucasians.

Even in the Sistine Chapel, Michelangelo's representation of heaven on the ceilings does not show any other race of human being other than the Caucasian.

'Michelangelo also dressed the New Testament figures in his pictures in the clothing of his own contemporaries. He took pimps, prostitutes and street urchins [small, mischievous boys] into his studio to pose as sensuous, sometimes naked models for the saints.'[8]

This was an important part in reinforcing the spiritual and moral rights of the colonizers. White religious imagery played a central role in the stripping of Africans of their culture and history, laying them bare and defenceless, against the will of the colonizing European nations. European Christianity, one of Livingstone's three Cs — Christianity, commerce, and civilization — were necessary to open up Africa to white exploitation, even though in the long run the fourth C, conquest using military force, was probably the most determining factor. In the long-term, it can be argued that the insidious effect of the imbibing of the Western form of Christianity had much more of an effect in creating the foundations of African colonial and neo-colonial dependence.

It was through European Christianity that the colonizers built up a sufficient number of subjugated black Africans, who acted on behalf of the colonizers to help break down African culture and unity by creating deep divisions between tribes and nations. Psychologically, white Christianity set their African converts an impossible task; psychologically, the only way to achieve the same favour in 'God's eyes' was to be white, which the Africans could never achieve.

Developing an inferiority complex was the only default position available to African converts to European Christianity.

The Roman Catholic Church used white religious imagery and censorship of the spread of knowledge with the central main aim of not only controlling the masses but to keep a grip on monarchy as well.

'European painters and sculptors by their use of white models to typify biblical characters have falsified tremendously the physiognomy of the ancient Jews.'[9]

As the influence of the Roman Catholic Church and other religious sects declined across Europe, it fell to the Western governments and media to create and maintain a veil which controlled not just the passage of information and knowledge but influenced the opinion of the masses they sought to control.

Steven Levitt aptly described the power of information:

'Information is a beacon, a cudgel, an olive branch, a deterrent — all depending on who wields it and how. Information is so powerful that the assumption of information, even if the information does not exist, can have a sobering effect.'[10]

In modern times the Western mass media has become highly skilled in the use of information as a means of deception and a diversion of the people. When the First World War broke out, the media played a crucial role in mobilizing the British masses to fight the Germans. To this end, the British developed the Ministry of Information, whose main aim was to get the United States into the war on behalf of Britain, who did not possess the military power to face the Germans on their own.

They fabricated stories of German atrocities in a propaganda war, to target American intellectuals who were the most gullible and most likely to believe the propaganda.

The British Ministry of Information always had the aim of controlling the minds and thoughts of the entire world. Without American backing, it is likely that the British would have lost both the First and Second World Wars.

Therefore, before the First World War, one of the biggest problems for British war planners was that in 1916, America was outwardly a 'pacifist' country. President Woodrow Wilson had been elected on an anti-war platform. 'Peace before victory' was his election slogan. However, the reality was that President Woodrow Wilson was no pacifist. During his tenure, he invaded Latin America and Russia, and was able to take his people into the First World War after he had used a major state propaganda program to whip up anti-German sentiments.

For the Second World War, a committee on public information called the Creel Commission, was set up.[11]

Even the Germans were impressed with the British and American propaganda programs, and Hitler strongly believed that British and American propaganda had cost Germany the First World War.

Even though the Nazis were unable to match the worldwide reach of the British and American propaganda, they used negative propaganda to deadly effect against the Jews. In order to carry out the Jewish solution. Julius Streicher, a Nazi officer in charge of propaganda, used his newspaper to demonize the Jews and whip up so much anti-Semitism that many Germans unwittingly became players or silent collaborators, in the execution of the Jewish solution.

Most people are aware of the Vietnam war but the vast majority will not be aware of the false flag event called the 'Gulf of Tonkin incident' that was used by America to escalate the war.[12]

Following the Second World, France reoccupied its South Asian colonies triggering of the French and American war against the Communists lead by Ho Chi Minh. This battle saw France being kicked out of its former South Asian colonies and the splitting of Vietnam into North and South by the US.

The North Vietnamese were communists while the capitalist supporters of France and the US fled to South Vietnam.

America provided economic and military aid to France and South Vietnam and continued covert hostilities towards North Vietnam.

On August 4th 1964, a US destroyer, the USS Maddox, was allegedly attacked by North Vietnamese torpedo boats in North Vietnam's Gulf of Tonkin. The USS Maddox was covertly enagaged in aggressive intelligence gathering and coordination of attacks by the South Vietnamese and Laotian Airforce against targets in North Vietnam.

Despite receiving intelligence that no such attack took place, President Lyndon Johnson went on national TV to lie about the Gulf of Tonkin incident and announced a bombing campaign to 'retaliate'. President Johson received overwhelming support from the US congress which approved the Gulf of Tonkin Resolution which authorised him to:

"take all necessary measures to repel any armed attack against the forces of the United States and prevent further aggression".

No approval or oversight of military force was required by congress to escalate the Vietnam war.

The cost of President Lyndon Johnson's lies and the collusion of the western media was significant. The US lost the Vietnam war, which failed to deliver its political and economic objectives. It cost the lives of over 2 million North and South Vietnamese lives and an estimated 59,000 American marines died.

Some members of the Creel Commission like Edward Bernays and Walter Lippmann became famous for their efforts to control the public mind through propaganda and the mass media.

Edward Bernays wrote a book called Propaganda in the nineteen twenties, and applying the lessons he learned from the First World War, he argued that it was possible to, 'regiment the public mind every bit as much as an army regiments their bodies'.[13]

Edward Bernays helped organize the public relations efforts behind the United States backed coup that overthrew the democratic governments of Guatemala. His other 'success' was the promotion of smoking in women, with massive media campaigns in the 1920s using models and movie stars, portraying these highly popular women as symbols of free and liberated women.

Walter Lippmann wrote progressive essays on democracy and in his case advocated a new art of modern democracy with the 'manufacture of consent', a 'self-conscious art and regular organ of popular government'.[14]

Another American, Harold Lasswell, was the founder of the field of communications in the field of political science.

Control of public opinion is the foundation of modern governments, from the most despotic to the most free. Western media and politicians have learned from world history and apply these techniques routinel, in the dissemination of information.

The situation has been further complicated by the concentration and polarization of Western media in the hands of a few corporate giants and media tycoons.

In 1983, 50 media corporations were dominant in the United States. In 1987, it was down to 29 and reduced further to 23 in 1990. In 1992, there were 14, in 1997 they had been reduced to ten and by 2000 to six. By the year 2020 only four news corporations owned all the media outlets that controlled most of the news in the United States.

In Italy, the former prime minister, Silvio Berlusconi owned most of the Italian press, while Rupert Murdoch, owner of Sky and multiple media outlets, owned most of the press in Britain and Australia. Due to massive media mergers, the Western media has been centralized and polarized. Some of the few remaining critical Western journalists questioned these mergers.

Mark Crispin Miller wrote:

'The implications of these mergers for journalism and the arts are enormous; it seems to me that this is, by any definition, an undemocratic development. The media system in a democracy should not be inordinately dominated by a few very powerful interests.'[15]

As a result of this polarization of the mass media, very few journalists in these 'democratic institutions' have the free rein to criticize the powers that be. It would not be prudent to bite the hand that feeds them.

'It is not even necessary to construct a theory of intentional cultural control. In truth, the strength of the control process rests in its apparent absence.'[16]

The net result is that the education of Western journalists and other media professionals have inbuilt penalties and rewards for doing what is expected. Norms presented as objective rules and the occasional, but telling, direct intrusion from above. The main lever is the internalization of shared values.

The fact that the vast majority of American, Australian and British journalists, reporters and editors work for just a few huge corporate employers encourages the culture of self-censorship. The culture of self-censorship makes it impractical for Western journalists to tell the public, their bosses and powerful politicians want they do not want to hear.

George Orwell stated:

'Early in life, I noticed that no event is ever correctly reported in a newspaper.'[17]

Indeed, the sad fact is that as A. J. Liebling pointed out:

'Freedom of the press is only guaranteed to those who own one.'[18]

The elite Western media organizations set the agenda and the framework in which all the smaller outfits operate. The big players include heavily financed organizations and papers, like the New York Times, the Washington Post, Financial Times, CNN, Fox, Sky News, ITV and the BBC, for example. These organizations work closely with political institutions and universities, like the American Enterprise Institute, Carnegie Institute, and universities like Harvard, Yale, Oxford and Cambridge. They set the agenda and inform the elite media outlets, who then filter the information and propaganda to the public as news.

Many Western universities collaborate with the big corporations, as they receive a lot of funding and support from them.

These colleges and universities, in turn, reward conformity and obedience and punish 'troublemakers'. The end product of all of this is highly politicized information and opinions couched as news, with the sole aim of manipulating the minds of the target audience, into lines of thought and subsequently action.

For instance, when the occupying American forces in Iraq handed over 'power' to the makeshift interim Iraqi government, the BBC repeatedly claimed that 'full sovereignty' had been transferred to the Iraqi government. The reality was that a puppet Iraqi regime was being fronted, to divert the masses from the fact that a brutal occupation of Iraq was still in progress. The first task the new Iraqi 'government' implemented was to grant the Western occupying forces an indefinite stay in Iraq at a time when it was clear that an overwhelming majority of Iraqis wanted the Western coalition forces out of the country.

When the key critics or pundits set the agenda, everyone else follows. Once musical, artistic, or political ideas are given the nod from above, everyone else follows. Thus, some music, books and films become 'classics' and others languish, not from lack of excellence but from lack of Western elite acceptance.

On August 8th 2017, President Donald Trump issued a 'fire and fury' nuclear threat to North Korea in response to a US intelligence report that alleged that North Korea had acquired nuclear capabilities.

Donald Trump's presidency was plagued by misrepresentations and lies from the start and the 'nuclear diversion' came conveniently at a time when his links to Russia were under intense scrutiny. Given the enormity of the nuclear threat and the risk of triggering a Third World War, it was surprising that the main Western media outlets did not demand that the White House provide clarity and verify Donald Trump's claim.

Sometimes, stories that meet the traditional standards of journalism are withdrawn and renounced — not because they are inaccurate or false, but because they are true.

In 1970, when CNN carried a true story about the use of nerve gas against American deserters in South East Asia, they were forced to retract the story and apologize for it.

In 1993, the former head of the BBC, Greg Dyke and the British reporter Andrew Gilligan were hounded out of their jobs for carrying the story that the British government 'sexed up' the Iraq War dossier. These assertions included Tony Blair's claim that Saddam Hussein could deploy weapons of mass destruction in 45 minutes. It is now publicly known that these claims were lies, yet Andrew Gilligan lost his job and Greg Dyke was forced to resign. The new head of the BBC immediately went on air to issue an 'apology' to the Blair government.[19]

When frightened editors do not want to publish certain material, they 'raise the bar' and demand an admission of wrongdoing, preferably written from an official government source, which they know they are unlikely to get.

Thus young aspiring Western journalists soon learn not to publish articles without official government confirmation. They cease to be proper journalists and simply echo popular opinion and the hidden agenda of politicians and the owners of the mass media.[20]

Western media is very adept in playing on the proverb 'give a dog a bad name in order to hang it'. They select characters, people, religions, countries, and in the case of Africa, a whole continent, to demonize, which in turn justify actions which can only be classed as depraved.

In the Machiavellian world of Western media and politics, the aim always justifies the means.

Malcolm X warned:

"If you're not careful the media will have you hating the people who are being oppressed and loving the people who are doing the oppressing."[21]

The far-reaching media and mass communications business now have the capacity to reach and deeply penetrate diverse cultures like never before.

Today, Western media promotes Western ideology as no colonizer or missionary ever could.

Through the illusion of fairness and impartiality, deep-seated views about the West are seeded into the minds and psyche of millions of people around the world who listen to Western news, radio, and watch their films and documentaries in an unquestioning manner.

Most people absorb Western spin and hype as if it was the gospel, when even slight scrutiny would have revealed the truth.

Ever since the Second World War, Western nations have increasingly manipulated public opinion through the media. After John F. Kennedy's assassination, the CIA issued a memo to the media, advising them on how to counter criticism about the 'magic bullet theory'. Mainstream publishers and pundits suggested that anyone who did not believe the unreliable Warren Commission Report on John F. Kennedy's assassination, was 'financially interested' or 'hasty' and inaccurate in their research.[21]

The comment that 'no new evidence' has emerged was repeated several times as directed by the CIA. The CIA and the New York Times have long worked together. After the Second World War, the Office of Strategic Services arranged for the wholesale US importation and legal immunity for hundreds of German scientists under 'Operation Paperclip'. Allen Dulles, head of the OSS, recruited E. Howard Hunt to run a worldwide program of pro-capitalist, pro-American propaganda and named it 'Operation Mockingbird'.[22]

An ex-chief of the CIA, Frank Wisner, boasted that the CIA was able to play and sway public opinion anywhere in the world. Through a front called the Congress for Cultural Freedom, the US through the CIA funnelled millions of dollars to US friendly publications in Britain, South Africa and Latin America. When the Observer newspaper in London discovered the propaganda war, they referred to it as a 'literary Bay of Pigs'. Magazines like 'Time' and 'Life' have rubber-stamped CIA propaganda for over 50 years.[23]

In 1970 the CIA campaigned to undermine elections of the Chilean leftist Salvador Allende. In a move that exposed the influence of global businesses in politics, a leaked internal memo from the International Telephone and Telegraph Corporation urged action from President Nixon, who promised finances and American military to keep Allende from taking power.[24]

The close working of the American military with the media was also exposed during the course of Iraq conflict when CNN hired 'interns' who were unpaid and were there to learn the intricacies of the operations within CNN.

The United States Army Intelligence unit, the 4th Psychological Operations Group stationed at Fort Bragg in North Carolina, also employed interns.

When uncovered by Dutch newspaper, Trouw, an army spokesperson said:

"Psychops personal soldiers and officers have been working in CNN's headquarters in Atlanta through our program working with industry."[25]

Their job was to help the production of the news, and to this end, spread handpicked information while keeping other bits of the news quiet. Many people are still unaware that the satellites controlling the GPS in their cars like 'TomTom' or on their mobile phones are owned by the US military. The US army also wants to control the Internet and wage electronic warfare against disobedient media and control commercial satellites.

In November 2001, demonstrating the reach of the American army, the US army switched off Internet access to the whole of Somalia after listing them as a terrorist state.[26]

Massive news agencies like the Associated Press [AP] are a service that sends stories to over 15,800 media outlets around the world, and reaches over an estimated one billion people every day. Founded in 1848 it employs over 3,500 people and changes articles within minutes on receipt of new information.

On July 5th 2000 the European Parliament voted to expand a probe after finding out they were being spied on by Echelon, a US based communications network that monitors phone calls faxes and emails worldwide.[27]

The Western media has always cooperated with their governments to present misinformation, or support highly aggressive and exploitative foreign policies. Western media outlets beat the path for war for their respective governments.

They are crucial to the Western militaries in demonizing their proposed victims. They prepare their captive audiences with simplistic jingoistic biased news coverage that tests the people's appetite and will for the proposed conflict. They often present the proposed military intervention as a humanitarian necessity to free the oppressed people from their brutal dictors or leaders.

For a long time the United States government had pursued a campaign to break up Yugoslavia, the only Eastern European country that would not dismantle its welfare state and public sector economy. Much to US annoyance, Yugoslavia remained independent of NATO.

Western media, through one-sided reporting during the Yugoslav war targeted the Serbs, the largest nationality opposed to the break-up of Yugoslavia. Even though both sides committed atrocities, only Serbian atrocities made it to the press. Many of the atrocities were exaggerated, and some even fabricated. This war paved the way for NATO aggression against Yugoslavia. The vast majority of Kosovo Albanian refugees expelled from Yugoslavia only began after the NATO bombings.

A Western news crew asked an Albanian woman, crossing the Macedonian border, if Serbian police had forced her out, she answered:

"There were no Serbs — we were frightened of NATO bombs."[28]

The vast majority of the refugees in the Kosovo War were caused by the NATO bombings. Newspapers and media carried misleading reports given to them by NATO. Many experts accused NATO of running a propaganda campaign. The US state department reports of mass graves of 100,000–500,000 missing Albanian men were criticized as ludicrous according to independent critics.[29]

US newspaper Newsday reported that Britain and France considered commando assaults to break up Serbian massacres of Albanians. The State Department also reported organized rapes and crimes, but on closer inspection, there was no verification of these atrocities.

The United Nations High Commissioner for Refugees spokesperson spoke of mass rapes and hundreds of killings. When pressed for more precise information by Audrey Gillian, a British reporter, he reduced it drastically to five or six teenage rape victims and had not spoken to any witnesses and had no way to verify the reports.[30]

On the April 19th 1999 NATO bombings, the State Department announced that up to 500,000 Kosovo Albanians were feared dead, and the media did not challenge the figures. However, on June 17th, just before the end the war, the former British foreign minister, Geoff Hoon, contradicted them by saying some 10,000 ethnic Albanians had been killed, a drastic reduction from the American figure of 100,000–500,000 quoted by US officials.[31]

Such is the cognitive dissonance created by the Western media, that most Westerners are unable to equate dropping over 15,000 cluster and carpet bombs on civilians as terror, but recoil in horror when stories of suicide bombers and terrorist attacks by small groups of people, result in relatively few casualties. Westerners and those exposed to their culture have been completely brainwashed into accepting the characterization and stereotypes of Caucasians as the 'good guys' everyone else as 'bad guys'. Of course, sometimes, the white 'good guys' are the 'bad guys', like the Nazis. However, when Caucasians commit heinous crimes against humanity they do not get hammered like non-white people.

Non-white people are often merely guilty of living on land naturally blessed with resources. Some going as far as trying to defend themselves or resist the Western invasion or exploitation.

Western brainwashing starts in childhood, including cartoons, children's stories and computer games all the way to adulthood and the 24–hour news streaming via media outlets on television, newspapers and on the internet.

As a result, many Westerners loathe and are terrified of Africans and Arabs. Africans have been vilified in the West almost since Western civilization began, and Arabs in their more recent history. Today, even Africans and Arabs are scared of each other based on their Western socialization or exposure to Western propaganda!

Many in the West have so bought into their socialization that acts of genocide committed by Western nations or capitalist interests like multinationals does not elicit any empathy or horror as long as it is carried out by the 'good guys' against the 'bad guys'.

Take a perceptual anomaly in the West, like former British

Prime Minister, Tony Blair. To the average Briton, it is abhorrent that a professing Christian like Tony Blair, brought death and suffering to millions of people in the minds of many Westerners. The UK/US no fly zone and bombing of Iraq had already accounted for over 500,000 Iraqi deaths prior to their 2003 invasion and occupation. His record of invading foreign countries under false pretexts would have made Genghis Khan green with envy and the ever-increasing number of civilian deaths in Iraq and Afghanistan would have humbled the likes of Julius Caesar and Adolf Hitler.

Yet, Tony Blair is clean-shaven and wears sharp suits. His invasions made billions of pounds for Britain, his Western partners and multinationals. His foreign policy exploits during his premiership have also secured him a nice personal fortune. He speaks eloquently and nimbly and avoids all questions about the elusive weapons of mass destruction in Iraq. When interviewed by the British media, they let him dribble his way out of answering difficult questions, better than Diego Maradona did the English football team in the 1986 World cup; yet they rate his performance very highly on style...and the substance is studiously ignored.

The truth is, despite Tony Blair's terrible crimes against humanity, it is still difficult mentally to see him on parade, jostling with other bloodthirsty leaders like Idi Amin, Suharto, Saddam Hussein and others, because of our Western brainwashing.

Should Tony Blair risk growing a beard and wear Muslim attire he would rapidly shoot to the top of the most wanted terrorist lists around the world and risk being detained by security forces at airports. If he dared put on traditional African attire, he would find himself before the International Criminal Court in the Hague.

Such is the power of the brainwashing in the West that Osama Bin Laden may still be alive today if he had only shaved off his beard and put on a sharp Armani suit.

In America, the land of great conspiracy theories, truth is often stranger than fiction. In July 1969, watched by 600 million people worldwide, Neil Armstrong took one small step for man and a giant one for mankind… but was it on the moon or faked in a Hollywood set? Controversy about this historic landmark in the history of man has divided opinion for over 40 years. Calls for NASA to release the original footage to finally put the claims of the conspiracy theorists to bed, were shattered when on August 14th 2006 NASA claimed that they had mislaid the original tapes in their vast archive.[32]

In another great American conspiracy theory, investigators into the assassination of President John F. Kennedy had to conclude that he had been killed by a 'magic bullet', because the trajectory of bullet based on the position of his alleged assassin, Lee Harvey Oswald, was ballistically impossible.

Finally, and most worrying, are the conspiracy theories surrounding the events of September 11th 2001. This event gave President Bush his reason to launch his endless 'war on terror', and invade Afghanistan and Iraq on the additional pretext of weapons of mass destruction.

The neo-conservative led Project for the New American Century, PNAC, had called for another 'Pearl Harbour' to galvanize the American people into war frenzy as far back as 1996. Several reports released after September 11th 2001 have alleged that the CIA met with Osama bin Laden in a Dubai hospital. Routine procedures to shoot down the second and third planes were not followed. Members of the bin Laden family were allowed to fly out of the US, when all other aircrafts, except military, had been grounded. Eyewitness reports from several people reported seeing unmarked military planes crash into the Twin Towers, in fact, even CNN and Sky News reporters carried this story in the initial minutes after the first attack. Built to withstand a tsunami, earthquakes or a bomb placed at its base, the Twin Towers had an inner shell of reinforced steel. When the Twin Towers collapsed, it simulated a controlled demolition of skyscrapers and initial reports of several explosions going off on several floors was also carried on live TV. A fire on one of the higher floors could not have melted the inner steel framework of the Twin Towers so that it collapsed in the manner it did in under 30 minutes.[33]

In addition, to date, no clear footage of the plane or names of the casualties of the plane that crashed into the Pentagon were released. When under pressure, the Pentagon finally released some CCTV footage, it was of a blurry orange blast of less than five seconds long.

In another twist to the conspiracy, the plane crash in the Pentagon also wiped out the department that was investigating the mysterious loss of over a trillion dollars, along with the evidence that Donald Rumsfeld had announced the day before, on September 10th 2001.

Like the mystery of Saddam Hussein's weapons of mass destruction, the controversy surrounding September 11th 2001 continues to swirl.

In today's world, computers and the internet have revolutionized information technology. The ease of access to information and improvements in communication have brought the information age into full swing. Western media and revisionists now have at their disposal powerful means and tools for creating and disseminating information like no others before them. One such means of creating and revising known history has been the development of three-dimensional computer-generated imagery or CGI. Historical events and people imagined or real, can be brought to life, using advances in CGI. Today, Level D Flight Simulators, the highest level available in the airline industry, are regularly used to simulate real flying conditions to significantly reduce the risks and actual flight time used to train pilots. Most Western militaries employ the use of simulators as routine to create lifelike conditions for training their personnel before deploying them into actual combat.

Hollywood movies now use three-dimensional CGI to create scenes and doubles for their actors, which are so real that they are virtually indistinguishable from reality.

In a TED talk, Sinan Aral, a Data Scientist, warned about the increasing dangers of increasingly blurred lines between fake and real news.[34]

Fake news triggered off the genocidal killing of the Rohyinga in Burma and mob killings in India.

On April 23rd 2013, Syrian hackers infiltrated the Associated Press's twitter feed and posted fake breaking news about two explosions at the White House and that President Obama was injured. The fake tweet was retweeted over 4,000 times in under 5 minutes and then went viral. The

Artificial Intelligence automatic trading algorithm responded to the news and started trading lower.

As a result the Dow-Jones stock index saw $140 billion wiped out in a day.

Sinan also warned of the rise of synthetic media from robotic artificial intelligence (AI) sources called General Adversarial Networks which required modulation and democratisation from another set of AI. Using these techniques the Trump White House was able to revoke the pass of a CNN reporter, Jim Acosta, by making his actions appear more aggressive on video. However, the broadcaster CNN, were able to prove that the White House manipulated the video and successfully sued to reinstate their journalists pass.

The Western denigration of Africa and Africans has gone on for centuries. All Africans must develop a multi-dimensional approach to processing information, as to its factual accuracy, depth or substance and strategic aims. Africans must learn to read between the lines and understand the subliminal messages the West is trying to project, rather than be taken in by the hype.

Many Western headlines are high on presentation but low in content, to obscure facts or bury inaccurate or even fictitious information that mislead people who do not seek to understand its deeper meaning. By adopting this approach, it is possible to decode the hidden meanings, agendas and symbolism of white supremacy and avoid the social programming which lies beneath.

In an article on the American use of war pretext to start wars, Richard Sanders wrote:

"It is vitally important to expose this latest attempt [9/11] to fraudulently conceal the largely economic and geostrategic purposes of war. By asking who benefits from war; we can unmask its pretense and expose the true grounds for instigating it. By throwing light on repeated historical patterns of deception, we can promote scepticism about the government and media yarns that have been spun to encourage this war.

The historical knowledge of how war planners have tricked people into supporting past wars, is like a vaccine. We can use this understanding of history to inoculate the public with a healthy dose of distrust for official war pretext narratives and other deceptive strategems. Through such immunization programs we may help to counter our society's susceptibility to 'war fever'.'[35]

CHAPTER SIXTY SEVEN

GLOBAL CHESS GAMES

> *"Turkestan, Afghanistan, Transcapia, Persia, — to many these names breathe only a sense of utter remoteness or a memory of strange vicissitudes and of moribund romance. To me, I confess that they are the pieces on a chess board upon which is being played out a game for the domination of the world."* **Lord George Nathaniel Curzon,** British Viceroy of India in 1898.[1]

The beautiful game of chess remains as awe-inspiring as it ever was. Anatoly Karpov, former chess world champion once said, *'Chess is my life'.*

This view would resonate with many chess players because there are so many ways chess reflects life. To emphasise the complexity of chess — there are over 288 billion possible moves after only four moves apiece by each player. Therefore, across the 64 squares of the chessboard, there are a myriad of ways a chess player can play the game or respond to the threats their opponent has created. Fortunately, despite the fierce competitiveness the chess game breeds, there are limits. Thankfully, it is unheard of for battling chess players to stand up and trade punches or exchange gunfire across the board separating them. This type of behaviour tends to occur frequently in real life rather than in chess games!

Real life is infinitely more complex than chess. In life, there is a constant battle not only against the nature's elements but also between human beings as well. However, unlike chess, life has always been a competitive team sport for humans and always will be.

When trying to understand Africa's predicament, people often concentrate — as they are trained to by the Western politicians and media

— on the 'pieces' [African leaders] and the board, [African countries, Third World countries and their natural and human resources], instead of on the real players, [Western governments, multinationals, and non-governmental organizations]. It is worth noting that in life, as on the chessboard, the chess pieces are nothing without the players.

Chess is played on many levels. From the beginner, who simply moves their pieces reactively to counter immediate threats, to the super grandmasters, who not only consider the immediate consequences, but also the far-reaching consequences of outwardly simple moves.

At its highest level, chess is a strategic game that graduates from simple threats to deep tactics and a concrete knowledge of many tried and tested openings and systems. Strategy overrides the opening, middle game and the end game. If the overall strategy is wrong, the tactics and combinations are likely to be flawed. When the overall strategy is correct, everything else seems to work beautifully.

Apart from the racial discrimination and the inferiority complex that Western misinformation breeds in Africans and their diaspora, one of the biggest factors holding back Africa and its diaspora has been apathy and the failure to engage as individuals, communities and nations, in the strategic global game of chess of geopolitics.

Ever since the transatlantic slave trade until the present day, Africans, their land and their resources, have been played as pawns in the Western great global chess game. Africans have been fought over, exchanged, promoted, demoted, sold, bought, and killed, in the great European chess game for global world domination.

Unfortunately, too many Africans have only been concerned about the immediate and short-term results of their actions and have paid no heed to the global machinations around them, or indeed, the short or long-term strategic consequences of their actions.

Just as it is impossible to play a good game of chess without knowledge of the rules and systems top players use, it is similarly impossible to be a truly global player without a working understanding of the objectives and strategy employed by your opponents.

Many Africans have fallen into this trap of short-termism and have enriched themselves and perhaps their immediate family, to the detriment of their people as a whole, without grasping the real significance of their actions.

By capitalizing on the human weaknesses of fear, selfishness and greed, the West has opened Africa up, time and time again, using African people who value immediate gratification above all things, even their own lives. This is the same selfishness and greed that drove the Europeans to Africa, and motivated their African intermediaries, and resulted in vastly different outcomes for the people of Africa and Europe.

From the slave trade to present-day neo-colonialism, many Africans unwittingly and some consciously continue to play this role.

The transatlantic slave trade only succeeded because sufficient numbers of black Africans worked with the white slavers, to provide local knowledge of resources and help them acquire slaves. During colonization, the colonial masters recruited relatively a large number of Africans, who seemed convinced of white superiority, and never questioned the real reasons the Europeans had shown up in Africa. Unfortunately, these misguided African people have colluded with the West to bring incredible suffering to their own people all over the world.

After the Treaty of Tordesillas, the Catholic Church divided the non-European world between Spain and Portugal for conquest and plunder. The pretext was the spread of Christianity, but the real aim was personal and national enrichment.

The treaty was made to prevent the two leading Catholic nations at the time from warring over foreign lands and the spoils of plunder. Spain and Portugal were still to converge on each other like the pincer action of the crab's claws, with Africa and Africans finding themselves in a vice-like grip between European nations; a grip which Africa and its diaspora have yet to work themselves free from today.

The Portuguese started off looking for gold but were soon diverted to the equally lucrative business of slavery. They established themselves as slave traders across the West African coast and the East African coast. However, they were soon to use force and deception to fuel the slave trade. When the Portuguese reached the East African coast, in 1493, they found, the thriving Kingdom of the Kongo. As was the usual practice, without the backing of sufficient military force and not knowing the lay of the land fully, the Portuguese established peaceful relations with the people of the Kongo and supplied missionaries and artisans to familiarize the Kongo people with Portuguese culture. They traded goods for slaves, but as the demand increased, they employed and financed pombeiros [peddlers], who traded bought slaves for them from the major slave markets. Evidence that a commercial slave trade did not previously exist in the area, is the fact that these new types of slaves were referred to as 'persons of nzimbu' or people acquired with Kongo shell money, the local currency at the time.

The slave trade led to local wars in the area and when the people of Jaga invaded the Kongo Kingdom, they were only saved by the intervention of the Portuguese army. This encouraged the Portuguese to colonize the area formally and form Angola, with its harbour at Luanda.

From the relative trickle of slaves in 1493, the slave trade had topped 7,000 slaves a year by the 1560s.

When Christopher Columbus reached the Americas, he noted the ornaments indigenous Americans wore and just like with the Portuguese in Ghana, the Spanish realized there were vast deposits of precious metals nearby. The lush vegetation also excited interest in agriculture, especially the production of sugar, which was experiencing an increased demand in Europe. However, the Spanish had not come all the way to the Americas to dig the mines for gold and work the plantations by themselves. They immediately set about using the indigenous people as slaves. Aside from the brutal treatment the Spanish meted out to them, the native Americans died in large numbers from the diseases, mainly smallpox and measles, which the Spanish had brought with them. Unwilling to do the work themselves, the death of the native Americans in their thousands created a vacuum for productive workers, which needed to be filled.

This is where African slavery first met with America's slavery. The African slaves were physically stronger, and had some acquired resistance to measles and smallpox. They did not succumb to disease like the Indians. Some Africans already had African agricultural skills and coped better with the demands of cultivating commercial crops. When Spanish priests argued that Indian slaves who converted to Christianity were not to be enslaved, it accelerated the use of black slave labour. While the Catholic church was preoccupied with the plight of its Indian converts, they were not bothered about the welfare of black African slaves. The African slaves were viewed to be too savage to be converted to Christianity.

Like the Spanish, when the Portuguese reached Brazil in 1500, they soon set about using the indigenous Native American population as slaves, and like in Hispaniola, the results were the same. Vast numbers of Native Americans died from immigrant diseases and ill treatment. Already entrenched in the African slave trade, they began importing black African slaves to Brazil. The Portuguese were well placed for the triangular slave trade, as they had already established colonies on either side of the Atlantic. The Spanish who had been preoccupied with expanding their American empire now had to depend on slave treaties dominated by the Portuguese, Dutch, French and English for slaves.

Europeans developed a system of licenses, or asientos, which they granted to foreign slave traders, who were contracted to supply them slaves within a stipulated period. The quantity of slaves was termed 'piezas de India' or 'pieces of India', which represented units of potential labour in the 'Indies' of America.

Every 'piezas de India' represented an adult male in prime physical condition. Females, children, adolescents or older males were valued as parts of the standard unit. The dehumanization of black slaves was a necessity to keep the business of slave trading going, as to recognize their humanity would make the business unsustainable. Black skin became identified with an inferior status and bondage all over Europe. Black African people were not only property, but were property that could procreate itself. Like domesticated farm animals, the children of female African slaves became property themselves from birth to death.

Once the framework of the European exploitation of Africa was established under the guise of Christianity and civilization, it is not surprising these European nations arbitrarily partitioned Africa and it people during the colonial scramble for Africa.

Long before this, the Greeks had colonized Egypt and ruled for several centuries. Under the Greeks, it is called Ptolemy. This was a crucial time for the Greeks and Europe, as it was at around this time that Africa's civilization began to be ascribed to the Greeks, by Western scholars, as starting the European civilization.

By the mid-19th century most of Africa was still fairly much a mystery to the West. Only a relatively small area of Africa was colonized; the Portuguese had trading posts in Ghana and Angola, which were taken over by the Dutch and then the British. Most of these European outposts were confined to the West African coastline from Sierra Leone to Cameroon.

However, in the space of twenty years, between 1880 and 1900, Europeans would scramble for territory and resources in Africa, transforming African kingdoms into 40 European controlled states. By 1914 only Ethiopia and Liberia, an American slave colony, remained nominally independent.

Napoleon Bonaparte led the first modern European bid for African territory and occupied Egypt in 1798. However, he was decisively defeated in battle at Aboukir Bay by the British.

Later, the French became active again in Africa, and as early as 1830 the French army had invaded Algeria and had occupied the land. Within seven years, French investors prospected in Egypt and Turkey. A Frenchman, Ferdinand de Lesseps, designed and built the Suez Canal, using Egyptian slave labour. The idea of the Suez canal was to create direct access for ships carrying goods to India. This meant that Europeans did not have to sail around the Cape of Good Hope, known for its treacherous waters. Many European ships had already been lost at sea in this area.

The French had supported the puppet Egyptian leader at the time, Mehmet Ali, who was keen on using French influence to overthrow the Ottoman Sultan's powers.

The British were not impressed by the French influence and insisted that the future of the Ottoman Empire was a matter to be decided between the five European powers, not just Britain and France, but also Russia, Austria and Prussia.

After the governments of both Egypt and Turkey became bankrupt, the British prime ministers, first Disraeli and then Gladstone, took action in order to give Britain the edge in the Middle East. When the Khedive of Egypt offered just to sell his shares in the Suez Canal Company for £4 million, Disraeli raised the money through Rothschilds, in order to give Britain some control of the Suez Canal.[2]

For a time there was a multinational commission, established in England, in which England, France and Italy, all equally represented, ran Egypt's finances. It had an Englishman as finance minister, and Frenchman as minister of public works.

When the Khedive dismissed the international government in 1879, the European governments of Egypt responded by deposing in him and installing his son Tewfik.

This arrangement would not last, as anti-European sentiment was high and the Egyptian military, led by Arabi Pasha, overthrew the weak Egyptian leader Tewfik, another European puppet.

British Prime Minister Gladstone and his European allies became nervous about their investments in Egypt, and decided to overthrow the government led by Arabi Pasha. In September 1882, General Wolseley led an invasion force, which defeated Pasha's army and took him prisoner.

Egypt was occupied by the British, and indirectly ruled through a puppet Khedive. The real power was in the hands of the British agent and consul-general, for 40 years between 1882 and 1922.

To avert clashes between the great powers in Europe vying for African territory, the German chancellor, Otto von Bismarck, called for the Berlin conference, between November 15th 1884 and February 26th 1885. It is of note that no single African representative was present at the conference that was to ensure 'free trade' in Africa.

The German chancellor cleverly used this conference to set Britain and France against each other while diverting attention at home away from his policies. He stated that his map of Africa was really a map of Europe. Britain and France fell into this trap and in the subsequent decade they clashed repeatedly in Egypt, Nigeria, Uganda and in the Sudan.

With Africa sliced up like a cake, the European powers set out in earnest to stake their claim to African territory. All the while, the African leaders and people were unaware of the true intentions of the Europeans, who came across and welcomed them warmly. The Europeans used every method at their disposal to win the trust of the people and when they understood the land, the people and resources, moved in with military force to consolidate their claims.

This process was repeated all over Africa in one form or another by all the European nations involved in the scramble.

This was not just a scramble for Africa; Europeans effectively scrambled Africa. As Europeans struggled for territory, they erected borders which did not take into account where African people lived, their language or resources. Today the partitions, which were erected and later called countries, have continued to foment trouble between the African people. Through puppet leaders, the British indirectly ruled, typically using minorities as the power base against the larger majority. While this formula made it easier for indirect rule, it always disadvantaged the majority, and following colonial independence, these fault lines remained. The Western-empowered minorities clung on to power and sought their support from Europeans, allowing them to be used as a conduit through which Europeans could continue to exert control over the countries.

By that end of the European scramble for Africa, most of the African continent would be under British and French rule.

Despite of all the omissions and revisions authored by Western historians, it is quite clear that colonization has been even more destructive in Africa than transatlantic slavery. Millions of Africans died in the process of colonization. The death toll is not easy to compute but when you read between the lines of the revised Western history of Africa and infer from the omissions, it is obvious that the Western colonization of Africa was an exceedingly bloody affair.

Joseph Chamberlain stated:

'You cannot have omelettes without breaking eggs; you cannot destroy the practices of barbarism, of slavery, of superstition... without the use of force.'[3]

In the Belgian ruled 'independent state' of Congo, 'free trade' was simply a euphemism for the abuse of human rights and the use of slave labour, the profits of which went directly into the coffers of King Leopold II.

'The Belgian King Leopold II had a voracious appetite for territory, even by imperial standards, as he sought control of the last African acreage still unclaimed by Britain and France...In 1855, the king had issued an imaginatively criminal decree making twenty million Africans, by the stroke of a pen, tenants in their own country. Africans were systematically maimed and murdered both as warning and punishment for "trespassing" on the crown's domain.'[4]

The natives of Congo were forced to pick rubber which was in great demand in industrialized countries. Those who refused to collect rubber were shot, and their hands amputated by the Belgian soldiers who presented them as proof of proper use of the ammunition.

Under the rule of the Belgian king an estimated ten million Congolese people died from murder, starvation, disease and reduced fertility. Almost half of the Congolese population was exterminated by this bloody regime.

The horror visited upon these Africans by the Belgians, was exposed by Joseph Conrad's book, 'Heart of Darkness'.

In Namibia, when the Hereros resisted brutality from the German colonists, the German lieutenant-general, Lothar von Trotha, issued an annihilation order, Vernichtungsbefehl, declaring that every Herero should be shot whether armed or not. In the space of three years, the Herero population was reduced from 80,000 in 1903 to about 20,000 in 1906.

The Maji Maji uprising against the Germans was equally brutally repressed.

When the British general, Lord Kitchener, fought against the Sudanese at Omdurman, on the banks of the Nile, Winston Churchill, then a young war reporter witnessed the massacre of the Sudanese.

Winston Churchill vividly described the massacre:

'The maxim guns exhausted all the water in their jackets and several had to be refreshed from the water bottles of the Cameron Highlanders before they could go with a deadly work. The empty cartridge cases tinkling to the ground formed small but growing heaps beside each man. And all the time out

on the plain on the other side bullets were shearing through flesh, smashing and splintering bone; blood spouted from terrible wounds; valiant men were struggling on through a hell of whistling metal, explosion shells and spurting dust —suffering, despairing, dying……the charging Dervishes sank down tangled heaps. The masses paused, irresolute.'[5]

In the space of five hours, the Dervish army suffered close to 95% casualties, losing over 45,000 men. Not satisfied with the bloodshed, Kitchener had ordered the destruction of Mahdi's tomb and according to Churchill, 'carried off the Mahdi's head in Kerosene can as a trophy'.

Churchill also deplored 'the inhuman slaughter of the wounded' because after the battle, the British soldiers had gone among the wounded and killed them.

Africans would not only find themselves dispossessed of their land and resources, they were also used to fight European wars. All European sides used Africans — nearly all — as carriers of supplies, weapons and wounded. Over two million Africans served in the First World War as auxiliaries, and were the most exposed frontline troops in Europe.

Over a fifth of Africans employed as carriers died, many of them victims of the dysentery that ravaged the colonial armies in the tropics.

In East Africa, 3,156 whites in British service died in the line of duty; of these less than a third were victims of enemy action. However, if casualties amongst black African troops and carriers were included, the total losses were over 100,000.[6]

A German doctor in the German East African army, Ludwig Deppe wrote:

'Behind us we leave destroyed fields, ransacked magazines and, for the immediate future, starvation. We are no longer the agents of culture; our track is marked by death, plundering and evacuated villages, just like the progress of our own and enemy armies in the thirty-year war.'[7]

Despite African troops primarily being used for the most hazardous task of ammunition carrying and being unduly exposed to danger; they were also racially abused by British officers.

In 1918 a Trinidadian sergeant complained:

'We are treated neither as Christians nor British citizens but as West

Indian "Niggers" without anybody to be interested in or look after us. Instead of being drawn closer to church and empires are driven away from it.[8]

African troops also played a crucial role in the liberation of France from Nazi Germany in the Second World War. Their contribution, concealed by France through racism and political manipulation, was brought to light by a film in 2006, 'Days of Glory'.

In 1943–1944, over half of the French liberation army that fought in Italy and France were of African origin. The French Army numbering 550,000 men in 1944 included about 300,000 recruited from African nations. Over a quarter of the French soldiers who died in the Second World War were from France's 'African Legion'.

Unfortunately, not only was the African contribution airbrushed from French contemporary history and films many of the 'African Legion' troops had their pensions frozen. French newsreel footage and newspaper pictures endeavoured to exclude the African contribution and depicted the conquering French troops as white only.

On the contrary, the official French memory of the war did not similarly 'forget' the contributions of American, British and other white troops that helped liberate occupied France in 1944.[9] France commemorates and celebrates the sacrifices and contribution of their white allies every year, since the end of the Second World War.

The West is far from done with Africa. Western imperialist forays into Africa continue until the present day. The botched 'Wonga Coup' attempt by wealthy influential Westerners including Mark Thatcher, son of former British Prime Minister Margaret Thatcher, shows that the even Western individuals still intervene negatively in African affairs. Organized by a private military contractor, Simon Mann and 65 other coup plotters, they were bankrolled by wealthy Westerners in South Africa and Europe, including Mark Thatcher. The coup was a brazen attempt for white expatriates to grab a slice of Equatorial Guinea's oil riches.[10]

While Simon Mann's lawyers fought and succeeded in freeing him, preventing his extradition to Equatorial Guinea to face charges, thousands of 'terror suspects' are held in Guantánamo Bay, Western prisons and detention centres all around the world, without charge or access to lawyers.

Africans continue to be played like puppets on European strings. Africa is now firmly established as a source of raw materials to the rest of the world, while Africans have simultaneously developed a voracious appetite for consuming European goods. While corrupt African leaders carry a large share of the blame for the reverse development of Africa, coercive Western policies actively undermine and destabilize the continent and prevents true economic and social growth.

Any change in Africa must come from Africans themselves, who must move from the position of pawns, to true global players, if there is to be any meaningful development in Africa.

CHAPTER SIXTY EIGHT

THE DEATH MERCHANTS

"Throughout the world, on any given day, a man, woman, or child is likely to be displaced, tortured, killed, or "disappeared," at the hands of governments or armed political groups. More often than not, the United States shares the blame." Amnesty International. 1996.[1]

"Onwards chartered soldiers onto the Heathen lands
Prayer home books in your pockets, rifles in your hands.
Take the glorious tidings where trade can be done,
Spread the peaceful gospel — with a Maxim gun.

Tell the wretched natives sinful are their hearts,
Turn their heathen temples into spirit marts.
And if to your teaching, they will not succumb,
Give them another sermon with the Maxim gun.

When the Ten Commandments they quite understand,
You their Chief must hocus, and annex their land;
And if they misguided call you to account,
Give them another sermon — with a Maxim from the Mount."
Hymn sung by Cecil Rhodes' men, as a tribute to the men who had slaughtered the Matabele during imperial expansion in South Africa.[2]

War is a central theme of the ideology of imperialism, as it creates the instability required for the West to exploit. The business of war is one of the most lucrative to the West, whether it is conducted directly or 'subcontracted' out to warring parties all over the world. Imperialists see every flashpoint in the world as an opportunity to exploit the vulnerability of the region or people, sell military equipment to both sides or justify 'intervention' to decide the outcome in their favour. The arms Western puppets buy are good enough to kill each other with but are inadequate protection against invasion and occupation by superiorly armed Western governments who sold the arms to them.

Subcontracted war is the most common form and cause of war in the Third World, contributing to the chronic instability and poverty of these regions. In the Western world, the immediate effect of this is to intensify the arms race among Western rivals driving the whole world closer still to the prospect of annihilation in a nuclear war. The net result is that Western nations are obsessed with war and the development of ever more destructive weapons.

War, the tried and tested way of dispossessing people of land and resources, creates the cheap labour much sought after by imperialists and capitalists. War is the logical outcome of the drive of imperialism, as no one anywhere in the world would turn over their people, land and resources without a struggle. This necessitates the use of force to meet the particular needs of imperialism. It is very difficult to wage war against the different people of the world simultaneously. Therefore, it creates the need to instigate wars, arm the opponents, and profit from the instability and division it creates. This is patently a dangerous strategy but it is quite old and highly effective. However, it requires the imperialists to be better armed and in control of the manufacture, sale and distribution of arms for it to work.

During the slave trade, European slave traders sold arms to the African intermediaries as a means of destabilizing the region through war, to create new sources of slaves. Only through this means could slave trade have been as destructive to Africa and as lucrative to the West as it was. Most of the weapons sold to Africans were obsolete, ineffective or duds, ensuring that when the time came to disarm and subjugate their African vassals, they could do so without significant loss to themselves.

The slave trade and the European arms trade were inextricably interwoven. In the 16th century the Portuguese, apart from starting the Trans-Atlantic slave trade, became the main conduit of firearms from the West to Asia and Africa. The Portuguese arms trade generated enormous profits in addition to the profits they were making from the slave trade itself.

Despite several papal bans on sale of weapons to non-Christians, the arms trade from flourished. The first papal ban was issued in 1179, and many more papal bans followed but they were simply ignored. By the 17th century the Dutch took over from Portuguese as the leading Western arms dealers. Most of the European weapons traded were old and out-dated, but were highly effective in creating the strife and chaos they needed to perpetuate the slave trade.

Private English arms exports to Africa started in London in the 1690s. In 1698, Birmingham overtook London, after completing their first order for 'slave trade guns'. By 1754, Birmingham was manufacturing 25,000 — 30,000 guns a year for the West African market.

By the late eighteenth century it is estimated that Europe was exporting 283,000–394,000 firearms to Africa annually. Between 1750–1807, England accounted for 47% or nearly half of the African arms trade.

By 1907, the Belgian city of Liege had overtaken Birmingham and accounted for 67% of the African arms trade.[3]

The British invented the modern arms trade in the 1860s when a lawyer from Newcastle upon Tyne, William Armstrong set up in competition with the German arms manufacturer, Alfred Krupp.

The Maxim gun was an American invention, and its inventor, Hiram Maxim, had always targeted the British market. When he tried his prototype in Hatton Garden in London, among the dignitaries present were the Duke of Cambridge, the then commander in chief, the Prince of Wales, Duke of Edinburgh, Duke of Devonshire, Duke of Sutherland and the Duke of Kent. Hiram Maxim told them, "My gun is especially useful in stopping the mad rush of natives".[4]

The Maxim Gun Company was established in November 1884. Lord Rothschild was a member on its board. In 1888, Rothschild's bank financed the £1.9 million merger of the Maxim Company with the Nordenfelt Guns and Ammunition Company. Through his association with Cecil Rhodes, it ensured that the white South African imperialist was always well armed and financed.

The most famous arms dealer of all was Sir Basil Zaharoff who popularized the term 'merchant of death'. He made his millions through arms sales to warring factions after Vickers had paid him £86,000 as their chief sales representative in 1905. He was quick to understand the connections between arms and power, diplomacy, spying, bribery, and flying the flag, regardless of whose flag it was. He boasted, "I made wars, so I could sell arms to both sides. I must have sold more guns than anyone else must have in the world."[5]

The West's policy of arming all sides is thought to have triggered the First World War. Today, Britain's days as a leading exporter of manufactured goods have long passed. Britain has sold off its iconic car factories, which produced the likes of Mini, Jaguar and Rolls-Royce to Germany. However, in 2013 Britain ranked as the fifth largest arms exporter in the world behind Russia, America, China and France. In 2008 the British company BAE systems, became the world's leading developer of arms.[6]

British arms sales have always been run behind a wall of secrecy and euphemisms which divert the public away from its murderous activity. Today, the arms business is conducted largely by government officials, for governments, rather than privately.

Arms exports in Britain rose from just £470 million in 1975 to £4.7 billion in 1995, a massive increase, even accounting for inflation. Britain has a long and disgraceful record of selling arms to war zones for centuries. Britain is a major arms supplier to at least five countries with internal conflict, where the combined death toll runs to almost a million people.[7]

British arms trade includes sales to apartheid South Africa, where British made Saracens were used in the Sharpeville Massacre. British

Centurion tanks were used in the 1982 Israeli invasion of Lebanon, which claimed over 20,000 lives.

For twenty years Britain armed the Indonesian army in East Timor, where British Hawk aircraft was used in the genocidal campaign against the East Timorese.

A British company MIL-TAC armed the genocidal Hutu militia in the former Zaire. Idi Amin, former Ugandan dictator and mass murderer, used British telecommunications to track down his victims.[8]

Harold Wilson's government not only sold arms to the racist apartheid regime in South Africa, they also supported the Nigerian military regime to crush Biafra in the Nigerian-Biafran War.[9]

Saddam Hussein, supported by America and Britain, came into power in one of the bloodiest takeovers in Middle Eastern history and was soon the recipient of millions of dollars' worth of Western arms. In 1981, Douglas Hurd, then a junior foreign office minister tried to sell Saddam Hussein an entire British Aerospace system which, 'would be the biggest sale of its kind ever achieved'.[10]

A month after the gassing of the Kurds at Halabja in Iraq, Tony Newton, minister from the Department of Trade, flew to Baghdad to offer Saddam Hussein £340 million in export credits. These were to be used on 'machine tools', with a dual use. In plain English, they were used to assemble weapons.[11]

The arms trade in Britain has always been shrouded in euphemisms which the industry representatives use to camouflage their activities. For instance, arms sales are called 'defence procurement', which sheds no light on the true nature of the activities of the arms traders.

Lady Margaret Thatcher negotiated one of the biggest arms deals in history, the £25 billion, Al-Yamamah arms deal with Saudi Arabia, while she was Prime Minister. In the mid-eighties it was described as the 'biggest ever sale of anything to anyone by anyone'.[12]

There were allegations of bribery and corruption surrounding the deal and the National Audit Office, supposedly independent and audited government finances on behalf of the public, wrote a report on the deal, but John Major the Prime Minister at the time suppressed it. When Tony

Blair became Prime Minister and New Labour came into office, they promised to publish it, but they too withheld the publication.

In the manifesto of Tony Blair's Labour government, they stated categorically their 'pledges for a responsible arms trade'. One of these pledges was a firm commitment not to export licenses for the sale of arms to regimes that use them for internal repression or international aggression.

Under Prime Minister Tony Blair, the British arms industry boomed after September 11th 2001. BAE even sold a £40 million air defence system to Tanzania, one of the world's poorest countries. Tanzania had a GDP per capita of $250.00 a year in 1997, half the population had no clean running water and one in four children died before their fifth birthday. Even though this sale was even opposed by the World Bank Prime Minister Tony Blair gave it his personal backing, no doubt in the spirit of his evangelical speech to the Labour Party conference in which he called Africa's poverty, 'a scar on the conscience of the world'.[13]

In 2002, Britain and America steered the world inevitably towards conflict in Iraq, over alleged weapons of mass destruction. At the same time, India and Pakistan, both real nuclear powers, had faced off with each other once again, over Kashmir. Tony Blair travelled to India on a peace mission, however, while he talked about Britain 'exerting a calming influence' his government was simultaneously attempting to seal a massive, £1 billion arms sale of Hawker Siddeley Harrier jets to India.

A study produced by the World Development Movement in 1995 revealed that the British taxpayer paid at least one fifth of the total value of British arms exports in hidden subsidies. It also found that the British government spent ten times as much promoting arms as civil exports. Nearly £5 billion of taxpayers' money has been pawned against arms sales in the late 2010s.[14]

Eighty per cent of British arms exports go to poor and developing countries. In 1988 Margaret Thatcher's trade minister, Alan Clark, set up a little known, special fund of £1 billion. This fund was used by the Export Credits Guarantee Department of the Department of Trade and Industry to finance indebted countries that wanted to buy British arms.[15]

A £1.3 billion arms deal of mainly Hawker Harrier jets to Malaysia was concealed in an 'aid package' financing the Pergau Hydroelectric Dam, which was being built by British firms.[16]

Western governments and arms dealers have exploited every global area of tension as an opportunity to sell arms. Britain armed both sides when tensions rose between India and Pakistan, Russia and Georgia, Greece and Turkey, and in 2011, during the ousting and later murder of Colonel Gadaffi in Libya, a British arms company, MBDA, armed all three sides in the conflict.

In keeping with the imperialist policy of disseminating arms to stoke tensions and create chaos and instability to exploit later, in recent years, Britain has armed countries it went on to go to war against, including the Falklands war in Argentina, the Gulf wars against Iraq and the NATO military intervention in Libya.

Also in 2011 at the height of the 'Arab spring' during the popular unrest in Egypt, in order to remove the long-time incumbent leader, Hosni Mubarak, the British prime minister David Cameron flew to Egypt with a planeload of arms dealers, to steer the popular uprising towards the Egyptian military with strong Western ties.

Despite all the protests and suffering of the beleaguered Egyptians, they found themselves manipulated back under military rule after the popular Islamic leader was arrested and General Assisi, who served as a second in command to Mubarak for nearly 40 years, took over power in a coup.

In addition, some of David Cameron's arms found their way to Libya where they were used to foment the unrest that eventually toppled Gadaffi.

It is also thought that US and British weapons have been funnelled through the chaotic Libya to another regional menace, Boko Haram.

In March 2014, while answering Prime Minister questions, David Cameron defended his arms sales stating:

'I was criticised by the Labour party for taking defence contractors on trade missions overseas; that party does not think it is appropriate, but I think it is. I think we should be standing up for our defence industry and defence

jobs'.[17]

The United States is by far the world's largest military spenders. At least 40¢ in every taxed dollar goes to the Pentagon. The United States spends more than a whopping 25% of its total GDP on its military. At the end of the financial year, 2001/2002, military industries had spent more than $400 billion.[15]

It is the fighting and the sustaining of war that maintains America's military industry. During the Gulf War, American arm sales increased by 64% and after NATO attacked Yugoslavia it resulted in an extra $17 billion worth of arms sales. The US military's biggest supplier, Lockheed Martin, saw its sheer volume rise by 50% following the September 11th attacks in 2001. The company had record sales of more than $25 billion, and it received more than $12 billion in Pentagon contracts. Six weeks after the September 11th attacks, Lockheed Martin had secured the biggest military contract in history as a $200 billion contract to develop a fighter aircraft.[18]

In 2011, the US sold a record $66.3 billion in overseas weapons alone. [19]

Like Britain, at least 80% of United States aid is military in nature, and over 50% of this is spent on sustaining the oil industry. The majority of its aid goes to strategic 'allies' as bribes or rewards in order to maintain US economic hegemony and strategic influence rather than meet the targets for poverty and needs of the people who require the aid.

Western aid always comes with extremely stringent conditions attached, including the opening up of the target countries economy for foreign investments, called 'liberalization' and 'privatization' and the passage of Government control to the US treasury.

Practically every African country receives International Military Education and Training [IMET] funding from the United States. The majority of these countries are receiving over $100,000.00 in spite of clear evidence of human rights violations. Some of these countries receiving over a hundred thousand dollars include Nigeria, Cameroon, Democratic Republic of the Congo and Angola. East Africa, Ethiopia, Kenya and Tanzania receive higher levels of US military aid.[20]

Much like the West African frontier force that was used during the colonial era to subjugate the native people, the United States Special Forces and Britain have trained over 8,000 troops from countries all across Africa through the African Crisis Response Initiative started in 1996.

In 2004 after a trip to Sudan, Tony Blair announced the formation of a 60,000 strong African intervention force, which would intervene in African affairs directly, with or without the mandate given by African countries, the African Union or United Nations. In effect, these AU troops would be the African face of the neo-colonial Western forces wishing to achieve by force whatever their objects were.[21]

Through double standards in trades and disbursement of loans, Western governments have placed trade barriers and tariffs in the way of African governments, preventing them from investing in Western economies while at the same time through liberalization, and privatization forced African economies to open up and become a dumping ground for Western arms and goods.

According to a Christian Aid report, one in five of the world's small arms [about 100 million] are circulating in Africa.[22]

Between 1979 and 1989 the major global powers transferred weapons to the value of $60 billion to Africa. In the Democratic Republic of the Congo, an estimated $10.4 billion of their foreign debt is due to military expenditure.[23]

Kenya, a key US ally since the Cold War era, has been used as a base for US anti-terrorist operations against Somalia. In February 2002, over 3,000 US Marines took part in large-scale military exercises with Kenyan troops.[24]

The British government claims that it is effective at controlling arms exports but continues to licence the sale of arms to countries with a track record of human right abuses.

In 2011, a committee of British MPs whose brief is to overlook and scrutinize UK's arms exports acknowledged the contradiction between the British governments stated commitment to human rights, and its continued sale of arms to human rights abusing regimes.

Africans need to see through the façade and Western hypocrisy. It is time for Africans to realize that what unites them is far greater than the legacy of division created during the colonial era, and these divisions continue to be exploited in the neo-colonial era.

The incessant wars, instability and poverty that it creates and fosters are the ideal environment for imperial exploitation and are now being used as the retrospective reason for recolonization by imperial powers.

'In short the Security Council and its agents will become the last, altruistic and positive of all the imperial powers, restoring to the word colonialism the good name it once enjoyed— in Mediterranean antiquity no less than the nineteenth century.'[25]

'The second time around, Europe might stay a little longer and do the job right...Control can only be achieved by the return of colonial power operating under the aegis of the United Nations, and with popular consent expressed through a referendum. Now that independence has proved a cruel illusion in countries such as Mozambique, the population of that territory would without question welcome the return of Portugal as the presiding power backed by the UN.'[26]

CHAPTER SIXTY NINE

WEAPONS OF MASS DESTRUCTION: THE USE OF DEBT AS A WEAPON AND THE GLOBALISATION OF POVERTY

"The foreign aid program is the best weapon we have to ensure that our own men in uniform do not go into combat."
Robert McNamara, Former United States Secretary of Defence and President of the World Bank [1968–1981].[1]

"I think the economic logic behind dumping a load of toxic waste in the lowest–wage country is impeccable, and we should face up to that."
Lawrence Summers, Former Chief Economist for World Bank [1991], Secretary for the Treasury [1999].[2]

Traditionally, when weapons of mass destruction are discussed, predictably people tend to think about nuclear weapons, biological weapons and other weapons which bring about the mass killing of people. However, a weapon is defined as any tool or means used to maim or kill. Any 'weapon' or any means used to bring about mass killing and suffering is a weapon of mass destruction.

It is the pervading misconception that capitalism is a non-lethal process that allows one of the most devastating weapons of all — the globalisation of poverty and indebtedness — to continue unabated.

UNICEF estimates that 22,000 children die daily due to poverty. The World Resources Institute has stated that the worldwide toll of globalisation is approximately thirteen to eighteen million deaths of children every year.[3]

"When you consider that one hundred million have been killed in all form of wars of the twentieth century," wrote Michael McKinley, *"why are they to be privileged in comprehension over the annual death toll of children from the structural adjustment program since 1982?"*[4]

He quoted Lester C. Thurow's view that:

"the tragedy afflicting humanity was neither metaphor, nor simile, of war but war itself".[5]

In truth, the globalisation of poverty and debt has been the most devastating weapon of mass destruction — used in Africa or indeed anywhere around the world. Not even the combined effects of the atomic bombs dropped in Japan during the Second World War can match the destruction Western economic policies have caused in Africa. There are no historical precedents or parallels to the number of people killed or disenfranchised and impoverished by globalisation.

Africa, has been disproportionately hit by the effects of capitalism and even more so in its most recent reincarnation, globalisation. Unfortunately, after over twenty years of Western manipulation since independence, Africans are only now just waking up to the true level of the destruction of their economies, the erosion of political independence and the terrifying magnitude of the health problems like the AIDS epidemic and the Ebola virus, that face them.

CHAPTER SEVENTY

THE GEOPOLITICS OF DEBT

In 2010 the World Bank stated that 414 million people live in extreme poverty, i.e. on less than $1.25 a day, in sub-Saharan Africa while, ironically, European cows are subsidized to the tune of over $2.20 a day.[1]

Since Africa was sapped and structurally adjusted into poverty, economic growth and development have been stagnant. In 2014 the CIA worldwide fact book stated that nine out of the top ten countries with the highest infant mortality rates in the world were African countries. In 2015 one in three people living below the poverty line lived in Africa. The World Bank predicted that very few of the world's poorest countries would meet their 'poverty reduction targets' and that their foreign debt would continue to grow.[2]

Through global institutions, the United States maintains control over underdeveloped countries and sets the agenda in which international commerce takes place. While these global institutions are outwardly multilateral institutions, it is common knowledge that the United States Treasury Department controls the world's financial institutions. The World Bank is subordinate to the International Monetary Fund [IMF] and all other lenders, including the governments of most Western industrialized powers and much of the private sector, are under the financial control of the IMF — which is in turn controlled by the US.

In most African countries, all the Western aid received flows back to the West to repay debts racked up by Western-backed puppet, corrupt, unelected, repressive, authoritarian regimes — many long since gone. For instance, the Democratic Republic of the Congo spends about 37% of its GDP repaying debts largely accrued — and pocketed by —the shockingly corrupt regime of Mobutu Sese Seko.[3]

Trying to understand the world's economy without taking into account the complex geopolitical background that determines it is about as foolhardy as trying to understand a fish's behaviour out of water. Nevertheless, many extremely well paid and erudite Western economists make a living by churning out dazzling mathematical projections that attempt to support the false thesis that the economic fortunes of Western nations somehow stand alone and have nothing to do with their plunder of Third World countries.

A few examples will dispel any doubt about the link between world politics and the world economy. Oil today is the most important natural resource and the price of oil is a good indication of the state of world economics — much as gold was in the past.

In 1973, following the Yom Kippur War, oil prices surged upwards to 400% almost overnight. Within a year of oil prices rising in the 1970s both the US and UK had slipped into severe economic recession. During the war on Iraq, the lack of a steady oil supply and increased world demand saw oil prices rise to levels seen during the economic crisis of the 1970s and created a severe economic crisis in 2008 which the West has not yet fully recovered from. The US's military, political and social infrastructure, like its automotive use, public transportation and road networks area, are a living reflection of its heavy dependence on crude oil.

Western nations have peddled all kinds of economic solutions to Third World countries, like Structural Adjustment Programs, privatization and deregulation. It is instructive to note that none of the leading nations in the West ever took their own medicine, especially not while they were relatively underdeveloped. The real secret to the success of Western economies has been their ability to acquire essential resources for nothing, or next to nothing, whether by guile or by brute force. Western economic success is based on their ability to plunder, economically and militarily, the resources they needed. In the final analysis, Western economic success owes much more to the ancient law of plunder, 'might is right', than sophisticated economic principles. Today, the world stock markets rely on their 'confidence' in the Western military and political support rather than any backed securities.

The US's real power and most potent weapon of mass destruction has been the subjugation and domination of the world's economy— at a huge price to the world's poor. It has used devastating economic policies to attain and maintain its position as superpower and richest nation in the world today.

The hidden hand of the market will never work without the hidden fist. McDonald's cannot flourish without McDonnell Douglas, the designer of the F-15.[4] And the hidden fist that keeps the world safe for the Silicon Valley technologies is the US army, air force, navy and marine corps. Today, the US controls over a quarter of the world's resources and spends a quarter of all its resources on its military.

The foundation of America's economic hegemony was established at the Bretton Woods Conference in the US in 1944.[5] At this conference, the US military and corporations achieved almost unlimited access to minerals and resources all over the world. The main financial institutions like the World Bank, the IMF and the World Trade Organisation [WTO] were all created at Bretton Woods and are all controlled by the United States. These institutions are used to determine the economic and political policies of most countries in the world. It was also at Bretton Woods that seeds of debt as a weapon and the globalisation of poverty were sown.

Though outwardly multilateral organizations, their unilateral nature is underlined by the fact that the United States is the only country with an effective veto.[6] IMF and World Bank voting rights are directly related to the size of a country's GDP. The richer a country is the more voting rights they are entitled to.[7] Low and middle-income countries have a less than 40% share of the votes. The president of the World Bank is unelected, always appointed by the President of the United States and he is always a an American. The US treasury department and the World Bank control the IMF, and other 'multilateral' organizations like the WTO are subordinate to the IMF. All other lenders, including the governments of most Western industrialized powers and much of the private sector are under the control of the IMF.

When Paul Wolfowitz, the former head of the World Bank, was

appointed, it drew cries of outrage from countries all over the world. Wolfowitz was a well-known neoconservative Republican, a member of the organization called the Project for the New American Century and also a chief architect of the war on Iraq. The outcry did nothing to deter President George W. Bush from approving his appointment.

This institutionalized power asymmetry between rich and poor countries at the IMF, World Bank and the United Nations, has been the main reason why these institutions have persistently 'failed' to deliver for the weak and voiceless people of the underdeveloped world, who have been disproportionately affected by their policies. Seemingly by accident, these agencies run by Washington have used nefarious programs like the Structural Adjustment Programme [SAP] to widen steadily the wealth gap between the rich and poor nations, with a small elite group controlling over 80% of the world's riches.[8]

The World Bank — i.e. United States — is the largest source of finance for the Third World. Therefore, the World Bank's actions have the greatest effect in Africa because aid makes up a much larger share of African economies than it does elsewhere in the world.

Global funds and non-governmental organizations [NGOs] are generally donor-dominated. In the World Bank and the IMF, African countries have only two of the 24 constituencies, each of which has 20 members.[9]

Through these global institutions, the United States can maintain control over the economies of developing countries and set the agenda in which international commerce takes place. Through this concentrated financial power, the IMF can coerce most governments into adopting its policies by being able to deny them credit from almost all other sources. This most concentrated power is greater in efficacy than all the might of the US military.

Via the IMF/ US Treasury Structural Adjustment Programs, the US has been able deeply to undermine the economic, political and social structures in most former Third World countries. For instance, in Latin America, income per person grew by 75% from 1960 to 1980 but from 1980 to 2000, it grew by only 7% owing to IMF and World Bank policies.[10]

The only countries to buck the trend were countries like China and India, which developed economic policies independent of those recommended by the US's IMF treasury cartel.[11] China and India did not borrow money from the IMF and World Bank but used bespoke programs to implement their own development. Today, both these countries have emerged as economic superpowers.

In many cases, the IMF acted as a debt collector for major Western banks and financial institutions, which by themselves are not able to enforce the high interest rates they impose and which strangle economic growth in other countries such as Russia, Brazil and Argentina. They regularly recommend fiscal austerity even in the face of severe recession or depression.

To contextualise the power of this concentrated economic hegemony, one only needs to look at what happened to Russia during the early to mid–1990s. The Cold War had been won in the market place. Russia was not defeated by the US militarily or strategically; it was subjugated economically. Through economic manipulation the United States looted over $300 billion from the Russian economy.[12] It is thought that Russia lost about half of its national income in an economic failure which was declared to be the worst on record — outside of wars and natural disasters.

Historically, it was also economic power, not military that stimulated the break-up of the British Empire. Even the British, with their far-flung colonies that covered 70% of the globe, could not withstand the economic power of the US. After the Second World War, Britain was deeply indebted to the tune of over $40 billion. In their last imperialist throes, Britain and France launched a desperate unilateral attack on Egypt in direct contradiction to the United Nations and against the wishes of US, which feared a generalized Arab backlash. Britain and France occupied the Suez Canal in order to prevent the Egyptian leader, Colonel Nasser, from nationalising it. Due to severe domestic economic pressure, the heavy debt owed to America and the need for massive US aid, the British were forced to leave Egypt unconditionally, before the US could arrange a billion-dollar rescue package from the IMF and the Export-Import Bank.

Many people fail to appreciate the extent of the damage caused by the IMF/World Bank, as many people do not grasp the importance of economic growth and stability. Under Clinton's administration, the Treasury Secretaries Robert Rubin and Larry Summers aggressively opened up new foreign markets for capital and multinationals. They used the IMF to precipitate the Asian financial crisis in Thailand, Indonesia, Malaysia and the Philippines. Once achieved, the IMF conditioned its loans on the removal of restrictions to direct foreign investment into what had been protected national markets.[13]

Argentina's economic collapse in 2002 was largely a result of failed IMF policies, which were financed with billions of dollars from Washington. New loans went to pay official creditors, and the fiscal and monetary conditions attached to them prolonged and worsened the severe economic depression.[14]

Most countries, lacking access to international funds, were forced to accept damaging conditions associated with IMF and World Bank loans. Poor countries have been especially vulnerable to the ravages of concentrated global economic power. Due to their dependence, poor countries are only given relief if they conform to the rich world's set of rules, basically the Structural Adjustment package.

The United States gives its foreign aid more out of self-interest than with a view to assist the poor or suffering. It tends to reward allies, often brutal fascist regimes, and the aid always comes with strings attached — structural adjustment programmes — and 80% of it requires purchases from major US companies and the rest is military.[15]

The Yemen was punished by the US for voting against the First Gulf War. It cancelled a $70 million aid project. Yemen, one of the world's poorest countries, had a life expectancy at the time of only 46 years.[16] In 2003, the US withheld military aid to countries that refused to exempt US soldiers from being taken to the International Criminal Court.[17] Senegal was denied debt relief because it refused to privatise its peanut industry and the IMF demanded that Zambia privatise its national bank and threatened not to provide $1 billion in debt relief if they didn't.[18]

However, Pakistan, which had at one point been blacklisted by the

US and Western allies, was given financial reprieve for supporting the US's invasion of Afghanistan. This was done beside the fact that Pakistan was the only country in the world which staunchly supported Al–Qaeda and the Taliban in Afghanistan, sold or passed on nuclear weapons and information to North Korea and it was led by an unelected military dictator. President Musharraf became America's closest ally in its war on terror and in the hunt for al-Qaeda in Afghanistan US Subsequently, for supporting US's 'war on terror', Pakistan was removed from its list of 'rogue nations', had its debt cancelled and received substantial military and logistical support from the US and the UK.[19]

It is important to note that the US did not of course by any means practise its own or the IMF's preaching about economic reform but on the contrary took drastic steps to protect its own economy against global market forces. At the Bretton Woods conference after the Second World War, it was agreed that gold should be adopted as a monetary standard to back national currencies and to fix an international standard of an ounce of gold to $35. All other national currencies were fixed to the dollar and the dollar pegged to gold. After World War Two, the US had about half of the world gold reserves so it appeared to make good sense to peg the world's currencies to the dollar.

However, by 1966, central banks around the world held about $14 billion in gold reserves and the US only $13.2 billion. In addition, by 1971 the US was experiencing significant inflation and rising debt and had suffered a series of economic crises. President Nixon, in a move called the 'Nixon Shock', decided unilaterally to to remove the dollar backing to the international gold standard in order to prevent a run on the dollar.[20]

In so doing, President Nixon rendered the Bretton Woods agreement unworkable and reduced international currencies to 'fiat' money. Fiat money is defined as currency which derives its value from government regulations or law rather than being backed by gold or other assets. So by 1973, the gold standard had de facto been replaced by freely floating fiat currencies, which still is the system in operation today. This move paved the way for the US central bank to adopt 'quantitative easing' or simply printing more dollars when the need arose. Quantitative easing renders the dollar completely useless as legal tender if the US economy were to collapse.

Another important area of US foreign policy is the extension of US patents and copyright law to the rest of the world. This is one of US's most important foreign policy advantages. This policy denies poor countries access to essential medicines for desperately ill people because of a lack of adequate drugs and resources, including over 40 million people affected by HIV/AIDS in developing countries. The enforcement and extension of intellectual property protection, including patents, copyright and royalties, causes an enormous drain on the resources of the Third World and increases the capital flight from poor to rich countries, matching the total developmental assistance from North to South.[21]

This was the reason why the Clinton administration opposed South African and Brazilian laws which would permit them to produce their own generic drugs. Brazil and South Africa only won the fight due to the adverse publicity created by organised protests and international opposition.[22]

The world's poorest countries continue to pay the West over $60 million an hour in debt repayments. Since the Heavily Indebted Poor Countries initiative [HIPC] in 1996, they are still paying more on debt service than on health and education and, even so, have to meet the stringent conditions attached to the loans.

There is no reciprocity with regard to other countries opening up their economies to free trade and Western penetration. Through double standards in trades and disbursement of loans, Western governments have placed trade barriers and tariffs in the way of African governments, preventing them from investing in Western economies while at the same time through liberalization and privatization forced African economies to open up and become a dumping ground for Western arms and goods.

Despite the United Nations' decision that rich countries should give 0.7% of their gross domestic product in genuine aid to poor countries, Britain only gives 0.34% while the United States gives a paltry 0.19%.[23] The majority of US aid goes to strategic 'allies' as bribes or rewards in order to maintain US economic hegemony and strategic influence rather than meet the targets for poverty and needs of the people who require the aid.

Even though Africa's debt has many causes, both internal and external, the main reason Africa accrued its foreign debt was the Cold War and not just corruption, as the world is made to believe by the West.

The Cold War was political high drama and geopolitical intrigue to Western observers. However for Africans, the reality was a 'hot' war by proxy, between the world's superpowers. Unlike the First and Second World Wars, during the Cold War most of the combatants and casualties were the African people, their land and sovereignty. Millions of Africans died directly because of the Cold War and many more were forced to starve and become refugees as they tried to escape from neverending conflicts. The terrible legacy of the Cold War remains across Africa as many wars and conflicts with their roots stemming from this period still rage across the length and breadth of the continent. The economic fallout was that Africa was made yet more unstable and further underdeveloped.

The Cold War period did provide Africa with a wider means of securing funds and support for the fledgling independent states that were trying to establish political and economic independence. However, the military nature of most of the aid and the destabilising effects of persistent conflict precluded any meaningful development. The African Research Bulletin summed up the economic situation following the Cold War as follows:

The Cold War's demise...has proven a setback for black Africa. Super power rivalry once gave crucial purchase to poor lands with prized real estate for military bases, or a grip on maritime "choke points," or large reserves of materials...Africa's leverage has markedly weakened.[24]

In 1965, a US National Security Council memorandum recommended:

"US aid should be used as a political weapon with major assistance going to African friends of the US."[25]

Unfortunately, America's list of 'friends' is also a roll call of the top ten most brutal, vicious and corrupt regimes to terrorize, impoverish and kill innocent Africans. They included Mobutu Sese Seko of Zaire [now Democratic Republic of the Congo], Idi Amin of Uganda and Sani Abacha of Nigeria among many others.

Murder, torture, widespread human rights abuses and corruption by dictatorial rulers with a total lack of interest in human rights and democracy did nothing to deter the West from bankrolling these regimes and keeping them in power by providing them with all the military assistance they required. Many were the Western loans given during this period in the name of freedom, peace and security, which were actually used mainly to further the strategic interests of the superpowers and in real terms created and sustained conflicts, which brought much suffering to African people.

In fact, most of the loans and grants went directly to finance weapons acquisition from the Cold War superpowers and their allies rather than to the poor, starving and sick. This gave the West added impetus to increase the sale of all sorts of arms to Africa. America's greatest African ally, fondly referred to by the US State Department as their 'friendly tyrant', Mobutu Sese Seko, stole millions from the IMF, which he brazenly used to acquire property in Europe and build opulent palaces at home. Zaire received half of all US aid to the whole African continent in the late 1970s.[26]

The French provided the highly repressive Habyarimana regime in Rwanda with loans which were used to acquire weapons for internal suppression, in a bid to maintain its influence in French-speaking Africa. It is more than possible that these weapons could have been used in the genocide in Rwanda in 1994.[27]

In the unipolar world that followed the end of the Cold War, the African continent remains the continent most economically dependent on the whims and caprices of the IMF and World Bank in the world. Such are the levels of dependence on aid and loans that it now forms a significant part of the budget of many poor African nations. Since the Cold War period, Africa's debt problems have worsened dramatically under the careful guidance of Western financial institutions. Despite the economic ravages their policies have brought to Africa, the IMF and the World Bank have literally stuck to their guns and continue to dispense the same toxic medicine to African nations, albeit slightly altered in name only from time to time.

The World Bank's own evaluations of their project performance over the last ten years in Africa and Asia have shown them to be a resounding failure. It is estimated that between 60–70% of World Bank funded projects have failed.[28] Detailed studies of the performance of IMF programs showed that their single most consistent effect was to redistribute wealth away from the workers, leading to a massive flight of capital from the poor to the rich and from Africa to the West.[29]

As if their failure rate was not bad enough, they have managed to disburse most of their funds to tyrants, military governments and junta, providing these undemocratic and unelected governments with finance, military support and legitimacy in the West. This has been the main reason why the African electorates have found undemocratic leaders almost impossible to remove.

During the apartheid period — between 1948 and 1966 — the South African regime borrowed $250 million from the World Bank, making them their biggest clients at the time. When the South African apartheid regime ceased to be in 1994, the debt did not. The World Bank insisted the debt be paid and in this way those who had suffered under apartheid were forced to pay back for the debt bequeathed to them by the regime which oppressed them.[30]

In 1986, the same year that the repressive regime of Colonel Mengistu Haile Mariam was accused of having the worst human rights record in the world by the Economist, the World Bank lent Mengistu $100 million.[31]

Nigeria's Sani Abacha and Babangida, internationally known for corruption, were still able to borrow millions of dollars and pounds from the World Bank, which then found its way back to their personal US, UK, German and Swiss accounts.

The IMF and World Bank do not hide the fact that they are not daunted by the traits of cruelty, tyranny, and dictatorship. In fact they prefer these 'hand-picked characters' as they are friendly to the designs of the West and are seen as 'better credit risks' than democratically elected rulers.Ruthless dictators were better at imposing the unpopular economic reforms and conditions the IMF/World Bank imposed on its desperate customers. The vast majority of the electorate did not benefit from unnecessary loans and debts acquired by their puppet leaders. Nor were they enriched by deals which sold off and privatized national assets for next to nothing, and left their countries as virtual economic colonies for the Western nations and investors to do what they liked. Some IMF and World Bank loans had over a hundred preconditions attached that had to be meet on receipt of the loans.

The main conditions for Western loans were privatizing national assets, trade liberalisation by reducing trade barriers, devaluation of the country's currency and deregulation of the labour markets. All these conditions made the country easy prey for huge Western multinationals from the same countries, like the US and the UK, to swoop in and on a feeding frenzy, like a pack of hungry lions descending on its immobilized and helpless prey.

The IMF and World Bank blame corrupt African leaders for the 'failure' of their programmes but these claims are without basis as it can be clearly seen that their preferred clientele were corrupt, brutal dictators, without popular mandate. Also it is important to note that even their 'star pupils' who applied a SAP [Structural Adjustment Programme] to the letter, failed dismally. For instance, despite Bolivia adopting one of the most severe structural adjustment programmes to date, between 1985–1986, it remains one of the poorest countries in South America.[32]

The IMF and World Bank are clearly aware of the effects of their nefarious policies. In 1987, a G24 working group which included four executive directors of the IMF and three executive directors of the World Bank, wrote in a report: *"IMF SAP programmes had led have to a decline both of output and rates of growth, increased unemployment and adversely affected income distribution in developing countries."*[33] Their report recommended that SAP *'needs to be achieved by means that are consistent with other objectives such as growth and income distributions'.*

Despite this report, further SAP loans totalling $118 billion had been disbursed to seventy-one debt-burdened countries by 1990.[34]

CHAPTER SEVENTY ONE

IT TAKES A THIEF TO CATCH A THIEF

Corruption is one of the most common allegations the West has levelled against African leaders. While it is true that African politics is riddled with corruption, it is also true that without the assistance of their Western cohorts, they would be out of business overnight. Indeed, the breathtaking hypocrisy of Western politicians and media does not take into account the natural cycle of crime and corruption.

In 2005, while Tony Blair was chairing the Commission for Africa and delivering speeches about Africans eliminating corruption, his government awarded Halliburton's British arm, Kellogg, Brown and Root, a huge loan despite its being at the centre of a bribery investigation. KBR had received a British government loan for a large gas plant deal in Nigeria and had been accused of corruptly paying a $180 million in kickback to Nigerian officials. The NGO Action Aid remarked:

'The UK government requires African countries to take measures against corruption, yet UK government agencies use tax payers' money to support British companies accused of bribing their way into winning contracts.'[1]

On May 10th 2016 the British Prime Minister, David Cameron described Nigeria and Afghanistan as fantastically corrupt countries at a UK Anti-Corruption Summit in London.[2] In a conversation with the Queen, Cameron warned her: *"We've got some leaders of fantastically corrupt countries coming to Britain…Nigeria and Afghanistan, possibly the two most corrupt countries in the world."*[3]

However, the cycle of crime and corruption merely starts with the acquisition of stolen goods and money. It is usually completed when thieves find fences to buy their stolen goods from them and others to help them launder their stolen money. As the African parable goes: "As you point your accusing finger at others, the remaining four fingers of your hand point back at you."[4]

Point a finger at Africa and the remaining four fingers point at the West, the provider of dubious loans and grants to corrupt African governments, provided in the full knowledge that they are corruption and prone to mismanagement. They provide corrupt African politicians with the incentive, support, avenues and means to steal and bank their countries' money and assets in the West.

Much of Africa's stolen billions nestle in Swiss, British, US and German banks. Britain is notorious for providing safe passage for money launderers and illicit tax-havens. Since the 2001 US/British-led invasion of Afghanistan the amount of opium produced in Afghanistan has increased over threefold. A Labour official stated that: *"A Tory government hosting an anti-corruption summit is like putting a fox in charge of the chicken coop"*.[5]

Dr Folarin Gbadebo-Smith, a US-educated dentist and businessman, summed up the implicit role of the West in African corruption:

'A man who receives stolen goods is called a fence, but what do you call a country that receives stolen goods? They lend Nigeria money, somebody in Nigeria steals the money and gives it back to them, and then they leave these poor Nigerians repaying what they never owed. The role of these Western powers has been totally disgraceful'.[6]

An article from the Mail Metro stated:

'Corrupt African governments are not the cause of poverty in Africa. The governments of the West with their huge multibillionaire companies, rip off their own citizens and exploit third world producers'.[7]

In African states, the situation was not just a simple matter of the acquisition of loans from 'friendly' superpowers. A wide variety of underhand practices were employed to aid the disbursement of dubious funds to developing countries with the sole aim of creating crippling indebtedness and allowing Western governments to open up these countries and demand access to their natural resources, military cooperation and political support.

John Perkins in his book, Confessions of an Economic Hit Man, wrote:

"*Economic hit men are highly paid professionals who cheat countries around the globe of trillions of dollars. They funnel money from the World Bank, US agency for international development [USAID] and other foreign 'aid' organizations into the coffers of huge corporations and the pockets of the few wealthy families who control the planet's resources.*

The tools include fraudulent financial reports, rigged elections, payoffs extortion, sex and murder.

They play games as old as empire but one that has taken on new and terrifying dimensions during this time of 'globalisation'. Once the developing country saddled by crippling debts, defaults, the American government moves in like a mafia with a list of demands, which usually includes access to cheap natural resources or oil, setting up of military bases or even control over their votes in the United Nations all other so-called multilateral institutions.

There is never any real intention to collect the debt, as this would take away their leverage. The World Bank and IMF are usually on hand to offer more debt to pay existing debts, in the form of debt rescheduling, which only leads to an increase in the debts burden and further loss of sovereignty.

The disingenuous nature of the scam is that, however large the loan the bulk of the money is returned almost immediately to the multinationals and countries that gave them, as it never, in essence, left the United States but was transferred from one bank in New York to an engineering firm in San Francisco. The net effect is to leave the developing country with massive debt repayments from the principal and interest.

The role of the EHMs is to create a global empire by utilizing the huge multinationals, financial institutes like the IMF and World Bank, and Western governments to underwrite massive loans to developing countries for a wide variety of projects and schemes while at the same time obscuring the link between these dubious disbursements and Western governments.

If the deals turn sour, the Western governments can always blame the private sector, and this is one of the reasons why Western politicians and media go on about African corruption because their own tracks have been covered.

Subtlety and cunning are the key to success of these loan sharks.

...the subtlety of this modern empire building puts the Roman centurions, Spanish conquistadors, and the eighteenth and nineteenth-century European colonial powers to shame. We EHMs are crafty; we learned from history.

Today, we do not carry swords; we do not wear armor or clothes that set us apart.

In countries like Ecuador, Nigeria and Indonesia, we dress like local school teachers and shop owners. In Washington and Paris, we look like government bureaucrats and bankers. We appear humble, normal. We profess altruism, talk with local papers about the wonderful humanitarian things we are doing.

We cover the conference tables of government committees with the spreadsheets and financial projections and the lecture at Harvard business school about the miracles of macroeconomics.

We are on the record, in the open. Or so we portray ourselves and so are we accepted. It is how the system works. We seldom resold to anything illegal because the system itself is built on subterfuge, and the system is by definition legitimate.

However — and this is a very large caveat — if we fail, an even more sinister breed steps in, ones which we EHMs refer to as Jackals, men who trace their heritage directly to those earlier empires. The jackals are always there, lurking in the shadows. When they emerge, heads of states are overthrown or die in violent 'accidents'. And if by chance the jackals fail, as they failed in Afghanistan and Iraq, then the old models resurface. When the jackals fail, young Americans are sent to kill and die."[8]

Karl Ziegler was undoubtedly the 'economic hit man' that roped Nigeria, when a fledgling nation, into America's global empire with the $1.4 billion loan made to the country in 1975. It was the biggest loan made to Nigeria at that time and accounted for up to 75% of Nigeria's debt in the 1970s.

As was characteristic of many EHMs, Karl Ziegler was young, aggressive and inexperienced in international banking. He was only 29 years old when he brokered this deal on behalf of his bank, First Chicago. Even though it was common international knowledge that corruption was rife in Nigerian politics and that a huge and public scandal had embroiled the deal, it went through regardless.

Karl Ziegler's job was to make money by selling money and, because of geopolitical considerations, it did not matter if the deal was corrupt, plans were wrong, inappropriate and inadequate for the local conditions in Nigeria. Nor did it matter that Nigeria's general populace and environment would be lumbered with paying the loan back for decades. However, it was, of the utmost importance that the country took the bait.

As the lead bank in the syndicate, First Chicago made $3.5 million up front or 0.25% of the $1.4 billion loan, risk free, as soon as Nigerian politicians signed on the dotted line. A Salomon Brothers report, published in 1976, revealed that the thirteen largest US banks had quintupled their earnings from $177 million to $836 million during the first half of the 1970s, with a significant share coming from developing country loans.[9]

By 1976, Citibank was earning 72% of its income abroad, Bank of America 40%, Chase 78%, First Boston 68%, Morgan Guaranty 53% and Manufacturers Hanover 56%. In the 1970s, Banque National de Paris, one of the world's largest banking houses, profited more from its various African affiliates than its extensive branch network in France. Nigeria alone came to account for 20% of the bank's after-tax profits in the late 1970s.[10]

Export credit agencies [ECAs] are another means by which Western countries are able to give loans to developing countries and fund all sorts of nefarious projects. Very much like a credit card company, they provide credit to developing countries as long as the developing countries buy their goods and use their facilities. Sixty-five percent of all the debts owed by developing countries to Western nations were accessed via export credit agencies.[11]

To give some indication of the kind of numbers that export credit agencies support, between 1982 and 2001 they supported a staggering $7,334 billion worth of exports and $139 billion of foreign direct investment, primarily to countries of the developing world. Export credit agencies in the US and Europe are the largest source of public finance for private sector projects in the world.

Historically, rather than bankroll projects to support economic crimes, they have tended to pay bribes to support to tyrannical and dictatorial regimes or support environmentally unsound and socially undesirable projects US. Countries like Gabon, Nigeria and Algeria all owe more than 50% of the total debt to export credit agencies.[12] About 95% of the debt owed to the UK government by developing countries is in export credits debts.[13] In the United Kingdom, up to 30–50% of all export credits are allocated to facilitate sales by UK arms exporters to sixty-three of the poorest countries in the world.[14]

The developed world uses its ECAs to subsidize its exporters yet, in the name of free trade, demands that developing countries do not protect their producers in any way all.

In the early 1970s the US carried out one of the biggest swindles in the history of world economics. In 1973, OPEC increased the price of oil and invested the excess money in commercial banks. These banks and Western governments invested these 'petrodollars' in Third World countries that were being used as pawns in a chess game between the Soviets and the West. Many African nations and Third World countries were offered huge loans at low interest rates and some very low concessional rates. After America's debacle in Korea and Vietnam and, owing to the high oil prices, the United States adopted very tight money policies to decrease inflation, producing its own domestic recession.

After the fall of the Shah of Iran, between 1970 and 1987, interest rates were increased dramatically from as low as 0.5% for commercial loans to over 13%, creating an unpayable debt burden in most Third World countries. The situation was further aggravated when President Reagan began his 'Star Wars' weapon defence program and borrowed heavily from the World Bank and the IMF, which further increased interest rates.

Many Western governments, multinationals and companies that had given soft loans to repressive Third World regimes supported by the West now faced prospects of not being able to recoup their money as these countries were now unable repay the debts. So former US Treasury Secretary, James Baker devised the Structural Adjustment Program [SAP[, which has been discussed previously. Through the SAPs money could be squeezed out of these poor countries, not only allowing the Western creditors to regain their money but also force African leaders to hand over the reins of government to the IMF/ US Treasury, called the 'Washington Consensus', a neo-liberal programme which stressed the untrammelled operation of the Free Market and the reduction of state involvement in the economy — all very convenient for US business. Needless to say, projected investments that were promised towards meeting poverty reduction targets, money to fight the AIDS epidemic and stimulate development, did not materialize.

Africa's total debt is estimated to be about $353 billion. The original debts have been repaid over three times and continue to rise. In the late 1970s, Nigeria borrowed $2 billion from the international community. Since then it has repaid $28 billion and still had outstanding debts of $33 billion by 2000.[15] Nigeria pays $3 billion annually to the United States alone though it only earns $11 billion annually. It thus accounts for nearly one third of its GDP.

The result has been African economies have the slowest growth rates in the world in spite of the highest rates of borrowing from Western governments. The ratio of Africa's GNP to debts has become the highest in the world and Africa's total debt to total export earnings is rising rapidly and has become the highest in the world since 1987. Compared to Latin American countries Africa depends more on official borrowing rather than commercial borrowing.

Africa's problems have been compounded by natural disasters — drought, floods, epidemics, market forces and, in particular, wars. An estimated eight million Africans have died directly due to conflicts since 1987.[16]

The AIDS epidemic continues to plague Africa with sub-Saharan Africa accounting for 28 million people living with HIV and AIDS. Also many African countries rely on the weak commodity markets, which have declined 50% over the last 20 years. As many as seventeen African countries rely on primary commodities like coffee, cocoa, sugar and cotton for 75% of the export earnings.[17]

Several initiatives have been made to try to relieve Africa's debt problems. Some of these include the Brady initiative by commercial creditors and the Paris Club rearrangements by sovereign creditors. The Highly Indebted Poor Countries initiatives [HIPC] and Poverty Reduction Strategy Papers [PRSP] by the World Bank and IMF have all been unrealistic and ineffective. But what is remarkable is that thirty-four out of the forty-two highly indebted poor countries are African and because of conflicts, at least ten are ineligible for debt relief.[18]

The solutions proposed by creditors like the Paris Club are undemocratic as the creditors make all the rules and maintain that debtor countries are solely responsible for the debt crisis. Of course, this leaves Western lenders the opportunity to continue to make imprudent loans as they are always guaranteed repayments.

But how legal are the majority of these loans? Many were given to repressive regimes and corrupt leaders who used the money to strengthen their positions and line their own pockets. This problem is not a new one. It was recognised in Biblical times and captured in the concept of Jubilee.

The king of Babylon proclaimed in the Code of the Hammurabi, circa 1780 BC:

'If a man owe a debt and the storm god inundate his field and carry away the produce, or if through a lack of water, grain has not grown in the field in that year, he shall not make any return of grain to the creditor, he shall alter his contract-tablet, and he shall not pay the interest for that the year.'[19]

In 1927 Alexander Nahum Sack, a former politician in the tsarist Russian state and later a Professor of Law in Paris came up with the idea of 'odious debts'. He hoped to redress the problems faced by states or countries that had gained their independence from repressive and despotic regimes that had put them into heavy crippling debts, which prevented the countries from developing freely. He wrote two books, The Effects of the Transformations of the States in their Public Debts and Other Financial Obligations and the Succession of the Public Debts of the State.

Sack was of the opinion that the liability for public debts not created in the interests of the state should be that of the despotic regimes and their creditors and not that of the population that had fought to free itself of the regimes. This kind of debt he referred to as 'dette odieuse'. He wrote:

'If a despotic power incurs a debt not for the needs or in the interest of the state, but to strengthen its despotic regime, to repress the population that fights against it, etc. this debt is odious for the population of all the State.

This debt is not an obligation for the nation; it is a regime's debt, a personal debt of the power that has incurred it; consequently, it falls with the fall of this power.

The reason these "odious" debts cannot be considered to encumber the territory of the State, is that such debts do not fulfil one of the conditions that determines the legality of the debts of the State, that is: the debts of the State must be incurred and the funds from it employed for the needs and in the interests of the State.

'Odious' debts, incurred and used for ends which, to the knowledge of the creditors, are contrary to the interests of the nation, do not compromise the latter — in the case that the nation succeeds in getting rid of the government which incurs them — except to the extent that real advantages were obtained from these debts. The creditors have committed a hostile act with regard to the people; they can't. Therefore, expect that a nation free from a despotic power assume the "odious" debts, which are personal debts of that power.

Even when a despotic power is replaced by another, no less despotic or any more responsive to the will of the people, the "odious" debts of the eliminated power are not any less their personal debts and are not obligations for the new power....

'One could also include in this category of debts the loans incurred by members of the government or by persons or groups associated with the government to serve interests manifestly personal interests that are unrelated to the interests of the State.[20]

For creditors to expect any protection in their loans to foreign states their loans must be utilized for the needs and interests of the state, otherwise the loans belonged to the power, which contracted them, and were therefore, 'dettes de régime'.

Obviously, the doctrine of odious debts is open to abuse. To avoid arbitrarily repudiated debts, Sack proposed that a new government be required to prove that the debt ill-served the public interest and that the creditors were aware of this. Following these proofs, the onus would be upon the creditors to show that the funds were utilized for the benefit of the territory. If the creditors could not do so, before an international tribunal, the debt would be unenforceable.

In an ideal world, it may be expected that the perpetrators of this injustice, leading to the death or disablement of millions around the world, might cause some to rethink their position in order to end the suffering of many. But this is merely a dream. The onus is on every African to recognize for themselves the immense danger to themselves and their future generations posed by Africa's debt crisis and take appropriate measures to end it.

Many empathetic people in the developed countries recognize that the open wounds of slavery and the effects of neo-colonialism and imperialism in the world today simply amount to the conscious genocide of a vast number of under-privileged people all around the world, not just in Africa. Noreena Hertz wrote that a country may choose to exercise its right to waive its debts *'if the country is unable to guarantee its citizens, subsistence levels of food, water, clothing or shelter, if in order to service debt it is forced to destroy and degrade the environment, and if it is unable to guarantee the most basic human rights'.*[21]

African debts looted by undemocratic governments, military regimes or officials should be regarded as personal debt and not a national obligation. Thus the majority of African debts acquired illegitimately, should be cancelled. *"When the power falls, the debt consequently, falls with the power."*[22]

A case in point is the US's model of democracy, Kenya. In the Congo, the first democratic government of Patrice Lumumba was overthrown by the help of the CIA, and replaced by the brutal and repressive dictatorship of Mobutu Sese Seko. Mobutu not only killed and repressed his own people, but also looted a large proportion of the country's finances, which he stashed away in Western banks. While the country was crippled by staggering debt repayments, the money he stole accrued interest in Western banks.

This was much the same with General Sani Abacha in Nigeria, who enjoyed Western support and personally looted well over $3 billion.

Professor Adebayo Adedeji, former Executive Secretary of the United Nations Economic Commission for Africa, stated: *"Debt is tearing down schools, clinics, hospitals and the effects are no less devastating than war."*[23]

The crippling debts of African governments have rendered them simply debt-servicing and vital resources that could have gone to solve the serious health, hunger and infrastructure issues, are servicing the interest of debts which they never incurred.

It will take more than biennial reminders like Red Nose Day in the UK or the efforts of charity organizations to counter the effects of the actions of Western governments on the lives of millions of hapless African people. Unfortunately, these are not facts that Western governments want their people to know or understand as it would change the way many white people think about Africa, her problems and the solutions to the problems that affect her.

From an imperialist's point of view, Africa's debt crisis as engineered through the structural adjustment program was a tremendous success. It freed up new markets, provided investments for multinationals with cheap labour, tax cuts and switched control, even up to fine detail, from African governments to the Washington consensus. It created a net flow of wealth from the poorest nations on earth to the richest, especially the United States. So devastating has been the effect of Western debt in Africa that the US has rarely needed to use its military to intervene directly in African affairs in order to influence policies in its favour, as it has done elsewhere like in the Middle East. The brain drain from Africa to the West is also a symptom of the harsh economic conditions that prevail in Africa.

Incessant wars in Africa have maintained what one can only describe as controlled anarchy — ideal conditions for Western exploitation. Africa has provided the West with outlets for inappropriate sales of military equipment and systems for huge profits in exchange for crippling debt and debt repayments.

In theory, the structural adjustment program was supposed to stimulate a trickle-down effect for wealth distribution from rich countries to the poor. However, the only thing it 'trickled down' down upon the poor was bullets, suffering, disease and more poverty, unleashed, by the brutal, unelected, undemocratic puppet regimes supported by the Western governments in order to sustain Western hegemony.

Africa's wealth is being redistributed to the richest Western nations in the world. Africa has had to pick up the bill for the corruption of both immoral African leaders and colluding Western governments, bankers and businessmen.

Today, the poorest people on earth live on less than a dollar a day, still pay the West £60 million a day and are crushed by debts incurred by corrupt undemocratic African leaders who bought these weapons to kill them with.[24] Broken down further, many people in sub-Saharan Africa, who live on less than a dollar a day, owe the West, through their governments, about $134 a day, more than they earn in a year.

Any African leader or government that puts a single citizen before debt repayments is not worthy to lead its people. Legitimate debts should be repaid using timescales and amounts that reflect common humanity. The debts that African countries acquired from Western governments, who gave loans to corrupt leaders and dictators, should be written off. Western governments do have the capacity to recoup many of these bad loans, as these dictators did not save their money in African banks but in Western countries, usually the same countries that gave them the debts in the first place.

At the World Summit on Sustainable Development in 2002, Professor Jeffrey Sachs, a Columbian academic and leading economist, urged the participants to *'defend your people. It's untenable to be paying debt that could be used to fight the [Aids] pandemic. It's imperative to channel those funds to AIDS, given this holocaust'.*[25]

After World War I, Germany was forced to make reparation of up to 15% of its exports, and this was considered so excessive that it severely restricted Germany's ability to reconstruct itself following the war and was seen as an important cause of World War Two.

When the Allies negotiated a new debt repayment agreement with the then-new Federal Germany in 1953, Germany was only required to pay up to 3.5% of exports.

Britain, also devastated by the war, and heavily indebted to the USA, also negotiated a deal that limited debt repayments to 4% of exports to allow them to rebuild following the war. Britain's post-war debt was only finally repaid to the USA and Canada in late 2006.

Why then were the people of South Africa and Mozambique, the victims of aggression from the white apartheid regime and imperialists, unlike Nazi Germany, who was actually the aggressor in the Second World War, asked to repay the debts of their oppressors at a rate of 12–20% of exports?

Under the World Bank and IMF HIPC initiative, poor countries are expected to make debt repayments equivalent to 20% of their export earnings. Under this agreement, Mozambique had to pay 17% of export earnings in 1998, falling to 13% in 2000. South Africa paid up to 12% in 1996.

It is precisely for this reason that Nelson Mandela's ANC was unable to deliver the economic reforms as promised, in their pre-election campaign. The economic power in South Africa remained in the hands of the supremacists.

Unfortunately, the dazzling array of acronyms and euphemisms used by Western governments to conceal their true intentions in Africa and the true extent of the damage done by debts, is not appreciated by most Africans, who have not in turn held their governments accountable. Since the slave trade, the West has perfected the use of euphemisms and acronyms to cover their bloody trail of exploitation around the world. The fact that many African countries have not yet been subjected to bombing raids by American B-52 bombers or strafed by Apache helicopter gunships does not mean they should not be discerning enough to understand the effects the unpayable debt is having on Africa.

Jeremy Seabrook, author of the book, The No-Nonsense Guide to World Poverty, wrote:

'Poverty is not a question of the laggards and the left-behind of globalisation, but remains an inescapable structural necessity — required to justify continued growth and expansion beyond sufficiency.[26]

To continue to rely on the creditors' nations for solutions or debt cancellation is foolhardy and only undemocratic governments or puppet governments can continue to do so. Africans have tried to campaign to drop the debts for several years now without any significant success.

In 2000, General Olusegun Obasanjo, ex-president of Nigeria, presented the United Nations with twenty-two million signatures from the Drop the Debt campaign. In 2000 and 2002, the Jubilee South and the Jubilee North campaign to Drop the Debt presented the UN with a further twenty-five million signatures.[27]

The United States has spent well over $3 trillion on the illegal war and occupation of Iraq and the war in Afghanistan; this is several times over the total sum of money owed by all African nations to the West. This point illustrates that it is possible for the West to drop the illegitimate debts without incurring any untoward economic side effects. The sad truth is that there is no political will to do so.

Applying the principle in international law known as 'force majeure', which stipulates that a change in the conditions of the contract may render it invalid. This can be applied to the debt crisis of the 1980s, which saw the United States increase interest rates from 3.7% to 10% worldwide, creating a global economic crisis. On a personal level, a rise in interest rates of this amount may mean financial ruin, through repossession of your property due to unpayable mortgage rates or perhaps credit card bills.

As noted above, in the 1970s Nigeria's debt was about $3 billion with interest rates of about 3%. Over 40 years later, after paying the debt at least three times over, Nigeria still owed about $33 billion to the United States, which constitutes an interest rate of over 3500%. The figures make it immediately apparent that the debts are not just dubious but can never be repaid.[28]

Nigeria's petroleum industry employs about 1,000 skilled expatriates, even though people with similar skills within the African diaspora could be found. Instead of developing its own manpower resources, Nigeria prefers to, or is obliged, to contract out its oil exploration, despite the staggeringly high price of having to concede over 40% of its profits to foreign oil companies. Since political independence in 1960, Nigeria has relinquished over 40% of its oilfields and $200 billion to the US and European stockholders.[29]

That the debt/poverty syndrome impacts on health in Africa has been have highlighted by a number of economists:

Up to 70% of childhood cases of diarrheal diseases, malnutrition, measles and lower respiratory infections in the developing world — the big killers — are due to poverty-related malnutrition.[30]

Increased prostitution from forced urbanization because of poverty has increased the spread of HIV and AIDS in Africa. There has been an increase in deaths from preventable diseases like diabetes, epilepsy, malaria, sleeping sickness and Chagas disease due to poverty. Co-infection with tuberculosis, malaria and parasitic infections has been shown to decrease immunity and lead to high levels of viraemia and the high viral loads are associated with an increased risk of transmission of HIV and AIDS.

Absolute poverty reduces the chances of adequate health care and thus the deadly cycle of poverty and disease is very hard to break. As Nelson Mandela observed: *"AIDS kills those on whom society relies to grow crops, work in the mines and factories, run the schools and hospitals, and govern countries."*[31]

The most recent World bank statistics on African debt reveal that Africa's money problems have not gone away. They show that Africa's debt has risen to $493.6 billion and in 2019, many African nations spent more on debt servicing than on health. In 1990, Africa's unsustainable debt stood at $255 billion to official lenders and $28 billion to private creditors.

In 1996, 31 HIPC African countries had their debts forgiven but the private creditors did not relinquish their claims. This created the opportunity for speculators called 'Vulture Funds'.

The Africal Legal Support Facility — a branch of the African Development Bank — describes Vulture Funds as entities that purchase distressed debt on the secondary market, where it trades significantly below its face value, and then seek to recover the full amount, often through litigation.[32]

These entities, usually Western, buy the debt at deep discounts with the intention of suing the debtor for full recovery in an influential country like the US and particularly in New York.

For example, Vulture Fund speculators bought 'distressed debts' from Zambia, Democratic Republic of Congo, Ethiopia and Uganda very cheaply. They then demand that the countries met their contractual obligations and pay them in full. They then sued the countries that refused. They grind down the poor countries with prolonged cycles of litigation referred to as 'Champerty'. The litigation is usually taking three to ten years to "settle". This cold-blooded strategy earned them returns of between 300–2000%.[33]

Unfortunately, it is not only Western Vulture Funds tearing chunks out of Africa. In August 2019, a British judge granted an Irish company called Process and Industrial Developments LTD (P&ID), permission to seize up to $90 billion (£7.4bn) in assets from the Nigerian government over a botched gas deal from 2010.[34]

This amounts to about 20% of Nigeria's foreign reserves and, if allowed, will have a severe socio-economic impact on millions of suffering Nigerians. These developments hightlight issues around African sovereignty. How can courts in the UK and US hold so much power over sovereign African nations? Should matters like these not been judged in an unbiased international court?

Africa is caught in the deadly trap of the debt-poverty cycle, arising directly from its psychological inferiority complexes and its physical dependence on the white supremacy power structure. It is imperative that the African people and their diaspora unite as one to break free from the mental and physical slavery that this system imposes upon them. Failure to break free can only lead to perpetual slavery.

CHAPTER SEVENTY TWO
HUMANITARIAN IMPERIALISM

"Britain controls today the destinies of some 350,000,000 alien people, unable as at yet to govern themselves, and easy victims to rapine and injustice, unless a strong arm guards them. She is giving them a rule that has its faults, no doubt, but such, I would make bold to affirm, as no conquering state ever gave to a dependent people"
Professor George M. Wrong, 1909.[1]

"Our real task in the coming period is to devise a pattern of relationships, which will permit us to maintain this position of disparity [US military – economic superiority]... without positive detriment to our national security.
To do so, we will have to dispense with all sentimentality and day dreaming; and our attention will have to be concentrated everywhere on our immediate national objectives.
We need not deceive ourselves that we can afford the luxury of altruism and world-benefaction." **George Kennan,** policy planner, US State Department, 1948.[2]

Historically, the West has always needed a façade to disguise its real intentions when intervening in Africa. According to Europe, spreading Christianity justified the transatlantic slave trade and providing civilization to the African natives justified colonization. Today, Western intervention in Africa is justified by globalisation and humanitarian intervention. The 'strong arm' of the West, led primarily by the US, France and Britain, now offers the former Third World countries humanitarian imperialism.

The concept of humanitarian imperialism is not new. The British philosopher John Stuart Mill [1806–73] was the first to articulate Britain's foreign policy in a series of essays.[3] His essays on liberty reflected the strongly held belief in British cultural and moral superiority over other Europeans and especially over the 'barbarous people in the colonies'. He believed that the English had a civilizing mission as they were of a higher civilization and that barbarous people needed to be ruled for their own benefit.

In 'Essay on Liberty' Mill described England as 'a novelty in the world' and a remarkable nation that only acts 'in the service of others'. Mill also wrote about social liberties in detail yet he was quite clear on the racial boundaries that the English must not cross with the 'barbarians' and wrote:

"...the conquered and the conquered cannot in this case live under the same free institutions...these less advanced people must be governed as subjects."[4]

On the issue of individual liberties and economic policies, Mill stated:

"Restrictions on trade, or on production for the purposes of trade are indeed restraints; and all restraint... is an evil."[5]

Mill further stated that England was 'dedicated to peace' though if 'the aggressions of barbarians force it to a successful war, it selflessly bears the cost' while 'the fruit it shares in fraternal equality with the whole human race,', including the barbarians it conquers and destroys for their own benefit.[6]

Today, even though John Stuart Mill has been criticised by some for his conflicting views, he still reflects accurately Britain's modern foreign policy complete with its doublespeak and conflict of interests.[7] It is amazing to note that while Mill was pontificating on the superior morality of the English, they were enslaving Africans, colonizing India and invading China to force the Chinese into buying opium.

In the 17th century, European countries smuggled tobacco and opium for smoking to the Far East. By 1729, via the East India Company, Britain was trafficking in the region of 200 chests of opium to China. By

1838, this had increased to 200,000 per year.

Alarmed by the growing number of Chinese opium addicts, Emperor Daoguang demanded an end to the opium trade and seized cocaine stores and blocked British vessels from docking. However, following John Stuart Mill's dictum about the 'evils' of restricting British trade, Britain declared war on China and in 1839 sent an expeditionary force from India. British naval bombardments killed an estimated 20–25,000 Chinese and China ceded Hong Kong, thus paving the way for the expansion of the opium trade in terms of the Treaty of Nanking. The Chinese refer to this period as the 'Century of Humiliation'.[8]

In Africa, Western humanitarian imperialism is always allied to a 'noble' cause which, given Africa's poverty and chronic instability, are many. Today, the West frequently intervenes in Africa for humanitarian causes like 'peacekeeping', food distribution, conflict resolution, aid distribution and so on. Unfortunately, in most cases the underlying reasons for the need for assistance can also be traced back to the West.

The new face of colonialism in our time is its economic and humanitarian guise. Imperialism has not just caused wars in Africa, through its structural adjustment program, privatization and trade liberalization, it has waged a continual and persistent war against Africa via economic means. With controlled anarchy the desired outcome and war the means of producing anarchy, the economic devastation across Africa is not just an outcome of war but indeed its very aim. These are wars which produce mass migration and increase poverty and hunger with no chance of economic stability or growth. The increased societal pressures imposed by intense poverty lowers the threshold for conflict and infighting for meagre resources. Once local conflicts have become internationalised, Western governments and agencies provide resources and arms to both sides — thus prolonging, escalating and widening the conflicts.

The key to understanding Western intervention in Africa is always to look at the balance sheet of net loss to Africa and net gain to the West. All historical precedents indicate that Africa has been the clear loser in virtually all its interactions with the West.

Following the Second World War, especially since the 1980s, humanitarian intervention by the West has been developed into a fine art. However, it is not just an art which is good politics. It is a cracking good business as well. In 2005 Britain made a handsome profit of over £5 billion from the sub-Saharan region of Africa alone, after their investments, charities and aid were deducted. Yet, in the same year, the sub-Saharan region was officially designated the poorest region of the world and a place riddled with political instability, economic disasters and lack of development and basic infrastructure.

A Christian Aid report from June 5th 2006, stated: *"'Despite all the good intentions and billions of pounds of aid and debt relief, more money flowed out of poor African coffers into Britain last year than the other way round.'"*[9]

Another Christian Aid report into the financial relationship between Africa and Britain in the twelve months following the 2005 G8 summit of world leaders in Edinburgh showed that the UK economy gained over £11 billion in total or the equivalent of £187 from every African in the sub-Saharan region.

As Dr Claire Melamed, Christian Aid's senior trade analyst explained: *"These figures show that even in a year when Africa was high on the agenda thanks to Tony Blair's Africa Commission and aid and debt pledges at the G8, the underlying truth remains that we in the rich world are taking out vastly more resources from sub-Saharan Africa than we are putting in."*[10]

Exploiting tax loopholes and banking secrecy, large Western corporations and rich Western individuals raked in £22 billion in profits and capital flight from sub-Saharan Africa in 2005 alone.[11] While millions of Africans languish in poverty and disease, with many more desperately risk their lives and limbs to emigrate to the West, Western governments and their large multinationals are smashing down the doors to get into Africa.

During the West's 'halcyon' days of colonial imperialism, the heavy military hand of its gunboat policy was clearly visible as the main facilitator of the imperial process and a deterrent to African people who aspired to self-rule and determination. Today, the neo-colonial imperialism of globalisation requires much more subtlety. Even though it is a direct linear progression of the old colonial process, its most visible projection today is as an economic process and not a military one. The staple weapons of globalisation, including structural adjustment programs, privatization, trade liberalization and intellectual property rights are projected as economic programs designed to help the Third World. Since they do not require open military conquest, they are assumed to work through peaceful means only.

In old-style Western 'gun-boat diplomacy' Western countries openly aimed to seize African territory and govern while plundering the human and natural resources. Today's neo-colonial imperialism aims at 'governance' not government and seeks to control its neo-colonial economic policies and political agenda remotely. Neo-colonialism generates capital flight from Africa to the West far in excess of what was achieved under the old-style colonial arrangements.

If one were to strip away the razzle-dazzle of modern information technology and all the euphemisms and acronyms of globalisation, it would be clearly seen that Africa is steadily being steered back to its colonial role as a primary source of raw materials, natural and human resources to the West. Despite the Western promises that the structural adjustment programs were designed to boost productivity, eliminate inefficiency, and improve Africa's competitiveness on the global stage, they have achieved the exact opposite and most African countries have stagnated — just as they did in the colonial period — to mineral and export-oriented agriculture that leaves the majority of the African people in abject poverty.

African countries are severely disadvantaged in the world trade markets as they cannot determine the prices of their own mineral and agricultural produce, leaving them dependent on the West for vital finance, necessary to feed and develop their countries.

The great military theorist, Carl von Clausewitz, coined the phrase 'war by other means'.[12] The destructive processes of war are the basis of Western humanitarian imperialism. War creates the necessary environment for humanitarian intervention while at the same time creating the ideal conditions for the capitalist acquisition of human and natural resources. The creation and sustenance of conflicts in Africa has not just been a consequence of the globalisation process of Western capitalism; it has also been the way of facilitating it.

Since the SAPs were implemented in the 1980s, Africa has experienced an outburst of violent conflicts. This is due to the African ruling classes attempting through the acquisition of state power to politicise tribalism and fighting over the right to pawn off national assets internationally. War remains the underbelly of globalisation. In 1999, out of the 75 countries around the world experiencing some form of war, 33 were found to be in Africa.[13]

Capital flight, induced by globalisation, has led to soaring levels of poverty. The crushing poverty tears apart the societal fabric, such that many unemployed youths who would otherwise be employed on farms or urban centres have instead become the child soldiers of Africa's many complex tribal and religious wars. These conflicts are rooted in the terrible socio-economic and political conditions people have been forced to live in.

In Africa, where communal land tenure is still very widespread, wars drive the people from the land and allow capitalists to reclaim it for use by their huge multinational agribusinesses. It also boosts the production of a cash crop and export-oriented economy, which leads to food shortages and famines. This in turn increases African dependence on the importation of foreign food, like rice, to survive. Wars, too, disrupt the family and social networks necessary for people to effectively resist capitalist 'market reforms' that promote dependence.

Another key and dangerous feature of neo-colonial imperialism in contrast to its predecessor, colonialism, is the lack of responsibility for the disasters it causes. The political and infrastructural arrangements they had created in their acquisition of African territory under direct colonial rule physically tied Western imperialists down.

This also clearly identified who the perpetrators of the many injustices of the colonial period were too. For example, the German colonialists were directly responsible for the genocide of thousands of the Hereros in southern Africa. King Leopold of Belgium had personal responsibility for the deaths of millions of Congolese people in the Congo. However, in the neo-colonial system, even though millions of Africans are dying yearly from the effects of globalisation, the causes of their deaths, as well as the perpetrators, remain invisible and no one is held responsible for it.

The central theme of neo-colonialism has always been the undermining of the African political infrastructure and the creation of dependence on Western governments, financial institutions, and multinationals. The installing of puppet dictatorial regimes, wars through proxies, the odious debt burden, illegal arms sales, steep trade barriers and tariffs, and many more insidious methods, have been applied in a multifaceted approach in order to exploit Africa and maintain its African dependence. However, one method, which remains largely overlooked is the use of food aid as a form of stealth warfare.

On a continent where 70% of the population depends on subsistence farming, it is entirely logical to assume that any effective attack on the food supplies of the African people can significantly break down societies, creating the conditions necessary for globalisation to thrive. Food aid has become a major weapon for the neo-colonial war machine because it has not just created African dependence on the West for food supplies but has also allowed many African nations to become effectively re-colonized by Western governments through their Non-Governmental Organizations and multi-nationals. It has allowed entitled Western international organizations like the Red Cross and many others to claim the right to intervene in areas of conflict in Africa, claiming to be providing relief. This 'right' was enshrined in law when in 1988 the UN passed a resolution asserting the right of donors to deliver aid.[14] It was under the auspices of this resolution that the US military invasion and occupation of Somalia in 1992–1993 [Operation Restore Hope] was justified. Silvia Federici stated:

'It is well known that even when food aid is not delivered by occupying troops it only acts as a form of political and military intervention as it prolongs the war by feeding the contending armies [more often than the civilian population], it shapes military strategy, and helps the stronger party… the one

best equipped to take advantage of food distributions ... to win.'[15]

Before the intervention in Somalia, the US had already used food aid in the past to shape the outcome of African conflicts, as in Sudan and Ethiopia in the 1980s, where the provision of food aid by the US, UN and NGOs like CARE led them to become major protagonists in their wars.[16] Food aid to Africa therefore is war by stealth.

In the 1980s, the British rock musician Bob Geldof focused the attention of the world on the Ethiopian famine, in which over 50,000 people died, with a massive musical concert. However, the real cause of the famine was not the drought, overpopulation, or improper land use, as widely claimed, but the Ethiopian government's war against the Eritrean People's Liberation Front [EPLF] and Tigrayan People's Liberation Front [TPLF] and their forced resettlement program of hundreds of thousands of people.

The food relief provided by the US, UN and various Western NGOs, totalled almost $3 billion between 1985 and 1988, but essentially went to the Ethiopian government to fund its war efforts. Such was the complicity and cooperation between the US, UN and NGO personnel, that they hid the real causes of the famine from the public. They hid the diversion of food aid to the Ethiopian military [only 15% went to the civilians and the rest went to the army] and the human costs of the resettlement scheme. Western countries accompanied the Ethiopian Army 'to gain access to famine areas' and they even complained that their, 'humanitarian efforts were being hindered when the rebel fighters, EPLF or the TPLF recaptured territory'.[17]

The effects of food aid have been well studied since the 1960s, and it is commonly said, 'you don't help people by giving them food but by giving them the tools to feed themselves' [exactly what Mengistu was trying to do]. Food aid contributes to the displacement and relocation of rural communities around the food centres created by the NGOs. It undermines local agriculture by causing the price of local produce to crash and can create a new source of warfare, with the prospect of appropriating large food supplies and selling them locally or internationally. Even under famine conditions, it has been shown that people are better off when they preserve their ability to farm.

For the Western countries, the delivery of food aid by the multibillion-dollar US agribusiness, ensures that they profit twice. Firstly, they profit from the development of the African nation's dependence on food aid — and again, from having an outlet for the huge food surpluses that they produce.

Large US food agencies, like Cargill, profit twice from the suffering masses by delivering food aid in such a manner that it prolongs conflicts rather than shortens them.[18] Flooding Africa with food helps the United States and other Western countries to get to rid of their own agricultural surpluses and reap the profits from the dependence of African countries on Western food aid. Ghana, for example, has imported rice since the 1980s, despite rice being the main produce of its own farmers.

Mozambique is held up by social critics as one of the best examples of how a country can be re-colonized using war and humanitarian relief.

For almost a decade, between 1981 and 1990, the US and apartheid South Africa waged a war by proxy against the socialist government of Mozambique via a rebel group called Renamo or MNR [Resistência Nacional Moçambicana]. The West's intervention in Mozambique epitomised a process of societal destruction and creation of dependence which contains all the key elements of the neo-colonial process of globalisation.

The first step of the process was the destruction of the country's political, social and physical infrastructure in order to provoke a production crisis and enforce economic and political subordination. This was achieved by a systematic war of terror against the civilian population via massacres, enslavement and the infliction of horrendous mutilations. Over one million people were killed in the Mozambique war. Infrastructure like roads, railways, trains, bridges, hospitals and schools were destroyed, and their agricultural base undermined. The terror squads also prevented people from farming. In addition, over a million landmines created an artificial famine situation because of the risk to life and limb on the farms.

The second step was the use of 'food aid', delivered to the displaced people and the victims of famine, to ensure compliance with economic conditions and to create long-term food dependency.

The final step was the transference of decision-making from the state to international organizations and NGOs. So thorough was the attack on Mozambican sovereignty that once it was forced to seek Western aid, the Mozambique government had to accept that the NGOs be given the green light in the management of relief operations, including the right to enter any part of its territory and distribute food directly to the population at any place of their choice. Some right-wing NGOs, like World Vision, openly used the relief distributions for political and religious propaganda and while other NGOs, like CARE, were suspected of collaborating with the CIA.

Finally, the Mozambique government had to accept the imposition of 'peace conditions' and 'reconciliation' with its irreconcilable enemy, Renamo, the bandit proxy which was responsible for the countless atrocities and massacre of over one million people. The uneasy truce that resulted created the potential for permanent destabilization.

Sadly, Mozambique's situation is not unique in Africa. Silvia Federici puts it like this:

"...most African countries are practically run by US-supported agencies and NGO's; the sequence ...destruction of infrastructure, imposition of market reforms, forced reconciliation with murderous 'irreconcilable' enemies — destabilization— is found, in different degrees and combinations, everywhere in Africa today, to such a point that countries like Angola and Sudan are in a state of permanent emergency, where their political viability as political entities is now in question."[19]

No African country has been exempt from some form of Western intervention, past or present, and to comprehend the extent of Western humanitarian intervention or imperialism in Africa, it is necessary to review some of their interventions over the last 50 years.

ANGOLA

After the loss of the slaving ports and Elmina Castle to the Dutch and the British, Angola became Portugal's main slave trading port of eastern Africa. Following their independence from the Portuguese, Angola became one of the main battlegrounds of Western superpowers during the Cold War as their Civil War became internationalized.

When an invasion by apartheid South Africa backed by the US came close to overthrowing the newly independent government, Fidel Castro's Cuba sent troops who, together with the soldiers of the Angolan armed forces, the South West African People's Organisation [SWAPO] and Umkhonto we Sizwe [the armed wing of the African National Congress/ ANC], repelled the invaders, much to the annoyance of the US and the South African apartheid regime. Che Guevara, the Cuban icon, made his name defending the newfound freedom of Angola.

Attempts to secure a peaceful solution were scuppered by Henry Kissinger, who did his best to smash the MPLA freedom depredations of another proxy force, the National Union for the Total Independence of Angola [UNITA]. This lead to years of war and over 500,000 deaths and famine. As a result of this, Angola is saturated with landmines and has the highest amputee rate in the world. The late Princess Diana was famously referred to as 'a loose cannon' by the British press because of her campaign against the use of landmines in Angola.[20]

Such was the toll in lives and infrastructure that the South African apartheid regime was alleged to have caused over 1.5 million deaths and $60 billion worth of damage in the newly liberated Portuguese colonies of Angola and Mozambique.21 A UNICEF study estimated the death toll of infants and children in these two countries at 150,000–850,000 in 1988 alone.22

It was only in 2002 when UNITA's leader, Jonas Savimbi, Washington's client, was killed in combat by Angolan government forces in the area, that Angola achieved some kind of stability.

GHANA

Ghana gained its independence on March 6th 1957. Kwame Nkrumah became the first black African leader of the postcolonial period. A staunch Pan-Africanist, Nkrumah declared that Ghana's independence was meaningless unless it was linked up with 'the total liberation of the entire African continent'.[23] Kwame Nkrumah was also outspoken about the fact that there can be no real democracy without economic equality.

He devoted his political life towards creating a union of African states as he saw this as the only way for Africa to develop and acquire the requisite economic and military power to protect itself against imperialist subversion.[24] It was partly due to Kwame Nkrumah's efforts that within three years of Ghanaian independence twenty other African nations became independent and the Organization of African Unity was formed at a meeting of thirty two African countries in Addis Ababa, Ethiopia on May 25th 1963.

Kwame Nkrumah stressed the need for urgent action on a number of issues, namely: a framework for the Constitution for a Union of governments of African States, a common continent-wide program of economic and industrial development, a common African market, a single currency and African monetary system, a common African foreign policy and diplomacy, a common system of defence and common African citizenry.

Nkrumah embarked on an ambitious and extensive project of infrastructure development, including schools, hospitals, housing, motorways and telecommunications. He tried to build an economy based on agriculture and industrialization. Nkrumah attempted to kick-start the Ghanaian economy by the building of the Aswan Dam to utilize Ghana's vast aluminium ore reserves and supply electricity to most of West Africa.

On paper, this was a very good plan but it relied heavily on the previous colonial masters, Britain and the US, who constantly frustrated his efforts. Eventually, he was forced to accept a very bad deal from a US company, which refused to utilize Ghanaian aluminium ore and preferred to ship its own aluminium all the way from the United States. Frustrated by all of this, Nkrumah tried to reduce his country's dependence on the West by strengthening the economic and military ties with Eastern bloc countries. Unfortunately for him, this prompted the West to set about openly undermining him at every opportunity.

Corrupt European politicians and business persons bribed members of his government. The Western media publicly slated his government as being exceedingly corrupt and they constantly undermined Nkrumah's political authority. In the end, a CIA-organized and backed military coup deposed him from power and forced him into exile by Britain, from which he never returned.

In 1997 declassified CIA documents released revealed that the CIA was in close contact with the military coup plotters and had been reporting to Washington up to the day before the coup.

SOUTH AFRICA

Black South Africans were subject to the apartheid system, set up by the British and taken over by the Boers, for over a century. The African National Congress [ANC] and Nelson Mandela led the fight against the apartheid system. The ANC became the principal focus of the CIA, and the UK and the US declared Nelson Mandela a terrorist. According to a 1988 Pentagon report, Nelson Mandela's ANC was described as 'one of the more notorious terrorist groups'.[25]

In the eyes of the West, Nelson Mandela's remarkable success in becoming the President of a free South Africa could in some ways be likened to Osama bin Laden becoming the President of a democratic Saudi Arabia. Nelson Mandela only had his status as an international terrorist revoked by the US following his 90th birthday — many years after retiring from political office.[26]

The CIA helped the South African apartheid intelligence to suppress internal dissent and provided them with specific warnings of planned attacks by the ANC and information on the whereabouts of ANC members residing in neighbouring countries. This led to South Africa sending death squads into neighbouring countries like Mozambique and Botswana to assassinate CIA-fingered individuals. A CIA informant was responsible for the capture of Nelson Mandela while disguised as a chauffeur for a white man, resulting in him going to jail for 40 years.[27]

Throughout South Africa's white apartheid rule, successive British and US governments repeatedly vetoed UN resolutions to impose sanctions on apartheid South Africa. The UK and the US went even further. They illegally supplied arms and provided valuable diplomatic support for the white apartheid South African regime. The Reagan administration and Margaret Thatcher's Tory government steadily increased trade and conducted an illegal arms trade with apartheid South Africa.[28] British Saracen armoured cars took part in the Sharpeville Massacre in South Africa in 1960 and in other incidents for years after.

In 1995, studies on race inequality showed that in South Africa, whites who made up 13% of the population, earned about 61% of the total income, while all black groups [Africans, Coloureds and Indians], who made up 87% of the population, earned only 39% of the income. Africans made up 75% of the population but they receive only 28% of the income. The same study found the lifespan of the black South African to be nine years less than the white South Africans.[29]

SOMALIA

Before he decided to invade Ethiopia, the dictatorial leader of Somalia, Siad Barre, was supported by both the US and the Soviet Union. With the invasion, the Soviet Union ceased their support and assisted the socialist regime in Addis Ababa. Somalia was defeated in the war and this led to rising opposition, culminating in his overthrow. After Barre's downfall, the country was torn apart by inter-clan warfare and the secession of Somaliland in the north and Punt in the north east.

In 1992, Somalia was ravaged by a severe famine and the United States saw an opportunity for a military occupation disguised as 'humanitarian intervention'. US Marines made an unnecessary beach landing, consciously staged for the benefit of the Western media in an intervention they called, 'Operation Restore Hope'.

However, behind the scenes, four US oil giants who held exploratory rights to large areas of land in Somalia were keen on putting an end to the chaos that was affecting their investments and the Pentagon was looking for an opportunity to impress Congress, who were trying to cut down the post-Cold War military budget.

Of little importance to the US was the fact that the famine in Somalia had already peaked before their troops arrived. Soon after their televised landing, they got on with the real business, which was to control and dominate the political situation by eliminating the most powerful warlord, Mohamed Aidid, and his followers.

For several months, US special forces backed by Apache helicopters made 'smash and grab' operations to kill or capture Aidid's men. On several occasions, they machine-gunned Aidid supporters and fired missiles at them. Many Somalian civilians were killed in these attacks. In October, 1993, a daring attempt to capture two leaders of Aidid's clan resulted in the bloody and now famous battle, which left between 500–1000 Somalians dead with many more wounded. The US lost 18 dead, 73 wounded and five helicopters. In an attempt to obfuscate the truth, the one-sided battle was covered by a series of newspaper articles that were turned into a book and then a film called Black Hawk Down.[30] Despite all the media attention given to it by the West, very little mention was made of the death and suffering the Somalis endured. According to official CIA estimates, Operation Restore Hope resulted in the deaths of between 7,000–10,000 Somalians.[31]

In order to administer collective punishment on the Somalis for their rejection, the US closed down its largest bank and telephone service provider, cutting off communications, which included in the region of $500 million sent yearly in remittances by Somalis living abroad. They also cut off Somalia's internet links, monitored their international flights and sent naval forces to barricade the coast.[32]

In a surprising twist, the US, as ever, willing to adopt strange bedfellows as long as it fulfils their ultimate strategic interests, collaborated with Mohamed Aidid's son, the leader of the Somalia Reconciliation and Restoration Council [SRRC] in identifying and locating possible terrorist bases in the period after September 11th 2001.[33]

SUDAN

The humanitarian crisis in the Darfur region in Sudan has been played into the consciousness of the Western public as a reason of Western intervention, particularly by Britain and the United States.

While they attempt to internationalize the battle in Darfur over local resources, which probably dates back several centuries, they omit to tell their Western audience that their interest really lies in Sudan's vast oil reserves, probably as vast or even more than those of Saudi Arabia.

China beat the United States into Sudan and currently controls the oil mines in Sudan. For over a decade, Sudan was listed as a 'rogue state' by the United States and US companies were banned from prospecting in Sudan. However, in this age of humanitarian military intervention, all this may be about to change.

It was alleged that Osama bin Laden was based in Sudan from 1991 to 1996 and his operatives were involved in the deadly attack on US Marines in Mogadishu in 1993. In 1998, President Clinton ordered a missile attack on the Al Shifa pharmaceutical plant in Sudan, claiming it was a 'chemical weapons facility'. This was the source of 90% of the basic medicines in the Sudan, one of the poorest countries in the world.[34]

It was clearly an act of international terrorism. It was followed up by sanctions against Sudan which prevented them from filling the wide medicines gap that was left when the pharmaceutical plant was destroyed. Jonathan Belke of the Near East Foundation, a humanitarian organization, said: *"Tens of thousands of people, many of them children, have died from malaria, tuberculosis and other treatable diseases...* [35] as a result of the bombing.

Sudan requested a United Nations investigation into the US actions, labelling it an act of terrorism. Washington blocked the request. Eventually, Colin Powell brokered a 'peace deal' between the Sudanese government and the US-backed rebels in the South led by the late John Garang, as they tried to increase their influence in the region.[36]

PART TWELVE: AFRICA'S SOVEREIGNTY AND HEALTH

CHAPTER SEVENTY THREE:
RECOLONISING AFRICA

The African continent was never fully decolonised. The coastal Morrocan cities of Ceuta and Melilla remain under Spanish autonomous control. As of present day, in 2020, Morroco, considers both cities under Spanish foreign occupation.

French speaking African countries have not fared much better as their political leaders, economies, resources and therefore their development is firmly under the control of their former colonial masters, France.

Most other African countries, though nominally free, remain firmly attached to their previous colonial masters and continue to supply much needed raw material and human resources to them and other Western partners.

Unfortunately, the avarice of Western capitalism is such that it can never be satisfied with a slice or two of the Africa's resources, it needs the whole pie.

Thus, the need for 'humanitarian intervention' in Africa by the West has never been greater than at present. As the world's available supplies of oil dwindle, largely due to increased demand from the West and emerging industrial giants like China and India, and with the unrest and war in the Middle East, oil prices are set to rise steadily and with that the cost of living in the West.

In 2001, the US Vice-President Dick Cheney projected in his National Energy Policy Development Group reported that Africa would be one of the fastest growing sources of oil and gas for the US market. The chairman of the House Subcommittee on Africa, Ed Royce, buttressed this view:

"African oil should be treated as a priority for US national security post 9-11, and I think that post 9-11 it's occurred to all of us that our traditional sources of oil are not as secure as we once thought they were"[1]

In 2002, the New York Times also noted the increasing importance of African oil:

"Africa, the neglected step child of American diplomacy, is rising in strategic importance to Washington policy makers, and one word sums up the reason, oil."[2]

In recognition of this increased strategic importance, the African Oil Policy Initiative Group [AOPIG] was created in 2002. This group is composed of Washington policymakers, members of Congress, industry executives, consultants and investors who have drawn up a blueprint for US energy and mineral resources interest in Africa.[3]

In June 2002 Secretary of State Colin Powell was dispatched to visit all oil-rich African countries. Significantly, he avoided Nigeria, their most important African oil supplier because of the widespread and popular resistance against oil companies in the Niger Delta region. Former President George W. Bush made a trip to Nigeria to reinforce US ties on Nigeria's oil wealth.

In July 2003, Bush toured African countries in an attempt to strengthen ties with pliable African states. While George Bush endeavoured to be photographed hugging AIDS orphans, and his wife, Laura Bush shed tears for them, his administration refused to back The Global Fund to Fight AIDS, Tuberculosis and Malaria. They set up their own organization, which is subordinate to US interests. At the same time, back home, his Republican-controlled senate cut back funding pledged for the $15 billion AIDS initiative by about $1 billion a year.[4]

Currently the United States imports 15% of its total oil requirements from Africa, namely Nigeria, Equatorial Guinea, Angola and Gabon, and this was predicted to rise to 25% by 2020 according to the US National Intelligence Council.[5] Nigeria is the sixth largest oil supplier to the United States at present.

The Bush administration had quietly increased its military ties with Nigeria and pressured the Nigerian government to pull out of the

Organization of Petroleum Exporting Countries [OPEC]. It has always been the United States' long-term strategy to weaken OPEC by pressuring weaker countries to leave the organization thus reducing its hold on the oil markets. President Bush's African policy was described as, *'build the military and extract the oil'*.[6]

Plans to increase US presence in Africa have been underway for decades, including construction of a pipeline linking southern Chad to the Atlantic ports. It has increased the number of its military bases all over Africa, including a naval base at Sao Tomé and Principe close to the strategically important Atlantic oil-bearing basin of the Gulf of Guinea. The US is also working through proxies in Africa, especially Nigeria, where the US has trained five battalions of troops.

A New York Times report on July 5th 2005 stated: *'The US is seeking to expand its presence in Africa through new basing agreements and training exercises'*.[7]

Longstanding military ties with allies like Morocco and Tunisia are being enhanced. Long-term military bases in countries like Algeria and Mali are being sought. Aircraft refuelling agreements with Senegal and Uganda are being expanded.[8] The US European Command will rotate troops into 'bare-bones' camps or airfields in Africa while 1,800 Marines continue to be stationed in Djibouti for 'anti-terrorism operations' in the Horn of Africa. General James L. Jones, Head of US European Command explained that he envisaged a 'flexible' family of bases from which operations ranging from small special forces interventions to brigade-size operations can be mounted.[9]

While the African continent battles with the AIDS pandemic, poverty, conflicts and natural disasters, the United States and its Western allies are steadfastly focused on Africa's natural resources under the guise of their phoney 'war on terror'.

During the Cold War, US aid and alliances to Africa were aimed at reducing Soviet and Chinese influence. Since the Cold War with Russia has ended, Africa has less direct US foreign investment than any other region in the world. In fact, less than 1% of the total US investments around the world went to Africa in 2001 and more than half of that was spent on the oil industry.[10] Since 2002, the $700 million the US pledged for the heavily indebted countries initiative has yet to be disbursed. The US made a relatively negligible contribution of $200 million to the UN global AIDS fund, which needs $7–$10 billion.[11]

The African Growth and Opportunity Act [AGOA] was established and signed into law by Bill Clinton and enacted in 2000 by the US congress to assist sub-Saharan African countries to export to the US. However, there was little African involvement in its creation and 90% of the export to the US has been oil. It also contravenes WTO rules on trade and contains a clause that requires participating African countries not to oppose US foreign policy.

It also deflects attention from the fact that the US continues to subsidise its farmers by up to $200 billion a year to the detriment of African farmers.

The picture could not be clearer — America and its Western allies' strategic interests in Africa are primarily focused on oil, mineral resources, and militarizing the continent rather than tackling any humanitarian crises like AIDS and poverty.

In 2004 British Prime Minister Tony Blair proposed a 15,000-man strong EU African intervention force. At the time, he stated that Britain would train up to 40,000 African troops, over four years. The US had already been providing training for an African force since 1997. This 'African' force would be the new face of Western intervention in Africa in the years to come.

Crucially, Tony Blair also stated that this Western-controlled intervention force would intervene in African matters, as the West chose, with or without the agreement of the African Union or the African country involved.[12]

Since January 2014, there has been a sharp rise in the number of Western countries building up troops in Africa. The US Africa Command [AFRICOM] was created by George Bush's administration. Owing to resistance from African nations it had its headquarters in Stuttgart, Germany. Only Liberia expressed a desire to host AFRICOM on African soil. Despite this, the quiet build of Western troops and bases in Africa is alarming.

The US now has a military presence in 38 out of the 54 African nations. The US has increased its drone strikes in Somalia and in January 2014 killed an alleged Al-Shabab militant aged between 4–5 years old.[13]

France is particularly active in Africa, with significantly increased Franco-US military cooperation despite their outwardly prickly relationship. During the Tuareg rebellion in Mali in 2012 France participated with about 4000 troops. Another 1000 troops were sent to the Central African Republic to suppress a Muslim take over. According to Associated Press, France planned to deploy 3000 permanent French soldiers in the Sahel region and pre-position their fighter jets in Chad.

Other European countries, like Germany and Britain, have agreed to supply a rapid deployment force of about 600 troops to bolster the French efforts in the Central African Republic.

President Obama despatched some of the US's elite forces to Sierra Leone in 2014 to assist in the fight against the Ebola virus. They are allegedly helping to build the infrastructure and hospitals needed to fight the virus. However, the 101st Airborne is an elite division of combat troops trained to kill people and has no specialist experience or training in providing medical treatment for the Ebola virus.[14]

The British Prime Minister, David Cameron, as expected, also dispatched British troops to assist the US marines fight the Ebola virus. He could have sent highly trained medical staff and financial support to the UN and WHO's efforts to fight the Ebola virus but could not resist the opportunity to put more Western boots on the ground in Africa.

In May 2017 President Trump became embroiled in the fallout from the killing of four American servicemen and several Nigerian troops in an ambush by Isis-affiliated Islamic fundamentalists in Niger. President Trump has been unable to clarify what American troops were doing in the region.[15]

In the April 2000 summit, the Non-Aligned Movement [NAM], representing 80% of the world's population, unanimously rejected the West's neo-colonial gunboat approach to international affairs. It issued a detailed critique of the neo-liberal social-economic policies, called globalisation in the West, and firmly rejected the West's 'right of humanitarian intervention'.[16]

Such is the plight of Africa, that it has fallen to old rock stars to highlight the rocky state of affairs. Bob Geldof and Bono both appear genuinely committed to poverty reduction and have successfully mobilized millions of people around the world and raised millions of dollars for good causes in Africa. There is however, unfortunately, a caveat. Save for an insignificant 'slap on the wrist' the old rock musicians have not challenged the root causes of Africa's plight or the same Western governments and multinationals that are directly behind the orchestration and maintenance of world poverty. Indeed, Western media have even portrayed people like George W. Bush and Tony Blair as the saviours of the Third World.

When the World Bank approved another debt relief package laden with the usual pre-conditions of liberalization and privatizations and many more that have wreaked so much havoc in Africa, Bob Geldof praised it as 'a victory' of millions of people in campaigns around the world'. Bono referred to it as 'a little piece of history'. Their refusal to highlight the negative effects of the neo-liberal policies of the World Bank and Western governments in Africa has provided the Western governments and multinationals a convenient cover for their nefarious activities — so much so that they wish to identify with the rock stars and in this way promote their own appeal to wider audience. For example, after the G8 summit of 2005 Tony Blair collaborated with Bob Geldof in the establishment of the Commission for Africa and other issues, thus lending credence to the notion that Blair's policies were beneficial to Africa.

In effect, Bono and Bob Geldof gave legitimacy to the heartless exploitation of Western power in Africa: *"Their campaign portrays the enemies of the poor as their saviours"*.[17]

A critic of US policy in Africa, Bill Martin, argued:

'Bill Clinton broke new ground by forcefully applying free-market policies to Africa and, often unnoticed, by placing Africa on the US foreign policy map by casting it as a transnational security threat... Secretary of State, Madeline Albright, was blunt in 1999: 'Africa is a major battleground in the

global fight against terror, crime, drugs, illicit arms-trafficking, and disease."[18]

Bush's discourse and web of military engagements after 9/11 have turned these democratic policy statements into concrete actions, sustaining corrupt allies in the hope they can contain local unrest and resistance to corrupt local states, international capital and imperialist interventions. The discourse of internal and international terrorism is thus not simply being used as a substitute for the Cold War but it is forging new military and ideological networks capable of repressing internal dissent in the guise of pursuing 'foreign' terrorists.[19]

The scale of US continent-wide military planning in Africa is truly alarming. The US military has earmarked about $700 million to develop a 75,000-strong 'UN' peacekeeping force, with $480 million dedicated to African soldiers, the African face of Western imperialism. In 2004 during an interview with the BBC Charles Wald, a US Army General in control of the Africa Programme of European Command, told the BBC that he aimed to have five brigades with 15,000 men working in cooperation with regional partners including South Africa, Kenya, Nigeria, and two others yet to be chosen.[20]

It is important to start joining the dots to appreciate the unbroken chain of Western imperial activity that runs across political affiliations, parties, and countries — the 'Africa programme of European Command'; Clinton's Democratic policies concretised by US, British and French military bases springing up all over the continent. Today, African coastal waters are permanently patrolled by US and British warships.

Western aid to Africa is very often a leading headline in Western papers. Millions of pounds and dollars are pledged and stories carried in Western papers as if the money has already changed hands. However, spin money is not legal tender. Over half the money pledged on the news or in the newspapers is never given — and much of that which does, eventually ends up back in the hands of Western multinationals and expatriates.

An Action Aid report stated that up to a quarter of the aid provided by rich countries — up to $20 billion a year — goes to funding expensive and often ineffective Western consultants, research and training, rather than going to the African people in need. The vast majorities of these expatriate consultants are British and they can earn up to $200,000 a year. According to one report, in Ghana even relatively inexperienced expatriate consultants were earning per day what Ghanaian government officials earned a month.[21]

Some Westerners have tried to liken Western aid to Africa to the Marshall Plan used by the US to reconstruct Europe after the Second World War. Nothing could be farther from the truth. The US invested about $13 billion in post-war Europe. The Marshall Plan was not all altruism. It help reversed the effects of the Wall Street crash and the prolonged economic depression that ravaged until the Second World War. It cemented the US's place as the leading economic giant in the world and helped America to create a huge market for its goods, outlets for surpluses and tremendously boosted their industry.

As the Cold War settled in favour of the West, several initiatives aimed at refocusing attention on the true aims and benefits of aid to Africa were started. In the 1970s and 1980s the Brandt Commission produced a report to show the way forward with aid.

Mass movements like Live Aid led by Bob Geldof in the 1980s and Jubilee 2000 in the late 1990s showed Western politicians that there was an advantage to be gained by appearing to take the issues of world poverty seriously.

However, September 11th provided the West with the opportunity to swing away from liberal ideals, back to the rightwing Cold War policy, as President Bush clearly stated, 'You are either for or against us'. During the Cold War, aid was an essential weapon in the arsenal of the US. Funds were usually dispensed in the following order — military aid first and reconstruction programs to follow. Ex-colonial powers like France and Britain negotiated numerous aid agreements with their previous colonies as aid became a means of protecting self-interest and maintaining their influence.

In 1978 the UK Minister of Overseas Development, Judith Hart, summed up the importance of aid contributions to Britain's industrial strategy:

'There are two basic ways in which the aids programme helps British

Industry. By helping foster income creation, it increases the overseas markets for British goods. In the process, it also provides opportunities for aid-financed exports both under bilateral and multilateral aid agreements."[22]

Communist countries like the Soviet Union and China also sought to gain influence and maintain their strategic interests in Africa. In 1949 the socialist countries formed the Council for Mutual Economic Assistance [Comecon], through which they offered subsidised oil, technological assistance, grants and loans, all tied to the purchase of Eastern Bloc goods.

In brief, aid was good business. Right from the very start, poor countries were paying more to their donor countries than they were receiving in aid grants, loans, and technical assistance. In reality, aid has simply been another way of maintaining political, economic and military hegemony over underdeveloped countries. Western aid also provides outlets for surplus production. David Dollar of the World Bank stated: *"The direction of foreign aid is dictated as much by political and strategic considerations as by the economic needs and policy performance of the recipients."*[23]

Africa's abundance of natural and human resources coupled with the defenceless and dependent nature of the continent make it the prime candidate for all sorts of deleterious Western interventions in the years to come. Robert Cooper, foreign policy advisor to Tony Blair in 2002, set out the mission for 'enlightened states': *"The need...for colonization is as great as it ever was in the 19th century to bring to the rest of the world the principles of order, freedom, and justice to which 'Post-modern' societies are dedicated".*[24]

In light of the above, this move can only be interpreted as a further implementation of the West's covert plan to re-introduce colonialism in Africa in the face of stiff economic competition from China and other emerging economies.

The West's humanitarian intervention in Africa is in fact a gradual covert re-colonization of African countries which currently in full swing. It walks hand-in-hand with their other efforts to undermine Africa's most essential and precious commodity yet, its health.

CHAPTER SEVENTY FOUR

MONKEY BUSINESS: HIV AND AIDS

The scourge of the Human Immunedeficiency Virus (HIV) and the associated Autoimmune Deficiency Syndrome (AIDS) that is ravaging Africa is one of the most serious problems facing Africa today. Like most untoward things, the West alleges that HIV and AIDS originated in Africa. However, there are more unanswered questions than answers — about the origin and spread of AIDS. No matter how eloquently and convincingly Western scientists have put forward their arguments, AIDS is a world pandemic that disproportionately affects Africa.

AIDS is a socio-political problem as well as a medical one, as African children, youth and young adults are mostly affected. In 2019 UNAIDS estimates that were about 37.9 million people live with HIV worldwide.[1]

Sub-Saharan Africa alone accounted for 70% of people living with HIV and the same percentage of all AIDS deaths; 62% of all the world's HIV carriers aged 15–24 are in Africa.[2] Worldwide, AIDS has killed over 25 million people and has incapacitated many more.[3] HIV rose from 40 million carriers worldwide to about 60 million in 2015.

Given how developed the world is today, it is truly shocking that only 28% of the world's AIDS patients are on retroviral drugs and just one in ten pregnant women with AIDS gets treatment to prevent transmission to their unborn children.[4] Dr Brian Gazzard of the British HIV association said: *"The HIV epidemic is essentially uncontrolled, uncontrolled in Africa, uncontrolled completely in Asia right now."*[5]

The scourge of AIDS devastates three generations: the patient, the children and the care-givers, often grandparents, who have to provide for orphaned children even though they may need care themselves. Africa has an estimated 52 million orphans. AIDS was responsible for about 3 million of these in 2001. This figure rose to 5 million by the year 2016 and seems set to rise even higher in the next decade.[6]

The primary mode of transfer in Africa is heterosexual and young women appear to be disproportionately affected. Some suggested reasons are earlier sexual activity, greater biological/physical vulnerability, powerlessness to insist on condom use and lower socio-economic status.[7] According to development charity, Action Aid, over the past two decades the average life expectancy for Africans has fallen by 15 years as a direct result of HIV/AIDS. Currently, 161 children out of every thousand will die before their fifth birthday. In places, Niger for example, this figure is possibly as high as one in four.

Mike Rowson, Executive Director of an organization challenging health barriers, Medact, stated:

'It's partly due to HIV, but there's also lack of public trust and confidence in the health system, and widespread evidence that health care costs are pushing people into poverty.'[8]

People just need painkillers so that they can die without pain, and they don't even have paracetamol. It is symptomatic of the total degradation of society. Africa is falling off the edge of the world economy.

It is has been estimated that 40% of the population of Botswana live with HIV and life expectancy in Zambia is under 35 years due primarily to AIDS.[9]

Given the gravity of the AIDS pandemic it is essential to get to the root cause of this pandemic, and in so doing, garner a deeper understanding of it. This is the very reason that scientists do research. Medicine has only progressed to where it is today because of a logical, evidence-based approach.

In 2000, at the seventh Conference on Retroviruses and Opportunistic Infections, a study by Dr Bettle Kober of the Los Alamos National Laboratory suggested that the first case of HIV occurred in West Africa, with a plus or minus 20-year margin of error, meaning that HIV could have been in Africa from about 1919–1959.[10] Furthermore, in October 2014, researchers from Oxford University, England claimed to have successfully reconstructed the genetic history of the HIV-1 group M pandemic. They claim that the common ancestor of the HIV group M is 'highly likely to have emerged in Kinshasa around 1920.'

They also stated that various strains of HIV have jumped from primates to humans at least 13 times but only one such transmission event has led to the global pandemic. They claim that the spread of HIV was aided by a 'perfect storm of factors', including strong railway links during Belgian colonial rule, and changes to the sex trade which combined to see HIV emerge from Kinshasa and spread across the globe between the 1920s and 1950s.

The senior author of the study, Oliver Pybus, of the Department of Zoology, Oxford University stated:

"For the first time we analysed all the available evidence using the latest phylogeographic techniques, which enable us to statistically estimate where a virus comes from. This means we can say with a high degree of certainty where and when the HIV pandemic originated."[11]

However, this is not consistent with available medical data and statistics as the leading causes of death in Africans between 1950 and 1990.

The World Health Organisation (WHO) has been collecting and analysing the leading causes of death from all countries and continents around the world since 1950.

In 1996, a WHO report titled: Emerging and re-emerging infectious diseases stated this about HIV/AIDS:

'At least 30 new diseases have been scientifically recognised around the world in the last 20 years. The existence of HIV, the virus that causes AIDS, was unknown barely a decade ago.'[12]

That same year, researchers Adetunji, J. A. C. J., Murrary and T. Evans presented a papercalled the "Causes of Death in Africa: A Review" to the Population Association of America in May 1996.

The study reviewed information from 21 studies and identified 3,818 deaths due to maternal causes.

It also documented 3 sources of data on causes of adult mortality; 2 from vital records in Lagos (1977), Abijdan (1987-92), and the Adult Morbidity and Mortality Project (AMMP) in Tanzania in 1992.

The data from Lagos predates the HIV/AIDS pandemic and records accidents and violence as the leading causes of death (26.3%). The data from Abijdan, that falls within the HIV/AIDS period, shows that hypertension (31%), diarrheoal disease (11%) and HIV/AIDS (10.5%) as the leading causes of death.[13]

We must not forget that the simian virus in monkeys has co-existed with the human population in Africa for millennia. Despite the explanations given by Western scientists it appears more logical that given their explanation that the first Western country to become infected should have been Belgium, the former colonial masters in the Congo, rather than the US. Nor have they have provided an explanation as to why HIV was apparently latent from the 1920s until it was first identified in the USA.

In 1981, Center for Disease Control (CDC) in the US, published a report about 5 previously healthy homosexual men who became infected with Pneumocystis Jirovecii and Carini, normally harmless fungi that usually live as commensals in the human body.

The CDC noted that these fungi almost never affected people with normal immune systems.

On May 11th 1982, The New York Times published a shocking article about a new immune system disorder which had affected 335 people, mostly homosexual men and had killed 136 of them.

At this time this mysterious disease of the immune system was called the gay-related immune deficiency disease or GRID.[14]

The deadly 1918 flu pandemic that killed 500,000 worldwide was named the 'Spanish flu' by the Western media for political reasons; because it was largely carried by the Spanish newspapers and the fact that Spain had remained neutral during the First World War. In fact, it is thought that flu may have originated in Kansas, USA and was spread by US troops into Europe and then around the world.

Between 1981 and 1990, the largely US based immunodeficiency disease, GRID, largely affected the homosexual community and killed high profile victims like the famous actor Rock Hudson and British singer, Freddie Mercury.

Therefore, the fact that Africans are now dying of AIDS in large numbers does not necessarily mean AIDS started in Africa. The main reason for Africa's high mortality and morbidity rates is because of inadequate prevention and lack of access to life-saving medicine. The death rate in itself is not proof of its origins.

These are some of the main facts concerning AIDS as they are known. The human immunodeficiency virus or HIV is part of a family of viruses called the Lenti virus. They are found in non-human primates as well where they are known as simian [monkey] viruses. Current thinking is that there are two main types of HIV; types 1 and 2. HIV may be a descendant of the simian virus found in the green monkey, which is found in most of West Africa.

The earliest strain of HIV is thought to have been transferred from animals to humans [zoonosis] by the eating of monkey meat. Professor Paul Sharp of the University of Nottingham and Dr Beatrice Hahn of the University of Alabama supported this theory in 1999 and published a paper postulating that chimpanzees were the source of HIV.[15] HIV was supposed to have been found in the plasma sample of an adult male living in the area now known as the Democratic Republic of the Congo in 1959!, the blood of an American teenager in St Louis in 1969 and the blood of a Norwegian sailor in 1976.[16]

Given these assertions, it is paradoxical that the first clearly documented cases of AIDS occurred in the USA in 1981. In April 1984, Robert Gallo at the National Cancer Institute claimed to have discovered the HIV/AIDS virus in the US and at about the same time there was a counterclaim by Luc Montagnier in the Pasteur Institute based in France. In both instances, these viruses were only discovered while scientists were experimenting on biological weapons.[17]

A further complicating factor in the origin of AIDS is the controversial polio vaccine that was given to over a million people in Africa from 1957–1960. The affected areas, like the Democratic Republic of the Congo, correspond to the same regions in Africa worst hit by AIDS today. The poliovirus was grown [cultured] on monkey kidneys, which may have been contaminated with SIV, and were not screened for the monkey virus until 1984. Another monkey virus, SV40, is known to have been transmitted through the polio vaccines after a specific pool of Koprowski vaccines were reviewed.

To facilitate the transfer of the virus from one species to another it is necessary to reduce the immunity of the host so it does not destroy the vaccine or give it to infants under a month old whose immune systems are not yet fully developed.

Thus the majority of the Koprowski vaccines were given to infants less than a month old and in one trial, some infants were given fifteen times the standard dose to ensure effective immunization.[18]

If HIV was first found in the blood of an African in the Congo in 1959, it appears to coincide with European disseminated use of contaminated vaccines to millions of African children at the time. It is possible that these immune systems of these children were rendered more susceptible to acquiring HIV by the polio virus.

Historical precedents show that it was not just the HIV/AIDS viruses that have caused problems in humans or have been suspected of iatrogenic transfer to man. Several other viruses implicated in human cancers and diseases have been iatrogenically transmitted from contaminated live vaccines used widely in humans. In 1999, researchers found the SCMV monkey virus in damaged human brain cells. The virus has also turned up in brain cells from people with a wide variety of diseases, including Parkinson's, Alzheimer's, mental disorders like anxiety, depression and schizophrenia and others like autism, unexplained encephalopathy and chronic vegetative states. The SCMV is known to come from the African Green monkey, the same ones used by SmithKline Beecham. SmithKline Beecham uses the kidneys of African Green monkeys imported by a Belgian company to make the live polio vaccine. Both the UK and US governments have admitted that the polio vaccine introduced in 1955 was contaminated with the SV40 rhesus monkey virus.

The SV40 virus is known to inactivate the p53 gene that prevents multiplication of aberrant cells and is the key genetic human defence against cancer. The SV40 virus has also turned up in many brain cancers. In the 1970s the SV40 virus was found to occur in one third of all human bone cancers. In the 1990's, the SV40 virus was found in 80% of childhood tumours and 80% of a form of lung cancer called mesothelioma by researchers.[19]

Thus, it appears that theareas where the poliovirus was experimentally developed in central Africa are the very same areas that AIDS devastated initially. Over 400 chimpanzees were held in a farm where their kidneys were harvested and used to produce CHAFF or chimpanzee live attenuated vaccines. The monkey version of HIV — SIV — was only officially screened out of polio vaccines in 1987, over 30 years after the vaccine was produced.[20]

Asian monkeys, like their African cousins, were also found to be infected with an HIV-like virus. However, there has been no evidence to show that they displayed any ill effects. While the macaque virus has many similarities to HIV-2, its gene sequence has been shown to be up to 40% different to human HIV-1. In fact, the closest variants of the macaque monkey virus to the human variants have only been found in Asian macaques born in primary centres in the US and have never been detected in Asian monkeys caught in the wild.[21] According to the leader of the Primate Research Center, Professor Ronald C. Desrosiers, who sequenced the virus, it may be 'an artefact of captivity acquired from other species'.[22]

If HIV/AIDS was endemic in Africa by 1959, as claimed by Western scientists, why was it not killing off an African population living under the nightmare of slavery, colonization, war and mass displacement, amongst the other diseases like malaria and tuberculosis known at the time?

Why did it wait until after 1984 to take hold in Africa? In fact, there is no known AIDS epidemic in Africa until the early 1990s, nearly six years after it was discovered in America.

Undisputed methods of spread of the HIV virus prior to the African and worldwide pandemic have been as follows: through blood transfusions — following the increase in blood transfusions in the 1960s, especially after the Vietnam War, haemophiliacs, who were transfused with factor

VIII and victims of trauma transfused with unscreened blood and blood products from donors, intravenous drug use — the use of heroin rose dramatically after the Vietnam War and with it sharing of contaminated needles and blood borne diseases and homosexuals — the HIV/AIDS virus and the associated conditions were first described in homosexual white males in the United States.

Today heterosexual transmission is the most important mode of spreading the disease around the world and the major difference in the outcome for Africa in contrast to the West has been the availability of multidrug regimes, treatment and greater awareness.

The theory of a zoonosis, transferring the HIV virus from monkeys to humans, is all well and good, However, it then begs the question as to how the white male homosexual population in California, USA became the first clearly documented population affected by HIV. Did white homosexual males in California eat green monkey meat? The first reported AIDS cases, the natural history of the disease and its clinical presentation were clearly described in the white male homosexual population long before heterosexual transmission of AIDS became the most important mode of transmission of the virus not only in Africa but all around the world.

Perhaps Western scientists should also put forward a 'green monkey meat theory'. Following the logic of Western scientists, it is possible then that the so-called patient zero, a Canadian flight attendant, Gaëtan Douglas, who is claimed to have spread the HIV virus worldwide, may have eaten or brought back contaminated green monkey meat from Africa to the United States — the green monkey meat which was eaten by the US homosexual population and HIV then spread sexually and through contaminated blood products and needles throughout the world, and back to Africa.[23]

Officially, the possibility of HIV being deployed as a biological weapon is widely considered to be in the realm of conspiracy theories, however, historical precedents do not support this naive view. Human beings have practiced biological warfare throughout history. Deliberate contamination of food and water supplies with poison and other contagious material has been used in warfare by people for millennia.

The earliest recorded use of a biological weapon is in Hittite texts from 1500–1200BC. The Hittites drove victims of tularaemia into enemy lands causing an epidemic.[24]

Poison-tipped arrows were used in ancient Greece around 590 BC and around 130 BC Roman Commander Manius Aquillius poisoned the wells of besieged cities.

Millions of Native Americans died owing to lack of immunity when exposed to European diseases like smallpox. However, European colonizers were not ignorant concerning their lack of immunity and there is evidence to suggest that the British exploited the vulnerability of the Native Americans to their diseases and deliberately spread the virus in order to exterminate them.

During Pontiac's Rebellion of 1763–1766, the British colonialists handed out smallpox-infected blankets to native American Indians with the aim of spreading the disease.[25] A historian, Francis Parkman, references letters from June 29th, and July 13th, 16th and 26th 1763, between a British Commander, Lord Jeffrey Amherst and Swiss British Officer, Colonel Henry Bouquet, who discussed the topic of deliberately infecting native Americans during the conflict. Lord Amherst wrote on July 16th 1763:

'P.S. You will Do well to try to Inoculate the Indians by means of Blankets, as well as try Every other method that can serve to Extirpate this Execrable Race. I should be very glad your scheme for Hunting them Down by Dogs could take Effect…'

On July 26th 1763 Henry Bouquet replied:

'I received yesterday your Excellency's letters of 16th with their disclosures. The signal for Indian messengers, and all your directions will be observed.'

It is noteworthy that Australian Aborigines have also always maintained that the British deliberately spread smallpox in 1789.[26]

In the 20th century sophisticated bacteriological, virological and chemical techniques allowed many developed nations to produce and stockpile biological and chemical weapons. Commonly known biological agents for warfare include anthrax, Brucella and tularaemia while viral agents include smallpox and viral haemorrhagic fever and toxins like botulinum and ricin.

The exponential development of weaponisation techniques allowed developed countries to deliver these deadly viruses covertly and overtly so as to infect or poison large numbers of a civilian population in a short space of time. For instance, after the Second World War, the US developed a biological aerosol in a bursting bomblet to aid the delivery of biological weapons. It was estimated that a B-47 bomber using an E 120 spraying spherical bomblet [SUU-24 A dispenser] could infect 50% or more of a population in a sixteen square mile radius with tularaemia.[27]

The US has carried out unethical human experiments for many years. In the 1840s, Dr J. Marion Sims, considered the 'father of gynaecology', performed surgical experiments on female African slaves without anaesthesia. Most of his victims died of infection contracted during his experiments. In another experiment to test his theories on Trismus, or lockjaw, he used a shoemaker's anvil to remove the skull bones of babies from enslaved African women.[28]

In 1846, Dr Walter F. Jones of Petersburg, Virginia, described in his journals how he poured boiling water onto the backs of naked African slaves afflicted with typhoid pneumonia at four hourly intervals because he thought this might 'cure the disease'.[29]

In the 1940s, the Statesville Penitentiary was used for a controlled study of the effects of malaria on its prisoners. The study was carried out by the Department of Medicine at the University of Chicago, the United States Army and the State Department until 1969.[30] In 1946–1948 President Truman collaborated with the Guatemalan President Juan Jose Arevalo, US researchers and with Guatemalan officials, to infect prostitutes deliberately with syphilis and other sexually transmitted diseases. About 1500 people, including prison inmates, insane asylum inmates and Guatemalan soldiers were involved in the tests in order to gauge the efficacy of penicillin in treating sexually transmitted diseases. It is estimated that up to 5,500 Guatemalans were involved in the study which was led by John Charles Cutler, who later took part in the Tuskegee syphilis experiment, financed by the Pan American Health Sanitary

Bureau [now the World Health Organisation], the Public Health Service, the National Institute for Health and the Guatemalan government. In 2010, President Obama officially apologised for the Guatemalan study on behalf of the US.[31]

It is particularly surprising, or perhaps typical, that several human experimentation studies carried out by the US after the Second World War, including the Tuskegee syphilis experiment, were ongoing while Nazi doctors were being tried at the Nuremberg trials and later executed for their own grotesque human experimentation studies. In fact, at the Nuremberg trials, Nazi doctors cited the precedent of US malaria experiments as part of their defence. The Nuremberg trials led to the promulgation of the Nuremberg Code prohibiting doctors from carrying out unethical human experiments.

From the 1950s to 1972, mentally disabled children at the Willowbrook State School in Staten Island, New York, were deliberately infected with viral hepatitis. Their parents were promised enrolment into the Willowbrook School in exchange for signing a consent form for alleged 'vaccinations'.[32] These procedures involved deliberately infecting the children with viral hepatitis by feeding them an extract made from the faeces of patients infected with viral hepatitis.

In 1956 and 1957, the US army carried out a biological warfare experiment in Savannah, Georgia and Avon Park, Florida. They released millions of yellow fever and dengue fever infected mosquitoes to see how the disease would spread. Hundreds of people fell ill with fevers, encephalitis and typhoid fever. Respiratory problems and still births were recorded and several people died. Army researchers pretended to be public health workers so that they could record symptoms, photograph and perform tests on their victims.[33]

Human experimentation was also carried out in the military and their Secret Service departments looking to develop new physical and psychological torture techniques. After the Cold War started, unethical human experiments were heavily funded by the US government in a bid to develop more effective interrogation and torture methods.

In 1957, Dr Ewan Cameron of the Allan Memorial Institute,

Montreal, Canada, began a covert CIA-funded program called MKULTRA Subproject 31. Dr Cameron designed experiments to completely erase a subject's mind and memory of his victims and then re-pattern them in a manner of his choosing. First, he would break them down psychologically to the level of an infant and then attempt to rebuild their personality into what he liked. He used drug and insulin cocktails, induced comas, high voltage electric shocks, sensory deprivation, hooding, humiliation and sexual abuse amongst other techniques. Dr Cameron regularly travelled around US military installations to lecture and teach his interrogation techniques.[34]

Given this background, it came as no surprise when in 2001 Dr Frank Donoghue, CEO of the Physicians for Human Rights [PHR], reported a series of war crimes and instances of human experimentation following George W. Bush's invasion of Afghanistan.

In November 2001, US forces and their Afghan collaborator, the warlord Abdul Daustam, while on the payroll of the CIA, massacred over 2000 Taliban fighters who had surrendered to them in Dashte-e-Leili in Afghanistan. Many prisoners perished of suffocation and thirst when they were packed liked sardines into the 'convoy of death'. Some survivors recounted licking the sweat off each other just to survive. Most of the Taliban fighters who died were buried in mass graves but some of the survivors were transported to Guantanamo Bay prison where, as in Abu Ghraib in Iraq later, they were tortured with sleep deprivation, water-boarding, stress positions, isolation, humiliation, sexual abuse, electric shocks and much more.[35]

The Germans were the first to use chemical weapons in World War One. They released vast quantities of chlorine gas and hoped that the wind would carry it up to the Allied trenches. In retaliation, the French weaponised their artillery to contain phosgene gas. In 1919, with the approval of Winston Churchill, the British used mustard gas in aerial bombardments in Mesopotamia, modern day Iraq. In 1935, fascist Italy also used mustard gas in their invasion of Ethiopia resulting in an estimated 150,000 deaths from chemical warfare alone.[36]

Biological and chemical warfare developed rapidly and by the Second

World War weaponisation techniques to cause mass casualties were perfected. The Japanese, led by Shiro Ishiri, started a biological weapons research facility in 1930 at the Tokyo Army Medical School. It is estimated that they killed as many as 600 prisoners a year in human experiments in just one of their 26 centres.[37] During the war they bombed Ningbo, China with ceramic bombs full of fleas carrying the deadly bubonic plague. Modern Chinese historians estimate that 400,000 Chinese people died as a direct result of Japanese field testing and operational use of biological weapons.[38] Following the Second World War, the US granted Japanese biological weapons researchers from the infamous Norberto Institute immunity from prosecution in exchange for information on their human experiments.

The US first developed their biological and chemical weapons facility at Dugway Proving Grounds in Utah. In 1971, President Nixon merged the cancer research and biological warfare units, based at the US Army's bio warfare department at Fort Detrick, Maryland.[39]

In the 1970s Henry Kissinger oversaw a CIA biological weapons program called MK:NAOMI. This coincidentally was the same time that the Rockefeller Population Council was urging third world depopulation.[40] It is highly coincidental that Henry Kissinger was also a leading adviser to Merck pharmaceuticals, whose president, George W. Merck, also had been America's lead biological weapons director following World War Two. Many scientists allege that SIV was transformed into HIV in the early 1970s. In a further twist, Henry Kissinger also worked with a weapons contractor, Litton's Industries, whose president was serving as an overseer of Litton's medical subsidiary, Bionetics.[41] Bionetics was responsible for running the National Cancers Simian Cancer Program and the biological weapons testing centre at Fort Detrick, Maryland. In the 1970s, Bionetics was once responsible for supplying all the chimpanzees, monkeys, monkey viruses and primate cell lines for US government-funded virus cancer research, biological weapons development and HBV vaccine manufacturing.

A leading medical doctor and public health specialist from the University of Harvard, Dr Leonard Horowitz, deeply implicated Bionetics in his theory about the dissemination of contaminated HBV vaccines and the possible transformation of HIV into eleven deadly strains.[42]

While evidence about biological warfare is circumstantial and shrouded in secrecy, it is no secret that the US has been concerned about world population control since the 1920s. Prior to the Second World War and in anticipation of the establishment of the US as the sole superpower, an extremely influential body in the US, the Council for Foreign Relations [CFR] led by the Rockefellers and the American Eugenics Society urged the US government in its 'War and Peace Study' to implement worldwide population control even down to a genetic level.[43] The CFR foresaw the US's post-war role as an imperial giant. Rather than directly controlling colonies around the world, like the previous colonial masters, they argued for controlling their economies and exerting influence instead.

The Rockefeller Foundation, through the Council for Foreign Relations, saw the production of genetically modified foods as the ultimate tool for social engineering and control. They aimed to use genetics and food technology to exert control over the biologic essence of human beings down to their reproduction, hormones, psychology and genes. Contraceptive corn, containing in-grown contraceptives, was later provided as food aid to Third World countries by the US and its subsidiaries.

The Rockefeller Foundation concentrated its efforts through two separate arms, the Rockefeller Population Control and its agricultural arm which deals with food production and control through food. The first president of the Rockefeller Population Council, Frederick Osborn, was also a member of the American and British Eugenic societies. The American Eugenic Society was a staunch supporter of Nazi Germany and advocated the cataloguing of the infirm, poor and black Americans for extinction and life-long segregation. Since the 1920s, the Rockefeller Foundation have invested billions of dollars into research population control using anti-fertility agents and genetic research since the 1980s into genetically modified food crops.[44] Sperm antibodies and fertility agents have been grown into GMO foods. Oral contraceptives were tied to loans and aid to Third World countries.

In the early 1970s, Henry Kissinger requested and received a National Special Security Memorandum 200, a document that allegedly highlighted the urgency of dramatically reducing African populations. In 1974 Henry Kissinger signed Security Memorandum 200 to use food as a population weapon.[45] Since the Second World War food giants like Cargill and Monsanto now control virtually all the seed and crop production in the world.

Given all the above, it is entirely possible that HIV was produced in US laboratories, not just as a part of research to fight diseases in humans, but in an effort to create devastating biological weapons. Ever since the First World War, Western nations and the US, in particular, have experimented with biological weapons of mass destruction. Anthrax, which has been extensively experimented on, has been modified in the laboratories and deployed on the battle field by many Western countries.

Anthrax was used to deadly effect by the US. against the Japanese during the Second World War. Today, though it is officially illegal, most Western nations have biological and chemical weapons as a standard part of their arsenal. Saddam Hussein was alleged to have accumulated large amounts of anthrax supplied by countries like Britain and the US before he stopped being useful as their friendly dictator in the region.

For those not conversant with the history of European biological warfare there are many recent historical precedents. The Tuskegee syphilis experiment was started in 1932 by the US Public Health Service and ran until 1972 when some members of staff leaked it to the press. The story broke in the Washington Star on July 25th 1972, in an article written by Jean Heller of the Associated Press, and she wrote:

'For 40 years, the US Public Health Service has conducted a study in which human Guinea pigs, not given proper treatment, have died of syphilis and its side effects. The study was conducted from the autopsies what the disease does to the human body'.[46]

Nearly 400 illiterate black African male sharecroppers, infected with syphilis, were enrolled from Macon County, Alabama. They were never told they had syphilis, nor were they treated for it. They were tricked into enrolling in the study by the lure of free medical services, meals and burial insurance, which was significant in those days. They were told they were being treated for 'bad blood', a colloquial term used to describe several illnesses, including anaemia, fatigue and syphilis.

By 1947 even when a cure for syphilis was found in the form of penicillin they were not offered treatment because the Tuskegee scientists wanted to study the natural history of how syphilis spreads and kills its victims. Some of the ravages of tertiary syphilis include heart disease, tumours, paralysis, blindness, insanity and eventually death. Dr John Heller, the head of the Tuskegee Syphilis study, had publicly advocated the use of penicillin to treat syphilis as simple and effective and his own study showed a 20% reduction in life expectancy without penicillin treatment. However, despite this, the organisation he headed, the American Public Health Body, went to great lengths to prevent their African American subjects from getting proper treatment.[47]

By the time the Tuskegee experiment was stopped, 128 men had died from the direct effects and complications of syphilis, 40 women were infected and 9 children were born with congenital syphilis.[48]

The National Association for the Advancement of Colored People [NAACP] filed a class action suit through Fred Gray, a lawyer who had previously defended Rosa Parks and Martin Luther King. A $10 million out of court settlement was won for the men and their families. It took the American government until 1997 to issue an official apology through President Clinton, who stated:

"What was done cannot be undone, but we can end the silence… we can stop turning our heads away. We can look you in the eye, and finally say, on behalf of the American people, what the United States government did was shameful, and I am sorry."[49]

On the legacy of the Tuskegee syphilis experiment Borgna Brunner had this to say:

"In 1990 a survey found that 10% of African Americans believed that the US government created AIDS as a plot to exterminate blacks, and another 20% could not rule out the possibility that this may be true. As preposterous and paranoid as this may sound, at one time, the Tuskegee experiment must have seemed equally far-fetched".[50]

Despite the extensive damage and the high percentage of Africans affected by HIV/AIDS, Western nations have refused to relax patent laws which would help African nations mass-produce cheaply and make available drugs to treat people with the HIV virus. President Bill Clinton's administration repeatedly blocked attempts by South Africa to produce cheap drugs, which would have gone a long way to reduce the morbidity and mortality of millions of AIDS suffers in Africa. Brazil was also barred but went ahead anyway, in the face of US sanctions. The result today is reduced mortality and morbidity from HIV and AIDS in Brazil.

Given the US government's track record with biological weapons, it was pure Western hypocrisy when the 'Tree Woman', Wangari Maathai, the first African woman to win a Nobel Peace Prize, was pilloried after she accused the West of using HIV/AIDS as a biological weapon of mass destruction against Africa. More importantly, a universal, clear, scientifically backed and well critiqued thesis on the origin of HIV/ AIDS has not been put forward.

The effects of AIDS in Africa is devastating but this is more to do with the lack of resources available to tackle the condition and does not in itself constitute proof that AIDS originated in Africa. The combination of poverty and AIDS is lethal and many Africans die, largely from lack of access to treatment. A chillingly cost-benefit per life assessment was made by even in wealthier African countries like South Africa:

In even relatively prosperous South Africa, an early death for millions was the outcome of the state and employer reaction to the AIDS epidemic, with cost-benefit analyses demonstrating conclusively that keeping most of the country's 5–6 million HIV positive people alive through patented medicines costs more than the people were 'worth'.[51]

However, it has not all been doom and gloom, and some African nations like Uganda and Zimbabwe have reversed the HIV/AIDS trends in their countries. InKampala, the capital of Uganda, HIV infection rates among pregnant women fell from 31% in 1993 to 14% in 1998.[52]

They promoted condom use and marketing, sex education programs, same-day HIV kits, self-treatment kits for sexually transmitted diseases and displayed a strong political will to involve all sectors of the society.

Africans do not have to die needlessly from AIDS and African governments must take the firm decision to put the lives of their people above anything else and take the decision to mass-produce the drugs by doing whatever it takes to acquire the technology and expertise. The simple and cheap practice of safe sex cannot be overstated and sex education is necessary to prevent more people from contracting this disease.

Unfortunately, while Africa was been struggling to come to terms with the devastation of the HIV virus and AIDS deaths another deadly viral epidemic, the Ebola virus, emerged on the African continent.

CHAPTER SEVENTY FIVE

BATS IN THE BELFRY: EBOLA AND CORONAVIRUS

EBOLA

The Ebola virus belongs to a viral family of Filoviridae causing viral haemorrhagic fevers and is one of the most serious public health threats of the 21st century. Like the SIV, the Ebola virus is thought to be endemic in Africa. It uses fruit bats as carriers and is deadly to primates and humans. Mirroring the HIV virus, it is not entirely clear how the Ebola virus made the jump to human beings. Like HIV, the Ebola virus and other viruses causing haemorrhagic fevers and have been present in their carrier animals for millennia.[1]

In 1996, the WHO report on Emerging and re-emerging diseases commented on the Ebola virus stating:

'The Ebola virus was unknown 20 years ago. The Ebola haemorrhagic fever outbreak in Zaire in 1995 was fatal in 80% of cases. The natural host of the virus remains a mystery.'[2]

It has been postulated that the Ebola virus may have been transmitted via the contact with infected fruit and the eating of contaminated bush meat by locals.

The Ebola virus kills 25–90% of all those infected with an average mortality rate of 50%. The highly contagious Ebola virus is transmitted via contact with an infected person's bodily fluids, particularly mucous membranes, and remains infectious in corpses for several weeks after death. Symptoms typically present 2 days to 3 weeks following contact. It presents with sore throat, fever, headaches, generalised muscle and joint pains, nausea, vomiting and diarrhoea. It attacks the central nervous, immune and clotting systems in the body, leading to disseminated clotting of blood and internal and external haemorrhage. The victims are highly contagious, particularly in the late stage of the disease.

There is no known cure for Ebola disease at present and treatment is largely symptomatic — replacing lost body fluid and blood products until the patient either succumbs or recovers.

Ebola can survive in the semen of survivors for up to seven weeks and can therefore also be transmitted via sexual intercourse. However, people who are fully recovered are not infectious and their blood contains protective antibodies which may, in time, provide a means of treating infected people with a vaccine.

Prevention and treatment involves rapid detection, contact tracing, social distancing, proper disposal of the dead and de-contamination of any objects that may have been infected. The proper handling of bush meat is vital to prevent spread to humans from contaminated animals.

Filo viruses are amongst the most virulent and the most transmissible viruses in the world and the US Center for Disease Control [CDC] classes Ebola as a category A bioterrorism agent and biosafety level 4 pathogen on the basis of its transmutability, high mortality rate and potential to cause significant public health damage.[3]

As expected, the lethal nature of the Ebola virus did not escape the attention of Western bio-warfare researchers and extensive research has been carried out on transforming the Ebola virus into a lethal biological weapon in the West. Biopreparat, a Russian biological weapons company, is alleged to have genetically combined the smallpox and Ebola viruses to create Ebolapox. Ebolapox has the potential to kill large segments of human populations. Fortunately, they also stated that the human specific Ebola viruses are difficult to aerolize and degenerate quickly on contact with air, making it difficult to weaponize.[4]

The Ebola virus was first identified in South Sudan [Ebola Sudan] followed by Ebola [Zaire] in the Democratic Republic of Congo in 1976. Until the West African outbreak, the most deadly form of the Ebola virus was the Ebola [Zaire] virus which had a mortality rate of about 90%.

In 1989, Ebola [Reston] was identified in a US laboratory in Reston, Virginia, USA.

It was deadly to their research rhesus monkeys but non-pathogenic to accidentally infected researchers. The Ebola [Reston] was found to have been transmitted by airborne infection as it was picked up in the respiratory passages and lungs of the infected monkeys on autopsy. They concluded that the Reston Ebola virus can be aerolized.[5]

In 1994 a single case of Ebola [Ivory Coast] was identified after a female researcher accidentally became infected and she was transferred to Basel, Switzerland, where she made a full recovery. In March 2014, the World Health Organization reported a major Ebola outbreak in Guinea, West Africa. The Ebola outbreak rapidly spread to Liberia and Sierra Leone. Poor infrastructure and lack of adequate medical facilities and funds in these war-torn countries meant that contact tracing and isolation of infected people was poor.[6] Culturally sensitive embalming and burial of Ebola victims also led to the spread of the virus in countries like Sierra Leone.

By October 25th 2014, WHO reported the Ebola outbreak to have exceeded 10,000 people infected and over 4,922 deaths. Only twenty-seven documented cases occurred in the three worst hit countries; Liberia with 2705 deaths, Sierra Leone with 1,281 deaths and Guinea with 926 fatalities. Eight deaths were reported deaths in Nigeria, one in the United States and one in Mali.

West Africa, Senegal, Nigeria and Liberia have now been declared Ebola virus free by WHO. So has Sierra Leone but with the warning of possible re-occurence.

Sensationally, on October 17th 2014 two doctors — a Liberian doctor, Dr Cyril Broderick, a scientist and former professor of Plant pathology at College of Agriculture and Forestry, University of Liberia, and Dr Francis Boyle of the University of Illinois, claimed that the US Department of Defence, [DoD] was funding Ebola trials on humans, which started weeks before the Ebola outbreak in Guinea and Sierra Leone. Dr Broderick alleged that the US DoD gave a Canadian pharmaceutical company, Tekmira, $140 million to conduct Ebola research that involved infecting or infusing healthy humans with the Ebola virus.

The Ebola viruses lethal potential for bio warfare along with similar viruses like the Marburg virus and Lassa haemorrhagic fever-causing viruses had already been explored by major world powers in their search for the ultimate biological weapon. Dr Boyle also stated that one of the epicentres for the Ebola epidemic was a US research laboratory in a town called Kenema in Sierra Leone. Boyle, an expert in biological warfare, drafted the Biological Weapons Anti-Terrorism Act of 1989 and was responsible for helping the US implement the 1972 Biological Weapons Convention.

In an interview with a Global Research journalist, Dr Boyle stated that the USA had been using West Africa as an offshore site to circumvent the convention on Biological Weapons and do bio-warfare work for many years.[7] In 1988, the Los Angeles Times had reported that the US Army was carrying out bio-warfare germ research worldwide across one hundred and twenty sites since the 1980s.[8] Tulane University researchers and researchers from the US bio-warfare centre in Fort Detrick have been carrying out bio-warfare research in West Africa for many years.

The US bio-warfare researchers from Tulane University, under contract with WHO, carried out their research under the Mano River Union countries [Sierra Leone, Liberia and Guinea] to develop national and regional prevention and control strategies for regional diseases. They were also specifically looking into the threat of bioterrorism using the Ebola virus.

Dr Boyle questioned the appearance of the lethal Ebola [Zaire] virus from its primary site to West Africa over 3500 km away. Dr Boyle also claimed that the Ebola virus from the original breakout in 1976 was transferred to Britain's main bio warfare centre in Porton Down, from where it was sent to bio warfare labs in Fort Detrick, USA, and then back to bio-warfare researchers in West Africa. Prior to 2014 there has never been an outbreak of Ebola in West Africa. Boyle believed that accidental release of the Ebola virus led to the West African outbreak.[9] On the face of it, it is entirely possible for accidental contamination or release of dangerous genetically modified biological germs to be released. Richard

Ebright, a bio-safety expert at Rutgers University, New Jersey stated that:

'More than two hundred incidents of loss or release of bio-agents from US laboratories are reported each year.'

However, this may be an optimistic view given America's long history of unethical human experimentation and use of biological, atomic and nuclear type weapons like material like depleted uranium. It is extremely worrying to note that as far back as the late 1980s, the white South African apartheid regime carried out a secret bio-warfare program called 'Project Coast' with the aim of developing ethnically sensitive biological and chemical agents that would selectively kill or at least sterilise black Africans.

Dr Wouter Basson, known as 'Dr Death' by South Africans and the media, headed the nefarious biological and chemical warfare programme and many comparisons have been made with Josef Mengele of the Nazi regime. Dr Basson alleged that he had assistance from the UK and the US.[10] In an interview for a documentary with Joel Cohen, Dr Basson stated that he met with the UK's top bio-weapons expert, Dr David Kelly. Dr David Kelly was found dead subsequently under mysterious circumstances after he had leaked to the media, in his other role as a nuclear arms inspector in Iraq, that Tony Blair's claim that Saddam Hussein had weapons of mass destruction was false. The Mail Online claims that Dr David Kelly was aggressively interviewed by British Intelligence, MI5, a week before his alleged suicide. It is thought that Dr Kelly was also planning to do an exposé on the UK and US links to the South African bio-weapons program, Project Coast.[11]

Basson, a cardiologist, was the personal physician to the former white apartheid president, P.W. Botha. He received over $10 million dollars investment a year at the time and boasted that he recruited over 200 top bio-warfare researchers in the West whom he had approached for help on developing genetically modified killer diseases specifically for black Africans.

Project Coast was known to have worked on the Ebola, Marburg and Rift Valley haemorrhagic fever viruses, also Anthrax, cholera, salmonella, botulism, thallium, E.coli, ricin, organophosphates, necrotizing fasciitis, hepatitis A and HIV.[12] It is alleged that it had managed to weaponise Ebola in South Africa in the 1980s.

Basson and his associates created toxins for military and police use and genetically engineered extremely dangerous and new organisms as biological weapons.[13] Project Coast continued its biological and chemical warfare research in direct violation of the Biological Weapons and Toxin Weapons Convention [BWTC] which was the first multilateral disarmament treaty banning an entire category of weapons in 1976.[14] They were alleged to have supplied a 'lethal' triple cocktail of powerful muscle relaxants which was used in the systematic killing of two hundred SWAPO prisoners, who were injected with the lethal cocktail and then dropped into the ocean from helicopters in 'Operation Duel'. Basson was also alleged to be have been involved in assassinations and attacks against members of anti-apartheid movements.[15] Neighbouring countries like Mozambique and Zimbabwe accused the apartheid South African Government of using lethal biological agents against their troops.

Project Coast only came to light when Dr Basson was arrested in a sting operation in 1997. He was found to be in possession of 1000 extremely potent ecstasy tablets and papers relating to Project Coast. He was taken to court and faced 153 witnesses and 67 charges before South Africa's Truth and Reconciliation Commission relating to assassinations, 229 murders, conspiracy to murder and theft, drug possession, drug trafficking, embezzlement of R36 million and use of illegal biological and chemical agents. Dr Basson refused to seek amnesty from the Truth Commission. He defended himself without witnesses and threatened to expose his bio warfare recruits and contacts in the West. Remarkably, despite the weight of evidence against him, he was acquitted of all charges and was discharged from the military with full pay in 1999.[16]

In a truly surprising move, Dr Basson or 'Doctor Death' was rehired by the Mandela government under pressure from the UK and US, and put in sole charge of dismantling Project Coast. Towards the end of the white apartheid regime, Dr Basson had covered the tracks of Project Coast by privatising it. Even after the program officially ended in 1994 there has been no independent verification that the bio-warfare agents Project

Coast created were ever destroyed. The order to destroy the bio-warfare stockpile by the UK and the US went solely to Dr Basson.[17]

THE CORONAVIRUS PANDEMIC

In late 2019, news started to emerge from China about a viral epidemic that had broken out near the 'wet' markets of the city of Wuhan. By December 31st 2019, the World Health Organisation (WHO) reported that the outbreak was a novel coronavirus, SARS-CoV2. It took some time to sink in but as the infection continued to spread globally it has become apparent that the world has been hit by the worst viral pandemic since the 1918 'Spanish Flu'. On March 11th 2020, the World Health Organisation declared that the novel coronavirus infection was now a pandemic.

Coronaviruses are so-called because of their appearance of wearing a crown under the microscope. There are about seven types of coronaviruses known to affect humans. Some are known to cause the common cold in humans like the 229E, NL62, OC43 and NKU1. Other coronaviruses cause severe illness in humans like MERS-CoV, the Middle Eastern Respiratory Syndrome (MERS), SARS-CoV causes Severe Acute Respiratory Syndrome (SARS) and SARS-CoV2 causes COVID-19.

The coronaviruses causing severe illness in humans are also know to infect animals and are thought to have the ability to evolve in animals and then re-infect humans with deadlier versions.

In a February 2020 report, the WHO stated :

'Bats appear to be the resevoir of COVID-19 virus.'

In China, bats, particularly the Horseshoe bat, have been sold in wet markets for many years. Wet markets are places were live animals are sold for food. These bats are thought to also infect pangolins which are also considered a delicacy in China.

The last viral pandemic amongst humans was the SARS outbreak of 2002. The pandemic lasted about 8 months, spread to 26 countries, infected over 8,000 people and about 800 people died. SARS was suspected to have started from Horseshoe bats in a 'wet' market in Guangdong province, China, while the COVID-19 virus appears to have originated from bats in a wet market in Wuhan, China. In a further twist, Horseshoe bats do not live in the wild near Wuhan. A Chinese researcher Huabin Zhao from the Department of Ecology, Hubei Key Laboratory of Cell Homeostasis, College of Life sciences, Wuhan University pointed out in an interview with Science that:

"COVID-19 was linked to Horseshoe bats, which do not hibernate in cities in China."

However, they are used in biomedical reseach in two major facilities in Wuhan. The Wuhan Institute of Virology is a Level 4 biosecurity facility — the highest for biocontainment. The Wuhan Centre for Disease Control is a Level 2 facility located near the wet market. It has been reported that researchers from these facilities had been studying the coronavirus in bats and had been collecting specimens from the wet markets.

In a further twist Dr. Anthony Fauci, a lead member of the US coronavirus task force and lead physician at the National Institute of Allergy and Infectious Diseases, allegedly funded the Wuhan Institute of Virology to the tune of $7.4 million.[18]

Like the Ebola virus, coronaviruses are common in animals and rarely jump from animals to humans. This constellation of strange coincidences has raised the question of whether the novel coronavirus was bio-engineered or occurred naturally. Conspiracy theorists allege that the Chinese were involved in gene splicing experiments with bat coronaviruses and also postulate that the virus could have accidentally escaped the Wuhan facilities and infected humans.

At present, the consensus from virologists around the world and the US military is that there is no evidence of the coronavirus being engineered. Virologists have stated that genetic studies of the disease spread and of the genetic material of the novel coronavirus has not produced any evidence to support a bio-engineered virus.

However, it is worth noting that in 2015, researchers from the Wuhan Institute of Virology, US and Switzerland demonstrated the ability for bat coronaviruses to thrive in human cells.

In a paper published in the journal 'Nature Medicine' they described how they had created a chimeric SARS-like virus out of the spike protein of a coronavirus found in Horseshoe bats called SHC014, and the backbone of a virus that could be grown in mice. In the petri dish, the chimeric coronavirus could infect and replicate in primary human airway cells. The virus was also able to infect the lung cells in mice.

At the time some virologists like Dr. Simon Wain-Hobson at the Pasteur Institute in Paris voiced their concerns about this type of experimentation and considered the risks to outweigh the benefits.

He noted the fact that the chimeric virus "grows remarkably well in human cells" and added that "if the virus escaped nobody could predict its trajectory."

In 2018, the Washington Post reported the concerns raised by science diplomats from the US embassy in Bejing who had visited the Wuhan Institute of Virology and were so concerned by the lack of safety and proper management at the laboratory that they sent two official warnings to the US.

According to the Washington Post's columnist Josh Rogin, in a cable dated January 19th 2018 the officials stated:

'During interactions with scientists at the WIV laboratory, they noted the new lab has a serious shortage of appropriately trained technicians and investigators needed to safely operate this high-containment laboratory.'[19]

Both SARS and COVID-19 appear to be transmitted from person to person via physical contact. However, while SARS caused more severe illness, COVID-19 appears to be easier to transmit person to person, via droplets that are expelled when a person coughes or sneezes. COVID-19 is also spread by touching contaminated surfaces and then touching one's eyes, nose and mouth. The COVID-19 virus has been shown to be able to live on contaminated surfaces like plastic and metal for up to twenty-four hours.

The SARS and COVID-19 symptoms are similar and both start with high fever and a dry cough. In SARS, this is followed with shortness of breath and diarrhoea. The severe cases of SARS progress rapidly to pneumonia, requiring hospitalisation and ventilation.[20]

With COVID-19 infection most people will experience mild to moderate symptoms, however some will progress to pneumonia with severe breathing difficulties and some requiring ventilation. Reported evidence from COVID-19 patients from around the world has shown that not all patients present with the classic symptoms. Some patients do not have a high fever and may experience headaches, abdominal pain and diarrhoea.

One of the reasons the COVID-19 virus is easily spread is that it has a long incubation period between infection and the development of symptoms. The average COVID-19 patient develops symptoms between 5–6 days and can be spreading the disease during this period. However, this can range between 1–14 days.

Unlike the Spanish Flu that had a predilection for young adults, the COVID-19 virus tends to be more serious in older people and those with underlying medical problems like hypertension, obesity, heart disease, respiratory problems and diabetes.

As of May 2020, approximately 3.4% of people with reported COVID-19 infection globally have died compared with the seasonal flu that generally kills less than 1% of those infected.

Once a person is infected with the COVID-19 virus a fierce battle ensues between the host's body and the virus which needs the host cells in order to replicate. The body mounts a multi-step immune response that takes about 1–2 weeks to establish itself. The first reaction is non-specific in which the white blood cells like macrophages, neutrophils, dendritic cells battle to slow the progress of the virus into the cells of the host.

On the other hand, COVID-19 virus has an affinity for cells in the airways and lungs and docks on Angiotensin Converting Enzyme (ACE2) receptors on the lung tissue. The COVID-19 virus then hijacks the cells' internal processes to generate genetic material and replicate itself rapidly. In response, the immune system produces inflammatory substances called cytokine to help send extra blood, fluid, white blood cells, and fibrin to wall off the virus and attack the human cells infected by the virus.

In the non-specific adaptive response to the virus the human body deploys specific Y-shaped proteins called antibodies or immunoglobulins to bind the virus, effectively marking the virus and cells containing viruses out for destruction by the immune system. The body also mounts a cellular response in which white blood cells called B-cells and T-cells are produced. The function of the B-cells and T-cells is to recognise the viral antigen and destroy and human cells infected with the virus. Some of the B- and T- cells persist as memory cells in the body and can help mount a more specific and stronger response to the same virus up to a decade on.

Unfortunately in some people, for reasons still not known or understood, the body's immune reaction or 'cytokine storm' is so severe that it ends up destroying much needed healthy lung tissue and effectively drowing the COVID-19 patients with their own secretions.

It is this cohort of patients that require ventilation to assist the patient to push oxygen through their flooded and damaged lung tissue to the rest of the body. Given the severity of the bodies inflammatory reaction, it becomes clear why patients with underlying conditions or elderly people without sufficient physiological reserves struggle to survive with a severe COVID-19 infection.

The current thinking is that people need a good non-specific and cellular immune response in order to beat the COVID-19 viral infection.

CURRENT TREATMENT:

At present, there is no known treatment for infection with the COVID-19 viral infection. Much of what the doctors do is supportive management to assist the body's immune system in overcoming the infection.

However, a few things have been shown by various studies to be promising avenues of investigation.

Firstly, re-purposed medication like combination anti-viral therapies using known drugs like Beta–interferon, lopinavir, ritonavir and ribavirin have been trialled.

Other studies have shown well known drugs like Chloroquine and Remdesivir to be promising in the treatment of COVID-19 patients.

The next line of attack against the COVID-19 infection is immune therapy utilising antibodies from recovered COVID-19 patients or genetically engineering antibodies in a laboratory to help assist the patient's own immune system in appropriately fighting off the viral infection. This line of treatment is still experimental and there have not been any large trials to test the efficacy of this approach. In April 2020, warning against the concept of COVID-19 'immunity passports' for recovered COVID-19 patients, the WHO stated that:

'No study has evaluated whether the presence of antibodies to SARS-CoV2 confer immunity to subsequent infection by this virus.'

Finally the development of a controversial COVID-19 vaccine has been touted as a cure for the virus but could take at least 18 months to produce. The basic idea of a vaccines is to attempt to co-opt the hosts immune sytem into providing long-lasting immunity against pathogens like bacteria or viruses. Vaccines are broadly divided into two main types: live attenuated vaccines or inactivated vaccines. There are also subunit vaccines which include: recombinant, polysaccharide, and conjugate vaccines and toxoid vaccines. The most common vaccines in use are live attenuated vaccine in which the virus or bacteria is weakened but kept alive in order to trigger a strong non-specific and adaptive immune response.

Inactivated vaccines are made by using 'wild' viruses or bacteria in which have been grown in a culture medium, killed by heat or gamma radiation in a culture medium and then included in a vaccine.

This is a safer vaccine and can be used in immunocompromised and older patients but is less effective and may require several booster doses to provide the immunity required. Subunit vaccines are made by using a protein or polysaccharide fragment of the virus/bacteria or a toxin produced by them as an antigen.

Traditionally, the production of safe vaccines is a slow and arduous task that generally takes between 10–15 years to produce. The first stage involves laboratory research and development to isolate an antigen from the bacteria or virus that can safely be presented to a human being in a test vaccine without causing the disease. The stage may involve animal tests and can take several years to complete. The test vaccine then requires approval from overseeing governing bodies, like the US Food and Drug Administration in America, before human testing can begin.

Once a test vaccine has been cleared for further investigation it then undergoes three phases of clinical trials.

Phase 1: Tests are conducted on a few healthy human volunteers to work out dosages and find out the smallest dosage of the vaccine that produces the strongest immune response without unwanted side effects.

Phase 2: The test vaccine is now given to hundreds of volunteers who are the people it is intended to protect. For example in COVID-19 it would be people above age 60, health and key workers and people with underlying medical conditions.

Phase 3: In this phase, the vaccine is rolled out to tens of thousands of people. This is perhaps the longest phase because the vaccine is now evaluated on how it works under 'natural disease conditions'.

Throughout all these phases, the safety and efficacy of the vaccine is carefully monitored and if there are too many side effects or the vaccine is not seen to produce the required immune response it will not meet the standards for approval and use by the general public.

This traditional and meticulous approach has produced many relatively safe vaccines that are in use today. The result is that the fastest time in which a safe and efficacious vaccine has ever been produced has been 5 years.

THE CONTROVERSIAL COVID-19 VACCINE

In 1796, an English physician, Edward Jenner, inoculated an 8-year-old boy with cowpox as a means of developing immunity for smallpox. Edward Jenner is now credited as the father of immunization and vaccination when in fact, inoculation or variolation, terms used interchangeably at the time, was most likely practised in Africa, India and China long before the 18th century, when it was introduced into Europe.[21]

More importantly, direct experimentation on human subjects or Human Challenge Studies of this kind would now be considered unethical.

A COVID-19 vaccine is most controversial for many reasons but has been promoted as a possible cure for the pandemic by western governments, big pharmaceuticals and others including the billionaire philanthropist, Bill Gates. In an interview with CNBC, Bill Gates argued that the world will need 7 billion doses of vaccine eventually, with healthcare workers having priority access, followed by low-income countries.

He added that the COVID-19 vaccine will likely become part of newborn immunization schedules. In addition, he stated that a coronavirus vaccine only needed to be 70% effective in order to stop the vaccine spreading globally.[22]

In order to make this vaccine a reality, Bill Gates has partnered with, and championed the Coalition for Epidermic Preparedness Innovations (CEPI).

CEPI was set up as a response to the lack of scientific progress on the Ebola virus. The UK government has already donated £250 million to CEPI. According to CEPI, they are developing at least eight potential vaccines for COVID-19 which they claimed will be ready by the end of May 2020. Bill Gates is also the founder of another organisation called the Global Alliance for Vaccines and Immunisation (GAVI) which he created in January 2000. The GAVI Alliance includes the WHO, UNICEF, World Bank, Bill & Melinda Gates Foundation, many donor nations (mostly western, including the UK) research agencies, vaccine manufacturers, private sector partners, civil society organisations and implementing country governments.

However, despite all the good intentions and philanthropy, everybody knows that there is no cure at present for the common cold. The common cold is actually caused by over 200 viruses which mutate frequently. The most common viruses implicated in the common cold include the Human Rhinoviruses (160 strains), Adenoviruses, Coronaviruses and the Para-influenza viruses. The Flu jab is at best on average 40–60% effective against the influenza virus and needs to be taken yearly for life.

In addition, there are clear dangers associated with conducting human trials for a virus using live attenuated vaccines because of the risks of infecting healthy people and creating an epidemic or even another pandemic.

Moderna, one of the companies racing to produce a coronavirus vaccine have been conducting human trials on a RNA vaccine. By employing genetic engineering techniques researchers are trying to insert pieces of the genetic code of the COVID-19 virus — also called

Plasmids — into a vaccine which when taken will become part of the host's (Human) genetic make up and in theory provide them with life-long immunity to the COVID-19 virus.

In addition to this complexity, most genetic engineering today usually involves the use of pieces of DNA or plasmids as transmitters of the genetic code, not RNA. A COVID-19 RNA vaccine will be a first and a step into the unknown without all the tradition safety nets and checks that have been built into the production of safe vaccines over several decades.

This vaccine embeds the genetic code of the coronavirus into all the cells of the body, and supposedly helps the body's immune system learn about virus and produce antibodies. Hypothetically, this could also have the dire consequence of the body producing a cytokine storm against all the vital organs in the body at the same time instead of just the lung tissue as in the COVID-19 infection or the pancreas in acute pancreatitis.

It is indeed worrying that most of the western countries peddling the idea of a vaccine have their eyes on the African continent and other third world countries as human guinea pigs in their attempt to produce a vaccine in under two years.

Most of the safe vaccines in use have produced against viruses and bacteria that have been known to medicine for over 50 years. The novel coronavirus is a completely unknown and new virus. Coronavirus has been shown to be unpredictable and has already undergone significant mutations since the COVID-19 pandemic began.

Matthew Memoli, an immunologist at the US National Institute of Allergies and Infectious Diseases, who also stages human challenge studies, warned against the onward rush towards producing and disseminating a COVID-19 vaccine globally, bypassing all health and safety standards.

Dr Memoli stated:

"When you are going to give somebody a virus on purpose, you really want to understand the disease so that you know that what you're doing is a reasonable risk."[23]

In other words, a new RNA COVID-19 virus vaccine that is produced at breakneck speed and has bypassed all the usual safety checks and controls for safe vaccine production, could bring a disaster of biblical proportions to the African continent. It is particularly worrying why the West would want to vaccinate millions of Africans first when they generally do not fall into the cohort that are severely affected by the coronavirus and the epicentres of the COVID-19 pandemic are in Europe and America, and not in Africa.

DOES THE CORONAVIRUS HAVE AN AFFINITY FOR BLACK OR BROWN PEOPLE?

Another worrying picture to emerge from the gloomy statistics of the COVID-19 pandemic has been the over-representation of black and other ethnic minority people. Figures emanating from the UK and US have shown that black and ethnic minorities have been worse hit by the coronavirus than their white counterparts. The first 19 NHS staff to die due to COVID-19 infection in the UK where from Black and Ethnic Minority backgrounds (BAME).

While in-depth research into the behaviour of the SARS-CoV2 virus is awaited, statistically it would appear that the poorer socio-economic background and historical bullying and pressure within the structure of the NHS may be contributory factors causing disproportional BAME deaths.

In April 2020, Dr. Chaand Nagpaul, the head of the British Medical Association called on the British government to urgently investigate if and why black, Asian and minority ethnic people are more vulnerable to COVID-19, after the first ten doctors in the UK named as having died from the virus were all BAME.

These figures are disproportional even allowing for the over-representation of BAME staff in the NHS — 44% of medical staff compared with 14% of the population of England and Wales. In April 2020, the BAME population made up a third of the patients in the intensive care units.

Dr. Nagpaul speculated that several things could be contributory factors, such as BAME doctors felt less able to complain about inadequate Personal Protective Equipment (PPE), a recurring complaint among healthcare workers during the COVID-19 pandemic in the UK. He also noted that BAME staff often felt more bullied and harassed than their white counterparts and would be twice as likely not to raise concerns because of fears of recrimination. He also highlighted the higher prevalence of diabetes, heart disease and kidney disease compared to their white counterparts.

Dr. Nagpaul stated:

"Previous inequalities will be greater at a time of crisis. This [coronavirus] may be bringing into focus the inequalities facing BAME communities."[24]

The UK statistics on the coronavirus supports the notion that BAME key workers would have felt impelled by their difficult socio-economic situations to face the risks of working and contracting the virus than of self-isolating when they felt exposed. Many BAME staff cannot not afford the luxury of working from home like their white counterparts.

Updated figures from the Office of National Statistics (ONS) published in May 2020 stated that male security guards, chefs and taxi drivers were most likely to die with COVID-19 infection based on figures calculated by the ONS from coronavirus deaths in England and Wales registered up to April 20th 2020.

The highest rate of deaths was among male security guards: about 45.7 per 100,000 people.

Male chefs were calculated as 35.9/100000 and male bus and coach drivers were 26.4/100000. One in five of people in these jobs were aged 55 and over and one in five of them were from a BAME background.

By the ONS calculations, a BAME nurse was 4.3 times more likely to die than their white counterparts. When BAME deaths were adjusted for poor socio-economic backgrounds and underlying health issues the ONS figures revealed that BAME people where more than twice as likely to die from COVID-19 infections than their white counterparts.

The figures in the UK are fairly consistent with the statistics emerging from the US. Even though the coronavirus can infect anyone as proven by the infection of the British PM Boris Johnson and Prince Charles, it is clear that black people are being disproportionately affected.

The figures from the US show that places with large African American populations were reporting the highest numbers of deaths and infections. In April 2020, Chicago, a city in which black people constitute 30% of the population, reported that African Americans accounted for 70% of all the coronavirus cases in the city and more than half of its deaths.Historic and structural socio-economic inequalities like facility closures and caps on public health insurance plans like Medicard and Medicare has meant that African Americans who live in high density urban areas and work in essential industries have far more exposure to the virus and less access to adequate medical services.

Unconscious racial bias may also be a contributory factor in determining unequal health outcomes in the US. The Century Foundation found that healthcare providers located within majority African American or Latino neighbourhoods tend to provide lower quality care.

Kriten Clarke, the Committee President and Executive Director of the Layers Committee for Civil Rights stated:

"We know that black Americans are particularly vulnerable. This is a social, economic and racial justice issue."[25]

Another interesting fact that has emerged from the information about COVID-19 patients in Europe and North America is the role vitamin D is playing in the severity of the COVID-19 infection. Vitamin D deficiency amongst black people in the UK and US is thought to be endemic as the higher levels of melanin prevent the absorption of UVB sunlight and reduce the production of vitamin D in the skin.

Vitamin D helps regulate the amount of calcium and phosphate in the body. Vitamin D is naturally produced in the skin from ultraviolet light (UVB) from sun exposure. It is carried from the skin to the kidneys and liver where it becomes activated and helps in the absorption of calcium from the guts and the maintenance of adequate blood levels of calcium to prevent osteoporosis.

Vitamin D is also known to support the immune system in various ways. A vitamin D receptor is expressed on immune cells; B-cells, T-cells and antigen. Thus vitamin D can modulate the non-specific and adaptive immune responses. In addition to this vitamin D is thought to help modulate the body's response to bacteria or viruses and prevent the 'cytokine storm' or severe inflammatory response of the immune system that can be fatal.

Vitamin D deficiency has been linked with an increased risk of upper respiratory infections, autoimmune diseases like multiple sclerosis, diabetes, rheumatoid arthritis, inflammatory bowel disease and systemic lupus erythematosus.[26]

A study by researchers in Trinity College, Dublin, published in May 2020, highlighted the association between vitamin D levels and mortality. The main finding was that vitamin D deficiency is a significant factor in determining the severity of the COVID-19 infection and a recommended mandatory vitamin D supplementation of 400iu daily as an adjunct to any treatment of COVID-19.

It is not clear whether this advice will be relevant in treating patients in Africa where adequate sunlight is available all year round but it does suggest that vitamin D levels should be checked and any deficiency corrected as part of the patient's overall management.[27]

AFRICANS AGAINST COVID-19

In April 2020, the EU Commission President Ursula von der Leyen announced a €15 billion fund to help poor countries fight COVID-19.

She stated: *"We will only win this battle with a co-ordinated response."*

Her comments were primarily aimed at African countries and were unanimously supported by EU nations and the UK. When her comments are taken against the backdrop of European countries like Italy, Spain and Britain struggling to contain the virus in their own countries and not having enough resources to provide Personal Protective Equipment to their medical staff and key workers, one may be forgiven for being perplexed.

So far, the fears that Africa would be overwhelmed by the COVID-19 pandemic have been unfounded. Weak healthcare systems, corrupt governments and large slums which make social distancing next to impossible were cited.

Nigeria, the 'Giant of Africa' is supposed to have about 169 ventilators for a population of over 200 million people.

The Financial Times reported that Sierra Leone had just one ventilator for 7.5 million people, which is statistically still better than Nigeria considering that many ventilators do not work and there may be no electricity to run those that do. The Central African Republic was reported to have three machines while Burkina Faso had eleven.

Despite the dire state of affairs of the health systems across Africa, as of May 2020, most African countries were reporting relatively fewer cases of new infections than in Europe or the US which is now the epicentre of the COVID-19 pandemic.

This may be due to limited testing of patients but the hospitals are not over-run with COVID-19 as was seen in Italy and Spain.

This led Darren McCaffey, a Political Editor to state:

"Africa, a continent of 1.3 billion – accounts for barely 1% of the number of infections and even less than one percent of the deaths."

It is true that the demographics across Africa have helped. Africa has a relatively young population with about 60% of all Africans aged below 65-years-old and the coronavirus disproportionately affects older people.

However, it is also true that many African countries locked down early and hard, like Rwanda and Uganda.[28]

Perhaps it is also worth comparing African countries with Greece, which is indebted and does not have the healthcare resources of countries like Italy, Spain or Britain but has fared much better. It is clear from the historical precedent of the 1918 'Spanish Flu' that social distancing and maintaining good hygiene works. Greece locked down quicker and harder than richer European countries and has reaped the benefits of few infections and deaths. The British government led by Boris Johnson and President Trump in the US made disastrous costs assessments and dithered while crucial time was lost and the virus spread through their respective populations. The historical lessons from the 1918 'Spanish Flu' were available for all to use. It is quite clear that this was the route African countries need to follow given their fragile healthcare systems.

It was essential that nations put the people first and dealt with the economic fall-out later. Even so, African nations must do more to make the lockdown bearable and effective by making sure that the people have access to much needed resources like adequate meals and medical services to reduce suffering. The more effective the lockdown, the better it is at stopping the virus from being transmitted through the population. Smart leaders will be repaid by being able to kickstart their economies earlier while others continue to struggle with the virus.

All Africans must remain extremely vigilant about bioterrorism and it is important that African governments across the continent close down all clandestine Western test laboratories due to the real potential of catastrophic loss of life to their people.

PART THIRTEEN:
FREEDOM AND SACRIFICE

CHAPTER SEVENTY SIX
REPARATION

Slavery, segregation and racism are among the worst examples of man's ongoing inhumanity to man. It is an impossible task accurately to assess the full extent and damage that these depraved practices has caused as most historical accounts today only represent the tip of the iceberg.

The transatlantic slave trade destroyed the fabric of many African societies and displaced millions of Africans within the African continent. Many African communities became nomadic as a result of slavery and the legacy of the bitter intertribal wars that were fought is a sense of deep-rooted mistrust among the African people. The transatlantic slave trade set the development of African people back several hundred years because of the strife that ensued and still continues. It is known that prior to the transatlantic slave trade the development of many African communities was on par, if not more advanced in many respects than their European counterparts,

In 1999, the African World Reparations and Repatriation Truth Commission, in its first international conference, met in Accra, Ghana, and called for the West to pay $777 trillion to Africa within 5 years.[1] The commission had calculated the reparation figure based on an estimated number of human lives lost in Africa during the transatlantic slave trade as well as an assessment of the worth of diamonds, gold and other minerals taken from Africa during the colonial rule.

However, when the social, cultural and psychological impacts of the transatlantic slave trade are included and the fact that institutional racism continues to exact a significant financial cost to Africans all over the world till present day is taken into account, the $777 trillion claimed by the

African World Reparations and Repatriation Truth Commission could fall well short of the actual cost.

It is an undeniable fact that the global white capitalist apartheid system is based on a system of white financial privilege, opportunity and advantage on the one hand, and black financial disadvantage, lack of privileges and opportunity on the other hand.

However, reparation must not only be seen simply as a means of making a financial reimbursement of the damage inflicted on African peoples and their descendants but also as a way to get the West to take ownership and responsibility for the central role they played in stripping African people of their humanity. Reparation must also be seen as a way of engraving into the consciousness of all people to come, the dangers of imperialism and racism, ensuring that this dark chapter in the history of mankind is not repeated. Reparation is not just about financial compensation but also about the return of the dignity of the descendants of slavery, return of stolen property and the correction of the historical lies in all areas of human activity that have been used to maintain the white supremacy system of exploitation.

No amount of money or land or any other reparation for slavery can bring back or compensate for a single one of the millions of lives lost. Nor can it replace the lost dignity or sovereignty through slavery and colonialism. But it would be a start in the right direction in stopping today's tragedy of African mental and economic slavery.

It would also be a step in the right direction towards equalising the opportunities in real terms of the lives and aspirations of African people all over the world. Western governments legalised slavery and colonisation and the former British Prime Minister, Tony Blair, went on record to state that slavery was legal at the time as a defence of their atrocities. But then so was the Nazi holocaust in terms of Nazi German law.[2]

Even though many Europeans and North Americans descendants strenuously argue that they did not directly benefit from slavery, this is fallacious argument. Several generations of Europeans have benefited immensely from the industry and infrastructure that were built from the proceeds of the transatlantic slave trade and slavery itself. Logically, it can therefore be argued that if they inherited the proceeds of slavery, they also inherited the liabilities too.

Nobody would argue that an apology can undo the wrong that has been done. But an apology would acknowledge it. The very act of taking ownership and confessing responsibility for wrongdoing, followed up with a genuine attempt to redress the patently obvious effects of whatever harm was done, acts as a means of closure to all the parties concerned. Till today, neither of the two main protagonists — the United States or Britain — have officially apologised for the genocide of the slave trade. Instead many pathetic excuses have been tendered as to why reparations for slavery, debt cancellation following colonisation and neocolonisation cannot be allowed.

Some argue that it was too long ago to be relevant. In response, it is worth reiterating that the affluence and infrastructure Westerners enjoy today was built with the blood and sweat of slavery and colonialism and in actual fact the same infrastructure continues to be sustained by the economic slavery of white supremacy in other forms.

The fact remains that in Europe people are compensated for things which are completely trivial when compared to the genocide that Africans endured. In Western countries where one can be compensated for tripping on uneven pavements or for becoming obese after years of eating fast food or for lung cancer after a lifetime of smoking, it seems absurd that Africans cannot be compensated for the greatest and longest crime of genocide and inhumanity that the world has ever known.

The families of the Lockerbie plane bombing were compensated over ten years after the incident. The British police are still seeking redress and compensation for the murder of a British policewoman, Yvonne Fletcher.

Another common argument is that there are too many people to pay reparations to and so pay nothing at all. Anyone unfortunate enough to be unfairly dismissed from work in the West will appreciate the negative impact it has and rightly seek some form of compensation. Not one individual will accept the excuse that their company or employers have laid off so many people that already, as a reason to be excluded from any form of compensation at all. In addition, African countries are still being stripped of their resources and manpower. African, African American and West Indian communities are still suffering daily discrimination at schools, work, with housing, funding, politics and trade between African nations and the Western nations.

It is worth looking at how Western governments spend their money to assess whether their inability to pay reparation for slavery is due to a lack of available funds or a lack of morality. The US government alone has spent trillions of dollars on maintaining and improving its military. According to an article in Newsweek magazine the US has spent six trillion that killed half a million people since September 11 2001.[3]

The US has instigated and fought many wars since the Second World War for no reason other than to extend its influence and manipulate poorer countries into accepting unsavoury deals, trade conditions and prices so that the average US Americans can maintain their standards of living. Billions of dollars has been spent unnecessarily financing wars, the arms trade and luxury goods in the West that could have been put to good use in so many ways.

In a nutshell, Western nations have the financial means to pay reparation several times over. Illegal and bad debts which are crippling most poor nations can be written off within an hour if that was the will of Western governments. Rather they stand by and watch the poorest of the world die of hunger, diseases and lack of infrastructure while they debate about world debts. A reparation of $777 billion rather than $777 trillion would alleviate many problems in Africa. Clearly, it is better for the West to pay some reparation rather than nothing at all. Instead, the white global apartheid system continues to widen the gap between rich and poor and if unopposed the exploitation can only result in poorer countries spiralling deeper and deeper into debt and poverty.

There are several precedents where international compensation or reparation has been paid. After the First Word War the victors forced the loser Germany to pay colossal reparations. Germany compensated the Jews for the holocaust. The Native Americans and Japanese Americans were compensated for the crimes committed against them by the US government. Unfortunately, in Africa's case, the West obscures the issues and refuses to face the facts. They peddle misinformation about reparation.

It is a grotesque fact that the British government paid £20 million compensation to British slave traders and owners for loss of business and 'loss of property'.[4] In the region of three thousand slave-owning families were recompensed after the emancipation of slave ownership in 1833. This is equivalent to £21.4billion by 2018 in today's money according to the Historical UK inflation rates and calculator.[5]

Former British Prime Minister, David Cameron's family received about £3 million to compensate them for the 202 African slaves on their Grange Sugar Estate in Jamaica.[6] To further rub salt into the African slaves' open wounds, following the abolition of slavery and to appease slave owners for the abolition of slavery, the British government promised to enact vagrancy laws under which slaves attempting to leave the plantations would be penalized and landownership beyond the size of a garden plot would be illegal for freed slaves.[7] Under the British government's Slavery Abolition Act only children under six years old were freed with immediate effect. Adult slaves were regarded as 'apprentices' who would, in exchange for free board and lodging, have to work for their 'owners' for forty and a half hours a week for no remuneration for 7 years until 1840.

Perhaps just as shocking a fact that the £20 million paid by the British Government as compensation for the losses of the slave trade went to British slave owners, is the fact that the British tax payer only paid off the debt on February 1st 2015, nearly 200 years later.

In 1834, the British Government raised the £20 million (40% of the government's yearly income at the time or the equivalent of £300 billion today) by taking a £15 million loan from Nathan Mayer Rosthchild and his brother in law Moses Montifiore to which the British government added £5 million.

In effect, this means that the African and West Indian descendents of slavery who have never been compensated for slavery help to pay compensation to wealthy former British slave owners, like David Cameron's family.

This information was inadvertently released to the public by a tweet from HM Treasury on February 9th 2018. The tweet stated: *"Here's today's surprising #FridayFact. Millions of you helped end the slave trade through your taxes. Did you know?"*

The tweet was quickly deleted after it generated an angry backlash.[8]

In Belgium, King Leopold II received 50 million francs in compensation after his Congo Free State was handed over to the Belgian government. King Leopold's reign of terror in the Congo wiped out almost half the native population.[9]

France made Haiti pay the modern equivalent of $21 billion from 1804–1947 — nearly 150 years — for the losses France sustained from the Haitians' abolition of slavery and for liberating themselves from French slave traders and owners.[10] Today, France continues to appropriate the natural and human resources of its former African colonies via its CFA colonial arrangements to the tune of $500 million per year, more than seventy years on from colonial independence.

In the words of Brother Mbandaka :

"If someone invaded your home, murdered your father, raped your mother, stole valuable property, kidnapped you and your siblings and waxed himself rich, having worked, whipped and raped you daily; then said sorry years later, without mention of compensation for your trauma and stolen legacy; would you forgive him?"[11]

The Church of England benefitted immensely from the slave trade and the West Indian plantations. The permission of the Church was required to embark on a slaving mission and many ships were captained and christened by clergymen. Sir John Hawkins, who captained a slave ship called 'The Good Ship Jesus', is accredited with introducing Britain to the slave trade and inventing the triangular Atlantic slave trade.

The clergy provided the moral and theological basis for the African holocaust that was slavery and endorsed some unconscionable deeds such as horse-whipping, severing of limbs, raping of women and girls, buggery of men and boys and mass murder — all in the name of Jesus Christ.[12] The Church of England officially apologized for profiting from slavery — two centuries after some of its members helped bring about its abolition.

However, the Church of England's dishonest claim to have played a vital role in the abolition of the slave trade in 1807 and its emancipation in 1834 is shameful. The Church and thousands of clergy slave owners were handsomely compensated for 'loss of [their] property'.[13]

Till the present day, Africans and their descendants have received few apologies, still less any form of compensation. This is logical, of course. How do you apologise to, or compensate people you are still exploiting?

Some prominent Africans, including President Obama, have argued against the payment of reparation for slavery. Other Africans and some in the diaspora have declared that reparation for slavery is pointless…I disagree. What does it say of an African's psychological state of mind when they cannot stand up for themselves and claim what is an inalienable right of freedom and equality?

What does it say of people who have endured the world's greatest and longest period of man's inhumanity to man, to maintain that they do not require even an apology, less talk of reparation?

It is possible, by a stretch of the imagination, to conceive that the Jews may have forgiven the Nazis for the Holocaust, but perhaps not while it was still going on!

It is, in my opinion, a sign of mental slavery, when black African people argue against a white apology or reparation, as compensation for crimes against humanity as terrible as slavery and colonization.

When white people argue against it, they usually have racist or paternalist views and usually do not know enough about the subject matter in order to come up with the strong opinions that they do. It is not usual for robbers of any race or colour to voluntarily give up all the loot the have stolen without being persuaded to do so by the law.

When these people, black or white, argue against African reparation because of its cost, or because it was in the 'past', then they must also to argue against the compensation the Jews received for the Holocaust or the Native Americans received after their near-total decimation at the hands of white American settlers.

In the Western world where people are compensated for comparatively trivial things it does expose one's moral compass and psychological state of mind when you hear people argue fiercely against reparation for the crime against humanity like slavery.

The failure of Africans and their diaspora to claim reparation not only confirms their sense of powerlessness but also demonstrates a lack of self-confidence and a tacit acceptance of permanent second class citizenship. Many miseducated Africans cannot stand up for themselves, their communities or their people. Rather, they help the white community circulate the tired excuses why Africans are unfit for an apology, which is free, never mind compensation for an obvious wrong.

In March 2014 the heads of state of fifteen Caribbean countries got together in St Vincent to unveil a plan demanding reparation from Europe for the enduring suffering inflicted on them by the transatlantic slave trade. Chaired by Sir Hilary Beckles, the reparations task force unveiled a 10-point plan on March 10th 2014 at the meeting of the Caribbean Community [CARICOM] Regional Political and Economic body. They aimed to request an formal apology from the US and Europe and to seek financial redress in the form of reparations.[14]

The lawyer leading CARICOM's claim, Martyn Day, stated:

"Current consequences of race discrimination, resulting from the slave trade in the past, still exist today".[15]

For over 400 years Africans were classified in law as non-human, chattels, property and real estate. They were denied recognition as members of the human family by laws and practices derived from the parliaments and policies of Europe. This history has inflicted massive psychological damage upon Africans and Africans by descent and is evident daily in social life. Only a reparatory dialogue can begin the process of healing and repair.[16]

The US and Europe have continued to refuse any admission of guilt for African slavery therefore negating the need to issue an apology. Perhaps, the most significant reason for the West not acknowledging responsibility or paying reparation for slavery is that it is ongoing. However, they may soon pay a high price in the form of extremism as people become painfully aware of the vast inequalities in wealth distribution and the reasons why.

History has repeatedly shown that peaceful protests to end continuing white oppression will most likely end up in violence, as there is no man on the face of the earth who will accept as his lot in life perpetual subservience to another. Human beings crave freedom and oppressed people will eventually fight for their rights. US Americans fought the British to gain their independence and the West, including Britain, fought the fascism of Nazi Germany. Africans, if not given their rights, will have no option but to take them.

Reparation is about the value humans beings show each other for their lives and especially how much we value ourselves as people. In terms of restoring value for African lives and property, reparation for slavery and the crimes of colonization is a necessity for Africa and its diaspora. An apology and redress, is an important psychological requirement for all human beings, in order to obtain closure for wrongdoing by someone else. It is the same principle that guides us to offer a simple and honest apology when we have wronged others or want to receive an apology and some validation when others have wronged us. African people, whether they are on the continent or part of the diaspora, must seek reparation for the inhumanity of slavery and colonisation in order to help achieve closure on this terrible stain on the collective human consciousness.

CHAPTER SEVENTY SEVEN

THE PSYCHOLOGY OF FREEDOM

"During my lifetime I have dedicated myself to this struggle of the African people. I have fought against white dominion. I have cherished the ideal of a democratic society in which all persons live together in harmony, and with equal opportunities. It is an ideal I hope to live for and achieve. But if need be, it is an ideal for which I am prepared to die." **Nelson Mandela.**[1]

'And ye shall know the truth, and the truth shall make you free.' **John 8:32.**[2]

"You are not free until you can exercise the full extent of your human rights to be who you are in society." **Thomas Jefferson**[3]

"If my mind can conceive it, and my heart can believe it—then I can achieve it." **Mohammed Ali**[4]

All human beings are born free, and it has only been in freedom that people can attain or experience rich and fulfilling lives. No human being can give or take the natural freedom that is bestowed upon us at birth by God. Blessed with great imagination and intellect, human beings have the capacity to be anything they want…or be nothing at all.

However, this God-given freedom can be severely restricted by circumstances, the environment and by other people. The enslavement of a human being is perhaps the greatest limitation of the psychological and physical expression of human freedom that can be achieved.

As human beings are at the apex of the food chain among mammals, only another human being can significantly prevent them from experiencing their natural God-given right to freedom of expression and living. The denial of other human beings of their natural right of expression is at the very core of white imperialism, which seeks to control and deny others this natural freedom as they aspire to dominate the world's human and natural resources. The result of this quest are unending worldwide cycles of violence as the imperialists seek to dominate others, their victims struggle to break free.

The Socialist Papers on Racism state :

'Human beings need to be free as birds need to fly. The need to be free in spirit, mind and body, is an integral part of the human spirit and when wilfully denied by others, will inevitably lead to conflict...The process of human slavery is ultimately a psychological process by which the mind of the people is gradually brought under the control of the captor. They become imprisoned by the lack of consciousness [awareness] of themselves.'[5]

It is only in this understanding of mental slavery that the plight of Africans and its diaspora becomes clear. The loss of higher-level human awareness and functioning meant that Africans went from building great civilizations to becoming completely dependent and subservient to their white masters. Many Africans have wrongly sought acceptance into the white community instead of seeking equality and their full complement of human rights.

Miseducated Africans have been brainwashed by the West into seeking the ultimate ideal of full integration into the white community and devaluing their own culture and identity instead of seeking their freedom and true equality. The impenetrable barrier of institutionalised white racism has uniformly rebuffed them all. Unfortunately, many Africans — miseducated into psychological inferiority and physical dependence — cannot see any other way to progress as a people and are destined to persist in trying to integrate themselves into Western culture and societies — to no avail.[6]

In settling for less than their full complement of freedom, human rights and true equality, generation after generation of Africans in the diaspora have lived in Western societies without validation. The vast majority of the African diaspora start their lives as virtual nobodies and eventually die as virtual nobodies in Western societies, whose rigid social hierarchy defines them as their dysfunctional inferiors from birth. These Western societies subject them to a multitude of negative life experiences from birth up until death in their designated role of the dysfunctional inferiors regardless of their true level of abilities.

By residing in the Western paradigm and not taking account of the effects institutional racism has on their lives, many in the African diaspora have reacted slowly and ineffectually to the barrage of blows the white community rains upon them like a blindfolded boxer who only ducks after being hit.

Blind materialism has also played a very important role in the miseducation of the Africa as many have falsely associated the mere acquisition of material wealth with nominal equality in the white global apartheid system that cuts across all areas of human activities, including economics. Materialism has an immensely powerful appeal to all human beings regardless of their race or colour and, unfortunately, many Africans have paid and are still paying a very high price for blind materialism and consumerism in Western societies. It is sad that that they fail to realize that in a fair and equal society, they would probably be ten to even one hundred times wealthier.

To be free one must have a clear understanding of what freedom means. The Oxford dictionary of current English defines the state of freedom as: *'The condition of being free or unrestricted'*.[7] Freedom from psychological mental slavery for Africans only occurs when the slaves regain full awareness or full consciousness of who they really are. One is only self-conscious as long as one is aware of one's identity and dignity and live in their own paradigm.

Because mental slavery operates largely in the subconscious or unconscious mind, it is not dependent on how materially wealthy or how deprived or poor one. Mental slavery does not distinguish between the highly literate but miseducated Africans and illiterate and poorly educated Africans. The highly literate but miseducated Africans simply function as higher-level servants or slaves to the Western capitalist system.

No matter how rich or poor, no matter how accomplished or unaccomplished Africans are, as long as they continue to define themselves by Western culture, depend on the West and seek to remain unequally yoked with the white supremacy system and culture, they will remain forever their slaves.

It is amazing just how quickly Africans forget that a high price in blood has been paid for every freedom that they enjoy today in the Western paradigm, both in Africa and in the diaspora. Less than 250 years ago, not quite five generations ago, African slavery was practiced freely all over the West. Under seventy years ago, racism was legal in America until the Civil Rights Movement dismantled legal segregation and secured African American voting rights. South Africa's apartheid regime, the bastion of white supremacy in Africa, only handed over power to Nelson Mandela's ANC in 1994.

The modern mutations of African slavery or economic slavery, colour discrimination and institutional racism are all very much alive and well today. In fact, there are arguably more modern-day economic African slaves today than there were African slaves in actual physical bondage during the height of the transatlantic slave trade. Unfortunately, many Africans have not bothered to join all the dots to appreciate the truly global nature of the African's plight.

The real cause for this pandemic of institutionalised racism and its effects has been the smooth social transmission of racial ideology in the West. This white global apartheid system is unprecedented in human history and has been subtly transmitted globally, penetrating deeply due to the power of modern media and information technology.

Cognitive dissonance is the uncomfortable inner tension that comes from having to hold two conflicting thoughts or ideas at the same time. In the modern expression of mental slavery, Africans in the diaspora and the white communities they live in find themselves having to find an uneasy balance where the Africans try to ignore or justify the real situation they inhabit. Africans have to ignore their obvious oppression while the white majority justifies its privileges and camouflages its oppression.

Some Africans take it even further and are desperate to be like their white masters. They develop what can only be described as a 'Transatlantic Slavery Syndrome', which, like the Stockholm Syndrome, sees the victim identifying and even falling in love with his or her oppressors. While the Transatlantic Syndrome would have developed as a survival and defence mechanism in kidnapped slaves, in its modern expression it disables the minds of miseducated and Western indoctrinated Africans such that they can see no wrong in their white masters and oppressors.

Human beings have an enormous capacity to adapt and adjust to prevailing situations in order to survive. Western imperialists, in the furtherance of their desire to dominate and exploit others, have cleverly exploited this natural psychological 'elasticity'. All human beings are psychologically malleable and can be manipulated emotionally and intellectually if the right stimuli are provided. The only way African slaves were brought under heel was the calculated distortion of their psychological responses and values by pure terror through their dopamine reward systems. As the African slaves were stripped of their identity and culture by their white slave masters enslaved Africans were left with no identity or culture to draw strength from.

Mental slavery in its starkest form saw African slaves permitting themselves to be enslaved in order to survive rather than die. According to Hegel's Phenomenology of the Mind, the master-slave paradigm is defined by the recognition of the master by the slave and the lack of recognition of the slave by the master. However, what is also important in this philosophy is the means by which the slave's recognition or compliance is obtained by the master. African slaves had to physiologically adjust to the conditions of slavery in order to preserve their physical lives. In many they then died a psychological death.

In the 1940s–1950s, renowned psychologist Abraham Maslow developed the 'Hierarchy of Needs' model that largely remains valid today for understanding human motivation. He provided one of the clearest models of the physical and psychological elasticity of human beings in the face of their prevailing circumstances. Even though survival is the key motivational driver to human behaviour, human beings have evolved, over tens of thousands of years, many other motivational needs. These needs are inborn and form the basis of how human beings interact and create societies. Maslow's hierarchy of needs states that we must satisfy each need in turn, starting with the first, which deals with the most obvious needs for survival before we deal with the higher motivational needs of influence and personal development. In other words, when the lower-order physical and emotional needs are met, we raise our expectations and concentrate on the higher psychological need. Conversely, we do not concentrate on the higher-order needs when the primary object is to survive.

Maslow's original model, for most people the most definitive, was published in 1954 and consisted of five needs: biological and physiological needs, safety needs, belongingness and love needs, social needs, esteem needs and self-actualization needs.

The first needs therefore are things like air, food, drink, shelter, warmth, sex, sleep. Next come protection from the elements: security, order, law, limits, stability. Then work group, family, affection, relationships, followed by self-esteem, achievement, mastery, independence, status, dominance, prestige, managerial responsibility and finally realizing personal potential, self-fulfilment, seeking personal growth and peak experiences.

The needs must be satisfied in order, according to Maslow. Once one set is satisfied, the aims and drives always shift to the next higher level.[8] Today, the sad fact is that millions of Africans subsist at the most basic level of Maslow's hierarchy. The African diaspora in the West, in addition to typically subsisting at the lowest level of Western social hierarchy, have regressed to the deepest psychological phase of mental slavery, where integration into the white society that marginalizes them is valued more highly than their individual or collective freedom. The Transatlantic Slavery Syndrome sees the African victims become emotionally attached to the white perpetrators and express their love and admiration for them. Miseducated Africans are cut off or ignorant of their true history and culture and plagued by an ingrained fear and worship of white people upon whom they also depend for their livelihood.

This combination of lack of independent thought coupled with the reality of their psychological and physical dependence creates inferiority complexes and frustration that are acted out in various cyclical self-destructive patterns of behaviour. Unmitigated and unimaginable physical and emotional abuse was the key to the development of mental slavery. One of the founding fathers of American democracy, Thomas Jefferson, exhorted his fellow slave masters to use force and violence.[9]

Having already acquiesced to slavery owing to their fear of death, the African slaves were faced with never-ending acts of gratuitous violence in all areas of human activity. Their slave masters used constant physical and emotional abuse as a means of instilling the 'fear of freedom' into their slaves. Thus the alleged 'inferiority' of the slave became internalized as well and thus was easily transmissible down the generations of the descendants of slavery and colonisation.

Once the fear of freedom and the devalued image of self-had been internalized, the slaves faced an even greater problem — 'intropression' or the oppressor within, from their internalized negative and devalued self-identity and the living death of the daily reality of slavery imposed by the slave master. This is the stage that neo-colonial Africa and many of the descendants of transatlantic slavery in the diaspora and in the West find themselves today. The internalization of the denigrated and devalued self-image given them by the white colonial slave masters is an advanced stage of the process of neo-colonial slavery and is characterized by the slaves mal-adapting to their socio-economic circumstances to meet the demands of their white slave master and the yearning of the slaves to become 'white' like their masters.

An eminent psychologist, Hussein Abdilahi Bulhan, wrote:

"The slave has thus every reason to overcome slavery. To overcome his bondage, he first overcomes his fear of death and embraces liberating work. Originally, he became a slave because he did not risk his life for recognition and freedom. Having become a slave, his fear of death persisted and was incarcerated in the person of the master."[10]

Since the freedom to be self-determining and actualising comes with the responsibility of self-reliance, many miseducated Africans, who have for years depended heavily on their white masters, find it difficult even to imagine independent thought, never mind independent action and self-reliance.

Thus the paradox that faces Africa and their diaspora today is their abject poverty and deprivation in the midst of plenty. Caught up in the intricate Western spider web of white misinformation, inferiority complexes and poverty and cut off from their own African paradigm by an ignorance of and lack of knowledge of their own history and culture, they subsist in a denigrated fashion on the lowest rungs of the global white social hierarchy.

Several psychologists have shown unequivocally that the social phenomenon called racism can be artificially created but it can also be destroyed. Human beings are not born racists but rather become socialised to be such. The fabricated nature of Africa's suffering and the fact that racism is a man-made, socially transmitted disease, has been clearly demonstrated. Many social engineering experiments have been carried out to buttress this fact but one of the most famous examples is not from an esteemed psychologist but rather from a schoolteacher named Jane Elliott.

Jane Elliott was a schoolteacher for third graders in a school in Iowa, USA. Martin Luther King had been their 'Hero of the Month' in February 1967. When Martin Luther King was assassinated in 1968, she wanted to try and help her pupils understand the significance and the enormity of his death. Her pupils lived in a small white community with little contact with African people and where racial attitudes and stereotyping was rife. When she asked the white children what they thought of black people, many negatives came back — they are dirty, they steal, they riot' etc.

She decided to carry out the 'Brown eyes, Blue eyes' experiment in which she divided the class into those with brown and blue eyes and arbitrarily conferred 'privileges' on the children with blue eyes and stripped the brown-eyed ones of theirs. Even though it was just an experiment, the behaviour of the children involved changed dramatically. The children in the blue-eyed side became aggressive and arrogant while the brown-eyed children became withdrawn, ashamed and angry. When she reversed the privileges, the children's behaviour changed accordingly. After her experiment, Jane Elliott concluded:

"A person who has been raised and socialized in America has been conditioned to be a racist...we live in two countries, one black and one white."[11]

Since Jane Elliott carried out her experiment, several psychologists have carried out social engineering experiments to buttress the conclusion that racism is a reversible socially transmitted disease. About thirty years later an identical experiment was carried out in adults — with essentially the same results.

Most human behaviour is the product of a complex combination of several factors, including genetics, biology, social learning and the environment. For instance, the ability for members of a particular family to speak the same basic language in the same accent and intonation is a clear sign of socially transmitted behaviour. A child is equipped to speak and learn any number of human languages if his or her socialisation requires it. For instance, a Chinese child brought up by Nigerian parents in a Nigerian setting will speak a Nigerian language, in a Nigerian accent.

Past human behaviour is the best predictor of future human behaviour. Once socialized, a person will follow a generally predictable life pattern and most importantly so will that person's children. Most people socialised as dysfunctional inferiors will act this out in their own lives and unfortunately so will their children.

Human behaviour is significantly modified by rewards, the lack of rewards and to a lesser degree by punishment. This is how the physiological dopamine reward system deep within our brains, moulds our subconscious desires to ensure the survival and the procreation of the human race. It is well known that rewarding bullies by pandering to their demands or attempting to bribe them or pay them off usually only backfires, as the bullies get the reinforcement of their negative behavioural pattern they sought to achieve in the first place. For example, it is tempting to shout and scream at an obscene phone caller but this only gives them the attention and recognition they crave. Not rewarding the bullies or hanging up the phone quietly on the obscene caller deprives them of the sensation of power, the attention and recognition they desire. It is also well known that unrewarded human behaviour rapidly becomes extinct when the motivation for behaviour is unrewarded or punished.

Most bullies use a hard exterior to mask their deep psychological insecurities and fears and they tend to become bored with and scared of people they are unable to bully because their feelings of dominance and importance or the material gain they seek is unobtainable.

So powerful is this human system of rewards in modifying our behaviour that most child psychologists recommend that parents employ a sensible system of rewards, encouragement and minor punishments to modify their children's behaviour. They advise positively reinforcing good behaviour in children with encouragement and occasional rewards but not bribes. Depriving them of some simple pleasures like their toys or outings to show displeasure or negative behavioural traits in a consistent manner can dramatically change a child's behaviour and strongly influence their future adult behaviour in a positive way.

Even if you do not believe in an underlying psychological imperative for the white global system of domination, you cannot argue with the material benefits of the white superiority system.

Materialism revolves at the core of the global system of white domination, and be it gold, silver, sugar, slaves and now crude oil the West has sought after the immense financial rewards the capitalist system provides them without any moral compunction, to the exclusion of everything else and by any means possible.

When this simple human motivation towards the presence or absence of rewards is taken globally, it becomes clear that if capitalism provided no material or psychological rewards, it is highly unlikely that it would be pursued in such a frenzied bloodthirsty fashion.

Capitalists do not overtly or covertly invade or occupy any country without any significant material or strategic significance. When genocide engulfed Rwanda and nearly one million Tutsis died, an open Western invasion and occupation of Rwanda was very low on the agenda. Without a clear opportunity to acquire or annex lucrative material gains like oil wells, gold or diamond mines, the unfolding genocide in Rwanda provided no incentive to the West to intervene. The Belgian and UN forces stationed in Rwanda refused to intervene to stop the massacre even though they could see the violence developing around them. Their stated function was to protect and evacuate the foreign nationals stationed in Rwanda. However, it is not coincidental that Western-backed Rwandan rebels took over power following the assassination of the Hutu President and political elite. The US-backed Rwandan and Ugandan invasion of the Democratic Republic of Congo eventually was intended to yield the usual material benefits in the form of precious minerals like coltan, gold and diamonds.

While it is difficult to use the word 'reward' when describing the material and psychological benefits Africans in general have received from Europeans ever since the holocaust of the transatlantic slavery, we must not forget that the African miseducation in Western culture severely distorted the African value systems, not just of themselves but towards each other too.

If a 'reward' is any object or feeling highly desired or highly valued by an individual then in the distorted paradigm of the miseducated African they may feel rewarded or valued by things that may at first appear strange and illogical to an unbiased observer. During the slave trade, African intermediaries laboured under a psychological inferiority complex and sold their fellow African citizens into slavery for the 'rewards' of glass beads, guns and rum. Later, these African slave trade intermediaries would reincarnate as corrupt African politicians and leaders whom in a bid to outdo their predecessors, sold their country's resources along with millions of their own people into economic slavery for a relative pittance.

Many miseducated Africans are unaware that they, along with their countries' resources, are being sold out by their African puppet leaders and, even in the full knowledge of this, are very apathetic towards it. The reason being that they value, identify and define themselves by the Western culture they are trying to emulate more than fighting for their true freedom.

The miseducated African typically is self-centred and individualistic in his or her approach to life and towards other Africans. Most Africans do not believe the European tale that slavery was undertaken to spread Christianity to Africa more than they believe the tall story that the 'white man's burden' of colonization was to bring civilization to Africa. It would be an equally hard sell to convince many Africans that the ravages of globalisation, across Africa today, were borne out of an altruistic need to spread Western democracy and freedom in Africa. However, miseducated Africans buy into Western culture and ideology because they consciously and subconsciously define themselves by the Western system.

Many Africans in the diaspora remain at best apathetic to the plight of fellow Africans, at the worst are even complicit in bringing about the poverty and suffering of their own people. It is not because they do not see through the hypocritical claims of Western aid and charity but because they do not value themselves — or other hapless Africans like themselves — enough to galvanize themselves into positive action.

The news of millions of deaths from HIV and AIDS-related illnesses in Africa may elicit very little reaction among these types of Africans. This is possibly due to an intrinsic lack of self-worth and its projection on to other Africans or due to apathy and shame. However trivial the gossip or information about Westerners may be — reality television, the European football scores, celebrity gossip columns and Western soaps — it is sure to get them really excited.

The psychological reward for a miseducated African — whether in the diaspora or in Africa — is the acknowledgement of their outward shows of Westernization. In the African diaspora it is their acceptance and acknowledgement by the Western society in which they reside or aspire to. The clothes they wear, their hairstyles, the language they speak and the way they speak it, what they eat and feed their children, even where they claim to be from, all revolves around their drive to be accepted and integrated into their chosen white society.

In the diaspora, miseducated Africans even choose nutritionally unhealthy European foods, high in fat and calories like full English breakfasts, or burgers and fries, over healthy nutritionally balanced African meals just to demonstrate how Westernized they are. They are very proud to be the 'only black' man or woman in a job, because to them it means they were the only Africans apparently good enough for their white counterparts. They are proud to be isolated from other African families and like to boast about being the only 'black people' living in the mainly white populated areas, or how their children are the 'only black' children in the school. They do not seem to realise that their self-imposed isolation is a clear sign of their own inherent weakness and vulnerability.

Given how hard they try to integrate, the white supremacist recognizes that some of these African 'coconuts', will readily act like puppets of the white masters, over their African people without need of any further grooming or encouragement. Therefore, some are occasionally elevated to high office, albeit with diminished powers and roles when compared to their white counterparts.

Some of these African people also consciously or unwittingly become part of the 'First black Syndrome' in Western societies. The miseducated Africans love to be used in the 'First black Syndrome' of the white supremacy system. The West is very keen to emphasize the efforts some miseducated Africans make to integrate themselves into the white community. Every now and then, they are featured in the Western media, which is quick to point out their 'first black' status.

In Britain, they are sometimes rewarded with medals, like the Officer of the Order of the British Empire, OBE and Member of the Order of the British Empire, MBE, which are in fact highly symbolic awards in recognition of Britain's dominion, exploitation, genocide and slavery of their African parents, grandparents and the wider African collective.

In Africa, the monetary rewards of psychological slavery and subordination to their white masters can be immense for a select few. These African intermediaries have conspired with the West to rape and pillage their own people for personal gain for over 400 years. Overall, even though they represent less than 1% of the total African population, the effects of their greed have determined the lives of millions of Africans in Africa and in the diaspora for generations.

While many African puppets have become obscenely wealthy relative to the suffering masses and lead opulent lifestyles, at the core of their personalities — perhaps masked by their greed, empty pride and intense selfishness — lies a deep and enduring psychological inferiority complex and self-hatred, such that they cannot see anything of real value in their own people. Many people would baulk at selling their pets into slavery never mind another human being and the fact that they could willingly sell and impoverish their own people displays an acute poverty of morality. These African intermediaries have reincarnated today mainly as corrupt military dictators and politicians who use the guise of politicized tribalism and nepotism to sell off the wealth of their nations to the West, plunging millions of their own people, even members of their own families, into abject poverty.

Paradoxically, the problem is that they derive their support not just from the West but also from many of their deeply divided and conflicted people. Apathetic from years of predatory colonial regimes and corrupt African leaders, they do not see their government as their own and they support the corruption that impoverishes them. They may also simply envy it.

Keeping the African continent and its diaspora abroad in a constant state of chaos and flux prevents stability and development. The white imperialist must manipulate the socio-economic situation such that their African intermediaries remain unassailable and unaccountable to their people while they continue to control the resources of their countries. As such, African intermediaries are heavily supported with money and military aid by Western powers in order to prevent their captive people from ever breaking free.

Ironically, the same brutal African leader on the Western payroll is portrayed in the Western media as an example of Africa's inability to find suitable leaders or manage its own affairs.

Using their African intermediaries, the West can strip African countries of vital natural and human resources resulting in widespread poverty and the economic dependence.

When physical deprivation and poverty combine with the continual stream of negative imagery and information from the West, it helps to cement ideas of psychological inferiority and dependence in the minds of unsuspecting Africans who are exposed to, or live with, the Western paradigm. It feeds the African mind with the necessary negative physiological and psychological stimuli of numerous images of African poverty and stark prostration necessary to build the inferiority complexes that completely paralyse them.

The esteem needs of African nations and their diaspora comes up daily against the glass ceiling of second to tenth class citizenry in the Western paradigm and ensures that self-actualization and self-determination are not realized. In the West, to realize their personal potential and gain some self-fulfilment, Africans are funnelled into very narrow areas like sports and music, through which they can seek their own personal growth and peak experiences.

To achieve this, Western society places innumerable obstacles in the path of ethnic minorities making it exceedingly difficult and in most cases almost impossible to achieve comparable success in many mainstream careers — hence the very poor social mobility in the two Western countries with the largest black populations; the UK and the US. Thus, the alienating effects and inequality of Western capitalism are felt more acutely in African nations and diaspora, including the communities, families and individuals.

Mental slavery is simply a state of mind. It is a prison with an open door. To break the chains imprisoning one and escape the confines of the prison you need the knowledge of where the boundaries are. Only true knowledge of self and history can lead one through the open door of mental slavery. If a prisoner wanted to escape jail, he would have to know the prison perimeters. To attain freedom, one has to understand the constraints on your freedom. Only when adequately armed with this knowledge can you break free successfully. No matter how disingenuous the imperialists, they have never been able to fully imprison the human mind and the soul is totally free.

However illogical racism might seem to the objective and intelligent onlooker, as long as this noxious behaviour is rewarded, it will continue. This is the reason Caucasians find it hard to do right by the black countries and communities they come across, because they stand to lose the potential rewards Africans provide. Africans, through ignorance of their own history, continue to fight over trifles and issues created by the West as diversionary tactics to keep Africans divided against themselves and thus easy prey.

The most worrying thing of all is that Africa and its diaspora, despite centuries of oppression, remain largely dependent on the West for their economies, industry, medicine, jobs and their militaries.

The condition of the Africans and their descendants abroad is that they are nominally free in the body only. They remain in the grips of their white oppressors in spite of all they have had to endure because they remain mentally enslaved. Unfortunately, many miseducated Africans have not yet worked out that they are mentally enslaved and many who suspect that they are, have not worked out what the constraints to their freedom are.

African miseducation largely revolves around ignorance of or limited knowledge of African culture and history; the fear and psychological inferiority complexes generated due to this mental isolation; the acting out of inferiority complexes; low expectations in a myriad of self-destructive ways; and, finally, crippling dependence.

During the Western colonization of Africa, their African subjects were educated in the history, ways and manners of their colonial masters. Very little time, if any, was spent studying their own culture, history, achievements, or people. To make matters worse, European scholars generally wrote Africa out of history. Western references to Africans in their literature were patronizing at least and often denigrating. The net result is that the 'well' miseducated African usually knows very little about his own people and does not care to know, as his white professors, books and media taught him to believe that Africans do not amount to much. Miseducated Africans end up in a bottleneck as they come to realize in time that they are never going to be fully accepted in Western society on account of their colour and background. All they have ever learned about Africa from Europeans or read in books, in newspapers and watched on the news about black people tends not to be flattering at all.

Many African people still fall headlong into the trap and hold their Western miseducation as their accepted truth. As they cannot see a way out for Africans, they follow the path of least resistance and join the bandwagon of African critics. They may even exploit other Africans if given a chance and readily fall in line with demands of their white counterparts who use them in positions of pseudo-leadership to continue to suppress the aspirations of other Africans. Some Africans end up resenting both white and black people and others eventually slip into a state of chronic depression. It is important that Africans realize the need to re-educate themselves as white superiority is not based on facts. It relies on the continual exploitation of the less privileged and the flaunting of the ill-gotten wealth and opportunities as trophies which Africans obviously lack and are supposed to read into as a sign of their own inferiority.

Even when Africans are fully aware and conscious of the situation they still have to deal with the reality of the ethnic penalties and disadvantages that have been woven into the fabric of Western societies. For many Africans their predicament becomes almost overwhelming to deal with. This is precisely where they and their descendants have gone wrong as they have tended to adopt an individualistic approach to a collective societal problem. The individualistic approach to racism is doomed to failure as no one person can solve the problem of racism alone. Africans and their diaspora, whose plan is not to get involved, ignore racism and just live their lives, will unfortunately come up against the stonewall of institutionalised racism time and time again. While personal wealth and high social standing may provide some cover, it is ultimately insufficient protection for individual Africans or their children, against a concerted attempt by the white system to bring them down from their isolated position.

Michael Jackson — or 'Jacko' as he was sometimes known — was not really as 'wacko' as people think. It is alleged that he tried to change himself from black to white with the help of plastic surgeons. His desire to change his skin colour and appearance may have been borne of a deep-rooted insecurity that being a black man in white American society fosters. Unlike many black African people, the difference was that Michael Jackson had the money to attempt it. Unfortunately, for black people, even money cannot buy acceptance into a racist white society.

Knowledge empowers people, and the wrong kind of knowledge can paralyse people and make them incapable of responding adequately to situations around them. The miseducation Africans have received is Eurocentric in origin and has justified exploitation, slavery, segregation and institutional racism.

Over 50 years ago the famous pan-Africanist, W. E. B. Du Bois wrote:

"It is worse than stupid to allow a people's education to be under the control of those who seek not the progress of the people but their use as means of making themselves rich and powerful.

It is wrong for the University of London to control the University of Ghana. It is wrong for the Catholic Church to direct the education of black Congolese."[12]

The various methods with which many Africans and their descendants have chosen to cope with white imperialism has varied widely but can but grouped under a few main themes.

On the African continent and in the diaspora many Africans, consciously or subconsciously, remain very apathetic to the situation around them and refuse to engage the system in which they live. They abdicate and leave the responsibility of their countries socio-economic fortunes to politicians they do not trust, their children's education to teachers and the wider society, their religious and spiritual development to their pastors; their health to their doctors and their money to their banks. While it is all well and good to take advantage of the services modern civilization and technology provides, these services were meant to be monitored by the person most affected by them: you.

Some other Africans have responded by becoming what they call 'coconuts'. 'Coconuts' are physically black or brown on the outside but psychologically white on the inside. They have totally imbibed Western education and culture. They consciously or subconsciously reject and look down on everything African and to do with Africans. They rigidly and slavishly defend every move and action of their white counterparts and are loath to criticize or see anything wrong with the West. They are often very well versed in Western culture and etiquette, in some cases even more so than white people are. On the other hand, they are very quick to find fault in black African people and criticize them at will. If given a chance, they will put down black African people and their aspirations, not just for the recognition they get from the white community but primarily because they genuinely have a very negative opinion of the black race — their own race.

In reward for their efforts, they are sometimes elevated to prominent positions and are used as figureheads, whose real aim is the quenching of black aspirations. African coons or 'coconuts' all too often argue strenuously to put black counterparts out of jobs and positions and will tacitly turn the other way when the white networks secure jobs and positions for their own people.

Another type of black African person you come across are those that, quite justifiably, feel very proud of the positions they have reached through years of hard toil and a lot of self-sacrifice and biting down in Western societies. Their point of view is quite simple: if I could suffer and make a way through, then so can you, even when this achievement has taken them on average about ten years longer than it has taken the average white person in a similar job or position.

While there is nothing wrong with hard work and self-sacrifice, there is a lot wrong with being unsupportive of fellow Africans who try to follow their example. There is no pride or honour in being unhelpful or even being obstructive to fellow Africans simply because you had a hard time of it. In fact, Africans must strive to be as helpful to one another as possible in order to reduce their collective suffering. This is one of the most disappointing aspects of the Africans' social oppression, which promotes individualism rather than a collective approach to their socio-economic problems. As Africans try to lift themselves upwards against the odds, the Western society has put in place an individualistic and selfish approach that does nothing to uplift the community in general.

The main reason for this kind of behaviour is the constant negative referencing that many miseducated Africans indulge in. Instead of looking forward to and comparing themselves to their white counterparts, they continue to look backwards to the black African people, or the African communities they have managed to escape from, who are downtrodden from years of oppression and suppression and thus they lose any real objective assessment of their actual position. Perhaps it is rather too painful to come to an objective assessment, as this would reveal that while their white colleagues ghost through the system, Africans take, in general, about ten years more to reach the same position — if they ever do — than whites. In many cases, the African people they like to reference themselves against have in general had very limited opportunities to advance their careers.

Some African people have given up all together. The situation around them looks bleak and they cannot see a clear route out of their predicament. They literally stop trying. Children, who as mentioned earlier learn a great deal from observation, see and perceive this sense of hopelessness all around them and lose the will to strive for themselves as well. They concentrate on the present and seek only quick money and immediate gratification. Predictably, this slippery slope leads nowhere fast and can lead to a life of crime or the fringes of crime. They do not plan for the future because they see none; they live fast and die young.

Unfortunately this group of African people unwittingly also perform another function; that is creating and maintaining a source of negative referencing the white communities love to propagate as in their view it justifies the atrocities they have committed or will then proceed to commit. These Africans unwittingly create a negative reference point for the black communities, propagating feelings of low self-esteem and the self-hate that has locked these communities in the poverty trap that they find themselves in.

Whenever discussing racial inequalities it is important to base discussions on well researched statistics that tell the whole story and not the individual anecdotal stories that do not really reflect the true situation. This is a favoured method of diversion of the West when dealing with race and equality matters, and it is up to the oppressed to read the writing carefully and not then be satisfied with personal gain, either financial or positional when the majority of the African people are languishing in abject poverty.

Therefore, Africans cannot be satisfied with having a tiny minority of a few iconic and wealthy individuals at the expense of the impoverished collective.

Colin Powell and Condoleezza Rice were visible black US politicians but they did not represent the opportunities that are available for African Americans. Not even having Barack Obama as a black American president was sufficient in itself to improve the lot of African Americans and Africans everywhere without a concerted effort from all Africans. Rich, flamboyant African leaders and celebrities showing off their jewellery, clothes and cars do not represent the reality of the poverty and depravation of the vast majority of Africans. Africans must endeavour to avoid the myopic and selfish view of seeing the world only through their own eyes or personal construct or through the jaundiced view that the West has of Africa. Without a global outlook and position, Africans will fail to appreciate the gravity of the situation they face, both on an individual level and collectively as people.

Conversely, it is obvious that the West sees itself as individuals as well as a collective and this leads to greater cohesion in these societies and therefore, makes them more effective and purposeful, for good or bad. Africans, on the other hand, tend to see themselves only as individuals and in trying to avoid the European label of inferiority, tend towards dispersion and less societal cohesion.

The selfish and individualistic approach has got miseducated African people nowhere. In Africa, individualism and tribalism are the bedrock on which corruption thrives. People driven by poverty and suffering and misled into feeling inferior by Western propaganda, have decided that only one person matters — themselves. Corrupt African politicians have taken to stealing each successive government blind. Their captive populace, instead of bringing the corrupt regimes to book, rather choose to devise means whereby they too can either get into positions in government where they can steal the taxpayer's money for themselves. Their motto being: "If you can't beat them, join them."

The net result is that African countries, rich in people and natural resources, are impoverished in real terms. The wealth of the country is usually nestled in the Western accounts of an ever-growing number of corrupt leaders.

In Africa, many people are languishing in abject poverty. They are in darkness because there is no electricity, they have no petrol to drive their cars and no roads to drive on if they have a car. Inexplicably, they do not to make a firm link between their desperate poverty and the politicians who are siphoning their countries' funds to accounts in the same European countries that have exploited Africa for hundreds of years now. Corruption in Africa continues unabated because these unscrupulous leaders are largely unchallenged by their longsuffering people and their agenda of self-aggrandizement before the wellbeing of millions of poor people dying daily of disease and hunger across Africa.

Effective African leadership would immediately and dramatically improve the lives of millions of Africans and would inevitably attract even more wealth to the countries as it would foster confidence in investors, indigenous and foreign. However, the situation is such that many African societies worship affluence, no matter how it comes about. They only care about themselves, and find it easier to support the corrupt leaders in the hope of benefiting somehow. As a survival strategy too, this approach has failed. The African majority usually does not get a dime and most people who sell their communities out for small change, find themselves still trapped in poverty.

The same principles apply to the African communities living in Western societies. Frustrated by lack of opportunity and poverty, African youth in diaspora tear themselves apart over trifles, completely missing or ignoring the point, namely, that their social issues are largely not of their own doing but are part of a wider scheme of open and covert white racism that keeps them divided and penned down in poverty.

Institutional racism is one of the most insidious forms of racism. Institutional racism ensures that white privileges and black ethnic penalties are enshrined in white societies. It has allowed racism to become so casual in Western societies that socialized racists simply act out racist ideas and agendas without a second thought to their actions. There does not need to be a deep collective conspiracy to be racist. It suffices that white Westerners simply act out what they have been socialised to be — which is racist — much in the same manner as African people are socialised to accept lower standards and positions. White people expect to get jobs without competing fairly with ethnic minorities. They expect their schools and housing to be well funded. They expect the police and courts to treat them fairly — and inevitably they do.

This is the reason why many white employers employ and treat their staff differently. A white employee can expect to get away with more, work less hard, earn more money and find it easier to be promoted than someone from an ethnic minority. This is the predetermined inherent white privilege woven into Western societies.

CHAPTER SEVENTY EIGHT
THE FIRST STEPS TOWARD PSYCHOLOGICAL FREEDOM

"If there is no struggle, there is no progress. Those who profess to favour freedom, and yet depreciate agitation, are men who want crops without plowing up the ground. They want rain without thunder and lightning. They want the ocean without the awful roar of its many waters. This struggle may be a moral one; or it may be a physical one; or it may be both moral and physical; but it must be a struggle. Power concedes nothing without a demand. It never did and it never will."
Frederick Douglass[1]

Psychological freedom is a two-step process. The first step is developing a clear knowledge of self. The second is the exercise of the freedom of self or self-determination and self-actualization. It is very important to note that the elimination of white racism is not a prerequisite for the liberation of the African mind from mental slavery on any level, individual, community or national. It is unrealistic to expect the white supremacy system that thrives on the exploitation of African resources and manpower to be the same system that selflessly hands out freedom and equality to Africans.

The first step towards full freedom and equality is a clear understanding of what the limitations and constrains of black freedom are. Any black African who does not appreciate that the white supremacist/imperialist is waging a broad-fronted attack on him or her, using every means possible and in all areas of human activity, may find that he or she falls short of actualizing true freedom and equality. It is only when this realization has been made and accepted internally that concrete steps can be taken to address the problem.

Apart from true African knowledge, one of the biggest impediments to the freeing of the African is the African's fear of freedom and the fear of death. The fear of death was the key reason why Africans and other non-white people succumbed to Europeans as slaves and colonized people. Frantz Fanon asserted that the risk of life is a precondition for the freedom of the slave.

It is important to note that when one analyses Hegel's master-slave paradigm, it is essential that both the master and the slaves lives for either one to be recognised. Therefore, the slave master also has a vested interest in preserving his own life. Otherwise their sacrifice and preparedness to die for their cause is rendered illogical.

Freedom, therefore, requires the risk of life as well as the conquering of the fear of physical death. What motivates the slave master therefore, and guides the amount of risk they are prepared to take, is the size of the rewards they can reap and the ability and the willingness of their potential victims or slaves to resist oppression.

Practical examples of this behaviour can be seen everywhere because the white supremacist does not lightly intervene in the affairs of people who know who they are and are prepared to do whatever it takes to defend themselves. White supremacists as a rule prey mainly on the weak and defenceless people of the world. Where the people have internalized ideas of their own inferiority from their colonial masters and have been made apathetic, impotent and defenceless by the machinations of the white supremacists, they invariably suffer most.

Bulhan wrote: *"As long as the colonized accepts servitude for fear of death, so long as he is unwilling to die for freedom; the ; the colonizer is tyrannical and violent without limit."*[2]

Fanon recognized the need for reciprocal recognition for human life and relatedness. He argued that without reciprocal recognition, there could be no identity, no self-worth, no dignity. He concluded that recognition is unattainable without struggle and that the struggle entails the risk of life.

'I am not merely here-and-now sealed into thingness. I am somewhere else and for something else. I demand that notice be taken of my negating activity, insofar as I pursue something other than life; insofar as I do battle for the creation of a human world- that is, a world of reciprocal recognition. He who is reluctant to recognize me opposes me. In a savage struggle, I am willing to accept the convulsions of death, invincible dissolution, but also the possibility of the impossible.'[3]

The fear of freedom while also encompassing the fear of physical death, stems more from 'intropression' or the internalized desire of the self to actualize themselves as caricatures of their white masters than from their fear of the 'unknown'. Miseducated Africans have lost the ability to be self-actualizing and self-determining, after many years of dependence on their slave and colonial masters.

Many Africans in the diaspora are terrified of the prospect of being self-determining because self-determination involves taking responsibility for their own lives and the lives of their families and communities without having to rely on their white masters for food, infrastructure, and direction.

Since the official abolishment of slavery the descendants of the African slaves have lived almost entirely within the paradigm set for them by their white masters and have been happy to define themselves by, and identify themselves with, a system of white supremacy that was set up to exploit them from the onset.

Most African countries slumped into abject dependence on the West less than ten years after their 'flag independence' from their colonial masters.

They rely on the West for their food, socio-economic infrastructure, political direction, and the health of their people. Many desperate African people rely on Western charity and aid donations to maintain the basic needs of their survival, like food, clean water, medicines and the education of their children.

Since Western aid is woefully insufficient to meet even these basic needs of Africans, and the same Western countries sap out the natural and human resources at a much faster rate than they provide aid, the result is the predictable rise of poverty and disease, year in, year out, with the steady erosion of any claims to sovereignty as time passes.

As political instability, poverty and chaos spread across Africa, it drives an increasingly desperate African people into forced migration westwards, and into crime and corruption. Hundreds of African migrants perish at sea in their desperate bid to reach Europe every year. It is indeed to the credit of the evil genius of white supremacy that the suffering African masses cannot work out the true source of their woes, never mind have the focus to come up with constructive solutions.

The more the oppressed African people sink to the level of basic living, and concentrate only on food, water and shelter, the more vulnerable they are to the predations of white supremacy.

Bulhan noted that oppression always takes root when the fear of physical death exceeds the will to live and wrote:

'Whenever fear of physical death gains prominence, tyranny and exploitation flourish. The individual who places a premium on biological survival becomes uprooted from his community's ideals, history, and destiny. And the more the oppressed seek physical survival, the more their oppression deepens and the more frequent the betrayals.'[4]

As all human beings are mortal, they all will, after, hopefully, a long and productive existence, die and have to meet their maker. Physical death can only be postponed at best…it cannot be avoided.

While many Africans submit to the ever-worsening conditions of white socio-economic slavery in order to cling on to their ever-shortening and increasingly poor quality physical lives, they are, in fact, already suffering a degree of psychological and social living death.

The logic of this surrender into slavery is flawed because violence and premature death, from a myriad of preventable causes, is a persistent feature of the African people and their diaspora experience all over the world, wherever they are within reach of white imperialists or supremacists.

The poor quality of life and shortened life expectancy of Africans are a consequence of their enslaved and dependent position and not the reward of the white slave master, which makes it necessary to dig deeper into their psyche to expose the internalized inferiority complexes and the reason why many Africans remain blind to this fact.

It is the internalized inferiority complexes coupled with the fear of physical death and the fear of freedom and the lack of self-reliance and determination, which combine to lock the Africans into the Western paradigm.

Many miseducated Africans in diaspora are too scared to live and too scared to die, and instead find solace in a myriad of pointless and self-destructive circular activities that distract them from the reality of the precarious living situation and their lack of linear progression on an individual level and as people.

The short-term solution is sought after in disregard to the long-term consequences, and they turn to drugs, alcoholism, gambling, crime and corruption in droves.

Many others turn in desperation to the churches and the mosques in search of miraculous solutions to their socio-economic problems; poor health, no jobs and no money, and for a glimmer of hope to explain their desperate and desolate existence.

Unfortunately, like a flock of sheep being led by a pack of wolves, many more fall headlong into the traps set for them by their predatory religious leaders who fleece them in the name of the Lord.

Africans must redefine themselves as a matter of urgency. In Caucasian lexicon, the word 'black' is simply an adjective and strictly speaking, it is inaccurate to refer to Africans as black because, in reality, Africans come in all shades and colours from dark complexions to white. Despite being semantics, it is similarly inaccurate to refer to Caucasians as white, because strictly speaking they are not white but shades of pink and light brown. Africans in the West are referred to as black Caribbeans, black Americans, black British, black other, etc. in contrast to people from other races who are referred to in relation to the land mass or geographical area from which they descend, for instance, Asians, Indians, Europeans and South Americans.

There is, however, a more important reason why all Africans and their descendants must reject out of hand the appellation 'black', and these are the powerful deeply symbolic and negative connotations it is associated with in the Western world.

It is no secret that the word 'black' in Western society embodies everything negative the Western or Caucasian thinks about the world. Hence, the popular description of black Monday, black widow, black Death, black moods and many more. In medieval times, the grotesque and evil, the devil and his flock of demons were depicted as black men.

Clearly, the negativity is directed at African people, because we do not see a similar response towards owning flashy black cars or expensive black tuxedos and evening dresses.

The term Negro is simply Spanish for black, and is a more polite form of the word Nigger. When Africans allow Westerners generally refer to them as black, we allow them to continue to apply this highly negatively symbolic description to them, it is practically no different than calling Africans Niggers or Negroes.

Racism is so widespread and prevalent in the West because it is so easily transmitted in the highly codified symbolic language that permeates all aspects of their lives and readily invokes strong negative emotions and thoughts consciously and subconsciously.

Any African who has suffered racism first-hand or vicariously knows that Westerners do not need to communicate verbally with each other to provoke the words or actions we define as racism.

True African knowledge is the key to mental freedom for both the recipients of racism and the racists. When true knowledge of self is actualized, the focus, determination and direction become clear and the journey to freedom can begin. It will also help liberate the minds of Caucasians, who through their socialization have come to the firm but unfounded belief in their own innate superiority over all Africans.

The key to knowledge is not just the accumulation of knowledge, which in itself is an act of vanity, but the application of knowledge.

To have knowledge of true African history and identity but not to apply that knowledge practically is simply another form of mental slavery where in most cases, the main inhibiting factor is the fear of white supremacy reprisals. Financial wealth alone is not a prerequisite for freedom from mental slavery; the application of true knowledge is.

In order to break the self-regenerating cycle of socialized inferiority it is important to read and imbibe the right information about Africa and its diaspora knowing that the main source of our information about themselves, Caucasians, is covertly and even openly hostile.

The African child is the key to Africa's future, and their parents, extended family and community in ensuring that they are fed the right information about themselves from the start must expend every effort. You cannot teach what you do not know and even as we try to teach our children, we must re-educate and reorientate ourselves from the miseducation given to slaves and the colonial masters, and is perpetuated by the Western media and Western institutions of learning. Africans will find that their increasing knowledge, self-confidence, courage, conviction and positive orientation will also naturally rub off on our children.

Chinweizu wrote:

"Euro-imperial universalists oppose the Africanisation of curricula in Africa because an African child who is first given a thorough grounding in the African cultural tradition, before being exposed to those of other lands is not likely to be intimidated into awe of European culture, and is far less likely to be inducted into servility towards European culture.

'Knowing African nursery songs, ancient African epics, drama, fables, stories, parables, and a correct appreciation of their worth, would fortify him against hegemonist propaganda. He would display a cultural confidence born of sound knowledge of the glories of his African civilization, and be less prone to genuflect to the culture of Europeans, Arabs or whoever else.'"[5]

In the West, the black family unit is particularly prone to the negative effects of institutional racism. Every effort must be expended to build and support the black family unit. The single African mother and rarely the single father parenthood or 'survival' units under the intense pressure of institutional racism are a recipe for failure.

The family is the centre of the universe for every child. Children are like sponges and learn from society as a whole and not just from their parents or families. Whatever the African parent fails to teach their child the wider society will fill that gap with some lessons of their own. This may involve learning about sex, prostitution and drugs from peer groups, television, and schools and not from their parents.

Driven out of their homes by the alienating effects of Western capitalism and in search of money, in particular, the socialization vacuum created in the African child's life is filled by television, temporary nannies, friends and peer groups.

The alienation that Western capitalism produces moves the psychosocial centre of an individual from within an individual towards outward goals of materialism, status quo and narcissism.

The miseducation many an unfortunate African child in diaspora receives is largely from a system set up to exploit and denigrate them and not just from their parents who may have fallen short from their natural role of educating and nurturing their children in the pursuit of money.

All Africans must attempt to understand about themselves, they must seek to know the white global apartheid system inside out. Only then would they grasp that the amorphous shape shifting institutional racism of white supremacy/imperialism works, in all areas of human activity. Armed with this knowledge, Africans will be in a position to be effectively to counter their frequent and savage attacks.

There must be no more 'mindless' acceptance of Western propaganda and all sources of information must be appraised and assumed to contain a nugget of disinformation, which must be taken with more than a pinch of salt until proven otherwise. Without this discipline, it is much better to switch off the television or not read the newspapers when one is tired, so you do not allow the subconscious mind to soak up subliminal misinformation uncritically, and form the basis for further actions or behaviour.

It is important to seek the right information, whether written, audio, or visual to help build up your psychological wellbeing. The African child should be the main focus of our attention, and Africans should not only seek to re-educate themselves but also read to, teach and learn from their families and friends.

Africans must no longer over indulge themselves in time-wasting circular and negative dysfunctional knee-jerk reactions to the oppression they face. Africans, must as a matter of our survival and wellbeing, immediately adopt a linear and progressive problem-solving approach to our life problems, the majority of which are a direct and indirect product of white supremacy, be it slavery, colonialism, neo-colonialism, or globalization.

With the renewed confidence realized from the knowledge of self, the low self-esteem and low expectations of the children of miseducated Africans will be a thing of the past. Better life choices that enhance the individual and their families, rather than the bank accounts of their white puppet masters, will help break the poverty-disease dependence cycle that reinforces their physical dependence and feelings of psychological inferiority.

Africans have been problem solvers for millennia. Human civilization in Africa, science, mathematics, astrology, medicine, technology and the arts all developed as by-products of the linear progressive thinking and problem-solving of our ancestors in response to nature's challenges.

From our birth to our inevitable death, life follows a predictable pattern for all human beings. From dependent babies, we become children who then grow into teenagers, independent young adults, middle-aged adults, older adults and ultimately dependent elderly. For every life stage, there is general age-specific behaviour and achievements that demonstrate that stage or progress through life.

In prehistoric times, if a man-eating lion was on the prowl, or a rogue elephant with a predilection for killing humans was on the rampage, linear thought leading to concrete action, dictated that the tribe or people would try either to escape, trap or kill the beasts. They would at the very least leave the vicinity where they were at their most vulnerable. Hanging around waiting for the beasts to be miraculously struck down or pretending that the threat does not exist are examples of circular thought leading to a dysfunctional non-progressive response.

The biggest threat to the psychological and physical wellbeing of all Africans and their diaspora wherever they may be, are the greatest predators of all… man… and in particular, the white imperialist or supremacist.

Ignorance is no excuse, whether you do not know or do not care to, the result is the same. Inaction in the knowledge of the true situation is not much use either. For most Africans living in extreme poverty, it will translate into a short life of severe hardship, which could end prematurely, due to a myriad of preventable means.

Africans who have the intelligence and the foresight to begin to counter the deadly paradigm of the white supremacist, may experience all sorts of fabricated difficulties, designed to force their heads back down. Africans, who know who they are, and what is going on around them, will find that their motivation to secure freedom and material equality and their will to succeed, is exponentially increased by the white supremacists' attempts to impede them.

In the Serengeti, when the herds of gazelle have to make the seasonal but perilous river crossing in search of greener pastures, they must face down their fear of the rapids, hungry crocodiles and prides of lions that await them at the banks of the river and in the river itself. Every year, in spite of all the dangers that face them well over 90% of the herd will reach the greener pastures and live on to perpetuate the species. Refusing to seek greener pastures or cross the river due to fear means certain death not just for the individual gazelle but also for the whole herd.

Even though our human predators, the white imperialists, represent clear and present danger just like their counterparts in the Serengeti, they are still crucially only a thin white line. Much of what they do to Africans and their diaspora largely requires the cooperation of Africans in some form or another.

While a relatively small percentage of Africans, have acted directly on behalf of their white masters against the African collective, it has been the widespread ignorance and passivity of Africans in general that has cemented the deleterious effects of Western intervention in Africa.

The passivity is a result of a combination of ignorance, inferiority complexes and fear, all by-products of the Western education we were given with the subtle aim of creating this dependent psychological state. Once the ruling African elites and middle class are indoctrinated, the reach of the supremacist is extended to the whole country and beyond. This is why the lives and wellbeing of so many Africans, and their diaspora are negatively affected because they remain and even seek to belong to the Western paradigm and are therefore remain, directly and indirectly within their killing fields or zones.

By understanding institutional racism and all its manifestations, slavery, colonization, globalization, we can see and appreciate the severe effect it had on the lives of millions of Africans, in the past, the present and potentially in the future.

Armed with the right knowledge, Africans will seek freedom and equality. They will no longer be moved by mindless materialism. They will no longer seek the acceptance and approval of our slave masters at any personal or general price to their people. Africans will no longer look to the authors of their problems for the solutions to their problems. Africans, who have empowered themselves with true knowledge will no longer be satisfied with meaningless platitudes or accolades. By seeking first freedom and equality, all other material trappings many Africans seek in vain will come naturally.

When Africans understand that their survival into the next day depends in part on a deep understanding of the global machinations of the institutional racism of the white supremacy system, they are ready to make the crucial paradigm shift.

Linear activity is any activity that directly answers, firstly, nature's simple but crucial question of survival before anything else. Linear activity is therefore goal and results oriented. For instance, if the object of a football game is to score goals to win the match, then linear activity is every activity that is carried out to score that goal. On the other hand, circular activity while sometimes temporarily useful psychologically to reduce stress does not address the primary and crucial question of survival and must not supplant linear activity as the main expenditure of our energy.

Using the game of football again as an analogy; teams that continuously dribble and pass the ball aimlessly between themselves expend a lot of energy, but usually do not score any goals.

Circular human activity is just about any activity in any human area of social interaction that deflects one's mind away from the primary and crucial question of survival. While circular activities are useful in reducing stress and anxiety, ultimately, they are ineffective in providing direction. Circular activity could be alcohol dependence, drug abuse; it could be sports, television or even religion. Because today we live in the world where many seek to thrive and not just survive, the crucial survival question is only masked. As consumerism is the key driver of capitalism, the need to search for and acquire material goods inordinately occupies the minds and the time of many in the developed world and even in the Third World where they are exploited by capitalism. However, for millions of the world's poorest whether they live in concrete or actual jungles, they have to find food, water and shelter on a daily basis to ensure that they see the next day.

Many Africans simply obey Maslow's first law of survival. They engage in repetitive, circular and ineffective behavioural patterns in response to external stress. They seek only the seek food and water, to feed their hunger and slake their thirst, in the short term. However, as part of linear thought pattern followed by concrete actions, they should not only seek food and water, to feed their hunger and slake their thirst, in the short term, they should also seek to tackle the cause of their famine and lack of good drinking water.

Instead of looking for temporary shelter and safety, they should also seek to fight the cause of poverty that prevents them finding or affording decent accommodation. Instead of taking up arms to join another senseless Western instigated war that further destabilizes the region and exacerbates the already severe poverty, they should recognize that they are playing into the hands of the imperialists and ultimately would be the only losers.

It is extremely important to note that the easiest way to extinguish any noxious human behaviour is not to reward it. It is as simple as that. Unless Africans or their diaspora have some vested interest in perpetuating the deprivations and suffering imposed upon them by this global system of white supremacy then each, and every African individual must be prepared to resist and not reward racism on every level and in every area of human activity, be it on a personal level, family, community, national and global levels. While it is undoubtedly true that a collective push towards the eradication of racism would be helpful, those who are waiting for global cohesion to take place first before they sort out the day-to-day problems that this nefarious system imposes, are mistaken. Little drops of water make an ocean, and it is imperative that everyone contributes first their own little drop before they can contemplate many grander schemes.

In this technological information age, it is important for Africans to develop, produce, disseminate and control information about themselves.

They must fight to change the curriculum in schools in Africa and the diaspora to reflect true African history and culture.

All Africans must endeavour, through re-education with the right knowledge, to break the inferiorization cycle and failed psychosocial development of our children by taking primary responsibility for our children's education.

Africans must stop grooming their children, indeed their future, to take up roles as low-skilled workers or as surplus labour in the white supremacy system and rather grow them for a promising future in Africa and for the African diaspora. All African nations must undertake to provide and prioritize the basic needs of their people above all else. Every African nation must endeavour to feed their people and ensure that the health, safety and education of their people are their primary priorities before the service of any odious debts.

It is crucial that the poor, disenfranchised and hungry African people to make the realization that their surest route to obtain the basic needs of life, food, water, shelter; access to medicines and adequate medical care resides in a good government of the people by the people.

It is remarkable that millions of African people perish for lack of basic life needs when in actual fact only a very small statistically insignificant minority of people, the super-rich will not be significantly better off materially, if the world's wealth was redistributed more equitably.

Most African people, even up to the level of multimillionaires, would enjoy an appreciable increase in wealth and standard of living if corruption were significantly reduced.

This analogy also applies to the diaspora living in the West where the dismantlement of institutional racism would improve access to good schools, housing, jobs opportunities and business opportunities. This would increase social mobility and enhance the nation as a whole, not just the black or ethnic minority communities.

All African nations as a unit should stop as a matter of urgency, paying and servicing odious foreign debts, which sap the life and resources out of the countries. These lost resources must be redirected towards the health and education of their people to help rebuild the country up from the grass roots.

Eradicating poverty will support the rehabilitation from mental slavery and produce generations of Africans who have the self–confidence to become the very best in their chosen endeavours.

The widespread practice of bribery and corruption has to be eradicated at all levels, again even though it is theoretically quicker and easier to achieve this from the top down, pragmatically it will only be achieved when a larger percentage of the population begins to take personal responsibility to stop giving, demanding or receiving bribes and bring pressure to bear on their politicians to do the same.

Corruption acts as a drain on African nations and deprives the nation of essential resources just as a baby is deprived of a meal when his/her or her mother empties her babies' milk or food down the drain.

The white supremacy global system of institutional racism needs and feeds of the corruption of African nations or rather corrupt African politicians and if Africans become organized, they will be less exposed to their ravages.

As corruption begins to die a natural death across the continent, many Africans will find it translates almost immediately into material, and socio-economic gain, better and regular pay, better roads, schools, hospitals, good roads and communication facilities.

It will also make the continent more attractive to foreign investment that can be tailored to meet the needs of the people without destroying the environment.

One of the ways the Europeans stripped Africans of their identity was through changing their names and next his language.

A language is one of the key building blocks of any society and people. It not only promotes social cohesion by uniting the people who can speak and understand a certain, language; it is a means of projecting a culture and people for beyond the physical borders of where they inhabit.

Frantz Fanon argued that cultural deracination was the intellectual and emotional counterpart of economic enslavement and was essential to facilitate exploitation and wrote:

"To speak a language is to take on a world, a culture."

Fanon continued:

"The fact of having to speak nothing but the other's language when this other was the conqueror, ruler, and oppressor was at once an affirmation of him, his world view, and his values; a concession of his framework; and an estrangement from one's history, values, and outlook."[6]

Still on language, Kassahun Checole in an interview for the New African magazine in June 2004 stated:

"It is a tragedy in our history, that, as Africans, we have not noticed the relationship between language and civilization or even between language and economic development. No civilization has developed with a foreign language."[7]

No people can develop without their culture and history, more so, especially in the Machiavellian world of white supremacy.

Frantz Fanon warned:

"Colonialism…. Is violence in its natural state, and will only yield when confronted with greater violence."[8]

Africans everywhere must cease to reward white supremacy through their fear, apathy, ignorance, and impotence and unite around the common cause of freedom and equality in all areas of human activity, especially politics, economics, science and technology in order to shake of the bondage of mental and economic slavery imposed on them by white supremacy. It is the only way to attain a decent quality of living for the vast majority of Africans, whether on the African continent or in the diaspora.

"The wellbeing and progress of Europe have been built up with the sweat and dead bodies of Negroes, Arabs, Indians, and the yellow races. We have

decided not to overlook this any longer." Frantz Fanon.[9]

The global power structure of white supremacy is the single most important reason why Africans suffer, be it poverty, disease, crime or corruption.... Toto ignore this is tantamount to committing physical and psychosocial suicide or agreeing to join the multitude of the living dead; the poor, denigrated and exploited people of the world. Worse still, the intergenerational life sentence of mental slavery locks their children into a lifetime of servitude as well.

Once the African collective, Africans and their diaspora, realize that African empowerment is directly related to the adoption of correct behaviour patterns, organization, behaviour discipline and control through the right knowledge and not through mindless materialism or craved acceptance into the white community, the core of the African problem is solved.

It is worth reminding people that materialism is only a facet of our existence on earth. 'Money does not make a man'. We were all born into this world, naked without any material trappings. When we eventually depart into the next life, we will not be taking a single material thing with us either. The core essence of a human being is multifaceted and is not defined by materialism alone.

While acknowledging that money and materialism is an important part of life, especially within the Western paradigm, the true essence of man, our souls, love, and charity cannot be bought or sold. This is why the intrinsic value of all men remains the same, rich or poor, white or black. Linking your intrinsic self-value to the amount of money and material trappings you possess or do not have is a recipe for a lifetime of misery.

In the end, freedom is taken and not given, it is time for African people read the writing on the wall, and make a conscious decision to take charge of their lives to become self-determining individuals, families, communities and countries. Nobody will hand you equal rights if you do not fight for them or grant you freedom if you do not first seek to be free.

To be free you have to first think free, and this can only be achieved by re-educating your mind and then actually implementing this new Afrocentric paradigm as a way of life for you and your family. Africans must learn to be African, buy African, think African and live African. Only when Africans live in their own paradigm can they hope to reach the pinnacles of human achievement again.

CHAPTER SEVENTY NINE
AFRICANS WHO SACRIFICED FOR FREEDOM

Every freedom enjoyed by Africans under the Western paradigm has been hard fought for. Many Africans and indeed, many white people have devoted their time and even their lives in the pursuit of true freedom and equality for all.

Africans who sacrificed everything for their people are too numerous to name, but in recent popular history certain African people stand out quite clearly.

HARRIET TUBMAN

Harriet Tubman was born into slavery between 1815 and 1825 in Maryland, USA. There are no records to pin down the day of her birth.

Harriet was only 5 feet tall and but she is remembered as an American hero and a giant icon of African freedom.

She is the best known African American abolitionist who guided hundreds of African slaves out bondage using the 'Underground Railway'.

The 'Underground railway' was not an actual railway but a covert network of people, black and white, who collaborated to help African slaves escape slavery from the slave owning Southern states of America.

Tubman was born to slave parents who named her Araminta Ross at birth. She was also known by the nickname 'Minty'. After she escaped slavery she adopted her mother's name Harriet and later used her husband's last name, Tubman.

Harriet Tubman's great mother was thought to be an Ashanti from

Ghana or Senegal who was kidnapped in slavery.

Under the harsh conditions of slavery, Tubman was set to work as a childminder aged only 5 years old. Her job was to watch over her mistress's baby. She would be whipped everytime the baby cried leaving her with scars on her neck for the rest of her life.

As a young girl, her suffering under the terrible slave conditions continued. She had her skull fractured when she tried to aid a runaway slave. She stood between the fugitive slave and her white master's who threw a heavy metal object at fugitive slave which hit Tubman on the head smashing in the side of her skull.

A devout Christian, it appears that this incident was a turning point in her life and Tubman claimed to have had visions and messages from God that gave her the conviction and courage of beliefs and her guided her in her expeditions to free slaves from their bondage.

Between 1851 to 1860, Harriet Tubman became the most famous conductor of the Underground Railroad. Over 9 years, she made 19 trips into the slave owning south and freed around 300 slaves, including her parents, relatives and friends.

She risked her life on every trip and proudly told another famous Afro-American activist, Frederick Douglass, that she had never lost a 'passenger' on her expeditions.

In addition to being a conductor on the Underground Railroad, Harriet Tubman worked as a cook and a nurse during the American Civil War and doubled up as a spy and a scout.

Tubman was the first woman in the civil war to lead an armed assault. Harriet Tubman, helped the Combuhee River Raid in which over 700 slaves were freed.

Harriet Tubman continued to fight for freedom after the American Civil war ended and was a vocal supporter of women's suffrage giving speeches in Washington, New York and Boston.

Harriet Tubman died of pneumonia on March 10th 1913.[1]

MARCUS GARVEY

Born in Jamaica in 1887, from a Jamaican family of the maroons, Marcus

Garvey left for the United States in 1916. There he formed a massive black organization, the Universal Negro Improvement Association, UNIA, which sought to restore the dignity of downtrodden blacks who were held only in contempt and pity by their white owners in the United States.

In his newspaper, the Negro World, he thundered:

'Two hundred and fifty years, we have been a race of slaves, for 50 years we have been a race of parasites. Now we propose to end all that, no more fear, no more sycophantic begging and pleading; the Negro must strike straight from the shoulder for manhood rights and full liberty.'[2]

He was also a contributor to other black papers like the African Times and Orient Review.

Marcus Garvey believed that blacks were the chosen people of God, a view that held many similarities to Zionism.

The U.N.I.A. was the first significant black nationalist movement that responded to the needs of blacks in economic, political, religious, social, cultural, and recreational areas. In Garvey's theology, blacks were the chosen people of God. Garveyism so resembled Zionism that Garvey actually called his followers 'Zionists'.

Garvey belonged to a long tradition of Africans scattered abroad who had been trying to reconnect with the African continent. They include African Americans such as Bishop Henry McNeal Turner, Paul Cuffee and Martin R. Delaney, and Afro-Caribbeans such as Edward Wilmot Blyden, who eventually settled in Liberia, and J. Albert Thorn.[3]

When Garvey was still a boy, Thorn was advocating a back-to-Africa movement in Jamaica. As the experiences of Garvey and others show, Westerners become paranoid when blacks begin to speak of themselves as Africans.[4]

Recently published documents and statements from the records of the US Department of Justice reveal a concerted effort, beginning in 1919, to undermine Garvey and his movement. By 1927 these federal officials, led by J. Edgar Hoover, had succeeded in bringing about Garvey's deportation. Without the leader, the movement became wracked with dissension. It never re-established itself as a significant force in the campaigns for African American political, social, or economic advancement in the United States.

Even after his deportation to Jamaica from the US he formed the People's Political Party.

In 1935, he left Jamaica for Britain where he died in 1940.

MALCOLM X

Malcolm X was only six years old when his father, a black activist influenced by the views of Marcus Garvey, was lynched in Lansing, Michigan. He drifted into Harlem's hustler culture and ended up in jail charged with robbery, prostitution and drugs offences.

In 1946 he was arrested for robbery and sentenced to jail for seven years. It was while he was in jail that he underwent a transformation. In 1933 he became a convert to the black Muslim movement, the Nation of Islam, founded in Detroit in 1930 and led by Elijah Muhammad, formerly called Elijah Robert Poole.

Malcolm, who had been a promising law student, was impeded in his intended profession by racism. He was an eloquent and passionate speaker and he soon became one of the leading figures in the Nation of Islam. He loved to speak in parables and is famous for saying black Americans never landed on the Plymouth Rock like the white American settlers; the Plymouth Rock was landed on them. He said,

"If I go home and find my child has blood running down her leg and someone tells me a snake bit her, I'm going out and kill snakes, and when I find a snake I'm not going to look if he has blood in his jaws."[5]

His strong views brought him much criticism from the white community. It also brought him into conflict with Martin Luther King Jr. who was simultaneously advocating non-violent, peaceful protests based on principle and religious grounds.

In November 1963, after President John F. Kennedy was assassinated, Malcolm X called it a case of 'the chickens coming home to roost'. This caused a media furore. Elijah Muhammad suspended him from the Nation of Islam for going too far. He left the organization altogether in March 1964 and formed Muslim Mosque, Inc. in New York.

In 1964, Malcolm X visited Mecca and West Africa and began to develop a softer, more rounded view of the world. He had experienced seeing free black men living in dignity as first class citizens in West Africa and in Mecca saw white and black people interact freely and with equality while observing their pilgrimage. However, he did not veer too far away from his true beliefs and while giving a speech in Harvard in December 1964, he declared:

"We don't believe that Afro-Americans should be victims any longer…we believe that bloodshed is a two-way street, that dying is a two-way street, that killing is a two-way street."[6]

In his last days, Malcolm X lived life with the certainty of death hanging over him. He prophetically predicted his own death to his autobiographer, Alex Haley.

On February 21st 1965 he was gunned down while addressing an audience that included his wife, in Upper Manhattan. Even today, a fog hangs over the circumstances and who may have killed him. Even though it is widely asserted disgruntled members of the Nation of Islam killed him, there are those who feel the CIA was involved.

However, his legacy lives on. He taught and offered black African people a strategy of survival, self-reliance, self-defence, self-respect and self-determination.[7]

STEVE BIKO

In South Africa in the 1960s and 70s, a new breed of black activists arose out of the Black Consciousness Movement [BCM]. Steve Biko, a medical student from the Eastern Cape became an articulate spokesman on Black Consciousness for the ANC.

Steve Biko was of the opinion that the problem with black oppression was first and foremost a psychological one. He hoped to break this psychological bind by promoting black pride and capabilities, black achievements and black self-sufficiency. black people should counter the negative image they had about themselves and replace it with a more positive one. He was disparaging about the submissive and cowed attitude of some of the black population and in 1970 he wrote in a student newsletter:

"The type of black man we have today has lost his manhood. Reduced to an obliging shell, he looks with awe at the white power structure and accepts what he regards as the 'inevitable position...

In the privacy of his toilet, his face twists in silent condemnation of white society but brightens up in sheepish obedience as he comes hurrying out in response to his master's impatient call. In the home-bound bus or train he joins the chorus that roundly condemns the white man but is first to praise the government in the presence of the police or his employers...All in all; The all, the black man has become a shell, a shadow of a man, completely defeated, drowning in his own misery, a slave, an ox bearing the yolk of oppression with sheepish timidity."[8]

In 1972, Steve Biko left medicine to become a full time political organiser. As self-determination was their goal, they did not seek or want help from whites, especially what he called 'pink liberals'. He saw them as part of the problem. The BCM motto was 'Black man, you are on your own'.

It was not long before the South Africa apartheid authorities were on to him. In 1973, Steve Biko and seven colleagues were issued banning orders. He was forbidden to speak in public, write for any publication or to be in the presence of more than one person at a time.[9]

The security forces harassed him continually and over a three-year period he was arrested and detained 29 times. In spite of his banning order restricting him to King William's Town, he continued to write, campaign and travel. In August 1977 he was arrested at a police roadblock outside Grahamstown on his return from a secret meeting in Cape Town. He was stripped naked and savagely beaten by a group of white policemen until he collapsed comatose from head injuries.

Chained hand and foot, incoherent, naked and bleeding from obvious head injuries, he did not receive any medical attention for over twenty-four hours and when an apartheid doctor was called, he reported that he could find no apparent injuries. His condition deteriorated and the following day it was decided that he should be transferred to a prison hospital in Pretoria, 700 miles away.

Still naked and in chains with only a blanket for cover and a bottle of water to drink, he was taken to Pretoria where he died a few hours after arriving at the prison hospital, aged only 30 on September 12th 1977. At the inquest into his death the South African Police were cleared of all blame.

THOMAS SANKARA

Thomas Sankara is perhaps the greatest leader and visionary the African continent has ever seen. He was a captain in the Burkinabe [Burkino Faso] armed forces that swept to power in a popular coup d'état in the former French colony known as Upper Volta in 1983, aged only 33 years old.

He became President and remained so until 1987. Once in power, Thomas Sankara launched the most ambitious programme of economic and social change ever seen in Africa. What Thomas Sankara achieved in his short spell in power and his life is nothing short of remarkable.

He renamed the country Burkina Faso meaning 'Land of Upright Men'. He aimed to eliminate corruption from society and break the dominance of their former colonial master, France. He refused all foreign aid arguing: "He, who feeds you, controls you."[10] He insisted his people had thc capacity to feed themselves. He explained Western imperialism to his people in the simplest of terms and urged them to see Western neo-colonialism as the imported food like the corn, wheat and millet on their plates and the imported clothes on their backs.

In an effort to improve food security he redistributed land from feudal landlords to peasants. Wheat production in Burkina Faso rose from 1700kg per hectare to 3800kg per hectare, making Burkina Faso fully food-sufficient in just four years. To prevent famine caused by the desertification of the Sahel, Sankara successfully organised the planting of ten million trees.

He spoke out about Western neo-colonial penetration in Africa through trade, aid and finance at the Organization of African Unity and called for a united African front to cancel all 'odious foreign debt'. He argued that the poor and exploited had no obligation to pay the rich and exploiting. To neutralise the power and influence of the IMF and the World Bank he nationalised all land and mineral wealth in Burkina Faso.

Thomas Sankara recognised that people's health was their wealth and launched an equally ambitious program to improve the health and wellbeing of his people using the motto: 'A healthy mind equals a healthy body'. The programme received recognition from the World Health organisation for vaccinating 2.5 million children against meningitis, yellow fever and measles.

Sankara's administration in Burkina Faso was the first African country publicly to recognise the AIDS epidemic as a major threat to Africa. The revolutionary regime in Burkina Faso organised national literary campaigns to bring the people with them.

Thomas Sankara was one of the first world leaders to promote women's rights and ensure that women were equally represented throughout his administration.[11] About women's rights, Thomas Sankara stated:

"The revolution and women's liberation go together. We do not talk of women's emancipation as an act of charity or because of a surge of human compassion. It is a basic necessity for the triumph of the revolution. Women hold up the other half of the sky."[12]

He banned female genital mutilation, forced marriages and polygamy. He promoted contraception and encouraged husbands to go to the market and prepare meals to experience for themselves the conditions their women faced at home.

Thomas Sankara was very tough on corruption; one of his first moves was to sell off the government fleet of Mercedes Benz cars and he made the cheapest car sold in Burkina Faso at the time, the Renault 5, the official service car of ministers. He reduced the salaries of well–paid public servants and forbade the use of government chauffeurs and first class tickets. He lowered his salary to $450 a month and limited his possessions to a car, four bikes, three guitars, a fridge and a broken freezer. He refused to use air-conditioning in his office because it was a luxury that most people in Burkina Faso could not afford.[13]

Thomas Sankara's ideology and progress stunned and alarmed Western powers, especially France. Several puppet French African leaders were very uncomfortable and did not want his ideology spreading to their countries. Prominent amongst Sankara's African detractors was the French stooge, Felix Houphouet-Boigny of Côte d'Ivoire.

His former close friend and compatriot, Blaise Campaore, backed by France and Houphouet-Boigny turned on him and plotted to kill him. Even though Thomas Sankara caught wind of the plot, he would not have Campaore arrested. A week before his murder, Thomas Sankara stated: *"While revolutionaries as individuals can be murdered, you cannot kill ideas."*[14]

On October 15th 1987 Campaore's guards stormed into Sankara's office, shot him dead and dismembered his body. He was buried hurriedly in a makeshift grave while his former compatriot, Blaise Campaore, took over power and set about dismantling Sankara's legacy and reinstating France and other Western powers and institutions like the IMF and World Bank in Burkina Faso.

PART FOURTEEN:
THE AFRICAN RENAISSANCE

CHAPTER EIGHTY
THE REWRITING OF AFRICAN HISTORY

"I stand before you a proud black man, honoured to be a black man, who would be nothing else in God's creation but a black man." **Hon. Marcus Garvey.**[1]

"Don't judge me by the colour of my skin but by the content of my character." **Martin Luther King Jr.**[2]

"Impossible is just a big word thrown around by small men who find it easier to live in the world they've been given than to explore the power they have to change it. Impossible is not a fact. It's an opinion. Impossible is not a declaration. It's a dare. Impossible is potential. Impossible is temporary. Impossible is nothing." **Mohammed Ali.**[3]

A journey of a thousand miles starts with a single thought not a single step. Since transatlantic slavery, colonization and now neo-colonization, the God-given gifts of self-determination and actualisation have been drained at source by the white supremacy global power system. Today, Africans are commuted into a self-regenerating cycle of inferiority complexes and dependence.

Africans have become divided amongst themselves and psychologically submissive to Western influences. Centuries of severe physical and emotional abuse, grinding poverty and the devaluation of their sense of identity and culture has taken its toll.

Given this background, the first step of the African miseducated in Western ideology is in the opposite direction towards the mirage of Western integration. Miseducated Africans develop inferiority complexes and become dependent on the white imperial power structure rather than take positive steps towards true freedom, self-determination, self-actualization and fulfilment.

Fortunately, the potential of metamorphosis from an apathetic, subservient and self-hating miseducated African into a conscious African remains feasible with the right re-education.

Europeans have sought to divide and rule over Africans using every means possible and every difference they can exploit, real or imagined. This is why the West works ceaselessly to suppress and distract Africans and the diaspora with conflict, poverty and mindless consumerism to prevent them remembering who they really are and blossoming. The revolving kaleidoscope of deformed and unrepresentative personifications of Africans presented by the West inhibits and suppresses the African psyche from birth to death.

All Africans, be they on the African continent or in the diaspora, must consciously navigate the kaleidoscope of negative paradigms Western supremacy creates, into true knowledge of self in order to rediscover themselves and know the right direction to follow. Failure to appreciate this self-evident truth leaves Africans exposed to further genetic and psychological changes that encourage Western subservience and condemn future generations of Africans to psychological and physical slavery.

Life as we know it began with Africans in Africa. Africans are the tree of all human life, which took hold in the African continent and branched outwards across the whole world. Africans developed the basis for all aspects of human life: science, technology, art and culture.

Given the whole human race originates from Africa, any misplaced claims of innate white superiority are delusional. Europe developed as a branch of the human tree that first grew in Africa. An African proverb states that the branches of a tree cannot claim to be superior to the tree from which it grows and depends on for its nourishment.

For millions of years our African ancestors faced down everything nature threw at them. They innovated, developed technology and organized themselves socially and politically into families, villages and countries. Self-determining for millennia, Africans cultivated the land, fed themselves and produced music, arts and sciences. Egypt, for all its marvels, was only the tip of the African pyramid of civilization.

Tragically now, in the 21st century, paralysed by psychological inferiority and physical dependence on the West, Africans cannot even feed themselves, never mind produce technology or keep up with peers. It is ironic to note that the only other people in human history to be totally wholly dependent upon the grace of another human to live have been slaves and servants.

African people are the heirs of glorious ancient civilizations, religions, science, and technology, dating back thousands of years, much further back than Western science can currently comprehend.

The African Egyptians practiced complex astronomy, astrology and medicine and understood about the earth's rotation and processional cycles around the sun. The Egyptians not only knew of, but also charted, the presence of planets in the solar system thousands of years before Europe had developed to the point where they mistakenly thought the earth was flat and the whole solar system revolved around it.

As with most ancient people of the world, Africans produced science and technology as a by-product of the struggle to survive nature's challenges and tried to understand their reason for being through religion. Much of the science we have today is built upon the basic concepts of science and technology developed by African people, with later contributions from civilizations from all over the world. The creation of a concept is infinitely harder than working out the different applications to which that concept can be applied.

For instance, man's creation and use of the wheel was the critical paradigm shift in human development and not the multitude of uses for which the use of the wheel has subsequently been applied. Virtually all ancient religions began as sun worshippers, believed in an afterlife, reincarnation and in a god. They all deferred to a higher force or intelligence and most record the presence and interaction with extra-terrestrials or god-like beings.

In ancient times, knowledge was sought after to elevate the physical, mental and spiritual states of man. The pursuit of knowledge was also driven by the need to communicate with God or their gods.

Ever since the European Renaissance and Western imperialism, there has been a macabre twist in man's search for and the application of knowledge. The West and the white man have primarily sought knowledge as a means to dominate, exploit and kill others. This is why today most of the advances in science and technology for civilian purposes are usually by-products of military research and weapons designed for the mass destruction and suffering of people.

European Christianity and Judaism have always tried to place the white man at the centre of the universe.

In the white supremacist's original model of the world and the universe, the earth was flat and all the other planets revolved around it including the sun. The white man created 'God' in his own image, and placed his 'white God-man' in the epicentre of their 'universe'.

Looking back on history, each of the last three dominant European empires that have ruled over large areas of the world — the Romans, the British and today the United States of America, have not only tried to define what the world was but also placed themselves strategically at its centre.

Today, the West is not trying to create a new world order; they are trying to maintain it. The global arms race is not simply driven by the threat of other developed nations acquiring arms and competing for resources, it is also aimed at creating and maintaining the ever-widening gap between the West and the 'rest' — between rich nations and poor nations. The world has become the oyster of rich Westerners who enjoy material luxuries, unimaginable to the vast majority of the global human population.

The white supremacist power system of global inequality is universal. Therefore it should come as no surprise that most Western powers, even traditional enemies, co-operate when determining and maintaining the political, economic and social order around the world. Institutions like the United Nations, NATO, the world's largest financial institutions like the World Bank and the IMF, despite their officially stated functions, help the West to create and maintain global inequality. They maintain the gap between the powerful and the powerless and between rich and poor nations. This is the unpublicized agenda of G8 summits and the meetings like the Paris Club between rich and powerful nations. Evidence of the New World Order abounds.

For example, it is an essential part of the Western imperialist structure that the Western media can broadcast virtually unopposed to most countries in the world while non-Western countries are denied similar access.

Financially, the West can manipulate the economies of most of the Third World countries, creating conditions that foster long-term dependence and exploitation.

When Western countries aggressively attack and occupy other sovereign nations causing widespread death and destruction, even these occupied countries rely on the Western media to find their voice. Ultimately, only the powerless and propped-up puppets of Western imperialism face international 'justice'. Statistically, it appears that the International Court of Justice is primarily reserved for deposed African leaders. The likes of former American President, George Bush, and former British Prime minister, Tony Blair, will never be summoned to the International Court of Justice to explain why they started the destructive and deadly wars in Iraq and Afghanistan, leading to the death of millions of people, based on premises they knew to be false. The US is not a signatory and has publicly stated that it is exempt from being tried in the International Court of Justice.

Western countries like the United States and Britain make international laws, break international laws and then hold other people and countries accountable for breaking the same laws. Militarily, the West has continued to mass-produce, proliferate and use weapons of destruction while simultaneously using 'multilateral' institutions like the International Atomic Energy Agency [IAEA] to prevent other countries from developing nuclear capability.

Much of Western foreign policy is based on the manipulation of the military, socio-economic and political wellbeing of Third World countries facilitating their exploitation through unrepresentative puppet governments.

Since Roman times, the West has widely utilised the principle of divide and rule to prop up undemocratic and usually unelected minorities against majorities. The instigation of internecine struggles in underdeveloped countries remains popular with Western powers. Tragically, as history has shown repeatedly, once Western powers set up these struggles between poor and downtrodden people the oppressed generally forget the role of the Western instigators as they squabble over the scraps of their own resources left over by their colonizers. They frequently go back to their white puppet masters in their new roles as mediators, arbiters and arms dealers.

Unfortunately, rather than unite, many Africans tacitly and openly accept their alleged inferiority in the face of Western technology and affluence. While it is undoubtedly true that the West has seized the earth's steering wheel from the other countries in the world — in what direction is the human race moving now?

For all the technological advances and modern conveniences human beings enjoy now, many basic questions that puzzled our forefathers remain unanswered.

Despite the advances of modern science and technology human beings still have no concrete answers as to who we really are, why we are here, or why we live and die. There is no precise scientific answer to the simple question: what time is it now?

One response would be to refer to the Christian calendar which much of the world commonly works to. However, the current Gregorian calendar is not exactly based on science and was adopted by Pope Gregory XIII in a papal bull on February 24th 1582 to correct the earlier Julian calender. Today's date is different depending on whose calendar you choose, be it Mayan, Jewish, Egyptian, or Chinese.

An old African parable, when translated, states that '*what the elder sees while sitting in his chair below a tree, even when young men climb to the top of the tree, they still cannot see it'*.[4]

Modern Western capitalism is undoubtedly intelligent but it is not wise as it pursues total hegemony and exploitation at the cost of total destruction of all life on earth. Unlike Europeans, our African ancestors appreciated the holographic and temporary nature of what we call reality and materialism. Our African ancestors could see beyond the realms and confines of the physical three-dimensional conscious mind we describe as reality. Thus, our African ancestors had a deep appreciation of the need for a harmonious existence with the environment and the inner spiritual self.

Possibly more due to arrogance than to a lack of intelligence, many Western scientists refuse to look at the multidimensional nature of life and continue to try to understand the whole universe from a single dimension or a purely physical standpoint. They look for signs of life as they know it on Mars rather than look for life as it is. They fail to appreciate that life, akin to our human physical being and spirit, need not necessarily be confined to the narrow realm that they can see or measure. If we look out across a clear starry night and appreciate that the millions of tiny dots we call stars are suns just like our sun which sustains life on earth, each one able to sustain a solar system of its own, then we may be humbled into understanding how insignificant we really are in the grand scheme of things.

Our African ancestors did not have complicated computers and other technology to work out quantum physics and additional mathematics but nor were they hamstrung by their egos and the delusion of being all-knowing and divining.

All people, regardless of race, colour or creed, must realise and accept the inherent flaws in their personal constructs, especially those created within the Western paradigm. In truth, our personal constructs are based on our incomplete appreciation of 'reality' by our conscious minds. It does not matter what forms the core of our personal constructs: religious, political, intellectual, scientific or cultural beliefs, or even a combination of two or all — every single one is inherently flawed and subject to manipulation. We must therefore keep an open mind and have enough humility and appreciation of others and our environment to continue learning from childhood until the day we die.

The white supremacists do have a superficial understanding of the holographic nature of our 'reality'. After all, they attack people's senses daily using every means and medium possible — information technology, air, food, water pollution and various medicines, in order to create and maintain alternate realities that make people vulnerable to suggestion and manipulation. In this way they try to stall the natural human reversion to the conscious appreciation of one's true self that will occur if allowed.

This is why virtually every means of communication in the West has a dual use as a means to covertly and overtly gather information, mass mind control, advertise and sell products, and identify and eliminate any threats to its hegemony.

Edward Snowden's exposé of the NSA's mass spying on enemies, allies and the general population was just factual confirmation of what many people already suspected.[5]

Another whistle-blower, Julian Assange, famous for WikiLeaks and wanted by the US, had earlier exposed how the US exploits and withholds information. Julian Assange's exposé revealed America's mass murder by special hit squads, renditions with kidnapping and export of suspects to countries with known human right abuse records for torture along with killing of innocent civilians all over the world, including in Iraq, Afghanistan and Pakistan, extra-judicial killing via drone attacks, bribery, corruption, collusion with repressive governments, and so on.[6]

Today, it would appear that the West has only one ambition — total global hegemony. To this end they will ceaselessly produce more lethal weapons of mass destruction and better means of mind control and assist their multinationals in seizing control of all the essentials of life — food, water and minerals.

Tragically, it is all to no avail. All the efforts of the West to achieve total hegemony are doomed to end in catastrophic failure. Human consciousness is conceived in freedom and cannot be constrained within the microscopic physical bandwidth humans define as reality. However, despite the ultimate futility of their quest, the Western global apartheid system still represents a the clear and present danger — to all life on earth. Violent convulsions from without and within, conflict and catastrophic damage to the environment, will inevitably ensue as a result of the misguided and futile attempt by Western supremacy to impose their hegemony over all.

Like a deer caught in the glare of the headlights, many Africans are physically and psychologically paralysed into inaction by the sweeping scientific claims, opulence and technological advances in the West. Some Africans are so resigned in the acceptance of their alleged inferiority that they are even offended by the thought of another African seeking equality and asking searching questions about the true state of affairs in the world.

Africans have been deliberately cut off from their true history and ignorance of Africa's great past and achievements is still widespread all over the world. The West has since filled this vacuum with misinformation about alleged Western superiority and the alleged inferiority of Africans. As a result, many Africans suffer abject poverty and a wide range of psychological and physical ailments purely from lack of knowledge.

However, acquiring true knowledge of Africa's great past is insufficient on its own. It is essential for the key learning points of the knowledge acquired to be practically applied in each and every African's life for it to make a lasting difference to Africa and its diaspora. Africans must not just strive to acquire knowledge for the sake of it. They must act on the basis of their knowledge to rise of up against Western economic slavery.

Psychologically, as a result of the vacuum of identity, many miseducated Africans have barked up the wrong tree. They seek acceptance into Western culture and communities rather than seeking true freedom and equality. Of this many Africans are guilty in varying degrees. Miseducated Africans usually seek to distance themselves from their own culture while copying and imitating Western culture. Since the best version of you is yourself, they would do much better trying to understand and enhance their own cultures by adopting a bespoke system that appropriates the best attributes of other cultures to enhance and improve their own.

Life for human beings has always been a team sport and that team usually consists of family, friends, your community and country. Unlike the fragmented African individual, the centred pan-African has extended his or her ideological reach much further to include the African continent and all its diaspora. In stark contrast to this, the fragmented African individual has elected to play the game of life alone. Worse still, he or she plays it as a tool in the hands of Africa's enemies.

Bishop Henry McNeal Turner wrote:

'Africa is our home, and is the one place that offers us manhood and freedom... Every man that has the sense of an animal must see there is no future in this country [America] for the Negro'.[7]

All Africans, black or white, belong to 'Team Africa' —whether they are aware of their illustrious history and are proud of it or whether they have been brainwashed by their Western miseducation and are ashamed of their African heritage and dark skin colour. It does not matter if one has been openly or covertly rejected by Western societies, the bottom line is Caucasians have uniformly defined Africans as the lowest common denominators in their societies and global hierarchy. It is worth remembering that the white slave masters even went as far as declaring that it took only one drop of African blood to make an 'African'.

A conscious African who is truly grounded in his or her own Africanism cannot be bought, sold, shaken or moved by Western imperialism. African individuals who know who they really are, are well centred. They will very often show clear leadership qualities. On their own, they are the equivalent of a small army. In a group setting, they work effectively as an integral part of a team.

Thus, the fight against racism and imperialism needs to be conducted firstly on a personal level, then as family groups, as communities, countries, continent wide across Africa and globally.

Racism, imperialism or globalisation must never be rewarded in any way shape or form as this feeds, strengthens and perpetuates the white imperial monster. Resisting imperialism in every area of human activity is the only way racism and imperialism will meet its natural end and it is only in this way that the suffering masses of the world will be emancipated.

All life is motion and the sensation of standing still is one of the biggest illusions our minds play on us. 'Time waits for no one' and Africa and its diaspora can no longer continue to get by with masterly inactivity.

There are many reasons for Africans and their diaspora to quicken their footsteps in recent times. The world's human population is exploding, rising above seven billion people in the last one hundred years. This population explosion creates direct pressure on natural resources, like food, water, and land. In addition, there is the growing and unsustainable demand for the modern luxuries of life, which in turn increases the amount of carbon dioxide produced by developed countries and accelerates the effects of global warming. Global warming further destabilizes the availability of natural resources and climate changes produce flooding, heat waves, and famine.

Thus the threshold for human conflict and social unrest under these conditions is greatly lowered and it does not require the genius of a rocket scientist to work out that the poor and dependent people will be the first and hardest hit of all.

Global shortages of basics, like food and water, already dominate the lives of billions of the world's poorest people. Grain, water and even the air we breathe, natural resources that human beings have taken for granted for millennia, have come under the control of Western imperialists, who will trade them on the stock markets to make billions of dollars out of the suffering of billions of people.

Many miseducated Africans feel confident that their white masters, who they depend on for all their material goods; cars, electronic gadgets, aircraft, and infrastructure, have all the answers to any global contingency — do they?

Till the present day, thousands of Americans, mostly black, remain refugees in their own country years after Hurricane Katrina wreaked havoc in August 2005. In 2011 the Japanese had no answer to the tsunami that killed over 120,000 people and created a nuclear catastrophe after nuclear stations damaged in the tsunami leaked radiation.

Currently, human beings do not have any answer to the earth being hit by a large asteroid, which could end life on earth as we know it. Even the ever present danger on earth in the form of a super volcano eruption cannot at present be effectively prepared for. There is super volcanic activity in the Yellowstone region in the US. The active Yellowstone super volcano erupts every 120,000–650,000 years. It last erupted about 600,000 years ago.

To emancipate themselves, Africans and their diaspora must collectively make imperialism and racism so futile, so psychologically and financially unrewarding that it ceases to be an option. When white imperialists experience a persistent lack of financial and psychological rewards, the natural human behavioural tendency to extinguish unrewarding behaviours and attitudes dictates that they will no longer seek the exploitation and denigration of others, especially Africans as a means of sustaining their own system.

A concerted approach against racism may even stimulate the West to build environmentally sustainable societies, which could in turn translate into a reduction in global conflicts, arms proliferation and environmental pollution.

From our journey through historical precedents, it becomes clear that racism and imperialism are simply different forms of the same thing and all Africans must be vigilant and aware enough to recognize it as it shape shifts so as to take advantage of the time, place and circumstance.

Standing up to racism requires organisation and therefore politics is an important tool by which a collective stance can be taken, articulated and implemented by Africans. Unfortunately, through a lack of awareness and lack of knowledge, many Africans and the diaspora have shown amazing levels of apathy towards politics.

Virtually all Africans are caught up in the vast global network of the white imperial or supremacy system. It is usually not a question of whether an African has been affected or miseducated by Western ideology — it is really a question of to what degree.

There are no miraculous cures to Africa's maladies. It has taken Europeans over 500 years of persistent exploitation and denigration to manipulate Africans into the position in which they find themselves today. It will also take time for the self-awareness and self-determination that the empowerment their Afro-centricity gives them to move Africans collectively to a position as a world force again. To be able to reawaken their own consciousness or awareness of self, all Africans must seek to achieve a degree of separation, both intellectually, psychologically and even physically, from the Western paradigm.

The only way to safely cross back into their own paradigm and remain there is to rediscover their true worth or intrinsic value through the gateway of Afro-centricity. A clear sign of recovery in a Westernised African is when he or she no longer see the need to identify and define themselves by the white supremacy system. A truly conscious African sees other Africans as a source of strength and a resource rather than a figure of hatred or derision. Conscious Africans are able to join the dots and can positively link each individual African with the collective on the African continent and Africans in diaspora.

The white supremacist/imperialist attacks Africans in every area of human activity. Africans must therefore be prepared to defend themselves in every area of human activity. The white supremacist never rests and continually plots how to bring down and destroy Africans using every means possible; Africans must therefore remain vigilant and be prepared to defend themselves and their people by all means available to them.

The white supremacists are well organized. Africans must also organize — from the grassroots up and from the leadership down so that a broad-fronted resistance protects the individuals from harm rather than fight as fragmented individuals who remain separate and therefore vulnerable. Remember the adage: 'United we stand, divided we fall'.

For all its vaunted strengths, white imperialism remains a thin white line and therefore needs Africans to co-operate in planning their own subjugation and exploitation. The fact that white supremacists have provided guns, drugs and money to African individuals, communities and nations does not automatically mean they must destroy themselves and other Africans with them. Only Africans labouring under their Western miseducation will see it necessary to encourage and support exploitative processes that ultimately enslave or destroy their people as a whole.

All Africans must strive to develop a balanced global perspective rather than just a limited personal one. A common tactic used by imperialists is to divert attention by focusing the mind on multiple minor issues or tactics, distracting the observer from their overall grand strategy.

It is important never to conclude on the words or actions of white supremacists based on a narrow personal opinion. It is critical to interpret their actions based on the actual or potential, immediate and long-term, the local and global effects of their actions on the African collective, in order to ascertain if it is indeed truly altruistic or just another diversionary tactic.

For instance, in Africa, it is not uncommon for, say, a Western charity to be digging a borehole to provide water for a small African community while a huge multinational from the same Western country is looting millions of dollars' worth of resources from the whole nation. Africans must individually and collectively evaluate the total effect of Westerners in Africa and among the diaspora from the actual net short and long-term effects rather than from the immediate personal gain.

All Africans must search their consciences to decide whether they are consciously or unwittingly playing a role in helping the global white supremacy power structure exploit and impoverish their own people. Denying white imperialists tacit and open support will significantly hamper the process of exploitation. white supremacists, have painstakingly miseducated millions of Africans on the African continent and in the diaspora for decades to perform this role.

This naturally leads to the next issue of how much Africans value themselves and other Africans like them. In reality it is fair to say that the West attaches very little importance to the lives and wellbeing of Africans and their diaspora. Don Cheadle, Oscar nominee and star in the movie, Hotel Rwanda, had this to say:

'One African life lost really doesn't mean anything. Thousands have to die before people take notice...It's hard to argue that the West doesn't view African life as cheap and irrelevant.[8]

When Ken Saro-Wiwa's son desperately tried to galvanize help from environmental groups in London to save his father from imminent hanging by Sani Abacha, they suggested he comes back when more people have been killed.[9]

However, the real question has to be not how much Europeans value African lives but how much value do Africans themselves place on their own lives and on the lives and wellbeing of fellow Africans. African individuals cannot deem themselves to be free until their families, communities and countries are free. No African must be left behind.

It is easy to understand why many Africans are disillusioned with politics. After all, along with Western Christianity, it has been the main tool used for decades by white racists, imperialists and corrupt African leaders to impoverish them and keep them down. But politics is the only medium by which timely, wide sweeping change can be brought to the suffering masses of the African continent.

In the 1960s Martin Luther King Jr. successfully led the civil rights fight against legalised racism in the United States and black South Africans only won the right to vote in 1993 after a protracted struggle. Clearly, only wide-spread democratic political organisation can secure for African people the psychological and economic freedom they need to express themselves and reach their true potential.

Even though politics has acquired a dirty name through the actions of dishonest, corrupt and morally bankrupt politicians, it is important for people to remember that politics in the broader sense is also simply the way we, friends and family, choose to interact with each other. Since prehistoric times, people have organized themselves into groups and indulged in social interaction and therefore in 'politics'. Therefore, politics has always been an essential part of human behaviour. The way we interact with our wives, husbands, family, friends, community and country all constitute a form of politics. Everyone knows about office politics, family politics and even relationship politics.

Many African communities still invest a great deal of effort in their local community politics that preserve the cultural rules and practices but unfortunately remain apathetic towards national politics that plays the most critical role in determining their economic, social and physical wellbeing.

In far too many instances, African politics has been about seizing power and self-enrichment by stealing national assets and selling them off to corrupt Western governments and multinationals. Ultimately, politics determines how rich or how poor Africans are, the availability and price of food and essential services, whether they get an education and what quality of education they get. Politics determines their health, and the availability of good hospitals and medicines to take care of themselves, and their loved ones.

Politics has determined whether Africans have stayed in Africa or have felt forced into risking their lives in economic and political migration to secure a living abroad. Even when Africans reach the West, Western politics have broadly decided where Africans live, what they can afford, what and how they eat, the jobs they get and this most importantly the future of their children.

The blind imbibing of Western values and consumerism coupled with a widespread lack of critical thinking, political awareness and apathy has allowed Africa and its diaspora to descend into the appalling level of poverty and suffering that pertains across Africa and the diaspora today. In the West, black African people and communities find themselves completely marginalized and only useful to pay taxes or fight and die in Western wars they did not start, understand or know nothing about. Psychologically, Africans in the diaspora inadvertently strengthen the white supremacists by providing them with a steady source of reinforcement of their negative stereotypes with regard to Africans as their social deprivations and crime begets more poverty and crime. Africans and the diaspora also form a growing section of the Western consumer market as many Africans tend to spend indiscriminately to acquire the much-coveted trappings of white consumerism instead of investing in their own communities.

Many African nations have policies in place that would provide their people with decent economic, health, education and security services if implemented. However, the problem has been not the policies but lack of implementation due to the unhealthy political environment in which these policies have been drafted.

Doubtless, a positive change in the political environment in Africa would bring immense benefits to Africa and the diaspora. This change can only come in the form of progressive democratic leadership and governments throughout the African continent. To this end, it is vitally important that this African democracy is bespoke, clear and distinct from Western-imposed democracy.

It must be a democracy by African people for African people. No other form of democracy will work in Africa, be it imposed or mindlessly copied from other countries. Many African communities have had 'democratic' political bodies and systems which organised their lives for many centuries now. The African communal spirit which ensured that everybody was taken care of in their community, can be extended nationally or even continent wide. In fact, without the existing African family and community social system, the poverty and suffering in Africa would be unbearable. Anecdotally, it is notable that the suffering of poor African people living in the cities or urban areas is far greater than those in the villages or more rural settings where certain remnants of African traditional culture are still maintained. Post-colonial African countries were left without a guiding national spirit, allowing tribalism and cronyism to rule supreme.

Owing to Western propaganda, most people often see democracy as a Western ideal only. However, true democracy is a human ideal and has been practiced in different forms, by different people all over the world for many centuries. Africans must use bespoke democratic systems for themselves in a way that would allow freedom for all regardless of sex, religion, race or creed.

Every African, whether in Africa or the diaspora must strive to have a 'global position'. It is time for every individual African to stand up and be recognised. All Africans must carefully consider the cause and effects of their actions or lack of action, not just on a personal level but also as part of their families, communities and country. To do this our personal constructs of the world must be factual, knowledgeable and broad-minded in order to be balanced.

Unfortunately, many African leaders appear oblivious to world politics and its machinations and have wilfully or unwittingly led generations of their people into decades of suffering and poverty by not understanding or caring about the implications of the long-term effects of their immediate actions. Even as the fledging African nations struggled to find their feet many of the long-term effects of Africa's debt and the effects of the structural adjustment program could easily have been predicted. It is crucial that Africans only elect leaders who demonstrate sufficient understanding and awareness of global politics and have the motivation and courage to push for changes which will benefit their people not impoverish them.

It is time for Africans to compare and judge themselves, not just against other suffering Africans or diaspora, but also with established world standards. Every African must make this assessment in order to understand what they have to do to reach this set of goals and to understand when they are being deprived access or prevented from reaching their goals. This means there can be no societal double standards or hypocrisy. What is good for the goose should also be good for the gander. Africans, both in the diaspora and on the African continent, should aim to produce a colour-blind, free and fair society in the West and progressive nations on the African continent, which strives to match and even surpass present world global development.

With this viewpoint, Africans should always strive for more rather than settle for less and stop obstructing each other's progress. Africans must choose to work together, cohesively, aiming towards progress for all.

As there can be no political sovereignty without economic sovereignty, Africa's economic situation is fully understandable because economically it remains dependent on the West. Crippling debts repayments and export-only based economies with colonial precedents is a major factor behind Africa's poor economic growth.

Even as Western aid and crippling 'odious debts' maintain a stranglehold on African economies and industry, it is no surprise that most Western pundits continue to recommend more aid, more debt and increased dependence as a solution to Africa's problems. However, for Africa to turn the corner, it must embrace self-sufficiency and self-reliance, with both arms. African leaders who continue to service these "odious debts" at the expense of their own people, cannot claim to have any legitimate rights to lead their people. If African leaders do not to stop paying the odious debts, no one will and the people must hold their governments to account. Immoral debt repayments must be stopped immediately and the funds made available to fight against poverty and diseases like AIDS and provide health and education for their own people. A redress of Africa's debt and trade situation would immediately stimulate African economies.

For decades, the West has presided over Africa's economic woes and watched on while millions of Africans have died from disease and poverty. Western economic policies like the SAPs have ravaged the already fragile African economies creating even greater poverty, suffering and death. African leaders who choose blindly to continue their dependence on the West once again act in the same role as African slave traders did during the slave trade. Many puppet African leaders benefit directly through the embezzlement of funds and illegal sale of national assets, paid for by the blood and suffering by millions of their own people, as well as that of future generations to come.

If dependence on drugs and alcohol destroys the individual's mind and body, African dependence on Western aid destroys African minds and bodies in their millions.

During the civil rights movement, African American leaders learned that the only way to keep up the struggle and manage their communities was by becoming self-sufficient rather than relying on what was clearly a hostile source for all their needs. Africa does not need Western aid, especially when it comes attached with conditions that clearly are detrimental to Africa's progress and even survival. That Africa needs help cannot be denied but like the physician's oath, if you genuinely want to help Africa: 'first do no harm'.[10]

African persons, communities and countries have been discriminated against for no other reason than their colour. Wherever it appears that an African person, or group of people has been favoured by the West, it has always been because they fulfil some open or covert strategic objective or the other for the West and not because they are in any way superior to the other African people who they have assisted in exploiting. Therefore, dark skin is the common denominator in racism and capitalist exploitation whether at an individual level or at the level of communities or even nationally. Western favours to black people are always temporary, conditional upon mindless and unquestioning servitude and are usually withdrawn at will depending on the prevailing circumstances.

This underlines the point that in whatever guise the Western governments come, be it humanitarian or through war, destabilizing the country through economic means or the installing of puppet governments, their primary aim is one and the same — to exploit the people and the land of their resources and the result is always a massive loss for the African people and its diaspora. For the African diaspora living in the West, the same principle is applied in a slightly different fashion. The African people in the diaspora are kept divided by the West seeking out and destroying good leaders and replacing them with 'puppet' men and women.

Puppet African leaders understand their subservient role in Western societies, and act as points of control through which the duplicitous white supremacists exert their control on ethnic minorities in the Western societies.

Ultimately, we are all one race: human. Genetically, all human beings are 'Africans' no matter your race, colour or nationality. We must recognise our common humanity, rather than the minutiae that makes us different. In truth, it should not matter whether one is black or white. Unfortunately, the reality today is that the West thrives on the division and subdivision of people into groups, cultures, and colours in order to facilitate their discrimination and exploitation.

CHAPTER EIGHTY ONE
AFRICAN ADVANCEMENT

The African child is the key to the resurgence of the African continent. Every African individual, society and government must see to it that the African child receives the right nurturing and education. This will help them to emerge healthy, well-balanced people who are confident and secure in themselves and are equipped to move their people forward to places Africans can only dream about today. Children who have the right upbringing and support will have the self-confidence to mould the putty of life into any type or level of success they can imagine.

Child poverty and death from preventable causes and disease must be eradicated across the African continent. Access to clean water, adequate housing and good education are all-important facets in providing them with the right building blocks for the future.

Miseducated parents bring up miseducated children. It is therefore imperative that African parents make an effort to understand Africa's problems so that they do not inadvertently handicap their own children, dooming them to repeat all the mistakes of the past. African parents' extended family and community must ensure that they are fed the right information about themselves from the start. You cannot teach what you do not know and even as we try to teach our children, we must re-educate and reorientate ourselves from the miseducation given to slaves and the colonial masters, and is perpetuated by the Western media and Western institutions of learning. Africans will find that their increasing knowledge, self-confidence, courage, conviction and positive orientation will also naturally rub off on our children.

Chinweizu wrote:

'Euro-imperial universalists oppose the Africanisation of curricula in Africa because an African child who is first given a thorough grounding in the African cultural tradition, before being exposed to those of other lands is not likely to be intimidated into awe of European culture, and is far less likely to be inducted into servility towards European culture. Knowing African nursery songs, ancient African epics, drama, fables, stories, parables, and a correct appreciation of their worth, would fortify him against hegemonist propaganda. He would display a cultural confidence born of sound knowledge of the glories of his African civilization, and be less prone to genuflect to the culture of Europeans, Arabs or whoever else'.[1]

Such are the times that we live in that it is almost heretical to mention the words, 'African technology'. Africa has long lost its 'Vorsprung Durch Technik', or advance through technology. It is not that Africa does not have scientists or professionals in all walks of life; the problem is that the vast majority of them work abroad in Western countries, while those who stayed at home do not have the financial or infrastructural support to implement change. With the right mindset and support, many African professionals and scientists who work in the West can collaborate with their African colleagues on the continent and begin to develop bespoke systems to advance science in Africa, an integral part of any developing society and the technological mainstay of the ancient African societies, their first gift to the world.

Such is the impotence of Africa that African people die in their millions from disease and poverty, as they look helpless and imploringly to the West, the architects of their suffering, aid, be it medicine to save the sick and dying, or food to eat to prevent people from simply dying of starvation.

Virtually all the technology that runs day-to-day African lives — electricity, water, factories, oilfields, mines — are imported. It is not surprising then that the price of the goods Africans sell to the West are dictated by the West. If oil prices get too high Africans are ordered to produce more goods at cheaper rates to keep the West happy, and at the same time, African traders are priced out of the global market by the same

Western powers.

African governments must use every opportunity to ensure that there is a mandatory transfer of skills and technology to their own people whenever they procure the help of expatriates to set up or run industry. This must be uniformly applied across all fields, whether it is science, arts or sports. This is the only way to develop their people in order to make their countries technologically self-sufficient.

Africans have come a long way and are probably the most resilient human race on earth. Africans have suffered much more, much harsher and far longer persecutions than perhaps any other race on earth. However, today, in every area of human endeavour, in spite of all attempts to suppress and extinguish the spark of creativity and excellence, Africans have succeeded and continue to break through, even when given less than half a chance. This burning will to survive and succeed, showcasing their strength of character and resilience, is not widely celebrated or acknowledged but cast your eyes on any field that has not precluded black people through prejudice, from music to sports, arts and science, even politics, you do not have to search too hard to find a successful black African person.

The political miracle, Barack Obama, sporting sensations like Tiger Woods in golf, the current six times Formula One world champion and best rookie ever, Lewis Hamilton, Usain Bolt in athletics, the Williams sisters in tennis and many more Africans in all works of life have blazed the trail in their respective disciplines, showing the intelligence, creativity, determination and discipline to dominate their chosen field against all odds.

African unity is imperative, as not only do Africans have far more in common than what divides them, they simply have nothing to lose by pulling together. The whole world will benefit from a progressive and productive Africa and diaspora.

Africans must develop a more integrative national approach to life simply because it is a tried, tested and reliable way for any group of people to progress into a more cohesive and relevant unit. Tribalism has no place on a global context and a 'no African left behind' approach to life will greatly enhance and enrich the lives of all who become involved.

However, it is important to teach unity rather than preach unity. The mere act of African individuals, families, communities and countries coming together, supporting each other and creating day-to-day interdependencies 'teaches' unity by example and is much more powerful than mere words.

Hell would freeze over first if Africans and their diaspora wait until the West had a change of mind and suddenly decided to stop profiteering from the exploitation that has lasted over 500 years. The only reliable way to change a particular human behaviour is not to reward it.

It is time that Africa and its diaspora lived up to its responsibilities. Without a shadow of a doubt, dealing with Africa's starving children, poverty, the AIDS epidemic and the wars which are tearing up Africa are the primary responsibilities of Africans. Unfortunately today, Africans have been carefully groomed into a state of almost helpless dependence upon the West. As long as Africans cede their responsibility towards their own children, land and future to others, Africans fortunes will continue to spiral downwards out of control.

Frantz Fanon said:

"Everything needs to be reformed, and everything thought through anew."[12]

Africa needs true leaders and not the Western-supported and imposed puppets who practise 'followership' not leadership. There is some truth in the statement: 'A people get the government it deserves'. Every Africans must realize that they are an integral part of their own governments, whether they like it or not. Without the people, there can be no government. It is not even the chicken or the egg conundrum. The people always came first.

A new form of African politics has to grow from the grassroots hand in hand with the distillation of good government practices. All African politicians must become salaried civil servants so that their decision to become politicians stems from a desire to serve their respective nations and people rather than seek the acquisition of wealth.

No matter how cruel and despotic a leader or regime or how

democratic or benign they are, all governments need their people. Herein lies the nascent power of the African people to change their situation. Even though African people have been severely traumatized by colonial rule and now by corrupt despots that act as puppets for neo-colonial dependence, the basic link between people and their governments or politics remains the same.

For over 90% of all Africans good leadership is the only way to guarantee food, shelter, good education, hospitals, good roads, jobs and security for themselves, their families and the wider society is through good government, whether on the continent or in the diaspora. Many misguided Africans, socialized into seeing their governments as completely distinct entities from themselves, need to engage with government and wider society rather than isolate themselves from it. The African diaspora is no less culpable as many disengage so much from the society around them that they can individually be trapped and caged like animals by the white supremacy system. They need to take an interest in local and national politics and economics both in the West, or in Africa. They must see news of injustices ranging from unlawful arrests, imprisonment, social and judicial violations and even murder of their fellow African citizens and people around the world as having everything to do with them — not just when they involve themselves, their family or their community.

Africans cannot sit aside quietly when African nations are openly invaded and pillaged by Western nations, comfortable in how far away the crisis is from them both in mind and body. It is important to remember what Martin Luther King Jr said:

"Injustice anywhere is a threat to justice everywhere."[3]

For instance, African nations needed unite and resist the US, UK and France's invasion of Libya with the murder of Gadhafi and the eventual dissolution of the country into chaos.

The sum total of the geopolitical awareness some Africans consists of a few sound bites, casually gleaned from right wing Western media or the newspapers, making them, especially prone to psychological manipulation. This must stop. They must become unaware of their own history and the machinations of geopolitics around them as if they remain ignorant they can easily be programmed by their white masters and end up lurching around like zombies, fire-fighting from one crisis to the next.

Conscious Africans on the African continent or in the diaspora can readily see that their shared history and many similarities far exceed their few interesting differences.

The conscious awakening of individual Africans and their diaspora is a prerequisite to the sustainable advancement of the the African people as a whole.

CHAPTER EIGHTY TWO
THE AFRICAN DIASPORA

Only the determined will of the people of Africa can lift them up from their prostrate position globally. The African diaspora has a no less important role to play in the renaissance of Africa. The African brain drain is a huge part of Africa's problem — and therefore they are also part of the solution.

The African diaspora consists about 30.6 million people according to researchers at the Brooking Institute. Africans who reside outside the African continent include a very high percentage of Africa's elite and intelligentsia. Although they are invisible as a nation, they are as populous as Angola, Malawi, Zambia or Zimbabwe.[1]

They are an important key in the solution of Africa's problems as they have a good understanding of both African and European politics and culture and are, therefore, ideally placed to help make a difference on the continent.

The World Bank and the IMF estimated that the African diaspora is the biggest group of foreign investors in Africa. The World Bank stated that the African diaspora remitted over $60 billion to Africa in 2012.[2]

The African remittance Outlook for 2019 was estimated at about $47 billion.[3]

It was projected that expatriate staff employment in Africa rose by 75% due to skills shortages in Africa by 2015. The World Bank estimated that the replacement cost of employing expatriates in Africa at about $5.6 billion as far back as 2009. A figure that is only set to rise despite the fact that some countries like Nigeria have enough skilled labour to fill the abandoned job positions.

According to the UN, African professionals working in the US contribute about $150,000 a year each to the US economy. However, for every $300 dollars sent home, they contribute $12,000 to the US economy. African professionals in the West are usually under-employed, and underpaid Western expatriates to Africa are often less qualified but paid far more than the African professionals they work together with in African countries.

As Emeagwali put it:

"Since a significant percentage of African doctors and nurses practice in US hospitals, we can reasonably conclude that African Medical Schools are de facto serving the American people, not Africa."[4]

The World Bank estimates that 70,000 skilled Africans immigrate to Europe and the US yearly. They help fill the gap created by the brain drain of 100,000 skilled Western expatriates to Africa who are paid higher wages than that prevailing in Europe than the Africans are hired to replace them on the lowest possible wages.

The impact of the African brain drain is most acutely felt in the health sector with most African countries suffering a severe lack of trained medical doctors to look after their people. According to the World Health Organisation WHO, the African average is 0.45 physician per 1000 people. This was calculated using the latest data between the period 2012-2016 for 26 countries.

In 2015, the number of African trained international medical graduates (IMGs) in the US alone reached 13,584 a 27% increase from 2005. This was described as the equivalent of one African-educated physician migrating to the US a day for a decade.

On average it cost each African nation between $21000 and $59000 to train a medical doctor. It is estimated that Africa losed about $2.0 billion through brain drain in the health sector alone. In contrast, the Western countries they migrate to make enormous savings on training costs.

As Richard Kweitsu stated:

'For instance, one in ten doctors working in the UK comes from Africa, allowing the UK to save on average about $2.7 billion on training costs.

Similarly, the US, Australia and Canada save respectively about $846 million, £621 million and $384 million in training costs from the African physicians they recruit'.[5]

The African Union Migration policy framework (2018-2027) has made several recommendations on how to reduce brain drain from the African continent.

These recommendations include gender–responsive economic development programmes to provide gainful employment, professional development and educational opportunities to qualified nationals in their home countries.

It is clear that these recommendations African countries will have to be support these measures by ensuring meritocratic recruitment procedures, the development of infrastructure and provision of incentives to attract and retain highly qualified African national.

At the G7 Summit in 2017, the President of the African Development Bank, Akinwumi Adesina stated:

'The future of Africa's youth does not lie in migration to Europe; it should not be at the bottom of the Mediterranean; it lies in a prosperous Africa. We must create greater economic opportunities for our youth right at home in Africa'.[6]

The reversal of the African brain drain is an important facet in the revival of Africa's fortunes. It is not enough to bemoan the fact that the brain drain exists. It is far more important to take steps to reverse it by addressing the root causes.

Africa cannot eliminate poverty without utilising and nurturing its intellectual capital. The brain drain reduces the collective intellectual capital necessary to fight corruption and mismanagement. Africa's renaissance requires the collective efforts of all Africans and their diaspora to deal with the problem.

CHAPTER EIGHTY THREE

THE CAUSE

"This is not the end; it is not even the beginning of the end, it is perhaps the end of the beginning." **Sir Winston Leonard Spencer Churchill.**[1]

An objective global perspective of the African lot, in all areas of human activity, reveals quite clearly that Africans and the diaspora are currently in a desperate fight for survival. This means that all Africans wherever they are must unite around a single cause, a single goal and a single destiny.

The cause is centuries of grievous inhumanity as propagated by the white supremacy system.

The goal is to free themselves from the deprivations of slavery, mental and physical and discrimination in the white supremacy system.

The destiny is to restore Africa to its former glory, not just for our future generations but to enrich the people of the world in general by making it a better place for all, regardless of race, colour, or creed.

Survival is the most important theme around which Africans should unite. Every African, individual, family, community, country and across the continent must realize that the need to survive today is as strong as ever whether they live in a concrete urban, suburban or natural jungle.

Africans must stop following the path of least resistance and begin to actively counter the white supremacists program of denigration and exploitation.

In Africa, it is for every single African and their families to decide if they want passively to accept being deprived, dispossessed and remaining poor while corrupt puppet African politicians act as conduits for the West to drain the continent of its resources while in pursuance of their own selfish ends.

In the West, the African diaspora must decide if they want to remain cheap, expendable labour for the white community while they continue to seek the mythical golden fleece of white acceptance and integration. The unlikely premise for true integration taking place is the total dismantlement of the white supremacy structure on which the white society depends for its economic and psychosocial wellbeing. All African efforts to fight for their independence from a position of psychological and physical dependence are all invariably doomed to failure.

It is worth remembering that it was only when segregated African Americans had more control of their finances, schools, and leaders, that they could start the civil rights movement that liberated many for over three decades. Now lulled into believing that the fight was over they have gradually lost the drive and the means to finish the battle, and the roll-back is on. In the US, African American men are being murdered on the streets in full view of the world yet the African American society largely feels helpless to stop the extra judicial murders by the white police officers.

Racially motivated murders of Africans anywhere should be the concern of all African nations and deserves a firm response to stop the killing and seek justice and reparations.

Fragmented African individuals who, even though an African ethnic minority, remain in search of the golden fleece of white acceptance and integration into a much larger majority of white who are socialized to hate and despise them will remain frustrated and isolated.

They will always be out of energy, time and position as they waste their best efforts and time trying to integrate into the white supremacy system instead of seeking true freedom and equality. They reject their African heritage out of hand based on ignorance, instead of accepting it as the main source of strength of black African individuals, communities, nations and the African continent.

In sharp contrast, Africans who follow the natural tide of life and align themselves through Afrocentric knowledge to the whole body of Africa and its diaspora from which they can derive everything they need to survive and thrive, will find true self-determination and actualisation. By aligning themselves with other conscious Africans they will find true self-fulfilment, self-determination, confidence and hope, even when white supremacists predictably and savagely do everything in their power to disrupt this natural process.

Africans who 'know' must also 'do', because knowledge without work is but vanity. Self-defence is necessity. Africans must not be afraid robustly to defend themselves, their families and their people whenever and wherever required. Pan-Africanism provides all Africans with a stable platform wherever they are in the world. The pan-African ideological stance immediately sweeps away a great multitude of artificial divisions created by the West to divide and fractionalise relationships between Africans everywhere.

It also makes available to the pan-Africanist a nearly homogenous African continent, rich in material and human resources, from which he or she can derive psychosocial and material wellbeing. It is also the best way to safeguard the individual and collective lives and wellbeing of as many Africans and their diaspora as possible.

While the concept of Afro-centricity is good, a purely Afro-centric stance without the global positioning of pan-Africanism will generate immense practical difficulties as it unrealistically expects Africans to live, express and identify oneself as a black African minority in a hostile and unaccepting world. Afrocentricity should complement pan-Africanism but not attempt to supersede it.

Pan-Africanism moves like a majestic ship sailing over a deep ocean of tribal and colonial differences and grievances. It allows for a unifying theme and creates a common ideology that supersedes all including that of the individual, the tribes, and even nations.

In order to fully understand and counter the effects and current plans of white supremacy, Africans must personally confront a terrible part of their history and must not be too ashamed or embarrassed to face it. Africans are still in many ways the victims and slaves of the white supremacy system and any shame or embarrassment must be on the perpetrators and not their victims.

Africans must re-educate themselves and correct the distorted and damaging images of Africa and the diaspora that is contributing greatly to the process of inferiorisation and dependence.

All Africans must become proficient and well versed in global politics and economics from an African perspective and not just from the point of view of their oppressors. They must develop their own media outlets and propagate their own independent thought and views. From a global standpoint, it is essential that all human beings, white and black, begin to liberate their minds by the study and understanding of true African history and the modern-day African history of the African diaspora in order to get a more global and rounded view of themselves.

It is important for Africans to experience and understand other Africans firsthand and not just through the Western media, and those Africans in diaspora who can afford to must travel to Africa, within Africa, and other places like the Caribbean where they can see different African cultures firsthand.

A well-known Afrocentric, Maulana Karenga, developed the Kwanzaa movement in America to give African Americans a uniting theme, Nguzo Saba, around seven strongly binding principles in order to rebuild themselves in the wilderness of a patently Eurocentric and hostile environment. It is worth knowing and imbibing these principles as it helps give Africans a clear idea and focus as to what they can do to emancipate themselves.[2]

The first and founding principle is Umoja or Unity. By building unified harmonious communities, starting at home with the father and mother, all other projects or aims have a firm foundation on which to rest.

His next principle is called Kujichagulia: Self-determination, achieved by re-establishing knowledge of self and projecting your own self-image.

Ujima or Collective Work and Responsibility help the family and community to build and maintain their community together without which the liberation struggle is impossible.

Ujamaa or Cooperative Economics helps African communities to invest and build together for mutual benefit to achieve economic self-reliance.

Nia or Purpose devotes the African collective to faithfully maintaining and building up their great African legacy as the present custodians.

Kuumba or Creativity encourages creativity in the African community with the aim always to leave the community more beautiful and better than what we inherited.

Imani or Faith encourages Africans to believe in their own people with all their hearts and to respect their parents, teachers and leaders. It states boldly the righteousness and the victory of our struggle and believes in a divine creator.

There is a saying that goes: "Whom the gods would destroy, they first make mad". However, there is a definite method to the madness of white imperialism, even as they blithely accumulate vast armouries of ever more destructive nuclear weapons and thrash the environment at an ever-increasing rate.

Martin Luther King Jr. noted this trend over 50 years ago when he remarked:

"Our scientific power has outrun our spiritual power. We have guided missiles and misguided men."[3]

However, to underestimate the imperialists and trivialise the importance of their actions would be foolhardy. Imperialism over the centuries has killed millions of people around the world and threatens the very existence of life on earth today. Understanding the method in Western imperialist madness is a necessity for any African individual or nation that wishes to be rid of the pervasive negative effects of imperialism and racism. This of course holds true all over the world wherever imperialism has taken hold and the people suffer.

Racism is illogical and irrational but even so it is a deadly component of imperialism. Without racism, imperialism itself would die a natural death as many of its actions would be deemed too barbaric and illogical in the cold light of day.

When racism and imperialism are exposed in their true form, it is a psychotic notion that an assumed sense of superiority gives one the license to kill, rob, and exploit others. Such ideation that can either get one detained as a dangerous psychopath in a high-security prison or sectioned off to a secure mental health unit for life. Unfortunately, this mindset was and is still prevalent among the arch-imperialists. They have never been detained or sectioned because of the vast material benefits they have realised.

Imperialism is anathema to the survival and wellbeing of the human race and the environment. Consistent with their policy of riches for a few and untold misery and poverty for the rest, the proponents of imperialism tend only to look as far as the immediate benefits and the lure of long-term hegemony.

This approach is unsustainable as it flies against the nascent and innate desire of humans beings to survive, thrive and be free. The imperial drive in itself is the origin of many conflicts that have led to wars all over the world. While the imperialists are forever seeking more vicious and ingenious ways to maintain control over their exploited masses, the oppressed people of the world buck violently in a bid to break free and thrive. As imperialism is the chosen path of the world's richest countries it is safe to say that, if unchecked, the world is well and truly on the path to total destruction.

It is time for the true Africans to stand up and claim their full inalienable human rights of freedom and the right to choose their own path in life. In doing so, Africans are not only saving themselves but in reality they will initiate changes that can pull the whole earth back off the track of total destruction the Western imperialists have set it on, back onto a path of worldwide integration and conservation. Frantz Fanon said:

"For Europe, for ourselves and for humanity, comrades, we must turn over a new leaf, we must work out new concepts, and try to set afoot a new man."[4]

Some Africans are awaiting a dramatic event or happening in order to spring into action. Unfortunately, there is no point in Africans furtively looking over the hills or through the windows waiting for Western imperialists to collapse. Procrastinators always unite tomorrow. African unity has to be taught, not just demanded. Only true Afrocentric knowledge can fill the gap and only then will enlightened Africans, who now see and appreciate the true global picture of events, realise that their immediate and long-term survival lies in uniting.

According to the biblical story of the Exodus, the Israelites left Egypt in order to end a lifetime of slavery and survived in the wilderness only by their faith in God and the strength of their convictions. The Europeans who became the founding fathers of white America braved stormy seas, unknown and wild terrain in order to dispossess and replace the Native Americans in a land they call home today. In contrast, African Americans seeking new frontiers only need to book a flight.

The imperialists have manipulated human beings by playing on the human weaknesses of fear, selfishness and greed but the human desire for freedom and the will to survive is infinitely stronger. Many Africans living in the Western paradigm are too scared to live and too scared to die. They are paralysed by their fear of white repercussions given their dependence. They are blinded by their inferiority complexes to the white man and lost in the circular activity of their day to day existence, consumerism, religious and tribal beliefs. However, I say to them, truly the only thing to fear in life, is fear itself.

The African plight is as much a tragic humanitarian disaster as it is an environmental one. Africa's main problem, similar to that of all other naturally resource-rich but poor people around the world, is that they inhabit the land the imperialist needs to destroy in order, to extract the resources they crave — be they natural or human. The human and environmental disasters wreaked by capitalism and imperialism walk together.

With the advances in information technology and air travel, the global human village has shrunk and become more accessible than ever before. Blinded by our minute physical and cultural differences, human beings have foregone the tremendous synergy and rapid development that working as a cohesive global unit could bring. If human beings were to survive another millennium, it would be incomprehensible to future generations why we persisted on this path of self-destruction for so long. Human beings have a terrible capacity to destroy things all around them yet, when united against threats to their survival, a tremendous capacity for creativity [kuumba] and progress.

The survival of all human beings is inexorably intertwined. Therefore, in our ever-shrinking world, all human beings — of every race, colour or creed — have a moral duty to fight racism in all its ramifications even as we try to slow down the global environmental catastrophe. As the earth is pushed closer and closer to the tipping point in the form of a catastrophic storm or cataclysmic man-made disaster, the imperialists still refuse to acknowledge the real effects of their actions while the majority of the world's poor and disenfranchised populations remain apathetic towards the refusal.

In all this, Africans remain the most vulnerable and unprepared people in the world, vulnerable to the effects of imperialists' increasingly desperate grab for resources and the destructive effects of nature's backlash.

The line in the sand has been drawn. Will the imperialists or the 'inhumans' succeed in creating total hegemony over the lives and resources of the rest of humanity, killing thousands, even millions, more in their bid to condemn them to mindless and endless servitude? Alternatively, will the rest of humanity have the courage to rise up to the greatest threat to their survival, liberties and freedom yet?

As an optimist and having a firm and resolute belief in a God who created all men equal, I believe that the strong and resilient human spirit that motivated our African ancestors, and the ancestors of all peoples around the world, will see us — Africans and all mankind — through in the end. I believe that the greater body of humanity and the stronger human instincts of survival and freedom will prevail over the inhumanity, selfishness and greed of the imperialist few.

Unfortunately, in our modern world, 'freedom' is not available for free. The real freedom Africans should fight for may never be realised in their present lives or even their children's. Nonetheless it should be fought for with all the strength they can muster. Africans must plan for the long-term total emancipation of all Africans wherever they may be and break forever the conditioning of generations into submission and dependence.

Place your trust in God. Find love in yourself. Embrace your inner African self.

That is the surest way to the light.

APPENDIX

Nelson Mandela wrote:

"I was not born with a hunger to be free. I was born free — Free in every way that I could know. Free to run in the fields near my mother's hut, free to swim in the clear stream that ran through my village, free to roast mealies under the stars and ride the broad backs of slow moving bulls. As long as I obeyed my father and abided by the customs of my tribe, I was not troubled by the laws of man on God.

'It was only when I began to learn that my boyhood freedom was an illusion, when I discovered as a young man at my freedom had already been taken from me that I began to hunger for it. At first as a student I wanted freedom only for myself, the transitory freedoms of being able to stay out at night, read what I pleased and go where I chose. Later as a young man in Johannesburg, I yearned for the basic and honorable freedoms of achieving my potential, earning my keep, of marrying and having a family – the freedom not to be obstructed in a lawful life.

'But then I slowly saw that not only was I not free, but my brothers and sisters were not free. I saw that it was not just my freedom that was curtailed but the freedom of everyone who looked like I did. That is when I joined the African National Congress, and that is when the hunger for my own freedom became the greater hunger for the freedom of my people. It was this desire for the freedom of my people to live their lives with dignity and self-respect that animated my life that transformed a frightened young man into a bold one, that drove the law-abiding attorney to become a criminal, that turned a family-loving husband into a man without a home, that forced a life loving man to live like a monk. I am no more virtuous or self-sacrificing than the next man, but I found that I could not even enjoy the poor and limited freedoms I was allowed when I knew my people were not free.

'Freedom is indivisible; that chains on any one of my people were the chains on all of them, the chains on all of my people were the chains on me.

'It was during those long and lonely years that my hunger for the freedom

of my own people became a hunger for the freedom of all people, White and Black. I knew as well as I knew anything that the oppressor must be liberated just as surely as the oppressed. A man who takes away another man's freedom is a prisoner of hatred; he is locked behind the bars of prejudice and narrow-mindedness. I am not a truly free man if I am taking away someone else's freedom just as surely as I am not free when my freedom is taken from me. The oppressed and the oppressor alike are robbed of their humanity.

'When I walked out of prison, that was my mission, to liberate the oppressed and the oppressor both. Some say that has now been achieved. But I know that this is not the case. The truth is that we are not yet free; we have mainly achieved the freedom to be free, the right not to be oppressed; we have not taken the final step of our journey but the first step on a longer and even more difficult road. For to be free is not merely to cast off one's chains, but to live in a way that respects and enhances the freedom of others. The true test of our devotion to freedom is just beginning.

'I have walked that long road to freedom. I have tried not to falter; I have made many missteps along the way. But I have discovered the secret that after climbing a great hill, one only finds that there are many more hills to climb. I have taken the moment to rest to steal a view of the glorious vista that surrounds me, to look back on the distance I have come. But I can only rest for a moment for with freedom comes responsibilities, and I dare not linger, for my long walk is not yet ended." [1]

REFERENCES

PART ONE: GLOBAL CONTEXT

CHAPTER ONE:
THE CALM BEFORE THE STORM

1. Einstein, Albert. "Albert Einstein Quotes." Brainy Quote.com. BookRags Media Network, 2001-4. Web. 28 February 2014.
2. "Bhopal Gas Tragedy." Wikipedia. Wikimedia, n.d. 28 February 2014.
3. "Savar Building Collapse." Wikipedia. Wikimedia, n.d. 28 February 2014.
4. Hartmann, Thom. "Globalisation is the Number One Risk Facing Humanity." OpEd News. Op Ed, 30 August 2012. Web. 28 February 2014.
5. Blatter, Sepp. "Racism? It Can All Be Forgotten in a Handshake." Daily Mail 16 November 2011.
6. Race Relations Act 1968.
7. "Obama Birth Certificate." Whitehouse.gov. White House, 16 September 2009. Web. 28 February 2014.
8. "Obama heckled in Congress." Wikipedia. Wikimedia, n.d. 11 March 2014.
9. "Shooting of Trayvon Martin." Wikipedia. Wikimedia, n.d. 28 February 2014.
10. Michael Brown shooting
11. Eric Garner's killing by New York Police. Wikipedia
12. Obama's interview with Fareed Zakaria CNN. (http://www.cnn.com/videos/politics/2016/12/08/obama-legacy-racism-in -office)
13. Ben Cardin on Sunday, April 9th, in comments on "Fox News Sunday". www.poliyifact.com. Congressional Research Service: Cloture Attempts and Historical Development Through November 20 2013. By Richard S Beth, Visiting Scholar, Elizabeth Rybicki, Specialist on Congress and Legislative Process and Michael Greene, Senior Research Librarian.
14. Mother Jones on filibustering President Obama compared to other US president. [MotherJones: 3 Charts Explain Why Democrats Went Nuclear on Filibuster by Kevin Drum and Jaeah Lee. November 22nd, 2013 11: 00 am]

CHAPTER TWO:
DISSECTING EUROPEAN RACISM

1. "Willie Lynch Letter: The Making of a Slave." Finalcall.com. FCN Publishing, 2014. Web. 28 February 2014.
2. Fuller Jr., Neely. The United Independent Compensatory Code/System/Concept. Self-published. 1971.
3. An African American Professor of Journalism at Colombia University, William Cobb.
4. Willie Lynch speech.
5. Triune Brain. Paul D. MacLean:
6. Holocaust Exposure Induced Intergenerational Effects on FKBPS5 Methylation in Biological Psychiatry Journal. Published Online: August 12, 2015.
7. Einstein, Albert. "Imagination is more important than knowledge". Brainy Quote.com. BookRags Media Network, 2001-4. Web. 28 February 2014.
8. Brain researcher, Dr. Win Wenger, Ph.D., suggested that we engage in over 90% of visual processing of information and less than 10% of verbal processing of information. We therefore underuse our brains by over 90% of its capacity most of the time. Internet.
9. "Human Echolocation." Wikipedia. Wikimedia, n.d. 28 February 2014.
10. Necker Cube, Kanza Triangle and Muller Lyer Illusions, 1832. Illustration.

11. The Influence of culture on visual perception: Segall M, Campbell D and Herskovits M.J, 1966.

CHAPTER THREE:
SUBLIMINAL PROGRAMMING

1. Mander, J. Four Arguments for the Elimination of Television. Quote by Dr. Krugman. William Morrow, Reprint 1 February 1978.
2. Ibid
3. Dr Erik Peper 211. . Austin, Suzy. "Your Brain is always One-Step Ahead." Metro 14 April 2008, natl. ed.: page 14.
4. Hogg, Tracy and Blau, Melina. Secrets of the Baby Whisperer. Vermillion, 2001.
5. Howard Bloom quoted by Kick, Russ. You are Being Lied To: the Disinformation Guide to Media Distortion, Historical Whitewashes and Cultural Myths. Disinformation Books/Razorfish Studios, 2002: page 12. 6
6. Brain changes in depression.
7. Howard Bloom, Op. cit., Kick, Russ.
8. Haynes, Prof. John-Dylan. "Unconscious Determinants of free decision in Human brain." Nature Neuroscience 13 April 2008, 10.1038/nn.2112.
9. Prof John-Dylan : Ibid

   UK spending on Advertising. Dohnert, John. "GroupM Predicts Digital Ad Spend Will Surpass £113 Billion in 2013." ClickZ 28 March 2013. Web. 2 March 2014. [Advertising spend to top £21.8 bn in 2019 by John Glenday. 03 June 09:17 am.

CHAPTER FOUR:
STOLEN DREAMS

1. Social skills acquisition by age 10. Erickson, Eric. "Erikson's Psychosocial Stages Summary Chart." PDF. Social Scientist. Web. 2 March 2014.
2. Cortisol implicated in Depression. "Chronic Stress Puts Your Health at Risk." Mayo Clinic. Web.
3. Dopamine implicated in Depression.

CHAPTER FIVE:
PUPPET MASTERS

1. 'The salons that hope you can't tell the goats and human apart': by Sam Piranty, BBC News. 10/10/2014.
2. The West African Frontier Force. Wikipedia.
3. The German Schutztruppe. Wikipedia.
4. Mohammed Ali quote.

CHAPTER SIX:
AFRICA'S CROSS: THE BURDEN OF WHITE SUPREMACY

1. "African Deaths from Preventable Causes." World Health Organization. Fact Sheet. Web. 2 March 2014.
2. "Mortality Rates." Wikipedia. Wikimedia, n.d. 3 March 2014.
3. "Life Expectancy, Africa." World Health Organization Report 2011. Web. 2nd March 2014.
4. Child Mortality: UNICEF DATA. https//data.unicef.org>child-survival In 2018, UNICEF reported that, approximately 84% of all the under-five deaths in the world occur in just two regions: sub-saharan Africa (54%) and South Asia (28%).[Child Mortality-UNICEF DATA. https//data.unicef.org>child-survival]
5. "Blair Blasted over Tanzania Deal." BBC, 31 January 2007. Web. 2nd March 2014
6. Prince, Rob. "The Real Story about Bush HIV/Aids and Africa." Counter Punch 14 August 2013. Web. 2 March 2014.

CHAPTER SEVEN:
IN THE BEGINNING: THE EVOLUTION OF HUMANITY AND WESTERN CIVILIZATION

1. Cicero, Marcus Tullius. "Marcus Tullius Cicero Quotes." Brainy Quotes. com. BookRags Media Network, 2001-4. Web. 2 March 2014.

CHAPTER EIGHT:
IMPERIALISM AND RACISM

1. "Joan of Arc." Wikipedia. Wikimedia, n.d. Web. 2 March 2014.
2. Chomsky, Noam Chomsky. Fascism in Europe.: page 67.
3. Ibid., 68.
4. Ibid., 68.
5. Ibid., 68.
6. Ibid., 68.
7. Ibid., 68.
8. Ibid., 68. See also "Fanta." Wikipedia. Wikimedia, n.d., 2 March 2014
9. Ibid., 68. See also "Operation Paperclip." Wikipedia. Wikimedia, n.d. 2 March 2014.

CHAPTER NINE:
APPROPRIATING WORLD HISTORY

1. Brown, Michael Barrett. Francis Bacon after Imperialism. Heinemann.: pages 26-7; 36.
2. Hitler, Adolf. "Adolf Hitler Quote." Mein Kampf. Boston: Houghton Mifflin and Co., 1925: page 231.

CHAPTER TEN:
CAPITALISM AND MILITARISM: THE RIGHT OF MIGHT

1. Welsing, Francis Cress. "Quote from Oliver Cromwell Cox." The Isis Papers: The Keys to the Colours. USA: Third World Press, 21 October 1994: page 1.
2. Bond, Patrick. Looting Africa: The Economics of Exploitation. Quotation by Rosa Luxemburg. Zed Books, 28 June 2006.: page ix.
3. Chomsky, Noam. Hegemony or Survival [Chomsky, p.60].
4. Noam Chomsky; Human Rights Watch.
5. Rendition flights by the US and the UK. [The Guardian: UK provided more support for CIA rendition flights than thought- Study. Ian Cobain and James Bell. Wed 22 May 2013] [The Guardian: Rendition – UK urged to tell all on US rendition flights. Jamie Doward. Sat 28 June 2014]
6. Privatising of Military in Iraq.
7. Libyan rebel leader sues Britain over rendition ordeal. Richard Norton-Taylor Monday 19th December 2011 13.03 EST
8. Chomsky,Noam. IBID Peasant Agriculture.: page 68.

CHAPTER ELEVEN:
THE HIDDEN PSYCHOLOGICAL IMPERATIVE OF GLOBALISED RACISM

1. Perkins, John. Confessions of an Economic Hit Man. Ebury Press, 30 September 2011.
2. Op. cit., Dr Welsing, preface/ii.
3. Ibid., 3.
4. Donald Trump's first speech to European leaders in Warsaw, Poland.
5. Ibid
6. Rise Above Movement (RAM) in Charlottesville riots 2017.
7. Ibid.
8. US GUN CONTROL: 'Dying of whiteness: why racism is at the heart of America's gun inaction. Lois Beckett in San Francisco Fri 9th August 2019 01.00 EDT
9. Neely Fuller from Isis Papers.

CHAPTER TWELVE:
GLOBALISING WHITE PRIVILEGE

1. "Official Estimates of the First World War and Second World War." Wikipedia. Wikimedia, n.d. 2 March 2014.
2. Bush, Time Magazine, Man of the Year, 2004.
3. Simms, Andrew. Independent Print Ltd. 22 November 2005. Print. Andrew Simms quoted in article by Philip Thornton: Iraq's Oil: The spoils of war. Independent/ UK/ Tuesday, 22/11/2005
4. www.telegraph.co.uk: Britain invasions by Jasper Copping. 9.30 am GMT. 4th November 2012.
5. Dr Gideon Polya. www.

countercurrents.org/polya. 5th July 2013

6. Contrast wealth of world's richest against poorest. Bill Gates' worth.

CHAPTER THIRTEEN:
DESTRUCTION OF THE ENVIRONMENT

1. Al Gore 'Inconvenient Truth'.
2. "In 2008, NASA geophysicist…" Pa.press.net., Press Association, 16 December 2008. Web. 3 March 2014.
3. "Heads of the Royal colleges…" PA.press.net., Press Association, 16 September 2009. Web. 3 March 2014.
4. IPCC report.
5. Deforestation.
6. Evaporation of Lake Chad and ice-caps of Kilimanjaro.
7. "Bush Drives a Bulldozer through Laws Protecting the Wilderness." Times 7 May 2005. Print.
8. Grusky Sr., Alexander N. "Clean Air Act? World Bank and IMF: Ringleaders of Globalization." News and Notices for IMF and World Bank Watchers, Centre for Global Concern.
9. Donald Trump on climate change. Trump: American citizens come first. www.bbc.co.uk
10. Maathi, Wangari. Caption. Nobel prize-winner planting trees.

CHAPTER FOURTEEN:
GLOBALISING POVERTY AND WAR

1. Structural Adjustment Programme.
2. Woodward, D. "Globalization and Liberalization: Effects of International Economic Relations on Poverty." UNCTAD. Inter-Agency Thematic Contribution to the International Year for the Eradication of Poverty. New York, United Nations 1996.
3. Bezruchka, S., "Is Globalization Dangerous to our Health?" Western Journal of Medicine 2000: pages 172, 332-4.
4. US poverty.
5. Castro, Fidel. "Opening Speech at the South Summit." Havana, April 12th 2000.

CHAPTER FIFTEEN:
THE AFRICAN HOLOCAUST

1. Professor Sachs quote on Africa. Bond, Patrick. Looting Africa: The Economics of Exploitation. Quotation by Professor Sachs. Zed Books, 28 June 2006.
2. Walker, Robin. When We Ruled: Quotation by Professor John Clarke. Every Generation Media, November 2005: page 7.
3. Chinua Achebe quote.

PART TWO: DECOLONIZING AFRICAN HISTORY

CHAPTER SIXTEEN:
AFRICA, THE BIBLICAL GARDEN OF EDEN

1. African Proverb.
2. Isaac Newton quote.
3. "African continent population." World Population Statistics.com, Web. 3 March 2014.
4. "Africa, Second Largest Continent." Encyclopaedia Britannica; Macropedia Ready Reference, 1995.: 131. 3 March 2014.
5. Ibid., 133-4.
6. "Toumai Skull: Is it Man's Earliest Ancestor?" Nhm.ac.uk. Natural History Museum, 8 April 2005. Web. 3 March 2014.
7. "Genetics: DNA Points to African Origins." The Washington Post 11 March 1996.
8. Van Sertima, Ivan. "The African Presence in Ancient America." They Came Before Columbus."
9. Ibid., 94-6.
10. Op. cit., Van Sertima, pages 24-7.
11. Von Daniken, Erich. Chariot of the Gods.
12. McRichie, "Ancient and Modern Britons."
13. Christopher Columbus and ancient mariners. Admiral Zheng.
14. McKissic Sr.,William Dwight. Beyond Roots: In Search of Blacks in the Bible.:

page 31.
15. Rare Chinese coin found by Illinois University Researchers.
16. William Dwight McKissic Sr.
17. Hansberry, William Leo. African History Notebook, Volume II, Africa and Africans Seen by Classical Writers. Ed. Joseph Harris.: pages 74-5.
18. Roberts, Dr Alice. Out of Africa. Documentary. BBC.
19. Finch, Charles S. Echoes of Darkland. Pages 28-31.

CHAPTER SEVENTEEN:
THE SHAPE OF AFRICA

1. Kaiser, Ward L. "Concept of Modern Africa since Suez Canal. Shape of Modern Africa, A New View of the World." A Hand Book of the World Map: Peter's Projection: pages 10, 12, 13.
2. Felder, Cain Hope. The Biblical Institute for Social Change Quarterly 3.1: page 2.
3. "Africa: The Beginning." African Heritage Study Bible: page 106.
4. Windsor, Rudolph, R. The Valley of the Dry Bones: page 52.
5. Van Sertima, Ivan. "Sabeans. Phoenician DNA 44 M76 North African gene found in 80% of Phoenician descendants."
6. Mazrui, Ali. World Culture and the Black Experience.: page 13.
7. Houston, Drusilla Dunjee. Quoted by Baldwin. Wonderful Ethiopians of the Ancient Cushite Empire.: page 126.
8. "Notes to Esther 1:1."African Heritage Study Bible.: pages 787-8.
9. Op. cit.,Van Sertima, Ivan, Sabeans.
10. Ibid.
11. Felder, Cain Hope. Troubling Biblical Waters: page 24.
12. Hansberry, William Leo. African History Notebook Vol. II, Africa and Africans as Seen by Classical Writers. Ed. Joseph Harris: pages 13, 24.
13. Ibid
14. Ibid

CHAPTER EIGHTEEN:
THE AFRICAN ORIGINS OF HUMAN CIVILIZATION

1. Walker, Robin. When We Ruled. Every Generation Media, November 2005: pages 139-143.
2. LeBombo bone . www.taneter .org
3. Ibid., 75-6. "Ishango Bone."
4. Mathematical concept of Ishango bone.
5. Ibid., Wadi Kubbinyani. "Agriculture and Cattle."
6. Thomas, Hugh. Slave Trade. Page 28.
7. Volney, Count and Diop. African Origin: pages 27-28.
8. Ibid, pages 27-8.
9. Deron, Vivant. Travels in Upper and Lower Egypt., Vol.1. New York: Arnos Press, 1973: pages 271-2.
10. Van Sertima, Ivan. Egyptian Skeletons.: pages 111-2.

CHAPTER NINETEEN:
THE CENTRAL SAHARAN CATTLE CULTURE

1. "Saharan Cattle Culture." Wikipedia. Wikimedia, n.d. 3 March 2014.
2. Ibid.
3. Ibid.
4. Ibid.
5. Op cit., Walker, Robin, When We Ruled. Citing Fabrizio Mori, Fabrizio and Uan Muhugging, Uan: page 142.
6. Central Saharan Cattle Culture.
7. Ibid.
8. Ibid.
9. Arkell, A J, British Historian.
10. Op. cit., Walker, pages 139-143.
11. Op. cit., Walker, "The Badri."

CHAPTER TWENTY:
AFRICAN SCIENCE AND TECHNOLOGY

1. "Euclid." Encyclopaedia Britannica. Micropaedia, 1995: page 590.
2. Jefferson, Thomas. Quote.
3. Jefferson, Thomas Ibid.
4. Professor Emeagwali.

5. Moscow Papyrus. www.taneter. org
6. The Rhind Papyrus. Ibid
7. Timbuktu Mathematical Papyrus. Ibid

CHAPTER TWENTY-ONE: THE FIRST SURGICAL TREATISE

1. "Kocher's Manoeuvre." Baily and Love Surgical Manual.
2. Medical eponyms.
3. "Medicine Timeline: From Cave Paintings to the Internet." History of Information.com. Web. 3 March 2014.
4. The Oldest Surgical Treatise, c.1,600 BCE. Edwin Smith Papyrus.
5. Ibid
6. "Egyptians used Toothpaste." Selected Bibliography and Medicine. Delta State. Web. 14 March 2014.
7. Wadley, Lyn. "Middle Stone Age Bedding Construction and Settlement Patterns at Sibudu, South Africa." Science 334.6061 (2011): pages 1388-91.
8. Nabta Playa and the Ancient Astronomers of the Nubian Desert/ Ancient Origins. www.ancient origins. net. Egypt-Archaeology Expert. www. archaeologyexpert.co.uk. By Grahame Johnston 30/10/2016]10. Late Neolithic megalithic structures at Nabta Playa by Fred Wendorf
9. Pyramid of Giza: Build
10. Procession Cycles
11. Ptolemy days of the week.
12. Al-Makkari. "History of Mohammedan Dynasties." Print.
13. Van Sertima, Ivan.
14. Ibid.
15. Hatch, John. "Leo Africanus."
16. Ibid.
17. Tuchscherer, Konrad. Quote.
18. Ibid
19. '15 things You Did Not Know About The Moors of Spain: Black history Studies'.
20. Day of All Saints.
21. Queen Elizabeth and Isabella expel Africans.

CHAPTER TWENTY-TWO: AFRICA: THE DARK CONTINENT

1. David Hume, English philosopher.
2. George Kimble (Geographer, b.1912) (www.africaourafrica.com: interesting quotes about Africa.
3. Op. cit., Walker. Citing Dr Victor Robinson.
4. Ibid
5. St Clair Drake. "Black Folk Here and There.:" preface XVI.
6. John Hatch. "White slaves?" in North Africa.
7. Op. cit., Walker. Citing Thomas Hodgkin: page 4.
8. Op. cit., Walker. Citing Koumbi Saleh, Koumbi: page 26.
9. Thomas Wyndham on Oba of Benin.
10. Thomas Wyndham . Ibid
11. Ibid. Dutch man in Benin.
12. Op. cit., Robin Walker. Citing "Defensive Benin Wall:" page 335.
13. Op. cit., Walker. Citing "Nok Culture.:" 313.
14. Igbo-Ukwu Culture. Walker, Robin. Ibid.
15. Frobenius, Leo. "Black Diaspora."
16. Eredo: The Largest City in the Ancient World- Black History Studies. www. blackhistorystudies.com. Wikipedia.
17. Op. cit., Walker. Citing Shona Zimbabwe.: page 513.
18. Op. cit., Walker: Mansa Musa.: pages 375, 377-80.

CHAPTER TWENTY-THREE: THE AFRICAN COMMUNAL

No quotes

CHAPTER TWENTY-FOUR: AFRICA'S DECLINE

1. Op. cit., Walker. Citing Ivan Van Sertima.: page 549.
2. Subsidised training. Cost of UK trained doctors compared to foreign doctors.
3. The Kings Fund is making the difference: Diversity and Inclusion

in the NHS. By Authors: Michael West, Jeremy Dawson, Mandip Kaur December 2015.

4. The King's Fund: Ethnic minority deaths and Covid-19: What are we to do? Authors: Suzie Bailey, Michael West 30 April 2020
5. High trade tariffs for Africa.
6. "When Others are Grabbing Their Land." The Economist, The Economist Newspaper Ltd. 5 May 2011.
7. Ibid.
8. The Bamako Convention: www. Unenviroment.org.
9. Trifigura Found Guilty of Exporting Toxic Waste. BBC News, 23/07/2010].
10. Dumped in Africa: Britain's toxic waste. The Independent 18/02/2009].
11. Greenpeace investigation
12. Where Do 50 Million Tonnes a Year of Toxic e-Waste Go? By Baher Kamal. www.ipsnews.net 2017/09].
13. John Pilger: The New Rulers of the World. Page 102
14. Ethiopians who cook water.

PART THREE: THE EUROPEAN INTRUSION

CHAPTER TWENTY-FIVE:
THE SLAVE TRADE

1. Kick, Russ. You are Being Lied To: the Disinformation Guide to Media Distortion, Historical Whitewashes and Cultural Myths. Disinformation Books/Razorfish Studios, 2002. Citing Christopher Columbus.
2. ILO definition of slavery. (ILO and Kevin Bales, Freetheslaves.net).
3. CNN exposes slave auctions in Libya. [Slave auctions in Libya are the latest evidence of a reality for migrants the EU prefers to ignore: by Simon McMahon, December 5, 2017 10.37 am GMT: theconversation.com]
4. "Serfs/ Slaves." Encyclopaedia Britannica.
5. Op. cit., Walker. Citing Mansa Musa.: pages 377-80.
6. Hatch, John. The History of Britain in Africa: prologue, page 21.
7. IBID: John Hatch
8. Portuguese in Abrodi – The Africans Who Wrote the Bible.
9. "Ghana Castle of No Return." New African June 2004.: page 31
10. Ibid
11. Black Diaspora.
12. Ibid: Dutch occupation of the Elmina Castle. New African, June 2004
13. Treaty of Torsedillas.
14. David Basildon; Historian. The African Slave Trade: page 79.
15. British profits from slavery.

CHAPTER TWENTY-SIX:
THE SLAVE EXPERIENCE

1. Thomas, Hugh. "David Livingstone."Equiano, Olaudoh. "Interesting Narrative of the life of Olaudoh Equiano." National Museum of American History. Web.
2. Oluadoh Equiano served in British Navy. Olaudoh Equiano (c.1745-1797): The Former Slave, Seaman & Writer. The Abolition Project. Olaudoh Equiano. Abolition.e2bn.org. See also Timeline-Equiano Society. www. equiano.net.>timeline.]
3. Equiano Olaudoh recruited by British Government to repatriate black poor to Sierra Leone.
4. Op. cit., Equiano. Capture and enslavement.
5. Ibid.
6. Equiano terrified of white captors.
7. "The screams of the women..." Equiano describes conditions on slave ship. (From lost Ndigbo, Emeagwali).
8. Equiano suicidal.
9. "The screams of the women". (From lost Ndigbo, Emeagwali).
10. John Newton's diary on his slaves.
11. Olaudah Equiano Grieves for sister and is force fed.
12. Equiano on slave's terror on arrival to America.

13. "Black Diaspora." Chesapeake.
14. Equiano: Slave families split and sold on.
15. When will Britain face up to its crimes against humanity? The Guardian. By Kris Manjora 29th March 2018 06:00 BST
16. "Slave Rape; Treatment of slaves." Wikipedia, Wikimedia, n.d. 3 March 2014. Genetic studies show that Afro-Caribbean's have 25% of European genes from slave raping.
17. Equiano on miscegeny
18. Melanated and Illustrated Media 05/05/19. [Atlas Obscura: The Extraordinary autobiography of an enslaved muslim man; by Jonathan Carey January 25th 2019]

CHAPTER TWENTY-SEVEN: SLAVE RESISTANCE

1. Op. cit., Walker. "Slave Revolts."
2. Armistad.
3. Black Diaspora.: page 92.
4. Ibid., 94.
5. Op. cit., Walker. Quote from Prof. Nascimneto.
6. Ibid.
7. Klein, Herbert S. African Slavery in Latin America and the Caribbean. New York: Oxford University Press, 1986: pages 202-3.
8. Black Diaspora.
9. Ibid.
10. Ibid.
11. Ibid. [The Black Diaspora by Ronal Segal, page 119].
12. Korngold, Ralph. Citizen Toussaint. London: Gollancz, 1946: page 145.
13. Ibid.
14. Ibid.
15. Black Diaspora.
16. Ibid.
17. Williams. Columbus to Castro. Pages 196-97.
18. Koromantyn. Black Diaspora.: page 18.
19. Ibid., "Surinam and Jamaica."

CHAPTER TWENTY-EIGHT: ABOLITION

1. In an 1858 letter, Lincoln said, "I have declared a thousand times, and now repeat that, in my opinion neither the General Government, nor any other power outside of the slave states, can constitutionally or rightfully interfere with slaves or slavery where it already exists." In a Springfield, Ill., speech, he explained, "My declarations upon this subject of negro slavery may be misrepresented, but cannot be misunderstood. I have said that I do not understand the Declaration (of Independence) to mean that all men were created equal in all respects.
2. " Debating with Sen. Stephen Douglas, Lincoln said, "I am not, nor ever have been, in favor of ... making voters or jurors of Negroes nor of qualifying them to hold office nor to intermarry with white people; and I will say in addition to this that there is a physical difference between the white and black races, which I believe will forever forbid the two races living together on terms of social and political equality."
3. Abraham Lincoln's quotes.
4. Slaves Emancipation proclamation. Dred Scott.
5. Alexander Stephens, the Confederate-Vice-President speech following the secession of Confederate States in 1861.
6. Casualty rates of the American civil war.
7. Sir Walter Raleigh quote.
8. The Zong incident. African slaves drowned for insurance money.
9. "Memoirs of Granville Sharp." Memoirs. London, 1820: chap. VIII. Print.
10. Ibid
11. Ibid
12. Ibid
13. British Abolition of slavery, 1807. "Slave codes." Black Diaspora.

14. ILO definition of modern day slavery.
15. Ibid
16. Number of modern day slaves.
17. Ibid

PART FOUR: COLONIALISM

CHAPTER TWENTY-NINE: COLONIZATION: CRIMES AGAINST HUMANITY

1. Thomas Hughes on Churchill.
2. Okonkwo in 'Things fall apart' by Chinua Achebe. (Chinua Achebe. www.goodreads.com)
3. Encyclopaedia Britannica.
4. Dr Emeagwali.
5. Carmichael, Stokely. Land and Power, Modern Black Nationalism.: 204.
6. Headrick, Daniel R. The Tools of Empire: Technology and European Imperialism in the Nineteenth Century. : page 3.
7. Theodore Von Leutwein, German Governor in Namibia.
8. German Genocide: State of Africa. page 3.
9. Ibid. Herero Massacre.
10. Shark Island massacre.
11. British Tasmanian Genocide. Channel 4. TV.
12. Flinders Island Aborigine resettlement. Channel 4. TV.
13. Khosian and Maori massacres.
14. Colonial Expansion deaths: British Indian Famine.
15. King Leopold of Belgium and Henry Morton Stanley: Valley, Paul. "Forever in Chains." Quote. Independent Print Ltd. 28 July 2006, spec. ed.
16. King Leopold declares the Congo as Terra Nullius in 1885.
17. Valley, Paul. "Forever in Chains." Quote. Independent Print Ltd. 28 July 2006, spec. ed.
18. Ibid
19. Ibid
20. Ibid
21. Ibid
22. Ibid
23. Ibid
24. Edmund Dene Morel. Book- Red Rubber
25. Casement Report.
26. King Leopold compensated by Belgium.

CHAPTER THIRTY: AFRICA SCRAMBLED

1. Berlin Conference, November 1884. "100 Years of Partition - Centenary of the Berlin Conference." Africa Now, March 1985.: page 25. Print.
2. Ibid. "African History as a Legacy of the Berlin Act." Africa Now March 1985.:
3. Ibid: Lord Salisbury quote.
4. Ibid: Queen Victoria quote: 'Let them each have a big mountain'.
5. Cecil Rhodes quote. Rhodes, Cecil. Quote. Imperialism: The Highest Stage of Capitalism. By V. L. Lenin.: page 79.
6. Lovell Jr., John. Black Song: The Forge and the Flame.: pages 31-2.
7. Portuguese in Benin: Cross and Sword approach.
8. British imposition of Hut Tax. Christopher Palin.
9. Niall Ferguson: Empire; 'Good and bad corn'
10. Ibid.

CHAPTER THIRTY-ONE: THE SHADOW BRITISH EMPIRE

1. Ibid. England profits from pirates.
2. Ibid. Sir Henry Morgan and Sir Francis Drake.
3. Niall Ferguson: Empire; Emperor Mughal.
4. Ibid: Translation of Bhagavat gita to English
5. Ibid: 'Nawab' to 'Nabobs.
6. Goldie Taubman.
7. British colonial India. Colonel Dyer.
8. Ibid. Amritsar massacre
9. Poverty in British Colonial India.
10. Legacy of British Colonial rule in

Kashmir.

CHAPTER THIRTY-TWO:
PALMGERIA: THE NIGERIAN EXAMPLE

1. Goldie, Taubman.
2. Jaja of Opobo
3. British gun-boats shelled Nigerian towns.
4. Tafa Balewa. State of Africa. : page 8.
5. Ibid: Awolowo
6. Martin Meredith quote:
7. John Hatch: Formation of Nigeria.
8. Ibid.

CHAPTER THIRTY-THREE:
THE COLONIAL IMPERATIVE

1. Railways to Parts of Africa: Commission for Africa.
2. French pull out of Guinea.
3. Niall Ferguson on Hitler
4. Ibid
5. Ibid: Hitler's "Shoot Indians." Quote.
6. Ibid
7. British Governor in Kenya. ? Niall Ferguson.
8. Ibid.

PART FIVE: SEGREGATION

CHAPTER THIRTY-FOUR:
THE LEGISLATIVE AND IDEOLOGICAL ORIGINS OF SEGREGATION

1. Rogers, J.A. Abraham Lincoln: Sex and Race.
2. Encyclopaedia Britannica. 3. Ibid.
3. Ibid.
4. Ibid.
5. Ibid.
6. Ibid.
7. "1/3 Human Being." American Constitution.
8. Article 38 of the Code Noir.
9. Black Diaspora.
10. South Carolina Slave Code
11. Virginia General Assembly Law 1680.6.
12. Scott vs. Sanford. Supreme Court. 1857.
13. Israelite Exodus from Egypt.
14. Isaac Le Peyere
15. Hale, Matthew. "Preadamites."
16. Agassiz lectures
17. Nott and Gliddon

CHAPTER THIRTY-FIVE:
THE EVOLUTION OF SEGREGATION IN THE UNITED STATES OF AMERICA

1. Vagrancy laws of 1866.
2. Commanding General Alfred Terry quote.
3. Convict leasing in Georgia. [Mancini Matthew J. (1996). One dies, Get Another: Convict leasing in America South, 1866-1928 page 1-2.]
4. 14th and 15th Amendments. Civil Rights Abuse.
5. President Ulysses Grant on Ku Klux Klan
6. "Lynch Laws." Wikipedia. Wikimedia, n.d. 3 March 2014.
7. Brown on typical lynching. Bennett Jr., Lerone. Before the Mayflower: A History of the Negro in America 1614-1964.: page 294.
8. Walter White on lynching.
9. Ibid.
10. Graph on lynchings.
11. Lynching stats.
12. Lynching quote.
13. 'A Portrait of the Lynching Era', 1880-1930
14. "Share Cropping and Peonage: Terror to Triumph."
15. Historical Overview on black vote.

CHAPTER THIRTY-SIX:
THE END OF LEGAL SEGREGATION

1. Uncle Tom, Uncle Remus, Jim Crow and 'Old black Joe'. D.W. Griffith's classic silent movie, The Birth of a Nation, released in 1915.
2. The Thirteenth Amendment, ended legal slavery.
3. W.E.B. Du Bois vs Booker T

Washington.

4. Ibid
5. A Death in the Delta: The Story of Emmett Till; by Stephen J. Whitfield. Pages 41-42.
6. Tyson, Tim, The Blood of Emmett Till
7. Brown vs. Topeka Board of Education.
8. "Terror to Triumph." Survey of America students.

PART SIX: APARTHEID

CHAPTER THIRTY-SEVEN: SOUTH AFRICAN APARTHEID

1. African Slavery in Boer controlled Cape Town.
2. Apartheid Group Areas Act.
3. Land Acts.
4. Bantu Homelands Citizen Act 1970.
5. M.C Botha quoted in Albert Louis(Albie) Sachs [1969].

CHAPTER THIRTY-EIGHT: THE BRITISH EXPROPRIATION

1. Paulin, Christopher M. "White Man's Dreams; Black Man's Blood."page 2.
2. Ibid. page 70.
3. Ibid
4. Ibid. Hut tax.
5. Lord Robert's quote on Boers.
6. Socialist Papers on Racism." Citation of Wilson, F. "Farming 1886-1966" Oxford History of South Africa: page 162.
7. Emily Hobhouse.
8. Dr Kendal Franks quote. "Boer women need soap."

15. COLONISING ZIMBABWE

9. Cecil Rhodes quote : "The first race in the world" and claimed that "the more of the world we inhabit the better it is for the human race". [Rhodes 1902, p.58]
10. The Rudd Concession.

16. THE WHITE ZIMBABWEAN LAND GRAB

11. Zimbabwe. A Country Study, p.137-153, Nelson, Harold]
12. "White farmers in Zimbabwe 1890-2005" PhD Thesis, University of Oxford p. 60 by Selby, Angus (2006)]
13. "Propaganda [sic]The Other Rhodesian War" by Robin Wright (17th May 1976).

17. THE RHODESIAN BUSH WAR

14. Ian Smith quote
15. The Lancaster agreement

18. LAND REFORMS

16. Between 1980 -1998, under the "Willing buyer, Willing seller" scheme white farmers had voluntarily given up about 3,498,44 acres of land. However, by 2013, 10,816,886 acres of white farmland had been expropriated by black Zimbabweans.
17. Tony Blair's Labour government renege on the "Willing buyer, Willing seller scheme". [The Independent: Mugabe's farm seizures: racial justice or catastrophic power grab? MacDonald Dzirutwe Friday 6 September 2019 14.21]

CHAPTER THIRTY-NINE: APARTHEID THROUGH BLACK AFRICAN EYES

1. Use of the sjambok
2. Nelson Mandela, Long Walk to Freedom, pages 27-28.
3. Ibid.
4. Ibid.
5. Institute of Criminology at the University of Cape Town report
6. Dr Hussein Abdilahi Bulhan. Executions in South Africa.: p.172. (In Psychology of Oppression).
7. South Africa: White Rule, Black Revolt by Ernest Harsch. 1980.: p 84.
8. Ibid
9. Ibid
10. Gini Co-efficient. [Black and White Income Inequality in South Africa and the US: John Campbell. September 12th 2014].

PART SEVEN: THE FORGOTTEN PEOPLE

CHAPTER FORTY:
AUSTRALIA'S FIRST INHABITANTS

1. Captain Cook declares Australia Terra Nullius.
2. Loretta De Pleritz and Larry Croft: "Aboriginality Under the Microscope: The Biological Descent Test in Australian Law (2003). 3 Quart. Law and Justice Journal 105]
3. Aborigine life expectancy compared to India and Central Africa. Ibid
4. Dr Keith Woollard. Australian Medical Association.
5. Australian black deaths in custody 13 times higher than apartheid South Africa in 1986.
6. Juveniles in detention.
7. Australian Royal Commission
8. Jew discriminated against during immigration to Australia.

CHAPTER FORTY-ONE:
HAITI: THE FIRST BLACK REPUBLIC

1. French soldier deaths exceed Waterloo.
2. Alexander Pétion
3. Simon Bolivar fulfils his promise to free slave in Gran Colombia.
4. Ammi Sarfo wrote: "If you want to see what unconstrained U.S. power looks like- look at Haiti." [Haiti: Past, Present &Future- From Freedom to Neo-Colonial Occupation-Never Forget]
5. [Windows on Haiti 2011].
6. Ibid.
7. "American Sweat Shop." Noam Chomsky.
8. Papa Doc Duvilier
9. Baby Doc
10. The UN military force[MINUSTAH] controlled by the US military maintains oversight in Haiti while an NGO created by Bill Clinton in 2010, the Interim Haiti Recovery Commission (IHRC) effectively administers Haiti's economy.

PART EIGHT: RELIGION

CHAPTER FORTY-TWO:
RELIGION: THE OPIUM OF THE PEOPLE

1. "The Criminal History of the Papacy." Extract. Nexus Magazine 14.3 (2007). Print.
2. John Hawkin. Quote.
3. The Times. 4 October 2005.
4. American Survey.
5. Dowd, Mark. Hallowed Be Thy Game.
6. Church of Diego Maradonna.
7. Bailey, Anglican Canon Edward. The Secular Faith Controversy.
8. Alex Ferguson on religion.
9. Blyden, E. Christianity, Islam, and the Negro Race. London: W. Whittingham, 1888: page 22.
10. Polybius. Letter to the Editor. 1 March 2007. "Faith, Atheism and the Battle for Today's Moral Desert." The Times.
11. Descartes. 'I think therefore I am'.
12. Authors of Gideon New Testament.
13. Ibid.

CHAPTER FORTY-THREE:
ANCIENT RELIGION

1. Ancient understanding of Summer equinoxes and winter solstices.
2. Durant, Will. The Story of Civilization: Caesar and Christ.: page 558.
3. Ibid.
4. Christian Calendar. The Perennial Dictionary of World Religions.: page 154. Print.
5. Op. cit., Kick.
6. Ibid.
7. Ibid.
8. Ibid.
9. Ibid.
10. Ibid.
11. Ibid.
12. Trinity: History of Trinitarian Doctrines. Stanford Encyclopaedia of Philosophy. https//plato.stanford.edu
13. Op. cit., Kick.
14. Ibid.

15. Ibid.
16. Ibid.
17. Ibid.
18. Ibid.
19. Ibid.

CHAPTER FORTY-FOUR:
BLACK AFRICAN CHRISTIANITY

1. Windsor, Rudolph R. The Valley of the Dry Bones.: page 53.
2. Felder, Cain Hope, The BISC (Biblical Institute for Social Change) Quarterly 3.1: page 2.
3. The Early Church in Africa: Dr John Mbiti.
4. "Tertullian." Wikipedia. Wikimedia, n.d. 3 March 2014.
5. Christ and Nubia.
6. "The Rights of the Ethiopian Orthodox Church to the Deir Sultan Monastery in Jerusalem." Jerusalem, 1986: page 14.
7. Leslau, Wolf, ed. Falasha Anthology.: ix.
8. "African Zion: The Sacred Art of Ethiopia." 17 October to 9 January 1994. Walters Art Gallery, Baltimore. Caption from Exhibition.
9. "Pope to View Poland's Sacred Black Madonna." Washington Post 4 May 1979, natl. ed.
10. "Ethiopian Paintings Stolen by British Soldiers." Metro newspaper 11th February 2005.

CHAPTER FORTY-FIVE:
PIOUS FRAUD

1. Ancient Sun Worship: YBLTo.
2. Church missionaries.
3. Wicca devotees celebrate the feast of Yuletide.
4. Sheryl Ann Karas: The Solstice Evergreen.
5. Jones, Charles. W. "Knickerbocker Santa Claus." New York Historical Society Quarterly 33.4 (1954): page 357.
6. Del Re, Gerard and Patricia. The Christmas Almanack. New York: Random House, 2004: page 131
7. "Nicholas, Saint." Encyclopaedia Britannica.: 99.
8. Del Re, Gerard and Patricia. The Christmas Almanack. New York: Random House, 2004: page 130.
9. "Pope Marches 40 Saints of Official Church Calendar." St Nicholas Center. org. UPI Wire Services, n.d. Web. 14 March 2014.

CHAPTER FORTY-SIX:
THE ICONOGRAPHY OF JESUS

1. God in Manger Story; [You are Being Lied To] by Russ Kick.
2. Ibid.
3. Ibid.
4. Ibid.
5. Durant, Will. The Story of Civilization: Caesar and Christ.: p.558.
6. Eddy, Patricia G. Rescuing Jesus from the Gospels.: pages 227, 236.
7. "Christianity." The Perennial Dictionary of World Religions.: p. 170.
8. "The Momentous Mission of the Apostle Paul." U.S. News and World Report 22 April 1991: pages 54-5.
9. "The Secret Family of Jesus" By Robert Beckford. Documentary. Channel 4. Television.
10. Ibid.
11. Acts of the Apostle 120 years after gospel.
12. "Identity of Jesus." Documentary. Channel 4. Television.
13. Shroud of Turin forgery.
14. Ben Ammi, Yeshua the Hebrew Messiah or Jesus the Christian Christ? :page 79.

CHAPTER FORTY-SEVEN:
ORIGINS OF MONOTHEISM AND THE TEN MISSING TRIBES OF ISRAEL

1. Epic of Gilgamesh; British archaeologists.
2. Epic of Gilgamesh.
3. Finch III, Charles S. Echoes of the Old

Darkland: Themes from the African Eden: page 131.

4. Clarke, John Henrik Clarke. Introduction. Alfred Butler, The Arab Conquest of Egypt and the Last 30 years of the Roman Dominion.
5. Encyclopaedia Britannica.: page 188.
6. Africans Who Wrote Bible.: page 64
7. Ibid page 17.
8. Ibid AWWB. Sir Wallis Budge. Op. cit., Africans Who Wrote Bible.: page 46.
9. Akhenaten decline. Encyclopaedia Britannica.: page 189.
10. Budge, Wallis. Egyptian Religion. 1994.: 37-40. See also: Brugsch. Religion und Mythologie: pages 96-9.
11. Encyclopaedia Britannica.
12. Encyclopaedia Britannica.
13. Africans Who Wrote Bible.: 59: See also: Ward, C.O. Ancient Lowly. 2 (1907): 76. Print.
14. "Moses." Encyclopaedia Britannica. 1996.: page 72.
15. Gary Greenberg. The Moses Mystery: The African Origins of Jewish people.
16. Ibid., Citing Sigmund Freud.: 60-1.
17. Ibid.
18. Ibid.
19. Ibid.

CHAPTER FORTY-EIGHT:
WHO WROTE THE BIBLE?

1. Livingstone, Lawrence. The BISC (Biblical Institute for Social Change) Quarterly, Vol.4.3: page 1.
2. African/Eden.: 110.
3. Paine, Gustavus S. The Men Behind the King James Version.: pages 1,3,4,10.
4. Ibid., page 77.
5. Fox, Robin Lane. Unauthorized Version.: Page 49.
6. Ibid.
7. Ibid., 100.
8. Africans Who Wrote Bible.: 1ST English Bible; William Tyndale.
9. Africans Who Wrote Bible.
10. Solomon. "Dark and Comely."
11. Nicene Council.

CHAPTER FORTY-NINE:
CATHOLICISM AND CAPITALISM

1. Pope Urban. "Address of Pope Urban in 1096, at Clermont, France, in Caldwell and Merrill." The New Popular History of the World.: p. 220.
2. Christian History, 12.4, Issue 40: page15.
3. The Africans Who Wrote Bible.: St Augustine.: page 163.
4. Williams, E. Capitalism and Slavery. London: Chapel Hill, 1944. Print.
5. Augstein, H.F. Race; The Origins of an Idea, 1760-1850. Bristol: Thoemmes Press, 1996. Print.
6. Polygenesis: Yeboah, S.K.: 59.
7. Ibid., 69.
8. Ibid., 70.
9. Africans Who Wrote Bible.: 166.
10. Ibid.
11. Poliakov, Leon. History of Racist ideas in Europe. 1996.: Page 220.
12. Constantine quote.
13. Black slaves bible as liberating dynamic.
14. South American Churches restricting reading and slave preaching.
15. Reverend William Montgomery Brown: 'How shall the colour line be drawn?.
16. Authors the of the Deakes bible: 'Races must stay separate, especially black and white'.
17. Bishop Deya trafficking children.
18. Bush inspiration from God: Libby architect of right Christian vote.
19. Bush inspiration from God: Libby architect of right Christian vote.
20. "Africa's Witch Children," Dispatches. Channel 4. Television.

PART NINE: SLAVERY ENTRENCHED

CHAPTER FIFTY:
EUROCENTRISM

1. Wayne. B. Chandler.

2. Kaiser, Ward L. A New View of the World - A Handbook of the World Map: Peter's Projection.: 10, 12, 13.
3. Ibid. Joseph Conrad's map of Africa.
4. 'Moreno blacks'
5. Friedman, J.B. The Monstrous Races in Medieval Art and Thought. Cambridge: Harvard University Press, 1981.: pages 108-17.
6. Monstra: Miles.R.: page 17.
7. Malik, K. The Meaning of Race History and Culture in Western Society. London: Macmillan Press, 1996.: 43.
8. Freedman, Paul. Images of the Medieval Peasants.
9. Omosegbun; 1995.
10. Septimus Severus, Black Roman in Britain.
11. From the Africans Who Wrote Bible: Quote by Alden Vaughan and Virginian Vaughan, in William and Mary Quarterly.
12. Karl Orfried Muller, a Germans scholar.: page 241.
13. Link between Egypt and Africa.
14. AWWB: Undermined African achievement.
15. Dr Emeagwali. Quote.
16. Aristotle. Barbarians. Quote.
17. Unification of Europe around demonization of Islam.
18. Gobineau, Joseph Arthur. "Tragedy of Conquest and the Racial Degeneration of Nations."
19. Ibid.
20. Ibid.
21. Ibid.
22. Ibid. Gobineau, Joseph Arthur.

CHAPTER FIFTY-ONE:
THE PSYCHOLOGY OF SLAVERY

1. Carter Woodson.
2. Douglass, Frederick Douglass. My Bondage and My Freedom.: Pages 250-1.
3. Black and white psychological experiment.
4. Dr Welsing, postulated in her "Cress-Colour Confrontation theory."
5. Ibid.Neely Fuller. **I cut the repeated quote.**
6. British Survey on tanning.
7. Mark Twain. Isis Papers.: 29. Quote.
8. Isis Papers: Burroughs, Edgar Rice, author of the best-selling Tarzan Series of the Apes in 1929.
9. Frantz Fanon.
10. Orlando Patterson.
11. Marx, Karl Max. Quote on alienation. "Economic and Philosophic Manuscripts of 1844."
12. Prevalence of depression in US and UK.
13. Ibid.
14. White man-god complex. Isis Papers.
15. Edward Blyden.
16. Lasch, Christopher. The Culture of Narcissism. Social critic, historian, and author.
17. Op. cit., Welsing. Quoting Brown 1954.
18. Isis Papers on Inferiorization.
19. Erikson, Erik H. Childhood and Society. Quoted in Isis Papers.: 253. Print.
20. Clary, Johnny Lee, later to become the leader of the Ku Klux Klan.
21. Clark, K. & Clark, M.P.. "The Development of Consciousness of Self, and the Emergence of Racial Identification in Negro Pre-School Children," Children of Social Psychology. 1939: 10: Page 591.
22. Welsing, Dr. Cress, describes the social process, through which the genetic potential of the black child, is destroyed, 'inferiorization'.
23. Clark, K. & Clark, M.P.. "The Development of Consciousness of Self, and the Emergence of Racial Identification in Negro Pre-School Children," Children of Social Psychology. 1939: 10: Page 591.
24. Woodson, Carter. The Mis-education of the Negro.: pref. xiii. Steel, Claude Steel and Aronson, Joshua. Study.
25. Claude Steel and Joshua Aronson

psychological tests.

26. Ibid: Psychological tests.
27. Hussein Abdilahi Bulhan wrote about the paradigm the oppressed people find themselves in.

CHAPTER FIFTY-TWO:
THE SEASONING PROCESS

1. Miller, John Chester. Thomas Jefferson. Macmillan press, 1977. Print.
2. Op. cit., Equiano.
3. Campbell, Horace Campbell. Rasta and Resistance: From Marcus Garvey to Walter Rodney.: Page 15.
4. AntiSlavery.org. Web. 14 March 2014. Slave breeding.
5. Doctor Benjamin Rush, one of the signers of the American Declaration of Independence, and the so-called, father of American psychiatry. Diagnosed 'Negritude' in black slaves.
6. Doctor Samuel Cartwright, went on to claim that runaway black slaves had a mental disorder called 'Drapetomania'.
7. Dysaesthesia Aethiopsis Ibid

CHAPTER FIFTY-THREE:
COLONIZING AFRICAN MINDS

1. Fanon, Frantz. Quote by Jean-Paul Sartre. Wretched of the Earth: Page 13.
2. Opening up Africa: This method, had already been described by leading British missionaries, in particular, Thomas Fowel Buxton and Henry Venn John Hatch
3. David Livingstone: Hugh Thomas.
4. Ibid., Lord Lugard.
5. Ibid.
6. Ibid., Ajayi Crowther.
7. Crowther, Ajayi. Quote.
8. Senghor, Leopold Senghor. State of Africa.
9. Ibid., 59.
10. Ibid
11. Chinweizu. "Decolonizing the African Mind.:" Page 4..
12. Kofi Busia Ibid., 3.
13. Ibid.

CHAPTER FIFTY-FOUR:
SOME LEGACIES OF MENTAL SLAVERY

1. Wilson, Amos N. "Black-on-Black Violence:" Pref. xiii. Para: 2.
2. Ibid.
3. Ibid
4. Ibid
5. Cost of prison in America.
6. Op. cit., Chinweizu 9.

CHAPTER FIFTY-FIVE:
YOUR COUNTRY NEEDS YOU BUT DOES NOT WANT YOU

1. Kerner Commission. "Summary of Report." Report of the National Advisory Commission on Civil Disorders. 1968.: 1
2. Hacker, Andrew Hacker. "Two Nations: Black and White, Separate, Hostile, Unequal.:" Pref. page viii.
3. Paul Gilroy.
4. Black slaves are 2/3rd a human being. US Const. art. 1 sec. 2 cl. 3. 1787.
5. Lord Kitchener Poster.
6. John Pilger aptly described them as 'non-people' in his book...
7. David Cameron. Calls immigrants swarms.
8. Freuke Petry, leader of the German far right party, ADP, described immigrants as 'compost'
9. Old Racism defined: 84.
10. "MacPherson Report on Steven Lawrence.:" page 85.
11. Racism redefined. 8.Ibid., 84.
12. Powell, Enoch Powell. "Rivers of Blood." Speech.
13. Mc Larren-Walter Act 1952.
14. Immigration anxiety.
15. Clement Attlee.
16. British Immigration anxiety: (Admiralty records: 1.585- Admiral Donnelly, 22nd February 1815)
17. Sabbagh, Dan. "David Cameron: 'Go Home' campaign; Could go National-No 10." Guardian News and Media Ltd. 30 July 2013: See also Jones, Stephen. "Home Office." Image. 2nd August

2012.

18. Former Imperial Grand Wizard of the Ku Klux Klan , David Duke: Did Racism help Donald Trump win? (http://www.aljazeera.com/programmes/upfront/2016/11/racism-donald -trump) 12th November 2016. 09:36 GMT. Donald Trump, United States, Racism]
19. Ibid
20. [Huffington post : 14 reasons why Donald Trump is a racist]
21. Griffin, John Howard. 'Black Like Me'.
22. Ibid

PART TEN: SOCIAL EFFECTS

CHAPTER FIFTY-SIX: SOCIAL MOBILITY

1. African communities in US and UK.
2. Updated OECD report.
3. February 2014, Gregory Clark, of Princeton University and author of 'The Son Also Rises'.
4. Donald Trump quote on black people.
5. Moore, Michael. Stupid White Men.
6. 2008 report on intergenerational social mobility from the Brookings Institute and Pews Charitable Trusts.

CHAPTER FIFTY-SEVEN: HEALTH, EDUCATION AND HOUSING

1. "Why Do Blacks Die Young?" Time 16 September 1991.
2. US Department of Health and Human resources, National Cancer Institute 1992 SEER Program Statistical Manual, NIH publication no. 92-2789.
3. Ibid
4. Ibid
5. Ibid. Early Childhood Facts." Children's Defense. Org. Web.
6. Smith, Lori Smith. Economic Human Rights.org. Quote. Web.
7. Lori Smith on Republican Senator Frist.
8. "Incarceration Figures in Afro Americans." Mental Health and Mental Institutions.
9. Roemer, John. US economist. Quote.
10. ECLS Data Researchers in the US.

CHAPTER FIFTY-EIGHT: CHILDHOOD POVERTY

1. Social Capital definition.
2. Guy Shrubsole quote on land ownership in the UK [The Guardian: Half of England is owned by less than 1% of the population(about 25,000 landowners) Rob Evans Wednesday 17th April 2019 20.29 BST]
3. 2003 UNICEF report.
4. UK report findings show that UK child poverty has doubled since 1979 and children live in homes earning less than half the national average ranged about 16%. 1. (BBC News. 14 February 2007).
5. A study conducted by economists, Richard Vedder, Lowell Galloway, and David C. Clingaman showed that the average income for a black American is 61% fewer pay years than the average white income that is the same percentage that it was in 1880!
6. In US African American families 1/10 assets of white families.
7. Updated OECD report from 2012.
8. Lyndon Johnson.
9. Heath, Professor Anthony and Cheung, Dr. Sin Yi. "Research Report No 341: Ethnic penalties in the Labour market: Employers and discrimination." Oxford University and Department of Sociology.
10. Metro article on confidence.
11. Gumbel, Andrew. "Poverty Gap in US has Widened under Bush." Independent Print Ltd. 27 July 2007.
12. Ibid
13. "Underachievement, How to Help Black Boys." Guardian, Guardian News and Media Ltd. 8 March 2005.
14. "Swann Committee." Guardian. Guardian News and Media Ltd.8 March, 2005.
15. "Diversity is the Best Policy, Race and Diversity Survey." RFO-Metro 23

February 2005.

16. The Institute for Fiscal Studies and the Resolution Foundation

CHAPTER FIFTY-NINE:
JUDICIAL SYSTEMS AND EMPLOYMENT

1. Over 1 million Afro-American males in jail.
2. Statistics on black people stopped by the police in the UK
3. "Racist DNA Scandal." Whirlwind Newspaper April/May 2006: page 3.
4. Ibid.
5. Guardian. Guardian News and Media Ltd. January 2006. Print.
6. Afro male executions for rape.
7. The Police officers dilemma: Using ethnicity to disambiguate potentially threatening individuals.
8. 'US police killing heads for 1,000 this year with Black Americans twice as likely to die.' June 1st 2015 13.38 BST by Oliver Laughland, Jon Swaine and James Lartey in New York]. Journal of Personality and Social Psychology , 83(6), 1314-1329. Correl J.,Park B., Judd,CM and Wittenbrink B. 2002]
9. [Miscarriage of Justice in US. BBC News 26th November 2019]
10. See: Marshal Project by Daniel Lathrop and Anna Flag 08/04/2017]
11. TUC paper.
12. Ibid.
13. Afro males combat deaths: Schexnider, 1983.
14. "Justifiable homicide." Robin 1963: page 54, Takagi, 1979.

CHAPTER SIXTY:
BROKEN FAMILY UNITS

1. "Children of lone parents are 70% more prone to psychological illnesses later in life." Times page 2. 1st March 2007. See also: Sieghaart, Mary Ann "Marriage Maketh man, but Labour Fears to Say So."
2. Brown, Yasmin Alibhai. Quoting Gunner Myrdal in "The American Dilemma: The Negro Problem and Modern Democracy." Independent Print Ltd. 5 September 2005.
3. Genuine Scouser. Quote. Sky News Online Edition, 6 October 2006. Web.
4. John Laidlaw.
5. Henry, Thierry. Quote. Guardian News and Media Ltd. 4 March 2005.
6. Gibson, Althea. Quote. The Black Diaspora.: Page 424.
7. Ibid.

PART ELEVEN: GEOPOLITICS

CHAPTER SIXTY-ONE:
FAILURE TO THRIVE

1. Mandela, Nelson. The Struggle is My Life.: Page 75.
2. Hilary Clinton on Muammar Gaddafi's murder.
3. Sarkozy, Nicolas. Quote. BBC Focus of Africa. Spec. Ed. Quarterly Quotes.: April-June 2008.: 8.
4. Morrow, Lance: "The Agony of Africa," Time 7 September 1992.
5. "African Losses." Christian Aid Report. 8 March 2005.
6. Ngugi, Mukoma Wa. "We Are in a State." Column. BBC Focus on Africa.
7. Op. cit., Bond. Walter Rodney quote. From Patrick Bond.
8. Op. cit., Bond. 96.
9. Fanon quote.
10. Ibid.
11. Ibid
12. Unilever
13. Wikipedia: Economic history of the United Kingdom
14. John Hatch: In 1937, North Rhodesia, was paid 5.5 million pounds in dividends and royalties from Mines the British government collected only 700,000 pounds.
15. Ibid.
16. Ibid
17. African rails to ports only. "Commission for Africa." 2005.
18. "EU/ US Attack African Unity at World Trade Organization." Whirlwind

Newspaper April/May 2006: page 7.
19. West subsidize agribusiness
20. Ibid
21. Ibid
22. NEPAD. Op. cit., Bond.: 98.
23. Kenya loses $60.2 because it supported WTO against the US.
24. African dependence on cash crops and subsistence.
25. Ibid.
26. Ibid.
27. "Free Trade has Robbed African Poor of 150 Billion Pounds." Quoted from Christian AID report. Metro, 20 June 2005.
28. Ghana: Ibid.
29. "Nigerian Gas Flowing." Guardian News and Media Ltd. 21 June 2005. Print. Referencing: Shell faces flaring lawsuit.
30. Nigerian Poverty rank.
31. Nigerian life expectancy
32. UNICEF: Infant Mortality
33. HIV/AIDS in Nigeria: UNIAD.
34. Christian AID: British made £5 billion from Sub-Saharan Africa/ Nigeria in 2005.
35. The East African Magazine: Sept 3rd 2001 www.theeastafrican.co.ke
36. Yusuf, Bilikisu. Epilogue: Nigeria in Crisis.: page 302.
37. Amadi, Elechi. Decolonising the African Mind.: page 242.
38. Ibid, Bilikisu 302.
39. Chinua Achebe: on corruption.
40. Former French President Mitterrand on Africa's relevance to France
41. Jacques Chirac on same.
42. Sekou Toure quote.
43. Mediapart blogs Jan 30th 2014
44. 14 African Countries forced by France to pay Colonial Tax for the Benefits of Slavery and Colonization. By Mawuna Remarque. Tuesday 28th January 2014at 3:41 pm
45. Ibid
46. French Minister of Finance, Rene Pleven on CFA. Wikipedia.
47. Mawuna Remarque.
48. The gilded cage: Who does the CFA franc really benefit? www.howwemadeitinafrica.com. By Simon Allison. 10/04/2015.
49. Ibid.
50. Ibid
51. Ibid
52. Poverty deaths in Sub-Saharan Africa. Update stats.
53. Over 50% of Sub-Saharan Africa lives on $1/day.
54. Seren Boyd, in the BMA News.
55. Ibid.
56. Commons International Development Select Committee on famine in Africa.
57. Ibid.
58. Ghanaian doctors in US.

CHAPTER SIXTY-TWO:
NEO-COLONIALISM

1. Okri, Ben. Guardian. Guardian News and Media Ltd. 20 January 1999.
2. George Kennan, US strategic planner, 1948.
3. Henry Kissinger, 1974.
4. Neo-Colonialism: The last Stage of Imperialism. Kwame Nkrumah.
5. Smithsonian National Museum of Natural History: Douglas Owsley, a Smithsonian forensic anthropologist.
6. Zabarenko, Deborah. "Starving Virginia settlers turned to cannibalism in 1609." Study. Reuters 2 May 2013.
7. Written accounts of cannibalism in an old letter from the president of Jamestown, George Percy, were reprinted in a Smithsonian magazine.
8. John Winthrop on American exceptionalism.
9. Britain urges American interest in world politics.
10. Monroe, President James. "Monroe Address to Congress." Monroe Doctrine. Ibid.
11. John O' Sullivan on Anglo-Saxons.
12. Natural superiority of Anglo-Saxon

race. "Anglo-Saxons." Wikipedia. Wikimedia n.d. Web. 12 March 2014. Ibid.

13. Senator John C. Calhoun of South Carolina . Ibid.
14. Stannard, David E.AMERICAN HOLOCAUST. Oxford University Press, 1992. Pp. 118-121.
15. George Washington: Noam Chomsky/ Pilger: The 'Indian' he said, have nothing human except the shape.
16. President McKinley stated.
17. Rudyard Kipling, "The white man's burden," subtitled "The United States and Philippine Islands".
18. William Jennings Bryan to write: "Destiny is not as manifest as it was a few weeks ago."
19. Marshall Plan.
20. European repatriation following WW2.
21. Francis Fukuyama of the US State Department.
22. President Bush, British PM Tony Blair and the Spanish PM José María Aznar threaten Iraq.
23. Allied invasion of Russia. Churchill quote.
24. Kennedy Cuban Missile Crisis.
25. "Right of access." George Kennan of the US State Department
26. New York Times. New York Times Company 6 August 1954.
27. Ibid
28. "New World Order." LA Times 1990.
29. Ibid.
30. Robert McNamara.
31. George Herbert W. Bush.
32. Paul Wolfowitz: an arch neo conservative and main architect of the Iraq war was appointed the head of the World Bank by George W. Bush.
33. George Weller, photo journalist, Nagasaki atomic bomb. "Nagasaki Bomb Story Gets Out, 60 Years On." Guardian News and Media Ltd. June 2005.
34. My Lai massacre in Vietnam.
35. Missing nuclear bombs or 'broken arrows'.
36. North Korea tests suspected nuclear bomb in 2006.
37. George Bush initiates 'Son of Star's missile program'.
38. US attempt to ring fence Russia with ballistic missiles. Tisdall, Simon. "Arms Race Fears Fulfilled." Guardian News and Media Ltd. 23 February 2007. Ibid.
39. US rendition flights. "EU countries 'turned a blind eye to rendition." Independent Print Ltd. 15 February 2007: page 22.
40. Joseph Padilla rendition. Klein, Naomi. "The US Psychological Torture system is finally on trial." Guardian News and Media Ltd. 23 February 2007.
41. Ibid.
42. Dr Ewen Cameron torture techniques. Klein, Naomi. "The US Psychological Torture system is finally on trial." Guardian News and Media Ltd. 23 February 2007.
43. 98 prisoners died in US custody. BBC Newsnight. Press Association: US psych torture.
44. Zorn, E. and Harvey, Paul. Citing William Blum. "Ah, Genocide and Slavery, Now that's a Good Day!" Chicago Tribune. 24th June 2005.
45. Ibid. US radio commentator, Paul Harvey

CHAPTER SIXTY-THREE:
AN ANATOMY OF MODERN WESTERN COLONIZATION: COLONIZING IRAQ

1. John Perkins on Iraq.
2. Observer: 3 November 2002.
3. Guardian News and Media Ltd. 30 October 2002.
4. Lord Curzon on vital oil sources.
5. Hitler on oil fields.
6. Hitler on Baku's oil.
7. John Perkins on strategic significance of Iraq.
8. Significance of Iraq compared to the Hudson river in American civil war.

9. T.E Lawrence, a flamboyant Orientalist.
10. US State Department on Middle East's oil.
11. Hitler planned to annex oil in Middle East too.
12. British suppress Kurdish insurgency using phosphorus bombs.
13. Churchill mused; "I do not understand this squeamishness about the use of gas.
14. Robert Fisk stated that 'Britain set up a colonial regime in Iraq after a long military campaign during World War I. In response to Iraqi resistance, including a country-wide uprising in 1920, British forces battled for over a decade to pacify the country, using airplanes, armored cars, firebombs and mustard gas. Global Policy.org. Web. 14 March 2014.

a. Sykes-Picot Agreement 1916. The French and British reached this secret agreement in 1916 dividing Mesopotamia into zones of British and French influence in the event of the collapse of the Ottoman Empire. This division of spoils - which also included a share for Russia - demonstrates the Allies' attitude towards the people of the Middle East and reflects their lack of sincerity when they promised self-rule. The British later ignored the agreement when they seized the oil-rich province in 1918.

b. Ibid. Air attacks were used to shock and awe, to teach obedience and to force the collection of taxes. Winston Churchill, as responsible cabinet minister in the early years, saw Iraq as an experiment in high-technology colonial control. Though officials in London sometimes had qualms about the violence, colonial administrators on the ground like Gertrude Bell expressed enthusiasm for the power of the imperial military enterprise.

15. John Kelly, the U.S. Assistant Secretary of State. Confirms US support for Saddam Hussein.
16. The Anglo-Persian Company, later know as BP takes over control of Iraqi oil.
17. Iraqi's only get 5% of their own oil reserves. Noam Chomsky on Iraqi oil distribution in 1920.
18. Henry Kissinger quote on Iran-Iraq war.
19. US/UK companies supply nerve gas to Iraq.
20. British companies supply anthrax to Saddam Hussein.
21. Covert arms to Saddam Hussein from Bush Sr.
22. Thatcher and Astra company.
23. Depleted uranium.
24. Human cost of the first Gulf war and sanctions.
25. Project for the New America Century (PNAC).
26. Millennium Project:
27. Ibid.
28. US/ British forces in Iraq use cluster bombs against civilians. "Cluster Bombs." Independent Print Ltd. 21 November 2005.
29. Ibid
30. White phosphorus used in Falluja.
31. Allawi. Ilyad Allawi: more human rights abuses and murders in Iraq, during the US and British occupation.
32. "Crude Designs." Independent Print Ltd. 22 November 2005. Print.
33. Ibid
34. Iran Resalat on Saddam Hussein.

CHAPTER SIXTY-FOUR:
PLUNDERING THE CONGO

1. Congo's humanitarian crisis in figures.
2. Congo's vast mineral resources. US heavily relies on Congolese coltan for its Nuclear and Space programmes.
3. Massive Congolese hydrocapacity.
4. Patrice Lumumba's speech in June 1960.
5. 11th July1960, Moise Tshombe, leader of CONAKAT declared the mineral rich Congo's southern province of

Katanga an independent state

6. Moise Tshombe, supported by US, Belgium and apartheid South Africa.
7. Belgian officers kill Patrice Lumumba and dissolve his body in acid.
8. US install un-elected Mobutu as a military dictator.
9. US played a role in the regional unrest that led to the Rwandan genocide.
10. President Obama was credited with the passage into law of Public Law 109-456 in 2006
11. Rwandan M23 rebels facilitate the stealing of Congo's coltan by Rwanda.

CHAPTER SIXTY-FIVE:
A WAR WITHOUT END

1. US opposes outer space treaty in 1967
2. William Blum: Rogue States.
3. Madman Philosophy.
4. Ibid.
5. Ibid.
6. Ibid.
7. Bradley Manning. Press Association. 31 July 2013. Web. 12 March 2014.
8. Marqusee, Mike. "A Four-Year Nightmare." Guardian News and Media Ltd. 4 November 2004. Quote: "...it is not anti-American to reject this imperial power."

CHAPTER SIXTY-SIX:
SMOKE WITHOUT FIRE

1. Tzu, General Sun. Quote. C. 500 BC.
2. Orwell, George. Quote .1984.
3. George Seldes.
4. John Pilger, The New Rulers Of The World, introduction.
5. "Time of Conscious Intention to Act in Relation to Onset of Cerebral Activity (Readiness Potential)- The Unconscious Initiation of a Freely Voluntary Act". Brain: 106(3): 623-642. Issue 3, September 1983. A Journal of Neurology].
6. Decoding the contents and strength of imagery before volitional engagement- Roger Koenig-Robert and Joel Pearson- Scientific Reports 9, Article Number: 3504 (2019). Published 05/03/2019].
7. Brainwave researcher: Dr Herbert Krugman. ? Isis Papers.
8. "Michelangelo." Newsweek 5 May 1986.
9. Ibid.
10. Levitt, Steven. Freakonomics: page 60.
11. Creel Commission. Noam Chomsky.
12. The Gulf of Tonkin incident: How to start a war: The American use of War Pretext Incidents: Global Research 19 August 2014. First published in May 2002. By Richard Sanders.
13. Edward Bernays: Noam Chomsky.
14. Walter Lippmann
15. Mark Crispin Miller
16. Herbert Schiller 1989
17. George Orwell.
18. A. J. Liebling
19. Greg Dyke of the BBC and Andrew Gilligan lose their jobs over Tony Blair's false 45 minute claim.
20. Self -censorship by aspiring journalists.
21. Malcolm X quote.
22. Warren Commission Report on John F. Kennedy's assassination.
23. 'Operation Mockingbird' Ibid.
24. 'literary Bay of Pigs'.
25. Carlos Allende.
26. US Army Intelligence working with CNN.
27. BBC News: US shuts down Somalia Internet: Friday, 23 November 2001. news.bbc.co.uk/2/hi/Africa/1672220.stm)
28. Echelon spying on Europe.
29. NATO Bombing. San Francisco Guardian.
30. Ibid.
31. Ibid.
32. NASA conspiracy.
33. Twin Towers conspiracy.
34. Sinan Aral, TED X CERN November 2018: How can we protect the truth in the age of misinformation.

35. Richard Sanders quote: How to start a war: The American use of War Pretext Incidents: Global Research 19 August 2014. First published in May 2002. By Richard Sanders.

CHAPTER SIXTY-SEVEN:
GLOBAL CHESS GAMES

1. Lord George Nathaniel Curzon, British Viceroy of India in 1898. Quote. Rashid id: page 145.
2. Niall Ferguson: British occupation of Egypt. The Rothschilds, Disraeli and the Suez Canal
3. Joseph Chamberlain had said. "You cannot have omelettes without breaking eggs."
4. Levering, David Lewis. The Race to Fashoda: pages 34, 92.
5. Churchill massacre in Sudan.
6. African Troop losses.
7. German doctor, Ludwig Deppe.
8. Trinidadian Soldier.
9. African Legion.
10. "Wonga trial brings fresh humiliation for Thatcher." Independent Print Ltd. 19 February 2007: page 23.

CHAPTER SIXTY-EIGHT:
THE DEATH MERCHANTS

1. Amnesty International 1996.
2. Hymn sung by Cecil Rhodes men: Ferguson/Hugh Thomas.
3. "Merchants of Death", The International Traffic in Arms by Jonathan A. Grant. Vol. 6, issue 2. December 2012
4. Hiram Maxim Gatling Gun: Pilger
5. Gun merchant Sir Zaharoff. Ibid.
6. BAE largest arms developer in world.
7. British arm sales to war zones.
8. British arm sales to Idi Amin.
9. British arms in Biafra.
10. Douglas Hurd Middle East arms sales.
11. Tony Newton
12. Thatcher Al-Yamana arms deal.
13. Blair arms to Tanzania.
14. British tax payer arms subsidies.
15. 80% of British arms to poor and developing countries. Alan Clark set up £1 billion exports fund for arms sales.
16. Pergau Hydroelectric Dam deal. Concealment of arms deals as dam funds.
17. David Cameron on arms sales to Egypt and Libya.
18. US world's largest arms dealers: Lockheed contract. Ibid. Pilger
19. Arming all sides: CAAT
20. IMET force.
21. Tony Blair's Intervention Force in Africa.
22. Small arms circulating: Christian Aid
23. Congo arms sales.
24. US military exercises with Kenya.
25. Article: Johnson, Paul "Wanted: A New Imperialism." National Review 75" 14 December 1992. Pages 28-34.
26. Article: "Is the Time Right for New Imperialism?" European 14 May 1992.

CHAPTER SIXTY-NINE:
WEAPONS OF MASS DESTRUCTION: THE USE OF DEBT AS A WEAPON AND THE GLOBALISATION OF POVERTY

1. Robert McNamara, Former United States Secretary of Defence and President of the World Bank from 1968-1981. John Pilger.
2. Lawrence Sumners, Former Chief Economist for World Bank 1991, Secretary for the Treasury 1999. John Pilger.
3. Ibid.
4. Ibid.
5. Ibid.

CHAPTER SEVENTY:
THE GEOPOLITICS OF DEBT

1. European cow subsidy. marginalrevolution.com. How much does a European cow earn? 18/Aug. 2014).
2. World Banks 2015 projections.
3. Congo Debts = Mobutu debts.
4. MacDonald and MacDonnell Douglas;

Pilger.

5. Bretton Woods: Chomsky.
6. Unilateral-multilateral organisations.
7. Institutional power asymmetry. African Members; richer country = more votes.
8. Small elite control 80% of the world's wealth.
9. African countries have only 2 of the 24 constituencies in the World Bank and the IMF.
10. US aid to friends not causes.
11. China and India buck the trend.
12. Concentrated US power was financial. Russia looted.
13. IMF in Far East, Asia.
14. IMF in Argentina brought about financial collapse.
15. 80% of US aid for military use.
16. Yemen punished.
17. US withholds aid for ICC votes against U.S exemption.
18. Zambia and Senegal punished.
19. Musharraf/Pakistan. Taken off terror list and given aid for supporting war against the Taliban.
20. Nixon Shock : President Nixon: The man who sold the world Fiat money. By Ron Rimkus, CFA Economics. Blogs.cfainstitute.org/President Nixon.
21. Financial drain on poor countries due to western patents.
22. Clinton and US opposes cheap AIDS drugs for South Africa and Brazil.
23. Slavery legacy. Patrick Bond
24. African Research Bulletin.
25. Ibid.
26. Mobutu aid.
27. French arms to Rwanda.
28. 60-70% failed World Bank projects.
29. Capital flight.
30. Apartheid regime debts.
31. Menghistu debts.
32. Bolivia and SAP fail.
33. 1987, a G24 working group report.
34. Ibid.

CHAPTER SEVENTY-ONE:

IT TAKES A THIEF TO CATCH A THIEF

1. NGO Action Aid on KBR bribery allegations in Nigeria. [The Guardian: UK backs oil firm despite bribery inquiry ; Halliburton arm gets $10 DTI loan guarantee David Leigh Mon 20 June 2005 21.24 EDT].

See also –Probe into KBR role in Nigeria Bribe case |Financial Times 7 AUG 2006. UK Solicitor Pleads Guilty for Role in Bribing Nigerian Government Officials. 11 Mar 2011. www.justice.gov

2. David Cameron on fantastically corrupt nations.[Afghanistan and Nigeria 'possibly most corrupt countries', Cameron lets slip - PM heard talking of 'fantastically corrupt countries' as he speaks to the Queen at an event to mark her 90th birthday. Anushka Asthana and Jamie Grierson Tue 10 May 2016 18.19 EDT
3. Ibid
4. African parable
5. Mayer, Karl. Nigeria in Crisis. Quote by Dr F Gbadebo-Smith.: Preface page xxii..
6. Dr Folarin Gbadebo-Smith,
7. Mail. Metro Section. 20 June 2005.
8. John Perkins on economic hit-men.
9. Karl Zeigler: Perkins.
10. Salomon brothers: IOU.: page 68.
11. Export Credit Agencies.
12. African debts to ECA.
13. Ibid.
14. Ibid.
15. Nigerian debts spirals out of control. Ibid.
16. 8 million Africans died directly due to conflict since 1987.
17. African countries rely on weak commodity markets.
18. Africa debt ratio. 34/42 ineligible for debt relief.
19. Babylon Code of the Hammurabi, circa 1780 BC:
20. Alexander Nahum Sack.

21. Noreena Hertz quote.
22. When power falls/debt falls.
23. Adedeji.
24. Africans pay west $60 million/day in debt payments.
25. Professor Jeffrey Sachs: Columbian academic and leading economist urged the participants to "defend your people."
26. Seabrook, Jeremy. "Comments and Debates." Guardian 27 July 2006.: 29. Print.
27. Drop the Debt Campaign.
28. NGO taking over African governments.
29. Nigerian oil revenues lost to US..
30. Debt-poverty link
31. Mandela, Nelson. Quote.
32. Vulture Funds in the Foreign Debt Context: The African Legal Support Facility]
33. Vultures, Doves and African Debt: Here's a way out. Danny Bradlow, University of Pretoria. May 5, 2020 2.13 SAST
34. CITY A.M INTERNATIONAL P&ID CAN SEIZE $9BN IN Nigerian assets, British court says By August Graham 16 August 2019

CHAPTER SEVENTY-TWO:
HUMANITARIAN IMPERIALISM

1. Professor George M. Wrong, 1909. Niall Ferguson.
2. George Kennan quote
3. Mill, J. S. Essays.
4. Op. cit., Mill. Mill's Essay on Liberty. P96
5. Ibid.
6. Ibid
7. Chomsky, Noam. America's Quest for Global Dominance.: page 45.
8. Opium wars against China. The Opium Wars: When Britain made war on China. By Anne Gibson, BBC history. www.bbc.co.uk/history/0/20428167. 03/12/2012
9. Christian Aid reports.
10. Christian Aid reports.
11. West exploiting tax loopholes and banking secrecy loot Africa.
12. War, globalisation and Reproduction by Silvia Federici: Paraphrased Carl Von Clausewitz to call structural adjustment "war by other means".
13. Ibid: African wars: Effie 1999.
14. Ibid: McCrae and Zwi. "Right to Intervene.:": 1194a. page 11-2.
15. Ibid: Duffield. "Food Aid." 1994: page 60-63.
16. Ibid.
17. Ibid.
18. NGO's like World Vision collaborating with the CIA. See papers.
19. Silvia Federici

ANGOLA

20. Angola: Land mines and Diana.
21. UNICEF study in Angola.
22. UNICEF death toll in Angola and Mozambique.

GHANA

23. Nkrumah aim.
24. Blum, William. Rogue State. Citing: CIA catch Nelson Mandela.

SOUTH AFRICA

25. Pentagon Report: Nelson Mandela classified as a terrorist.
26. Mandela US terrorist status revoked when 90 years old.
27. CIA informant helps arrest Nelson Mandela.
28. Illegal arms to apartheid South Africa. Mandela jailed for 40 years after CIA tip off.
29. Social Papers on Racism.

SOMALIA

30. Black Hawk Down
31. Operation Restore Hope.
32. US shut down Somalia's largest bank and telephone provider, al-Barakat bank.
33. US work with Aidid's son in 2007.

SUDAN

34. Clinton bombs pharmaceutical factory.

35. Jonathan Belke of the Near East Foundation,
36. Colin Powell brokered a 'peace deal' between the Sudanese government, and the rebels in the South led by the late Paul Garrong.

PART TWELVE: AFRICA'S SOVEREIGNTY AND HEALTH

CHAPTER SEVENTY-THREE: RECOLONISING AFRICA

1. Ed Royce
2. New York Times
3. African Oil Policy Initiative Group (AOPIG) was created, in 2002.
4. Talbot, Chris. "Bush's Tour of US Imperialism designs on Africa." World Socialist Website. Web. 12 March 2014.
5. US National Intelligence Council
6. Bush African policy.
7. US is seeking to expand its presence in Africa 'through new basing agreements and training exercises'.
8. Ibid.
9. General James L. Jones, Head of US European Command.
10. Low US African investment.
11. Ibid.
12. Blair African Invasion force.
13. "Saviours of the 3rd World." Guardian 2005: See also "Bards of the Powerful." Comments and Analysis. Print.
14. President Obama and David Cameron send troops to fight to West Africa the Ebola virus [See also- www.vox.com : Why Congress and the Pentagon are tussling over US troops in West Africa; " The mission is worth it," one expert told Vox. By Alex Ward on February 18, 2020 5.50 pm]
15. Trump unable to explain American troops in Chad. [www.vox.com: Why were US soldiers even in Niger? America's shadow of wars in Africa explained; American troops are fighting in multiple African countries without anyone back home really noticing. By Phillip Carter and Andrew Swick on October 26, 2017 9.00am]
16. .Non-aligned movement (NAM) rejects West's gun-boat policies
17. "UK backs oil firm despite bribery inquiry." Guardian 21 June 2005. Print.
18. Looting Africa. Quote from Bill Martin 114. Print.
19. Ibid., 116. US Africa military planning.
20. General Charles Wald. Ibid., 114. Continent wide 'African UN peace keeping force.
21. Expats earn more in Ghana: Action Aid. Web. 12 March 2014.
22. Christian Aid Report. Judith Hart, in 1978.
23. Christian Aid Report. Quote. David Dollar,
24. Cooper, Robert. Observer 7 April 2002.

CHAPTER SEVENTY-FOUR: MONKEY BUSINESS: HIV AND AIDS

1. UNAIDS: Global and AIDS statistics-2019 fact sheet.
2. 62% of all the world's HIV carriers aged 15-24 are in Africa.
3. "World losing fight against AIDS." BBC. BBC News. 23 July 2007. Television.
4. Only 28% of AIDs patients on retroviral medication.
5. Dr Brian Gazzard.
6. Africa has an estimated 43 million orphans of which, AIDS was responsible for about 12 million.
7. Heterosexual transfer.
8. Mike Rowson, executive director charity Action.
9. Botswana life expectancy.
10. Dr Bettle Kober of the Los Alamos National Laboratory
11. Oliver Pybus, of the Department of Zoology, Oxford University. HIV Origins traced to Kinshasa in 1920's. AFP- Jean –Louis Santini. 03/10/14
12. 50 facts from WHO report: Emerging and re-emerging diseases: https//www.who.int/whr/1996/media_centre/50facts/en/-71k

13. Adetunji, J.A.C., J. Murray, and T. Evans 1996 "Causes of Death in Africa: A Review".
14. [The NewYork Times: NEW HOMOSEXUAL DISORDER WORRIES HEALTH OFFICIALS. By Lawrence K. Altman 11th May 1982]
15. Dr. Beatrice Hahn [You are Being Lied To] by Russ Kick.
16. Blood of a Norwegian sailor.
17. AIDS/HIV discovered in lab.
18. Koprowski polio vaccines.
19. SV40 virus supresses gene.
20. SV40 virus in cancers.
21. Steinbrook, Robert. "Research refutes that Human AIDS originates in Monkeys." LA Times 2 June 1988.
22. Professor Desrosiers.
23. Patient Zero, Canadian, Gaeten Douglas.
24. Biological warfare with Tularaemia.
25. British colonialists hand out small pox blankets.
26. Aborigines maintain smallpox was used by British in Australia.
27. Biological Weaponization techniques. Wikipedia.
28. Unethical human experimentation in the US. Wikipedia
29. Ibid
30. Ibid
31. President Obama apologises for Guatemalan study.Ibid.
32. Mentally disabled children at the Willowbrook State School in Staten Island, New York were deliberately infected with viral hepatitis.
33. US release Yellow fever and Dengue fever infected mosquitoes in Florida.
34. Dr Ewan Cameron of the Allan Memorial Institute, Montreal, Canada, began a covert CIA funded program called MKULTRA Subproject .
35. Afghan prisoners tortured and killed in 2001/2002.
36. British use mustard gas in Iraq and Italians used mustard gas in Ethiopia.
37. Tokyo Army Medical School establish biological warfare unit in 1930. Wiki.
38. Chinese death toll exceeded 400,000. Ibid.
39. President Nixon merged the cancer research and biological warfare units, based at the U.S Army's bio warfare department at Fort Detrick, Maryland.
40. Population Council was urging third world depopulation.
41. Henry Kissinger requested and received a National Special Security Memorandum 200; a document that allegedly highlighted the urgency of dramatically reducing African populations.
42. Bionetics implicated.
43. The Council for Foreign Relations (CFR) on world population control.
44. Rockefeller Foundation invested billions of dollars in anti-fertility agents in 1920's.
45. In 1974, Henry Kissinger signed Security Memorandum 200; to use food as a population weapon.
46. Tuskegee Syphilis experiment.
47. Democracy Now: From Tuskegee to Puerto Rico. Interview with medical historian. Professor Susan Reverby.
48. Human cost of Tuskegee experiment.
49. 1997, President Clinton's apology for Tuskegee experiment.
50. Borgna Brunner: Legacy of Tuskegee experiment.
51. Bond, Patrick. Looting Africa. Section quoted: Cost-Benefit assessment in South Africa.: page 8.
52. Ibid. AIDS infection rates falling.

CHAPTER SEVENTY-FIVE:
BATS IN THE BELFRY: EBOLA AND CORONAVIRUS

EBOLA

1. Ebola virus.
2. 50 facts from WHO report: Emerging and re-emerging diseases: https// www.who.int/whr/1996/media_centre/50facts/en/-71k

3. The U.S. Center for Disease Control (CDC) classes Ebola as a category A bioterrorism agent and biosafety level 4 pathogen.
4. Russian company produce Ebolapox.
5. Ebola Sudan first recognised in 1976.
6. WHO report Ebola outbreak in West Africa. (www.bbc.co.uk/.../world-africa-2976978...).
7. Global Research: Dr Cyril Broderick, a scientist and former professor of Plant pathology at College of Agriculture and Forestry, University of Liberias, and Dr Francis Boyle of the University of Illinois', claimed that the U. S. Department of Defence, DoD, was funding Ebola trials on humans.
8. L.A Times report on US worldwide biological warfare research from 1980's.
9. Dr Francis Boyle. Ibid Global Research.
10. Dr Wouter Basson, known as 'Dr Death' by South Africans.
11. Dr David Kelly and 'Project Coast'.
12. Project Coast. Wiki.
13. Ibid.
14. Ibid
15. Ibid.
16. Ibid
17. Ibid.

THE CORONAVIRUS PANDEMIC

18. [New York Post: Dr. Fauci backed funding for controversial Wuhan lab studying the origin of coronavirus.By Joe Tacopino April 29, 2020|1:14 am]
19. [Wuhan Lab says there's no way coronavirus originated there. Here's the science :By Jeanna Bryner. Contributions from Rachael Rettner Live Science Senior Editor. www.livescience.com]
20. [See; Biospace: Compare: 2003 SARS Pandemic Versus 2020 COVID-19 Pandemic. Published: April 03, 2020 By Gail Dutton. Biospace.com]
21. .[Gross CP, Sepkowitz KA. The myth of medical breakthrough: small pox, vaccination, and Jenner reconsidered. Int J Infect Dis. 1998; 3:54-60. [PubMed] [Google Scholar]
22. [CNBC: Bill Gates says this is what you need to know about a coronavirus vaccine]
23. [Science: Speed Coronavirus vaccine testing by deliberately infecting volunteers? Not so fast , some scientists warn. By Jon Cohen|Mar 31, 2020, 5.20 PM. Posted in: Health, Coronavirus doi: 10.1126/ science abc0006]
24. [THE GUARDIAN: HIGHER PERCENTAGE OF BAME STAFF DYING OF COVID-19. By Haroon Siddique, Friday 10th April 2020. 12.53 EDT]
25. [The Guardian: It's a racial justice issue: Black Americans are dying in greater numbers from COVID-19. By Kenya Evelyn in Washington Wed 8th April 2020 12.00BST]
26. [Journal of Investigative medicine: the official publication of the American Federation for Clinical Research: Vitamin D and the Immune System. Cynthia Aranow, MD, Investigator. Ncbi.nlm.nih.gov]
27. [SCITECH DAILY: Vitamin D determines severity in COVID-19: Researchers Urge Government to Change Advice. By Trinity College Dublin May 13 2020. ["Vitamin D and Inflammation: Potential Implications for Severity of COVID-19." By E Laird, J. Rhodes and R.A. Kenny. 11th May 2020]
28. [EURONEWS: Analysis: Africa's unexpected COVID-19 figures. By Darren McCaffrey, Political Editor, 12/05/2020]

PART THIRTEEN: FREEDOM AND SACRIFICE

CHAPTER SEVENTY-SIX:
REPARATION

1. Niall Ferguson on reparation costs.
2. Tony Blair: Slavery legal at the time.
3. [Newsweek: US HAS SPENT SIX TRILLION ON WARS THAT KILLED

HALF A MILLION PEOPLE SINCE 9/11 REPORT SAYS by Tom O'Connor on 11/04/2018 at 2.13 pm]

4. Manning, Sanchez. "Britain's Colonial Shame: Slave Owners Given Huge Payouts after Abolition." Independent Print Ltd. 24 March 2013. Discussion: British paid slave owners compensation.
5. Historical UK inflation rates and calculator: inflation.iamkate.com
6. David Cameron's family profited directly from the slave trade.
7. Land ownership beyond a garden plot was illegal for freed slaves.
8. The Guardian: When will Britain face up to its crimes against humanity? By Kris Manjapra
9. King Leopold of Belgium compensated for Congolese Holocaust.
10. French collected reparations from Haiti because they became free and still collects colonial tax from 14 CFA countries.
11. Brother Mbandaka, Alkebu-Lan Nommo, Whirlwind Newspaper.
12. Clergy encouraged slavery.
13. Church compensation for slavery by government.
14. Fifteen Caribbean states demand compensation for slavery. The Guardian March 2014.
15. The lawyer leading Caricom's claim, Martyn Day quote.
16. "Babylonian Text about Debt." IOU.

CHAPTER SEVENTY-SEVEN: THE PSYCHOLOGY OF FREEDOM

1. Mandela, Nelson. Quote.
2. John 8:32. Bible
3. Jefferson, Thomas. Quote.
4. Mohammed Ali quote.
5. The Socialist Papers on racism wrote.
6. "Breaking the psychological chains of slavery..." page 7.
7. Oxford definition of 'free'.
8. Maslows Hierarchy of Needs.
9. Op. cit., Miller. Thomas Jefferson.
10. Op. cit., Bulhan 104.
11. Jane Elliott experiment.
12. Africanist W. E. Du Bois wrote.

CHAPTER SEVENTY-EIGHT: THE FIRST STEPS TOWARD PSYCHOLOGICAL FREEDOM

1. Frederick Douglass
2. Bulhan quote: Bulhan wrote: "As long as the colonized accepts servitude for fear of death, so long as he is unwilling to die for freedom; the colonizer is tyrannical and violent without limit."
3. Frantz Fanon quote
4. Bulhan
5. Chinweizu
6. Frantz Fanon on languages.
7. Kassahun Checole in an interview for the New African magazine in June 2004.
8. Frantz Fanon: Fanon, Frantz. The Wretched of the Earth. Quotation: "Colonialism .... Is violence in its natural state, and will only yield when confronted with greater violence."
9. Ibid

CHAPTER SEVENTY-NINE: AFRICANS WHO SACRIFICED FOR FREEDOM

HARRIET TUBMAN

10. www.harriet-tubman.org. www.pbs.org, Harriet Tubman-PBS.org

MARCUS GARVEY:

1. The Black Diaspora. Quote by Ronald Segal.: page 256.
2. "African Diaspora in Search of Roots," South July 1987: page 115.
3. Franklin, V.P. Black Self Determination: A Cultural History of African American Resistance.: page 201.

MALCOLM X:

4. Black Diaspora. Quote by Malcolm X.
5. Ibid. Op. cit., Malcolm X "Death a two way street."
6. Black Diaspora by Ronald Segal.

STEVE BIKO:

7. State of Africa.: page 418.
8. Ibid. Black Diaspora.

THOMAS SANKARA

9. Wiki. He who feeds you
10. Sankara promoted women in government.
11. Sankara's quote on women.
12. Thomas Sankara on corruption.
13. 'While revolutionaries as individuals can be murdered, you cannot kill ideas' Thomas Sankara.

PART FOURTEEN: THE AFRICAN RENAISSANCE

CHAPTER EIGHTY:
THE REWRITING OF AFRICAN HISTORY

1. Garvey, Marcus. "Marcus Garvey Quotes." Brainy Quotes.com. BookRags Media Network, 2001-4. Web. 12 March 2014.
2. Ibid., Martin Luther King Jr.
3. Mohammed Ali quote: 'Impossible is nothing'.
4. African parable.
5. Edward Snowden.
6. Julian Assange.
7. Bishop Henry McNeal Turner, "The Negro Has Not Sense Enough." Speech. 1 July 1900.
8. Don Cheadle on Rwanda.
9. Ken Saro-wiwa: Page 96, Crude, THE STORY OF OIL.
10. Physicians' oath: 'First do no harm'.

CHAPTER EIGHTY-ONE:
AFRICAN ADVANCEMENT

1. Chinweizu quote
2. Frantz Fanon quote: Ibid., Fanon. Wretched of the Earth.
3. Martin Luther King Jr. quote.

CHAPTER EIGHTY-TWO:
THE AFRICAN DIASPORA

1. African diaspora population
2. Ibid., IMF: African Diaspora remittance to Africa. African Diaspora Remittances are Better than Foreign Aid Funds by Adams. Bodomo. 04/03/2013
3. MIGRATION AND REMITTANCES Recent Developments and Outlook World Bank Group KNOMAD December 2018 www.worldbank.org Remittances for 2019.
4. Emeagwali quote
5. Brain drain: a bane to Africa's potential 9th August 2018. By Richard Kweitsu
6. President of African Development Bank Akinwumi Adesina citation.

CHAPTER EIGHTY-THREE:
THE CAUSE

1. Churchill, Winston. "Winston Churchill Quotes." Brainy Quotes.com. BookRags Media Network, 2001-4. Web. 12 March 2014
2. A well-known Afrocentric, Maulana Karenga, developed the Kwanzaa movement in America to give African Americans a uniting theme. "Maulana Karenga." Wikipedia. Wikimedia, n.d. 12 March 2014.
3. Martin Luther quote.
4. Frantz Fanon.

Appendix:

1. Nelson Mandela: Long Walk to Freedom.

Printed in Poland
by Amazon Fulfillment
Poland Sp. z o.o., Wrocław

62275463R30463